P9-BJM-774

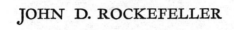

JOHN D. ROCKEFELLER

John D. Rockefeller.

A photograph taken when about forty-five.

John D. Rockefeller

THE HEROIC AGE OF AMERICAN ENTERPRISE

BY

ALLAN NEVINS

Volume One

NEW YORK

CHARLES SCRIBNER'S SONS

1940

KRAUS REPRINT CO.
New York
1969

Reprinted from the original edition in the
Wesleyan University Library

Reprinted with the permission of the author
KRAUS REPRINT CO.
A U.S. Division of Kraus-Thomson Organization Limited

TO

MARY RICHARDSON NEVINS

Preface

THE CAREER of John D. Rockefeller is one of the most interesting and significant in American history. Stretching over a span of almost one hundred years, it is in many respects unique, and in some of monumental importance. Indeed, it may be said that our industrial history since the Civil War can hardly be understood without a clear grasp of the principal facts of Rockefeller's work. Yet by far the greater part of the material in print upon this career is violently controversial, and almost none of it is unbiassed. The few attempts which have been made to present an objective and impartial account of Rockefeller's life have been too limited in scope to deal with the subject thoroughly. There has plainly been great need for a biography which should review all the transactions of his life both candidly and carefully, without prejudices or preconceptions.

This book is an attempt to meet the need. It is an effort to illuminate, without fear or favor, all aspects of the work of a remarkable innovator, who left a deep imprint upon both the industry and philanthropy of the nation, and who has been both bitterly assailed and warmly defended. The biography was undertaken in a spirit of impartiality, and under circumstances which assured the complete independence of the author. Every effort has been made to consult the leading critics of Rockefeller, and also to reach his principal surviving friends and defenders. The author has carefully reviewed the immense mass of material uncovered by legislative and Congressional investigations and by judicial suits. He has gone through the almost endless list of pamphlets, magazine articles, newspaper reports, and other publications bearing upon Rockefeller. Files of journals from Cleveland to New York and from Washington to Boston have been searched. The author has had the benefit of the

Rockefeller family papers, generously placed at his disposal by Mr. John D. Rockefeller, Jr.; he has also used the papers of some of Rockefeller's chief opponents. Many men who took part in the struggles in which Rockefeller engaged, both for him and against him, have been interviewed. If the author brought any bias to his work, it was that of a convinced believer in a free competitive economy.

Readers of these volumes will find that at numerous points it traverses the views of Rockefeller and the Standard Oil taken by previous writers. Sometimes the conclusions are adverse to Rockefeller; sometimes they are favorable. Though the author is much more intent upon *understanding* Rockefeller and his activities than upon either defending him or indicting him, he has not hesitated at many points to express his opinion frankly. Readers will also find that the volumes contain much material upon Rockefeller, the Standard Oil, and the great benefactions which here appears for the first time; and that some of it is of vital importance to a comprehension of the man and his labors. At various points the author has gone into controversial topics somewhat more fully than he would have preferred. But he has done so because previous writers have given these topics an artificial prominence which cannot be ignored.

No biography of this character could be carried to completion without the aid of a multitude of interested people. At the end of the second volume an effort is made to list some of the most important of the hundreds of friends and well-wishers who have generously given their help. Any merits the work may have are in large part due to them; but for its defects the author assumes full responsibility.

A. N.

New York City
August 1, 1940

Contents

BOOK I

THE RISE OF JOHN D. ROCKEFELLER, MERCHANT [1839–1869]

I.	"I REMEMBER THE BROOK"	3
II.	BOYHOOD AT OWASCO	28
III.	FAMILY DISASTER	49
IV.	"I WAS NOT AN EASY STUDENT"	64
V.	YOUTH WHOSE HOPE IS HIGH	80
VI.	A FOOTHOLD IN LIFE	101
VII.	CLARK & ROCKEFELLER	129
VIII.	BLACK GOLD	147
IX.	A VENTURE IN OIL	172
X.	BOOM AND DEPRESSION	192
XI.	WIFE AND HOME	217

BOOK II

THE MAKING OF THE GREAT TRUST [1869–1883]

XII.	BUILT ON OIL—AND REBATES	247
XIII.	THE BIRTH OF STANDARD OIL	276
XIV.	THE SOUTH IMPROVEMENT SCHEME	306

XV.   WAR, OPEN AND UNDERSTOOD   338

XVI.   THE CONQUEST OF CLEVELAND   361

XVII.   THE TIDE ROLLS ON   387

XVIII.   ROCKEFELLER AND THE PRODUCERS   413

XIX.   LEVIATHAN   433

XX.   THE CRUCIAL TWELVEMONTH: 1874–1875   451

XXI.   SWEEPING THE BOARD   484

XXII.   A BATTLE OF GIANTS   520

XXIII.   THE REGIONS CHALLENGE ROCKEFELLER 547

XXIV.   THE PIPE-LINE REVOLUTION   575

XXV.   THE FIRST GREAT TRUST   603

XXVI.   CITIZEN OF CLEVELAND   623

XXVII.   THE GREAT MACHINE   649

Illustrations

John D. Rockefeller   *Frontispiece*

FACING PAGE

Mrs. Lucy Avery Rockefeller, John D. Rockefeller's grandmother, at two different periods in her life   18

Eliza Davison Rockefeller and William Avery Rockefeller,
John D. Rockefeller's parents   19

The supposed Rockefeller birthplace, Richford, New York   56

Three boyhood homes of Rockefeller   57

Early American 1838 timetable of the Ithaca & Owego Railroad   *Page* 59

The Academy at Owego, New York, before and after remodelling in the eighteen-fifties   70

The Rockefeller children in Cleveland   71

Letter announcing the Clark, Gardner, Rockefeller partnership sent to customers in 1860   *Page* 137

Two heroes of the discovery of oil: Uncle Billy Smith and
Edwin L. Drake   164

The house occupied by "Colonel" Drake in Titusville   164

First Standard Oil Refinery in Cleveland   165

Pithole, Pennsylvania—the oil regions city which vanished   182

FACING PAGE

A model of the first Standard Oil Refinery in Cleveland set
up in the Field Museum, Chicago   183

A refinery of a later date   183

Oil barges in the Allegheny River in the later sixties   204

Kier's advertisement of petroleum as a patent medicine   205

A housewife cleaning and filling lamps   205

A page of a ledger showing gifts made by Rockefeller in the
first months in which he was employed   226

Lucy Spelman and Laura Celestia Spelman   227

Laura Celestia Spelman and John D. Rockefeller before they
became engaged   232

Rockefeller and his wife on top of Mt. Washington on their
wedding trip   233

John D. and William Rockefeller in youth and middle age   270

Early office buildings used by Rockefeller in Cleveland   271

Facsimile of the Articles of Incorporation of the Standard
Oil, 1870   Pages 290 and 291

Early trunk lines tapping the oil regions   Page 360

Rockefeller writes a firm of oil buyers   " 389

The Titusville Oil Exchange, 1883   452

Early tank cars with horizontal metal tanks   452

Illustrations

FACING PAGE

Rockefeller on the Isle of Wight 453

John D. Rockefeller, Mrs. Rockefeller and their daughter Bessie
in England 453

Five leaders of the Standard Oil: Joseph Seep, S. V. Harkness,
Charles M. Pratt, John D. Archbold and Charles Pratt 478

Ambrose McGregor and William Rockefeller 479

A Rockefeller family group at Forest Hill 624

Rockefeller on vacation in the Far West 625

Rockefeller swimming and bicycling at Forest Hill 632

Views of the house at Forest Hill 633

Rockefeller's New York house 660

Rockefeller jesting with John D. Archbold 661

Rockefeller sleigh riding in the Adirondacks 661

Rockefeller with his son John and some other young people 674

Rockefeller on a mountain-climbing jaunt 674

Mrs. John D. Rockefeller 675

BOOK ONE

THE RISE OF JOHN D. ROCKEFELLER, MERCHANT [1839-1869]

If we command our wealth, we shall be rich and free;
if our wealth commands us, we are poor indeed.

EDMUND BURKE, *Letters on a Regicide Peace.*

I

"I Remember the Brook"

EW REGIONS have ever been given a richer and more variegated beauty than western New York, and in 1839 that beauty was still largely unspoiled. Dense forests, high hills with cloud-mottled slopes, calm blue lakes, rocky streams, broad sweeps of plain, were as yet but lightly touched by the hand of man. All along the new Erie Canal stretched a thickening band of settlement. But the slopes of the highlands southward were still sparsely inhabited. Here lay the Finger Lakes, fringed by noble woods of beech, maple, and oak, making a country of which the German poet, Ludwig Fulda, said years afterward that it combined the charms of the Swiss lakes with those of the Black Forest. Here flowed the upper waters of the Delaware, Susquehanna, and Allegheny, all at first winding west as if to seek Lake Erie, and then suddenly dropping south into Pennsylvania. Here were stony uplands, deep chasms like Watkins Glen, and fertile valleys like the Genesee. Much of the country was less seductive to practical farmers than the easily tilled lands of the Ohio and Illinois regions. Ever since the canal had made water-transit easy, the main stream of emigration had ceased to spill into upper New York, flowing on westward to the prairie regions. This was why, beautiful as the area was, its hillier parts remained half wild; a country of crooked miry roads, of fever and ague, of wolves and occasional bears, and of backward communities of pioneer type, with only rarely a progressive township or ambitious little city.

In 1839 the rural community about Richford, a hamlet in the northeast part of Tioga County, midway in the "southern tier" of New York, was distinctly one of the backwater spots of the region. The main currents of emigration and settlement which were sweeping steadily westward passed it by. Like most of upper New York, this district had once been a possession of the Iroquois. Land-hungry

3

New Yorkers and Yankees had dribbled into it after the peace of 1783, seizing the fields of the Six Nations, who had unhappily staked their fortunes on the success of British arms. But Richford did not stand in the most promising part of this new territory, and its first settler, Evan Harris, had not arrived until near the end of Jefferson's second administration. Lying nearly twenty miles north of Owego, the village was encircled by the high hills, running up to two thousand feet above sea level, that served as watersheds for the Ontario basin to the north and the Susquehanna to the south. The soil of this rough country was too thin to be attractive; access to markets was difficult; the winter climate was severe. Settlers had seized first upon the more accessible lands about Auburn and Syracuse to the north, and around Owego and Elmira to the south. The first tavern had not been built until 1811, and Ezekiel Rich, the most prominent early citizen, had not opened his tannery until 1821. He was an energetic man who also manufactured gloves and mittens, stocked a general store, built and kept a hotel, and dealt in land. The army of western emigrants was building up new States beyond the Mississippi before the town was formed by act of the legislature April 18, 1831. At first it was called Arlington, but within the year a new enactment changed the name to Richford.[1]

Its disadvantages of land and situation might by 1840 have made it evident to discerning observers that Richford would never be more than a village, and that the settlement about it would be essentially static. Yet its very newness gave the hamlet a certain bustle and energy. The census of that year showed 822 people in the township. It boasted of several sawmills and gristmills, stores, a whiskey distillery, a schoolhouse, a prosperous Congregational and a struggling Episcopalian church, and a hotel. Doctor Elijah Powell, arriving in 1823 to practise medicine, had a doctor's office and drugstore in a large three-storied brick building that he had erected at the northeast corner of the public square. The principal general store was now kept by James Robbins, successor to Rich.[2] Some hopeful citizens

[1]Leroy W. Kingman, *Our Country and Its People: Memorial History of Tioga County;* H. B. Prince, *History of Tioga, Chemung, and Tompkins and Schuyler Counties, New York.* Kingman's volume is a superior piece of local history.

[2]Ezekiel Rich's son, Chauncey Leroy Rich, clerked in Robbins's store, and in 1845 purchased it, becoming the most prominent citizen of the township. A portrait and sketch are in Kingman, *Tioga County,* 789 ff.

still dreamed of a railroad and factories. The settlers were busy cutting timber in winter, and widening their fields of timothy, wheat, and potatoes in summer. Pioneering conditions of life were slowly yielding to a better era. Clapboard houses had supplanted most of the log cabins; some homes were even built of brick. Though a few dwellings were yet heated by fireplaces alone, most of them had stoves. Flint and tinder had been replaced by matches; flour was no longer made from rye, but of wheat; less and less cloth was spun and woven at home. The number of people who had been inside a bank and seen a railway train was steadily increasing, while not a few citizens had visited New York City, which by wagon-road was well over two hundred miles distant.[3]

Richford lay in the center of its shallow valley basin. Leading north and west from the diamond-shaped village green, well shaded by maples, from Robbins's store and Doctor Powell's dignified little office, and from the comfortable, rectangular-shaped hotel, its two stories painted a cheerful yellow, that faced the green, a stony road rose into the hilly country. The forest hung above it, occasionally giving way to pleasant patches of meadow or grain, with a weather-beaten little farmhouse. About four miles from the village, on a high knoll facing south between two brooks that met to form Owego Creek, stood a small unpainted dwelling, most of which has since disappeared. It was built in the style or lack of style common with country carpenters; a stiff, boxlike main structure of a story and a half, joined at one side by a single-story ell containing kitchen and woodshed. It had a solid frame, neatly clapboarded, with a low-pitched shingle roof. Two large barns rose not far distant, while halfway down the knoll was a well; a ring of apple trees had been planted about. The two windows and door at the front looked out upon the road and a pleasant view of hills and trees. Here at the beginning of July, 1839, on a fifty-acre farm, William Avery Rockefeller was living with his young wife Eliza and a daughter of seventeen months named Lucy; they had a hired girl, and a hired man came frequently to work.

Unlike his neighbors, William Avery Rockefeller had not settled in Richford township as a farmer. He was an itinerant trader and

[3]Paul D. Evans in Alexander C. Flick, ed., *History of the State of New York*, V, 167 ff., gives a vivid account of changes in frontier civilization in this period.

medicine-vender, and his principal reason for coming here was that his father and mother lived half a mile up the road. Indeed, a considerable number of Rockefellers resided in the country about the three villages of Richford, Harford, and Harford Mills, and could give companionship and protection to his wife and child while he was away on long trips. But July 8 found him at home, for a new baby was expected. When that evening the mother was suddenly seized with labor pains, he did not ride to Richford for Doctor Powell, but after the country fashion hurried a farm hand for a neighbor—Mrs. Hannah Hamilton, less than half a mile distant. Within a few minutes she was heating water and preparing bandages for Eliza Rockefeller, who lay in the groundfloor bedroom, a small apartment ten feet long and less than eight feet wide, with a low ceiling. We can imagine the anxious bustle in the flickering candlelight, the worried father outside trying to keep the baby sister quiet; doubtless his father and mother, Godfrey and Lucy Rockefeller, hurried in. Before midnight a son had been born.[4]

Richford and Harford Mills probably took little interest in the advent of the child soon to be named John Davison Rockefeller, for babies were numerous and the family were not prominent members of the community. Godfrey, grandfather of the baby, was a quiet, industrious, commonplace farmer who had come to the township only four or five years earlier—the date is uncertain—and who was destined to live out his life there inconspicuously, and be buried in Harford Mills Cemetery in 1857. The grandmother, Lucy, was an energetic, strong-minded, helpful woman. William Avery Rockefeller, the father, possessed a far more arresting and colorful personality than either, and was fast making a deeper impression. He returned in dashing style from long trips which he liked to make mysterious to the villagers. He drove fast horses, wore fine clothes, and carried himself with an air of command. He was a tall, handsome, quick-moving young man, who won the liking of many

---

[4] I spent much time in Richford in 1937 gathering what local materials were available. Mr. W. O. Inglis in July-August, 1917, visited Richford, Moravia, Owego, and other points in the boyhood environment of John D. Rockefeller, interviewing every one who had information. His notes, later partially worked into a MS biography, are in the Rockefeller papers and afford much valuable material.

observers by his ready, friendly talk, and aroused the suspicion of others because he was markedly individual. But Richford as a whole had not yet decided what to make of him.

America in these years was a young, fast-growing country, with marks of adolescence upon all aspects of its society. Martin Van Buren was in uneasy power in Washington; at Albany William Henry Seward was giving the State its first Whig administration. In nearly every field of endeavor institutions were still sufficiently plastic to be moulded by men of strength. When John D. Rockefeller first saw the light in the poorly furnished Tioga farmhouse, other children who were to place their mark upon American life were in their infancy. J. Pierpont Morgan, Grover Cleveland, and William Dean Howells were all youngsters of two, in Hartford, Conn., Caldwell, N. J., and Martins Ferry, O., respectively. Andrew Carnegie and James J. Hill, both born under the British flag, were four years and one year old. An infant in Philadelphia was christened Henry George only a few weeks after Rockefeller's birth. In Boston, Henry Adams was a little more than a year old, while not far away, on a farm of the western Catskills, John Burroughs was just past two. John Hay had been born the previous year, and Charles W. Eliot five years earlier. Few of these came into an abode as humble as Rockefeller's, and most of them had early advantages far greater than he received. Yet none of these men, not even Cleveland or Carnegie, was to place a more weighty impress upon the nation than he.

And none was to illustrate, in the circumstances of his early and later life, a more impressive change in the fabric of American society. A dramatic contrast might be drawn between the half-tamed hills and vales of Richford, the placid elemental rural existence of the township in 1839, and the pattern of industrial concentration and specialization which Rockefeller helped to place a few decades later upon a far more crowded, far more urbanized, far wealthier republic.

II

Had the villagers of Richford been able to make a study of Rockefeller's ancestry, they would hardly have discerned in it any promise of special distinction. His father's family had dwelt in America for more than a century. Johann Peter Rockefeller, emigrating to the colonies from Sagendorf in Rhenish Germany between 1720 and 1723, had first settled in Somerville, N. J., and then near Amwell on a branch of the Raritan, where he built a gristmill. He brought not only five children by a first wife, dead in Germany, but a second wife who was to bear more children in America. His son Johann Peter 2d, born of the first wife, remained at Amwell, married, and in 1750 became the father of William Rockefeller. This William married a remote relative, Christina Rockefeller, the daughter of Diell or Diehl Rockefeller, who had been born in the Palatinate and had settled in Germantown, N. Y., about 1734, becoming owner of about six hundred acres. The marriage thus united two distinct branches of the Rockefeller family in America. From it sprang a son named Godfrey, born in Germantown on September 24, 1783 —the same Godfrey Rockefeller who had come to Richford about 1834, and who was the father of William Avery Rockefeller.[5]

Nobody in the prolific and widespreading Rockefeller family had yet reached a position of note in America. But the middle name of William Avery Rockefeller represented an important new blood strain, a family which had already attained distinction and power in New England and New York, and was destined to attain more. Even in the earliest years of the Rockefellers in America, British blood had begun to mingle with the German stock. The first wife of Johann Peter 2d was a Mary Bellis, whose name would probably be spelled Bellows today, and his second wife was Elizabeth Peterson.[6] Christian was probably of pure German descent. Godfrey Rockefeller was apparently therefore of one-fourth English blood. His sister Hannah had married Henry Avery of Great Barrington, just across the Massachusetts line from Germantown, N. Y., and as a visitor in her house he shortly met pretty Lucy Avery, Henry's niece, whom he married in 1806.

This Avery line in America had begun with Christopher Avery, who was born in Devon, the son of a kersey weaver of Newton Abbott, married a Margery Stephens in 1616, and crossed the ocean to Massachusetts about 1630 as part of the great Puritan migration.

[5]Henry Oscar Rockefeller, ed., *Transactions of the Rockefeller Family Association, 1910–14.*

[6]Peters and Peterson were and are common English names, and at that date in the colonies the name was far more likely to be English than Scandinavian.

He was of unusual character and energy, and dared to stand out in Gloucester, where he settled, against a harsh Puritan minister. His son James, who had been born in England about 1620 and had migrated to America with his father, was a still abler man, who settled in New London, Conn., and acquired influence as magistrate, Indian fighter, and landowner. Six sons and three daughters were born to him and his wife, Joanna Greenslade. From the middle of the sevententh century the Averys flourished like a mighty oak, putting forth new branches—sometimes many—in every generation. Like most Puritan families, they had character, brains, and energy. By the Revolution their lines, even more prolific and widely ramified than those of the Rockefellers, had spread outside New England and had produced businessmen, clergymen, soldiers, politicians, and community leaders of a dozen other types. The Averys fill many pages of the *Dictionary of American Biography,* nearly all tracing a descent from the original Christopher. When this vigorous family united with one branch of the Rockefellers, it gave the quieter, more plodding German stock an immediate accession of energy.[7]

John D. Rockefeller's mother, Eliza Davison, was of Scottish descent. In his veins the original German blood had therefore been diluted to three sixteenths or less. The tracing of ancestral traits is always hazardous. But after recording the indisputable fact that his ancestry was purely British and German, with the British strongly predominating, we are tempted to venture the statement that the most important part of his heritage was derived from his Puritan forbears. His career showed more of the shrewd, enterprising character of the Averys than it did of the patient, jovial Rockefellers, or of the industrious, economical Davisons.

Both his New England and German lines of ancestry have found thorough chroniclers. The records of the Averys fill two stout volumes—*The Groton Avery Clan, 1616-1912.* A reader of this work cannot but be impressed by the serried lists of magistrates, educators, engineers, soldiers, ministers, editors, and other substantial men, scattered from Maine to California, contained in its tables. As for the equally numerous Rockefeller family, early in the twentieth century they developed a keen interest in their past. A coat of arms

[7] Two thick volumes compiled by Elroy M. Avery, *The Groton Avery Clan* (that is, the Averys who sprang from the first forbears in Groton), trace the Avery genealogies in accurate detail.

was discovered in 1904. A year later the Rockefeller Family Association was formed, holding its first meeting in July, 1905. This group grew within thirty years to a membership of very nearly one thousand. John D. Rockefeller from the first took a courteous interest in it, sometimes extending the hospitality of his Pocantico Hills estate to the annual gathering, and in 1914 joining the Association. His sister, Mrs. Rudd, became a member in 1909, and his brother Frank in 1916. The group have published the proceedings of their yearly meetings, conserved family records, issued an interesting magazine called *Rockefeller Family News,* and published an exhaustive *Rockefeller Genealogy.*[8]

The research of the Rockefeller Family Association has been carried far back into the European past. In 1906, at the suggestion of its officers, John D. Rockefeller erected a monument at Ringoes, N. J., to Johann Peter, founder of the American line. At Rheinbrohl, Germany, the Lutheran pastor read a newspaper account of this event. He wrote the minister at Ringoes. Certain Rockefellers still living at Sagendorf in the Rhineland believed themselves related to the American family, he reported, adding: "You may confer a favor upon Mr. John D. Rockefeller by calling his attention to this notice." The letter was duly forwarded. John D. Rockefeller gave it to his brother William, who in turn sent it to Doctor Aaron R. Lewis of New York, the genealogist who had traced the American lineage. Doctor Lewis went to Germany, and in the fall of 1907 reported that he had carried his quest back for more than seven centuries, to Carolingian days—900 A.D. He had found in southern France, near Lodève in the Cevennes, a family named Roquefeuille (Italian Rocafolio; English Rockleaf), which had owned a château and a great estate. "Away back in the Middle Ages I learn they had money, coins, bearing their name," the enthusiastic Doctor Lewis told the Rockefeller Association. He was able to show pictures of these coins of the "Seigneuire de Roquefeuil," marked with an imposing R. Then he traced the family down through French history, giving it a connection with Admiral Coligny, the Huguenot martyr of St. Bartholomew's Eve; and described the Roquefeuilles, who

[8]For additional information, see H. O. Rockefeller, ed., *Transactions of the Rockefeller Family Association, 1910–14,* and the same *Transactions, 1915–25.*

were Protestants, as finally migrating to Germany to escape persecution.[9]

What was of real importance to John D. Rockefeller, and to present-day students of his career, was his immediate ancestry—his grandparents and parents. What chances had they been given by life, and how had they made use of them?

Some of the Averys, a true pioneer stock, had been early to arrive in what is now called the Rockefeller country. Just after the Revolution Massachusetts claimed lands in western New York on the basis of her royal charter, and in 1786 a body of commissioners agreed that in return for surrendering all pretensions to sovereignty there, she should be compensated by a grant of property in certain areas. One of the tracts was a block of 230,400 acres between the Chenango River and Owego Creek, north of the Susquehanna, lying partly in Tioga County. The following year this block, popularly called the "Boston Ten Towns" or "Boston Purchase," was transferred to a group of men from Berkshire County, Mass., headed by Samuel Brown. A number of them lived within a short distance of Great Barrington, the home of many Averys. Having paid 12½ cents an acre for the land, subject to whatever title the Indians might have, they at first sold it to actual occupants at 25 cents an acre, but soon advanced it to $1, and later still to $5.[10] In 1801 John Humphrey Avery, a cousin of Lucy Avery's father, migrated to Owego, N. Y., seventeen miles south of Richford, and continued to dwell there until his death two years before John D. Rockefeller was born.

The country was undoubtedly well known by report to all the Averys in the Great Barrington district, and through Lucy Avery Rockefeller to her husband Godfrey. Alluring tales of its beauty were circulated, for the early comers were much struck by its attractiveness. While the Six Nations still held western New York, their lordly expanse of forest, cliff, lake, and winding river had delighted the eyes of wandering travellers. This was a country much like the

[9]For inquiries which seem to disprove this tale of French ancestry and trace the line back to a Tonges Rockenfeller of Bonefeld, Germany, see "Oil King a German," by La Marquise de Fontenoy, Boston *Herald*, Aug. 7, 1909.

[10]Kingman, *Tioga County*, 46 ff., gives the history of the "Purchase" in full.

wilderness of Cooper's Indian romances, and indeed lay not a hundred miles from Otsego Lake. The cornfields of the Indians bore so abundantly that the soldiers of Clinton and Sullivan—men from New Jersey, New York, Connecticut, and Massachusetts—returning from the expedition of 1779, astonished their friends by the ears of maize they brought back—"the finest," wrote Clinton, "that I ever saw." One of his officers drew the long bow to assert that some ears measured twenty-two inches. Large numbers of western Massachusetts people came into the area early in the century.

Of Godfrey Rockefeller we know little save that he was a plain, kindly, easygoing farmer who married a wife much abler than himself. He was of medium height and weight, strongly knit, good-looking, and of sociable temperament. He had bluish-gray eyes, brown hair, and regular features; as a farmer he was competent and hard-working, save when love of good company and the flowing bowl led him astray. He had never accumulated much property. Tradition states that when he left Germantown, N. Y., to marry Lucy Avery, he was regarded with disfavor by her relatives, for they knew that he drank and was unstable; but then that was a drinking age. It is certain that Lucy had the keener mind, the stronger character. She was the daughter of sturdy Miles Avery, who had been born at Norwich, Conn., and who had fought on various Revolutionary fields—Germantown, Monmouth, Stony Point —attaining the rank of sergeant. He was justice of the peace for thirty-four years in a day when it meant something to be a squire, and Pittsfield deeds refer to him as "gentleman." We know that Lucy obtained a fair education, for she had been a schoolmistress. She was taller than her husband, broad-shouldered, stalwart, and alert. With her clear blue eyes, set far apart, her firm chin, and her look of energy and decision, she had a commanding personality.[11]

They had good reason for their removal. After their marriage, they had first settled in Great Barrington, where Godfrey farmed with some energy, and gained sufficient popularity to be elected sheriff of Berkshire County. But the Berkshire land is stony and unproductive; children came one after another, till ten in all (Wil-

[11]Mr. W. O. Inglis obtained much information on Godfrey and Lucy Avery Rockefeller from John D. Rockefeller and others. Mr. Inglis's valuable notes of conversations with Rockefeller will hereafter be cited as "Inglis, Conversations with Rockefeller."

liam Avery being the third, born in 1810) pressed hard upon his means; and he and his wife looked about for ways of bettering their lot. By 1809 the family was living at Grangerville, N. Y., near Saratoga Springs. They soon moved back to Ancram, N. Y., a little south of Germantown; then to Great Barrington again; and finally to Livingston, N. Y., still closer to Germantown. It was at Ancram that William Avery was born.[12] Throughout all these removals Godfrey remained poor, and the rich lands of the West must have seemed more and more attractive to the household.

By 1830 there was much talk of the new settlements in northern Ohio and southern Michigan, and Godfrey lent a ready ear to tales of the latter territory. A daily boat was running this year between Buffalo and Detroit. Lumber, minerals, and fertile soil at $1.25 an acre were at the disposal of those who ventured into the West. An emigrant song of the period enthusiastically celebrates the crops, scenery, fish, game, and not least the girls, of Michigan, and exuberantly predicts that

> With little prudence any man
> Can soon get rich in Mich-i-gan.

Though Godfrey was nearing fifty, he did not feel too old for a new start. He and his wife, who dreaded taking a large family into the wilderness, doubtless discussed the matter with care. From the uncertain family legends we gather that Lucy finally dictated a compromise on her own terms. They would go west, but only to Tioga County, where she had relatives and would have trustworthy, industrious New England people around her. One family account states that Godfrey traded his Livingston farm for a tract in Richford which he had never seen. It is much more probable that he bought at the low ruling prices. In his good-natured way he gave the family compromise a wryly humorous interpretation. When asked, on leaving Livingston, if he were Michigan-bound, he gayly chanted to the tune of the song: "No, Tioga County in this State will be my Mich-i-gan." And when the new farm was reached, the story runs that he wistfully climbed the northernmost hill of his property and remarked: "This is as close as we shall ever get to Michigan." The slope soon became known as Michigan Hill, and this in turn became

[12]So William Avery Rockefeller states in a note in the autograph book kept by John D. Rockefeller, Jr., as a boy.

the designation of the neighborhood containing the Rockefeller farms and those immediately adjoining.[13]

The move to the new country was in a covered Conestoga wagon, drawn by oxen. Into this the household goods were piled, and Mrs. Rockefeller and the younger children sometimes rode inside, sometimes walked. They followed the four-rod "Susquehanna Turnpike" which, commenced in 1805, now crossed the State from Catskill Landing on the river to Ithaca, passing through Richford. The journey, since fifteen miles was a good day's trip, probably took almost a fortnight. It led through country much of which was wild, and in Tioga County still infested by bears, wildcats and an occasional highwayman. According to family tradition, Godfrey Rockefeller first used the little house in which John D. Rockefeller was later to be born, presently removing to a red-painted building on Michigan Hill. This larger house seems to have been erected about 1837 by one Avery Rockhill, whose name indicates that he may have been a relative of Lucy Rockefeller.

All the old inhabitants of Richford who have furnished evidence upon Godfrey's family since John D. Rockefeller became famous agree that Lucy Avery Rockefeller was the dominant spirit. Her husband farmed his new acres with somewhat spasmodic energy. Where industry and initiative are concerned, the tales are all of what Lucy did. A stone wall was needed near the road winding over Michigan Hill. She briskly supervised its construction, directing the workmen and bringing small stones in her apron; and it still stands, straight and firm. Her father had told her of his Revolutionary exploits in Colonel John Durkie's regiment, and she used to gather her children about her and recount his adventures. She herself showed militant traits. "My grandmother," once said John D. Rockefeller,[14] "was a brave woman. Her husband was not so brave as she." Her old neighbors remembered, long after she died, her religious fervor and her goodness to those about her. Her children were devoted to her. To the end there was a high and bold spirit in this New England woman.

She had courage, and she also had tact. John D. Rockefeller has

[13]Mr. W. O. Inglis, MS Biography of John D. Rockefeller, 3. Written for the family, this manuscript is in the Rockefeller papers.
[14]Inglis, Conversations with Rockefeller.

told how she heard noises in the barn one night as she was sewing. Instantly running out, she found a man stealing oats. She seized him, but he struggled, and she realized that he would soon get away. Snatching the scissors from her apron pocket, she clipped a piece of cloth from his coat before he escaped. Threshing was under way at the time, and several neighborhood hands who were on the crew came to the house several days later for meals. One had a jagged hole in his coat. Lucy Rockefeller exclaimed: "Why, Mr. Blank, what a bad gash in your coat-sleeve! I happen to have a piece of cloth that just matches it. I will fix it for you." She brought out the cloth from the thief's coat and sewed it into the gap. It fitted. The embarrassed thresher said nothing, and neither did Lucy. But there were no more attempts to steal oats from the Rockefeller barn.[15]

IV

William Avery Rockefeller had come of age in 1831. According to family tradition, he had studied medicine with some doctor as a youth, and at twenty-one lost no time in leaving his father's farm and setting up in business for himself. It is uncertain when he appeared in Richford. But legal papers in Tioga County show that a deed was recorded September 21, 1835, by which Thomas Astley of Philadelphia, through James Pumpelly of Owego, sold to William A. Rockefeller of Richford fifty acres of land in lot 550 of the Boston Purchase for $151.[16] This would indicate that he came to the township at about the same time as his parents—certainly not long afterward. The following spring (May 27, 1836) he deeded ten acres of the tract to his mother for a mill site.[17] Then at the beginning of 1836 (January 20) he bought half of lot 549 of the Boston Purchase, about 120 acres, for $480. His holdings when John D. Rockefeller was born thus amounted to about 160 acres.

The family tradition assumes that he arrived in Richford with his parents. But a neighborhood legend credits him with a more spectacular advent. According to this story, he appeared at Richford some time after Godfrey had occupied his new farm. He clattered into the village square, a tall, frank-faced young man in well-cut clothes, astride a handsome horse. Reining up before some of the

[15]Inglis, MS Biography, 6.
[16]Tioga Deed Book 32, 119.   [17]Deed Book 48, 252.

idlers lounging on the hotel stoop, he gravely saluted them. Then he drew a small slate from inside his coat and wrote upon it:

"Where is the house of Godfrey Rockefeller?"

When the idlers replied, he made signs that he was deaf and dumb, and motioned them to write their directions on his slate. They did so, pointing out the road he must take, and wonderingly watched him ride off. At home he continued the same pretence, to the amazement and horror of his family, until suddenly he could contain himself no longer and burst out laughing.

It is hard to believe this story wholly apocryphal; it is not the kind of tale that men invent. And whether true or not, it accurately suggests the audacity, humor, and eccentricity of the most colorful of all the Rockefellers. In that ante-bellum era, P. T. Barnum was one of the most typical of all Americans, and there was a pronounced strain of the Barnumesque in William Avery Rockefeller. No one could look at him without seeing that he was a remarkable character. Nearly six feet high, deep-chested and muscular, he was as swift and supple as an Indian.[18] A heavy mass of chestnut hair fell across a broad, high forehead. His blue eyes could be merry and twinkling, or piercing and threatening, according to his mood. His mouth was broad and sensuous; his chin and jaw were strong. Later in life he took on a heavy aspect, but at this time he was a spare, stripped athlete, able to outrun, outjump, and outswim any competitor. He had a will that brooked no opposition. Though kindly, hearty, and jovial, he suffered no restraints. As observers later testified, he acted precisely as he pleased, and was a law unto himself. He felt no compulsion to justify himself; if men did not like what he did, they could simply go hang.[19] Vibrant with energy and exuberant in spirit, full of the joy of living, supremely self-confident, he was a marked figure in any gathering. Life became brisker, heartier, and merrier wherever he appeared.

As a young man of twenty-four, he was already busy with the

[18]The story above was repeated to me by various Richford people in 1937. Legends in the Binghamton area, told me by Doctor Carlton J. H. Hayes, state that one of William Avery Rockefeller's cronies picked up and often used in that district the pretense of being deaf and dumb. John D. Rockefeller testified that William Avery was "the strongest and liveliest" of Godfrey's sons; Inglis, MS Biography, 6.

[19]Mr. George Welwood Murray, who saw a good deal of him about 1890, so stated to me in May, 1938.

trading expeditions and the herb- and patent-medicine vending which were to occupy him for most of the next half century. He had all of the Avery enterprise and shrewdness, and all of the Rockefeller love of society and fun. He had roamed far before the family ventured west to Richford, and may even have visited this district before his parents came. Our first information shows him already much occupied with his various undertakings and prospering in them.

In those days the peddler of medicines could assume in many communities a semiprofessional status. Medical schools in America were still few and for the most part abysmally weak. There were not enough graduate physicians to meet the needs of the fast-growing country, and pioneer settlements were too poor anyway to pay for expert services. The situation that existed during William Avery Rockefeller's early manhood may be gathered from the census of 1850. This revealed that the United States, with 23,300,000 people, had 40,755 physicians and surgeons, and 6139 apothecaries and druggists. The catalogues of all the medical colleges (some of them beneath contempt) showed that the number of their graduates to the end of 1850 did not exceed 18,000, dead and alive! Several thousand American practitioners might have received their training abroad in Edinburgh, Paris, or London. But even estimating the number liberally, they would not raise the roster of professionally schooled men to one half the "physicians and surgeons" returned by the census. The other half had picked up a little knowledge by working in some doctor's office, compounding medicines with a druggist, or other means.[20] Many were dangerous quacks; many dealt capably with the simpler ailments. But quackery then did not mean what it does today. In an age when even the Harvard Medical School gave abominably inadequate training, and, as President Eliot later declared, turned out some graduates who killed as often as they cured,[21] and when the principal teacher at the medical school of the University of Michigan recommended heavy doses of chlorate of potash (ruinous to the kidneys) "for all sorts of symptoms,"[22] the line between quackery and

[20]The N. Y. *Tribune* for 1851 made this the subject of editorial comment.

[21]Charles W. Eliot, *A Late Harvest*, 35 ff., describes the low estate of Harvard's medical training.

[22]Doctor Norman Bridge, *The Marching Years*, 81–89, explains how much misinformation was inculcated in the Michigan medical school.

honest medicine was hard to draw. William Avery Rockefeller was in due time to join the great army of amateur doctors as an "herbal physician"; at this period, however, he was simply a distributor of drugs and patent nostrums.

Such a man found it necessary to be well dressed, well outfitted, and self-confident. Travelling from town to town, he would hire a suite at a good hotel; send out a boy with handbills advertising "Doctor So-and-So, the Eminent Specialist"; interview the local editor; and spend from several days to a fortnight seeing credulous patients. Such travelling "doctors" and drug-dispensers were numerous until late in the century stringent State laws killed their activities. Doubtless William Avery Rockefeller made a good deal of money by selling nostrums and "cancer cures." Public faith in patent cure-alls was enormous, and the press teemed with advertisements of Old Jacob Townsend's Genuine Townsend Sarsaparilla, which "does wonders in the cure of Consumption, Dyspepsia, Liver-Complaint, Rheumatism, Scrofula, Piles, Costiveness, all Cutaneous Eruptions, Pimples, Blotches, and afflictions arising from Impurity of the Blood"; Trask's Magnetic Ointment; Ayer's Cherry Pectoral; and dozens more.[23] "Big Bill" Rockefeller also, when opportunity offered, dealt in salt, furs, horses, and land. Sometimes he penetrated far to the west—to Ohio, Michigan, Illinois—and came back with wonderful tales of his adventures.

In these varied, bold, and doubtless sometimes sharp enterprises, he always appeared with a spanking team, a spick-and-span wardrobe, and plenty of ready money. He would not touch liquor, and declaimed energetically—as befitted a man whose business was to keep people well—against its dangers. But he liked the jovial crowd at the tavern fire or game of horseshoes; he shot like Hawkeye, and could whip a trout stream like Izaak Walton; he was full of fun. He liked to talk of trading with the Indians, and of clever shifts by which he had outwitted Yankees who tried to trick him. David Harum would have found him a kindred soul. Everybody agreed that he was magnetic, that he was as keen as a Sheffield blade, that he most faithfully paid his debts. But an air of mystery hung about him. This was inevitably created by his long disappearances, the uncertainty surrounding his income, and his shrewd ways. He encour-

[23]I have copied these names from Auburn, N. Y., newspapers of the period.

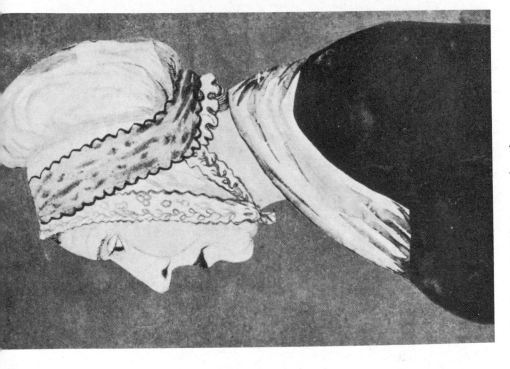

Mrs. Lucy Avery Rockefeller and Cynthia Selover, John D. Rockefeller's grandmothers.

Eliza Davison Rockefeller and William Avery Rockefeller, John D. Rockefeller's parents.

aged the conjectures because it suited his odd temper to mystify people. In the end, he was to mystify the entire country, and to pass from the stage of human ken so much a mystery that his burial-place today is unknown.

Because of the mystification, a thick cloud of legend arose in his wake which still casts a fog over much of his life at Richford and Moravia. We can be certain of a few definite facts. One is that in 1836, the year after he bought his fifty acres, he spent some time trading in Cayuga County, about twenty miles north of Richford. In Niles Township he met Eliza Davison, daughter of John Davison, a precise, cautious, prosperous farmer. She was a spirited young woman, with the red hair not uncommon in the Scottish stock, and dancing blue eyes; "a beautiful girl and smart around the house," a friend later recalled.[24] Several accounts make her a schoolteacher, but John D. Rockefeller has denied this, and the misspelling of her letters indicates a slender education.[25] She was kindly, helpful, and, like her father, very strait-laced in all matters of ethics. She was also deeply religious, and sang in the choir of the Niles church, which was called Dutch Reformed, but was attended by people of various Protestant denominations. Here a Scottish minister, Archibald McNeal, gained a wide reputation by his powerful two-hour sermons. She had an older brother named George and an older sister named Mary Ann, the former already a substantial farmer, the latter married to Peter Van Duyne, who was also prosperous. Altogether, it was a family of character and position. William Avery Rockefeller and Eliza felt the attraction of opposites. The courtship was brief, and on February 26, 1837, they were married. They settled immediately on the Richford farm, where a daughter was born February 21, 1838, and the subject of this book in 1839.

These facts are clear and indubitable; but the mytho-poetic process has woven a tissue of fable about them which may or may not contain threads of truth. One story concerns the courtship. It is said that William Avery Rockefeller breezily knocked at the Davison door as a peddler, and got out his pencil and slate—which may actually have been an habitual device to ensure sympathetic attention. Eliza, struck

[24]Brookyn *Daily Citizen*, Jan. 2, 1910, interview by J. V. Knight with Mrs. Bevier of Plymouth, Ohio, girlhood friend of Eliza Davison.

[25]Descendants of the Van Duynes in Moravia possess letters which they have kindly allowed me to copy.

by his handsome face, fine clothes, and obvious cleverness, saucily exclaimed:

"If that man were not deaf and dumb, I'd marry him!"

He then—according to the story—laughingly claimed her, and she was soon glad to keep her word.

Other stories deal with the marriage itself. The family tradition is that William and Eliza were married in John Davison's parlor. But one neighborhood legend states that while Eliza was much in love, her stern, careful Baptist father distrusted the gay and expansive suitor, and opposed the match. However, he did not actually forbid it—indeed, he had no right to, for Eliza was twenty-three—and William drove up, claimed his bride, and took her to the house of a friend, where they were united without the father's blessing. This version in the course of decades received a good deal of embroidery, as may be gathered from a history of the marriage published in the Elmira *Telegram* some seventy years later:[26]

He [William Avery Rockefeller] was a wandering Ishmael, travelling from home about Cayuga and adjoining counties, pretending to be deaf and dumb, performing sleight of hand, sometimes gambling; a regular nondescript, but whatever he did he returned home with his pockets full of money. In his peregrinations he struck an old hard-shell Baptist farmer in the town of Moravia, with a susceptible daughter. His finesse, good dressing, and gentlemanly demeanor made him a conqueror of the fair sex. He had, about this time, made enough to build a battened house in the woods, which had been taken up by the Rockefeller colony, furnished it with mahogany furniture, and installed as housekeeper a young woman of the vicinity. He made such a glitter with his money that marriage with the Moravia girl soon followed. People of the countryside from Moravia to Harford Mills recall the wedding journey through the valley to Groton, Dryden, and Harford one March winter's day. In a capacious gooseneck sleigh, shining and bespangled with ornaments, drawn by two handsome blacks, caparisoned with a gold-mounted harness, costly black robes covering the inmates of the sleigh, the moving spectacle was the astonishment of country beholders.

The bride made the best of her disappointment on reaching the abode of her husband. She became a power for good in the colony. She provided a home and marriage for the housekeeper and her two children. She and Mother Rockefeller exerted full control of the neighborhood until she took her husband and growing family back to the Moravian farm.

There are such glaring inaccuracies in these florid paragraphs—for

[26]Undated clipping, Rockefeller papers.

John Davison lived in Niles, not Moravia; William Rockefeller did not gamble and never furnished the house with mahogany; and the family never went back to the Davison farm—that we are disposed to deny it any evidential value whatever. Yet some parts of the story are accurate. The description of William accords with other accounts of him; Niles lies near Moravia, and the Davison farm is between the two towns; the house of the bridal pair was clapboarded if not battened, and was in or near the woods; and since the marriage took place in late February, the ride home in March seems possible. The tale at least indicates the striking impression that William made in that part of western New York.

The most significant sentences in this account are those which state that Eliza became "a power for good in the colony," that she provided for the housekeeper (otherwise identified as Nancy Brown, and still recalled in that district) and her children,[27] and that she joined hands with Lucy Avery Rockefeller to exercise a certain control over the Michigan Hill neighborhood. We can well believe this. Of Eliza's firm traits of character we have the fullest knowledge. Her deep piety and strong will were accompanied by a remarkable serenity, which she handed on to her son. She was frugal, reticent, and the soul of order and discipline. Her ideas upon morals were precise to the point of intolerance; a certain narrowness and severity, the natural result of her rigid upbringing and lack of educational advantages, sat heavily upon her. She was not given to fun; wrapped up in her household and her religion, she was as deeply introverted as her jovial, adventurous husband was extroverted. She was self-contained and dignified. To some people she seemed too austere to be lovable. But as a devoted mother, determined to bring up her children in a straight and narrow path, as a helpful, unselfish neighbor, and as a self-sacrificing worker in her church, Eliza Rockefeller had many fine characteristics.[28] The lessons in the duty of giving that she

[27]In 1937 I was told something of Nancy Brown by Mrs. John Willcox, daughter of Jacob Rockefeller and cousin of John D. Rockefeller, residing at Richford. She was emphatic as to the kindliness and ability of Mrs. William Avery Rockefeller. She also repeated the neighborhood story that William Avery Rockefeller was the father of two children by Nancy Brown, and in later life made financial provision for them; both becoming women of character and usefulness. It has been impossible to verify or disprove this tale.

[28]Numerous people still living knew Mrs. Rockefeller, especially in Cleveland, and have expressed to me their admiration for her.

impressed on her son were destined to make history. She and her mother-in-law, Lucy Avery Rockefeller, were alike in their strength of character, religious faith, and belief in thrift, industry, and order. On the other hand, she and her husband were never made to understand each other, and in time grew far apart.

John D. Rockefeller inherited much from his mother in self-discipline, reticence, patience, inner equanimity, and a somewhat unlovable austerity. He inherited much from the Rockefellers and Averys in enterprise, adventurousness, energy, and tenacity. It was a remarkable blend, and we shall find in him some contradictory qualities.

v

The child born on July 8, 1839, was not long to remain at Richford, and once he left was seldom to return. John D. Rockefeller retained only a hazy memory of the neighborhood. "I remember very clearly the brook that ran near the front of the house," he said as a man, "and how careful I had to be to keep away from it."[29] His mother instilled this caution. He remembered still more clearly the brook in front of his grandmother's door, and the grandmother herself in her red-painted house, an indication of her strong personality.

The supposed Richford birthplace, as we have said, no longer stands, though tourists are sometimes shown a structure mistakenly said to be it.[30] The clapboarded house faced south when the Rockefellers occupied it. The main structure measured twenty-two feet six inches in breadth, and sixteen feet seven inches in length, while it was eleven and a half feet from ground to eaves.[31] It was solidly built of timbers axe-hewn from the neighboring woods. The one-story extension to the left, facing the road, for stable and woodshed, was about three quarters the size of the house, and helped to cut off the cold westerly winds. All the rooms were small and low-ceiled. The

[29]Inglis, Conversations with Rockefeller.

[30]Correspondence in the office of John D. Rockefeller, Jr., shows that in 1936 part of the alleged birthplace, taken to New York and placed in storage there, was offered for sale to John D. Rockefeller, who was not interested. It had been bought of Mrs. Carrie Rockefeller, a cousin who owned it and lived in it, by a resident of Brooklyn, allegedly to be set up at Coney Island. When this plan was given up, it was sold to another holder. John D. Rockefeller revisited Richford at various times, but with characteristic modesty rejected all ideas of preserving any memorial of his birthplace.

[31]Mr. W. O. Inglis made careful measurements while the house still stood; MS Biography, 9, 10.

front door opened into the bedroom already described as the scene of John D. Rockefeller's birth. It was lighted by one four-paned window facing south, and another lesser window looking east up the half-mile slope of Michigan Hill. To the rear was an even smaller bedroom. A combined living-room, dining-room, and kitchen occupied the remainder of the first story. The low attic furnished lodging for the hired girl, and storage space. Water was brought in from a door-yard well, and fuel from the woodshed. The house had two stoves, one in the kitchen and one in the main bedroom. A brick chimney was built from the attic floor up, which one biographer regards as a pathetically amusing effort to give passers-by the impression that a broad and comfortable fireplace was to be found within.[32] But country people in that day were not so much concerned over appearances! The half-chimney had a strictly utilitarian purpose, for a stove was placed in the bedroom below, and its pipe, passing through the ceiling into the upper room, was connected with the half-chimney above by an elbow. Thus while the stove gave heat downstairs, the pipe at least mitigated the winter temperature above.

Beyond doubt it was a bare little house. It could have boasted of few pictures or knickknacks, and still fewer books—for neither parent cared for reading. At night its only illumination, in 1839, would have been by tallow or sperm candle. Yet country life is seldom dull or empty, for it offers too many tasks to perform. The cellar was kept full of apples, potatoes, and canned fruit. In winter, herbs, seed-corn, peppers, and glistening yellow pumpkins would give color to the kitchen. Somewhere—probably in a dry, vermin-proof room of one of the two big barns which stood then, as long afterward, near the house—was an ample supply of salt pork, hams, shoulders, side meat. Somewhere also dried fruit would be stored, and perhaps a barrel of sweet cider for drinking and vinegar. The house was full of the life which young children give every home. Two other dwellings were within sight of the door. Frequent visits were paid by Godfrey Rockefeller and his stirring, cheerful wife, by Egbert, Jacob, and other brothers of William Avery Rockefeller, and by neighbors. In summer, with doors and windows open, the ripple of the brooks filling the ear and the soft green hills delighting the eye, the cottage was light and cheery. In midwinter, when the valleys

[32]John T. Flynn, God's Gold: The Story of Rockefeller and His Times, 20.

were choked with snow, its small, low-ceiled rooms were snug and comfortable. At district school No. 10 near by, placed on a quarter-acre lot for which William Avery Rockefeller sold the land from his farm,[33] church services were held nearly every Sunday.

When the child could toddle out of the front door, he looked down on a grassy slope to where the two brooks met, and, as Owego Creek, flowed on to Harford Mills. The streams were cold and clear, the haunt of trout which William Rockefeller, on his visits home, sometimes snared for supper. Apple trees shaded the open ground near the house. On either side hills rose nearly a thousand feet above the high level of the house itself; hills heavily wooded with pine, hemlock, beech, and maple, for the greater part of the farm was still covered with primeval forest. Probably William Avery Rockefeller had bought his last 120 acres for lumbering. Trees also dotted the rolling valley, and broke the cornfields and pastures. The creek, after bending northwest a few miles, turned southward to join the Susquehanna some twenty miles below. A part of the Rockefeller holdings was cleared land worth tilling. In summer the hired man kept up the fences, helped tend the horses and cow, grew some grain for the animals, chopped wood, and hoed the garden. Rockefeller himself had little time or taste for manual labor.

This new country to which the family had come held all the picturesqueness as well as rigor of the primitive. Motorists today can run within a few hours to many points of scenic interest—to beautiful Lake Seneca, and still more beautiful Skaneateles Lake; to the Rainbow Falls in Watkins Glen; to the sulphurous waters of Clifton Springs; to Taughannock Falls, and the heights above Cayuga Lake where Ezra Cornell raised his university. The world the Rockefellers knew was far more circumscribed, but it had something of the charm caught in the old Currier & Ives country scenes. No urban note jarred upon its rural quality. When Godfrey and William Avery Rockefeller settled on this rough tableland, the broad expanse of Tioga contained only 33,900 people. In 1836 Chemung County, a large rectangle, was carved from the western side of Tioga. This left the latter, when the next census was taken and John D. Rockefeller was

[33]Tioga Deed Book 25, 176. The quarter-acre was formally conveyed for the nominal sum of $5, under date of October 9, 1845, the school having been built earlier.

one year old, with only 20,527 population. Owego was the largest town in the county, and even Owego had not been founded until 1800. While the Rockefellers did some marketing in Harford Mills, they went for most purchases to Richford; and Richford, its site a wilderness in 1810, had not achieved its village square until 1821. The "Susquehanna turnpike" connecting the district with the Hudson, and another road running north to Auburn and south to Owego, were its principal connections with the outside world. Heavy wagons carried away lumber, potatoes, buckwheat, butter, cheese, calves, and pigs, and brought in drygoods and groceries. Nearly all the people about were first settlers, or children of first settlers.

Richford was much such a village as Franklin, not far to the south in the future "Oil Regions" of western Pennsylvania, where Samuel C. T. Dodd, later counsel for the Standard Oil, was born a few years before his chief, John D. Rockefeller, and which Dodd has vividly described for us. "The streets in wet weather were deep with mud, and in summer were grass-grown. It was a pleasure to run in our bare feet on the grass, except when the bees were in the clover, and many times we suffered from stings." Both villages were familiar with stagecoaches passing on their regular routes. Both felt a moment of excitement as "the driver merrily tooted his horn as he came over the hills," and in both the people "soon gathered at the post office to hear the latest news." Both saw occasional Indians drift through the streets. Both heard tales of bears and panthers shot, and saw hunters bring in deer and wild turkeys. Both were used to the crescendo shriek of the sawmill, and the steadier buzz of the gristmills, turned in Richford by the rushing waters of Owego Creek. Indeed, logging along this creek was one of the principal industries of the township. Both Franklin and Richford were familiar with the flights of passenger pigeons, with the autumn smoke of great forest fires west and north, and with emigrants or "movers" passing in files of covered wagons to new homesteads beyond the sunset.[34]

Communications were gradually improving, population was slowly thickening. The Erie Railroad, after preliminary public meetings at Monticello, Owego, Jamestown, and other points, came into existence in 1832—though it was to be seventeen years before its first engine puffed into Owego. The Cayuga & Susquehanna Railroad, between

[34]*Memoirs of S. C. T. Dodd, Written for his Children and Friends,* 6-9.

Owego and Ithaca—its line running a good many miles west of Rich-ford—had begun operations in 1834. It was doubtless the first railroad that John D. Rockefeller ever saw. To the north the Erie Canal, DeWitt Clinton's "Big Ditch," had been completed in 1825, and along its busy channel such towns as Syracuse, Rome, Rochester, and Lockport were thrusting their mushroom growth into areas still largely forest. All about them miles on miles of blackened stumps and half-cleared farms testified to the feverish energy with which the new population was subduing the wilderness. "There are certainly more houses, warehouses, factories, and steam engines than ever were collected together in the same space of time," wrote Mrs. Trollope of Rochester in 1832; "but I was told that the stumps of the forest are still firmly rooted in the cellars."

Another English traveller, Joshua Toulmin Smith, passed with his wife through this western country in 1837-1838. They were horrified by railroads "laid on wood—*very* shaky—dreadfully noisy and very unpleasant on account of the sparks from the engine. This arises from the burning of wood instead of coal." The stagecoaches they found even more uncomfortable, for the highways were full of ruts, mud-holes, and rocks. They ate "horrid" food, watched uncouth election parades, and were disgusted by the universal tobacco-spitting. Some towns, notably Buffalo and Auburn, with their New England set-'tlers, had handsome houses built in beautiful settings, but the fur-nishings were in general tasteless—"all here is for show." The imper-tinent curiosity of staring people, and the violent manifestations of mob opinion, also shocked the Smiths. They saw the frothy excite-ment and intolerance which accompanied Seward's election as gov-ernor over William L. Marcy, and they did not like it. "Liberty of opinion exists not," Smith concluded, "and without this the name of freedom is a mockword."

Naturally the small boy in the house near Michigan Hill had no sense of the greater land growing up beyond his woods and meadows. Sometimes he must have been taken into Richford, for his father loved to drive about in his smart buckboard behind spirited horses, and Eliza Rockefeller, starved for society, would have been eager to visit the town. It is likely that the parents travelled the seventeen miles to Owego in the fine fall weather of 1840 to see the great Har-rison and Tyler parade held there. This was the year of America's most picturesque campaign. The universal depression which followed the panic of 1837 had produced a popular uprising against Van Buren and the Democrats. In every town log cabins rose, with barrels of hard cider inside; great balls were set rolling along the highways. But the boy John was too young to know anything of this. Living on a remote farm, he probably learned nothing of public affairs until the stirring days of the Mexican War came on—the first of four wars through which he was destined to live.

II

Boyhood at Owasco

JOHN D. ROCKEFELLER was almost four when, in 1843, his parents forsook Richford for Moravia in the Finger Lake country. This removal to a richer farm in a more populous neighborhood promised to better the family in every way—in comfort, material opportunities, and social surroundings.

Some evidence exists that John's mother had never really liked the Richford neighborhood. She had married a gay, finely dressed husband, full of talk and bustle, exhaling an air of success. But the house in the wooded hills often seemed lonely when, between the ordeals of her successive childbirths, business took him away for long absences. Nobody ever knew just when he would return, and she must frequently have gazed up and down the road longing for his appearance. She also felt a wearing financial uncertainty. The ledger kept in Robbins's store, later Rich's, still exists in the Pierce store in Richford.[1] It shows that when William Avery Rockefeller was absent his family had supplies on credit, and whenever he returned he footed the bill in a lump payment. Probably he did not feel like coming back until he had gained enough to discharge the debt and cut a flourish in the village. During the late winter and spring of 1843 he was gone month after month, till the bills reached nearly a thousand dollars— a tremendous sum for that time and place.[2] An occasional letter would not greatly alleviate his wife's loneliness and anxiety.

Moreover, Eliza, brought up in a religious, thrifty, scrupulous family, wished her own household to follow the same pattern. Though she had been a fun-loving girl, years and responsibility brought out the Scotch severity in her temperament. With her stern piety, she

[1] It existed there in 1937, when I inspected it. [2] Robbins's ledger.

28

could have felt little liking for some of the Rockefellers living on Michigan Hill; a group which, with the last of Godfrey's ten children growing to independence, really deserved the name of colony.[3] All the Rockefellers were "smart," and men like Egbert were of fine character.[4] But neighborhood stories suggest that some were no great churchgoers and were "worldly" in a way that she reprobated. They were fond of taverns, turkey-shoots, barn dances, raccoon hunts, and other boisterous frontier amusements; they liked horse dickers and games of chance. Several, far from being industrious and saving, were easygoing and improvident. William Avery Rockefeller was a teetotaler, but at least one of Godfrey's sons shared his father's conviviality. Chauncey Rich, the clerk in Robbins's store who soon became its owner, or perhaps Robbins himself, once bet Jacob Rockefeller, a charcoal-burner living in Robinson Hollow, that he could not keep a temperance pledge for a stated period. If he kept it and came to the store sober, he would be forgiven part of his debt. He won the wager, for the ledger bears the entry:

"Allowed Jacob Rockefeller, for not drinking, five dollars."

Nor did Eliza like the general moral tone of the Richford community. It had too much frontier crudity, turbulence, and laxity. Her native town of Niles had been settled years earlier, largely by New Englanders who showed all the thrift and moral principle of their ancestors, and she longed for its sobriety. Long after John D. Rockefeller had become rich, he told his Cleveland minister, Doctor C. A. Eaton, that he was glad he had left Richford when young, for it was a loose and irreligious place. The daughter of Chauncey Rich took him to task for this verdict,[5] but whether just or not, it reflected a conviction that he had evidently absorbed from his elders. Liquor from the local distillery was cheap, drinking was general, and after prolonged and exhausting labors, the country blades liked rough amusements. The Congregational church was too far away for Eliza to leave her young children and attend, especially in bad weather.

[3]Of the ten children one died in infancy; the others were five sons and four daughters. The four sons born after William Avery, and growing up in Richford when John D. Rockefeller was an infant, were Norman (b. 1812), Jacob (b. 1816), Miles Avery (b. 1821), and Egbert (b. 1827). *Transactions of the Rockefeller Family Association, 1905–9*, pp. 252, 253.

[4]"I never knew a Rockefeller who wasn't smart," one aged citizen of Richford told me in 1937.

[5]She so told Mr. W. O. Inglis in 1917; Inglis, Notes.

Still another of Rockefeller's impressions may have come from his mother. "It is unfortunate for my ancestors that they settled in Richford, where the land was poor," he said.[6] "The country there is beautiful, but the settlers wasted their energy in trying to get the stumps out of the ground, and trying to make crops grow in the poor soil." He was perhaps thinking of an uncle, David Rockefeller, who lived in the neighborhood till his death in 1890 at ninety-one, or another relative, David, who died there in 1882 and is buried in the Harford Mills cemetery. Eliza doubtless talked of Richford in such terms, for in contrast with the rich valley about Niles, it seemed to her a stony district of marginal land in the backwoods. Moreover, she realized that the school facilities were wretched. The Teachers College Library at Columbia contains a notebook used by the county superintendent of schools for Tioga County in 1841–42. His report on Richford District No. 10 refers to the school as being near the residence of "Mr. Rockefellers." The note goes on:[7]

Feb. 28, 1842. Visited the school alone only six pupils present School House built of logs very open & inconvenient a mere *shanty* wholly unfit for a School House School small and backward. District contains only about 7 or 8 families. Teacher poorly qualified.

For several years William Avery Rockefeller probably had financial reasons for not moving. A third child was born on May 31, 1841, and named after the father. Even in a new country three children are a financial burden. The hired man and girl cost money. But when the medicine peddler returned from his long absence in 1843, it was with full pockets. As usual, he drove a new team and told gleeful tales of his trading. Apparently it had been an especially successful trip, for even after he had paid the thousand-dollar account at the store, he had money to spare—enough of it to take his family to a new and better home.

In peddling medicine and trading, "Big Bill" had explored western New York with some thoroughness. He had noticed opportunities for timber-cutting on Lake Owasco. Now he let it be known that they were going to a farm near Moravia, which stands at the southern end of the lake as Auburn stands at the northern; a farm not far from Niles, where Eliza's father and many girlhood friends were still liv-

[6]Inglis, Conversations with Rockefeller.   [7]Page 64 of notebook.

ing. Early summer of 1843 found the girl and man who had ridden down the valley six years before as bride and groom riding back as sedate parents of three children, with two wagons full of furniture and other belongings. They left behind them Godfrey, now sixty, who lived fourteen years longer, and Lucy, who survived the Civil War, dying at eighty-one. Both parents lie along with many other Rockefellers at Harford Mills.[8] Eliza was now twenty-nine, William thirty-three. They might well have felt triumphant and hopeful. Their children were bright and healthy—Lucy a girl of six, John almost four, William completing his second year. They had left a farm at Richford which they were to sell two years later to Peter and Henry Decker of that town for $1700.[9] Moreover, they were entering the Owasco Valley with sufficient ready funds to establish themselves. Surely John Davison could no longer doubt that his daughter had done well for herself.

II

The new home of the Rockefellers, more than thirty miles from Richford, was not reached till the third day. The family travelled north and slightly west through Harford, Dryden, Freeville, and Groton into Moravia. As they went the hills dropped lower and lower until they died away altogether, giving place to gently rolling country, with blacker soil, larger barns, and more prosperous-looking houses. On every side they met indications of a richer, pleasanter country. Their destination was a ninety-two acre farm four miles north of Moravia, and about three miles southwest of John Davison's place. William had bought it on October 29, 1841, of Gilbert and Elizabeth Roseboom of Niles, paying $1000 down and giving a mortgage for $2100 more.[10] It lay near the southern end of Owasco, one of the smaller Finger Lakes, above the rough road that skirted the lake on the east.

The region had long been famed for its deep, rich soil. The Cayugas and Senecas, occupying the district in common, had farmed

---

[8]The gravestones show that Godfrey Rockefeller died September 28, 1857, aged 74; that his wife, Lucy, died April 6, 1867, aged 81. Other inscriptions commemorate David Rockefeller, who died July 23, 1890, aged 91; and William H. Rockefeller, who died May 5, 1882, aged 64.

[9]Cayuga Deed-Book 44, p. 33; sale made Oct. 29, 1845.

[10]Cayuga Deed-Book 65.

here, growing corn as fine as that which amazed James Clinton's soldiers.[11] It was in Cayuga County that Jethro Wood nearly twenty-five years earlier had patented his famous cast-iron plow, the best then made. Legends of the Iroquois, called the Romans of the Indian tribes for their skill in government and prowess in war, gave the district a romantic past, an atmosphere of its own. Owasco Valley had been filled by settlers soon after it had been surveyed into townships in 1790, and by 1843 had taken on a maturity and stability that Richford had never attained. People already said that it was a singularly wholesome country, healthful for Indians and whites, livestock and game. It gradually gained a reputation as a land of big men and big trees, surviving to be old men and old trees. Today some elms in that country are said to be 350 years old, and in 1918 the town of Moravia boasted that, of its 2000 people, 195 were past ninety.

Eliza Rockefeller's family had been among the first settlers of Sempronius township, from which in 1833 the towns of Niles and Moravia were partitioned. Abraham Selover, her maternal grandfather, had bought 200 acres of land there in 1796, apparently from a land speculator, William Vredenburgh of New York City, who had earlier invested in the future of the new country. John Davison, her father, had made a similar purchase of 150 acres in 1801, and had married Abraham Selover's daughter Cynthia. His wife died about 1825, when Eliza was a child, and the older Davison girl, Mary Ann, then fifteen, had acted as a mother to Eliza until John Davison married again. Both Selovers and Davisons, according to tradition, had come from New Jersey.[12]

At the northern end of Owasco Lake, twelve miles long and from one half mile to two miles in breadth, lay Auburn, called after Goldsmith's "loveliest village of the plain," and home of the rising statesman William H. Seward. The wide elm-shaded streets, neat lawns, and thrifty houses gave it a New England look. Its domed courthouse, its old Western Exchange Tavern, with wide piazzas, its theological seminary, and its penitentiary were famous landmarks. Not many miles northward ran the Erie Canal. Syracuse and the salt-making settlement of Salina, soon to merge, stood not far to the

[11]See E. S. Storke, *History of Cayuga County, passim.*
[12]I have talked with a granddaughter of Mary Ann (Davison) Van Duyne, who showed me letters of Eliza Rockefeller to Mary Ann.

northeast, directly on the canal. Both Syracuse and Auburn were distributing points to a large agricultural population, and their access to raw materials and command of markets were fast making them manufacturing centers. William Avery Rockefeller had placed himself nearer the main currents of civilization. Yet the country about the new Rockefeller farm still had the marks of a new region. Game roamed the woods, and plenty of trout, bass, and perch were found in the lake. An occasional Cayuga Indian wandered down from the north. On the hills rose great tracts of virgin timber, which at first had been reckoned of little value, but since the growth of the towns to the north was now being cut and sold. As yet no school existed in the lake district where the Rockefellers lived, and this was a matter of concern to the parents. With "Big Bill" Rockefeller it was soon to become a matter for action.

The village of Moravia, which contained about seven hundred inhabitants, had been named for the Moravian or United Brethren sect, whose missionaries had preached among the Indians before settlement was permitted.[13] The chief activity of the town centered in a cotton mill—"the Stone Mill"—which employed about a hundred hands; it had been built about 1830, using water power from a dammed stream, and continued operations until after the Rockefellers left. The most conspicuous building was the "Brick Hotel," later the Moravia House, built about 1820, a great three-story brick-and-frame structure on the lake shore, which served as a community center. It had a bar and dining-room on the first floor, bedrooms on the second, and a ballroom on the third. Young people flocked to dances in this upper room, which was also used for lectures and political meetings. Tradition states that the elder Rockefeller once seconded a temperance speaker there—a total abstinence society had been active for years. Another pretentious hostelry near by was the Cascade House, a great yellow edifice overlooking small waterfalls near the southern end of the lake, and drawing many visitors in summer. Its owner was much interested in lumbering. The Rockefeller family traded at Jewett's general store; sometimes on Sundays Eliza, there being no Baptist group, went to the thriving Congregational church.

The Rockefeller house stood on a grassy knoll eighty feet above

---

[13]James A. Wright, *Historical Sketches of the Town of Moravia from 1791 to 1818.*

the Lake Road, and perhaps a quarter mile from the eastern shore. From the front windows the family could look through the framework of two great pines that shaded the lawn, past a barn and a carriage house on the opposite side of the road, to the sweep of blue water beyond. Every clear morning they saw the sun kindle it to a rosy blush; every afternoon the great hill which rose sharply behind them threw its black shadow first far out on the lake, and then clear across it. The green slopes of the opposite shore rolled off into woods and meadows, and the dark wash of forested hills in the distance. The lake itself was clear and cold, the stones on the bottom visible far from shore. A brook which curved about the knoll fell tinkling down the well-wooded slopes to the lake. It was a beautiful country.

The house when the family arrived was a small frame structure of five rooms, which William Avery Rockefeller with characteristic enterprise immediately enlarged by a front addition that became the main part of the building. When remodelled, the lower story contained a living-room about sixteen feet square, lighted by windows facing west and south, and another large room separated from the first by double-leaf doors. The original five rooms of the old part of the house had been converted into two—a large kitchen and a store-room.[14] The upper story of the addition contained three small bedrooms, which had no interior finish. Once more two stoves heated the whole house, one in the living-room, with its pipe passing through the sleeping chambers of the children above, and one in the kitchen. The upstairs bedrooms, with no plaster or panelling, let in the whistling winter winds and sifting snow, but were none the less healthy for that. The water supply was brought from the brook at the top of the knoll by a small wooden flume.

It is evident that this second residence of William and Eliza Rockefeller, which was destroyed by fire in 1926, but of which good photographs exist, was commodious and well built. For seven years it was the family home, and the Rockefeller children later testified to its comfort. Taken by itself, it constitutes a refutation of the old story that John D. Rockefeller's boyhood was passed in an approach to poverty. Mrs. William A. Rudd, his sister, has spoken scornfully of these persistent legends. "Such tales are very ridiculous," she said.[15]

[14] Mr. W. O. Inglis took measurements before the house was burned down. Postcard pictures of it are still sold in Moravia.
[15] Inglis, Notes of Conversation with Mrs. Rudd, 1917.

"We always had plenty to eat and wear, and every reasonable kind of comfort. We were not rich, of course—far from it; but we had enough to eat and use and save—always."

III

Of William Avery Rockefeller's financial position at this time, or at any time, it is impossible to speak in detail, just as it is impossible to say much of his pursuits. But the immediate rebuilding of the house argues prosperity. He still owned the Richford farm; he had paid $1000 down on the new place, and cancelled the $2100 mortgage on it at the beginning of 1848;[16] and he possessed a good deal of personal property. Some time in these years John Davison advanced him and Eliza $1500, taking his note—for what purpose we do not know. Possibly the money went into the lumbering venture, for "Big Bill" needed capital to buy timber, cut it, and transport it up the lake to Auburn. The elder Rockefeller also invested $50 (an amount greatly exaggerated by some writers) in a joint-stock company building an eighteen-mile plank toll road along the west side of the lake from Auburn to Moravia. Such roads were then popular ventures. The Auburn *Daily Advertiser* of December 13, 1849, announcing that this one was nearly completed, published a long editorial praising them enthusiastically. The sixteen-mile plank road from Auburn to Cato, it remarked, already finished and receiving tolls, had reduced the price of cordwood in Auburn from $7 to $3.50 a ton, and had raised land values all along its line. William paid his $50 in five instalments in the first half of 1849.[17] Meanwhile he still engaged in various kinds of trading and went on long trips afield.

The vibrant, jovial "doctor" soon became a prominent figure in Moravia. Men remembered him well more than sixty years later. "He was a big athletic man with bright eyes and a hearty laugh," said David Dennis, one of John D. Rockefeller's schoolmates, "and no matter where he went you'd see people turn to listen to him."

[16]Jan. 3, 1848; Cayuga Mortgage Book 30, p. 345.
[17]Papers of the Auburn and Moravia Plank Road Company are kept in the rooms of the Cayuga County Historical Society. Rockefeller took Share No. 51 of 600 shares of $50 each. He made two payments of $2.50, one of $5, one of $15, and one of $25. The road was sold at auction on Sept. 28, 1852, for reorganization, but so far as the records show, he failed to redeem his share.

Another Moravian emphatically declared: "He seemed to take command wherever he went." This was the masterful quality of the Averys. His love of mystification persisted. It was said that he invariably left on his long trips at night, and returned unannounced at night. To maintain a partial cloud about his affairs, he would talk freely of undated and unplaced adventures, but baffle all inquiries by an evasive retort or mocking laugh. Once Dennis's father asked where he had got a new vehicle and smart team.

"Don't think I stole 'em, do you, Sam?" William Rockefeller replied.

"Well, didn't you?" Sam Dennis returned, hoping to draw the trader out.

"He didn't answer a word," said Dennis's son in telling of the conversation in 1917;[18] and it is evident that he retained the feeling of doubt that he had felt as a boy, and that Rockefeller with inner amusement doubtless wished to create. The sense of a curtain drawn across part of his life seems to have given him much gratification. He liked to arouse wonder, and men would marvel all the more when he appeared out of the unknown with dashing horse, shining buggies, new clothes, and a bulging wallet. This instinct was to be transmuted years later into pure reticence in his son. John D. Rockefeller was to show all his parents' taciturnity, and nothing whatever of his father's sense of showmanship.

This showmanship, if neighborhood stories have any truth, took picturesque forms. Dennis tells us that William liked to keep large sums of money in his house. "There I've seen it—ones, twos, threes (we had three-dollar bills then), fives, tens, twenties, fifties, all corded like wood and the bundles tied with twine." He records also that "Big Bill" exhibited to his father and some others a three- or four-gallon pail apparently filled to the brim with gold pieces. He spoke as if a bucketful of money had been one of his ambitions. "There! I've been after it a long time and now I've got it!" Though we may be sure no three-gallon pail was filled with gold, this story may have some foundation. After the widespread bank crashes of 1837 many businessmen with far more capital than the elder Rockefeller—Peter Cooper was one—refused to trust banks, and kept their funds in home

[18]Inglis, Notes of Conversations in the Moravia Neighborhood, July-August, 1917.

or office.[19] John D. Rockefeller asserted that his father often had large sums about his person. "He made a practice for many years of never carrying less than $1000, and he kept that in his pocket. He was able to take care of himself, and was not afraid to carry his money."[20]

Certainly "Big Bill" had perfect faith in his strong right arm and sledgehammer fist, in his tremendous natural energy. "He was a big, powerful man," says Dennis, "as quick as a flash, and afraid of nothing." Like Abraham Lincoln at the same time farther west, he prided himself upon being the best athlete in his neighborhood—though he was more of a Denton Offut than a Lincoln.[21] "I heard from Cyrenus La Monte," declares John D. Rockefeller, "that my father could stand beside a fence and jump over it backward." He was known throughout the countryside as a crack shot. In the woods he always carried a gun, and frequently brought back game. He owned several rifles, one a remarkably fine piece with telescopic sights. He set up targets on an old pine in one of the meadows, and fairly riddled the tree; he could hit swallows and hummingbirds on the wing. Once, it is said, he won a bear cub at a marksmanship contest, and used to put it through various tricks with enormous gusto. Just before Christmas in 1850, according to Aaron K. Clark of Moravia, another schoolmate of John's, he bought chances of a hotelkeeper at Locke Pond (now Lake Como) who set up turkeys to be shot at, and hit three in succession at thirty rods—"Yes, rods!"[22]

According to other neighborhood legends, the elder Rockefeller used his marksmanship at public gatherings to help sell his medicine. To draw a crowd he would set up a manikin, place a clay pipe in his mouth, stand off two hundred paces, and shatter the pipe to fragments. He made a standing offer of ten dollars to anybody who could duplicate the feat. Once at a county fair in Cortland a humorous incident took place. Rockefeller propped up his manikin, a large crowd assembled, and he stepped back to take careful aim. A curious bystander not far from the target was calmly puffing away at his

[19]Cf. Allan Nevins, *Abram S. Hewitt, With Some Account of Peter Cooper.*
[20]Inglis, Conversations with Rockefeller.
[21]It will be recalled that Denton Offut, whose boat Lincoln got over the Sangamon dam, wore in public a sash of varicolored ribbons from shoulder to hip; advertised himself as a veterinary surgeon; and professed to have a secret way of whispering in a horse's ear by which the most vicious brute could be controlled.
[22]Inglis, Conversations in the Moravia Neighborhood, 1917.

pipe. Bill moved his rifle imperceptibly, fired, and blew the pipe of the unsuspecting farmer to smithereens. Badly frightened, the man dropped as if he were shot. But Bill laughed, ran over to help him to his feet, and pressed a ten-dollar bill upon him. "Go and buy yourself a pipe," he said. "The temptation was too great—I couldn't help myself."

He was credited also with being a ventriloquist, and with amateur hypnotic powers—for interest in Mesmer was then keen. There is even a tale that he once met a farmer whose cutter was stalled in the snow, bet him $50 that he had a rooster in his sleigh which could pull the cutter free, and made the rooster do it—or seemed to. "I threw a mist over his eyes," was Rockefeller's explanation.

This man who showed such versatile energy, who "took command everywhere," is credited with mobilizing public sentiment in his neighborhood for building a schoolhouse. When the decision was made, Rockefeller suggested that the school be placed in the center of the district. The problem of finding the center having been delegated to him, he solved it by an ingenious device. He drove from the northern boundary to the southern, counting the revolutions of his wagon wheel. Then he drove from east to west. Finally, by driving half the revolutions in each direction, he fixed the spot where the school should stand. This turned out to be about a mile and a half from his own house, a healthful walk for Lucy and John. On Sundays the building was sometimes used for religious services, an arrangement in which Eliza Rockefeller was peculiarly interested.

William Avery Rockefeller gladly assumed other community responsibilities. For a time he was charged with collecting the school taxes, and he showed an iron will behind his hearty good nature. A farmer named Bowen would not pay his tax, although often and pleasantly requested to do so. He said he was too poor. But if he thought that the affable Rockefeller could be put off indefinitely, he had mistaken his man. Rockefeller marched into his barnyard one day and seized a cow as security for the district bill. There was a glint of steel in his blue eye when Bowen came to protest; no taxes, no cow—and the farmer quickly paid up.

Busy fathers are not always the best fathers, but William found time in these years to give careful attention to his children, and particularly the boys. It was a steadily growing family. Mary Ann, named after Eliza's motherly sister, was born August 24, 1843, and twins, Franklin and Frances, came on August 8, 1845. The father was at home on both occasions to make sure of the comfort of his wife. He made an affectionate head for the entire family, but naturally bestowed his shrewdest and most watchful tutelage on John and William.

He fostered his own ebullient spirit of play and liveliness in the boys. "He always wanted something going on at the house," said his eldest son in 1917, "singing or music of some sort." The house boasted a melodeon, on which the father and later his daughter Lucy played, while Eliza sang well. It was under his father's encouragement that John developed a love for song and music that followed him throughout his life. William rowed with the two boys on the lake and taught them how to fish. Seventy years afterward John could remember the perch they took, "fine big yellow ones, some of them as big as half a pound, and delicious to eat." At his own expense William stocked the lake with pickerel, a display of initiative which his son remembered clearly. "That's the kind of man he was; he'd get a thing done while his neighbors were beginning to talk about it."[23]

Once when they were out rowing—"it was cool and clear by the shore," said John D. Rockefeller in after life—little William kept expressing a desire to swim. He was a plump, lively youngster, not more than six, and had never attempted to paddle. But his father felt that such pertinacity should be both rebuked and rewarded, and chuckled: "Very well, my boy; you shall swim." Taking Will by the waistband, and swinging him clear of the boat, he dropped him into the water. As the boy rose, the father caught him by the collar and gave him his first instruction. John, quieter and more cautious, did not learn to swim until after he had left Moravia.[24]

But William was essentially a businessman, highly practical, whose main desire for his sons was that they become shrewd, alert businessmen. As they grew older, he gave them business lessons. He taught them something about lumbering, wood measurement, buying and selling; he laid down rules for driving a bargain. "Among other things," said Rockefeller later, "I was sent over the hills to buy cordwood for the use of the family, and I knew what a cord of good solid beech and maple wood was; and my father told me to select only the

[23]Inglis, Conversations with Rockefeller.   [24]Idem.

solid wood and the straight wood, and not to put any limbs in or any 'punky' wood. That was a good training for me. I didn't need my father or anybody else to tell me how many feet it took to make a cord of wood . . ."[25] He trained them also in habits of industry, punctuality, and thrift. It was all done in a gay, hearty, interesting way, but so effectively that it sank into their consciousness. They grew up to worship their father, who apparently could perform most practical labors better than anybody else, and who carried his power and magnetism about him as a kind of radiance. His influence was burned sharp and deep into his oldest son, with whom it remained even ninety years afterward as a living impulse, and was transmitted to his children as a family legend.

IV

Yet we may well question whether the father's part in the training of John D. Rockefeller was any greater than the mother's. If William's was the more spectacular influence, Eliza's was the more constant. She was drawn close to John by her husband's recurring absences, and by the fact that he was obviously more like her than any of the other children. As the man gradually went out of her life, the youngsters increasingly filled the void; and of them all, John impressed her as offering the firmest reliance and support. Will, even as a youngster, showed the carefree robustness and restlessness of his father. Later, as a man, he was to be the salesman and "mixer" when the two brothers were associated in business. John was more of a Davison. While he grew sturdily, he was thinner, more serious-faced and more conscientious than Will. Even at Richford he had shown the hard reticence of the mother and her steady persistence. He developed, too, as the years passed, a certain serenity of character, an unemotional patience that was like hers. He had her religious bent. "He was a quiet boy; he seemed always to be thinking," was the report of every one in Moravia who spoke of him later. By instinct he was receptive to Eliza's grim, careful training, and her influence was as potent with him as his came to be with her.

As a mature man John D. Rockefeller spoke of his mother's stern guidance and discipline. She fortified the father's teaching as to re-

---

[25]Speech to the Young Men's Bible Class of the Fifth Avenue Baptist Church, N. Y. *Evening Mail*, Oct. 21, 1905.

sponsibility and applied it to instill neatness, economy and industry. No child ever came into the Rockefeller house with muddy feet; mats lay at all the doors and they were for use. Nobody was permitted to make unnecessary work for others. "We children were not allowed to cut our nails here or there in the house, where some one would have to sweep up the scraps." Eliza had them go "to the proper place where they could be disposed of." Moreover, "she never tolerated any wasteful thing." She made them work. Drawing a string across the kitchen-garden, she said: "John, you take care on this side of the string, and Will, this side is yours. You will each keep your side clear of weeds and cultivate the ground."[26] And they did. Yet these chores were performed with little sense of hardship. Eliza had a way of getting things done easily—a way that her son was to inherit. "I never saw her cross or ruffled or out of patience with any one," testified David Dennis in describing her. "I never heard her scold the boys. She had a way of smiling and speaking quietly and making them do whatever she ordered, without any trouble. No matter how much her husband was away, she managed the farm, hired hands to do the farm work, and got along well! John had a good deal of her quiet way." Dennis was emphatic as to her fine qualities. "She was as fine a woman as ever lived. She was an angel upon earth."[27]

However, beneath her smiling taciturnity lay plenty of courage. When John D. Rockefeller revisited the house in 1919, he recalled an incident of those lawless times. Some thieves came one night when the father was away. "Mother had whooping cough and was staying in her room so that we should not catch it. When she heard thieves trying to get at the back of the house and remembered that there was no man to protect us, she softly opened the window and began to sing some old Negro melody, just as if the family were up and about. The robbers turned away from the house, crossed the road to the carriage house, stole a set of harness and went down the hill to their boat at the shore." Eliza could also show a severity that the growing boys seldom cared to challenge. She managed them by tact and encouragement when she could, but did not spare the rod when she thought punishment a necessity. John recalled being

[26]Inglis, Conversations with Rockefeller.
[27]Inglis, Conversations in the Moravia Neighborhood, 1917.

tied to a tree back of the house on several occasions for a sharp whipping. "I remember that when our dear mother would 'lay on Macduff,' she would say, 'I'm doing this in love,' but it hurt just the same. . . . On these occasions I made my protests, which she heard sympathetically and accepted sweetly—but still laid on, explaining that I had earned the punishment and must have it."[28]

Doubtless he did earn a few whippings. For with all his gravity and quiet industry, he showed an impish humor. His brother Will used to call from upstairs just after the two had gone to bed: "Mother-r! Won't you *please* make John stop?" In relating this, John D. Rockefeller would conclude with a quizzical smile: "Certainly I was not bothering him." His sister Mary Ann later recalled him as a tease. "He would plague us all with his jokes, always with a straight, solemn face. He kept after poor Will so much that a hired man who worked for us used to say: 'I hope to live to see the day when Will will turn on John and give him a good thrashing.' Well, he did. It may not have been a thrashing exactly, but Will took hold of John and gave him such a tussle that he was not plagued so much after that. . . . But he never got over being a tease until he was grown up. When I was still a small child in Cleveland I remember John pulling a sled I sat on. He managed to give it a twist so that it spun around and slid down a hole in our yard. . . . My! How polite and surprised he seemed to be!"

In these years the parents gave John his first opportunity to earn a considerable sum by turkey farming. The family kept both chickens and turkeys, finding the half-wild habits of the latter troublesome. Every spring several turkey hens "stole their nests"; that is, wandering to some distant weed-grown fence-corner, accumulated their eggs and hatched their broods. It was a perilous venture, for the eggs of small turkeys often fell a prey to cold, rain, weasels, rats, or foxes. One spring Mrs. Rockefeller knew from the sly disappearances of a turkey hen that she was laying a secret nestful of eggs. The boy was called in.[29]

"John," his mother told him, "if you can find that nest, save the eggs, and see that the chicks are safely hatched, I shall let you have them for your own."

[28]Inglis, Conversations with Rockefeller.
[29]Rockefeller told this story of the turkeys frequently: I have met various men who had it from him.

The boy set about his task with thoroughness. Next morning he watched the turkey as she sauntered out of the barnyard and up a weedy slope. He took a parallel course half the field distant. The hen was suspicious; she stepped cautiously, craning her neck about, and veering from her intended destination. John waited with tenacious patience. Little by little the hen approached the woods and dived into the brush, where he lost her.

Next day the maneuvers began again, and once more the hen eluded him; but he was not to be defeated. Finally he discovered the nest. Then, day by day as the eggs were laid, he carried them into the house, leaving a small collection of china knobs behind. When the hen was ready to set, she was brought into the barn, given all her eggs, and carefully shut up. Finally the shells broke and the beautifully marked birds, brown as quails, hatched out. John had a coop ready, and provided the turkeys with curds, bread crumbs, and water.

All summer the boy tended his brood vigilantly, keeping them out of the tall wet grass, guarding them against wild animals and hawks, and encouraging them to feed fat on grasshoppers. That fall he sold eight or ten turkeys. As he paid no overhead in this first business operation, a respectable sum went into the blue china bowl on the dining-room mantel which was his savings bank. Next spring he was able to buy three more turkey hens and raise their broods. His little hoard grew until it held gold as well as silver and copper coins —grew until it required a box. "I can still see, upon the mantel, the little box with the lattice top that I kept my money in, silver and gold," he said in later life.

As the money increased, he formed another habit which was always to be associated with his savings. He began to give. This was required by his mother as part of his attendance at the Sunday school in the little schoolhouse back on the hill.[30] Later he could hardly remember when he had not given away part of his little surplus. "From the beginning," he declared, "I was trained to work, to save, and to give."

The boy's father, when this venture with turkeys occurred, was apparently engaged in various enterprises near Moravia and Lake Owasco, especially lumbering. He bought growing timber, engaged

[30]John D. Rockefeller wrote the author in 1936 that from earliest childhood he had gone to Sunday school; and that in Moravia his teacher was a man who had been very profane but was converted into an earnest Christian.

workmen, and in the cold winter weather had the trees logged-off and piled on the lake shore. When the spring thaws came the logs were rafted up the lake to Auburn, where pine brought $5 to $8 a thousand feet. John D. Rockefeller later remembered how his father rose at four A.M. to go to work, moving through the cold house with a lighted lantern, and disappeared into the night, the runners of his sleigh whining sharply against the snow; and he remembered how after supper his parents talked over business details.

"I had a peculiar training in my home," Rockefeller said almost sixty years later to a group in New York. "It seemed to be a business training from the beginning. I was taught to do things—simple things such as a boy could do." He was enjoined to do them thoroughly, and to appreciate the dollars-and-cents value of labor. While still a small child he learned to milk cows. "I could milk a cow as well as a man could milk a cow." He was trained in other manual skills and in self-reliance. "I was taught at the age of eight to drive a horse, and to drive him just as carefully as a man could drive him. I remember very well the instruction of my father—'My son, hold very carefully going down hill. Don't let him stumble. When you are on the level road let him trot right along.' And I shall never forget that."[31]

The boy's first coppers had gone into the china bowl on the mantel when he was only seven years old. While he added to them, first small rewards for running errands and subsequently larger sums, his father was teaching him elementary business practice. He began with punctuality, alertness, and order, and went on to specific lessons in purchasing. "He used to dicker with me and buy things from me," said John D. Rockefeller on another occasion; "taught me how to buy and sell."[32] After such transactions, he would review the bargain, pointing out errors or commending his son for astuteness of judgment. The elder Rockefeller had a firm conviction that business would rule the future, and wished his sons to make their way with unerring tread. His children appreciated his pains, and though they knew he had faults, took literally the Biblical injunction that they should honor their parents.

[31]Speech to the Young Men's Bible Class, N. Y. *Evening Mail,* Oct. 21, 1905.
[32]Inglis, Conversations with Rockefeller.

V

The country school which John first attended was good enough, as schools of that rather primitive region then went. It had been built of lumber instead of logs. Possibly it kept in session for five months of the year, though many were open only three. Whether it was heated by a stove or open fireplace we do not know. Doubtless it was much like the school which Millard Fillmore had attended at Sempronius, as a preface to his two years of reading law and working at the fuller's trade in Moravia, and his subsequent climb upward in state and national politics to the Presidency. A homely, unsystematic education was given in these simple structures, where on cold days the ink had to be brought to the fire to thaw and the teachers were often mere youths of seventeen or eighteen, who had a hard time maintaining their authority against the "big boys." Each student usually brought his own speller, arithmetic, and reader, studied his own lessons, and was heard individually or in very small classes by the teacher or by an older child acting as monitor. These rough methods had their compensations. A brilliant pupil took his own pace through *Cobb's Spelling Book* or the *English Reader,* and ciphered rapidly to the end of the *Western Calculator,* beyond which, in the opinion of rural philosophers, there were no mathematical worlds to conquer.

John had three teachers in this country school—Day Lester, a Miss Hobart, and a man named Barber. We know little of them, save that Barber tried to awaken an interest in books, and that Miss Hobart was strict. A schoolmate records that she was first brought to the district by William Rockefeller's hired man, Hiram Odell.[33] He went for her, driving a spirited bay named Hornet; and arriving near home, Hornet ran away, "whirled round a corner, pitched Miss Hobart out, and blacked both her eyes so that she couldn't go to school for two weeks." This schoolmate, Aaron C. Clark, remembered John and Will as "pretty small boys then, very quiet." He thought them well behaved and well dressed. "John seemed to know his lessons pretty well," and at recess played ball with the other boys, "but he never seemed to be overfond of it."

David Dennis retained a clearer impression of John, who was

[33]Inglis, Conversations in the Moravia Neighborhood, 1917.

four years his junior. He too thought him "quiet." He studied hard. "He was lively enough when we were out at play, but in school he paid attention to business. He was a good-sized boy, well made, quick, and active when he wanted to be; but most of the time, as I recall now, he seemed to be going along quietly thinking things over." Apparently John, while not brilliant, was an exceedingly earnest scholar. Dennis even recalled him as a great reader. "Often when I'd go over to play I'd find him deep in a book." But if this interest ever existed it soon disappeared, for later John D. Rockefeller could not recall that he had read widely. He was particularly keen on arithmetic. Once Dennis solved a difficult problem in duodecimals for him. "He asked me if I was sure it was right. Then he took the slate to the teacher and asked him if it was right. The teacher said it was. John took it away and studied it over again. Then he rubbed it out and did it all over, just to make sure he had it."

This instinct for thoroughness cropped out in other ways. Dennis relates that they played checkers. John would ponder a move minute after minute until Dennis exclaimed:

"O, come on, John. Don't sit there all day studying."

And the younger boy, not looking up, would reply:

"I'll move just as soon as I get it figured out. You don't think I'm playing to get beaten, do you?"[34]

Various incidents in the Moravia period gave the boy a glimpse of larger horizons. One, in his eighth year, was a trip to Syracuse with his father who was buying a barge-load of salt. Syracuse at that time had about 20,000 people, but to John it might have been London or Paris. Father and son went to a hotel—"a first-class hotel that charged a dollar a day"—with a marble-floored lobby, tessellated in black-and-white squares. The metropolis awed John by its miles of houses set closely together, its paved streets over which wagons rattled crisply, and its wooden sidewalks. The main thoroughfares showed crowds of people, keen-eyed and hurrying; heavy boats crawled along the famous Erie Canal; trains coughed violet jets of smoke against the sky. It was a panorama of modern power impressing for the first time a boy who had heretofore fed his eyes only upon forest, lake, and farm. Thaddeus Stevens at about the

[34]*Idem.*

same age travelled from the rough Vermont hills to Boston, gazed upon its marvels, and then and there resolved that he would become rich! With John a part of the glory of the great city was borne away—on his feet. His father bought him a pair of patent-leather shoes, and seventy years later he still recalled the luxurious gleam and fragrant odor of the glossy leather.[35]

Other events, even at Moravia, suggested a wider world. In 1848 the news of California gold ran through the East like a wind across the tops of a forest. In Moravia itself G. L. Meade gathered $500, and joined seventy-nine other men in and about Auburn who formed the Cayuga Joint Stock Company. They collected a total capital of $40,000, chartered the bark *Belvedere,* and in February, 1849, set out on their voyage around Cape Horn.

Discussion meanwhile arose of a railroad from Auburn along the lake, and worried William Avery Rockefeller over the fate of the plank road in which he held a small investment. Wagons of emigrants constantly passed the house, and the boy who inquired where they were going was told stories of steamboats puffing on great rivers, of cities springing up in the wilderness, and of new States being carved out beyond the Mississippi. His father had travelled widely—doubtless much more widely than any other man in Moravia township. He knew something about Cornelius Vanderbilt and the Astors, Peter Cooper and Samuel Slater. He knew that joint-stock companies were more and more numerous. He could tell John that Pittsburgh was making iron and glass, that Buffalo was full of flour mills, and that Cincinnati already was famous as the greatest pork-packing center in the world. He could tell him that as he had driven through York State—and William Avery Rockefeller kept his eyes open when he drove—he had been astonished by the factories rising on every hand. Had not the last census, when the effects of the depression of 1837–39 had hardly worn off, shown scores of woolen mills alone in the State? Did not Troy turn out stoves enough to heat the whole country, and boast that her horseshoes marked the highways of the globe? Was not the establishment of Zadock Pratt, over in Greene County among the Catskills, the largest leather tannery in the world? Was not Cohoes, which he could remember as once a sleepy village, now simply alive with the hum

[35]Inglis, Conversations with Rockefeller.

of machinery—cotton mills, carpet mills, and what not? Were not
Johnstown and Gloversville known all over the East for their shoes
and gloves, and turning out more every year? The profits of these
establishments, as William Avery Rockefeller knew, often amounted
to 10, 15, and even 25 per cent annually. They were filling the
land with wealthy men.

The Machine Age was already advancing. The boy John, self-contained, unemotional, intensely earnest, still lived in the Rural Age, a
hard and limited life. Every morning his mother called from the
foot of the stairs: "Come, son; it's time to get up and milk your
cow." From spring to late fall he would run barefoot over the hills
back of the house, working alone or playing with other boys. "Sometimes I'd stub my toe and get a stone bruise, sometimes a splinter
or the scratch of a thistle," he wrote later. On cold mornings, to
warm his feet, he stood on the ground from which the cow had just
sleepily risen. On winter nights the wind roared in the pine trees
along the lake shore, while the snow often sifted through the cracks
of his unplastered upstairs bedroom. He did not resent the work
and the cold; he appreciated the natural beauty of the region. "That
was a lovely home," he later exclaimed of the house by silvery
Owasco. Yet increasingly he learned of the existence of a far more
complex and exciting world—of gas-lighted streets, rumbling factories, rushing trains, men living with greater power and energy.
Was his future to be there, or among the fields and forests? If he
did not consciously ask the question, he at least felt the contrast.

III

Family Disaster

AD William Avery Rockefeller prospered as steadily in Moravia as he at first promised to do, the career of his eldest son might have been materially different. Beyond question, early adversity did much to mould and toughen John's character. For evident reasons, he said nothing in later life, even to his children, of the family difficulties which had cast a shadow over his boyhood. Yet these troubles, when viewed in due perspective, were probably an important element in his training. It is a truism that an early taste of the hard battles and bitter mischances of life, an acceptance of anxious responsibility, an acquaintance with buffets and slander, do more to strengthen the will and deepen the understanding than a softer schooling. John D. Rockefeller was to spend most of his active years in grim fighting. He was to be more widely hated, attacked, and reviled than any other man of his generation. It* was no real misfortune that, at an age when most boys are carefree, adversity hastened his maturity, taught him wariness, patience, and fortitude, and hardened his temperament.

For some years the prospects of the elder Rockefeller in his home overlooking Owasco seemed sunny enough, but a series of misfortunes struck him. One was the fatal illness of his daughter Frances, born the summer of 1845. The historian of the Cayuga County Medical Society possesses the faded daybook of Doctor William Fenimore Cooper of Kelloggsville, seven miles from Moravia, a cousin of the novelist and graduate of Bowdoin, who was family physician to the Rockefellers. He was a successful practitioner, cul-

tivated, urbane, and as an oil portrait shows, handsome. At one time
he was coroner, and at another postmaster.[1] Beginning on November 10, 1846, he records a long series of visits at a dollar each to the
home of "William Rockefellow." He was there on the 22d, the 25th,
the 29th, and the 30th of November; fourteen times during December; and eight times during January, 1847. Sometimes he charged
an additional fifty cents for medicine. The visits continued at intervals of a week or less until July 11, 1847, when they broke off
abruptly. No details are given, but clearly somebody underwent
a serious and protracted illness. We may conjecture that this assidu-
ous attendance, about seventy visits in all, was upon Frances, for she
died in 1847.

This protracted illness was evidently a serious matter. At the same
time Rockefeller's lumber business naturally diminished with the
forests. It is possible that some of his investments, like the $50 put
into the plank road, turned out badly. And finally, the popularity
which he had at first enjoyed in his neighborhood was impaired in
various ways. A man who "takes command everywhere" is sure to
create friction. Perhaps because he had outwitted competitors in his
trading operations, perhaps because he made his lumbermen do a
full day's work and was merciless with slackers, perhaps because his
flamboyant ways aroused irritation, enemies appeared. Since his
powerful physique, commanding air, and dynamic energy made
him dangerously attractive to women, he had too ready an eye for
a pretty girl. According to David Dennis, rumors of an intimacy
between him and Charlotte Hewitt, sister of his neighbors Earl and
Lew Hewitt, aroused the hostility of the two men.

It appears that the first evidence of this growing antagonism was
a charge of horse-stealing. In that rich country many fine horses
were raised for the city markets. Some farmers near Moravia who
had lost their animals looked suspiciously about for the thief. Not
far away in Madison County operated a dangerous band of outlaws,
the six Loomis brothers, whose exploits in horse-thievery, counter-
feiting, robbing houses, and arson are still a legend in upper New

---

[1]This book is in the possession of Doctor Cornelius F. McCarthy, historian
of Cayuga County Medical Society, who also has a painting of Doctor Cooper.
Two blacksmith-made obstetrical forceps which Cooper used were exhibited
in the New York State Building at the New York World's Fair in 1939. Doctor
Cooper's last call on the Rockefellers was apparently made June 16, 1848.

York.[2] One or two stock-growers, seizing upon the fact that William Avery Rockefeller would drive away with one team and later unexpectedly reappear with another smart pair, hinted that he was connected with a gang of this kind; that he received missing horses, and after running them off through a deep gully still seen near the site of his house, found a market for them on his long trips.[3] This was ridiculous; William Avery Rockefeller's honesty was never otherwise impugned, and all questions of honesty apart, he was too shrewd a man, and ordinarily found legitimate money-making too easy, to be implicated in any such perilous traffic. It appears that before long the real culprits were found. Three men of the vicinity, among them one Joshua Rosekrans, were arrested, tried, and sent to prison.[4] Tradition has it that William was a leader in obtaining the indictments; that he had heard the whispered charges against him, knew that his hired man, Scott Brower, was more definitely named, and in resentment quickly tracked Rosekrans down. The author has been unable to verify this story from the incomplete legal records of the county. All he has been able to find is that on January 18, 1844, the grand jury in Auburn indicted Joshua and Conrad Rosekrans for petit larceny—which indicates that their honesty was open to suspicion.[5]

It is certain that Rosekrans became William's bitter enemy. Generations later a son, Melvin J. Rosekrans, assisted one Charles Brutcher in composing a crude piece of fiction, called *Joshua, A Man of the Finger Lakes Country*, which combined a whitewashing of Rosekrans with a bitter attack upon William. It is a wonderful blood-and-thunder yarn, garnished with secret tunnels, trap doors, caves, rattling chains, and paths through dangerous swamps. It tells how a mysteriously sinister "Big Bill" Rockwell, coming from "Richport," settled down near the farm of the virtuous Rosecamp [Rosekrans] family. With two hired men, both possessing criminal

[2]Carl Carmer, *Listen for a Lonesome Drum*, 229–239.
[3]These stories persist in the region, told vaguely and with almost universal disbelief; Ida M. Tarbell gave them wider currency in *McClure's Magazine*, XXV (1905), 228.
[4]Flynn, *God's Gold*, 36, 39.
[5]Criminal Records, Cayuga County Courthouse, Auburn. On motion of L. O. Aiken, counsel, trial of the Rosekrans brothers was put off till the next term of court. From *Joshua, A Man of the Finger Lakes*, it might be inferred that this indictment was for the theft of logging tools, possibly from Rockefeller.

records, he not only ran off large numbers of horses, but when pursued succeeded in fastening the evidence of another theft upon the guileless Joshua and effecting his arrest. The story culminates in a tremendous courtroom scene in Auburn, in which poor Joshua is about to be sentenced to the penitentiary, when his most influential friend, Doctor William Cooper, enters and dramatically exposes Rockwell as author of the foul plot against the lad; the malefactor flees from the courtroom, hotly followed, to make good his escape; and "on that same night numerous farmers' barns in that locality burned down." This fantastic attempt at a literary revenge has deservedly become a collector's item in upper New York.[6]

But the book, however puerile, does show that one family had sworn undying hatred of William Avery Rockefeller. The bitterness growing out of the Rosekrans feud may or may not have had something to do with a far more serious charge against the trader. In the spring of 1848 a girl named Anne Vanderbeak was assisting Eliza Rockefeller with the housework. William was at home at the time, but soon left on one of his trips. Stories began to be heard of an improper connection between them. On July 23, 1849, the Court of Oyer and Terminer was sitting in Auburn, with Justice John Maynard of the Supreme Court, Judge John P. Hulbert of the County Court, and Justices Edgar W. Bateman and Samuel E. Day of Special Sessions on the bench. Among the indictments offered that day by the grand jury was one against "William A. Rockefeller" for rape, and one against the physician, William F. Cooper, for assault and battery with intent to ravish. Cooper was present and furnished $500 bail to appear at the next sessions court; Rockefeller was not there, and on motion of the district attorney his case was sent to the same tribunal. None of the evidence placed before the grand jury survives, nor did the judges express any recorded opinion of it. A search of newspapers fails to reveal any report or comment. Neither case ever came to trial. Rockefeller apparently avoided arrest, while Doctor Cooper's indictment was quashed, and he continued in honorable practice at Kelloggsville until his death in 1884.[7]

[6]Published 1927; no printer named.

[7]Criminal Records, Cayuga County. The historian, James Wright, pointed out that the indictment, unlike others on file, bore no endorsement to indicate its disposition. He believed that if the district attorney had believed in its validity he would have made some note on the subject. Legal writers on evidence emphasize the importance of a prompt complaint in rape cases.

Since the case against William Avery Rockefeller was never tried, it is impossible to determine whether the charge was true or false. It should be noted that although Anne Vanderbeak alleged a criminal attack upon her in April, 1848, the indictment was not returned until nearly fifteen months later. It may also be noted that one of the Hewitts was on the grand jury. And we have clear evidence of hostility against Rockefeller on the part of his father-in-law, John Davison. As we have seen, Davison had lent William $1500. When the Circuit Court sat in Auburn on February 5, 1850, to hear civil cases, his attorney, B. F. Hall, immediately filed notice of a suit against Rockefeller. The latter was absent. "On reading and filing proof of the summons in this case," runs the court record, "and on affidavit that the defendant has not appeared therein nor caused any answer to the plaintiff's summons to be served," the court took summary action. It ordered its clerk to accept proof of Davison's claim, and fix the amount to be paid him. Next day, after hearing the clerk's report, the court gave Davison a judgment for $1210.75, with $40 additional for costs.[8] Some of the Rockefeller clan in upper New York have said that this was a friendly suit—that it was simply a means of keeping a relative's hand upon the Rockefeller property. But this view is negatived by other evidence of the same general date.

John Davison had made his original will in the spring of 1847, dividing his property equitably among his widow and three children. After stating that he had advanced about $1500 to Eliza following her marriage with William Avery Rockefeller, "for their benefit and settlement in the world," he ordered his executors to deduct that sum from her share of his estate. This was a simple and fair provision. But now, on November 15, 1850, he added a codicil. In this he directed that all his personal property be valued. One half should be transferred without restriction to his daughter Mary Ann. The other half was to be placed in the hands of the executors, "whom I hereby constitute trustees of said fund so by me placed in their hands, to be by them securely invested or loaned, and the annual legal rate of interest of aforesaid equal half as above named, they shall annually pay to my daughter Eliza during the term of her natural life for her use and benefit. Provided, however, that if they become satisfied that the interest aforesaid is insufficient for her support, then my said

[8]Civil Records, Cayuga County.

executors may yearly pay over to her from the principal in their hands such a sum as in their opinion shall be necessary for her relief."[9] It is clear that shrewd John Davison was making certain that William should not lay hands on any part of his estate. It is also clear that he was making what provision he could against a situation in which William Avery would possibly contribute nothing whatever to Eliza's support.

William seems to have been hard-pressed financially at the time, and was perhaps beset by other creditors. On July 13, 1850, he sold his farm, now described as one hundred acres or thereabouts, to his neighbor, Lewis M. Hewitt, for $4173, taking a mortgage of $3000 in part payment. It is significant that both sale and mortgage were executed not in Cayuga County but in Tioga, where William and Eliza appeared in person before a justice of the peace to sign the instruments.[10] The mortgage, it may be noted, was duly discharged in three annual payments.[11] If Davison collected his judgment of $1250, this mortgage probably represented nearly all that the Rockefellers had left.

Whatever the precise facts surrounding the indictment, it is clear that William was absent from Moravia at the time and refused to return, or disappeared before he could be arrested. His absence was not necessarily a confession of guilt. If unable to obtain bail, he might have had to spend a weary period in prison.[12] He may also have felt that his enemies had created so much prejudice against him that he would have to face a hostile jury, and that with the girl giving her word against his, he would assuredly fare hard. It is somewhat curious that when John Davison's estate was finally settled, $50 was found owing to Anne Vanderbeak. When fifty years later, in July, 1905, Ida M. Tarbell collected what facts she could about William Avery Rockefeller for *McClure's,* she found plenty of people in Cayuga County, where the mytho-poetic process had flourished mightily, ready to tell stories to his discredit. She wrote that although "the universal verdict was that he was a good

[9]Probate Records, Cayuga County. The will was probated Aug. 9, 1858, with George Davison and Peter Van Duyne as executors.

[10]Cayuga Deed Book No. 80, p. 29. Lewis Hewitt went to Tioga to sign the papers.

[11]Cayuga Mortgage Book No. 40, pp. 490, 491.

[12]John T. Flynn writes that Davison refused to supply bail; *God's Gold,* 38.

fellow, jolly, generous, and kind," yet he possessed "all the vices save one." But it at once appeared that William had his defenders. James A. Wright, the cultivated historian of Moravia, wrote the New York *World* that, as a lifelong resident of the town, who was twelve years old when William had left it, and who had talked with many older neighbors, he could enter a sweeping denial. "I can say that there is absolutely no proof of the charges made by Miss Tarbell, or of the vices to which she refers." The accusations originated, he added, from the "false stories and foolish gossip of irresponsible persons. These gossipers can be found in any community. They are swift to speak evil of their fellow men, but never of their better qualities."[13]

Miss Tarbell also wrote that William had left Moravia "under compulsion." But John D. Rockefeller indignantly denied this. "I was a boy of eleven then—or thereabouts," he said. "If he had left 'under compulsion,' as she says, I would have known something about it. There was nothing of the sort. We moved over to Owego, and if we were fleeing from justice that wasn't very far."

Of course it is obvious that a boy of ten would *not* be told anything of the scandal or of his father's indictment; it would be carefully kept from him. Apparently William, after remaining absent the latter half of 1849, sent word to his family early in 1850 that he had found them a new home near Owego, the county seat of Tioga, some distance to the south. This time there was no farm, and he rented the house instead of buying it. It is true that Owego was only sixty miles distant from Auburn, that good roads ran between the two towns, and that a letter from the sheriff of Cayuga to the sheriff of Tioga could have been delivered within a week. The Rockefellers could not long conceal their place of residence, and William was certainly there in midsummer of 1850 to sign the deed of sale for his farm. But it is significant that in Owego we encounter a new set of traditions describing William's early appearances as few, short, and furtive. He is pictured as coming home, at first, in

---

[13]*McClure's Magazine*, XXV (1905), 229–233; Wright, *Historical Sketches of Moravia*, 362. Rockefeller had a long talk with Mr. W. O. Inglis about Miss Tarbell's article at Pocantico in December, 1920, a record of which is in the Rockefeller papers. He defended his father as a man of integrity, pointed to his scrupulous honesty in business affairs, and noted that the school district had entrusted its affairs to him. His indignation was intense.

the dead of night, throwing pebbles against his wife's window, and stealthily entering at the rear to avoid notice.[14] It is likely that he kept very quiet until the storm had blown over.

It is a mysterious matter, this indictment, and no clear judgment can be delivered upon it. We do not know what part was played in the affair by the antagonism of the Rosekrans and Hewitt families. We know nothing of Anne Vanderbeak; she may have been genuinely wronged, or may have been a hysterical, vindictive imaginer of wrong. We know nothing of the rôle of John Davison, who now apparently hated his son-in-law. Perhaps the indictment represented a real crime; perhaps it was cooked up to get William out of the neighborhood. The author must confess that he knows all too little of William Avery Rockefeller. He is convinced that no one now alive knows more. This picturesque, powerful, self-willed man seems, in his mixture of strength and weakness, and above all in the disproportion between his abilities and the work he found to do, essentially a pathetic figure. All observers have agreed upon his ability. Even the authors of *Joshua, a Man of the Finger Lakes Country,* paid unwilling tribute to him. They described him as "a splendid specimen of manhood, well over six feet tall and built in proportion," as "truly a commanding figure, with strength and will-power written all over him," and, with his kindly smiling face and shrewd piercing blue eyes, "a born leader of men."

But whatever the inner truth of this affair, to the family it represented a terrible disaster. Only those acquainted with rural communities can comprehend the stunning force with which these blows must have fallen on Eliza. A criminal indictment, with all the dread visions of prosecution and the penitentiary which it called up, was alone bad enough. It spelled irretrievable disgrace in the eyes of family and friends. The suit by John Davison and the hasty sale of the farm were other blows only less severe. They threatened poverty, and poverty also was a disgrace. The kindly yet cruel inquisitiveness of the Moravia neighbors would have been intolerable. We may be sure that a great deal of quiet weeping, interrupted by heartfelt prayer, went on in the upper chamber occupied by Eliza Davison Rockefeller. We may be sure that removal into another county, to which reports of the family troubles would not penetrate,

[14]Flynn, *God's Gold,* 47.

The supposed Rockefeller birthplace, Richford, N. Y.   A photograph taken in 1921.

Three boyhood homes of Rockefeller.

Top: House on Lake Road near Moravia, N. Y. *Center:* First house occupied near
Owego, N. Y., in 1850. *Bottom:* Second house occupied in Owego, 1850–53.

was accepted with fervent relief. We may be sure that while a proud front was maintained before the world, the mother must have kept a Spartan grip upon herself if she did not occasionally let her children see how deep was her anguish, how apprehensive her outlook upon the future.

But Eliza did have a Spartan temper; her son John, insofar as he felt the blow, developed a Spartan quality. And in those days American families were always making fresh starts, for in a new country such starts were easy. The early spring of 1850 saw all the portable goods of the household packed into a wagon. The helpful daughter Lucy; grave-eyed John, growing tall and thin; chubby, restless Will, Mary Ann, and Frank, were all installed in another vehicle by their mother. The hired hand said "Giddap," the horses trudged off southward, and slowly blue Owasco disappeared from view. Three days later found them all—doubtless with their bustling, cheery father in command—unloading the wagon before a small house on a secluded road near Owego. A fresh page of family history was being turned.

II

When John D. Rockefeller left Moravia, he bade farewell to childhood and entered upon adolescence. He passed his eleventh birthday not three months after that April day in 1850 when the family wagon drew up outside Owego. Increasingly, as the oldest of the three boys and the most responsible of the five children, he became his mother's principal reliance. She asked his advice and depended upon him for responsible tasks. Already he had assumed tacit direction of his lighthearted brother Will, and when his father was away—as William now was most of the time—he displayed a quasi-paternal authority over the entire brood. He thought anxiously of the future. His cousin, Mrs. John Wilcox, has described a visit by Eliza and her family to Richford several summers later. John drove the buggy, looked after the horse, and exercised an unobtrusive supervision over the rest; "he told the other children what to do."[15]

"What a beautiful place Owego is!" exclaimed John D. Rockefeller in later life. "How fortunate we were to grow up there."[16]

[15]Inglis, Notes, Richford, July-August, 1917.
[16]Inglis, Conversations with Rockefeller.

It was indeed an excellent place to stimulate a growing boy. As a community, it was definitely superior to Moravia. The family removals had in fact constituted a series of upward steps adapted to the advancing years of the Rockefeller children. In infancy, a home almost in the backwoods; in childhood, a better house, a farm in a thriving valley, and a larger village; now, with the need for more schooling, a rapidly growing town. Later, William Avery Rockefeller would lead his boys to a city. It was as if the shrewd "doctor" had planned to match the growth of his children with gradations from simple to complex communities. John D. Rockefeller came to feel that he had. "We left this home," he said of Moravia, "and removed to Owego, with its excellent academy and fine people and broader views. Then, in good time, the removal to Cleveland. . . . What if we had remained on the poor land at Richford, with the poor outlook? But father saw the situation and planned for our greater opportunities."[17]

The contrast between Moravia and Owego was that between a village and a small city. To be sure, even Owego retained a rural atmosphere and was primarily a country market-town. It stood at the head of navigation on the Susequehanna, whose clear waters were yet unstained by wastes or chemicals; it was embosomed by fields of corn, buckwheat, and hay, while luxuriant stretches of forest lay all about. The Onondaga name for the locality, Ah-Wah-Gah, meant "the place where the valley widens." Because the soil was rich and the river attractive, settlers had appeared by 1786, even before the Onondagas had gone, and had soon become numerous. There had been gentry in the place early in the century, for a dozen families held slaves and had accumulated modest wealth. The first inhabitants were predominantly New Englanders, at least at one or two generations' remove; they gave Owego a clean, prosperous New England look from the outset, and tended to look down upon the Pennsylvanians just to the south. The best houses offered happy examples of the New England architecture as modified by the classical influence so strong from 1800 to 1850, and some of them were furnished with elegance.[18]

After 1822, when Owego became a county seat, it had grown

[17]*Idem.*

[18]L. W. Kingman, *Some Account of the Early Settlement of the Village of Owego, Tioga County, New York, called Ah-wa-ga by the Indians.*

vigorously. In 1850 the township counted 7159 people; approximately as many as Rome, N. Y., and very nearly as many as Auburn and Schenectady, which both fell short of ten thousand. Even Rochester at this time, it should be realized, had only 36,400 people, and Buffalo only 42,260. Owego was a commercial center for as much

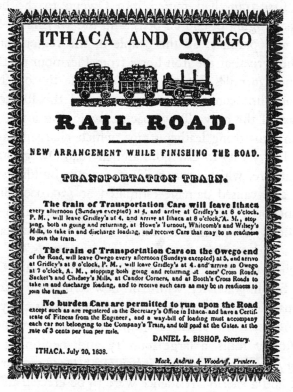

Early American 1838 timetable of the Ithaca & Owego Railroad. Though a locomotive appears in the picture, the trains were drawn by horses at this time

of the trade of the Finger Lakes district as drifted southward, and was the most important town on the Susquehanna north of Wilkes-barre. Large lumber rafts still went down the river. For a time its people had cherished hopes of a profitable commerce from upper New York, but the Erie Canal had blasted these dreams. Nevertheless, a steady rivulet of goods flowed over the Syracuse and Auburn highways and the Cayuga & Susquehanna Railroad from Ithaca, opened as a horsepower line with wooden rails, but now supplied with the crude locomotive "Pioneer," built by convict labor in Auburn prison, and able when the steam was good to keep up with a trotting horse. Moreover, just before the Rockefellers arrived, the Erie Railroad, creeping up from the east and south, linked the whole "southern tier" of counties with New York City. On June 1, 1849, the first train had puffed into Owego to the booming of cannon, the ringing of church bells, and the waving of hats, hand-kerchiefs, and parasols; all the people of the region having come to cheer the arrival of the iron horse from Piermont on the Hudson River, some 230 miles distant. But for a time the old New York-Owego stage line continued in business, and the Rockefeller boys saw the last of the heavy Troy coaches, weighing a ton each, their bodies slung on strong leather straps, which charged passengers $8 fare from Jersey City to Owego. Later in 1849 Owego had suffered a disastrous fire, which burned down seventy buildings "exclusive of barns" and caused damage estimated at $300,000. But this dis-couraged nobody. "The businessmen," writes a historian of the city, "without delay caused the erection of the present substantial brick blocks . . . and progress thereafter was continuous."[19]

Thus when the Rockefellers made their appearance Owego was a scene of bustling activity, with trim new structures lining its main streets, houses and stores still building, two railroads carrying freight and passengers, and a spirit of confident hope everywhere. It had taverns, lumber mills, a large foundry and, beginning in 1852, a shoe factory. As the county seat it boasted a large courthouse, while a new jail and a sheriff's residence were to be erected the following year. Maple-shaded sidewalks led past churches, an academy, hotels, and two newspaper offices.

One of the best-known American authors, Nathaniel P. Willis, had lived in his neighboring cottage of "Glenmary" on Owego Creek not many years earlier. Willis has celebrated in a series of essays, "Letters From Under a Bridge," the glassy peace of the Sus-quehanna, the beauty of the maples, pines, beech, and dogwood of the forests, the prosperous look of the fields of buckwheat, corn, and potatoes. He praised also the growing urbanity of the com-munity. He knew a dozen families who offered excellent dinners, and "twice as many who ask to tea and give ice-cream and cham-

[19]W. B. Say, ed., *Historical Gazetteer of Tioga County, 1785–88*, 386.

pagne. Then for the fashions, there is as liberal a sprinkling of French bonnets in the Owego church as in any village congregation in England. And for the shops . . . there is no need to go to New York for hat, boots, or coat; I mean the Owego tradesmen (if you are capable of describing what you want) are capable of supplying you with the best and most modish of these articles. Call you that 'back-woods'?"

Young Washington Gladden, later famous as preacher and writer, was working in these years as printer on the Owego *Gazette,* and contributing to its columns. In 1853 a coterie of Owegans were to establish the short-lived *St. Nicholas Magazine,* published at the *Gazette* office. The founders included Judge Charles P. Avery, who contributed a series of articles on "The Susquehanna Valley,"[20] and Thomas Collier Platt, a graduate of the local academy, who had recently returned from Yale and was destined to become Republican "boss" and Senator.

Judge Avery had been elected to the county bench in 1847, and was soon re-elected. Son of the before-mentioned John Humphrey Avery, who had served in the State Assembly, he and Lucy Avery Rockefeller had two great-grandparents in common. Had William and Eliza been inclined to court Owego society, they could easily have sought the acquaintance of the judge and his sister, Emily Eliza Farrington, whose husband later became county judge, or that of a score of other distant relatives. As many Averys lived in Owego at this time as in Great Barrington a generation earlier. But the Rockefellers never sought out these connections, and John D. Rockefeller in 1936 did not even know that any had ever dwelt in Owego.[21]

In fact, William Avery Rockefeller showed a very comprehensible instinct for retirement. With the Cayuga County indictment still hanging over his head, he would have been reluctant to claim the acquaintance of a kinsman associated with Tioga County justice.[22]

---

[20] 1853–54; copies of this magazine are now rare.

[21] Inglis, Conversations with Rockefeller.

[22] Judge Avery's aunt, Frances Avery, had married Charles Pumpelly of Owego in 1803; a prosperous merchant and lumber-dealer prominent in local politics. Their ten children bore exactly the same relationship to the Rockefellers that Judge Avery did. They belonged distinctly to the aristocracy of the town. One daughter married John Mason Parker, who became Judge of the State Supreme Court; one married Theodore Frelinghuysen, who became president of Princeton; and one married James Forsythe, who became president of

He selected a house about three miles east of town on the old River Road. The family, after living here a few months as tenants of the La Montes, then removed to a somewhat smaller building only a few rods distant owned by another neighbor, Buffington D. Montaigne. Standing about one hundred and twenty feet north of the River Road, it commanded a view across open fields to the Susquehanna, with Big Island lifting its crest of trees against the wooded hills of the opposite shore. The name of the island was later changed to Hiawatha, which, as several writers on Rockefeller have gleefully pointed out, means "He-who-seeks-the-Wampum-Belt."

As in his previous choices, William had selected a site commanding a fine prospect of woods and water. These successive homes planted in John D. Rockefeller a love of streams, lakes, and trees. He always remembered the two brooks at Richford, the long narrow lake at Moravia, and the smiling expanse of the Susquehanna at Owego. In later years his offices in Cleveland and New York looked out upon rivers, and he built his most attractive home beside one. As for trees, when he acquired money and leisure his greatest delight was to plant and transplant them, leaving prospects of hill and river between their green masses.

The new house, which still stands, was almost as large as that at Moravia, with a similar arrangement of rooms. Downstairs a wide entry-hall opened on either side into good-sized living-rooms, each with three large windows, while behind one of them was a small bedroom. A large open wood-shed stood near the house. No farm land was attached, but space in the rear permitted a garden. Here, too, were buildings for the family cow and for William's team when he was at home; for while he was away they kept no horse and had to borrow one to take any considerable trip. John was now primarily responsible for the garden and cow, for getting his brothers and sisters to school, and for a hundred other duties. With every passing year greater burdens settled upon his shoulders, and he was more

---

Rensselaer Polytechnic Institute. *The Groton Avery Clan, passim.* Even if William Avery Rockefeller was ignorant of the presence of these relatives, his mother, Lucy, must have written Eliza about them, or told her on one of Eliza's trips to Richford. If, as seems the fact, the Rockefellers moved among these and other kindred, some of them close friends of the La Montes, without revealing their relationship, it is indeed a commentary upon the family capacity for avoiding "publicity," and in John D. Rockefeller's later phrase, "sawing wood."

and more the head of the household. The relation between him and his mother grew closer, and the influence of her patient strength of character—the strongest influence in his early life—became heavier. His consciousness, too, of a distinctly more reserved and vigilant attitude toward the world, tended to mature him.

IV

"I Was Not an Easy Student"

WHEN the family settled in Owego, Eliza Rockefeller had become careworn and stern. She had borne six children, she had buried one, she had passed through harsh vicissitudes, and she could not but feel worried over the future. William Avery Rockefeller was forty, and she was thirty-six. They had reached a point in life where the question of their future was important, and it was of special concern to the forward-looking, conscientious mother, anxious to do much for her brood.

On their first arrival in Owego the family were apparently temporarily straitened for money. According to descendants of a neighboring farmer, George Danforth Higbee, the boys entered the district school in the fall of 1850 without books or any funds to buy them; and Higbee, hearing of this from his children, purchased the needed texts.[1] But the financial position of the family rapidly improved. Apparently William's next trips were successful, for within a few years he possessed not only the $3000 paid on the mortgage of the Moravia farm, but considerable additional sums.

John D. Rockefeller later recalled that his father kept funds in the Bank of Owego: "I remember well carrying a draft on the bank in the top of my hat." Within a few years William was to buy property, lend money, and give considerable amounts to his children. It should be realized that in 1850, $3000 was equivalent to at least five times as much today. As an indication of the value of money in that period and section, John D. Rockefeller later spoke of his Grandfather Davison as "a rich man." He added: "In those

[1]Miss L. M. Higbee of Willimantic, Conn., to the author, Nov. 1, 1938.

days one who had his farm paid for and a little money besides was counted rich. Four or five thousand was counted rich. My grand-father had perhaps three or four times that."[2]

Yet the future remained uncertain, and in the wife if not the husband the instinct for economy was powerful. Eliza was a frugal housekeeper, watched the pennies, and dressed the children simply but tastefully; all his life John cared little for clothes. They remained "country children" among the New York bonnets and haberdashery of more prosperous Owegans. Possibly their plain style of living was associated with William's temporary retirement from public notice, but more probably it was a matter of training; for Eliza believed that her children should be taught quiet tastes and acquire habits of industry and saving. In later life, John D. Rockefeller said he could still hear his mother saying: "Wilful waste makes woeful want." She quickly won the respect of her neighbors by her piety, responsibility, and neatness. A woman of great dignity, she always paid her afternoon calls, as her neighbor Cyrenus La Monte has re-corded, in the formality of a black silk dress.[3]

At home she governed her children with a strict discipline, touched with severity. Besides a girl in the teens and two adolescent boys, she had to manage the two youngest, Mary Ann and Frank, who were growing rapidly and beginning to assert themselves. Frank in especial showed an independent boisterous spirit that made him superficially even more like his father than was his gay, sociable brother Will. Eliza allotted the chores; she issued rules for conduct. Once she haled all five children into the house and threatened them with collective punishment for riotous play. John recalled that on another occasion when she lay ill, she discovered that he had not done some work assigned to him. She promptly sent him to the river bank for a willow switch. He prudently cut it with his knife so that it broke after the first few blows.

"Go and get another switch," his mother commanded, "and see that it is not slashed this time."

[2]Inglis, Conversations with Rockefeller. But it is clear that Davison never had as much as $15,000; records of the settlement of his estate, kept in the Rockefel-ler papers, indicate that it was not more than $10,000.
[3]Mr. W. O. Inglis collected in 1917 much data from members of the La Monte and other Owego families who have since died, while I have talked with old residents of the town.

He recalled also that once while being punished he succeeded in convincing his mother that he had not been guilty of the offense for which he was being whipped.

"Very well, son," she replied with grim humor. "But we have gone so far that we may as well proceed. It will be credited for your account the next time."[4]

One winter the Rockefeller boys had been expressly forbidden to skate on the river at night. But on a crisp moonlight evening John and William could not resist the temptation. While skating they heard calls for help, and discovered a neighbor boy who had broken through the ice and was clinging desperately to the edge, unable to crawl out. John got a long pole and they rescued him. Naturally they were full of their adventure and decided that, since they had saved a life, it would be safe to tell their mother. Never were they more mistaken. Eliza praised their resourcefulness and embraced them both. Then a light of justice came into her eyes, and she proceeded to punish them heartily for disobedience.

In summer the quietest pools on the river were full of young swimmers. John learned to paddle in a brook on the farm of George Smith, not half a mile away, and was then ready for the Susquehanna. He played ball in the spring, went nutting in autumn, and coasted in winter. Later he recalled an adventurous incident of these years. At the old River District school the children were permitted to study outdoors on hot days, and he climbed to the ridgepole with his book and sat astride it. Eliza unexpectedly appeared as a visitor and caught him. "I was taken to a council about it," he remarked. "I don't think it went further."[5]

This district school which all the young Rockefellers attended seems to have been even smaller than the one near Owego which Washington Gladden describes in his autobiography.[6] His schoolhouse was crowded with fifty to sixty pupils during the four-month winter term, their ages ranging from five to twenty. While they used any textbooks at hand, he had the benefit of a library of about 150 titles, chiefly history and travel, which was open to parents as well as pupils. But on the whole the River District afforded sound tuition, and John D. Rockefeller recalled it as "a good country

[4]Inglis, MS Biography, 36. [5]Inglis, Conversations with Rockefeller.
[6]Washington Gladden, *Recollections*, 27 ff.

school." One of his teachers, Waity Ann Soule, was particularly helpful. Her most famous pupil remembered a saying attributed to her: "Those three Rockefeller boys, with the large heads, will amount to something big some day."[7]

On Sundays the children went to both Sunday school and church in Owego, for Eliza was determined that they should have a religious training. Whereas William Avery Rockefeller, in the words of his oldest son, "was not a Christian man—but he respected it," religion was a passion with her. She asked Marcus La Monte, her nearest neighbor and a substantial farmer, to take the Rockefeller family to Owego along with his own in his roomy spring wagon. "You are a Presbyterian," she said. "You won't feel wrong about taking us to a Baptist church?" She firmly pressed money upon him for the service, which he of course refused. Thus the training begun at the Moravia Sunday school was continued without a break.

It was a training, obviously, with better teachers, larger resources, and more inspiring surroundings. The First Baptist Church—the earliest church with which John was associated—had been organized in 1831, and when the Rockefellers began to attend, the Rev. Charles Morton was filling the pulpit in the plain wooden building on Main Street.[8] His sermons played a part in John's education. So did the religious papers distributed in the Sunday school, for books in the Rockefeller home continued to be few. The boy made regular contributions from his savings, and joined in the social life of the congregation. Later, indeed, he remembered church and Sunday school as one of his principal concerns at Owego. He found the beginnings of what was to be his chief spiritual and one of his few emotional outlets as he rode every week in the La Monte wagon to the fervent services, and assumed his first obligations toward those who shared his mother's creed.

Little by little his savings began to amount to a considerable sum. Thanks to errands, to extra work for which Eliza paid him, and to the turkeys, the accumulation in the blue bowl grew steadily.

[7] Inglis, MS Biography, 34.
[8] L. W. Kingman, ed., *Owego Sketches by Owego Authors,* 100 ff. Material can also be found in Kingman's *Memorial History of Tioga County,* and H. B. Prince's *History of Tioga, Chemung, and Tompkins and Schuyler Counties.* Two other pastors to whom the Rockefellers listened were the Rev. Aaron S. Burlingame, 1851–52, and the Rev. J. M. Cooley, 1853–54.

His sister, Mary Ann, always remembered that he advised the other children to hoard too, "but none of us succeeded as he did in saving." After giving his brothers and sisters the benefit of his precepts, John took advantage of their weaknesses. "He used to buy candy by the pound and sell it to us by the piece and make a profit." And John never wasted his substance in idleness. Will sometimes paid Mary Ann a cent to milk his cow; she finally struck for two cents and got it. But John did his own work and kept his money. "Somehow he seemed to get through his tasks without help."

It was at Owego that he discovered how advantageously money could be invested. A farmer in the vicinity wished to borrow $50 for a year and was willing to pay 7 per cent interest. John's mother suggested that he furnish it, for he now had more than that sum in the blue bowl. He had learned the theory of interest in school and from his father's talk, but this was the first time that its practical significance came home to his bosom. He made the loan, and with it took a great stride into the adult world of business.

Toward the end of that year he was offered work by a neighbor, George Smith, in digging potatoes. It was back-breaking labor under a hot sun, and continued as it was for "at least ten hours" a day— so Rockefeller recalled, and it may well have been twelve—it taxed the strength of the thirteen-year-old-boy. He received three "shillings" or 37½ cents a day, and worked three days. Soon afterward the loan he had made fell due. The borrower walked promptly into the house with the $50, and an additional $3.50 for interest. John was impressed by the fact that capital earned money more easily than muscle did. It would have taken nearly ten days of gruelling labor at 37½ cents a day to obtain as much as his savings had brought him without exertion. If he had enough capital, a few thousands, it would earn more in a year than a laborer could make by working hard every day.

He came to a decision. "The impression was gaining ground with me," he said cautiously as he recalled the incident years afterward, "that it was a good thing to let the money be my servant and not make myself a slave to the money. I have tried to remember that ever since."[9]

Observers of the boy were early impressed by his steadiness and

[9]See pamphlet, "Speech Before the Men's Club, May 7, 1904."

seriousness. He worked earnestly at his studies, showing particular diligence in arithmetic. Apparently he was not much of a reader. But he was busy always, as in Moravia, pondering what he saw and heard. His family were disposed at first to think him indolent, and this was the impression he made on one boyhood associate, for then, as later, he disliked physical exertion. "John seemed a lazy boy," said this playmate afterward. "William was brisk and energetic. If he had something to do he would pitch right in and do it. But not John. If he was told to do something he would sit around and start figuring out the easiest way. He was lazy." Susan La Monte also recalled that "He used to walk slowly along, and often seemed to be thinking as he went." The meaning of this instinct for figuring out things was lost upon the playmate, but not upon Eliza Rockefeller. "I don't know what John is going to do when he grows to be a man," she remarked, "but I'm sure of one thing— he won't want. He is always studying." His sister, Lucy, put it more pungently: "When it's raining porridge, you'll find John's dish right side up."[10]

II

In August, 1852, John and Will entered the Owego Academy, while Lucy stayed at home studying music. The academy had been founded twenty-five years earlier with an endowment from church lands whose sale was authorized by the Legislature. Distant cousins of the Rockefellers, the Averys and Pumpellys, had been among the active founders, and James Pumpelly had been president of the first board of trustees. This was essentially a public high school, though the students paid tuition fees, and it had thriven. For three years now its principal had been a Scotch-Irishman of learning and vigor, Doctor William Smyth; a native of Ulster, and a graduate of the Royal Academic Institute at Belfast, who had later spent two years at the University of Edinburgh. Western New York possessed no finer scholar. In 1853, thanks in large part to his energetic administration, the academy numbered 358 students, of whom nearly two thirds were boys. Including Smyth, it had a permanent faculty of nine or ten, though several of the teachers were employed only part of the year. Charles R. Coburn taught mathematics, and

[10]Inglis, MS Biography, 34.

M. Eugène Marguerat the French language and literature. The heaviest burdens fell upon the principal and Miss Sophia M. Lathrop, "Superintendent of the Ladies' Department."

Doctor Smyth was a young man—he had been only thirty when he arrived in Owego—with a distinctly advanced attitude toward education. Though a master of Greek, Latin, and Hebrew, who taught his Presbyterian Sunday-school class from a Hebrew text, he had reflected to good effect upon ways of making education practical. He was an advocate of coeducation, for he held that "the powerful stimulus which the sexes mutually exercise over each other" was more efficacious than any other force "in developing the intellectual capacities." He believed also in making students think for themselves. As the academy catalogue stated:[11]

The analytic method of instruction is especially employed, leading to an investigation of every rule learned, and of every scientific operation performed. The student is thus enabled, not only to acquire a knowledge of the facts but also of the methods by which they can be applied to the practical business of life. The constant aim of the teachers is not only to supply the material, but to teach the pupil how to use it, and thus lead him to think and reason for himself.

Doctor Smyth insisted equally upon careful training in self-expression:

Original Composition is made a special study; every student being required to submit an essay once in fourteen days, which, after having its merits and demerits closely criticised, is afterward read in the presence of the whole school.

The practise of Oratory is considered a subject of the highest importance, and, therefore, the more advanced male pupils are required to prepare Orations, and to declaim before their fellow students and those visitors who may desire to be present. To secure readiness and facility in these branches, extemporaneous composition from Parker's Aids is frequently had recourse to, and short lectures are given embracing the principles of Rhetoric and its application to Composition.

The curriculum was broad and the tuition inexpensive. Reading,

[11]A copy of the catalogue for 1853 is in the Rockefeller papers; copies for other years of the early fifties, which I have used in Owego, differ little from it. Rockefeller told Inglis on December 1, 1920, that "I had perhaps two years in Owego Academy." It seems impossible to find school records which fix the exact date of his entrance and leaving.

The Academy at Owego, N. Y.

Top: Before remodelling in the eighteen-fifties. *Bottom:* After remodelling.

The Rockefeller children in Cleveland.

Above: John D. Rockefeller, Mary Ann, Lucy, Frank, and Will.
Below: Will, Mary Ann, and John.

writing, orthography, and mental arithmetic could be taken for
$3 each a term; English grammar, arithmetic, intellectual algebra,
and geography, with the use of the globe, for $3.50 each; algebra,
geometry, trigonometry, surveying, natural philosophy, chemistry,
history, physiology, and astronomy cost $4.50 apiece; and finally,
Latin, Greek, French, logic, moral science, political economy,
botany, mineralogy, and other natural sciences were available at
$5 each. Fuel cost each student 25 cents in the fall term and 30 cents
in the winter term. The Rockefellers probably took four or five
studies, and the cost to their parents would have been between $16
and $20 for each boy, a very modest sum even in those days. Doctor
Smyth's circular boasted of interesting scientific demonstrations and
lectures, free to all students:

As often as convenient, interesting experiments are made, illustrative
of Electricity, Pneumatics, Mechanics, and, during the past Term, a powerful Grove's Galvanic Battery has been procured, with which all the experiments connected with Galvanism can be shown, together with the operation of the Magnetic Telegraph.

Each morning John left home in time to report for school at 8:45,
doing his best to catch a ride for the three miles, and remained in
the quaint, square red-brick building, three stories high with a
central tower and bells, until four in the afternoon. Built some
twenty years earlier, it faced the public square in the very center
of town. At recess and noon he went to the "young gentlemen's"
playground. Here, under a teacher's eye, the boys were encouraged
in "such sports as are best calculated to refresh the body, exhilarate
the mind, and at the same time secure a good healthy physical development, without which, education is frequently more injurious
than useful."

Many of the students came from superior households in Owego
—households which sent their sons to Yale, Harvard, Union, or
Hamilton. Some of John's fellows showed promise, and were later
to win distinction. Benjamin F. Tracy, son of a farmer in the
vicinity, became Secretary of the Navy under Harrison; Frank
Hewitt multiplied his father's wealth, and ultimately gave $2,500,-
000 to the New York Postgraduate Hospital; Isaac S. Catlin, raising
the first company of Owego volunteers in 1861, became a general;
and George Worthington closed his life as Episcopal Bishop of

Nebraska.[12] The boy of thirteen was conscious of the quality of these companions.

"I doubt whether today you would find in any college a better lot of boys and girls," he exclaimed in 1917 as he surveyed a photograph of the student body taken in 1853.[13] "You can see," he explained, "what a fine environment it was for boys growing up, children of families of excellent principles and the best traditions; city people, association with whom was bound to benefit country boys."

But he added of this photograph: "No, my picture is not there. We were country boys." This remark is partly explained by an incident at another time, when John D. Rockefeller visited the son of his old academy principal, bringing a grandnephew. They looked at the same photograph, and the grandnephew vainly sought his uncle's face. Finally he said:

"Uncle John, I don't see your picture."

"No," replied the multimillionaire, "William and I had to remain out of it. We didn't have good enough suits."[14] Their clothes were probably homemade by Eliza.

III

The removal from the little country schoolhouse to the town academy must have been a confusing experience to the grave, silent boy. He had fallen behind town children of his years, and this intensified his reticence and reflective, brooding ways. He made little impression on his teachers, and the picture which persisted with his companions, when one persisted at all, was of a retiring lad who seemed in a brown study as he walked along. He applied himself earnestly to his books, but with no brilliant results. "I was not an easy student," he said later, "and had to labor diligently to prepare my lessons." So Cyrenus La Monte testified: "He kept trying and trying until he succeeded." Actually he had a remarkably

[12]In L. W. Kingman, ed., *Owego Sketches by Owego Authors*, 6–14, George S. Leonard writes on "Noteworthy Citizens of Owego." Boss Platt contributed a so-called poem to this interesting collection; Washington Gladden a half dozen pages of reminiscences, including an account of the Baptist Church which the Rockefellers knew so well; and Gen. Isaac S. Catlin a paper on "Owego During the Civil War."

[13]Inglis, Conversations with Rockefeller.   [14]Flynn, *God's Gold*, 45.

far-seeing and subtle mind, but his studies hardly gave it scope. He remembered several of his teachers vividly, but rather disagreeably. "We were all in fear of the man who taught grammar—great fear. Hardy, I think his name was. Coburn, who taught mathematics, was severe, but Hardy would think nothing of throwing a ruler, without warning, clear across the room. . . . He was very harsh."[15]

Adjustment to the pace of the better-schooled Owego children was no small feat for the Rockefeller boys. Their mother, dissatisfied with their early showing, realized that the La Monte children were making better progress. Asking Mrs. La Monte how they did so well, she was told that they studied every evening under Susan, the eldest, who about this time became assistant teacher of mathematics and English at the academy.

"I wonder if my children could come down in the evening and study with yours?" inquired Mrs. Rockefeller.

"They can if Susan says so," was the reply. "Susan's the head of this school."

An evening or two later John and William were submitting their textbooks to Susan and answering her questions. She testified in 1917 that only these two appeared and that her brothers gave them most of the assistance they received. She saw more talent in Will than in John. "William was much more active, and as I look back at them now I should say he appeared the more promising. . . . I have no recollection of John excelling at anything. I do remember he worked hard at everything; not talking much, and studying with great industry. He was just an ordinary well-behaved boy, plodding along with his lessons. There was nothing about him to make anybody pay especial attention to him or speculate about his future."[16]

However, in one subject he manifested particular interest—arithmetic. While other boys played ball, he preferred to keep the tally-sticks, and never made an error. It was part of the academy's analytical method to emphasize mental arithmetic; John was fascinated by this at Owego, while later in Cleveland and New York —like the financier George W. Perkins—he delighted in mental calculations. He thought the accomplishment of great practical value. He would sometimes test his secretaries or business associates

[15]Inglis, Conversations with Rockefeller. The catalogue lists nobody named Hardy. Perhaps Rockefeller referred to Edwin D. Bradley.
[16]Inglis, Conversations with Mrs. S. J. Life (Susan La Monte), 1917.

by rapidly stating a rather difficult problem, and asking for an answer without paper or pencil. If they met the test he was pleased. In his later years he declared that mental arithmetic had often saved him large sums:

"How well I remember when it helped me beat a Jew! I was buying a pipeline from Doctor Hostetter, the inventor of Hostetter's Bitters. He was an able man, a big man. It was a pipeline we had to have. I gave him a million dollars for it; no delay about that; but I had to keep him talking, talking half an hour while I was running over in my head calculations of the various plans for the payment of the interest. When we ended the talk he agreed to the terms I offered—and I had saved $30,000 on the interest by my mental calculations that had never ceased while we were talking."[17]

In Susan La Monte's reminiscences of John we find mention of the same reflective traits that struck others—"he walked slowly and seemed often to be thinking as he went along." But she recalled a second characteristic which no other observer of his boyhood noted, but which was subsequently remarked by those who knew him as a man: his affectionate sympathy for children, especially if small and pretty. "There was a little girl," said Susan La Monte, "a pretty little thing named Freer, with red cheeks and bright eyes and a sweet face. In after years Mr. Rockefeller would ask for her, and when she was left a widow in distress he aided her with a modest pension. And we had a little sister who died, a very pretty child: On the day she died John came to our house and stretched out on the ground and would not go away. He lay there all day. Even his mother could not coax him to go home to his meals."

The help which Susan gave the awkward country boy was always gratefully remembered, as was the friendliness of his district-school teacher, Waity Ann Soule. Whenever he came to Owego in after years he called upon these two. The visits to Susan La Monte, who became Mrs. S. J. Life, meant more than an expression of gratitude. They were opportunities to maintain a friendship with a remarkable woman who, after teaching in the academy, made a notable place for herself in the educational history of New York as founder and director of the Rye Female Seminary. She acquired a wide reputa-

[17]Inglis, Conversations with Rockefeller.

tion, taught the children of all three Rockefeller boys, and died in Owego, at the age of ninety-nine.

Though John later recalled with pleasure the walks to school through the beautiful Susquehanna Valley, his interest in outdoor sports was passive rather than active. According to Susan La Monte, the other boys had to prod him into helping pull their long sled up-hill in winter. A schoolmate relates that John would seldom play unless the game were one he had chosen. "He would not get mad. He would stand on the side and watch the game. But he wouldn't play." Cyrenus La Monte, her brother, recalled that while Will was always eager to join a ball-game, John seemed indifferent. He would play if needed. But "what he really liked to do was to keep the tally sticks, cutting a notch in the stick for every run that came in. . . . He never made a mistake." These fragmentary recollections give him an impresion of unobtrusive persistence, and Cyrenus La Monte attributes this characteristic to him in a superlative degree:

"Persistence! He had all the persistence there was!"[18]

Persistence, foresight, a cautious, subtle mind, love of system, and in all practical affairs, keen curiosity—these were his traits. Above all, the analytical quality of his deliberate intellect impressed careful observers. His curiosity was particularly aroused by the weekly scientific demonstrations at the school, which, given on Saturday afternoons in the principal's office, fascinated him. There, amid glass wheels for generating electricity, a galvanic battery, an awe-inspiring skeleton, and various chemicals in retorts and bottles, Doctor Smyth displayed such wonders of mid-nineteenth-century science as he could. "John was attracted by everything scientific," records Cyrenus La Monte, "and he would stand and ask questions and argue and tire you out." The telegraph was overspreading the nation, largely under the auspices of an Ithaca man, Ezra Cornell, and its possibilities excited John. "He was never done asking questions when experiments were being made in telegraphy at the laboratory."

Some notes in John D. Rockefeller's own recollections nearly sixty years later deepen this impression of a mind deliberate, reflective, subtle, and extremely canny, touched to constant inquisitiveness by glimpses of a fast-changing world. He kept a shrewd eye

[18]Inglis, Notes.

upon the shopkeepers and their changes in stock, and always re-membered the interest aroused when some one introduced the latest New York novelty, the sack coat. He similarly recalled a Frenchman who wore the first mustache that he ever saw.[19] He was keenly alive to chance meetings with "city people" from New York or Buffalo, the arrivals of Erie trains, the drays taking salt and plaster from the cars of the Cayuga & Susquehanna, the stringing of new tele-graph wires, and his father's tales of upspringing cities in the West, with banks, factories and steamboats. He meant to play a part in this urban world of incessant flux and growth; he meant to become important, like the local bankers and merchants whose wealth and character impressed their Owego townspeople.

An anecdote told later by a schoolmate illustrates this ambition. On the way to school they regularly passed the house of Gurdon Hewitt, president of the Bank of Owego and the town's richest citizen. Near it stood the homes of other wealthy men. One day as they were looking at this display of affluence the schoolmate demanded:

"John, what do you want to be when you grow up?"

John had long since come to his decision. "When I grow up," he stated emphatically, "I want to be worth $100,000. And I'm going to be, too."[20]

It was as if a present-day youngster announced—as multitudes do —his ambition to own a million. Later John D. Rockefeller said that at Owego he did not yet know what he wanted to be. But it is certain that just as he pondered many matters in his measured, care-ful way, so he pondered the power of money and of banks, factories, telegraphs, and railroads.

From his tenth to his fifteenth year, the most formative period of life, the boy found much in his surroundings to inculcate caution, reti-cence, forethought, and acquisitiveness. His mother, much-worried and hard-working, said little. His father—during his infrequent visits home—kept his own counsel on many of his activities. John doubtless learned enough about his father's unfortunate investments in the plank road at Moravia and elsewhere to understand that lack of foresight brings a heavy financial penalty. While he probably

[19]Inglis, MS Biography, 46.
[20]This story appeared in the N. Y. *World*, Jan. 15, 1899.

knew nothing explicit about the indictment, he was certainly aware that misfortune had befallen the family in Moravia, and that its results were still felt. All this had its effect upon his temperament. He schooled himself to distrust emotion, to repress his feelings. Then, too, his character was not left untouched by the straitened circumstances which followed immediately upon the sale of the Moravia farm and the removal to Owego—a period in which he and Will wore clothes "too poor" to appear in the school photograph. In those hard years saving was imperative; it became a habit, and as it grew habitual he learned how easily capital could be used to increase future gain. He meant to get ahead rapidly in the world, for he realized that his mother increasingly looked to him as her firmest dependence.

In brief, his training was excellent for his particular kind of future, and did much to make that future possible. It was not a training, unfortunately, which gave him a broad or rich view of life. He was too close to the pinching effects of the frontier; his life was too full of work—school tasks and home tasks; while his mind was too deliberate to absorb culture intuitively. Poetry, fiction, philosophy, science, painting, and even political ideas, all lay outside his interest and remained there, for he had no real opportunity to acquire a taste for them. The compensation for this misfortune was that it made him extraordinarily single-minded. It was a deficiency, moreover, that he shared with most Americans of his generation and that was therefore never obtrusive or painful. And while his training left him intellectually narrow, it should be noted that it did not have the supreme vice of making him hard. He was a very acquisitive member of a very acquisitive society, he was taciturn and impassive, but he was never cruel or ruthless. Many a boy has gone through the school of hard knocks to emerge with an instinct for trampling over everybody in his path. That tendency was early ingrained in Jay Gould, in Collis P. Huntington, in Russell Sage. They revenged upon society, with inexcusable additions, the miseducation that society had given them. But while Rockefeller went through a school of hardship, it was never really one of hard knocks; he was never cheated, humiliated, or abused, and while taught responsibility early, was not thrown out prematurely to fight his way among stronger men with his fists. He learned persistency and determination without learning a brutal aggressiveness. He always hated displays of emotion, but at bottom he was kindly. Angry as were the accusations brought against him in later days, nobody ever failed to see that this sharp line separated him from rougher, harsher, more unscrupulous leaders.

These early years gave religion a firm place among his habits and emotions. It offered partial compensation for the lack of richness in his life, gave existence a certain depth where it lacked breadth, and furnished one emotional outlet where he lacked any æsthetic outlets. His religion was as simple as it was fervent, quite untroubled by philosophic refinements or deistic questionings; the religion of most Americans then and since, emphasizing both faith and good works, and giving thrift, industry, and competitive enterprise a conspicuous place among the virtues of life. John D. Rockefeller thought of himself from these early years as a devoted Christian, willing to make sacrifices for his faith. We shall see that this sentiment had its effect upon both his code of business ethics and his program of philanthropy.

IV

With the second year at the academy this Owego interlude drew to an end. William Avery Rockefeller had transferred his operations farther west. His work of medicine-selling thrived best in new communities without fully-trained physicians. Necessarily, he was absent for long periods, and it is probable that he roved widely over Ohio, Indiana, Illinois and Wisconsin. After the first period of uneasiness, however, he began to appear freely in the Owego neighborhood. "He was the best-dressed man for miles around," later remarked Susan La Monte. "You never saw him without his fine silk hat." His capacity for arousing gossip and speculation was undiminished. Tongues wagged busily about this handsome, well-groomed stranger of dynamic ways who came and went so mysteriously while his family dwelt in frugal obscurity several miles out in the country. By 1853 he wished his home nearer his western field, while he realized that his children would have larger opportunities in some fast-growing city on the main trade routes. In the spring of that year he decided to remove to Ohio, the "New Connecticut" across the Alleghenies. Again Eliza Rockefeller faced the necessity of uprooting her family. She left with reluctance, and her neighbors, who respected her stern integrity, her devotion to her children, and her interest in church and school, were sorry to see her go. After regretful good-byes, once more the family belongings were packed and the Rockefellers took a westbound train on the Erie.[21] It was the last move for the family as a whole, though the restless father was destined to wander farther afield with the years, and finally to disappear beyond the Mississippi.

The Rockefellers were bound for Cleveland. Characteristically, William did not establish his household in the town itself. Arriving in September, he sent their goods to a little settlement named Strongsville on the prairie to the southwest. The farmhouse where the Rockefellers lived lies three and a half miles from Strongsville, and twelve or thirteen miles from the city. John D. Rockefeller thought in 1917 that they boarded at first with some cousins, the Humistons. It is certain that they did not work the farm.

The older boys were now past the facilities of any Strongsville school, and when fall came John and Will went to Cleveland to enter the high school. Their father, after due inquiries, selected a house kept on Erie Street by a Mrs. Woodin, who charged the boys a dollar a week each for board and room. In the fall of 1853 they resumed their studies. The first Central High School had just been erected, a one-story wooden building on Euclid Avenue in what is now the very heart of the city, and the superintendent, Andrew Freese, had planned a careful curriculum. William Avery Rockefeller opened an account in a Cleveland bank, and on his business trips to Cleveland bent a watchful eye upon his sons.

[21]Rockefeller wrote the author in 1936 that the family travelled to Cleveland by train; this contradicting John T. Flynn's statement in *God's Gold*, 49, that the family drove west.

V

Youth Whose Hope Is High

THE Rockefellers, as Franklin Pierce began his unhappy administration, had left New York behind them; they were in the West. Cleveland lay more than three hundred miles farther from the Atlantic than Owego. A small city, as yet little more than a town, it was growing fast. The railroad whistle was still a new sound to its inhabitants, for the line running southward through Columbus to Cincinnati had not begun running passenger trains until the spring of 1851, while it was later still that workmen drove the last spikes on the east-and-west line from Buffalo and Ashtabula. But with other railroads about to make their entry and a brisk lake trade, it was a lusty little place, full of enterprise and vigorous expansion.[1]

Indeed, it had already embarked on the second phase of its history. At the beginning it had been simply a commercial point on the lake, an entrepôt for sending goods into the Western Reserve, and a market town for country produce. Now men foresaw a larger future, for it was one of the logical points at which ore coming down the lakes from Michigan might meet the fuel from Ohio and Pennsylvania. This mystic union of coal, iron, and fire was to raise on the banks of the little Cuyahoga immense furnaces, rolling mills, and factories, whose chimneys would darken the sky of the city before the Civil War began.

Cleveland was still pretty in its semirural fashion, though the prettiness was fast vanishing. It was built upon a low, gravelly bluff, elevated forty to ninety feet above Lake Erie and falling off precipitously

---

[1] I have drawn much historical material upon Cleveland from the invaluable volumes of the Works Progress Administration, entitled *Annals of Cleveland;* a digest of the press, and especially the *Leader.*

in places to the water's edge, so that the streets nearest the harbor afforded fine views. The Cuyahoga River intersected this bluff or plateau near its western extremity by a deep, winding ravine. The generally narrow valley of its snakelike course was soon to be crammed with mills, railroads, and furnaces, and filled with suffocating soft-coal smoke; but as yet some of the reaches along the river, particularly those well back from the lake, were wooded and unspoiled. So far as the town's triangular site permitted—for it was caught between lake, river, and the river branch called Kingsbury Run—it had been laid out in rectangles as stately as Philadelphia's, and the principal streets were from eighty to a hundred feet wide. The green lawns were shaded by such an abundance of fine trees, chiefly maple, that Clevelanders later liked to talk of the "Forest City." Near the center of town, not far from the east bank of the Cuyahoga, was a square of ten acres which the erection of a statue to Oliver H. Perry in 1860 converted into Monumental Park. On the waterfront always rode a number of sidewheel steamboats, their tall chimneys smoking and their decks piled high with fuel and goods; near by lay white-sailed schooners, some of them speedy three- or five-masted boats; and fishermen sculled rapidly about. Despite the two new railroads, stagecoaches still rattled out daily to interior towns over the deep-rutted highways.[2]

In short, Cleveland looked in spots like a brash young city, and in other spots like a charming old town; for General Moses Cleaveland, agent and director of the first Connecticut Land Company, had brought the earliest settlers there while Washington was still President. The first sermon had been preached in 1800, the first ball held in 1801, and the first school taught in 1802. Growth had been slow until in Jacksonian days the three-hundred-mile Ohio Canal had been opened clear across the State to Portsmouth, connecting the lake with the Ohio; a silver ribbon almost as long as the Erie Canal. Although when the Rockefellers arrived the town counted 26,000 inhabitants, it had yet to pave its streets, install a sewerage system, and obtain a

[2]C. A. Urann, *Centennial History of Cleveland;* S. P. Orth, *A History of Cleveland;* and J. H. Kennedy, *A History of the City of Cleveland,* are useful works, but a fuller and better history, especially for the period after 1850, is much needed. Much can be gleaned from Ella Grant Wilson's *Famous Old Euclid Avenue of Cleveland,* and something from *Cleveland's Golden Story,* by James Wallen after data from Professor William M. Gregory. I have talked with many of Cleveland's oldest citizens.

central water supply. But all this was soon done. Its tanners, weavers, and dry goods and hardware dealers were busy supplying the emigrants who poured on into the prairie States. Superior Street, the principal business thoroughfare, was becoming lined with substantial office blocks and good shops. A Bohemian settlement west of the river was building up an extensive blanket industry. Barges laden with wool, wheat, corn, and coal came up the canal, and went back full of lumber, implements, and groceries. The Cuyahoga Steam Furnace Company, which after first using bog iron turned early in the fifties to Michigan ore, was producing large quantities of pig iron. In 1852 a small initial shipment of ore came down from Lake Superior, and three years later the brig *Columbia* brought 130 tons from Marquette in a single voyage. Cleveland had two newspapers, *The Herald* and *The Plain Dealer,* half a dozen banks, and an enthusiastic Board of Trade.

The two greatest cities of the Middle West at this time were Cincinnati, with its large pork-packing, flour-milling, and brewing establishments, and St. Louis, with its wealth from the fur trade and its central position as a Mississippi River distributor of manufactures to the South, and sugar, molasses, and coffee to the Northwest. They stood head and shoulders above the others, Cincinnati with 115,000 people and St. Louis with 77,000 in 1850. In the second rank Chicago, Detroit, Milwaukee, and Cleveland still ran almost neck and neck. Not one of them in 1850 was credited with 30,000 people; each hoped to be the future queen of the West. Clevelanders felt they had every reason for confidence. Was their city not the commercial capital of the twelve hustling counties of the Western Reserve, full of the energy and shrewdness of New England? Did its export and import trade not surpass Chicago's? Did not its position on several railroads, the canal, and the Great Lakes give it unique transportation advantages? The city had a bold and resourceful spirit, and its business leaders welcomed speculative ventures. Its enterprise and drive made it a perfect community for launching new businesses—an admirable place for ambitious young men eager to achieve a career.

II

The high school which John D. Rockefeller entered in the fall of 1853—the only one in Cleveland—stood on Euclid Avenue near Erie

Street, on the site now occupied by the Citizens' Savings and Trust Company. Its principal was Emerson E. White, later a college president, whom the boy liked. "Mr. White was a gentleman. He treated me like a gentleman—treated all the boys so," he said afterward.[3] "He made it pleasant for us to acquire learning. He was not a tyrant like Hardy." At the head of the city school system was Andrew Freese, an able Easterner of whom, as the leading figure in Cleveland education then and long after, John saw not a little; he sometimes visited the school and made speeches.

The boy's training was similar to that in Owego Academy. Latin interested him little, but he found excellent tuition in mathematics, and made the most of it. "I always got my mathematics first; arithmetic and algebra."[4] As at Owego, he received a severe drill in public speaking and in composition, writing essays on Education, Freedom, and St. Patrick which are still preserved. Much of the credit for his subsequent clear, accurate, and idiomatic use of English, surprising in a man who read so little, must be divided between White's training and the missiles of the choleric Bradley at Owego; but he inherited his mother's inability to spell. The high school failed to give him any great fund of general culture, and left his mind completely unawakened in various directions. But it did contribute to the development of his natural thoroughness, and to the habit of clear thinking which he showed as soon as he got into the world.

The two years he spent in the school, 1853–55, his fifteenth and sixteenth, were extremely sober and hard-working. The quiet, reserved boy had innate qualities which led him to take a serious view of life; and his shyness and staidness were increased by the fact that he was a countrified, awkward, poorly dressed lad living in a cheap boarding house with few friends and little pocket money. "From fourteen years of age to twenty-five I was much more dignified than I am now," he remarked as a man.[5] "I was very sedate and earnest, preparing to meet the responsibilities of life." Of his inner world we know little. At least subconsciously he was weighed upon by the uncertain family future, while consciously he was eager to make an early success. He was deeply impressed by the competitive hurry of the city, its energies all concentrated upon growth and moneymak-

---

[3]Inglis, Conversations with Rockefeller.   [4]Inglis, MS Biography, 56.
[5]Inglis, Conversations with Rockefeller.

ing. The dreams he had were naturally of business achievement, for business filled the atmosphere of the Yankee city. While the school boasted a collection of books, he cared little for reading. He was more interested in what Cleveland manufacturers and tradesmen were doing.

Outside his studies he had religious duties—church, Sunday school, midweek prayer meeting—and for a time piano lessons. Music was not neglected at the high school, and he was perhaps one of 300 city students who early in 1855 presented an oratorio, "The Festival of the Rose."

Though he had little gift for society, he found school companions as interesting as those of Owego. One was Timothy Radden, later justice of the Supreme Court of California.[6] Another was a stocky, combative Scotch-Irish lad, Mark Hanna, almost precisely of John's age, a son of the prosperous Cleveland grocer Leonard Hanna. The Hannas lived in a spacious, well-shaded brick house on Prospect Street, and at fifteen Mark had demonstrated his manly rashness by getting very seriously engaged to a young woman at his old home in New Lisbon, O. He was a positive, forceful, aggressive young chap, already thinking more of business than of books.[7] It is curious that John should have made so early an acquaintance with two great American "bosses." At Owego he had known Tom Platt, destined to be the unofficial ruler of New York State, and the involuntary maker of a President, Theodore Roosevelt, who would lead the most devastating of all the assaults upon the Rockefeller interests. In Cleveland he now knew Hanna, who was to become ruler of Ohio, and the principal maker of a President, William McKinley, who would prove far more to Rockefeller's liking.

As schoolboys, indeed, Rockefeller and Hanna were thrown into close association. One of their companions, Darwin G. Jones, recalled in 1922 that the three used to play and study together. Hanna, he remembered, was virile and athletic, of "a daring spontaneous disposition," while John was "reserved and studious, though always pleasant." One day the boys were kicking a football about, and John sent it over a fence into a yard where a painter was busy on a house. The

[6]Rockefeller referred to him in his conversation with Inglis as "Thomas Reardon."

[7]Cf. Herbert Croly, Mark Hanna, 36 ff. Croly makes it clear that Hanna always had a high opinion of Rockefeller.

ball all but knocked the painter off his ladder. He rushed into the street blustering that he would trounce the kicker within an inch of his life. "Now I never saw John in a fight," said Jones. "It was not his nature. He told the painter he had kicked the ball, and that he was sorry it had struck him, but the painter only flared up worse. . . . Before he could say much, though, Mark was on him like a tiger, and although he was just a boy, he gave that painter one of the worst whippings a fellow ever had."[8]

Cartoonists later would have given a good deal for this incident— John D. Rockefeller kicking a football labelled the common people and Mark Hanna rushing up to protect him! It offers some indication of their contrasting characters. John always detested personal altercations, and avoided quarrels because he felt them a useless waste of time, money, and nervous energy. Mark Hanna, on the other hand, delighted in a shindy. When in 1900 he made a speech in Bryan's own city of Lincoln, he began by reading one of Bryan's statements and declaiming: "I want to hurl it back in his teeth and tell him it is as false as hell!" Mark no sooner got into college at Western Reserve than he was suspended for insubordination. But John, as at Moravia and Owego, was quiet and restrained.

A fellow student, Lucy Spelman, found him "a studious boy, grave, reserved, never noisy or given to boisterous play."[9] She carried with her a corroborative image: "His most characteristic gesture . . . was to hug his slate to his chest as if it were a priceless possession." Both she and Darwin Jones were impressed by his scholastic record in mathematics. "In mathematics he was a figure. When questioned, he was ready instantly." By this time he had overcome most of the handicap of his meager training at Moravia, and cut a creditable figure among his classmates.

But if quiet, he was not without a sense of humor. The sly mischievousness which had led him to bedevil his brothers and sisters at Owego still cropped out. "He had a quick sense of humor," records Miss Spelman, "though one might say he was soberly mirthful. I do not recall him as ever laughing loudly. But I do remember the quick lighting up of his eyes and the dimple that showed in his cheeks when he heard or saw anything amusing." She recalled that he took little

---

[8]Interview with Jones in Atlanta *Constitution*, Feb. 12, 1922.
[9]Inglis, Conversation with Miss Spelman.

part in sports. In the public-speaking exercises he was restrained and subdued. "His declamations were so quietly given that they were quite unemotional, one might say unimpressive." Nevertheless, a gleam came into his eye when he spoke, and his classmates found one of his pieces humorously characteristic. Beginning "I'm pleased although I'm sad," it fitted the solemn lad so perfectly that the girls pounced upon it as a label; they nicknamed the grave young man "Old-Pleased-Although-I'm-Sad!"[10]

Yet behind this quaint, repressed, enigmatic manner there was plenty of activity and fire. In public discourse he could be unexpectedly effective. "I was on the debating team at high school in Cleveland," John D. Rockefeller recalled later. "I remember debating with Mark Hanna." Like Mark, in mature life he developed a certain aptitude in extemporaneous speaking. As an old man he referred to an occasion at the University of Chicago in 1901, when the decennial celebration required him to make three impromptu addresses in one day. Hanna was present and was struck by the vigor of these speeches. Forgetting their youthful association on the platform, he exclaimed: "Why, John, you're a born orator!" Rockefeller was pleased. "But I was used to public speaking from boyhood," he said.[11] Whenever his interest was aroused, he could rise above his quiescence and command his hearers' respect.

The Lucy Spelman whom we have quoted was almost two years older than John, but she had a younger sister who was to play a far more important part in his future. This was Laura Celestia Spelman, or "Cettie," as her friends called her and as she signed her letters. The Spelman girls were daughters of Harvey Buel Spelman, a prosperous Cleveland businessman who had been born in Granville, Mass., in 1811, of Puritan stock.[12] He had emigrated to Ohio as a young man, living for a time at Wadsworth, where "Cettie" was born,[13] and finally removing to Cleveland. His wife, whose maiden name was Lucy Henry, was of Massachusetts birth too. They had one son who

[10]John T. Flynn, *God's Gold*, 53.
[11]Inglis, Conversations with Rockefeller.
[12]I have used newspaper clippings on the Spelman family, and received information from residents of Cleveland.
[13]The Akron *Beacon Journal*, May 28, 1939, contains an article by Pauline Etter stating that Laura Celestia Spelman's parents removed to Kent, Ohio, soon after her birth in 1839, went in 1841 to Akron, and ten years later settled in Cleveland.

died at an early age. It was a New England family of the highest
type, industrious, thrifty, religious, and interested in culture. The
Spelmans were Congregationalists—indeed, Harvey Spelman had
helped establish a Congregational church in Akron, and twelve years
later another in Cleveland. They felt strongly—as most Western Reserve people did—on the slavery issue then beginning to convulse the
land. Mr. Spelman was active in the Abolition movement and in aiding runaway slaves to escape to Canada. He was in the State Legislature for a time, helping to establish a system of graded schools, and
was a member of the Board of Education in Cleveland. Mrs. Spelman
was known as a church worker and an adherent of the temperance
cause. Their daughter Cettie was a pretty girl, dark-haired, dark-eyed,
rather petite of figure, and full of vivacity, though she was religious
in temperament, and had a strong sense of propriety. She possessed
a will of her own; all the Spelmans did. When she completed high
school in the class of 1855—the first class to which diplomas were
given—she chose for the title of her graduation essay, "I Can Paddle
My Own Canoe."

It is uncertain how well she and John knew each other in the years
1853–55. Like John, she was fond of mathematics and distinguished
herself in arithmetic and algebra. They certainly had a speaking acquaintance. Lucy, indeed, knew him well enough to decide that he
was rather attractive. In conversation, "his appreciation was keen."
Perhaps Cettie knew him equally well. But it seems clear that the
stories that John fell in love with her at this time are mythical. Six
years later Cettie wrote her former music teacher, Mrs. Hawley, that
she was fancy free and had "no anxiety about leading a life of single
blessedness."[14] When she finally married John, many friends were
astonished by the news. As for John himself, in 1854 other objects
seemed more important to him and more within reach than the
smart young woman living in a handsome house, moving among the
best people of Cleveland, and making plans to go to Worcester, Mass.,
for further schooling. "Miss Spelman and her sister," he said later,
"were living in Huron Street, three minutes' walk from where we
were. But my mind was on other things just then."

By other "things" he meant primarily studies, home, and church.
There is no evidence that he was ever really interested in college, but

[14]Letters to Mrs. Hawley, Rockefeller papers.

he had taken to his school books with such purpose that his mother talked of sending him to one. That part of Ohio was proud of its educational facilities; Oberlin lay in the adjoining county to the west, and Western Reserve College was then at Hudson in the county just to the south. Either would give him a good training. Another of the "things" he referred to was doubtless his music. From practising on the melodeon at Owego he had now advanced to difficult piano pieces and was eager to become proficient. Years later, looking at an early photograph, he remarked:[15] "No wonder that I seemed so sedate in that picture. I was only fifteen years old, or less, when that was taken. I had not only my studies at high school on my mind, but I was practising six hours a day on the piano besides." He joined a singing class that met once or twice a week in a church basement on lower Euclid Avenue. And still another preoccupation was religion.

Cleveland in the fifties was a highly religious community, full of churches, looking up to the ministers as community leaders, and much given to revivals. James Ford Rhodes, who entered the city high school soon after John was graduated, and whom John knew well, has recorded that "moral and religious teaching was considered part of the duty of the public school teacher," and that the instructor who inspired him most, A. G. Hopkinson, was an ardent Congregationalist whose discourses "were tinctured by puritanical fervor." Young Rhodes witnessed a great religious revival in 1858. Evangelistic emotion pervaded the public schools of Cleveland, many of the pupils were swept away by it, and the future historian kept a vivid recollection of hearing the Congregational minister assure the youngsters that they were in danger of hell-fire if they did not embrace Christianity at once. "Prayer meetings were frequently held in the schoolroom after school hours, and were led by the minister and teacher."[16]

Perhaps John D. Rockefeller had his share in some such wave of revivalism. At any rate, he and Will continued the steady churchgoing which they had begun in Owego, becoming regular attendants at the Erie Street Baptist Church. This Erie Street Church had been organized in August, 1851, in what was evidently a very distinct sea-

[15]Inglis, Conversations with Rockefeller.
[16]M. A. DeWolfe Howe, *James Ford Rhodes, American Historian*, 30, 31. Rockefeller knew Rhodes's father, "Dan," a pioneer in the Ohio coal-mining industry, and described him to me as a rough-and-ready but very honest man.

son of grace; for its historians aver that during more than one hundred and fifty successive nights the congregation assembled in the building, listening to the pastor, and joining in prayer and song. The church had a youthful vigor and enthusiasm.[17]

And vigorously did John give himself to its work. He and Will joined a Sunday-school class taught by William V. Sked, an elderly Scot, a florist, and an exemplar of righteousness founded upon passionate study of the Scriptures. Sked, who had a garden and greenhouse on Perry Street, knew the Bible from Genesis to Revelation; he was stern, addicted to blunt truth-telling, and inclined to preach, but beloved for his Scotch rectitude. He soon became spiritual father to the young man and a close friend as well. Rockefeller later wrote of the severe drill which he gave his young people. "I remember that upon the very first occasion that I was ever asked to pray publicly, he stood up, looking around from his front seat, from which he always talked to us—he always had something to say, and always spoke from the Bible—he looked down upon me—I was frightened when he looked at me—and simply said: 'John, you will pray!' I had just come into the church and I was only fifteen years of age. When we prayed in those days we all knelt down."[18] Since the Sunday school had three hundred students, other friendships followed. The talented minister, J. Hyatt Smith, bent an approving eye upon the two young Rockefellers. When John was publicly baptized in the fall of 1854, a friend named Alfred Eyears, of whom we shall hear more, came in with him.[19]

Not long afterward John was made clerk of the church, an unusual responsibility for a mere youth, and indicative of the impression of maturity and responsibility that he gave to others. Before many years passed he was teaching one of the largest classes in the Sunday school.

III

The part which "Big Bill" Rockefeller played in his son's development was, as before, a double rôle, positive and negative. The negative side lay in the atmosphere of uncertainty which he threw about the life of his family. He still departed on long mysterious trips, and

[17]Cf. *Fiftieth Anniversary of the Euclid Avenue Baptist Church, October 16, 1901*, a 78-page booklet on church history.
[18]*Idem*, 31.   [19]Inglis, MS Biography, 54.

no one could predict when he would reappear. Mrs. Rockefeller could never feel sure that he would not turn up some day demanding a removal to some new town, as he had done thrice before. As a matter of fact, in 1855 he did move the household from Strongsville to Parma, a hamlet somewhat closer to Cleveland. Nor could the family place any certain dependence upon his earnings, his ability to avoid such antagonisms as had cost him dear at Moravia, or his business future. They knew all too well that he was sure, in his colorful, cheery, likeable way, to excite conjecture wherever he lived, and gossip of a kind that added nothing to their social standing.

John respected his father, who had admirable qualities. But we cannot too much emphasize the fact that the inevitable tendency of this family atmosphere of hazard and dubiety was to foster in him, the oldest son, Eliza's principal dependence in looking after the other children, a profound desire for certainty and dependability; for a stable home, stable earnings, stable resources, a stable place in society. His taste for order, thrift, and security was in part inherited—every true Avery had been stamped by a desire to push forward in the world and take a dominant place in his community. In larger part his traits were fixed by his mother's careful tuition; and they were accentuated by the unhappy results of William Avery Rockefeller's adventurous, unpredictable ways. By now John, of course, knew all about his father's principal calling. Every one in Strongsville did. John T. Flynn, inquiring in that town about 1930, found legends there of "Big Bill" Rockefeller which he wrought into a vivid paragraph or two:[20]

In Strongsville, as everywhere, the neighbors asked each other what Bill Rockefeller did for a living. Then one day Uncle Joe Webster, one of them, went on a trip, and his journey brought him at evening into the village of Richfield, Summit County, Ohio. Inside the hotel and on the wall his eye was fixed by a small sign reading: "Dr. William A. Rockefeller, the Celebrated Cancer Specialist, Here for One Day Only. All cases of Cancer Cured unless too far gone, and then they can be greatly benefited."

Could this be Big Bill Rockefeller from Strongsville? Uncle Webster did not have to wait long. For a little later a crowd gathered outside the hotel around the buggy of a big man in a long black coat and with a big dark red beard. Going outside Webster found Bill Rockefeller beginning

[20]*God's Gold,* 53.

to talk—his high pitch, as it was called then and still is. So this is what Bill Rockefeller did for a living. He was a pitch man. And he called himself Dr. Rockefeller! Uncle Joe called him Doc. And thereafter he was called Doc Rockefeller. Apparently he was doing well, too, for he charged $25 for a cancer treatment, though he sold his medicine in bottles for a smaller sum.

Even in the greatest American cities at this time, as we have said, medicine was at a deplorably low level. Most of the sixty medical colleges were contemptible; they did not turn out enough doctors to meet the needs of the country; professional standards were weak; and only three real colleges of pharmacy existed. Horace Greeley complained in 1854 of the all too typical operations of a journeyman tailor in New York City. This man, attacked by the cholera, then endemic in the city, kept the prescriptions which a physician gave him. When he recovered he gave up his shop, took the prescriptions, and began manufacturing an "invaluable and certain cure for cholera." Finally he hired an office, placarded it with advertisements, and hung out a bold sign, Dr. So-and-So! All along the frontier the Indian-herb doctor and peddler of home remedies flourished. If they sold enough quinine and not too much calomel, they might do more good than harm. Uncle Joe Webster, according to the Strongsville legend, learned that "Doc" Rockefeller was carrying his operations as far west as Iowa, and that in promising communities he also played the part of money-lender. He told of charging farmers 12 per cent for money, then and later a usual rate—in Populist days even 15 and 20 per cent were demanded—and of being glad to foreclose on well-improved land. He wanted people to know that he was a keen-witted money-maker.

But part of William Avery Rockefeller's influence on his son was direct. To this John bore ample subsequent testimony. If he ever felt any mortification over the half-furtive side of his father's activities, he did not confess it. Instead, he always emphasized the magnetic, high-spirited, expansive companionship that he found whenever he went home for week ends and vacations. The older Rockefeller still liked fast horses, good company, lively talk, and gay music. He still dressed in fine attire, carried plenty of money, and talked interestingly of the wonders of the West and his shrewd deals there. He loved hunting and the wide outdoors. Most people were irresistibly attracted to him. "What a bright smile my father had," said John D. Rockefeller more than sixty years afterward. "Everybody liked him. 'Uncle Billy,' they called him."[21]

But John found more in his father than a kindly parent and bright companion. He found in him a man keenly interested in affairs, a master of business precept, and a hard and enterprising worker. He was still anxious to teach his children thoroughness, vigilance, and promptness. He insisted on concentration. Sometimes they walked together in the streets of Cleveland. "If a crowd was rushing to a fire or any other excitement, father would say: 'Never mind the crowd. Keep away from it. Tend to your own business.'" Watching the boys' schoolwork and their tasks about home, he made it clear that there must be no compromise with accuracy and responsibility. He taught John, as the latter has recorded, how to draw up notes and other business papers. The boy saw that his father always paid his rent in advance, and that he was meticulous in all his business arrangements. "He was very scrupulous to carry out his contracts, particularly that they were clearly understood and carefully drawn; that is, committed to writing. And the training he gave me along these lines was very valuable, has proven so in all my life; and I have never forgotten his ideas of the sacredness of a contract, and I have never heard the question raised of my father doing just what he agreed to do in all his business affairs."[22]

This training made its impression even on Will, who had a more exuberant and carefree temperament than John. Soon after the Rockefellers settled in Strongsville, Will decided that he did not wish any more schooling. "Very well, Will," dryly replied the father, "I'll bind you out to a farmer until you're twenty-one." Will stayed in school. When subsequently the second son became a bookkeeper, he came home one night and told his mother that he feared he had made an error in a bill of lading. The matter preyed upon his mind so much that he finally tramped the long distance back to the wharf district, dangerous at night, went over the bill, and found the mistake. "It was only two or three dollars," said John D. Rockefeller afterwards, "but he could not rest until he found it. Dependable. That is the way father brought him up."

William Avery Rockefeller, like most of the hard, driving citizens

[21]Inglis, Conversations with Rockefeller, 1917–18.　　　[22]Idem.

of Cleveland, always had an aggressive conception of business. The world he moved in was one in which men consistently strove to get an advantage over each other, and he did not wish to see his sons victimized. Again and again he impressed upon them the necessity of driving careful bargains—if possible, hard bargains. His was the David Harum gospel: "Do unto others as they would do unto you, and do it fust." He was not brutal, but he was "smart" and keen, and proud to advertise it. John remembered, for example, his shrewd practice with laborers, anticipating a principle that has since been attributed to Henry Ford. "He would hire men to work for him; after a time tell them with a smile, 'I don't need you any longer'; then in a few days hire them over again. His 'policy of firing and hiring over,' he called it. It kept the men on tiptoe—no stagnation among them."

In his rough-and-tumble years of medicine-selling, horse-trading, lumbering, and money-lending, the elder Rockefeller had developed great astuteness. He inculcated it in his sons, systematically whetting both their defensive and offensive capacities. John always kept an amused but annoyed recollection of his father's cat-and-mouse loans, made in small ways at the time and more substantially when the boy went into business. Uncle Joe Webster said that "Big Bill" boasted to him of the merciless if good-natured training he gave the younger generation.

"I cheat my boys every time I get a chance," the "doctor" said. "I want to make 'em sharp. I trade with the boys and skin 'em, and I just beat 'em every time I can. I want to make 'em sharp."

It is highly unlikely that William Avery Rockefeller ever had any sympathy with the proposal to send his eldest son to college. Eliza would have liked it, and apparently John played briefly with the idea. He wrote an essay on "Education" in high school, in which he remarked:

When we look around us, and see the continual progress education is making, and also the great changes which have been constantly taking place since it began to rise, we cannot but think that everyone ought to endeavor to improve the great opportunities now offered them.

Had Isaac Newton been an unlearned man, on seeing the apple fall to the ground, would he not rather have eaten it than inquired why it fell?

But in 1855, when John graduated, his father announced that a college education would be too expensive. This was not quite accurate. The family means would apparently have been sufficient to maintain a son in Western Reserve or one of the many smaller colleges studding Ohio. What William really meant was that a college education would not be worth what it would cost. He looked forward to practical success for his boys, not book-learning. The decision mildly disappointed John, who long after spoke regretfully of what he had missed: "I hadn't the advantage of a college education."[23]

What John would probably have liked best, with his mathematical bent and practical mind, was a technical training such as the Case School of Applied Science later offered in Cleveland. As a man he was particularly impressed by engineering schools. In speaking of twentieth-century youth he said: "Better than a college education is the training that he gets in the technical schools that have sprung up all over the country." But he consoled himself by praising the advantages he had actually received. "I had a good mother and an excellent father, and I like to feel that whatever I may have lost through failure to secure a college education I made up in my home training."[24]

Considering both John's gifts and the conditions of the day, the father's decision was correct. John would have gained little from college. He always learned from life, not the printed page. He was the product not of an urbane and highly cultivated environment, but of a pioneer, restless, highly practical society; and as he was destined to business, it was important that he get into it as soon as possible. His father's decision thrust him into action at a time when business training and even a small business capital were strategically valuable. Four years more of study, with no opportunity to save and with some expensive new tastes, would have left him less able to profit by opportunities than he proved to be in the late fifties.

He turned cheerfully in the spring of 1855 to complete his preparation for a business post. Cleveland had an institution known as Folsom's Commercial College, then competing with Bryant, Lusk & Stratton's Commercial College but later merging with it, which late in 1854 had moved into "new and splendid rooms" in the Rouse

[23]Rockefeller told Mr. Inglis, Sept. 1, 1917: "While I was at high school in Cleveland I expected to go to college; but in a letter from my father I received an intimation; he conveyed an intimation that I was not to go."

[24]Flynn, *God's Gold,* 58.

Block at the corner of Superior Avenue and the Public Square. It was a "chain college," with branches in seven cities. E. G. Folsom, "professor of the science of accounts," headed a faculty of seven full-time teachers, aided by outside lecturers. Emphasis fell upon single- and double-entry bookkeeping and penmanship, but the school had a teacher of commercial history and the art of computation, and another of mercantile customs, banking and exchange. A lawyer of the city talked on commercial law; General John Crowell gave lectures on bills of exchange, to which the public was "respectfully invited"; and one of the best-known ministers, the Reverend J. A. Thome, held forth on commercial ethics.[25] John could also have gone over to the Bryant, Lusk & Stratton school to hear his former pastor, J. Hyatt Smith, lecture on "Elements of a Business Character." The charge for a full mercantile course, time unlimited, was $40. When John began we do not know, but it was probably ten weeks or so before he and Cettie Spelman received their diplomas at the high school commencement on July 16th; he said later that he gave three months to the course.[26] All the students worked hard.[27] Leaving early in August, he treated himself to a short vacation with the family at their new home in Parma. Then, late that month, he returned to the Erie Street boarding-house and began to look for employment.[28]

IV

It was hot in the newly paved streets of the little city. The now full-grown youth, with neat, dark suit, stand-up collar, black tie, well-brushed hair, and sober, earnest visage, began to make the rounds of such Cleveland houses as might need a bookkeeper and clerk. He was just past sixteen, but his tall, well-built figure and intent, serious face made him look several years older. It would have taken a keen observer to see that the quiet young fellow was unusual in anything

[25]See the frequent advertisements of the school in the Cleveland *Leader*, 1855.
[26]Inglis, Conversations with Rockefeller.
[27]Inglis in 1917 interviewed S. W. Andrus of Cleveland, a student about this period. He said there was no skylarking. "Everybody was there to learn something and we wasted no time."
[28]Rockefeller's own statement as to his place of residence, given to Mr. Inglis in 1917, is not quite clear. He speaks of the Woodin boarding house: "It was in Erie Street at first; then we moved to St. Clair Street, near Water Street; then to Hamilton Street, near the postoffice; from there to Miami Street. We were in Erie Street in 1853 and 1854. I was there in 1855."

except his earnestness. His high forehead and strong chin gave him a long, oval face; the eyes, set wide apart, had a keen, penetrating glance; his nose was long, broad-bridged, and aquiline; his mouth was broad, but his lips were thin, and in moods of concentration or determination he compressed them in a straight line. He had a dogged, reflective appearance, and any one who talked with him for five minutes would have been impressed by two facts: the simplicity and unity of his purposes, and the subtlety and foresight of his mind. He had not decided upon any particular business, but he had consciously put aside the idea of work in shops or stores; he did not wish to be a counter-jumper. He had his own ideas as to where the best opportunities lay, and meant to find a position within the flow of commerce.

"I went to the railroads, to the banks, to the wholesale merchants," he said later. "I did not go to any small establishments." Later still he spoke of a serious if vague ambition. "I did not guess what it would be, but I was after something big."[29]

He soon found that getting a job with the larger firms was not easy. Business was bad in Cleveland at the time. That May the Cleveland *Leader* had fulminated: "It is a most deplorable fact that a great many young men can find nothing to do. There is something associated with the idea of idleness which, in a manly bosom, excites a mingled feeling of pity and contempt." The inexperienced boy had no special entrée to commercial houses; he could only walk in, ask an interview, and state his qualifications. "I always asked for the head of the house, and, of course, saw any one who would see me." He had no important friends, and no smartness of manner or outward qualities of push and aggressiveness. Men who wished a hustler, full of snap and what Americans then called the go-ahead spirit, would be disappointed in his quiet, thoughtful appearance. The days dragged into weeks, and the weeks into more than a month. The Cleveland *Leader* again bewailed the shortage of jobs, and urged idle young men to go to the country for work. But John still went persistently about his search, undiscouraged by the sweltering weather or the indifference of employers. In such a small city he could call on most employers in a week. He went back a second time; then a third. His feet became sore with the weary trudging over hot stone pave-

[29]Inglis, Conversations with Rockefeller.

ments, but still he kept on. "It did not impress me as such a great ordeal to go looking for work every day for six weeks," he said long years after. "I had to get work. . . . I was not discouraged, because" (and here is a flash of practical philosophy remarkable in a youth of sixteen), "I was working every day at my business—the business of looking for work. I put in my full time at this every day."[30]

However, late in September his father discussed the situation seriously with him. John had then visited every possible office in Cleveland at least once, and was making his third call at many. William Avery Rockefeller concluded that he was wasting his time, and should wait a while before trying further. "It's all right, John," he said, as if failure must be confessed. "You go out to the country and I'll take care of you."

No remark could have done more to sting the young man to continued effort. He did not want to go to the country—perhaps to be supported by his father, perhaps to be bound to a farmer, perhaps to clerk in a village store. His whole future was menaced by the possibility. "It makes a cold chill run down my spine when I think of it," he declared as an old man. "What would have become of me if I had gone to the country?" He added doubtfully: "Perhaps I might have got a start in business later."[31]

Next morning, September 26, 1855, he went out with "desperate determination." The tang of autumn was in the air; Lake Erie on the north and the blue hills to the south were both veiled in a faint pearly haze; leaves were beginning to fall, and blackbirds in flocks were chattering in the yards preparatory to their migration. Winter would soon begin; the boy must find something quickly. His first inquiries were again discouraging. Finally he entered the three-story red-brick building on Merwin Street, a block from the Cuyahoga, occupied as warehouse and office by Hewitt & Tuttle, commission merchants and produce shippers. He told Tuttle, the junior partner, that he had been trained as bookkeeper, and perhaps the urgency of his request for work impressed the merchant with his earnestness and trustworthiness. Tuttle kept the books, but business was increasing, and he needed help. "Come back after dinner," he said. "We may have a chance for you then." Rockefeller departed gravely, but once around the corner broke into a skip of boyish delight. He went back

[30]*Idem.* [31]Inglis, MS Biography, 84.

to the Erie Street boarding-house for dinner in elation. After a hurried meal, he took the news to Deacon Sked, then sick at home. The
old Scot gave him some good advice upon diligence, probity, and
faithfulness to the church. Thus fortified, John reported at one
o'clock in Merwin Street.

Isaac L. Hewitt, the senior partner, saw him this time. He was a
man of enterprise, who had just put up a building on West Street
where mechanics of limited means might rent quarters for shops or
small manufactories.[32] This "Hewitt Block" was long a landmark in
Cleveland, and Hewitt himself a well-known citizen, whom we shall
meet later in the oil business. After an examination of John's handwriting, then a clear, bold Spencerian style, the partners told the boy
he would be given a trial as assistant bookkeeper. He was shown the
high desk where he was to labor, the letter-press for copies of the
firm's outgoing correspondence, and the blotter on which the day's
transactions were recorded. Forthwith he hung up his coat and set
to work. Nothing was said about salary; the firm would decide what
he was worth. "I cared very little about that," he said later. Feeling
that he had put his foot on the first rung and was part of the business world, he was enchanted. The place, he long afterward recalled,
"was delightful to me—all the method and system of the office."[33]
At six o'clock he walked homeward with the conviction that he had
arrived at manhood.

v

Thus far John D. Rockefeller's life had followed a pattern familiar
enough in the careers of nineteenth-century industrialists and financiers in America. Humble rural origins, boyhood hardships, a home
where thrift, thoroughness, and responsibility were constantly taught,
puritanical religious training, moderate schooling, early entrance into
a practical business environment—so the characteristic story runs.
New England and the Middle States were producing hundreds of
boys in these years who, though they lacked his ability, had precisely
John D. Rockefeller's advantages and handicaps, and who rose to
some degree of business eminence. Many incidents in Rockefeller's

[32]The Hewitt block is described in the Cleveland *Leader*, Sept. 26, 1855.
[33]Talk to Young Men's Bible Class, Fifth Avenue Baptist Church, N. Y.
Evening Mail, Oct. 21, 1905.

life could be matched by incidents from these other careers. He had made his first money selling turkeys; just so did Gustavus F. Swift, as a Cape Cod boy, make his first money selling chickens. At nine years of age Swift would walk into his grandfather's house and say, "Grandpa, I'll give you forty cents for the old white hen." He already had a purchaser at fifty!—and the bargain would be carried out. Just so Leland Stanford, on his father's farm near Watervliet, made his first money selling chestnuts. The hired man came from Albany with a report to the boys, who had gathered bushels of them, that chestnuts were high. "We hurried off to market with them," said Stanford later, "and sold them for twenty-five dollars." John's father, by his peculiar temperament and still more peculiar occupations, threw unusual cares on his son and brought him to early maturity. Other men were orphaned at an early age, like James J. Hill, or in some different fashion, like Henry Clay Frick and Collis P. Huntington and Peter Cooper, cast on their own resources.

Business—the development of the resources of the half-explored country—was then America's principal challenge to her young men. It offered the great main arena of endeavor. As energetic young Frenchmen in Froissart's time turned to war, as energetic young Englishmen in Elizabethan days turned to exploration, as energetic young Americans of 1800 turned to pioneering, so now the rising elite turned to business. It was much more than the road to wealth; it was the field to which the great majority of Americans looked for distinction, power, and the joys of self-expression. A whole generation pushed into it partly for money, more for the lust of battle and competitive effort, and most of all for eminence and authority. It was the central field of usefulness; it was the Great Game. Men were born by hundreds of thousands to play it. While the nation needed development, while growing multitudes pressed upon its resources for food, clothing, and the opportunities for a higher life, business was the great immediate necessity of the time. Three fourths of Rockefeller's youthful companions in Cleveland felt themselves destined to it; three fourths of the ambitious young Americans of the day plunged into it. The next generation in America was to produce few great statesmen—after Lincoln, none; its novelists and poets were small beside England's; its painters and sculptors did not compare with Europe's; but it produced more business genius than any country in the world had yet seen. Rockefeller himself in 1918, praising a man who spoke of his joy in work, referred to the Great Game:[34]

> That is it—accomplishment! That is the goal of every man who tries to do his part in the world. One builds a ship. It is of a certain size and power and model. He runs it in a certain way and makes money—but knows he will do still better with the next one he builds. Or one builds a railroad. It has 65-pound rails. His next railroad will have 100-pound rails, not iron but steel. . . . You remember the one hundred miles of dust on the Lake Shore road? Find the gravel-bed and make the road dustless. That was done. That's the thing—accomplishment, playing the game.
>
> Yet some say that because a man is successful and accumulates wealth,)all he is after is to get wealth and oppress. How blind!

The proud relief, the joy in financial independence, which the sixteen-year-old Rockefeller felt when he gained his first position, had their parallel in the lives of many another poor youth starting toward riches. Andrew Carnegie was twelve when he obtained his first employment as bobbin-boy in a cotton factory. "I cannot tell you how proud I was," he wrote long after, "when I received my first week's own earnings. One dollar and twenty cents made by myself, and given to me because I had been of some use in the world!" In such terms Rockefeller spoke later of September 26, 1855. "That was a momentous day to me, the getting of my first foothold, the chance to earn my own living." His feelings ran in narrower, deeper channels than those of Carnegie, and it was characteristic that he never failed to mark the day as a turning-point in his life. Along with the family birthdays and his wedding anniversary, it was celebrated as a festal occasion; when he came to have an estate the flag was hoisted in honor of the event, and old friends like Miss Sked, granddaughter of the beloved deacon, were invited to help keep its memory green.

[34]Inglis, Conversations with Rockefeller.

VI

A Foothold in Life

I⊤ ɪs ten months later. Noon hangs sultry in the offices of Hewitt &
Tuttle—noon of July, 1856. The partners have gone to midday
dinner, leaving their clerk in charge. A tall, fair young man in
clothes neatly brushed though of poor quality, he sits at his
desk making out a bill of lading. Before him stands a blue-clad,
well-whiskered captain of one of the little lake steamers. A look of
determination rests on the face of the serious seventeen-year-old
youth as he expostulates with the seaman.

"Now look here, captain," he is saying firmly, "I can't make out
the bill for that amount. It just doesn't tally with the actual cargo."

"Come, come, young man," replies the captain with burly authority. "You make it out the way I say. Nobody's ever going to
know. Why, everybody allows a margin like that."

John D. Rockefeller fixes him with his piercing blue-gray eyes.

"I am sorry to say no," he replies quietly. "But if the weight and
price are a certain amount, I must make my entries accordingly.
If I'm going to do right by you I can't begin by doing wrong for
somebody else, can I? If I did, you would soon be afraid that I
would cheat you too. Isn't that so?"

"Nonsense, you're too strict," says the captain. But he sees there
is no use pursuing the matter, and grumblingly takes himself off.[1]

Another year passes. In Brooklyn, a little town a few miles south
of Cleveland, John D. Rockefeller—now eighteen—sits in a buggy
outside of Wheelan's general store. He is talking with gruff old
Wheelan himself. His clothes are now better, and he looks more

[1]This story, with plausible detail, is recounted in the Cleveland *World News,*
Sept. 11, 1905.

mature. Tuttle, the junior partner, has recently quit the firm, and the young clerk has taken over most of his work. Part of his duty is collecting bills, and at the moment he is trying to close one of the most troublesome accounts on Hewitt & Tuttle's books. Tight-pursed Wheelan, with Yankee stubbornness, has been putting the firm off for months. Rockefeller talks pleasantly enough but refuses to let him go, returning steadily to the charge.

"You come around next month," growls the merchant.

"That's what you always say, Mr. Wheelan. It isn't fair; I still insist that we settle today. Then I shan't have to come again, and you won't have to be troubled."

"It won't hurt Hewitt to wait a little longer."

"But you know very well Mr. Hewitt has been waiting a long time already. I simply can't go back to him without the money."

For an hour the talk goes on, the merchant stubborn, the young man good-humored, but still sitting in his buggy, still pressing for his money. At last, half-irritated, half-amused, and wholly worn-out, the storekeeper gives up. "Here it is," he ejaculates. "I never saw such a pestering collector!"[2]

A long succession of such scenes might be described. We might picture young Rockefeller at the letter-press, carefully laying outgoing correspondence on the damp sheets which would take the impression; or entering the latest transaction in the blotter almost before his customer had gotten out of the door; or checking over bills presented by tradesmen. His experience at Hewitt & Tuttle's had been varied, the hours long, the work troublesome. For all he did the pay was small. On December 31, 1855, or thereabouts, Hewitt had called him aside and presented him with $50 as wages for the first three months and four and one-half days of work. It amounted to a little more than fifty cents a day. However, Hewitt had told him that with the new year he would be paid $25 a month, which was considerably better.[3] It was none too much, for if room and board were cheap, clothing and other necessities were not.

[2]Inglis, Conversations with Rockefeller.

[3]Rockefeller told Mr. Inglis in 1917: "About the only work I did that I recall as being like the work of an office-boy was to copy letters in the letter-press. . . . Before long I was put in charge of the cash, and of making entries in the blotter, the book of original record of all transactions. When you handle the cash and the book of original entry it is not long until you make the transfers to the other books."

Nobody doubted that the grave, thoughtful young man earned more than his salary. "I could not have done better for myself than I did for my employer," he said years later.[4] He was quick to learn, deft to execute, and above all, meticulously careful and methodical. His employers quickly realized that they could trust any responsibility of their small business to him and be certain of the result. He was soon writing their letters, making out their bills of lading, checking incoming shipments, and verifying charges against the firm. Inaccuracies or slack methods never got past this ominously quiet clerk. While he supervised the office, Hewitt & Tuttle paid exactly what they owed, got exactly what was due them, and delivered exactly what they had promised. "I scrutinized every bill," he said long afterward. "If it had ever so many items I went over each one, verified it, and carefully added the totals. The bill had to be accurate in every detail before I O.K.'d it to be paid." He was a new broom that swept clean.

But he was much more than a new broom dealing with accumulated dust, and much more than an automaton excelling in office routine. A devouring passion for business possessed him. All his waking thoughts were given to it. He threw himself into the duties of the little office down near the Cuyahoga as other young men would have thrown themselves into love, war, or adventure. Fifty years later he could remember the intensity with which he bent his whole heart and mind upon his first business tasks. "In dreams at night I find myself taking up that cash account, that first situation." Some of the dreams had a nightmarish tinge. As a multimillionaire he would occasionally awake fancying that he was still a clerk under Hewitt, and had just discovered a heavy shortage in his accounts! Or he would toss about imagining that he had just failed again to loosen some troublesome customer's purse-strings. "How many times I have dreamed now and then up to recent years that I was still trying to collect those old bills!" he recalled in 1918. "I would wake up exclaiming: 'I can't collect So-and-So's account!' "[5]

Any laxity, any slovenliness, shocked Rockefeller. He noticed with sharp disapproval that Tuttle sometimes neglected to make a record of petty cash that he took from the till for business purposes during

[4]"Speech to the Club, May 7, 1904" (pamphlet in Rockefeller papers).
[5]*Idem.*

the day. "I saw that he put in his check for the few dollars that were short later on"—but the method was careless. Once when young Rockefeller was visiting a busy neighboring office, he watched a plumber present a bill nearly a yard long to the head of the firm. The merchant glanced at it a moment, muttered "H'm, yes, . . . yes," and turned to his bookkeeper, saying: "Please pay this bill."

John threw a condemnatory look at the merchant. Recently he himself, going over some plumbing bills, had found serious errors. "I had trained myself to the point of view . . . that my check on a bill was the executive act which released my employer's money from the till and was attended with more responsibility than the spending of my own funds." The carelessness of the merchant revealed to him one reason why so many businessmen went to the wall. "I made up my mind that such business methods could not succeed."[6]

But for all his preoccupation with his work, he was happy in it. The tasks were sufficiently varied to be exciting, and to teach him a good deal about human nature. "My duties were vastly more interesting than those of an office boy in a large house today." He found the Hewitt & Tuttle office, with its upper windows looking out on the Cuyahoga and the constant stream of canal-barges and lake ships, very pleasant. His two employers, and particularly Tuttle, were kind: "a fine disciplinarian, and well disposed toward me." He felt the exhilaration of a neophyte who was learning a complete cult. "I wanted the position and . . . I enjoyed my work. I was happy in it. I had been taught to work from early boyhood, and this was so delightful to me, all the method and system of the office."[7] We may well emphasize the words "method and system"! They were to be the keynote of a great part of Rockefeller's business life.

And beyond the office, beyond his laborious grind, he began to see far horizons. Cleveland was growing by steady surges; it would count 44,000 inhabitants in 1860. New smokestacks were steadily coming into view up and down the Cuyahoga. A gas lighting system had been introduced, while every year more streets were paved. A railroad to the Mahoning Valley, which had been completed in

[6]Rockefeller, *Random Reminiscences,* 38, 39.
[7]Inglis, Conversations with Rockefeller.

1875, connected the Cleveland iron furnaces with immense supplies of cheap coal, and thereafter the position of the city as the principal iron center of the West was assured. Some very handsome fortunes were being made, and men were pointed out on the streets, like the short-bearded, keen-eyed banker Leonard Case, the railroad builder Amasa Stone, and the merchant W. S. Beckwith, who were rich by metropolitan standards. Young Rockefeller saw these wealthy men walking to lunch at the Stillman House, or the old Weddell House, from whose balcony Abraham Lincoln a few years afterward, when on his way to Washington, addressed the people. He was especially impressed by a leading citizen named Morris—apparently L. R. Morris, a shipping-merchant—"who was said to be worth $250,000! What a fortune for those days!" The meditative youth, always a lover of simplicity, was struck "by the way he walked, the way he looked, quite unaffected by his great riches. I saw other wealthy men, and I was glad to see that they went about their business without any display of power or money. Later I saw some who wore rich jewels and luxurious clothes. It seemed unfortunate that they were led into such lavish style."[8]

An incident at the office whetted his ambition to be a capitalist. As he recounted it to some Cleveland friends in 1905:

I was a young man when I got my first look at a banknote of any size. I was clerking at the time down on the flats here. One day my employer received a note from a down-State bank for $4,000. He showed it to me in the course of the day's business, and then put it in the safe. As soon as he was gone I unlocked the safe, and taking out that note, stared at it with open eyes and mouth, and then replaced it and double-locked the safe. It seemed like an awfully large sum to me, an unheard of amount, and many times during the day did I open that safe to gaze longingly at the note.

II

In his initial year of low-paid employment Rockefeller had to work out some difficult personal problems. First on $3.50 a week, then on $6, he must feed and clothe himself, save, and give. He devoted to these matters the same thought and system that he gave to the office of Hewitt & Tuttle. In fact, in 1855 he began a ledger of his own—"Ledger A." This document, still preserved, speaks eloquently of his early financial struggles.

[8]*Idem.*

The very cover tells something of his straitened circumstances. "When I found this book recently," said Rockefeller forty years later, "I thought it had no cover, because I saw that it had writing on its back. But I had utilized the cover to write upon. In those days I was economical, even with paper."[9] The size of a thin duodecimo book, it has neatly inked upon its leather cover the title "Ledger A," and below that, in Spencerian script upon a ruled line, his signature. Entries late in 1855 and early in 1856 show payments for board, with extra sums to his landlady for washing, and prove also that he was saving part of his little stipend. But he was no miser, for at the same time he was giving. From December to April he received less than $95 for four months' work. In addition to $1 pew rent, and smaller sums for a little religious paper, *The Macedonian,* he gave away $5.88, or about 6 per cent of his total wage. The Sunday school got one large copper on most Sundays, but sometimes five cents. "That was all the money I had to give for that particular object." Foreign missions were allotted at least ten cents a month; the Mite Society was given fifty; and the Five Points Mission, in New York City's most vicious slum area, twelve cents. The young Clevelander was sorry for New York! Additional gifts were made for needy members of the Erie Street Church, who included many casual laborers. One item runs, "to a poor man in church, .25," and another, "To a poor woman in church, .50."; while twenty-five cents went into a class present for the venerable Deacon Sked.[10] All this was a remarkable performance. On his meager income he had approached a literal interpretation of the Biblical injunction as to a tithe of a man's earnings. Most young men would have felt no obligation to give at all until they had established a comfortable margin between expenses and salary. But as Rockefeller had determined to get all that he honorably could, so he had determined to give all that he could.

The ledger indicates that in doing this Rockefeller used money that others would unhesitatingly have allotted to "necessities." In the same period that he gave away $5.88, he spent only $9.09 for clothing. Some $2.50 of this sum, entered for a pair of gloves, seemed

[9]See pamphlet, "Mr. Rockefeller's Ledger, Address Given March 21, 1897."
[10]The original of the ledger is kept at 30 Rockefeller Plaza, N. Y.; a reproduction is in the Rockefeller papers.

to him forty years later an unaccountable extravagance. "I remember that I used to wear mittens," he said dubiously, and indeed an early item was "three shillings" for mittens. But the $2.50 may have been a practical expenditure; bookkeepers needed supple fingers, and the fur gloves were a protection from the icy lake winds. It may even have been a gift to his father, who drove constantly. Most of the remaining $6.59 probably went for a cheap suit. "I could not secure the most fashionable cut of clothing," he remarked in 1897. "I remember I bought mine then of a cheap clothier. He sold me clothing cheap, clothing such as I could pay for, and it was a great deal better than buying clothes that I could not pay for."[11] He seldom bought his lunch, but carried it with him in a little box to the office.

The consideration that he was "as independent as Mr. Astor" (William B. Astor was then esteemed the richest man in America) kept him cheerful in his self-imposed regimen. He might have spent his $5.88 for further comforts. He might have drawn upon the little hoard, steadily growing in size and now amounting to several hundred dollars, that had lain in the blue china bowl. But he did not compromise with his Ben Franklin philosophy. "I did not make any obligations I could not meet," was his later comment. "I lived within my means."[12] When he received his first salary increase this country lad had a guilty feeling—"I felt like a criminal; like a capitalist." But he raised the scale of his personal expenditures only moderately. His life would nowadays seem singularly bare of amusements or recreation; but he was a self-contained young man who found that home, church, and singing-class provided enough social activity, and who got sufficient excitement from participation in the great drama of American business.

Home life did not long mean visits to Parma, for the Rockefeller family moved into Cleveland a year after John obtained his position. The old restlessness still possessed William Avery Rockefeller. He had lived in Strongsville for a time, then had come to Cleveland for a year in a house on Perry Street, then in 1855 had gone out to Parma, and after about a year had removed into town again! He and Eliza established a residence for the entire family in a brick

[11]Pamphlet, "Mr. Rockefeller's Ledger."
[12]"Speech to the Club, May 7, 1904."

house on the north side of Cedar Street—No. 35. It was a comfortable twelve-room house, and seems to have had that very distinct luxury for the fifties, a bathroom.[13]

All the Rockefeller children were growing up. Lucy was nineteen, a plump, sweet-faced girl, soon to marry. William, at fifteen a round-cheeked, light-haired, jolly youth, was in his last year of high school. Mary Ann, still short and dumpy, was thirteen, and boisterous, irresponsible Frank was eleven. The three brothers, as it cannot be too clearly understood, were almost totally unlike each other. A picture taken a little later, about 1858, shows all five children in a symmetrical group, three seated and two standing. All are dressed with great neatness and in good clothing; the two oldest boys have conspicuous watch chains, while Lucy's dress is obviously silk. Of the five it is Lucy, a comely young woman despite the severe fashion of her hair, and John, whose finely modelled and reflective face shows both determination and sensitivity, who arrest attention. All look older than their years, and John and Lucy as if responsibility had descended upon them at an untimely age—as by present-day standards it had. But part of their staidness may be attributed to the Victorian decorum then expected of young people, and part to the rigidity of pose required by long-exposure cameras.

Eliza Rockefeller was only forty-three in 1856; but the years, the frequent uprootings of the family, and the uncertainties of her life had aged her. She said little, she went little to other women's homes, and she lived within a narrow circle. But, independent in her tastes, she was not unhappy; letters written by her at a later period suggest a pleasant serenity and self-mastery. Her children kept her busy, while from 1856 onward she found an outlet for her additional energies in church work. Probably she had been a regular attendant at the Erie Street Church when the family took up its first residence in town in 1854; now, a member, she played an active part in its affairs, and served as vice-president of its Society for Women.

"Uncle Billy" Rockefeller, when at home, was as commanding, energetic, bustling, and likable as ever. He was prospering; and as he prospered, he became less and less a medicine-hawker and more and more one of the numerous irregular "physicians" of the day. He

---

[13]Miss Sked told Inglis, Sept. 26, 1917, that at the Cedar Street place the Rockefellers kept brown bantam chickens.

dressed more soberly, bore himself with more dignity, and went afield less frequently. The Cleveland *Directory* for 1857 lists him as "physician (botanic)." He may have built up a considerable practice among people who liked an herbal doctor better than a licensed medico, who preferred the glittering promises of patent medicines to the sober realities of a Latin prescription. The 1857 *Directory* gave John the same address and listed him as "bookkeeper."

John often made loans for his father;[14] and one evidence of the shrewd, headstrong "doctor's" prosperity appears in a loan of $1000 which he made to John's employer Hewitt. After the produce merchant had held the money beyond the term agreed upon, William Avery Rockefeller asked his son to tell Hewitt that it must be repaid. The young man did so several times, but unsuccessfully. "I couldn't go to my employer as I would to a stranger," he explained later. But his father was troubled by no feeling of delicacy. Marching down to Merwin Street, he asked to see the senior partner.

"Mr. Hewitt," he declared, "I'm sorry, but I must have that money —right away."

He was in an authoritative mood. Though he smiled, his jaw closed with a firmness that gave the produce merchant a subtle sense of danger. Hewitt got the money and discharged the debt. "When father looked at a man like that, the man was apt to do what he told him," remarked John D. Rockefeller, who had been present.[15]

Beyond question the canny "doctor" perceived John's business talent. In the spring of 1858 he called the young man to him one evening. "I have bought a lot at 33 Cheshire Street," he announced, "and I want a house built on it for the family. I want you to build that house. The money is ready. Draw up your plans and arrange to have the work properly done. Just keep within the amount I have allowed—everything else is left to you. I shall be away and must rely on your judgment."

John delightedly set about the task. He and Eliza planned the building.[16] He obtained a contractor—his account book contains an entry, "Names of Parties who want for job of Building House," with

[14]Rockefeller, *Random Reminiscences,* 48; John's landlady thought the "doctor" charged exorbitant interest rates.

[15]Inglis, Conversations with Rockefeller.

[16]So Rockefeller said on one occasion; but on another he told Mr. Inglis that his father left the plans.

eight names appended—and he watched the progress of the work morning, noon, and evening. "The builder lost money on his contract," said John's sister, Mrs. Rudd, years later. "It was his own fault, I suppose, for bidding too low; but I always felt sorry for that man." He had erected an exceptionally good house. Long after, when a manufacturer obtained it and planned to tear out some of the partitions, he found the construction so strong that he decided it was wiser to leave the walls as they were. The building, of dark red brick, ample in size, and like nearly all Cleveland houses, simple in line, bore the stamp of solid respectability. It was a source of great pleasure to the family—the best house they had ever had. In this same year John took charge for his mother of the estate business resulting from the death of John Davison.[17]

While usually engrossed in his own responsibilities and slowly shaping purposes, he still showed flashes of the droll humor which had been noted at Owego and in the Cleveland high school. One Cleveland friend recalls seeing him approach a group of girls preparing the lunch at a picnic—probably a church outing—to remark with a twinkle: "Girls, remember, if you eat slow you can eat more."[18] His brothers and sisters appreciated his teasing sense of fun. But on the whole he was a solemn young man; so grave, pious, methodical and unemotional that to some he seemed lacking in human qualities. He himself remembered how the son of a Cleveland merchant, discussing the personnel of Hewitt & Tuttle, exclaimed: "Oh, young Rockefeller—he's a stick!"[19]

Even Deacon Sked found a saturnine and disconcerting quality in him, though he was devoted to the old Scot. When the boy saw the downright florist just before starting work, the latter made a blunt statement. "Before I went away," recalled Rockefeller as an old man, "he remarked that he liked me pretty well, but that he had always liked my brother William much better. I could never think why he said that. I did not hold it against him, but it puzzled me."[20]

Most other people, while respecting John more than his associates and admiring his ability, liked jolly, sociable Will, or open-hearted,

[17]Documents relating to the Davison estate are in the Rockefeller papers.
[18]Miss Mary K. Tibbetts in Cleveland *Plain-Dealer*, July 13, 1905.
[19]Cleveland *Plain-Dealer*, Oct. 4, 1906.
[20]*Euclid Baptist Church Fiftieth Anniversary* (booklet), 30.

undependable Frank, much better. Mild and pleasant though John usually was, he hid behind an inscrutable exterior, always withholding part of himself. He detested unrestrained emotion, and outside very restricted circles showed little social warmth; while William, with nothing like his force of personality or piercing mind, was franker, more energetic physically, more gregarious. To be sure, beneath the subtle, reflective reserve of the oldest brother lay humor, patience, and though in early life he could show temper, a kind of sweetness. When some event suddenly tapped these qualities, men were surprised and impressed, though still baffled. But even when showing kindness to others, he often did it in an impassive, undemonstrative way which left a chill. "Don't be a good fellow," he warned one of his Bible classes in later years. "Don't let good fellowship get the least hold on you. . . . It is my firm conviction that every downfall is traceable directly or indirectly to the victim's good fellowship, his good cheer among his friends, who come as quickly as they go. We have to apologize every day for this class of men who fill our hospitals, our asylums, our poorhouses, and the very gutters of our streets. Look on them and don't be a good fellow." Here he had in mind the weakly convivial side of good-fellowship, and meant to insist that strong character is built upon discipline and the subjection of desire to will; but the remark had its broader significance as well.

While in some ways he was marked by breadth of view, in others he was distinctly narrow. Miss Tarbell's statement that he had "the soul of a bookkeeper" is absurd, for he had astonishing vision. "I liked bookkeeping," he later said, but in the same breath: "I had ideas. I wanted to get ahead." But it was a business vision, the vision of a one-track genius. In every way he disciplined himself. As he maintained his social independence, his aloofness from emotional relations, so he maintained an independence of human frailties. He felt few impulses to indulge himself in money-spending. Ordinary weaknesses of the flesh simply did not appeal to him. "I never had a craving for tobacco, or tea and coffee. I never had a craving for anything."[21] In the late eighteen-fifties his notebooks show only rare purchases of candy. He frequently bought nuts and apples, but that may have been for lunch. "He was always abstemious to a

[21]Inglis, Conversations with Rockefeller.

degree in everything," later recalled Mary K. Tibbetts.[22] Now and then he hired livery horses, for driving was soon to become his chief recreation, but as yet this too was rare. Neither at this time nor later did he show the slightest taste for the theatre. He read few books, and collected none. He did conscientiously attend lectures at the high school, church, and Y. M. C. A. (which he joined in 1857),[23] and his later writings and utterances show that he picked up from them and from sermons many a literary and historical fact. He bought a dictionary in 1857, gave $35 for a secretary-bookcase, and paid for a number of concerts.

He even disciplined his own industry. In a revolt against voluntary overwork, he wrote in his private ledger on June 25, 1858: "I have this day covenanted with myself not to be seen in No. 45 [Merwin Street] after 10 o'clock P.M. within thirty days. John D. Rockefeller." But of this he soon repented, for under the entry is written: "Don't make any more such covenants."

His detachment might have been broken down had he been thrown into a large business office full of lively young fellows, or been compelled to knock about for a time from city to city and job to job. But it remained intact, blending naturally with his ingrained caution, reticence, and tendency to ponder and reflect. He was quite aware, as he became older, that it had penalties as well as advantages, but he seems never to have understood why the world imposed them. With intimates, to be sure, his relations could be extremely close and warm, but even there he retained a certain taciturnity. Seldom have a father and son had a closer bond than that existing between him and John D. Rockefeller, Jr.; their devotion to each other was complete. Yet the relation, as the younger Mr. Rockefeller has said, was never expansive. "Neither father nor I possessed the temperament which gives itself freely. We talked about whatever we had to talk over—never discursively." In dealing with most men, the characteristics of Rockefeller which made for concentration of purpose and a single-minded grasp of business affairs engendered an isolation which faintly puzzled its victim. To a great army of employees his personality and policies came to command devotion, but except

---

[22]Cleveland *Plain-Dealer,* July 13, 1905.
[23]His ledger shows a number of entries for tickets.

among a small group of executives they never aroused warm affection.

III

When Rockefeller went to work the country was in the last phase of a world-wide boom promoted by railroad building, the stabilization of banking, the flow of gold from California and Australia, and other factors. Within two years the fruit and leaves of the green commercial tree were withering under the panic of 1857. But the blight proved brief. It was followed by another great war and post-war boom, carrying the industrial development of the nation irresistibly forward. Rockefeller had stepped upon the stage of American business at an advantageous time; a time of rapid transformations, multitudinous new beginnings, fast-increasing wealth and strength. He was just twenty-one—just attaining his manhood—when the prodigious war-time boom began.

To many people in the late fifties the slavery issue seemed all-engrossing; but actually the steady growth of industry and agriculture was the most important factor in national life. If slavery could only have been left alone, this growth in another generation would doubtless have revealed it for what it was—an anachronistic and economically unsound institution, confined to a limited section, and doomed to a slow but sure death. The nation was moving rapidly forward on three different but connected roads: it was on the move westward, on the move cityward, and on the move toward a complete industrial revolution. Edward Channing has pointed out that in the thirty years ending 1850, the people west of the Appalachians doubled with five millions to spare, while the people east of the Appalachians failed to double by two millions. In 1820 there had been only thirteen American cities with a population of more than 8000; but in 1850 there were eighty-five such cities, and in 1860 there were 144—with New York fast approaching a million, and Philadelphia already past a million. By that year even Cleveland had nearly 44,000 people. As for the industrial revolution, year by year it changed the face of American life.

Of all the manifold changes of the day, the swiftest and most spectacular seemed to be those in transportation. The railroad, so recently a dream, was now for every State a magical fact. When Rockefeller was born, transportation still remained for most of America just what it had been in Jefferson's time. People came together only by heroic effort: New Englanders tossing through Atlantic storms in little sloops and schooners, Georgians splashing on long horseback rides through red clay and dripping pines, Kentuckians working up over the Allegheny passes on long journeys of a month's duration. When Congress debated the Louisiana Purchase, half of its members believed that a great part of this new empire could never really be settled, and that it was too remote from the center of government ever to be securely controlled. Even in Rockefeller's boyhood, the West was a wilderness or semiwilderness showing little areas of tilled earth wherever men clung along the lakes and rivers, painfully grooving out their canals and hewing out their post roads, and waiting for the steamboat whistle and stagecoach horn.

But as Rockefeller had grown into youth Americans had seen iron rails slowly threading the interior of the continent, section linking to section until New Yorkers could travel overnight to Buffalo, and Philadelphians to Cincinnati or to Richmond. As he turned the leaves of his ledger in Hewitt & Tuttle's office the locomotive was penetrating even the remote parts of the West, bringing Iowa closer to New York Harbor than Boston had been when George Washington took the oath of office in Federal Hall. Twenty-three miles of rails in 1830; 2818 in 1840; 9021 in 1850; and in 1860 more than 30,600, or ten times the distance from Cape Cod to Frémont's Golden Gate. This was a revolution indeed—a revolution that levelled mountains and shrunk up the plains, built empires out of marshy prairie and buffalo ranges, and struck cities from the wilderness as the staff of Moses had brought water from the rock. No conqueror with legions of men had ever won so great a territory, or held it with such security and ease!

Cleveland itself by the end of the fifties had no fewer than five important railroads—the Cleveland, Columbus & Cincinnati, built at the very beginning of the decade; the Cleveland & Pittsburgh; the Lake Shore Railroad, connecting with both the Erie and the New York Central; the Cleveland & Toledo; and the Cleveland & Mahoning, which ran to Youngstown and the coal fields. Still another, the most important of all to Rockefeller's business future, was soon to be added—the Atlantic & Great Western. These, with the Great Lakes and the Erie Canal, gave the lusty city an almost unrivalled set of transportation facilities.

The young man in the wholesale-produce house was aware also of other changes. The telegraph wires which he had first seen at Owego were outrunning even the railways; and all about him were the evidences or astonishing rumors of other innovations. Inventors had taken out only 544 patents in 1830; in the decade that he entered business they filed 28,000. McCormick had patented his reaper in 1834, and by 1860 farmers were buying 4000 of them a year, chiefly in the Middle West. Rockefeller, driving out among the Ohio grain fields to make his collections, often saw their circling reels in the distance and heard the clatter of the vibrating sickles above his horses' hoofs. Steam had brought greater power to the textile mills, and improved machinery had quickened their productiveness. In consequence, cheap cottons and woolens could now be had everywhere, and men's clothing at $4 or $5 a suit—clothing that even young Rockefeller "could pay for." The anthracite fields had been linked by rail with the large seaboard cities, and Frederick Geissenhainer had shown that hard coal could be effectively used in the iron industry. Steel was not yet important in America; Bessemer's process was not invented until 1856, and it did not prove usable with most iron ores for years to come. Nevertheless, a stream of wrought-iron bolts, axes, moulded plowshares, springs, and wire was pouring from the mills at prices that delighted hardware and implement dealers, and that made the farmer abandon his forge. The friction match was no longer a marvel but an everyday object. Alarm clocks with standardized parts were legion. The sewing machine, invented in 1846, was steadily making its way into American homes, and even washing-machine patents were becoming common.

Tinned foods had become sufficiently cheap by 1856 to find a large market. Packing-houses, buying stock from the western farms, were smoking, salting, and canning their meats, though of course not yet refrigerating them. Photography, wood-pulp paper, manufactured leather goods, chemical by-products, cheap paint, cast-iron stoves, machine-milled flour, revolvers, parlor organs, penny newspapers from rotary presses, and a revolutionized postal service were some of the amazing new manifestations of the Machine Age. In the single decade before the Civil War the value of manufactured goods increased by 80 per cent, and in the latter year the nation's population, which in the childhood of many still living had been almost entirely rural, proved to be nearly one-sixth urban. The significance of these changes was widely recognized and indeed ecstatically hailed. The year he went to Cleveland, young Rockefeller had read glowing accounts of the Crystal Palace Exhibition in New York, where many of the wonders of the new industrialism were exhibited to curious crowds.

But other modifications of the older farm-and-wilderness civilization were not so far advanced and were less clearly understood. The accumulations of capital, the new transportation facilities, quantity production by means of machines, and thickening population had produced a natural tendency for men to unite in corporations. The joint-stock company was older than the Mississippi Bubble, older than the company which had financed the first permanent settlement of Virginia at Jamestown. But the corporation in the modern sense, the corporation with a great body of stockholders many of whom experienced no personal contact with the business, had just begun to flourish with vigor in America. Banks had been the earliest important organizations to use the new corporation procedure. At first bank charters, railroad charters, and manufacturing charters had been obtained by individual enactment of legislatures. But, following the passage of New York's general incorporation law of 1846, State after State permitted corporations to organize at will under a comprehensive statute. When the Beverly Cotton Manufactory had been incorporated by Massachusetts law in 1789, it had seemed to many an anomalous and disturbing organization; but by the Civil War such companies were becoming common. In the years 1820–23 more than five hundred corporations had been incorporated in America, chiefly in Massachusetts and New York; before Rockefeller went to work with Hewitt & Tuttle, all the northern and western States had passed comprehensive laws permitting incorporation, and the firms which had taken advantage of them were numbered by tens of thousands. In general, they were strictly forbidden to hold property outside the States in which they were chartered. Of course, partnerships and individual ownerships were still the rule; but everywhere observant men saw how rapidly the new corporate mechanism was growing, and what a sweeping effect it was bound to have upon American economic and social life.

The importance of the modern factory with its division of labor and its standardized product was also just being grasped. This type of factory had first appeared in America under Eli Whitney, who early in the century commenced making firearms with interchangeable parts for the government. Beginning in 1814, when Francis Cabot Lowell installed a power loom for the Boston Manufacturing Company at Waltham, that textile company had operated a factory with specialized labor, systematized methods of accounting, buying, and selling, and standardized output. After 1850 the Waltham watches were made in a similar manner. Cyrus H. McCormick had introduced an establishment of modern type in the West in 1847, when he built his reaper factory in Chicago and used specialized labor to turn out a thoroughly standardized machine with parts that could be supplied in any quantity and unvarying sizes. He was a pioneer also in carrying an elaborate organization outside the factory and into the market. His experiments with sales districts, field trials, guarantees of service, and the deferred-payment plan were to have a profound effect on American business. In Hartford, Samuel Colt's revolver manufactory was shortly carrying Whitney's processes of standardized production to a wholly new pitch of efficiency, and making machinery for gun-factories in England, Russia, and other parts of the globe.

Even in 1856 such factories as McCormick's, Colt's, and the Baldwin Locomotive Works were exceptional, and doing the work of pioneers. But the tremendous potentialities of their methods for industry in general had been demonstrated in a way that was easily visible to shrewd observers. The young man in Hewitt & Tuttle's was quick to observe, greatly given to meditation, and gifted with a mind of extraordinary force and grasp. He caught instantly the significance of an advertisement, a newspaper item, a chance word by a visitor to the office. He carried that significance home with him and thought it over carefully and intently. Little by little, as the months passed, he built up a clear image of the complex mechanical and commercial changes under way, and began to formulate certain theories as to the way in which they might be given a better pattern and greater power, the way in which the confusion and waste might be lessened.

IV

Rockefeller's first important display of initiative was in connection with the Erie Street Baptist Church. While Hewitt & Tuttle was a small, conservative establishment, in which he had little chance to do anything but collect bills and keep books, the church was a large, new, and very plastic institution. He was young, poor, and naturally quiet, yet he had qualities which made him a leader.

All our available evidence indicates that the Erie Street Church was a poor man's church.[24] The most prosperous sects in Cleveland were the Congregationalists and Episcopalians; that Western Reserve country had a strong New England tinge, and the Baptists had sat below the salt in every part of New England except little Rhode Island. The sect had shown especial vigor in sending missionary preachers into the new settlements of the West, and had grown rapidly, but its converts were seldom from the richer elements of any community. This particular congregation was new when Rockefeller joined it, having been organized about three years earlier by forty-four devout Baptists of the city. The members were largely poor clerks, artisans, and shopkeepers, and it had little money. It was essentially an offshoot of the First Baptist Church, some of whose communicants had noticed the "religious destitution" of the Erie Street neighborhood, a rapidly growing part of town, had opened a chapel there, and had finally purchased a battered Presbyterian meetinghouse and moved to the corner of Erie and Ohio. The room was small, uncarpeted, and bare of pictures or ornaments. The women sat on one side, the men on the other. Members of the congregation long swept the floor and washed the windows, for every penny counted. At the beginning the great asset of the church was its brilliant young minister, J. Hyatt Smith, who had originally been trained for the stage, and whose eloquent sermons drew people from all over town; "perhaps the most popular

---

[24]The booklet, *Euclid Baptist Church Fiftieth Anniversary,* contains much historical material; *see also* the W. P. A. Digests of the *Leader* and other Cleveland newspapers, and Ella Grant Wilson's *Old Euclid Avenue* and other volumes on Cleveland.

preacher in Cleveland at that time," said Rockefeller later. Paid a pitiful salary, eked out by "donation parties," he was too good for that poor congregation to keep and resigned in 1855 for a better pulpit. "Some of us young people," Rockefeller sardonically remarked afterward, "couldn't exactly understand why he should go off to those rich people and leave us, but we were told it was a call from God." The church reeled under the blow. Many feared it would break up. Next Sunday, anxious Deacon Ezra Thomas stood at the door and said to John, as to everybody else who entered: "Tell me whether you are going to stay. I want to know if you are going to stay."[25]

As a bright high-school graduate, a faithful attendant, a most staid and responsible young man, John soon took a prominent part in all church activities. He threw himself into them with characteristic single-mindedness. As we have said, the church offered this unemotional youth an outlet—until marriage, his most important expression of feeling; while it also offered his mother, brothers, and sisters the best part of what social life they enjoyed.

Indeed, it is difficult now for many Americans to realize how important a social institution the church—with its two Sunday services, its midweek service, its suppers, men's societies, sewing-clubs—then was in most towns of thirty thousand. Rockefeller repeatedly testified to the profit which his reserved, exacting nature found in this church connection. There alone he expanded; he let himself go with a sense of consecration and enthusiasm. He had no other place except his home, he said later, "where I felt so at ease." The inspirational preaching, the singing, the fervent baptismal ceremonies that could be traced back to John Spilsbury in early seventeenth-century England, the volunteer talks by those who had found religious comfort, the practical activity of missions and Sunday school, the "socials" at the minister's home, the picnics, gave him a sense of creative activity. After his toil over invoices and accounts, he found refreshment and release in his churchgoing; it imparted a higher meaning to his laborious life. "How grateful I am that these associations were given to me in my early boyhood, that I was contented and happy with this sort of work," he exclaimed as a man; "with the work in the church, with the work

[25]*Euclid Baptist Church Fiftieth Anniversary.*

in the Sunday school, with the work with good people—that was my environment, and I thank God for it!"[26] He looked upon the congregation as a sodality, all dedicated to the same high objects, and united by the bonds of Christian affection. "I cannot understand a church where people get up and march out," he declared later. "There ought to be something that makes a church homelike. Friends should be glad to see each other and to greet strangers. There should be something every time to make people want to come back." His favorite hymn was inspired by the text in Proverbs, "A friend that sticketh closer than a brother":

> I've found a Friend: oh, such a Friend!
> He loved me ere I knew him. . . .

Many people are Baptists, Methodists, or Catholics before they are Christians; but Rockefeller was a Christian before he was a Baptist. Of that fact his personal account book gives ample evidence. Even as a young man he was friendly toward other denominations. In 1860 and 1861, for example, he made contributions to the Methodist Church, a German Sunday school, a Negro church, and "Catholic orphans"—a remarkable list. A busy young Baptist in the Western Reserve who was then sufficiently tolerant and generous to give to Negroes and Catholics was an unusual young man indeed! For companionship he naturally preferred the members of his own church. He could have made a good many friends in high school, and later among young clerks and businessmen of the town. But he has explicitly told us that he liked best to mingle with the "earnest, inspired people" of the Erie Street congregation. The meetinghouse was his spiritual home; he trusted its successive prewar ministers, Smith, Alfred Pinney, and D. S. Watson, its deacons and other officers, and they trusted him. Some of his fellow members were later prominent businessmen in Cleveland; for example, Henry Chisholm, a Scot by birth, who became an organizer of great rolling mills there and in Chicago.[27] We should add that he became a warm friend of the minister of the First Baptist Church, whose

---

[26]"Speech to the Club, May 7, 1904."

[27]Friendship between the Rockefellers and Chisholms became fairly close; the Rockefeller papers show that Mrs. John D. Rockefeller frequently called on Mrs. Chisholm, and children of the two families saw much of each other.

son, Colgate Hoyt, was later to play a curious part in Rockefeller's life.

Rockefeller's devotion was proved by diligent service and constant giving. He attended faithfully. He gave increasingly from his small salary; the Sunday school contributions increased from one cent a week to three, to five, and then to greater sums, while his other donations rose in proportion. This money was badly needed, for heavy debts had been incurred in rebuilding the church, and much of the construction had been paid for by notes bearing 10 per cent interest. The minister was allowed only $800 a year and the sexton $100. We find in Rockefeller's little "ledger" the entry for July 30, 1858: "Extra Subscription for Erie St. Ch. $15," and there are others of like purport. He eagerly shouldered responsibilities. After serving as clerk from October 6, 1858, to October 14, 1859, he handed that duty over to his brother Will, doubtless with some supervision, and took charge of a Sunday school class. As clerk he set down in his ledger every expenditure for stationery and postage, and then cancelled it all by a red-ink entry, "Let it go." He helped the Rev. D. S. Watson, who was minister 1857–60, in various ways. And as the straits of the church increased, he was foremost in raising money.

Long afterward he told how the minister one Sunday announced from the pulpit that if a large sum were not raised immediately— as Rockefeller recalled it, $2000—the church building would have to be given up. He related that as soon as morning service was ended, he planted himself at the door. He stopped every member of the congregation, and begged for a contribution. As each one made a pledge, he put down the name and amount in a little book. Some could promise only a few cents a week; others offered twenty-five or even fifty. Young Rockefeller had then to pursue each member and collect the pledge, a task stretching over laborious months. At last the $2000 was accumulated and the debt paid.

"The plan absorbed me," Rockefeller recalled. "I contributed what I could, and my first ambition to earn more money was aroused by this and similar undertakings in which I was constantly engaged. The begging experiences I had at that time were full of interest. I went at the task with pride rather than the reverse, and I continued it until my increasing cares and responsibilities compelled me to resign the actual working out of details to others. I cannot understand why some men say, 'I am not a beggar.' Any man should be proud to beg in such a good cause."[28]

It is impossible to verify this story, which probably has more general truth than accuracy in detail. Indeed, Rockefeller gives another version, in which he describes himself standing in front of the church not to collect pledges, but to buttonhole members of a committee of twenty-five which had been selected to raise the money under his direction. Fortunately we do have some precise facts. Church records show that the panic of 1857 and ensuing hard times struck the congregation a disastrous blow.[29] It was carrying a heavy debt on its building, and another on a reed organ of which it was very proud—it paid an organist $50 a year! A contractor who was deacon of the church, A. A. Stafford, held a mortgage on the building, and in the spring of 1859 intimated that he would foreclose unless payment was made by a certain date. An extension was with some difficulty obtained; Rockefeller later said that he and Will, on the last night, went to Stafford's house and by throwing stones at his window woke him up to sign it. Energetic action was then required. A meeting of the trustees was called on July 18, 1859, to consider ways and means.

"The chairman," state the minutes, "made a few remarks relative to the immediate indebtedness of the church, and to his inability as Treasurer to meet the present demand. And stated that this meeting was called more particularly to consider what course to pursue in the premises and called upon the brethren present to speak fully upon the subject. Deacon Stafford said he had looked over the whole ground ever since the organization of the church and as all the projects heretofore resorted to for this object *had failed,* he would suggest the propriety of taking up a collection at every service on the Sabbath, assuring at the same time that it was customary in Eastern cities and [he] saw no impropriety in adopting the same course here. The brethren present expressed themselves freely upon the subject and it was moved by Brother Thomas and seconded by Brother Adams that a collection be taken every Sabbath . . . for the support of the gospel in this place."

[28]Inglis, Conversations with Rockefeller.
[29]A book containing the trustees' minutes for this period is in the Rockefeller papers.

The church embarrassments remained so heavy that on May 7, 1860, the trustees appointed a committee to examine ways of relieving them. Rockefeller was not a member of this body. Two weeks later it had been decided to sell the church property, and Brothers Chisholm and Deland were appointed to make arrangements. On June 6 the church was in such low water that the trustees voted to request the organist and sexton to discontinue their services. Meanwhile, the selling committee found no purchaser; and on August 8 it reported that it had deeded Deacon Stafford the church building and land in satisfaction of his claim. It had then leased the building for five years. So impoverished was the congregation that the cherished organ was advertised for sale. Nevertheless, the church was kept alive in its leased building by self-sacrificing gifts from members. Boxes were placed in the entry for contributions; a diligent canvass was conducted.[30] It was perhaps at this critical moment that Rockefeller took charge of the campaign for funds.

At any rate, it is significant that from the time of this crisis he became increasingly a leader in church affairs. He was elected one of the five trustees as soon as he attained his majority, taking his seat September 14, 1860. Despite his youth, men regarded him as the most sagacious member of the board. His brother Will continued to act as clerk. Under date of February 25, 1861, we find among the trustees' minutes: "Moved by Brother Rockefeller that a subscription paper be circulated among the membership of the church by the trustees to raise $118, this being a balance of indebtedness from current expenses to September 1, 1860, and balance due for repairs." By the end of 1861 the church was fairly stable again. A "grand Christmas festival" which John supervised raised money for a Sunday-school library, and was followed by others. He had been appointed to audit the treasurer's accounts, and beginning in 1862, the trustees met frequently at his house. The following spring he, Will, and ten others organized a Young Men's Society for helping clear away the debt, and despite the pressure of the war, they succeeded, with outside aid, in cancelling the obligation.[31]

By 1866 both John and Will were trustees, Will was treasurer of the church, and Frank and Mary Ann were prominent in all church

[30]Trustees' minutes. [31]*Idem.*

activities. By this time the congregation, some of whose members had done well in the war years, actually showed tokens of becoming a wealthy body. Beginning in 1867, trustees' meetings were held regularly in "Brother Rockefeller's office," he now being president of the body.[32]

V

Like everything else he did, his giving had an increasing amount of system. Sometime before the Civil War there fell into his hands a book published in 1855, which exerted a larger influence upon him than he then perceived. This was *Extracts From the Diary and Correspondence of the Late Amos Lawrence*. Lawrence, a great New England textile manufacturer and philanthropist, had died in 1852 in the plenitude of a well-earned fame. Many of his letters dealt with gifts. In one he asked his partner to direct a bank official to send over some money. "His beautiful bills find an exceedingly ready use. I shall be glad of one hundred in ones and twos, two hundred in fives, and three hundred in tens and twenties." Rockefeller found the volume absorbing. "He gave away more than $100,-000 to help mankind," he remarked later in life. "I remember how fascinated I was with his letters. I can see it, as if the type were before my eyes now, how he gave away crisp bills. 'Crisp bills!' I could see and hear them. I made up my mind that if I could manage it, some day I would give away 'crisp bills,' too."[33]

The "crisp bills" were not important. What was important, as the book made plain to every one, was the fact that Lawrence in the last decade of his life gave away five sixths of his whole income for that period; and above all, that he gave it away systematically, taking great pains to make his gifts appropriate and helpful.[34] He was no random philanthropist. The time was to come when Rockefeller would recall his planned giving in making his own benefactions.

We have a record of only one friendship of any interest outside the church in the years just preceding the Civil War. In the fall of 1857 Charles F. Browne, later famous as "Artemus Ward," a tall, cheerful stripling from Maine, joined the Cleveland *Plain-Dealer*,

[32]*Idem.*   [33]"Speech to the Club, May 7, 1904."
[34]*Extracts From the Diary and Correspondence of the Late Amos Lawrence,* (1855) edited by his son.

organ of the Douglas Democrats, as local editor at $12 a week. He saw to it that the local column twinkled with quips. Hewitt & Tuttle gave out daily market reports and other news, and Rockefeller was one of the young businessmen whom Browne, in that friendly little city, soon learned to know. In fact, Browne's predecessor, W. H. A. Bowen, brought him to Rockefeller's office during his first days on the *Plain-Dealer* staff. He was dragged in reluctantly, and stood in a confusion of embarrassment as Bowen announced: "Here's your new man, Mr. Rockefeller—my friend Charlie Browne!"

But Browne recovered at once and delivered some comic observations which broke Rockefeller's solemnity. "He was all angles and modesty," said the latter years afterward. "And funny! He could not help being funny. He saw everything from a queer, funny angle." Bubbling with merriment, full of original ideas, amusing even to look at with his quick eyes, violently Romanesque nose, and thick shock of hair, Browne soon became a general favorite. Many of the best things he ever wrote appeared in *The Plain-Dealer*. Early in 1858 he penned the first of his famous series of letters purporting to come from Artemus Ward, owner of the great travelling sideshow of wax works and "moral bears." Ward addressed it from Pittsburgh, which to gratify Clevelanders—rivalry between the cities being keen—he called "a 1-horse town." Expressing the business ethics of the period, he asked for free advertising and promised to have his handbills printed at the *Plain-Dealer* office. "You scratch my back and I will scratch your back also." Mutual back-scratching, as Rockefeller knew, was one of the first rules of business. In the fall of 1860 Browne went to New York and to fame. Rockefeller always delighted to recall him, laughed over his published works, and used to tell his children of a lecture he heard him give in Cleveland—a lecture midway in which Ward, growing thirsty, called upon the audience to appoint him and two friends as a committee to look at some "works of art" which he alleged were in the basement, and went out for a drink![35] Imitating Ward's drawl, he liked to quote one of his sentences: "I have a gigantic intellect—but I do not have it with me."

As the third year of his service with Hewitt & Tuttle closed in the

---

[35]Answering a written question, Rockefeller in March, 1936, sent me memoranda on his acquaintance with Artemus Ward.

autumn of 1858, the young bookkeeper, now nineteen, felt that he had completed his apprenticeship, and looked about with the object of bettering his position.

It had been a varied experience. To be sure, Hewitt & Tuttle had never been a thriving concern. They were almost waterlogged when the panic of 1857 struck American business, and the storm threw them on their beam ends. "The firm of Hewitt & Tuttle was really bankrupt," Rockefeller said sixty years afterward. "Mr. Hewitt's personal belongings were quite distinct from his interest in the business." Nevertheless, the partners' activities were sufficiently diversified to bring their clerk into relationship with the railroads, the lake steamships, the local merchants of northern Ohio, and the farmers. "My eyes were opened to the business of transportation," he said in recalling these years. The firm owned or managed dwelling houses, warehouses, and office buildings, and he used to collect the rents. He soon knew what had been done by Hewitt & Tuttle for years past. "I used to go over the old books . . . I soon found out how all the accounts were kept. This was not difficult, for I had always been methodical."[36]

The very smallness of the firm gave him the advantage of hearing the partners daily discuss their projects. "I was always present when they talked of their affairs, laid out their plans and decided upon a course of action." Then there were more and more transactions with men outside; railroad managers, lake captains, jobbers, and the like. After a time Rockefeller was given responsibility for rather complicated deals. "We would receive, for example, a shipment of marble from Vermont to Cleveland. This involved handling by railroad, canal, and lake boats. The cost of losses or damage had to be somehow fixed between these three different carriers, and it taxed all the ingenuity of a boy of seventeen to work out this problem to the satisfaction of all concerned, including my employers. . . . This experience in conducting all sorts of transactions at such an impressionable age . . . was highly interesting. . . ."[37]

His zest in the office work never failed him—he never let it become routine or drudgery; and since he was so keenly interested he ma-

[36]Inglis, Conversations with Rockefeller.
[37]Rockefeller, *Random Reminiscences*, 39–40.

tured rapidly. "The three years and a half of business training I had in that commission house formed a large part of the foundation of my business career," he later declared emphatically—and this is obviously true.

Undoubtedly his absorption grew out of the fact that he was looking forward to an independent career. At first his plans were tentative, for they depended upon the discoveries about the nature of business which he was reflectively making. But a further goal was always in his mind. "I had ideas," he said of his first months with the partners. "I wanted to get ahead." Of a slightly later period he remarked: "Even then I was preparing, getting ready for something big." He did not know what it would be, but he was diligently adding to the little capital he had saved, taking a larger and larger amount from his salary as the salary itself grew bigger.

His pay had been $25 a month for the first year. But at the end of 1856 Tuttle decided to part company with Hewitt. Rockefeller was ready to take more work, and Hewitt increased his salary to $500 a year, or more than $40 a month. His pay apparently went only to $600 during 1858, though he had now assumed practically all the duties of Tuttle, who had drawn $2000 a year. The clerk, still saving and still giving, began to wonder if he was fairly treated.

His discontent would have been greater had he not augmented his earnings through modest trading ventures. Such independent "fliers" became easier as he increased his acquaintanceship among merchants, who showed him opportunities in which Hewitt was not interested. His notebook for 1858 reveals two investments, both small. On September 6 he records "½ Profit 4 Bbls. flour," and two days later notes the expenditure of twenty-five cents for "drayage Flour and Hams."[38] Once he purchased eighty barrels of A1 pork, and sold it at a profit. With his ingrained caution, he undertook such ventures only when success seemed certain; but he was already showing that, having weighed a course, he could make a decision quickly and act on it with iron nerve. This combination of caution, precision, and courage attracted attention along the Cuyahoga waterfront. "Soon my employers noticed my methods of doing business," he said. "Other employers knew that I wanted to do the right thing;

[38]This notebook is preserved in the Rockefeller papers.

bankers then came to have confidence in me, and success followed step by step." Indeed, subsequent events prove that at least one banker in these early days was impressed by the young man. The fact that other men of affairs had shrewdly appraised his force and brains was also soon to become evident. He was preparing better than he knew for "something big."

VII

Clark & Rockefeller

So RAPIDLY did Rockefeller's discontent with his meager salary grow that in 1858 he asked Hewitt for a considerable increase. For doing just as much work as Tuttle he was receiving only one quarter of Tuttle's allowance (the junior partner taking a salary instead of a share of the profits). Moreover, he was getting less than his brother Will, also a bookkeeper-clerk in Cleveland, who was being paid $1000 a year. But when John asked for $800, Hewitt declared this impossible—which was no doubt true. "The firm was really bankrupt," said Rockefeller later. At one time it had made $6000 or $8000 a year, chiefly out of a flour-mill at Ogdensburgh; now it was losing. Hewitt, who had considerable property outside the firm, did raise his young assistant to $700, leaving the other hundred for future consideration.[1] Later, Rockefeller said that if he had been paid the full $800 he would have continued working for Hewitt. Early in 1859 the discontented young man began looking for something better. The effects of the panic of '57 were wearing off, Western trade was looking up, and he was anxious to strike into business for himself—to be independent.

Among his acquaintances in downtown Cleveland was a tall, broad-shouldered, attractive young Englishman (for Englishmen were numerous in the city), named Maurice B. Clark. He was working for Otis, Brownell & Company, grain and commission merchants at 9 River Street, and he had shown that he was self-reliance personified. Brought up near Malmesbury, Wiltshire, as were two other Cleveland men whom Rockefeller was to know well, Daniel

[1]Speech to Bible Class, Fifth Avenue Baptist Church, N. Y. *Evening Mail*, Oct. 21, 1905.

Shurmer and Samuel Andrews, he had begun life as a landscape gardener, and had knocked down an irascible employer who tried to chastise him. Fearing legal prosecution for the assault, Clark embarked for America, friendless and almost penniless—landing in Boston at the time of the great Bunker Hill celebration addressed by Daniel Webster. After several years of rough experience as farmhand, lumberman, teamster, and what not, he had arrived in Cleveland, taken the course at Folsom's Business College, and found a position. He was assisted by his friend Dan Shurmer, an earlier comer who had risen to be foreman of the firm of Hussey & Sinclair.[2] By industry and frugality Clark had saved about $2000, and was thinking of going into business for himself. Living at 36 Cheshire Street, he saw a good deal of the Rockefeller family near by, and knew John's reputation as a young businessman of more than ordinary ability and reliability.[3]

Clark, ten years older than Rockefeller, proposed that they form a partnership as commission merchants in grain, hay, meats, and miscellaneous goods, each investing $2000. They would collect farm products in northern Ohio and forward them to primary markets. The opportunity was attractive. John had saved only $800 or $900, but his father had promised that each child should have $1000 at the age of twenty-one for a start in life. John therefore proposed that the "doctor" advance him the $1000 at once, and that he pay interest on it for the sixteen months remaining before he came of age.

William Avery Rockefeller was quite willing. He had watched John closely, and took pride in his energy and capacity. But he enjoyed the old bargaining relationship that he had long ago established with his sons. They must realize that the world was strictly business, and grim, hard business at that.

"All right, John," he said. "But"—he held up a stern forefinger—"the interest will be 10 per cent!"[4]

This was the usual rate in Cleveland and other parts of the West —Lincoln's letters show that he insisted upon it for his stepmother's small funds; and John agreed. He was confident he could make

[2]Clark's grandson, Mr. Walter Teagle, has given me interesting information upon him.

[3]N. Y. *Herald,* Nov. 29, 1908.

[4]Rockefeller, *Random Reminiscences,* 40, 41; Bible Class Speech, N. Y. *Evening Mail,* Oct. 21, 1905.

the money bring that return. Accordingly, Clark and he pooled their funds, executed articles of partnership, and leased an office at 32 River Street. On March 18, 1859, though he himself later misstated the date as April 1, Clark & Rockefeller opened their doors with modest capital, abundant energy, and boundless hopes. The Cleveland *Leader* that day carried an encouraging news-item: "As experienced, responsible, and prompt businessmen, we recommend their house to the favorable consideration of our readers."

That night, and for many nights afterward, John D. Rockefeller, lying in bed, felt a thrill of pride. He was an independent man at last, a wholesale merchant with full opportunity to show initiative and brains. But he repulsed the exultant thoughts that crowded upon him, and after a habit he had formed, spoke sternly to his enthusiastic self.

"Now you are in business—true," he said to himself. "It is an opportunity. But be careful. Pride goeth before a fall. Nothing in haste, nothing ill-done. Your future hangs on every day that passes." This self-counselling was to become a habit. "These intimate conversations with myself," he wrote later, "had a great influence on my life. I was afraid I could not stand my prosperity, and tried to teach myself not to get puffed up with any foolish notions."[5]

II

The two young men had complementary qualities. Clark, a big, manly fellow, six feet tall and heavily built, was jovial, friendly, and fond of company; he had an extensive experience in directing workmen, buying produce and taking orders for goods, and made an excellent manager and salesman. He liked outdoor pursuits. While his character was excellent, he smoked and drank in moderation, relished a good story, and in general possessed robust tastes. He belonged to the Methodist Church, but as he confessed later, was "not strong on religion, but rather the reverse." He had some eccentricities; for example, an odd passion for attending auction sales. He would drive up to them, halt his vehicle on the edge of the crowd, and impulsively shout his bids over the heads of the bystanders. His grandson, Walter Teagle, who became president of the Standard Oil Company of New Jersey, remembered that the

[5]Rockefeller, *Random Reminiscences*, 46.

Clark attic was long stored with thousands of unsmokable cigars which his grandfather had obtained by a rash bid. Fond of the country and of horses, he shortly bought a farm near Cleveland and spent much time on it.[6] When he grew rich, he picked his business subordinates carefully, and then showed a decided disposition to hand over most business details to them. But in his late twenties, with his way still to make, he was industrious, energetic, and closely attentive to business.

Rockefeller brought to the partnership a thorough training in office work and a shrewd understanding of the grain and provision business. Clark, who had sought him because of his reputation for reliability and efficiency, was reluctant to recognize the range and solidity of his endowments, the dynamic strength behind his quiet ways. Taking full charge of the office, the junior partner gave its organization the same care that he had manifested at Hewitt & Tuttle's. "He was methodical to an extreme," Clark subsequently testified, "careful as to details and exacting to a fraction. If there was a cent due us he wanted it. If there was a cent due a customer he wanted the customer to have it."[7] Clark thought him too exact, but this preciseness was part of a thoroughness and probity which others instinctively admired. They trusted and respected the young merchant even if they smiled at his intense gravity. He was already "Mr. Rockefeller" to every one.

For a youth not quite twenty years old to assume the responsibilities of an independent business in a highly competitive field— a business soon handling carloads of produce and schooner-loads of grain—may seem to present-day readers remarkable. But business has its precocious talent no less than other callings, and Rockefeller had fully prepared himself. "By the time I was a man—long before it," he remarked later,[8] "I had learned the underlying principles of business as well as many men acquired them by the time they are forty." Nor was youthful initiative so exceptional in 1859 as today. In that period of unfettered competitive enterprise the earlier a man flung himself into affairs the better he fared. Jay Cooke had become an independent trader at sixteen, and a partner in a banking house at twenty-one. Jay Gould had amassed $5000 at the age of

[6]Mr. Teagle to the author.   [7]Interview by Mr. Inglis with Clark, 1917.
[8]Inglis, Conversations with Rockefeller, 1917.

twenty. In 1857 young Pierpont Morgan, only twenty, had established his own office. About the same time that Clark & Rockefeller was launched, a young Bavarian Jew, Nelson Morris, just a year Rockefeller's senior, was making a spectacular success as a trader in the Chicago livestock market. The year 1859 saw Andrew Carnegie, at twenty-four, manager of the Western Division of the Pennsylvania Railroad; and yet his rise was slow compared with that of his subsequent partner, Henry C. Frick, who at twenty-one was fast buying control of the Connellsville coke area. Years later James B. Duke would manage the hands in his father's tobacco factory at fourteen, and be a partner at eighteen.

One advantage of youth in business is that a young man can shift quickly from one field to another, as Carnegie shifted from railroads to iron. An equal advantage is that a young man can quickly repair initial failures, as J. Ogden Armour, for example, repaired them. This second advantage Rockefeller never needed, for he never failed at anything. The first advantage he did need, for he was destined to shift from grain and produce to a commodity of which he had probably never heard—which he certainly never dreamed would be important—when he became Maurice Clark's partner. The principal disadvantage of youth in business, even when it is joined with talent, industry, and experience, is that it inspires a certain distrust on the part of older men. It is difficult for youngsters to obtain capital or credit. Hence the initial value, to Rockefeller, of Clark's riper years. The senior partner was approaching thirty, he looked even older, and he was a man of the world. Unfortunately, Clark knew this all too well, and regarded his years and experience as more distinctly valuable than Rockefeller's contribution.

"He tried almost from the beginning of our partnership," said Rockefeller later,[9] "to dominate and override me. A question he asked several times in our discussions of business matters was, 'What in the world would you have done without *me?*' I bore it in silence. It does no good to dispute with such a man."

Actually Rockefeller was the better businessman of the two, and he also had credit facilities of value. When the firm opened their doors in March, 1859, their prospects seemed bright. But a frost soon blighted the crops of much of the Middle West, cutting down

[9]Bible Class Speech, N. Y. *Evening Mail*, Oct. 21, 1905.

the volume of grain to be handled. "My partner was much discouraged," Rockefeller tells us.[10] Moreover, when the partners had adjusted themselves to this difficulty, they found their $4000 capital insufficient. That fall large advances had to be made to shippers on their consignments, and more money became an imperative necessity.

In this crisis Rockefeller went first to a friend, offering his note. The reply was disheartening: "John, you know I would do it for you. But . . . I have an agreement with my brothers and we can't endorse paper." Thereupon John turned to his father, who gladly gave him some funds, taking a note. This tided the firm over the immediate difficulty. But a day or two before the note matured, William Avery Rockefeller appeared to claim his due. "Son, I must have that money," he declared. "I need it very much; I *must* have it."

John was annoyed, for he doubted if his father really needed the sum. "I was cross and did not like it," he has recorded. But business was business—and he knew the trader's ways. "Certainly, Father," he said, as if it were a matter of course; "I will send you a check."

He did so. In a few days the "doctor" returned, saying: "Son, I have some money left over. I could let you have a little."

John, sure now that he was being tested, dryly remarked that to accommodate his father he would borrow the money for a while. The loan was left for several months, and then the first episode was repeated.

"Sorry, son, I shall have to have that money."

"Certainly, Father; I'll send a check right away."

Each time, for this happened repeatedly, the robust "doctor" was delighted; his boy was shrewd and prepared for emergencies. John obviously had his affairs arranged so that he could raise cash without difficulty. Finally the father ceased these cat-and-mouse tactics and left the money permanently with his son. "That was a very great encouragement to me," said John D. Rockfeller in recalling this triumph, "for my father was a very able businessman."

The initial difficulties past, business flowed in so fast that still more capital was needed. Both partners were active in getting consignments of farm products for sale on commission. Rockefeller no

[10]Rockefeller, *Random Reminiscences*, 46, 47; Inglis, Conversations with Rockefeller.

longer spent all his time in the office, but began to travel through Ohio, soliciting business. Sometimes he made a direct appeal to farmers and local dealers, sometimes merely told them about the new firm.

"We are engaged in the business," he would say. "You may already have a commission house that is quite satisfactory to you. If so, I am not seeking your trade—I just want you to know about us. We are prepared to do the business, we hope we can do it as well as anybody else can do it, and if you make a change, won't you kindly give us young men a chance?" The results astonished him. The quiet force of his personality inspired trust. "I found that old men had confidence in me right away, and after I stayed a few weeks in the country, I returned home . . . and the consignments came in and our business was increased and it opened up a new world for me."

To finance this increasing trade it was necessary to turn to the banks, and Rockefeller approached Truman P. Handy, one of the most interesting figures in the city. Handy had come to Cleveland in the spring of 1832, when it was only a village of 1500 people, bringing his bride. He had a position awaiting him. George Bancroft, the historian, had become interested in the Commercial Bank of Lake Erie, which had failed in 1820 but the charter of which still had ten years to run; and he had induced eastern friends to pay off the debt and furnish capital. It reopened for business in 1832, with Leonard Case as president and Handy as cashier. Then as Cleveland grew, Handy in 1845 helped organize the Commercial Branch Bank, a successful institution of which he was at this time president and a principal stockholder. Dan P. Eells was cashier. Both men knew Rockefeller well. Handy—"a beautiful character," said Rockefeller later—was a prominent member of the Second Presbyterian Church, superintendent of its Sunday school, and active in various religious undertakings like the Y. M. C. A., and Sunday School Union, and in charities. Eells was secretary and treasurer of the Cleveland Bible Society, and also prominent in the Sunday School Union.[11] Both knew of Rockefeller's church work, had dealt with him as an employee of Hewitt, and had observed his punc-

[11]I have talked with numerous Clevelanders on both Eells and Handy; scattered material on them can be found in the W. P. A. Digest of the Cleveland *Leader* and other newspapers for the fifties, sixties, and seventies.

tuality as a depositor. They were anxious to see him succeed, for his account might well become valuable.

Rockefeller had no difficulty in stating his wants. "Mr. Handy," he said, "I must have more money for my business." The banker asked just how he expected to use it. Rockefeller gave an account of the firm's condition and ambitions. Handy looked thoughtful:

"Do you make any advance on merchandise unless you have the bills of lading or the property in the warehouse?"

"No, sir."

"Do you speculate?"

"No, sir."

"Do you promise, Mr. Rockefeller, that if we loan you money you will continue not to do so?"

When Rockefeller promised, the banker asked how much was required, and on being told $2000, said in conclusion: "Certainly, Mr. Rockefeller, certainly."[12]

The interview always seemed epochal to Rockefeller. As his first loan from a cautious banker, it put a stamp of approval on the work which Clark and he had done, and gave him fresh confidence in his ability to deal with large affairs. "As I left that bank my elation can hardly be imagined," he said long afterward. "He had asked for no more collateral than our warehouse receipts; that is, we were accepted as our own guarantors. I held up my head—think of it, a bank had trusted me for $2000. I felt that I was now a man of importance in the community." Other loans followed, for the business did not cease to grow. "I needed money," writes Rockefeller, "almost all the time, and all the money he had."[13]

At the end of the first year Clark & Rockefeller balanced their accounts with satisfaction. On a gross business of $450,000 they had made a clear profit of $4400, or almost 1 per cent. As a merchant, Rockefeller's income for the year was $2200, or more than three times the amount Hewitt had paid him as a clerk. The outlook was so bright that another young man who had been in the Otis, Brownell office with Clark, named George W. Gardner, put in some money and the firm name was temporarily changed to Clark, Rockefeller & Gardner.

[12]Bible Class Speech, N. Y. *Evening Mail,* Oct. 21, 1905.
[13]Rockefeller, *Random Reminiscences,* 42, 43.

Rockefeller's borrowings had taught him one important lesson. Something has been said of his discovery of the fact that his money

Cleveland, March 1st, 1860.

The undersigned have this day entered into a co-partnership under the style and firm of

CLARK, GARDNER & CO.,

for the transaction of a general Produce, Storage and Commission Business.

M. B. CLARK,
J. D. ROCKEFELLER, } (*Late Clark & Rockefeller.*)
G. W. GARDNER, (*Late of Otis, Brownell & Co.*)

Dear Sir:—Referring to the above notice of co-partnership, we respectfully beg leave to tender our services in the management of any business you may be pleased to entrust to our care.

Having Capital, and the command of facilities ample for the business we propose to undertake, we are prepared to make **Liberal Advances** **on Consignments of PRODUCE, &c.,** *to our address.* *Any business entrusted to us by our friends, will have our personal attention.*

Refer to Banks, Bankers and Business Men generally.

Yours, Truly,

CLARK, GARDNER & CO.

Letter announcing the Clark, Gardner, Rockefeller partnership sent to customers in 1860

could work for him; now he learned that the money of others could be put to work too. The full force of that discovery may be dated at the time he cast up the first year's accounts in the little River Street office. Superadded to all that Clark and he had contributed in work, brains, and $4000 capital was the contribution of his father and of Handy's bank in capital. Only that contribution had enabled the firm to make its $4400 profits; by obtaining more, by expanding, they could make still larger gains.

When he came home and told his mother what the balance had shown, he went to bed with a feeling of exhilaration. But he hastened to chide himself as before:

"Now a little success; soon you will be thrown down, soon you will be overthrown. Because you have got a start, you think you are quite a merchant. Look out, or you will lose your head—go steady!"[14]

III

Near the close of the firm's second year, the long-threatened secession of the cotton States made it evident that war was at hand. When Clark, Rockefeller & Gardner balanced another year's accounts on March 18, 1861, showing a profit of $17,000, the Confederacy had been established, Fort Sumter was threatened, and the North nervously awaited the first shots. In his unemotional and unexcited way John took a keen interest in the lowering conflict.

Entering manhood in a community heavily Abolitionist in sentiment, he had absorbed the doctrines of the Republican Party as a natural part of his creed. The Western Reserve, a transplanted bit of New England, had felt with deepening intensity on the slavery question ever since the Kansas-Nebraska Act of 1854. Rockefeller attended some of the public meetings which denounced Southern "aggressions" and Buchanan's course in Kansas. He knew Cleveland men who were officers on the "underground railroad"; he knew in 1859–60 that fleeing Negroes took ship for Canada close to his place of business on River Street. As a high-school student in 1854 he had written against slavery: "It is a violation of the laws of our country and the laws of God that man should hold his fellow man in bondage." His friends Celestia and Lucy Spelman, with their parents, were staunch Abolitionists. His friend Mark Hanna also felt strongly. In 1860 John cast his first vote for Lincoln, and was probably among the enthusiastic crowd which heard the President-elect, en route for Washington, speak from the Weddell House balcony.

[14]Inglis, Conversations with Rockefeller.

The firing on Fort Sumter and Lincoln's call for volunteers stirred him as it stirred almost every one in Cleveland. He and his brother Will both seriously considered enlisting. In September, 1861, Frank Rockefeller, though only sixteen, did go into the army. First he tried to run away from home, but the "doctor" caught him and said in his peremptory way: "Young fellow, if you want to enlist you will first say good-by to us in a decent way, and walk out the front door like a man!"[15] Then Frank chalked an "18" on the sole of each boot, and when the recruiting officer asked his age, replied, "I'm over eighteen." Serving as a private for three years, he was wounded at Chancellorsville and Cedar Mountain. But the two older brothers felt restrained by nearer responsibilities. Will had a promising position with Hughes & Davis, which later yielded him a junior partnership. John's firm had just got under thriving way, and already had a number of employees. The young man of twenty-two felt that he could not abandon this new venture. "I wanted to go in the army and do my part," he said later. "But it was simply out of the question. There was no one to take my place. We were in a new business, and if I had not stayed it must have stopped—and with so many dependent on it."

Those dependent upon it, he knew, might within a short time include his mother and sisters. His father was absent for increasingly long periods in the West. Presumably he still supported his wife and daughters, but the support must have seemed rather precarious, and while John prospered there was no need to worry.

However, Rockefeller contributed so that others might enlist. Captain Levi T. Scofield repeatedly told later how he came to the office on River Street one day with thirty raw recruits. Rockefeller saw what was needed, took a bag of money out of his safe, and gave each man $10. What impressed the incident on Scofield was that one recruit remarked: "God, he must be rich!" to which another replied: "Yes, they say he's worth as much as ten thousand!"[16] Rockefeller himself said of the war period: "I was represented in the army. I sent more than twenty men, yes, nearly thirty. That is,

---

[15]The three daughters of Frank Rockefeller gave me this anecdote in May, 1939.

[16]Also published in *Woman's Home Companion*, January, 1907, by a staff-writer who talked with Captain Scofield.

I made such arrangements for them that they were able to go."[17] His private accounts for 1861–63 yield no confirmation of this incredible statement. It shows contributions in 1861 to his brother Frank for flag, revolver, and "rifle company," a payment of $50 to the Fourth Ward War Fund, contributions to the purchase of revolvers for other men, and expenditures for substitutes. One entry in 1862 runs, "four substitutes for army, $20," and another "3 substitutes, $15." Still another item is dated October 22, 1862: "Families of soldiers from Fourth Ward, $20." He could now afford generous payments. But since his total listed disbursements for all war purposes in 1861–64 come to only $138.08, it is clear he unconsciously exaggerated the number of men for whom he "made arrangements." After all, no compelling moral reason existed why he should enlist, or assist others to enlist. J. P. Morgan, Philip D. Armour, and John Wanamaker did not enlist; Henry James, Mark Twain, William Dean Howells, and Henry Adams gave no service; Grover Cleveland and James G. Blaine kept out of the war.[18]

The war produced, or to speak more precisely, accelerated great changes in the commercial position of Cleveland. It cut off instantly the navigation of the Mississippi except for military purposes. The rich western traffic, which until the first shots had flowed in large part along the rivers—especially the Mississippi and Ohio—and much of which had been kept in north-south channels by the economic bond between the cotton States and the grain States, now changed its direction. The entire current of trade began to flow east and west. St. Louis and Cincinnati immediately dropped toward the rear. Chicago, Cleveland, and Buffalo advanced more rapidly than ever toward the commercial leadership of the West. The railroads and the Great Lakes became the main arteries of traffic, displacing the rivers; and the first years after the war found great trunk-line systems—the New York Central, the Pennsylvania, the Erie, the Baltimore & Ohio, and the Grand Trunk—being built up between the Atlantic seaboard and the Mississippi Valley. For seven months of the year, the Lakes and Erie Canal furnished a parallel route of commerce.

Inevitably Cleveland pushed forward as a trading and manufac-

[17]Inglis, Conversations with Rockefeller, August, 1918.
[18]A tabulation of Rockefeller's wartime expenditures is in the Rockefeller papers.

turing center, though in no such spectacular fashion as Chicago. The factor which now gave Chicago the undisputed sovereignty of the Northwest was the enormous increase of the States in the Upper Mississippi and Missouri Valleys in population and wealth. This vast prairie region rapidly became covered with rich farms, thriving villages, populous cities. The main arcs of a great network of railways all converged upon Chicago as a distributing and collecting center, while the shipping of Lake Michigan assisted in building up the metropolis. Cleveland, however, had no such great virgin hinterland to settle and exploit. It gained little in any direct way from the growth of the grain trade and its new east-west course. It remained above all else a lake city while Chicago was becoming above all else a railroad city—for Cleveland's rail lines were merely supplementary to its lake steamers. It had a custom house, where in 1865 imports were valued at $117,582,000, and exports at $96,572,-000; it had that year 155 lake vessels, and 177 canal boats. But even as a lake city it saw many of the great grain boats plow past it without transshipment, just as through railroad trains soon rolled over its switches without stopping. As the Middle West shot up to mighty stature in the war years, Cleveland found its chief opportunities in a new function.

The West was rapidly being industrialized, and the city became a center for assembling and re-routing the varied raw materials needed for the industrial expansion of the section. Brand Whitlock summed up the result in a telling phrase when, a generation later, he told how a foreign nobleman had married a Cleveland fortune—"coal, iron ore, and lake shipping." The merchants of Cleveland became middlemen in handling the basic products all about them. They brought iron ore from Michigan through the Soo, and distributed it to the mills of Pennsylvania and northern Ohio. They brought smelted copper from Michigan and sent it to the eastern metal works. They took long trainloads of soft coal from eastern Ohio and hard coal from Pennsylvania, selling both to western consumers. They built lake shipping to handle these products. They also set up mills of their own to forge iron and steel, to weave Ohio wool into worsteds, to make vehicles (and in time build the first automobile ever sold in America), to grind paints. Firms emerged which did a business enormous in volume and remarkable in diversity; firms like M. A. Hanna

& Co., which held iron and coal mines, owned vessels that carried iron ore down the Lakes and brought coal back, manufactured a variety of products, and cemented a firm alliance with the Pennsylvania Railroad in selling them. A careful enumeration in 1865 gave Cleveland a population of about 61,000.

IV

Like most others, the firm of Clark & Rockefeller prospered mightily during the war. Gardner did not remain long with it, retiring at the close of 1862; old-timers in Cleveland say that he and Rockefeller quarrelled, largely because he spent too much time and money on a boat that he kept in a yacht-basin near the mouth of the Cuyahoga.[19] Grain-growers and grain-traders alike did well in these years. With production stimulated by western settlement and the use of labor-saving machinery, the volume of trade was large. Prices were kept high by the necessity for feeding a great army, the rapid growth of manufactures and of an industrial population, the inflation produced by an expanding paper currency, and the heavy demand for foodstuffs from Europe and especially England, where the harvests of 1860, 1861, and 1862 were poor. Clark & Rockefeller were not in a position to get war contracts, avoided speculation, and did no profiteering; but they gained by the price-rise.[20] We do not have precise figures, but the $17,000 profit divided at the close of their second year was doubtless equalled and surpassed in every subsequent year. Their quarters expanded, until by 1863 they occupied Nos. 39, 41, 43, and 45 River Street; and when news of Appomattox came both partners were moderately wealthy men.

Their main business was in grain, but they dealt in other commodities as well. Thus we read in the Cleveland *Leader* for December 9, 1862: "The first considerable consignment, consisting of 1300 barrels of salt from the new Michigan Salt Works, was received yesterday from Saginaw by Clark & Rockefeller." In the summer of 1863 we find the firm advertising 500 bushels of clover seed, 800 bushels of timothy seed, and 200 barrels of mess pork. Most of their selling was done on commission, so that they took no risks from market fluctuations. In other ways Rockefeller continued to manage his office with

---

[19]Confidential Cleveland sources.   [20]Flynn, *God's Gold,* 103.

conservatism as well as energy. He felt that their success was largely founded upon his stringent avoidance of speculation and refusal to make advances or loans. He was much more precise and punctilious than Clark thought necessary, but his caution, as an early incident tellingly illustrated, paid.

One of their largest customers came in one day when Rockefeller was out. He said, in effect, to Clark: "I cannot continue my shipments to your house unless you advance me some money on the produce without waiting until you get bills of lading. You've got to trust me." Since he shipped regularly and in large quantities, the loss of his business would be a serious blow. Clark, in defiance of their strict rule against advancing money until the security was definitely in hand, intimated that the customer would have what he wanted. But when Rockefeller returned he set his foot down firmly. They had never yet given an unsecured advance; they had so assured the banks; and they would never do it while he was a partner. Clark expostulated that the customer would go elsewhere. But Rockefeller was adamant, declaring that he would see the man. Calling on the customer, Rockefeller explained that his request did not conform to sound business practice, and that the firm must maintain its rules. Later he recalled the tenor of his plea. "We can furnish you all the money you want," he said. "But it is impossible for us to do it in any other way than that which we have followed. I hope we shall not lose you. We will do our best to please you." The man flared up angrily. He had asked only a reasonable accommodation, he declared, and it was churlish to refuse. The junior partner returned to Clark disappointed, but unwavering.

Greatly to their surprise, the shipper continued to do business with them as if nothing had happened. He never referred to the matter again. Subsequently they heard that an old banker, John Gardener of Norwalk, O., who maintained close business relations with their customer, had been watching the affair. "I have ever since believed," wrote Rockefeller, "that he originated the suggestion to tempt us to do what we stated we did not do, as a test; and his story about our firm stand for what we regarded as sound business principles did us great good."[21]

[21]Rockefeller, *Random Reminiscences,* 44, 45; Bible Class Speech, N. Y. *Evening Mail,* Oct. 21, 1905.

Because their methods commanded confidence and they were known to be making money, expansion was not difficult. In borrowing money, Rockefeller's very manner inspired men with a sense of power and reliability. For some years a tall young man, he had grown broad-shouldered, and while he never had the rugged bulk of his father, carried a quiescent physical strength. "I have been strong always," he said many years later. "I come of a strong family, men of unusual strength. . . ." He was reserved in manner, but his piercing blue eyes gave an impression of force waiting only to be unleashed. A slight stoop, the result of his bookkeeping days, and a way of walking with his head thrust slightly forward, gave him almost a scholarly air. Those who saw him casually had at first an impression that his eyes were fixed on some distant object in abstract meditation. But when he talked with a man his gaze held him with steady concentration. Later he impressed some interviewers as looking into their very minds. His speech was clear and precise; the speech of one who had exhaustively considered what he said, and whose expertness gave it conviction. Already he possessed the reputation of a young man who, in business at nineteen, had thriven astonishingly. It gave him self-confidence. "How's that brother of yours," some one asked Mary Ann Rockefeller, "who can walk right up on a man's shirt-bosom and sit down?"[22]

He needed this self-confidence. It was on loans, more loans, ever new loans that Clark & Rockefeller built up their profits, making other people's money work for them. Rockefeller got most of these loans. Sometimes he resorted to a little stratagem. Clark always recalled with amusement how a Cleveland banker hurried into their office one day, saying that he thought he might use the $10,000 that Rockefeller had spoken of investing. "Great Scott!" cried Clark, taken unawares. "We don't want to invest $10,000. Why, John is out now trying to borrow $5000." Of course Rockefeller was chagrined to find on his return that Clark had spoiled his well-laid plan.

"But the funny part of it," said Clark in concluding his story, "was that John got the $5000 after I had made my blunder. Oh, he was the greatest borrower you ever saw!"

On another occasion, President Handy of the Commercial Branch Bank met Rockefeller on the street. Clark & Rockefeller had been

[22]Inglis, Conversation with Mrs. Rudd.

borrowing very heavily. The new president accosted the young man. "Why, Rockefeller," he said, half in jest and half in earnest, "do you know that we are worried by the amounts you have taken, and we wish you would come and explain it to the board of directors?"

Rockefeller was not abashed. "I thank you, I thank you," he said, straightening up and fixing the banker with a confident eye. "I shall be very pleased to come up and see them, because I wish to borrow much larger sums." But he never heard from them, and got all he wanted. James Ford Rhodes, who did business with him a little later, writes that two banks consistently supported him in his expansion.

As time passed a certain reserve, for distrust would be too strong a word, grew up between Rockefeller and Maurice B. Clark. At its bottom lay merely differences in temperament. Clark was a most likeable young man, frank, genial, hardworking, and honest. He was a member of the strictest branch of the Methodists. Widely respected, he was elected in 1862 a director of the Cleveland Board of Trade. But Rockefeller's precision in small matters and outspoken dislike of profanity or rough talk irked him,[23] while the young man's bold enterprise in large affairs sometimes made him apprehensive. John would come back from trips travel-worn and dirty, but jubilant over his new arrangements, and a wave of fresh commission business would flow in after him. Then to handle it, he would borrow large sums at high rates. Clark would have been satisfied with a more moderate, easygoing pace. He talked uneasily of the magnitude of Rockefeller's commitments; and though the results justified every venture, he still carried a feeling that this was partly a youngster's good luck. Rockefeller resented Clark's assumption of superior experience and acumen, which occasionally made him patronizing. He also disliked Clark's casual ways and lack of vision, seeing that he would never become one of the masters of American industry—and Rockefeller meant to be a master.

Rockefeller perceived, too, that currents of trade were changing their course. With the keenest business insight in Cleveland—not instinct but insight—he recognized that as agricultural dominion passed to the railroad centers farther west, the possibilities in handling grain, meat, and other produce at Lake Erie ports had become

---

[23]Rockefeller "heard me swear in the warehouse" when work got in a tangle, Clark told Mr. Inglis in 1917; Rockefeller thought not.

limited. A Chicagoan might make a great career in that field, for huge elevators were rising on Lake Michigan, and the Union Stock Yards opened in 1865; but not a Cleveland man. The flour-milling center would soon be Minneapolis. Rockefeller also saw that Cleveland must find its best prosperity in collecting and transshipping raw industrial materials, making the most of its position midway between West and East, and on both rail and water routes. He had begun midway in the war to look about for opportunities in this field, and he did not need to look far.

VIII

Black Gold

IN THE FALL of 1859, while Rockefeller and his partner were busy
with the autumn shipments of grain and hay, reports reached
Cleveland that a rich well of oil had been discovered in western
Pennsylvania, about a hundred miles distant as the crow flies.
Travellers brought word that a newcomer, "Colonel" E. L. Drake,
had actually bored into the earth for rock-oil, and tapped a hidden
source from which it could be pumped by the barrel, like water.

Word of this wonderful strike on Oil Creek also reached Cleveland through the press. The New York dailies, to be sure, for a time
ignored it. When about a month after the discovery the Philadelphia
Press published its first item, September 26, 1859, it garbled the facts
absurdly; stating that the find had been made in Connecticut by men
boring for salt, when actually the well had been sunk near Titusville,
Pa., by the agent of a Connecticut company, who was indeed using
the methods of salt borers but was looking for petroleum. On November 12 the weekly *Scientific American,* which had some Cleveland subscribers, carried a brief note about the opening of a "rich oil
spring" near Titusville. Six days later the Cleveland *Leader* published a suggestive statement that "the oil springs of northern Pennsylvania" were exciting considerable speculation, and that a rush had
begun to the "oleaginous locations."

Why this burst of speculation? Because it was just dawning upon
Americans that petroleum had extremely valuable uses both as a
lubricant and an illuminant. Why the rush, quickly rivalling the
efflux to the California gold-fields? Because the crude oil from
Drake's well, first ten barrels a day and later forty, sold during the
first four months at fifty cents a gallon, and came from a reservoir

that others might easily tap. Anybody could figure that 1200 gallons a day at half a dollar each meant $600, and any visitor could see that oil seeped out at numerous points in the district. In Pennsylvania scores of men, even hundreds, might dig their way to fortune!

II

Back of this sudden furor in Pennsylvania lay a fascinating story. While Rockefeller was growing up, while he was passing through school into Hewitt & Tuttle's office, two great processes had been imperceptibly converging upon one another—and upon his destiny. One was the process by which men discovered that great quantities of petroleum, a viscous, greasy, evil-smelling fluid long known in Europe and the Orient, lay close under the surface in Pennsylvania and western Virginia; so close that it could be tapped by easy borings, and pumped out. The other was the process by which, seeking better illuminants, men discovered first that they could distill a clear, inflammable oil from soft coal and shales, and next that they could distill it from petroleum. The two processes were carried forward simultaneously until they inevitably merged in the creation of a vast new industry; an industry which extracted oil in enormous quantities from the bowels of the earth and refined it to light the world's lamps and lubricate its machinery. Drake's discovery was important as a signal that this epochal merger had taken place—as a torch which illuminated that great fact.

It is possible that Rockefeller, interested in chemistry, learned something as a youth of the rudimentary steps in both processes. It is certain that when he launched into the commission business he was familiar, like everybody else, with lamps burning oil from coal, and with the fact of rock-oil deposits.

Of our petroleum reservoirs Americans had known something since colonial days.[1] In 1700 the Earl of Bellomont, royal governor of New York, instructed an agent to visit a spring "eight miles beyond the Senek's furthest castle, which they have told me blazes up in a flame when a lighted coal or firebrand is put into it," and to

[1] The best general works on the early history of petroleum in the United States are Paul H. Giddens, *The Birth of the Oil Industry;* J. T. Henry, *The Early and Later History of Petroleum, With Authentic Facts in Regard to Its Development in Western Pennsylvania;* James D. Henry, *The History and Romance of the Petroleum Industry;* and J. J. McLaurin, *Sketches in Crude Oil.*

fetch a sample. Sir William Johnson in 1767 saw some of the "curious oyl" taken from a petroleum spring at Cuba, N. Y. We might multiply historical references to these early deposits, which the Indians had known and used for medicine.[2] When late in the eighteenth century western settlers began digging or boring for salt along the Allegheny, Kanawha, and Cumberland, they found more or less petroleum, which struck them as a mere nuisance. Drilling wells became quite an art, and the use of wooden tubing through rock strata to reach pools of brine was introduced on the Great Kanawha while Jefferson sat in the White House.[3] Gradually a knowledge of the existence of oil springs, oil seepages, and oil-tainted salt wells became widely diffused among Americans; and they were too practical not to see that even crude oil might have its uses. Fortescue Cuming's *Tour to the Western Country* gave in 1810 a vivid picture of the collection of oil by farmers in the Muskingum Valley. And writing in the *American Journal of Science* in 1826, the learned Doctor S. P. Hildreth of Marietta, O., announced a discovery of petroleum on the Muskingum. A man hunting for salt had sunk a shaft about 400 feet, but instead of brine had found vast quantities of what was "vulgarly called Seneca Oil." Doctor Hildreth went on to say that "the petroleum affords considerable profit, and is beginning to be in demand for lamps in workshops and factories," and that it "gives a clear, brisk light, and will be a valuable article for lighting the street lamps in the future cities of Ohio."[4]

But for the most part the fluid was employed only as a medicine. As early as 1838 the elder Benjamin Silliman described the oil spring near Cuba, N. Y., where petroleum was collected by thin wooden skimmers. When heated and strained through flannel, it was used as a liniment for sores and bruises. Much larger quantities of such medicine, he added, came from Oil Creek in Pennsylvania. Doubtless Rockefeller's knowledge of petroleum, up to the middle fifties, was confined to this medicinal "Seneca Oil." In the Jacksonian era a tailor of Oil Creek named Nathaniel Cary carried kegs of it on horse-

[2] J. T. Trowbridge, "A Carpet-Bagger in Pennsylvania," *Atlantic Monthly*, June, 1869; Vol. XXIII, pp. 729 ff.
[3] See the historical statement by Patrick C. Boyle in *Industrial Commission Hearings, Standard Oil Combinations,* 1899, pp. 405 ff.
[4] Hildreth, imitating Jefferson, published a series of "Notes on Ohio," and wrote much for *Silliman's Journal;* Marietta College has his library.

back eighty miles down to Pittsburgh, where he sold it for a good price. Most of it was used for medicine; a little of it (when mixed with sperm oil) for lubricants. After 1848 the principal vendor of medicinal oil was Samuel M. Kier, a Pittsburgh shipper and canal-boat operator. He had joined his father and brother in leasing land at Tarentum, Pa., and had drilled two salt wells there. At a depth of four hundred feet oil rose in one of them—it was ruined! But the resourceful Kier knew that Americans were eager for balms and salves. In or about 1849, he opened an establishment at 363 Liberty Street, Pittsburgh, and began bottling his petroleum at fifty cents for an eight-ounce vial, brightly labelled: "Kier's Petroleum or Rock Oil, Celebrated for its Wonderful Curative Powers. A Natural Remedy."[5] As his market developed, he hired salesmen on commission, and sent gaudily painted medicine chariots from town to town. Advertising slips imitative of bank notes proclaimed that the oil came from four hundred feet below the surface, and bore pictures of the salt-well derricks.[6]

All this medicinal employment of oil was a mere red herring, leading men to overlook its true values. Perhaps George Washington had some shrewd if vague sense of its possibilities when in his will he commended his oil spring in western Virginia to the special attention of his executors. Ingenious men began to inquire after larger uses, and the refining process shortly came into play. Although petroleum had been known ever since the writer of Deuteronomy spoke of oil out of the flinty rock, and the fire-worshipers made their first pilgrimages to the flaming shrines of Baku, it remained but an inferior substitute for animal and vegetable oils until purified; and not until far into the nineteenth century was scientific purification attempted.

While Rockefeller was still a schoolboy in western New York, the Scottish industrial chemist, James Young, had established his position as the world's first petroleum refiner. In 1847 he learned of a petroleum spring in a mine at Alfreton, Derbyshire, and by destructive distillation obtained both lubricating and burning oils from it.

[5]Members of the Kier family, still prominent in Pittsburgh, have furnished me with documents upon his career. See also *Derrick and Drill,* arranged and edited by the author of *Ten Acres Enough,* which gives some interesting facts about Kier.

[6]J. J. McLaurin, *Sketches in Crude Oil,* pp. 26 ff.

The modern petroleum industry would have been born then and there had England possessed large petroleum supplies, but the Derbyshire spring was practically exhausted by 1851. As it dwindled, Young turned to the production of oil from coal, and in 1850 took out his basic patent for obtaining an inflammable oil from bituminous substances by slow distillation. On the basis of his work an important shale-oil industry soon arose in Midlothian.

Meanwhile, an ingenious Canadian, Doctor Abraham Gesner, had as early as August, 1846, distilled kerosene (a name he invented from the Greek *keros,* wax, and *elaion,* oil) from the coals of Prince Edward Island.[7] The manufacture of such oils can be traced at least as far back in history as the grant of an English patent in 1694 to three men for "a way to extract and make great quantities of pitch, tar, and oyle out of a sort of stone"—that is, out of bituminous shale. Gesner soon brought his process to the United States, taking out patents which he sold to a corporation called (after one change of name) the New York Kerosene Company. In 1854 it began the commercial manufacture of illuminants on Newtown Creek, the Long Island stream which separates Brooklyn from Queens; a waterway destined before long to be one of the world's principal centers of petroleum manufacture. Gesner's patents had to compete with those which James Young took out in Washington, and by the middle fifties various American manufacturers were using both.

Thus, while Rockefeller was working for Hewitt & Tuttle in Cleveland, coal oil or kerosene was becoming common. Together with lubricating oil, it was made from various carbons in various ways. Some used soft coal, some shale. New inventors of importance appeared. In 1852 two Boston chemists, Luther and William Atwood, began making lubricants from coal tar in Waltham, Mass., calling it "coup oil" after Louis Napoleon's recent *coup d'état.* Their manufactory was soon taken over by Samuel Downer, a prosperous whale-oil merchant, who erected new buildings in South Boston and employed Joshua Merrill, previously associated with the Atwoods, as superintending chemist.[8] He seems also to have sent Luther Atwood

[7]See Abraham Gesner, M.D., F.S.S., *A Practical Treatise on Coal, Petroleum, and Other Distilled Oils* (1860).

[8]I have used the interesting collection of Downer Papers in the Pennsylvania Historical Society, which refer chiefly to the refinery Downer later established in the Oil Regions.

and Merrill to England to superintend the erection of similar works there; and they returned with some important ideas drawn from English practice. Merrill, an inventive Yankee, tried many experiments with Trinidad bitumen and Cuban chapapote, with the result that in 1856 he and Downer obtained a new patent for making oil from bituminous minerals. They labored hard to perfect their process, and erected huge retorts, each capable of turning 1200 pounds of coal into 360 gallons of crude oil every day. Their South Boston manufactory, said to have cost half a million, was soon producing 650,000 gallons of refined oil a year, and justly attracted wide notice.

Of all American manufacturers of coal oil in the fifties, Downer was the most enterprising and important. Boasting that his distillates burned brightly and beautifully in patent lamps, he found a wide market. He and Merrill used not only large quantities of Trinidad bitumen, but soft coal from the Canadian provinces and cannel coal from Kentucky. For the "down east" trade, they soon erected extensive works in Portland, Me. Downer also sold lubricating oils to railroads and textile mills, finding a ready market. Meanwhile, others were emulating him; and so rapidly did the industry grow that when Rockefeller launched into business for himself in 1859, the country had between fifty and sixty establishments making coal oil. Twenty-five were listed in Ohio, and ten in Pennsylvania; indeed, the great majority were in these two States and Kentucky, where cheap bituminous coal lay close at hand. Most of the factories were small, but the Breckinridge Works at Cloversport, Ky., and the Lucesco Works in Westmoreland County, Pa., were big enough to attract national attention. The business, steadily expanding, was worrying the sellers of older illuminants like whale oil, lard oil, and camphene—a rectified oil of turpentine mixed with lard. Americans had read of the Mexican War by candlelight or sperm lamps, but they read of John Brown's raid by coal-oil wicks.

Probably Clark & Rockefeller handled coal-oil shipments. The Cleveland *Leader* pointed out early in 1859 that cannel beds, ideal for making oil, were numerous in the State, adding: "This business has become one of great importance in Ohio, and more than two million dollars are already invested in it."[9] Coal oil was then being

[9]May 5, 1859.

adopted in various public buildings of the city, notably the Cleveland Institute on University Heights. The principal wholesale dealer in coal-oil lamps, S. S. Barrie, who had a large salesroom on Ontario Street, was advertising the oil as a brilliant success, presenting four great advantages: "It is not explosive; it will not gum or smoke when burned in proper lamps; it is 50 per cent cheaper than lard or sperm oil; and it is 20 per cent cheaper than gas."[10] In December, 1860, he sold $20,000 worth of his wares—for a coal-oil lamp was a good Christmas present.[11] Yet it had its perils. Erastus Smith was shortly protesting in the *Leader:* "Allow me through your paper to say to the public that I am not the Smith that sold the coal-oil lamp that blew up and caused the death of Mrs. Kipp on December 5th. I say to the public beware of cheap oils."

When the war began Cleveland had at least four manufacturers of oil from coal, of whom Law & North operated on a large scale.[12] Evidence of the widespread use of the new illuminant appears in the second series of Lowell's *Biglow Papers,* written in 1861, which gives a picture of a rural evening in New England:

> The critters milked an' foddered, gates shet fast
> Tools cleaned against termorrer, supper past,
> An' Nancy darnin' by her ker'sene lamp. . . .

[10]Cleveland *Leader,* Aug. 23, 1859.   [11]*Ibid.,* April 2, 1861.

[12]The names of the other manufacturers were Cheeney, Watson, and Aaron Clark. Cleveland *Leader,* Jan. 4, 1866. For the price of oils at this time, see an advertisement in the New York *Commercial Advertiser,* Sept. 28, 1859. Also *Petroleum, a History of the Oil Region,* by Rev. S. J. M. Eaton, Philadelphia, J. P. Skelly & Co., 1866, p. 212. Both the advertisement and Eaton give tables showing the relative brightness of the flames produced by the various oils, their price, and cost per hour. The table in the *Commercial Advertiser* is as follows:

Material	Lamp	Intensity of Light	Quantity of Light from Equal Measure of Oil	Price per Gal.	Cost of an Equal Amount of Light
Kerosene	Kerosene	13.689	2.435	$1.00	$4.10
Camphene	Camphene	5.625	1.299	.63	4.85
Whale Oil	Solar	1.892	.833	1.00	12.00
Lard Oil	Solar	1.640	.706	1.25	17.70
Sperm Oil	Solar	2.025	.850	2.25	26.47
Burning Fluid	Large Wick	.553	.300	.87	29.00

III

But for years men were curiously slow in applying James Young's lessons upon the utilization of petroleum. The first American to show the requisite enterprise was Samuel M. Kier. When in 1848–50 he failed to sell his medicinal oil in satisfactory quantities, with in-born Scotch sagacity he consulted a Philadelphia chemist, J. C. Booth, who suggested refining by distillation. Using drawings made by Booth, Kier constructed a cast-iron still of one-gallon capacity, and obtained a refined product which he called "carbon oil." Though its odor was disagreeable, it burned well in camphene lamps, and he found a market at $1.50 a gallon. Kier himself devised, but did not patent, a four-pronged lamp-burner which would fit any lamp, gave a brilliant light, and sold widely in Pittsburgh. Building a five-gallon still, early in the fifties he set in operation a small but busy refinery on Seventh Avenue in Pittsburgh. He thus became the first known American refiner of petroleum for commercial uses. Since people feared an explosion, the city council compelled him to remove his plant to Lawrenceville, a suburb. Naturally, his shipments of "carbon oil" gradually attracted attention, and other manufacturers began thinking about petroleum.

Kier's inspiration was in part born of a greatly augmented supply of petroleum, which now came not in kegs on horseback, but in large quantities. Charles Lockhart, who became an important figure in the Standard Oil Company, stated many years later that he knew something of the origin of the refinery. Across the Allegheny River from Tarentum was a well which had originally been sunk for salt water, and which produced brine for several years. Then petroleum began coming up with the salt water. "A man named Isaac Huff operated the well, and I was clerking in Pittsburgh. Huff brought the oil to me, and I bought it from him, turning right around and selling it to Mr. Kier on my own account. In the following year I took Mr. Kip, of Tarentum, into partnership with me, and bought the Huff well, we running it as our own. I entered into a new contract with Mr. Kier." Under this contract, he began selling oil in large quanti-ties. For example, his account book showed a sale in March, 1853, of seven barrels of oil, at 62.5 cents a gallon. Once he even obtained 66.6 cents a gallon. Said Lockhart:

When I thus began selling Mr. Kier my oil, he found that he had more than he could market as a medicine. Mr. Kier knew that it had a certain value as an illuminant, but to make it entirely successful in that line it would have to be in some other than its crude state. With a surplus of petroleum on his hands, therefore, he got the idea of putting it through some process which would separate the medicinal part from the other, or . . . clarify it in some manner so that he might sell it both as an illuminant and a medicine. He went to Philadelphia and consulted a chemist there. . . .

The long-awaited pioneer in introducing American petroleum to the kerosene manufacturers on a large scale was Colonel A. C. Ferris, a man of means and abounding energy. A New Yorker, Ferris had gone to California in 1849 to dig gold, but returned home in discouragement the next year, and went into business. Visiting Pittsburgh in 1857, he happened to see a tin lamp which was effectively lighting the large basement of Nevin, MacKeown & Co., enterprising Scots in the wholesale drug trade; a lamp burning oil from the salt wells at Tarentum. The device riveted Ferris's attention. He knew that the New York Kerosene Company was making a similar oil from coal. Without loss of time he flung himself into the field of supplying refiners with crude oil and marketing the product.

Of crude oil very little was yet available. Ferris took steps to obtain most of the output at Tarentum. Here Samuel M. Kier, Lewis Peterson, Charles Lockhart, and a few other men owned wells—originally salt wells—which produced small but fairly steady quantities, one running two to ten barrels a day, and others two barrels each. Peterson enlarged an old well to yield five barrels. Ferris began making considerable sales in the East, disposing of his first barrel to a firm of grocers in South Brooklyn at 70 cents a gallon. The first considerable shipments, a dozen barrels or more, were made in December, 1857; and thereafter he sold chiefly to the New York Kerosene Company, which soon became enthusiastic over petroleum. MacKeown & Finley in February, 1858, agreed to furnish Ferris with two thirds of all their new product of "carbon oil" at 60 cents a gallon. Ferris in the spring of 1858 also began marketing some of Kier's "carbon oil," but found it less satisfactory.[13]

As the demand increased, the enterprising colonel began to search widely for supplies. He visited districts where crude oil was still

[13]J. J. McLaurin, *Sketches in Crude Oil,* 57.

gathered by the blanket-wringing method. When he heard that one J. M. Williams had opened an oil well in Ontario with pick and shovel, he hurried off to see him, bought his whole supply, and made an unsuccessful effort to persuade New York businessmen to purchase the oil-bearing trace for $26,500. At first Ferris shipped crude oil to New York in driblets—nine barrels of oil at one time, nineteen at another—but he gradually obtained larger quantities. He even bought considerable areas of land near Tarentum, and sunk a pit of his own for oil, without result. In 1858, the whole crude petroleum business in the United States amounted to 1183 barrels of 40 gallons each, and Ferris handled most of it. He also marketed lamps for burning kerosene—the best lamps at first being equipped with the so-called "Vienna burner" after a foreign model. His efforts had done as much as Kier's or Downer's to bring a great new industry to birth.

By the beginning of 1859 any shrewd and informed observer might have predicted the imminent advent of this industry. Advertisements of coal oil or kerosene were now familiar to every newspaper reader. Kerosene lamps, twice as brilliant as camphene and much safer, were seen in most towns and cities. Entries in Rockefeller's private account books for 1856–57 show several purchases of "burning fluid," doubtless some variety of camphene, carbon oil, or coal oil. On August 24, 1859, the New York *Commercial Advertiser* published a detailed account of the Long Island plant of the New York Kerosene Company. The works then represented an investment of several hundred thousand dollars, were producing 30,000 gallons a year, and were rapidly growing. Some of the other fifty-odd coal-oil refineries in the country were also becoming large. At the Chicago Fair in the fall of 1859, various kerosene lamps were displayed alongside reapers and threshers as an important branch of invention—for more than 200 patents had been granted on them.[14] In the New York district Colonel Ferris showed unremitting energy in popularizing the new illuminant. He had set up his first headquarters on Water Street, and when complaints that the oil was malodorous drove him out, removed to 191 Pearl Street. From here he sent out squads of canvassers who entered the shops of dealers with a lamp in one hand, a can of oil in the other. They would exhibit the new illuminant, and gladly take orders for a few lamps and a gallon or two of the oil,

[14]*Idem,* 56.

to be sold on commission. Ferris did much to better the quality of lamps, while the New York Kerosene Company steadily improved the process of refining.

The true uses of petroleum were being found. The market was ready. Year by year the nation's demand for illuminants and lubricants was increasing; in the early fifties the country was using nearly 500,000 barrels of whale oil annually, and about 600,000 barrels of lard oil and tallow oil.[15] As whales grew scarcer, the price of sperm oil had increased by 1850 to $2 or $2.50 a gallon, and threatened to reach $5! When would some one show how crude oil might be obtained not by one or two hundred barrels a month, but by tens of thousands of barrels a day? It was "Colonel" E. L. Drake, as immortal a discoverer as his great English namesake, who gave the answer.

IV

The train of events which brought Drake upon the scene began in 1854. Early that summer George H. Bissell, a graduate of Dartmouth College in the class of 1845, returned to the college community, which had also been his boyhood home, on a visit. He was an alert, enterprising Yankee who, though only thirty-three, had been a college teacher, a newspaper editor, and superintendent of schools in New Orleans, finally entering upon the practice of law in New York City.[16] One of his former acquaintances, Doctor Dixi Crosby of the medical faculty, showed him a bottle of petroleum which had recently been brought to Dartmouth from Cherrytree Run, a small tributary of Oil Creek in Pennsylvania—brought by another alumnus, Francis B. Brewer, whose father was senior partner in the lumber firm of Brewer, Watson & Co., which owned a large tract of timber land near Titusville, Pa. Crosby explained that he and the professor of chemistry and geology at Dartmouth had examined some of the oil, finding it a good illuminant.[17]

[15]Foster Rhea Dulles, in *Lowered Boats: A Chronicle of the American Whaling Industry,* gives a fascinating record of how whaling became big business, and was temporarily killed by the oil discoveries.

[16]See the sketch of Bissell by George H. Taylor, in *Dictionary of American Biography*.

[17]Various accounts give different details of this Dartmouth episode. I have followed Giddens, *The Birth of the Oil Industry*, 31, 32, though John T. Trowbridge in his *Atlantic* article is more picturesque.

It at once struck Bissell that if the oil occurred in any quantity, it offered commercial possibilities. He quietly sent Doctor Crosby's son, Albert H. Crosby, to the Oil Creek district that fall to make an investigation, and later found evidence of abundant deposits. On Oil Creek he and a companion stood near a famous spring, and, as the companion later wrote, "saw the oil bubbling up, and spreading its bright and golden colors over the surface." On November 10, 1854, Bissell and his law-partner, Jonathan G. Eveleth, bought from Brewer, Watson & Co. at Titusville about 105 acres, containing an "oil spring," on Oil Creek in Cherrytree township, paying $5,000. Oil rights in some 1100 acres of surrounding lands were included. On December 30, they organized the Pennsylvania Rock Oil Company, a New York corporation, with a nominal capital of $250,000, divided into ten thousand shares at $25 each. Their plan was to obtain as much petroleum as possible from surface pits and ditches on the property. Three barrels of oil were shortly sent to Bissell and Eveleth at their offices in the handsome new building of D. Appleton Company on Broadway. The drayman unloaded them in the hot sun before the fashionable bookstore, where the oil oozed out upon the sidewalk and filled the street with its overpowering smell. Appletons hastily loaded the barrels into a passing dray, with orders to take them away—anywhere, so long as it was a safe distance.[18]

But Bissell and Eveleth lacked capital to develop their oil lands. Indeed, they were such poor young lawyers that while launching their enterprise they could not pay personal bills and were once nearly thrown out of a hotel! At the very beginning, before signing the final papers for the purchase, they had visited New Haven in an effort to interest some capitalists there; and while of the six trustees of the company in 1855 four were New Yorkers and one was a Titusville man, the last was Anson Sheldon of Connecticut.[19] This fact seems significant. Sheldon may have known, or for that matter Bissell may have known, that in 1833 Professor Benjamin Silliman of Yale, then the most influential scientist in the country, had written

[18]Giddens, *The Birth of the Oil Industry,* 33, 34.

[19]See the valuable pamphlet, "New Haven and the First Oil Well," published in 1934 by James M. Townsend's nephew, Henry H. Townshend. James M. Townsend's papers are in the Drake Museum at Titusville, where I have used them.

a report on oil taken from the springs at Cuba, N. Y. At any rate, they shortly sent several gallons—some accounts say several barrels—of their surface petroleum to his distinguished son, Doctor Benjamin Silliman, Jr., professor of chemistry at Yale and principal founder of the Sheffield Scientific School. They and the New Haven men whom they had interested in their enterprise, notably the sanguine James M. Townsend, president of the City Savings Bank, eagerly awaited his analysis. Bissell and Eveleth had assured Townsend that the Pennsylvania tract contained mineral paint and metal ore as well as petroleum, and that the crude oil could be used for lubricants and lumber-raft flares even if Silliman's report proved to be unfavorable. Some skeptical observers, however, declared that the land for which they had paid $5000 was hardly worth its taxes.

Fortunately Silliman's verdict was enthusiastic. His *Report On the Rock Oil, or Petroleum, from Venango County, Pennsylvania,* was ready for delivery on April 16, 1855—though he withheld it until he could collect a bill for $526.08 from the impecunious promoters. Shortly published as a pamphlet, it has since been recognized as an epochal document in the history of the oil industry. Silliman showed, on the basis of elaborate experiments, that petroleum was a mixture of hydrocarbons essentially different in nature from animal or vegetable oils. He demonstrated that the application of fractional distillation, together with simple means of purification, would convert 90 per cent of it into a series of distillates, leaving only a 10 per cent residue. Of the distillates about one half—the intermediate half—were useful for illuminating purposes, giving better results in lamps than camphene or sperm oil. The high-boiling oils he described as especially valuable for lubrication because they did not freeze, did not tend to form a gum, and did not become rancid. From these high-boiling oils he also extracted paraffin, which, after it had been purified, he found to be an excellent candle material. Finally, he reported that when crude petroleum was passed through heated coke, it decomposed into a gas which burned in an Argand lamp with a clear, brilliant flame. All but a small part of the crude oil might be utilized by some of the easiest of chemical reductions. "In conclusion, gentlemen," Silliman wrote, "it appears to me that there is much ground for encouragement in the belief that your company have in their possession a raw material from which, by simple and not expensive process, they may manufacture very valuable products."[20]

In brief, Silliman discovered nearly all of the chief uses to which petroleum was to be put during the next half century, and indicated the principal methods of refining it for these uses. Few men outside New Haven read his report, however, and in the absence of large supplies of petroleum its immense significance was not at once evident.

The one immediate result of his favorable verdict was the formation of the Pennsylvania Rock Oil Company of Connecticut. It had eleven stockholders, one of them Doctor Silliman, was capitalized at $300,000, and took control of the Oil Creek land by a ninety-nine year lease—for Pennsylvania forbade outside corporations to hold land in fee simple. The certificate of incorporation was issued September 18, 1855, and sworn to November 26. Silliman became president, and New Haven was the headquarters of the company. At first Bissell and Eveleth controlled 4320 of the 12,000 shares, but their holdings were shortly reduced. For a time nothing but a little surface oil was gathered, much wrangling took place between the New York and New Haven groups of stockholders, and no real effort was made to develop the property.

Then in the summer of 1856 Bissell, stopping one day in the shade of a Broadway drugstore, was suddenly arrested by the sight of a bottle of Kier's Rock Oil in the window. He stepped inside and picked up one of the circulars. At once he was struck by Kier's picture of the salt-well derrick, and his statement about the 400-foot bore; and he conceived the idea of drilling for oil—an idea that had never occurred to Silliman. Eveleth heartily approved it. But it was then impossible to act. In fact, it was not until the autumn of 1857, just when the panic was at its worst, that the management of the company took a decisive step. The optimistic Townsend, who had become president, decided to send Edwin Laurentine Drake to look at the land. He tells us that this step met intense opposition from various stockholders. They would listen to his plans and shake their heads sadly, ejaculating: "Oh, Townsend—oil coming out of the ground, pumping oil out of the earth as you pump water? Nonsense! You're crazy!"

[20]The full text of Silliman's classic report is in Ida M. Tarbell, *History of the Standard Oil Company*, I, 265–275. See also J. T. Henry, *The Early and Later History of Petroleum*, 53.

Drake, who boarded at the Tontine Hotel with Townsend, was a sturdy fellow of thirty-eight. He had been a drifting, sociable, good-hearted jack-of-all-trades, railroad express agent, and conductor on the New York & New Haven Railroad. Doubtless many of the New Haven stockholders knew him well, for he had lived in the city since 1849; his first wife had died there, and he married a second wife in the city in 1857. He was tall, black-bearded, impressive looking, and a capital raconteur. His only bad habit of importance was an unconquerable improvidence. "I tell you," said a Pennsylvania stable-boy later, "we have a rich time up here when Colonel Drake comes; the way he pitches the quarters around to us boys is a caution."[21] Townsend confidently characterized him in 1857 as "the right kind of man for the undertaking, perfectly upright and honorable in all his dealings." Having bought 250 shares in the Pennsylvania Oil Company, he was a partner in a small way. The objects in sending him to Titusville seem to have been three: to straighten out certain legal tangles in the title to the land, to investigate its possibilities, and to look into the feasibility of boring for oil.

Drake made his journey in December, 1857. Before he left, Townsend asked whether he had a title of any kind to impress that half-wild country, and on learning that he had not, promptly created him a colonel. Mail was forwarded to "Colonel E. L. Drake"—with a flourish. On his way west he examined the methods of salt-well drilling near Syracuse, and left the railroad at Erie. Most of the forty-five mile road thence to his destination was "an extensive mud-hole." When he alighted from the stage at Titusville, which he described as "a small dilapidated Village of about 123 Souls of all descriptions," the friendly inhabitants greeted him with a cordial "How are you, Colonel Drake?" He remedied the legal defects in the land title; he found plentiful evidences of petroleum; and he inspected the saw-mills of Brewer, Watson & Co. to see how oil was used for lubrication and illumination. On his way home he visited the salt-and-oil wells of Tarentum, Pa., where he learned more about drilling. He returned to New Haven with an enthusiasm which immediately infected his associates—and especially the ardent Townsend.

A new company, the Seneca Oil Company, was now formed in New Haven in the spring of 1858 with a capital of $300,000, all in

[21]Townshend, "New Haven and the First Oil Well," 15.

the hands of New Haven men, and with Drake as president.[22] The property was leased to it for twenty-five years on a royalty basis, twelve cents to be paid for each gallon of oil produced; and Drake was appointed general agent with an annual salary of $1000, while he was allowed $1000 more for developing the land. In this new company he is credited with 8926 shares, but most of them were actually owned by other New Haven men, including Townsend, who did not wish his name to appear in so speculative a venture. Throughout this critical period in the history of the enterprise Townsend was the most energetic and confident figure back of Drake. Bissell and Eveleth had dropped to a position of impotence, though the former shrewdly kept in touch with all that was done. Full of hope, Drake brought his family to Titusville in May, 1858, settling them at the American Hotel. He was determined to sink a well until he reached the underlying reservoirs of petroleum, though the villagers assured him that the oil was merely "the drippings of an extensive coal field."[23]

Unfortunately, he spent his first year to such little apparent purpose that critics have unjustly assailed him as an enthusiastic, visionary procrastinator, lacking in practical capacity. Even J. J. McLaurin, who knew all the difficulties, states that his movements were "inexplicably slow." But it must be remembered that Titusville was a remote little village, with outgoing mails only once a week, and few materials for work; that after Drake gave up his initial plan of digging and decided to bore, drilling tools had to be made, not bought; and that workmen were hard to find, for they thought the whole plan "queer." Drake first hired laborers who with pick and shovel dug a well from which a mere quarter-barrel of oil a day could be pumped; and when they deepened it, water flooded in. He then determined to drill, and revisited Tarentum to engage help. The first well-employee whom he attempted to hire refused, but told him of a Tarentum blacksmith named William Smith, who made tools for boring salt wells, and of other men. Drake hired one of these other men. He then hurried back to Titusville, where in August he completed an engine-house and erected a thirty-foot derrick that his

[22]The best account of the Seneca Oil Company is in Giddens, *The Birth of the Oil Industry,* Ch. IV, based on the Townsend Collection and other sources.

[23]Drake's own account of the enterprise, written about 1870, is in the Drake Museum at Titusville, where I have used it.

workmen contemptuously called "Drake's yoke."[24] He waited for the driller—but he failed to come! Inquiry showed that he had regarded Drake as insane, and had promised to join him only to get rid of his importunities! Cold weather came on, and further work became impossible.

While some writers have suggested that the Seneca Oil Company was meanwhile giving the indomitable Drake half-hearted support, this view is refuted by the documents. Townsend, always loyal and cheerful, encouraged the "colonel" in his idea of drilling. "Go ahead, persevere, and directly you will see . . . the big augur going down and oil coming up." On September 2, 1858, the company voted to send its manager $500 at once, and $500 more at the end of a month —this evidently being the $1000 originally promised him for development. But this was only the beginning. Between April 20, 1858, and April 2, 1859, it sent him an aggregate of $2490.58 for his general operations; and between March 27, 1858, and August 31, 1859, it remitted an additional $2661.19 for specific purposes—boring tools, expert labor, and the like. This, a total of well over $5000 supplied in about a year and a half, was unstinted assistance for so small a corporation in so experimental a field.[25] As the summer of 1859 wore on, it is true, Drake's New Haven associates did run short of funds and manifested a certain impatience. In August, Townsend finally sent a last draft for $500, instructing Drake to pay his debts and come home; but the letter fortunately did not arrive until after the manager had struck oil. While from time to time Drake had borrowed money in Titusville, this was evidently in anticipation of payments from New Haven which soon afterward arrived.

In April, 1859, Drake effectively resumed his operations. Going to Tarentum, after arduous search for a driller he employed "Uncle" Billy Smith, paying him $2.50 a day. This veteran blacksmith, who had long worked for Kier and Lewis Peterson, was expert in forging the iron tools, including bits, augur-stems, and sinker-bars, used for deep bores. "I could not have suited myself better if I could have

[24]Drake writes: "I finally found a man who was willing to contract, to bore a round, smooth, straight five-inch hole, 1000 feet deep, for one Dollar per foot, the borer to draw no pay only enough to pay for the board of himself and Boy and his Tobacco until the work was completed." MS narrative.

[25]My figures are based upon the Townsend papers and the pamphlet by H. H. Townshend.

had a man made to order," wrote Drake. Before leaving Tarentum Smith made a complete set of boring tools, for which he charged Drake $76.50; tools so light that a man could carry them all on his back without trouble. He and his fifteen-year-old son arrived about May 19 and at once set to work, overseeing a considerable body of workmen. The site chosen was only about 150 feet from the bank of Oil Creek, and below its level. At this very spot, according to legend, the soldiers of General Benjamin Lincoln had halted during the Revolution to gather oil and apply it to their wounds and sore feet. First, beginning about May 20, a new pit was dug. Drake and Smith planned to use shovels to get down to bedrock, and then to drill, as in making all salt wells. But the loose earth caved in heavily, while the bottom of the pit filled with water. They therefore drained the spot, brought some cast-iron pipe from Erie, and with a heavy white-oak battering-ram drove it down, in ten-foot sections, through clay and sand to the solid bedrock. Then they began boring with a six-inch augur. This plan of operations, which proved excellent and was later used in most of the Pennsylvania oil wells, at once differentiated their undertakings from the old method of sinking salt wells. But the question whether Smith or Drake originated it seems to be insoluble.

After striking bedrock at thirty-six feet, the drillers went steadily down at the rate of three feet a day. Their oak battering-ram had been lifted by an old-fashioned windlass, but the drill was operated by steam power. Little attention was paid locally to their "wild" enterprise. On Saturday, August 27, they reached 69½ feet, and stopped work until Monday. But on Sunday afternoon Billy Smith and his son Sam left their neighboring shanty to examine the shaft. Sam, peering down the pipe, saw a viscous green liquid shimmering only a foot from the top. "Oil! Oil!" he shouted. It was a cry that was destined to echo around the world.

"Uncle Billy" gazed, believed, and sent the lad running to a neighboring sawmill camp crying, "We've struck oil!"

As the sawmill hands rushed up in excitement, they found Billy Smith eagerly dipping out the dark green oil. Every one looked, touched, and exclaimed. Hurriedly mustering some assistants, Smith connected a cistern pump with it and began to run the petroleum into whatever vessels he could find. Drake was absent and did not

Two heroes of the discovery of oil.

Lower Left: Uncle Billy Smith. *Lower Right:* The blackbearded Edwin L. Drake.
Above: The house occupied by "Colonel" Drake in Titusville when he struck oil.

First Standard Oil Refinery in Cleveland.

From a photograph by Mather in 1869 or 1870.

return until the next morning. He was greeted with a triumphant shout. The old blacksmith led him to the chugging pump and pointed to the iridescent stream, which had already filled barrels, washtubs, and buckets. "There's your fortune!" he exclaimed.

With good reason might Drake feel triumphant. He had written his name on an imperishable page of history. He was to come to want, and to die in poverty, relieved only by a meager pension of $1500 a year voted by the Pennsylvania Legislature. His grave was to go all but unmarked until, long after his death, H. H. Rogers raised a fitting monument above it. But he had made himself an unforgettable figure in the annals of American industry. He has been described as a dreamer, a bungler, and a time-waster, but these characteristics are inaccurate; for a careful study of the records shows that he was patient, industrious, resourceful, and indomitable. Unexcitable and tenacious, he had pushed his plans to fruition despite difficulties that would have discouraged most men.

To be sure, the idea of drilling for oil had been floating about the East for some years. Bissell had certainly been fired by it, and Kier and Lewis Peterson had probably entertained it. But the fact remains that Bissell had not interrupted his law practice to apply it; that Kier and Peterson, although receiving a very high price for petroleum, had done little with their wells. While various men had expatiated on the possibility of drilling, it was Drake who had gone to the Oil Regions, employed trained assistance, helped devise a workable plan, and put down the shaft. Although it took him a year and a half to do it, this was not because of procrastination but because of forbidding perplexities and obstacles. His record was one of striking celerity compared with that of the Pennsylvania Rock Oil Company. Incorporated in the fall of 1854, it and its daughter corporation, the Seneca Oil Company, had required nearly five years to get a hole 69½ feet deep drilled on its oil-bearing property!

v

Word of Drake's discovery flew like a Dakota cyclone. When Sam Smith hurried through the woods that Sunday afternoon to tell the operators of the Brewer & Watson sawmill that his father had struck oil and needed barrels right away, the boss of the gang, sagacious old Jonathan Watson, soon learned the news. He at once came over to look at the well, and meditatively watched the pump. Then, hastening back to get his horse, he snapped out to his head sawyer, William Kirkpatrick:

"Bill, I've got to go home on some business right away. You stay here and look after the mill until I come back."

Kirkpatrick stared after his hustling employer, pondered a few minutes, and then summoned Jim Tarr, his assistant.

"Watson wants me to take care of the mill till he gets back," he explained. "But I've got urgent business too. *You* look after the mill."

Watson galloped down Oil Creek, and hurriedly closed a bargain to lease the farms of Hamilton McClintock and John Rynd. Together with his partner, Brewer, he then began leasing land wherever he could find it along the Creek Valley.

The distrust and derision that had long surrounded Drake vanished like darkness before the dawn. Land which had possessed no value beyond its timber suddenly increased a hundredfold or thousandfold in price. Drake had rubbed an Aladdin's lamp, a lamp brimming with liquid gold. The McClintock farm which Watson so expeditiously leased was the very farm where Nat Cary had dipped his oil years before to sell it in Pittsburgh—a farm now worth a fortune. Billy Smith wrote his old employer, Peterson, in Tarentum: "For God's sake, Mr. Peterson, come up here. There's oceans of oil!" In New York George H. Bissell, who had arranged to be notified by telegraph of any discovery, bought up all the Seneca Oil shares he could acquire, and then hurried to the scene. Arriving four days after the first discovery, he began leasing farms in the vicinity whether they held surface indications of oil or not. Within a few weeks the news was leaking out of the little valley to Pittsburgh, to Philadelphia and New York, to Ohio and Virginia. Adventurers, investors, workers, vagabonds, all turned their feet toward what at once became known as the Oil Regions. Solitudes that had known only the hunter's shout and the woodman's axe soon resounded with the varied noises of men making roads, erecting derricks, and building impromptu towns; with the explosions of dynamite clearing away rocks, the yells of teamsters, the throb of engines driving bores deeper into the earth. The instinct of those who joined the rush was sound. Another California lay in those hills; a black or green gold that would make more and greater millionaires than Marshall's discovery at Sutter's Mill twenty-one years earlier.

On the very day the Drake well was pronounced a success a second one was begun by William Barnsdall, an English-born farmer who was quick to see the possibilities of the situation, and who allied himself with Henry Rouse, a shrewd merchant from Enterprise. Barnsdall was destined to found a great oil business, and to become well known to Rockefeller. He and Rouse struck oil in November, and when the yield proved to be only five barrels daily, resumed drilling. In February, they tapped a far richer vein. The third well, begun by David Crossley of Titusville, began to yield what was then counted an "enormous" flow of oil, about eighty barrels a day, in March, 1860. Then well after well, as the Oil Regions swarmed with eager speculators and diggers, was brought in. Drilling extended up and down Oil Creek, French Creek, and the Allegheny River, at first centering in the area between Titusville and Franklin—that is, in Venango County—but soon spreading beyond. The district hummed like an enormous beehive. Drake's well proved a small one; its output rose to forty barrels a day, and then before the close of 1859 fell to fifteen. But from the Barnsdall-Rouse well near Titusville, in the first four months after its completion, 56,000 gallons of oil were sold for $16,800.[26]

And after the spectacular Williams well was opened near Titusville in June—the first real gusher, called "the Fountain" from its geyserlike quality—new strikes became too numerous to list. Production for the year 1860 was estimated by competent judges at 200,-000 barrels (the standard barrel contained 42 gallons). *The Living Age* for September, 1860, published an article accurately entitled, "A Good Time Coming for Whales." In 1861 a number of other gushers were struck—the oil spouting high in air—and the first spectacular disasters occurred. Americans by the million talked of the Tarr farm, near Titusville, where one well flowed 4000 barrels a day for a time, and another 2500 barrels. They talked of the great spouting wells which, when friction produced a spark, burst into tremendous torches of flame, lighting up the countryside for miles around. They soon talked of creek bottoms flooded with oil, and of markets temporarily sagging to panic prices under the incredible output. The

[26]See the early chapters of Patrick C. Boyle, ed., *The Derrick's Handbook of Petroleum,* for a wealth of detail.

first thousand barrels from the Drake well were bought by Colonel Ferris and sold to New York refiners.[27] The government as early as 1860 closed a large contract for illuminating oil to supply lighthouses along the coast. Even in the exciting days when the Civil War began, and the whole country was agog over the first battles, the Oil Regions received an interested attention from the whole North.

VI

Rockefeller, laboring hard at his commission business in the winter of 1859–60, read and heard much of the great petroleum development. Since he was a dealer in numerous raw materials, this new industry assuredly aroused his curiosity. John G. Hussey, a prosperous commission merchant whose office was near Clark & Rockefeller's, and who had been Clark's employer for six years, went to inspect the oil district in the fall of 1859. Rockefeller knew him well. He may have known the object of his trip, though Hussey tried to keep it secret; he certainly knew of its results, for Hussey came back enthusiastic. Hussey & McBride, as the commission firm was known, promptly paid $20,000 for a one-fourth share of the oil found on the two McElhenny farms, 183 acres in Cherrytree township; and when in May, 1861, the first well ever put down to the "third sand" proved a gusher, they were jubilant. Hussey made more investments and did well in the Oil Regions. Other Clevelanders, visiting the fields in their infancy, came home full of excited observations and gossip.

By word of mouth or print Rockefeller doubtless learned all the more striking stories about the Pennsylvania field.[28] He probably heard how in November, 1859, James Evans, a blacksmith living at Franklin on French Creek, some eighteen miles southwest of the Drake well, decided that there might be oil in an old salt well at Horsecreek Furnace on the Allegheny River. The water in this seventeen-foot well had a faint odor of petroleum, and he determined to sink it deeper. A hardware dealer gave him iron for drill-

[27]Patrick C. Boyle, *Industrial Commission Hearings, Standard Oil Combinations,* 1899, p. 407.

[28]See Alfred Wilson Smiley, *A Few Scraps (Oily and Otherwise),* 44 ff. The development of the oil fields is described in dry chronological form, but with a wealth of statistical and other detail, and with general accuracy, in Patrick C. Boyle's above-mentioned huge volume, *The Derrick's Handbook of Petroleum.*

ing-tools on credit; he and his son forged them, rigged up a spring-pole, and "kicked down" a shaft. At seventy-two feet the tools stuck, and could not be extricated. Evans began pumping, and soon a dark green column of oil poured from the spout at the rate of twenty-five barrels a day. The town went wild. "Franklin had no such convulsion," writes one historian of the Oil Regions, "since the *William B. Duncan,* the first steamboat, landed one Sunday evening in January, 1828. . . . November court adjourned in half the number of seconds Sut Lovingood's nest of hornets broke up the African camp-meeting. Judge John S. McCalmont . . . decided there was ample cause for action. A doctor rushed to the scene, hatless, coatless, and shoeless. Women deserted their households without fixing their back hair." That night, Evans's daughter Ann greeted a visitor with jesting exuberance: "Dad's struck ile!" The words so accurately hit the homely but fantastic hopes of others that they were caught up, laughed over, and ran throughout the country and overseas. It is said that Miles Smith, Evans's son-in-law, returning years later for a visit to his boyhood home in England, was asked if he had ever really heard the phrase in America.

Rockefeller soon learned, again, how men were enriched almost overnight. William Barnsdall was shortly receiving, with his partners, $250 a day from the well that they sank. With some other associates he erected near Titusville in 1860 the first oil refinery in the Regions, a paying venture. He drove additional wells, was later the first to discover paying oil in the Bradford field northeast of Titusville, and became rich. Evans received an offer of $100,000 for the Franklin well which he had redrilled at an expense of only $200. But Rockefeller would have heard how other men found poverty and death in the fields. Many bankrupted themselves in digging dry holes. Some were blown up by the nitroglycerin charges which shortly came into use to "torpedo" failing wells. Some were burned to death in spectacular fires.[29]

In April, 1861, for example, a thrill of horror was sent throughout the East by the explosion and fire at Little & Merrick's gusher on a farm near the junction of Oil Creek and the Allegheny River, in

[29]William Wright, *The Oil Regions of Pennsylvania,* 35 ff., gives a vivid contemporaneous description of the Oil Regions. See also Alexander von Millern, *All About Petroleum and the Great Oil Districts of Pennsylvania, West Virginia, Ohio, etc.* (1864).

which nineteen persons lost their lives. An enormous vein of oil had been struck, and a crowd of spectators had gathered. Suddenly a spark set off the gushing oil, a neighboring well, a filled tank, and more than a hundred barrels of petroleum. A full acre of ground was converted into a veritable field of flame, enveloping workmen and bystanders. Victims rushed out with their oil-soaked clothes ablaze, looking, in the graphic words of an eyewitness, like "a succession of shots from an immense Roman candle." The most prominent of the burned men, Henry R. Rouse, groped through the circle of fire toward a ravine. In his pockets were valuable papers and a wallet containing a large sum. He jerked these loose and flung them far outside the flames; struggled half way out and fell, burying his face in the mud to escape inhalation of the fire; and then, recovering, fell again at the very edge, whence friends dragged him forth. Taken to a shanty, he survived for five hours, though his whole back was burned to a crisp. He remained conscious, and as water was given him by the spoonful after every few words, dictated a will leaving large gifts for public purposes.

In reading the daily quotations on grain and vegetables, Rockefeller's eye often fell upon oil prices. As early as November, 1860, the shadow of imminent overproduction darkened the petroleum industry. That month found 74 producing wells in the Venango County district, yielding 1165 barrels a day.[30] In December oil was selling at the wells at 22 cents a gallon; in January, 1861, coal oil brought $10 a barrel in Cleveland—a remarkable spread in prices. By April, the Oil Regions counted a total of about 135 wells, good and bad, with a production of almost 1300 barrels a day. About half of them were on Oil Creek, and most of the remaining half along the Allegheny River, but there were now nine wells at Franklin, from which point came the best heavy lubricating oils. By August 1 the Titusville *Gazette* reported about 800 wells along Oil Creek between Titusville and Oil City. That month and the next saw the great flowing wells come in on Tarr's farm and elsewhere; the Phillips well, with its initial gush of 4000 barrels a day, remained for twenty-seven years the champion of them all, while the Empire well, with 3000 barrels a day, was a good second. Another field was being

[30]Venango *Spectator*, Nov. 21, 1860.

opened up in southern Ohio and West Virginia, in the district about Marietta.

By the fall of 1861 so much oil was being produced that it seemed impossible to take care of it. Thousands of barrels simply ran away into Oil Creek; the surface of the Allegheny River gleamed and darkled with it for miles below Franklin. Many wells were being hastily plugged. Apprehensive men talked of an imminent exhaustion of the whole supply by the wasteful methods. But the world was eager for this oil. Exports from the United States in 1862 reached almost 275,000 barrels. Little refineries were being built in a score of cities—and not least in Cleveland. Rockefeller knew the city's pioneer refiner, Charles A. Dean. He had bought Watson's cannel-oil factory on the Ohio Canal; visiting the Oil Regions, he fetched back ten barrels of petroleum, and going to work with his foreman, John Alexander, turned it into kerosene. His first year's operations were decidedly profitable. Before the end of 1860 Hussey & McBride were putting up an oil refinery. During 1861 another was built by Backus, Williams & Co.[31]

And while these initial plants went up there reached out toward Cleveland a new railroad, the Atlantic & Great Western, which would connect the city directly with this area where speculators were madly selling sites, gangs were nailing up derricks, teamsters were swearing at struggling wagon-trains of mules, and the sight, feel, and smell of oil were omnipresent.

[31]Cleveland *Leader,* Jan. 5, 1866.

IX

A Venture in Oil

THE books of Clark & Rockefeller have perished. What would they tell us of oil from 1860 to 1863 if we could read them? The partners bought Ohio wheat, Michigan salt, Illinois pork. Did they deal also in Venango County petroleum? If they did, questions of supply naturally arose. Many Clevelanders visited the fields, and several described their experiences in letters—some vibrant with excitement—in *The Leader* and *The Plain-Dealer.*[1]

According to a tradition long kept alive by elderly businessmen in Cleveland, a group of dealers met soon after Drake's triumph to discuss the possibilities offered by oil. Some thought of buying land, some of handling kerosene, some of refining crude oil. Remembering that many who went to the Oil Regions lost their heads, they agreed to send a cautious investigator; and they chose Rockefeller as the man of greatest force and insight in their number. Whether this really happened we do not know; no records exist, and Rockefeller himself in old age could not remember any such visit. But it seems not unlikely that at some time before 1863 the alert young dealer, for his own purposes if not those of a group, inspected the oil country. If so, he probably took the Erie Railroad from Dunkirk on Lake Erie to its intersection with the Allegheny River at Irvine, just northeast of Venango County and the oil fields.

All this was still a wild district in 1862. Oil had been struck in an isolated region of rocky, forested hills, streams cutting through deep and heavily wooded ravines, and scattered valley farms. The Allegheny River enters Venango County from the northeast, and Oil Creek from the north, the two uniting at Oil City. A little farther

[1]For example, the letters of one Willard, in the *Leader,* March 1, March 5, 1861.

down, at Franklin, they are joined by French Creek. It was along these semiwilderness waters and about the villages of Titusville, Oil City, and Franklin, that thousands of men had gathered to search for oil. Even in the spring of 1862 no railroad had yet penetrated Venango County. The streams in that muddy country made the best highways. As late as 1864 a writer for *Harper's Magazine,* entering the Oil Regions by way of Irvine, found that the quickest mode of covering the fifty-odd miles of Oil City was by rowing a skiff down the Allegheny. Such roads as existed over the clayey, rocky hills and through the sandy bottoms were turned into sloughs by every heavy rain. It was doubtless a weary, battered, and muddy Rockefeller who first looked upon the Oil Creek territory.

II

The spring of 1862 found the Oil Regions suffering from a heavy slump. Demand had sagged, supply had become overwhelming. In January prices had fallen so low that a hastily formed combination of producers resolved to sell no oil at less than $4 a barrel, but this organization proved futile. Petroleum men were eagerly reading the Oil City *Weekly Register,* which had just begun publication. On January 27 it reported 30,000 barrels of oil awaiting shipment at Oil City, with prices of crude oil in New York 13 and 15 cents a gallon. Late that month export shippers made contracts with some Oil Creek producers for large quantities of crude, deliverable at wells during the year, for 35 cents a barrel, or less than one cent a gallon! This depression, fortunately, was temporary, for wartime demand soon caught up again with production.[2]

But Rockefeller would have been impressed in 1862 by the tragic evidence that innumerable small investors and well-diggers had been ruined by reckless ventures. News of Drake's strike had brought in thousands of men who were resolved to gamble for independence by sinking a shaft somewhere, anywhere, in the Oil Regions. Poor workingmen or clerks with a few hundred dollars were inspired by Barnsdall's and Evans's sudden wealth to sink oil wells at once and wait for a fortune to gush forth. As they could not afford engines, they "kicked down" their shafts by foot-power.

[2]Statistics of prices are given in Patrick C. Boyle, ed., *The Derrick's Handbook of Petroleum,* and in the daily press.

That is, they took leases on small fragments of river or creek front. Each group cut down rough timbers, perhaps forty feet high, with which they built a crude derrick to support the necessary "fall and tackle." A heavy post was driven deep into the ground some ten feet outside the derrick, and on it was poised a large beam. One end of this beam projected to the central point under the derrick, where it was attached to the drill, while the shorter butt was so weighted as to furnish an exact balance. The drill was of heavy iron with a steel cutting-face. It connected above with a stiff rod, on two sides of which were projections called stirrups, large enough for a man's foot. Two drillers, each placing a foot on the drill, kicked down with all their might, turning it as they did so; then, lifting their feet, let the weighted butt pull it up preparatory to a fresh downward stroke. This method sufficed for the slow drilling of shallow wells, tapping a few deposits near the surface. But it was soon found that the good wells had to be from 100 to 1200 feet deep. Most of the laborers and clerks lost all they had.

The wartime visitor caught glimpses on every side, in fact, of mingled riches and desolation. The sun glowed upon literally hundreds of derricks rotting in decay; it shone upon hundreds more that were centers of a frenzied and profitable activity. While some knots of men were lamenting the ruinous price of oil, others were talking eagerly of new wells and new fortunes. Everywhere along the muddy flats a mad energy was visible—but an energy disorganized, chaotic, and uncertain. The rivers and creeks were full of black and slippery oil scows. The roads were crowded with struggling wagons and swearing drivers. New villages of unpainted shacks and shanties had sprung up; the old villages had become dirty, unkempt little cities, without sidewalks, without grass, full of mud, pigs, and the stench of oil. Hotels like the Petroleum House in Oil City were jammed with speculators, chiefly New Yorkers, Philadelphians, and Pittsburghers. From the leafy forest came the scream of sawmills, and from creek banks the hammering of cooperage shops feverishly trying to meet the demand for barrels. On every side rose the steady "clip, clip," of engines pumping out oil. Piles of wood and coal were heaped near "locations." Mud-spattered horsemen abruptly came and went. Promoters hovered about like birds of prey, seeking money for their ventures, sometimes sound but more often gold-brick. A glint of madness lay deep in the eyes of many of the oil-obsessed men crowding the Regions, and the whole tempo of life was feverish with expectation, tense with the fear that a moment lost might cost a fortune.[3]

It was on the creek flats and not the hills that the derricks clustered most thickly; flats sometimes wide and sometimes narrow, but peppered with derricks as the New York and Liverpool docks were peppered with masts. For miles they stretched away with their vistas of black timbering, their puffs of smoke from throbbing engines. Everything within view was black. The soil was black, saturated with the waste petroleum. The engine-houses, pumps, and tanks were black with the smoke of coal fires. The shanties, for houses were still almost unknown, were black. The men who worked among the derricks, engines, and teams were white men turned black; some were millionaires and some were day-laborers, but all were sable in hue. Even the trees along the flats and ravines were black with the universal covering of oil and soot. The river and creeks, covered with a thick coating of petroleum, glistened with an ebony opalescence, sometimes stirred by ripples into rainbow hues. Here and there, as Rockefeller walked about, he might have seen one exception to the prevailing blackness; a bright green jet as some gusher lifted its column of oil into the sunlight against the dark hill behind.[4]

Transportation, as yet highly chaotic, accounted for by far the greatest share of oil costs. Storage facilities for the oil were naturally quite inadequate. Franklin S. Tarbell, the father of Ida M. Tarbell, was so impressed by the inefficiency of the early arrangements that he went into the business of building better tanks. The first receptacles were log or plank affairs, sunk in the ground or raised above it and rudely plastered with mud; much oil leaked away, and it was difficult to transfer the rest. Tarbell built excellent wooden tanks, hooped with iron, and to meet the demand opened tank-shops at four points in the district. But it was necessary to get most of the oil to market at once. It had to be transported by wagon to navigable points on the streams or by longer haul to railhead. For a time long

[3]Giddens, *The Birth of the Oil Industry,* p. 76 ff.
[4]Vivid pictures of life in the Oil Regions are furnished by John C. O'Day, M.D., in *Oil Wells in the Woods* (1905).

lines of carts and drays labored with the heavy barrels to stations as far distant as Erie, Pa., or Mecca, O. Far larger quantities went down the Allegheny by barges, rafts, and small steamboats; but even this route was difficult and freights to Pittsburgh were exorbitantly high.

As production rose, a large body of teamsters made the most of their monopoly of the transportation from wells to river or railhead. By 1862 no fewer than six thousand teams were regularly employed.[5] When roads were good the drivers raced furiously in a blinding swirl of dust, the air blue with their profanity and the ridges echoing to their blacksnake whips. When rain took the bottoms out of the roads, their wagons mired down hub-deep. Sudden rises and drops in the level of French Creek, Oil Creek, and the Allegheny complicated the problem. Sometimes barges and rafts would be left stranded, while the cursing producers impounded their petroleum in improvised reservoirs behind mud banks. In sheer despair they resorted, in 1863, to the doubtful device of artificial floods—"pond freshets." Midwinter ice sorely troubled the Oil Regions. In December, 1862, a great ice-gorge broke loose in Oil Creek, destroying scores of boats and some 30,000 barrels of oil. The frantic producers breathed more easily when in the following spring laborers began grading for a railroad from Meadville to Franklin.[6]

The tradition in Cleveland is that as Rockefeller saw the risks of production, he was equally impressed by the possibilities of refining. The difference between crude oil prices in the Regions and refined oil prices in the larger cities remained alluring in the extreme. Perhaps he went to the oil districts as early as the spring of 1862. If so, he then found petroleum selling at the wells at 25, 35, and 50 cents a barrel, while in seaboard markets refined oil was fetching 25 and 35 cents a *gallon*. This was of course an exceptional situation, produced by the sudden unmanageable flood of crude oil. But in the last weeks of the year, when conditions had become fairly normal again, Pittsburgh quoted crude oil in bulk at 31 and 32 cents a gallon, and refined oil at 80 and 85 cents, tax free; the

[5]McLaurin, *Sketches in Crude Oil,* 262. For the career of William Tarbell, see D. R. Crum, ed., *Romance of American Petroleum and Gas,* 335; Ida M. Tarbell, *All in the Day's Work,* 5 ff.

[6]Giddens has a good chapter on transportation; *Birth of the Oil Industry,* p. 101 ff.

corresponding figures in Cleveland were 31–32 cents a gallon for crude, and 80–85 cents for refined oil. Here obviously lay a glittering opportunity, for costs of refining were low. Some bold pioneers in the refinery business had made almost as much money as the first owners of gushers. Rockefeller may well have heard of J. F. Downing, a Bostonian who came to Erie, set up a small plant, bought crude oil from the Titusville wagon-trains, and was soon wealthy. He undoubtedly heard much of the Humboldt refinery at Plummer, and of others at Corry and in Pittsburgh. In the refining industry, as in producing, capital already counted. Small refineries were likely to be ruined by the terrific unpredictable fluctuations in prices, the alternations of glut and shortage; large refineries could breast these vicissitudes and make profits. But at their worst, the uncertainties of refining were fewer than those of producing.

III

While Rockefeller labored at his desk, while he made trips over northern Ohio to drum up shipments of grain, while he scurried to railroad offices, he kept his eyes open. He perceived, as we have seen, that in the grain-shipping, meat-packing, and general produce trade Cleveland could never equal Chicago, Milwaukee, and Omaha. He knew that Cleveland's real future lay in manufacturing and transportation. Comprehending this, and yet realizing that the iron business and the lake shipping business both required more capital than he commanded, he was especially interested in 1861–62 to see a number of little oil refineries going up on the banks of the Cuyahoga. Their scum discolored the river.[7] He perceived that the petroleum industry, growing by spectacular spurts, was throwing branches far outside the Regions and becoming of national scope.

Rockefeller knew that in New York the oil-export business was growing more important every month. He knew that every railroad president whose lines ran near the fields was eager to share in the new traffic; the Atlantic & Great Western, for example, was operating a line to Franklin in July, 1863, and the next month began building an extension to Oil City. Oil refineries went up in Buffalo and Pittsburgh, New York and Philadelphia, Boston and Baltimore.

[7]For the refining industry in Cleveland, 1860–66, see the W. P. A. press-digest, *Annals of Cleveland.*

The first pipe-line—a two-and-a-half-inch iron pipe extending three and a half miles from the Tarr farm near Titusville to the Humboldt refinery on Cherry Run—was throbbing in the fall of 1863 with a flow of from one to two thousand barrels a day. More and more money was being invested. Oil City by October, 1863, possessed twenty busy petroleum landings on the river front, and the firms owning them had tied up about ten million dollars in handling oil. In August, 1863, twenty refineries were busy in or near Cleveland, which that month produced 103,691 gallons of refined oil, nearly one fourth of it for export. The single Humboldt refinery in the heart of the Oil Regions still exceeded this entire Cleveland production. Nevertheless, the business seemed large to Clevelanders, and shrewd men could see that it would become far larger.

One of the first Cleveland men connected with refining was Samuel Andrews, already mentioned as an Englishman from the same Wiltshire town as Maurice B. Clark. He had come to Cleveland in 1857, an energetic young man with a flair for mechanics and chemistry. His friends Clark and Shurmer procured him a position in a lard-oil refinery owned by another Englishman, C. A. Dean, where he soon became a practical expert in oils, tallows, and candle-making. His employer was interested in new illuminants, and with the help of John Alexander, his foreman (also English-born), and Andrews, he began to make coal-oil from cannel coal in 1859. Probably this British-born group were well informed upon the English and Scottish methods of shale-oil refining. A year later, as we have seen, Dean was infected by the excitement of the oil rush, visited the Regions, and ordered an initial shipment of ten barrels of petroleum. From this he, Alexander, and Andrews made the first kerosene produced from petroleum in Cleveland. Alexander was always proud of having "put the first barrel through." All three, and especially Andrews, foresaw that kerosene from petroleum would quickly supplant derivatives of coal or lard as an illuminant. Dean manufactured it in increasing quantities, and Andrews continued to work for him. He was expert in the use of sulphuric acid in refining, and ingenious in utilizing former wastes.[8]

But by 1862 Andrews was eager to launch into business for himself. His income was meager and his wife took in sewing to aid

[8]See article on Andrews, N. Y. *Herald*, Nov. 29, 1908.

him.[9] The Cleveland directories listed him from 1859 to 1862 inclusive as "candlemaker," and he may have sold candles of his own, though Clark and Rockefeller later emphatically stated that he was merely "an employe in a refinery." He talked repeatedly with Maurice Clark about an independent refining business, for he knew that Clark had money; he talked also with Rockefeller, for he and his wife were Baptists and saw Rockefeller regularly at the Erie Street Church. It is uncertain which man he won over first.

Years later Clark stated that at first he discouraged Andrews, since "John and I together did not have more than $250 we could spare out of the business," but finally agreed that if John would go in, he would consent; and that Andrews then converted the junior partner.[10] But Rockefeller has given a different version. His recollection was that the firm possessed quite sufficient capital for the venture. "We had money. In those years I had funds I was willing to leave in the concern at 10 per cent. Clark made me take it out. I went and invested it in a railroad stock. Oh, I remember that well."[11] Clark, he added, had two brothers, James and Richard, who had followed him to America and were eager to engage in some paying business. "So . . . the two Clark brothers attached themselves to Andrews, and Maurice Clark affixed himself to me on the financial end, and I agreed with him that we'd go in and contribute one half the working capital and be the 'Company' in the concern, thinking that this was a little side issue, we retaining our interest in our business as produce commission merchants."

What is certain is that the refining firm of Andrews, Clark & Co. was organized in 1863. Rockefeller himself later said 1862, but he was evidently referring to preliminary discussions. It is of small moment whether Clark persuaded Rockefeller to embark in refining, or Andrews and Rockefeller jointly persuaded Clark. Both versions agree that Rockefeller said the decisive word. We may be sure that he investigated the venture thoroughly and entered upon it only when he decided that the prospects were bright. In coming to his decision he doubtless considered both the future of the oil industry, and the business capacity of Samuel Andrews. He of course recognized that his own caution and resourcefulness would con-

---

[9]Inglis, MS Biography, 95.   [10]N. Y. *Herald*, Nov. 29, 1908.
[11]Inglis, Conversations with T. J. Gallagher and Rockefeller, 1917.

tribute vital elements to the success of the undertaking. Convinced that careful accountancy was the foundation of stable business, and that the acquisition of large credit facilities was essential to steady expansion, in both fields he had become an expert.

A fact which cannot be too much emphasized is that the new railroad had suddenly placed Cleveland in a position to compete with any other refining center. The Atlantic & Great Western, a broad-gauge line projected long before Drake's discovery and financed by British capital, ran its first trains into the city on November 3, 1863, a great event in the history of northern Ohio. It was later celebrated by a munificent banquet tendered by the Cleveland Board of Trade to Sir Morton Peto, the English Liberal and capitalist who had built railroads in Austria, Peru, New Zealand, and Russia, and was now invading the United States. Rockefeller must have read the flaring accounts of the dinner, at which General Garfield, Henry B. Payne, and Amasa Stone praised the British builder. The menu included nine varieties of fish, six of game, nine of other meats, fourteen pastries, and unlimited quantities of "sparkling champagne." Extending westward from Meadville and Corry, Pa., the A. & G. W. not merely gave Cleveland, by virtue of its connection with the Erie Railroad, a direct and unbroken communication with New York City, through trains being scheduled at once. It not merely assured strong competition to the New York Central-Lake Shore system when that should be opened through northern Ohio. It gave Cleveland a broad-gauge line into the heart of the Oil Regions, for the Atlantic & Great Western had obtained a branch connection from Corry to Titusville in the autumn of 1862, and another from Meadville to Franklin the following summer.[12]

This road at once became the principal oil-carrier of the nation. In the two years 1863–64 it carried well over one and a half million barrels of petroleum—evidence of the immense value of oil freights. Most of this went to New York, but Cleveland had a goodly share, approximately one tenth of the whole. It was a piece of luck for

[12]Rolland H. Maybee, *Railroad Competition and the Oil Trade, 1855–73,* Ch. 1; E. P. Oberholtzer, *History of the United States,* I, 237; Sir Morton Peto, *Resources and Prospects of the United States, passim;* Cleveland newspapers, November, 1863; October, 1865. The A. & G. W. was without adequate terminals. Its eastern end was at Salamanca, N. Y.; its western ends were at Cleveland and Dayton. It connected with the Erie, and at Corry with a branch of the Pennsylvania.

Cleveland that the oil fields were first tapped near their northwestern border, and not to the south near Pittsburgh. It was a far greater piece of luck that this new railroad, planned without thought of oil, so quickly furnished cheap communication with the wells.

Refinery after refinery sprang up along the Atlantic & Great Western tracks. They were numerous but small, the owners having little money, great enterprise, and exuberant hopes. In 1863 Alexander, Scofield & Co. erected a refinery for $7000. Marshall, Barkwell & Co. opened another with no greater outlay. So did Outhwaite, Shurmer & Co. The refinery of Hanna, Doherty & Co., at first small, grew so rapidly that by the end of the war the invested capital was $100,000.[13] We shall meet some of the men here named—Hanna, Alexander, Scofield, Shurmer—later in our story.

While in 1863 it still required courage to go into oil, the industry showed more stability than in the two preceding years. With operations confined chiefly to the Allegheny Valley from Tidioute to Franklin, production was kept within reasonable bounds and prices rose. In February crude oil sold at the wells at a dollar a barrel, but quotations soon grew stronger. May found them rising from $3.50 a barrel to $4 and $4.50; and though Lee's invasion of Pennsylvania caused a sharp suspension of business, after Gettysburg crude oil touched $5 a barrel. September saw it selling for $6 at the wells, and on December 15 it still brought $4. One factor in this firm market was the steadily increasing use of kerosene in the United States. Even with the South cut off, in March it was estimated that the daily consumption of refined oil ranged from 1200 to 1500 barrels. By-products were also being discovered. Petroleum lubricants were proving invaluable, dyes were already being manufactured at the Humboldt refinery, and experiments were being made with naphtha fuel.[14] Finally, the European demand was growing rapidly. Great Britain had been the first country to import kerosene in large quantities, but now it was pouring into France and Germany. A merchant in Frankfurt am Main was reported in February, 1863, to have ordered 9000 barrels of refined oil, selling it all in a district of Germany which ten months earlier had never seen the product. The total exports of oil from 1863 amounted to 551,000 barrels, a

[13]The Cleveland *Leader,* in January, 1866, published a series of articles on the history and work of the Cleveland refineries.
[14]Von Millern, *op. cit.,* pp. 22, 23.

princely source of profit. No wonder that Secretary Chase wished to tax it heavily![15]

No wonder, also, that many young men were going into one part of the industry or another. In 1862 the enterprising young Scot, Andrew Carnegie, took time from his railway duties to journey from Pittsburgh to Oil Creek. He saw men kicking down wells, building shanties, and prospecting; he laughed at a sign over a chugging drill-engine—"Hell or China." He and some partners bought a farm, financed a company boring for oil, and reaped a handsome profit, a substantial contribution to the Carnegie fortune.

Andrews, Clark & Company built a refinery on the high south bank of Kingsbury Run, the still-wooded tributary of the Cuyahoga, about a mile and a half southeast from the public square of Cleveland. Lying near the point where the Run emptied into the Cuyahoga, it had water transportation to the Lake, while it abutted directly on the Atlantic & Great Western. At first they leased three acres with an option, then bought it. Early photographs show three lines of buildings on the red-clay slope: a big barnlike cooperage shop and a smaller warehouse near the top of the bluff; a battery of stills and furnaces, with two tall brick chimneys, farther down; and at the bottom shipping sheds of rough unpainted lumber, with barrels and boxes piled about. Huge trees scattered along the hillside tossed their branches in the lake winds that blew up the ravine. The steep incline of the bluff was initially an advantage in running oil by gravity, but later became a liability.[16] Men could stand then, as now, atop the hill and look over to the buildings of downtown Cleveland, distant a few minutes by fast horse. It was one of the best situations for a refinery in the city—perhaps, in its combination of water and rail facilities, the best. To this tract Rockefeller and his partners added rapidly; when the refinery passed to the Standard Oil Company in 1870, its buildings and yards (then in two groups, for another site at the head of the Run had been acquired) covered sixty acres, and eventually they spread over about one hundred.

Sam Andrews had charge of technical operations, with Richard

[15]For a good English view of this export trade in oil, see Sir M. Peto, *Resources and Prospects of America* (1866), 191 ff.
[16]The Standard Oil Company of Ohio still has a great refinery on this site, which I have carefully inspected. A few relics of the original plant survive, and the topography has not been radically changed.

The oil regions city which vanished.

Above: Photograph of Pithole, Pa., in the days of its glory.
Below: Part of the site of Pithole years later.

The Standard Oil Refinery.

Above: A model of the first Standard Oil Refinery in Cleveland, set up in the Field Museum, Chicago. *Below:* A refinery photograph of later date.

Clark assisting him. The process of refining was then cheap, simple,
and clumsy. Crude oil was emptied into long wooden troughs, sometimes with lumps of ice. After being strained into a wooden tank,
it was conveyed to a still to be boiled. The first distillate arising from
the boiling oil was gasolene, for which it was difficult to find uses;
then benzol or naphtha; then kerosene. At this time a barrel of
Pennsylvania petroleum ordinarily yielded 60 or 65 per cent of
illuminating oil, 10 per cent of gasolene, and 5 to 10 per cent of
benzol or naphtha, the remainder being tar and wastes. Five barrels
of crude oil thus gave three barrels of illuminant.[17] Andrews was
supposedly able to extract more and better kerosene than his rivals.
Rockefeller and Maurice Clark took charge of business affairs, while
James Clark acted as buyer in the oil fields. They were all enterprising and all worked hard. From the beginning the company
prospered.

IV

But almost from the beginning there was friction in the management. Rockefeller did not get on well with Maurice Clark's two
brothers. Even with Maurice he had moments of friction, for Rockefeller's combination of vision in planning and precision in management was not properly appreciated by the older man. It is clear
that his force of intellect and character had made him by 1863 the
dominant partner in the commission firm. But now the three Clarks
together threatened to be too much for him. Even when Andrews,
a steady, hardheaded young man, stood by him, they were outvoted.

Neither James nor Richard Clark was as reasonable and conscientious as Maurice, and James was actively obnoxious. "He was
a big, noisy, vulgar Englishman of bad habits," said John D. Rockefeller many years later. "He was in all sorts of speculations. Before
coming with us he had been with Hussey & McBride, and he used
to boast of the smooth way he dealt with Mr. Hussey and the tricks
he played behind his back. I left him no chance for favoritism or
any of his tricks. He didn't like it when I made him account for
every barrel of oil he bought, and for all his expenses."[18] Naturally

[17]See description of the refining process, Cleveland *Leader,* Jan. 4, 1866.
Manuel Halle, an early refiner, gave Mr. Inglis valuable information on the
subject in 1917; Notes, Rockefeller papers.
[18]Inglis, Conversations with Rockefeller.

James Clark was irritated by the stern oversight of this beardless youth of twenty-two, by his exasperating precision, his searching eyes, his quick grasp of every detail. Every instinct of the blustering buyer reacted against Rockefeller's quiet masterliness. He bristled under rebuke, sneered at the "Sunday-school superintendent," and scoffed at Rockefeller's industry. The clash of irreconcilable temperaments would quickly have ended in war had it not been for Rockefeller's patience and the profits which the firm was making.

Sometimes Jim Clark lost control of his temper. One day in Rockefeller's office, angered by some point of difference, he burst into a storm of profanity and abuse. Rockefeller sat calmly through it all with his feet on a chair. Finally he remarked:

"Jim, you may chop my head off, but you can't scare me—you can't bluff me."

Clark quieted down, but thereafter a truce was impossible. Jim continued to resent Rockefeller's unerring control of all aspects of the business. Rockefeller felt a deepening contempt for Clark's profanity, inaccuracy, and mendacity, for his gambling and other vices. He tolerated the man only for the sake of Maurice Clark and the business.

For Maurice still usually deferred to John, and together with Sam Andrews looked to him for initiative and advice. Rockefeller's sister has recorded that they used to come around to the Cheshire Street house at breakfast time and walk to the office with John. "They did not seem to want to go without him. They would come up to the side door of the house . . . and walk in and visit in the dining-room while John was at breakfast." This was at half-past six or earlier, for John followed his father's maxim: "If you want your business to succeed, be there early and start it yourself." They would be at the refinery by seven. The three talked of oil, oil, oil. "I got sick of it," says Mrs. Rudd, "and wished morning after morning that they would talk of something else." In the midst of the Civil War, it is strange that they never did! But this intense preoccupation with business was one secret of Rockefeller's quick mastery of it. It sometimes irked even his brother Will, who took life more easily; especially when Will, who slept with John, was kept awake by it.

Occasionally in the middle of the night John would nudge Will and ejaculate: "Listen to this! I've just thought of a scheme to do so and so." Will would remonstrate drowsily: "Keep your ideas till morning. I want to sleep."[19]

Within a few months the oil industry completely fascinated Rockefeller. Even when Andrews first talked with him he had been impressed by the possibilities of more efficient and more profitable refining. He soon saw that it would become enormously richer than the produce commission business; that all parts of it were in a much more formative state, and hence responsive to leadership; and that wealth in oil refining would depend strictly upon energy, resourcefulness, and skill. Most of the men who had rushed into the petroleum field were plungers, and an atmosphere of gambling hung over all the drilling there. But refining had attracted men of substance and conservatism. Samuel Downer, before mentioned as a manufacturer of coal oil at South Boston, in 1861 set up a large refinery, costing about $250,000, at Corry, Pa. This was at the junction of the Philadelphia & Erie and Atlantic & Great Western railroads, and crude oil was at first teamed to the plant from Oil Creek. Downer seems to have been the first to ship refined oil to distant points in tin cans—two five-gallon cans to the wooden case; a mode of shipment which soon became standard. In some later years he sent as many as a hundred thousand cases to Australia alone. The Humboldt refinery at Plummer, built by John E. Bruns and the Ludovici brothers in 1862, represented a still larger investment.

But all refiners, groping in a new field and lacking expert techniques, were wasteful in method and uncertain in result. Rockefeller abhorred waste. Like Lord Kitchener, he believed at this period that the secret of success was attention to details. A plumber brought him a bill for the new refinery, which required constant new installations and repairs. He found it full of errors, for the plumber was a ward politician who thought "mistakes" his rightful perquisite. Rockefeller said to Andrews: "Let us hire a plumber by the month. Let's also buy our own pipes, joints, and other plumbing material." They saved at least half on their plumbing costs.[20] Barrels soon became another problem. Coopers charged excessive prices—$2.50 for barrels not of the best quality—and were uncertain in delivery. In 1864 Andrews, Clark & Co. built their own cooperage shop, in which

[19]*Idem.*
[20]Inglis, Conversations with Rockefeller; Conversations with Mrs. Rudd, 1917.

they installed newly patented machinery; with the result that they were soon making excellent white-oak barrels, well-glued and painted blue, for ninety-six cents each. Rockefeller used to come to the shop at half-past six in the morning, and could be seen there, when help was needed, rolling barrels, piling hoops, or wheeling out shavings. The company soon bought tracts of white-oak timber. Instead of transporting the heavy green timber to the cooperage shop, as most manufacturers did, they dried it in kilns on the tract, and by carrying nothing but dried wood, saved materially on the cost of haulage. In a short time they acquired their own teams and wagons for hauling, a step which also reduced costs.

Meanwhile Andrews, with Rockefeller's encouragement, was making constant experiments in improving the refinery methods and utilizing by-products. Profits remained high. Later Rockefeller always emphasized the fact that this was an era of rich returns preceding an era of overcompetition and depression. When Congress levied a tax of 20 cents a gallon on refined oil, this was simply passed to the consumer. Little by little Andrews, Clark & Co. gained a place among the largest Cleveland refiners. Meanwhile, by the end of the war Cleveland was outstripping Erie and the Oil Regions towns as a refining center, and becoming a close second to Pittsburgh. And Pittsburgh, though nearer the source of supply, was dependent upon one railroad, the Pennsylvania; while Cleveland had two railroads, and in summer the Erie Canal route to New York as well.

v

Finally the friction between Rockefeller and the Clarks became unendurable. The situation reached a crisis late one afternoon in January, 1865, when Rockefeller brought Maurice Clark some papers to sign and found him in a belligerent mood. Grumbling when he saw another note, Clark put down his name reluctantly. Rockefeller has recorded his very words.

"We have been asking too many loans in order to extend this oil business," he said. "And the commission business, too. Why, altogether we have borrowed a hundred thousand dollars."

In his quiet, determined way Rockefeller defended his policy. "We should borrow whenever we can safely extend the business by doing so," he asserted. They discussed the matter, and finally

Clark laid down what might be construed as an ultimatum. He was against going any deeper into debt. "If that's the way you want to do business we'd better dissolve, and let you run your own affairs to suit yourself."[21] Perhaps he thought that, with two brothers holding important places in the business, he had Rockefeller at a hopeless disadvantage. The younger man said nothing, but filed the papers away in his desk.

As Clark left, Samuel Andrews entered. On his way home from the refinery, he wished to tell Rockefeller about the latest run of oil. After discussing it, Rockefeller related his dispute with Maurice Clark.

"He objects to my borrowing money," he said, in effect. "It's unreasonable; he knows, as you do, that I am very careful about loans. We have an opportunity now to expand, which may not last long. To be frank, Maurice has been very trying this past year. His brother Jim has a bad influence on him. They make progress difficult. From the way they interfere with necessary steps in the development of the company you would think that I was a child who did not understand business."

The refinery was the pride of Andrews's heart, and he also wished it to grow. "I don't like it either," he said. "They're too domineering."[22]

Rockefeller meditated upon the situation. He had endured the Clarks now for three years. They had constantly tried to make him feel, as he put it later, that he "was the straight-haired boy who grew up in Cleveland," ignorant of the outside world, a mere bookkeeper who should play a secondary rôle under their tutelage. He learned this month of the rich new strike just made at Pithole, and was convinced that oil-refining would become one of the greatest industries of the country.[23] He felt that he could make an important place in it; but only if he directed the business according to his own vision, his instinct for the future.

Turning decisively to Andrews, he spoke his mind.[24]

"Sam," he said, "we are prospering. We have a future before us, a big future. But I don't like Jim Clark and his habits. He is an

---

[21]*Idem.*   [22]*Idem.*
[23]Rockefeller, *Random Reminiscences,* 80.
[24]Inglis, Conversations with Rockefeller.

immoral man in more ways than one. He gambles in oil. I don't want this business to be associated with a gambler. Suppose I take them up the next time they threaten a dissolution. Suppose I succeed in buying them out. Will you come in with me?"

"Yes," said Andrews unhesitatingly. And the two Baptists shook hands.[25]

VI

One evening a few weeks later the five partners were assembled at Rockefeller's house on Cheshire Street. Again the threat of dissolution had been made by the Clarks. It was essentially a bluff, for Maurice meant only to frighten John; he always liked the younger man, and later followed his rise sympathetically. Nevertheless, the three brothers were determined to risk a break rather than admit Rockefeller's mastery in the company's affairs. If the rupture came, they believed that Andrews, as a fellow Englishman, would go with them.[26] They had met in Rockefeller's sitting-room to discuss company problems, and after a long debate their disagreement on the policy of rapid expansion remained unbroken.

"We'd better split up," said James Clark. He proposed that they sell the refinery business at auction. The buyer would take the entire oil investment; the loser would retain the commission business of Clark & Rockefeller.

"Is that your wish, Maurice?" asked Rockefeller. Maurice assented. "James?"

"Yes."

"Richard? Sam Andrews?"

They also assented. "Then there is a majority, regardless of me," Rockefeller remarked. "It is settled."[27]

The three Clarks went out into the night, convinced by Rockefeller's quiet manner that he dreaded the dissolution, and would recede in a day or two. Maurice Clark said as much, adding that he wished to keep John in the firm. Jim declared that he was tired of his "Sunday-school ways," and would let him go.[28]

[25]*Idem.*   [26]*Idem.*

[27]*Idem.* The account of the conference by Rockefeller includes the exact conversation about breaking up, and his memory in such matters was excellent.

[28]Inglis, Conversations with H. P. McIntosh, who knew James Clark well, upon James's attitude toward Rockefeller.

But before they reached their homes Rockefeller had taken his hat, hurried to the *Leader* office, and paid for the following notice in the next day's issue, February 2, 1865:

DISSOLUTION NOTICE

The firm of Andrews, Clark & Co. is this day dissolved by mutual consent. All persons indebted to the firm are requested to make immediate settlement at the office of Clark & Rockefeller.

M. B. CLARK
JOHN D. ROCKEFELLER
SAMUEL ANDREWS
JAMES B. CLARK
RICHARD CLARK

Maurice Clark read the notice at breakfast the next morning and rushed forthwith to Cheshire Street. Confronting Rockefeller, he pointed to it with indignation. "What do you mean by doing such a thing?" he demanded.

"Why, you all voted for it; and the law is that we must advertise to the community when a partnership is dissolved," explained Rockefeller.

"Do you really mean it? You really want to break up?"

"I really want to break up," replied Rockefeller quietly.[29]

The five shortly held a formal meeting to decide upon details of the auction. The Clarks had brought a lawyer, while Rockefeller had none. "I thought," he said when a multimillionaire, "that I could take care of so simple a transaction." The Clarks had now learned that Andrews had thrown in his lot with Rockefeller, and, while surprised, they remained a little contemptuous of these two, the "boy" and the "chemist." Two Clevelanders of English origin, Alexander and Scofield, had supplied the Clarks with money for the purchase. Rockefeller and Andrews for their part had arranged to borrow what they believed would be a sufficient amount for the plant and good will.[30] Somebody suggested that the auction be begun forthwith, and all agreed. The lawyer was asked to serve as auctioneer.

The young man who had made such hasty preparations to bid against the three brothers fully realized the momentous nature of

[29]Inglis, Conversations with Rockefeller. Again Rockefeller gave the exact words as he remembered them.
[30]Rockefeller, *Random Reminiscences,* 80.

the occasion.[31] He had served his apprenticeship with Hewitt & Tuttle. He had gone on with the aid of a partner to make a modest success; with the same partner he had entered a new field and set up a fast-growing manufactory. But he had never yet directed an enterprise free from interference. The time had not been ripe for that; now it was. This was his long-dreamed-of opportunity for "something big." "I look back on that day in 1865," he said long afterward, "and it seems to me one of the most important in my life. It was the day that determined my career. I felt the bigness of it, but I was as calm as I am talking to you now."[32]

Maurice Clark began the bidding at $500. Rockefeller raised it to $1000. The Clarks doubled this, and the price mounted. It crept up to twenty, thirty, forty thousand. Nobody had expected so high a figure, but still it went up.

"Fifty thousand." "Fifty-five thousand." "Sixty thousand."

Neither side was willing to yield. Gradually the bids rose to $70,000. This had been John D. Rockefeller's bid, and there was a pause.

"Seventy-two thousand," said Maurice Clark.

"Seventy-two thousand, five hundred," replied Rockefeller without hesitation.

Clark held up his hands. "I'll go no higher, John. The business is yours."

"Shall I give you a check for it now?" asked his partner.

"No," answered Clark generously, "I'm glad to trust you for it. Settle at your convenience."[33]

The first struggle was over; the heavier struggle lay before him. But with Andrews to administer the works, and himself in complete charge of business policy, he looked to the future with confidence. He had felt deeply the conduct of James and Richard Clark, their unreliability, sneers, and hostility. "The sufferings I went through in those years, the humiliations and anguish, I have not words to describe," he declared almost fifty years later. With Maurice Clark his friendship persisted. There was much in the man which he respected, while later he warmly admired his grandson, Walter Teagle. But even against Maurice Clark he felt a certain grievance.

[31]*Ibid.*   [32]Inglis, Conversations with Rockefeller.
[33]Rockefeller, *Random Reminiscences,* 80, 81.

Maurice had arrogated to himself most of the credit for their progress, and Rockefeller knew that this was unjust. "I made the firm's success," he told himself with pardonable pride. "I kept the books, looked out for the money."[34]

But all this was now past. In the Cleveland *Leader* for February 15 he inserted the following:

COPARTNERSHIP NOTICE—The undersigned, having purchased the entire interest of Andrews, Clark & Co. in the "Excelsior Oil Works," and all stock of barrels, oil, etc., will continue the business of the late firm under the name of Rockefeller & Andrews.

JOHN D. ROCKEFELLER
SAMUEL ANDREWS

The same issue carried an advertisement by Rockefeller & Andrews of carbon oil, benzine, and lubricating oils. On March 2, 1865, a dissolution notice of Clark & Rockefeller followed, "J. D. Rockefeller retiring." The young man was free from the restraint of plodding associates who lacked his penetration and resourcefulness.

"I ever point to the day when I separated myself from them," he declared in retrospect, "as the beginning of the success I have made in my life."[35]

[34]Inglis, Conversations with Rockefeller.   [35]*Idem.*

X

Boom and Depression

A T FIRST glance it seems astonishing that for the Clarks' share in a three-year-old refining company Rockefeller should give not only his half in the grain commission business, but $72,500 in cash, a sum that in 1865 represented a substantial fortune. It also seems astonishing that a man of twenty-five, already in debt to build up his business, could borrow a large sum merely to buy full control. But actually there was nothing strange in the purchase price or in Rockefeller's ability to borrow. The refinery, far from being small, was already the largest in Cleveland, and one of the largest in the world. We have noted various indications that Rockefeller possessed a high standing in Cleveland financial circles, and shall soon cite more. The business was worth all that he paid for it, though he later spoke of the price as representing a "bonus" to the Clarks;[1] and he could have borrowed still larger sums had they been needed.

This early emergence of Rockefeller's refinery to the foremost place in Cleveland is a fact of cardinal importance, yet it has been completely missed by writers on the subject. The evidence admits of no doubt. By 1865 all refineries paid a Federal levy on their product, and it was easy to compute the size of their businesses. Records show that the tax of $31,800.58 paid in November, 1865, by Rockefeller & Andrews, was the largest refined-oil tax levied up to that time in the Cleveland district.[2] The city then had about thirty refineries. The firm of Rockefeller & Andrews, as the year ended, had a capitalization of $200,000, as large as that of any and probably the very largest.

[1] Inglis, Conversations with Rockefeller, 1917.
[2] Cleveland *Leader,* Nov. 1, 1865. Records of the collector of internal revenue are not open to students.

A series of careful articles in the Cleveland *Leader* in January, 1866, describing the various plants, shows that four companies held an easy lead: Rockefeller & Andrews, Hussey, McBride & Co., Alexander, Scofield & Co., and the Pioneer Oil Works (Critchley, Fawcett & Co.). Of these Rockefeller & Andrews, with a business of $1,200,000 in 1865, far outdistanced Hussey, McBride & Co., with a business of about $500,000, and the Pioneer Oil Works, with a business of about $400,000. By January 1, 1866, the Rockefeller & Andrews works employed thirty-seven hands as against twenty-five employed by Alexander, Scofield & Co., and had a capacity of 505 barrels a day, or more than twice that of any Cleveland competitor.[3]

Moreover, just after Appomattox the oil business in Cleveland offered highly favorable prospects. It had been booming, and seemed likely to enjoy a steady expansion. The report of the Cleveland Board of Trade for the year after Rockefeller's purchase breathes an exuberant optimism:[4]

During the year 1866, there were received in Cleveland over 600,000 barrels of Crude Oil. About 400,000 barrels of refined oil were manufactured, and about the same amount shipped East, West, and South. These amounts were more than double those of the preceding year. In 1865, there were some thirty or thirty-five refineries in more or less successful operation. Now there are nearly fifty, large and small, with a capital of about three millions of dollars invested. The aggregate capacity of these works would be about 6000 barrels a day.

They have been run about three fourths of the time, say nine months in the year. If run to the full capacity during the nine months, this would give a capacity of 1,252,000 barrels of crude oil, about double the quantity consumed in this market during the past year, which was about 600,000 barrels. This crude oil when manufactured would yield at least 66⅔ per cent of refined oil, equal to 838,000 barrels.

During the year 1866, it is estimated that about two thirds of the oil manufactured in this city was shipped to New York and other ports for exportation abroad, leaving about 134,000 barrels for the home trade.

If the demand should warrant the manufacture of the refined oil to the full capacity of the present works, we should have a volume of 688,000 barrels to be forwarded to Eastern ports for exportation.

When Rockefeller took control of the refinery, American business was entering upon the great boom which followed the Civil War and

---

[3]Cleveland *Leader,* Jan. 4–20, 1866.
[4]Report of Cleveland Board of Trade, 1866.

lasted until 1873. In industry this was a period of multitudinous new ventures, multiform expansion, avid speculation, and fierce competition; the rapid formation of intersectional trunk-line railroads; the rise of great new industries like Bessemer steel, large-scale milling and meat-packing, and the manufacture of ready-made clothing; the first telephones and typewriters, the first talking machines, air brakes, and plastics. With immigration heavy and the West being rapidly settled, markets were expanding. For some years the pre-war tendency toward concentration in industry was checked by the inflation, the speculative confidence born of the war, and the new opportunities in business. These eight years were also a period of crass moneygrubbing, lavish display, the political scandals of the Grant régime, and debased business morality. In short, this was the Gilded Age, the era of the Great Barbecue. In 1860 the United States had 140,433 manufacturing establishments, with a capital of $1,010,000,-000; in 1870 it had 252,148 such establishments—one of them Rockefeller's—with a total capital of $2,118,208,769.

Many of these new ventures were mayfly affairs, perishing overnight, while even the strongest were tried as by fire in the grim depression after 1873. The panic of that year ushered in a dark period of contraction and deflation, so severe that 1880 was to find the number of manufacturing establishments held substantially at the level of a decade earlier. It must be borne in mind that, for American business as a whole, the first two decades after Rockefeller entered oil-refining were divided between a dozen years of exuberant expansion and seven or eight of remorseless contraction and consolidation. But as the oil industry had a wilder boom than most businesses, so depression smote it earlier and more harshly. It was a sick industry for several years before 1873, just as textile manufacturing, coal mining, and agriculture were sick industries long before the crash of 1929.

It is clear that Rockefeller took over the refinery because he had determined upon a swift and tremendous expansion, and was tired of the doubts and resistance of the Clarks. He turned back into the business nearly all its large profits. He borrowed as heavily as he could—"I had worn out the knees of my pants" begging credit at the banks, he said later.[5] He took decisive steps to strengthen all his

[5]Inglis, Conversations with Rockefeller.

departments. A tremendous confidence in the future of the Cleveland industry possessed him. The largest refineries were still in western Pennsylvania—the Downer works at Corry, the Humboldt refinery, and the works of Charles Lockhart in Pittsburgh. But Cleveland was gaining fast on the Oil Regions and Pittsburgh, for reasons which *The Leader* stated:

> Pittsburgh at the present time has more refineries than Cleveland; but Cleveland is destined to lead in this as well as in some other manufacturing pursuits, because of the natural and artificial advantages of its location; the Lakes furnishing means of direct communication with Europe, and the network of railroads bringing the oil and coal regions of Pennsylvania into close proximity with our harbor. Our nearness to and perfect system of railroad and water communication with the West and Northwest have already given Cleveland the preference in the market for oil consumers.

Since Rockefeller did nothing without careful planning, the speed with which he enlarged his business indicates that he had fully mapped his course before he outbid the Clarks. He and Andrews retained the name of the Excelsior Oil Works, and the old employees and equipment; in this respect "we continued as we were," Rockefeller later said.[6] But he quietly took over Maurice Clark's share in the general business management, assuming charge of all selling, and some of the buying. To assist in the latter work he sent John Andrews, Sam's brother, to the Oil Regions. Rockefeller also brought his own brother William into partnership, the two organizing William Rockefeller & Co. to build a second refinery, the Standard Works, at the head of Kingsbury Run. This was a firm, not a joint-stock corporation; "William was the head and Andrews and I were the company," said Rockefeller later. Before the end of 1866 another firm, Rockefeller & Co., was incorporated in New York to manage the export sale of oil. It had no president, consisted of the two Rockefellers and Andrews, and opened modest offices at 181 Pearl Street. The Cleveland offices of Rockefeller & Andrews were on the second floor of the new Sexton Block, a brick-and-stone structure on the banks of the Cuyahoga, reached by a muddy, ill-paved road. From the windows, just over a big fire-and-marine-insurance sign, Rocke-

[6]*Idem.*

feller could look out on the yellow stream and see his own scows of barrelled kerosene passing out to be loaded on lake boats.[7]

The selection of William as partner was a logical step. He and John had always been congenial, and he had become a very capable businessman. Like his older brother, he had received a strict business tuition from William Avery Rockefeller. Finishing high school while John was in his second year with Hewitt & Tuttle, he had been taken into their office as a bookkeeper under John's eye. When he became proficient, a prominent miller, Arthur Quinn, employed him at $350 a year. By 1859 he was getting a salary of $1000 from Hughes & Lester, a forwarding and commission house. Then he became a partner, first in Hughes, Lester & Rockefeller, then Hughes & Rockefeller, and finally in Hughes, Davis & Rockefeller. He was enterprising and shrewd, and, having saved his commission house profits, brought considerable capital to the refining business.[8] His gifts of personality were also worth much. A big man, genial, wholesome, with a humorous gleam in his eye and a kindly mouth, he always had something of the earth earthy about him; we are not surprised to learn that in his latest days he liked to go back to Moravia every year for a woodchuck dinner.[9] He made friends easily, and had become well known in Cleveland.

Rockefeller's invasion of the East to open up both the Atlantic Coast and export trade was a bold stroke. Up to this time no Cleveland refiner had made a systematic effort to cultivate the European market, for that meant competition with New York and Philadelphia firms possessing a distinct geographical advantage. The general reliance was upon jobbers and brokers. But the heavy capacity of the Excelsior and Standard plants required new outlets. It is impossible to say just when William reached New York. But we know that notice of his withdrawal from Hughes, Davis & Rockefeller appeared in the Cleveland *Herald* of September 18, 1865, that during the summer and fall the new Standard Works of William Rocke-

[7]*Idem*. New York and Cleveland directories. The Sexton Building had been completed in 1864 by David B. Sexton. It was four stories at the rear, on the river, and three in front. Rockefeller & Andrews had a large sign in front. For a reproduction of an old photograph of it I am indebted to Mr. M. G. Vilas of Cleveland.

[8]See sketch in D. R. Crum, ed., *The Romance of American Petroleum and Gas,* 247; also in *Dictionary of American Biography.*

[9]So old residents of Moravia told me in 1937.

feller & Co. were going up, and that this refinery began operations about December 1. Presumably he was in New York early in 1866. Here contacts had to be established with buyers in New England, New York, and Europe, prices watched, and arrangements made for wharfage, warehouse-room, lighters, and the repairing and refilling of damaged barrels. William worked vigorously, became intimate with oil dealers, and made friends with bankers—for money could be borrowed more cheaply in New York than in Cleveland.

The Cleveland *Leader* supplies us with a good account of the two refineries soon after Rockefeller took full command, its series of articles in January, 1866, naturally giving the older Excelsior Works the greater space. It states that during September, October, and November, 1865, they had produced more than 375,000 gallons of "burning fluid" and nearly 10,000 gallons of "benzole." They stood on the bluff at Pittsburgh Street, near the tracks of the Atlantic & Great Western, which ran a spur to their doors:

The warehouse for crude, forty-five by eighty-four feet, has doors for the unloading of eight cars now, and will be made to accommodate fifteen or sixteen when the switch is extended. There are two loaded warehouses on the premises—capable of holding about 6000 barrels—each about fifty by one hundred feet. The tankage for refined oil holds about 1500 barrels, for benzole 350 barrels, for crude oil 6700 barrels. In the still-house there are ten boilers of various sizes, the daily capacity of which is 175 barrels. There is one agitator, holding from 130 to 140 barrels.

This refinery was established in 1863, and employs thirty-seven hands at wages ranging from $45 to $58 per month. The capital invested in the business is in the neighborhood of $200,000.

It should be explained that the crude oil was pumped into heavy stills made of boiler-plate, where it was heated to 400° or 500° Fahrenheit by furnaces. The more volatile part of the oil rose as a vapor into overhead pipes, and was there cooled or condensed into a bluish-white liquid called distillate. This required further treatment before it became kerosene. It was conveyed into the lower part of tanks of water heated just below the boiling point; as it rose through the water to the top a waste vapor was generated and carried away, while the remainder of the distillate was piped off to a tank called the agitator. Here it was mixed thoroughly with sulphuric acid, which combined with the pitch that it held in suspension. The distillate was thus sweetened or purified; the acid and pitch sank to the bottom in a tarry combination known as sludge, while the oil was ready for further cleansing. This was received by a new water bath and the application of a solution of caustic soda to give it brilliancy, after which it was drawn into "bleachers" or "settling tanks" (large shallow vats). It was then barrelled as refined oil or kerosene.[10]

The Leader goes on to describe the new Standard Works:

> Directly on the other side, opposite the railroad track, is the new refinery of the above firm [William Rockefeller & Co.], which is made up in part from the firm of Rockefeller & Andrews—William Rockefeller, Esq., being of the late firm of Hughes, Davis, & Rockefeller. These works commenced running on the first of December last, and are now running only on half time, in consequence of the difficulty, at this season of the year, in procuring a sufficient and steady supply of crude oil. The establishment is not entirely completed. Tanks and a bonded warehouse will be built in the spring.

> The stills are ten in number, of thirty barrels each, all new. The agitator holds 134 barrels. Capacity of the refinery, 330 barrels [a day].

Rockefeller now had two partners whose tastes and abilities he completely trusted, and whose views chimed perfectly with his own. Andrews was the best superintending refiner in Cleveland; William Rockefeller soon proved one of the ablest export managers in America. No small part of Rockefeller's business genius consisted in the power to select gifted associates, and to make them work alongside him with absolute devotion. Even in 1866, as his business grew by leaps and bounds—for we have indications that this year it sold more than $2,000,000 worth of oil—he was scrutinizing other men, and was soon to enlist a new partner. His fervent faith in the future of the industry never flagged. He had staked his savings, his credit, and his energies upon it; and as he labored to drive his refineries into the lead in the Cleveland district, he imbued his associates with his own quiet but powerful enthusiasm.

II

And why not? The speculative boom which began in oil-producing in 1864 and continued through 1866 had spread to oil-refining, and there endured in 1867. This boom had been inaugurated in the Oil

[10]See the description in William Wright, *The Oil Regions of Pennsylvania,* 195, 196.

Regions by a great price rise in the first half of 1864. Stimulated by enlargement of the market, the advance in the value of gold, and a temporary slackening of output, the price of oil at the wells rose from $3 or $4 in the first weeks of 1864 to $13.75 in midsummer. It continued high. Well owners could pay all expenses and make profits of $3 to $7 a barrel. Many of them rolled in wealth. Men were feverishly boring fresh wells in old areas, and prospecting and "wildcatting" in new. Investors who heard that the Columbia Oil Company had paid dividends of $26 a share in the latter half of 1863 rushed to pour more money into speculative enterprises. Drilling rapidly extended up various "runs" emptying into Oil Creek and the Allegheny River, previously untouched but now worth exploration. In the summer of 1864 oil was struck in munificent quantities along Cherry Run, producing a quick new crop of millionaires, and in the first days of 1865 some diggers guided by a witch-hazel twig brought in a copious well on Pithole Creek. Great new rushes were the result, while the American public disgorged so much money for stocks that the Federal Revenue Commission estimated in 1866 that more than $100,000,000 had been applied to the purchase and development of oil lands.[11]

One group of four wells on Cherry Run yielded the original owners profits of about $2,000,000, and the entire valley with its steep sides was soon studded with derricks. But Pithole Creek, a tributary of the Allegheny, was the most spectacular of the early fields. The stream had been so named from pits or chasms near its mouth which emitted gas. On its upper reaches dwelt various farmers—the Copelands, Rookers, Holmdens—who eked out a backwoods existence by raising buckwheat and hunting deer. Here rose what John J. McLaurin has called "the meteoric city that dazzled mankind."[12] It was on the Holmden farm, seven miles upstream, that several employees of the Humboldt Refinery first struck oil with a well yielding 250 barrels a day. A succession of rich discoveries followed, drawing restless spirits from every quarter, until by September a town of about 15,000 people had risen in the wilderness. For a time its post office handled 5000 letters a day and did the third largest business in the

---

[11]*Report of the U. S. Revenue Commission on Petroleum as a Source of National Revenue,* House Exec. Doc. No. 51, 39th Cong., 1st Sess.

[12]*Sketches in Crude Oil,* 157.

State, next to Philadelphia and Pittsburgh. It boasted banks, churches, a daily newspaper, handsome shops, waterworks, a fire company, and more than fifty hotels, one of which had cost $75,000. Speculators and agents from the numerous oil companies swarmed into Pithole, purchased "acreage," and subdivided it into tiny fractions. Bits of land the size of a blanket sometimes sold for $300 and $400. Many would-be investors bought wells merely upon seeing water-color sketches of the district, and were often bilked. Shares in some companies sold as low as a dollar or half dollar each and were snapped up by clerks, workingmen, and servant girls. Meanwhile, Pithole had its roaring day of excitement and dissipation like Virginia City or Butte. Teamsters who made twenty dollars a day, diggers who had struck it rich, patronized the saloons, dance houses, bawdyhouses, and gambling dens. Then, as the wells failed, the town declined. Within a few years its glories had vanished; by 1874 it had only six voters, and when fire and flood completed its destruction, hardly a vestige remained to mark the site.[13]

But other upstart towns achieved more permanence; they remained on the map and were important centers for many years, until in the middle eighties the tide of oil discovery swept westward into Ohio and Indiana. Some are important today, for Pennsylvania still yields much oil. The situation as it was when Rockefeller bought sole control of his refinery has been vividly pictured by a correspondent whom the London *Times* sent to the Regions in the summer of 1865. He wrote:[14]

I am within the mark when I say that within a circuit of thirty miles around this Oil City there are more so-called cities and towns now existing than there were villages, or even farms, four years ago. Take one instance. Corry four years ago was a poor farm where the thinly scratched soil of cold clay land yielded so little that the whole place, buildings and all, might easily have been purchased at $8 or $10 an acre. It was a mere halting place for sportsmen *en route* to shoot deer in the now manufacturing regions of Petrolia. I was at Corry the other night. It is a fine rough city of about 10,000 inhabitants. The Atlantic & Great Western Railway, which has opened it up, has its great depot there, and has made it the central exchange of petroleum. It has nearly twenty banks, two newspapers, and the city is now building a large opera-house. The quotations

[13]Charles C. Leonard, *The History of Pithole* (1867).
[14]London *Times,* Oct. 18, 1865.

made in the oil-exchange at Corry, whether of oil, gold, or breadstuffs, influence Wall Street, and have infinitely greater weight on the trade of the country than anything done at Philadelphia, or indeed throughout Pennsylvania. Yet all this has been done within four years, and the site of the city which now transacts business to the amount of £3,000,000 sterling annually, and where the land sells almost as dear as in Cheapside, could all have been bought four years ago for less than £5000.

But Corry is only one sample out of many. Its position as the arbiter and ruler of prices between the oil regions and New York and Europe gives it, of course, great importance, though in reality the city is not larger than many others of Petrolia which are much younger. Rouseville, Plummer, Titusville, Franklin, are all the juniors of Corry by a couple of years, yet some of them are almost as important as Corry itself, and nearly as large. The city from which I write [Oil City] can scarcely be counted as more than three years old, yet . . . its extent, its squalid wealth and dirty evidences of incessant activity, its population, and its resources, all make it a phenomenon even in this land of hurried wonders. Oil City claims to dispute preëminence even with Corry. . . .

Methods of production had improved. Derricks by 1886 were nearly twice as high as when the first wells were sunk around Colonel Drake's shaft. The drilling machinery was much larger and heavier. Improved appliances pumped out the water and pulverized rock from the drill hole more rapidly, and a greater depth could be reached more easily. The torpedo, patented by Colonel E. A. L. Roberts, became an indispensable part of well equipment. These cylindrical tubes, filled with fluid nitroglycerine, were carefully lowered into stubborn or partly exhausted wells, and exploded by dropping a cast-iron weight upon them. The explosion shattered the rock walls at the bottom, and often brought a gush of oil and gas. The "torpedo man," travelling about the Regions in a cart with his tubes and cans of nitroglycerine, was long a famous figure, usually given a wide berth. Occasionally a heavy jolt of his vehicle or slip of his foot set free the terrible explosive, and man, horse and cart disappeared in a blinding flash, with only a burst of smoke and a gaping hole to show what had occurred.

Transportation had also been strikingly improved. As we have seen, at first teamsters dominated the situation. In rainy periods their wheels churned the roads into bottomless swamps, and as water pumped from the oil wells swelled the downpour from the skies, the sloughs turned into veritable creeks. Their brutality was appalling, and overstrained horses died by scores under the lash. When the mud was at its worst, barrels were "snaked" over the deepest holes one at a time, by horse and rope, and reloaded at the far side. One observer remarked that the Regions' mire "seemed but a covering to the bottomless pit, and a teamster who could swim possessed an advantage over one who did not." J. J. McLaurin describes the adhesive paste of oil and mud as "Wholly unclassable, almost impassable, scarcely jackassable!"

The constant losses and delays made men take the obvious step required to meet the situation. In midwinter the creeks and rivers were choked with ice, in midsummer they were often too low for navigation; and then the teamsters, waxing arrogant, charged exorbitant sums. At the height of their power they demanded $50 a day for team, wagon, and their own labor; emergency charges of even $300 a day are recorded, and one man declared that he would not turn his horses around for less than $10. As early as March, 1863 the *Scientific American* suggested laying a pipe along Oil Creek so that the petroleum might flow underground like so much Croton water. To be sure, at many points it would have to run uphill, while, being both lighter and less fluent than water, it might need propulsion even in descending gentle slopes. But a force pump would remedy this difficulty. The first oil pipe of any length, as already noted, was laid in 1863 from the Tarr Farm on Oil Creek to the Humboldt Refinery on Cherry Run. It was only a partial success, for the oil had to be driven by steam power over an elevation rising four hundred feet above the creek and no good pump was available. But it demonstrated what might be done, and the following year Henry Harley projected a longer line, beginning construction in the fall. The teamsters, who had shown marked hostility to the first pipe, attacked the second, not only cutting Harley's line but burning his collection tanks. Then the State authorities came to his rescue, and in the spring of 1866 he put into operation two pipe lines, with a daily capacity of 1500 to 2000 barrels each, from Bennehoff Run to Shaffer on the Oil Creek Railroad.[15]

Rockefeller doubtless heard how even earlier, in the summer of 1865, an oil buyer named Samuel Van Syckel ran a two-inch pipe, partly above ground and partly buried below ploughshare depth,

[15]Giddens, *Birth of the Oil Industry,* 141–149.

from Pithole to Miller Farm on the Oil Creek Railroad, and how two pumping stations swiftly carried the oil a distance of nearly five miles. He heard how Henry Harley's line also proved a complete success. A firm organized by Harley and W. H. Abbott soon took over the Van Syckel pipe, whose backers had fallen into financial difficulties, combined it with others, and formed the Allegheny Transportation Company, the first great pipe-line corporation. Various other enterprising individuals and firms entered the new field. For a time mobs of teamsters continued to tear up pipes by night, burn tanks, and threaten the lives of pipelayers. But by 1867 they were defeated, and the lines were on the highroad to dominance of all transportation between oil well and railheads. When J. T. Trowbridge visited the Regions in 1869, he found that almost the whole production, ten thousand barrels a day, flowed through pipes to the railroad centers, and that the cohorts of teamsters had disappeared. A great saving, he exclaimed, in expense, in whiskey, and in profanity![16]

As the network of pipe lines cobwebbed over the whole oil-producing district, tapping almost every well and converting a thousand streamlets of oil from as many subterranean reservoirs into a few great rivers and lakes of petroleum, an accurate system for measuring the flow also grew up. It was simple, cheap and efficient. When the tanks at an oil well became almost full, the nearest office of the pipe lines was notified. An agent promptly arrived with a measuring rod and book of receipts. He gauged the tanks, unlocked the stopcocks, and ran off as much oil as the owner desired. He then shut off the flow, measured the tanks anew, and computed the difference. The owner was credited with the proper amount of oil, 3 per cent being deducted for sediment and evaporation. If a small group of shareholders held the well, each might receive a document crediting him with his portion of the oil piped off. The earliest pipe-line companies were merely common carriers, and made no provision for storing oil, but as the boom increased, the production companies organized storage facilities with nests of tanks holding from five to twenty thousand barrels in a single place. At first the monthly storage charge was five cents a barrel or even more, but this fell rapidly.

[16]J. T. Trowbridge, "A Carpet-Bagger in Pennsylvania," *Atlantic Monthly,* XXIII (1869), 729 ff.

Throughout the boom period and for years afterward one great source of loss and peril in the Regions remained almost uncurbed—fire. Drake's well had been the first victim of a conflagration, for the enginehouse and derrick were destroyed in the fall of 1859, and work was halted for a month. Even when protected with the utmost care wells would sometimes burst into flames. A workman's pipe, a spark from the engine, the friction of a shoe nail on a stone, might ignite them; for the oil was often mixed with highly inflammable gas. The blazing fluid, shooting high in air and breaking in a shower of fiery pellets, might burn for days, a fountain of fire in the midst of the forest. As a character of Howells's *Hazard of New Fortunes* says, a flaming well sometimes turned midwinter into summer for a little patch of ground, so that trees budded and flowers bloomed in the grateful heat. Once in 1863 the Allegheny River caught fire; oil floating on the water leaped into flame, ran to rafts and barges, and burned up the bridge at Franklin. Signs appeared on trees, "Smokers will be shot," but men nevertheless smoked in the very midst of gas and crude oil. Burning oil tanks were sometimes emptied by cannon-shot to prevent their exploding and showering other tanks near by with flame.

The Titusville *Herald* published in July, 1866, a list of "the great oil fires of the past year." It enumerated nineteen, one of which had caused $200,000 damage. The very month in which this account appeared, a photographer was taking pictures of a group of wells at the mouth of Benninghoff Run. A thunderstorm was gathering, and he hastened to pack up his outfit. But while he was still busy the storm began, lightning smote one of the derricks, the fire spread to others, and within half an hour the whole scene was of charred, smoking desolation. Many lives were lost in these conflagrations. But the most memorable tragedy was that involving Henry B. Rouse and his friends, already recounted, which legend made a symbol of the fate of others in the Oil Regions. "Gentlemen," Rouse was said to have remarked as he eyed the gusher which had suddenly shot its dingy, wide-showering jet to the top of his derrick, "gentlemen" (puffing his cigar), "I am fifty thousand dollars richer today than I was yesterday." He stepped into the derrick house to give some directions, and was instantaneously wrapped in a pyramid of fire—

Photograph by courtesy of H. T. Morian.

Oil barges in the Allegheny River: probably in the later sixties.

From Mark Sullivan's "Our Times," Vol. II.

By courtesy of the Edison Company.

Rock oil and kerosene.

Kier's advertisement of petroleum as a patent medicine;
a housewife cleaning and filling lamps.

both he and his companions. The oil that had looked like miraculous wealth was in fact swift destruction.

During these boom years Oildom seemed half a region of gilded romance, half of violent melodrama. "Almost everybody you meet," wrote Trowbridge as late as 1869, "has been suddenly enriched or suddenly ruined (perhaps both within a short space of time), or knows plenty of people who have." He urged writers of sensational fiction to visit the Oil Regions and replenish their stock of ideas. As a matter of fact, it is remarkable that no novelist has ever given us an effective picture of this Pennsylvania Klondike. "Robberies, tragic deaths, bankruptcies, burning oil wells; fleets of oil-boats on fire, sweeping downstream in clouds of flame and smoke, destroying everything in their course; the rich reduced to want; vulgar families, the millionaires of a moment, tricked out in the unaccustomed trappings of wealth, like Sandwich Islanders in civilized hat and trousers; —walk up, gentlemen, and take your choice of subjects." He might have added to his panoply of picturesque incidents. He could have told of the Pithole audience, madly applauding the leading lady at "Macbeth" in the local theatre and tossing $500 in bills upon the stage; of Drake, the discoverer of this Eldorado, walking the New York streets in a nine-year-old coat, with sixty cents in his pocket; of a train of blazing oil-laden cars, the engineer speeding down the valley to a siding; of John Wilkes Booth visiting the district to pay $13,000 for a share in an oil well; and of an armed mob raiding Harley's tank farm and throwing fireballs into the tanks.

The figure whom the country accepted as typifying these early years of speculation was "Coal-Oil Johnnie," or John W. Steele. He was the adopted son of Mr. and Mrs. Culbertson McClintock, owners of a 200-acre farm about four miles north of Oil City. By 1861 several wells had gone down on the McClintock farm, and oil had begun to come up. One well flowed at the rate of 1200 barrels a day and others in generous measure, while the widow (for McClintock had died) stuffed her mounting royalties into a safe which she installed in her house. One morning in 1864, Mrs. McClintock, building a kitchen fire, poured some crude oil on her wood and kindling. Coals in the ashes exploded the oil and her clothing flared up. The house and safe were saved, but the widow died next day of her burns. Her adopted son, then but nineteen, a rough, uneducated, undisciplined teamster, inherited the contents of the safe and the ever-growing royalties, and soon attained nation-wide fame.[17]

For a short time Johnny idled, basking in the sun of his riches. "All I had to do," he remarked in retrospect, "was to loaf around, smoke good cigars, and let my bank roll swell." Then he began to make purchases, buying lots in Meadville and a fine team. Next came a taste of high life in New York, while in Philadelphia he met Seth Slocum, a sophisticated wastrel who showed him how to spend his money. Steele, hypnotized by Slocum, became the "Coal-Oil Johnnie" whose mania for spending startled city after city. With diamonds loading his shirt front and hands, and a resplendent carriage whose coat of arms showed an oil derrick, tank, and flowing well, he and his companion set out to see the world. They gave champagne parties to gamblers, pugilists, and chorus girls; rented a hotel for a day and turned it over to the public; bought a part interest in Skiff & Gaylord's Minstrels, with whom they paraded through various towns; distributed enormous tips and played astounding pranks. Steele later denied many of the exploits attributed to him, but admitted that he had not always been in a condition to know what he did. It was said that he wore dollar bills in his buttonholes for children to pluck, tossed a thousand-dollar bill to a Negro singer, knocked off men's hats when he did not like them and invited them to buy the finest headgear at his expense, and lost thousands in one night's gambling with the prize fighter, John Morrissey. Sharpers gathered about him like bees about spilled molasses.

But the flight of the coal-oil comet was as brief as it was spectacular. His oil wells slackened and became of little value; he was tricked out of much of his property; and he tossed away most of the rest. By 1867, having squandered perhaps a half million in all,[18] he was almost bankrupt. His wife had saved a little money from the wreck, and the two went west to Iowa and later to Nebraska. Here he became a hard-working citizen, and as railroad yardmaster attained a competence. But for a time he had been the symbol of Oildom.

Yet even in the boom period he was not quite a fair symbol. The area of order was gradually increasing. Trowbridge heard on every

---

[17]See John Washington Steele, *Coal Oil Johnnie: Story of His Career.*
[18]James Dodd Henry, *History and Romance of the Petroleum Industry,* 290.

side "that the day of extravagant speculation is over; that the thing has settled down into something like a regular business; and that they who really make anything by it are the men who stick to it as to any other business." Men of wealth and station had come to the Regions. James A. Garfield, writing in 1865 that "the fever has assailed Congress in no mild form," made an investment from which he reaped $6000 profit.[19] Simon Cameron promoted an oil company. Colonel W. T. Pelton, nephew and political associate of Tilden, became interested; so did some of the partners in Jay Cooke & Company; and so, it was said, did August Belmont and William B. Astor. Any real investment, as distinguished from a speculation, soon cost a large sum; a twelfth interest in the Coquette well near Petroleum Center sold for $225,000 and the owners of Phillips Well No. 2 paid $500,000 for a large well that interfered with the output of their own monster. The Oil Regions were less and less a place for the little fellow, more and more one for the big operator. Hard-headed and hard-fisted businessmen on every side—Dr. M. C. Egbert, William Phillips, John Fertig, and others—were becoming millionaires, and keeping their millions. Some of the big operators bought out farmers for trifling sums and then made fortunes from the land. The original investors in the Columbia Oil Company, among them Carnegie, received 4300 per cent on their money; and one of their richest areas was the Story farm near Petroleum Center, purchased for $30,000.[20]

III

It was inevitable that the boom in production should be accompanied by a boom in refining. The same factors of rising world demand, advancing gold values, and increased confidence in the future of the industry were at work. The speed with which the market for oil expanded astonished everybody. A commodity that had been a curiosity when Lincoln was nominated had become a necessity of civilization before he was murdered, the staple of a vast commerce. Houses, offices, and shops needed oil products for lighting; mills, factories, and railroads demanded them for lubrication; they became indispensable to paint manufacturers when war cut off the supply of turpentine. Every day some new use was presented. Kerosene, sup-

[19]T. C. Smith, *Life and Letters of James A. Garfield*, II, 822, 823.
[20]Burton J. Hendrick, *The Life of Andrew Carnegie*, I, 120, 123.

planting dim tallow candles, the dangerous camphene, the expensive coal oil, had become an invaluable friend to intelligence, culture, and social diversion. In millions of homes by 1865 it made the evenings bright and cheerful; it invited to reading and study, to games and merriment, to conversation and music. It was figuratively as well as literally one of the great enlightening agencies of the country.

Every one approved of the new industry, and was willing to lend it a hand. It had appeared when it was of peculiar economic value to the nation; when the Civil War swung the balance of trade against the United States, when gold was being exported, and when all the resources of the country were under a heavy strain. Land that had been thought valueless suddenly yielded a product which took an important place in our commerce. Nor was this all, for internal activity as well as foreign trade was benefited. Railways had a large new traffic, capital a field for lucrative investment, and labor an area in which it earned more than ordinary wages. The new industry, Sir Morton Peto wrote, was "a blessing bestowed upon the nation in the hour of her direst need."[21] At first many had watched the rise of oil refining skeptically, thinking it a temporary apparition. These observers prophesied that the mysterious Pennsylvania reservoirs would soon be depleted, and the gift of oil would vanish as quickly as it had burst from underground darkness. Even Rockefeller lay awake at night in the middle sixties and whispered admonishingly to himself: "You've got a fair fortune. You have a good property—now. But suppose the oil fields gave out!"[22] Fortunately these night-fears always disappeared with day. And although the yield of crude petroleum had fallen off in the three years, 1863–65, from the high figure of 1862, it swelled rapidly again in 1866. The new Cherry Run, Tidioute, and Pithole fields brought the production for that year up to 3,887,700 barrels. It was destined thereafter to rise steadily until in 1874 it reached a temporary record of 10,810,000 barrels; there was no danger of a shortage.

Prices in 1865–66 remained high. The yearly average quotation for kerosene per gallon, barrelled in New York, had been about 44 cents in 1863; it rose to 64 cents in 1864, was 58 cents in 1865, and remained

[21]Peto, *Resources and Prospects of America, Ascertained During a Visit to the United States in the Autumn of 1865*, pp. 205, 206.
[22]Inglis, Conversations with Rockefeller.

at 42 cents in 1866.[23] Profits for the early comers were large. Men could double their capital in two years, sometimes in one.

It is not strange that the number of Cleveland refineries leaped to fifty by the end of 1866. The Flats were now full of them. The air along the Atlantic & Great Western tracks was redolent of petroleum. Men complained that it spoiled the beer in the neighboring breweries; women that it tainted the butter and soured the milk. And the fires! They seemed incessant; the city fire fighters could hardly cope with them. One of the greatest blazes swept the works of Backus, Williams & Co. and Alexander Scofield & Co. in the summer of 1867, doing $65,000 damage.[24] Since everything was soaked with oil, any spark, any match set off a roaring conflagration. City ordinances compelled owners of oil tanks to dig moats around them for better fire protection. Grumblers proposed an ordinance to forbid refining within city limits, and refiners girded themselves to fight it to the bitter end. But everywhere men talked about oil, oil, oil.

As the plants grew in number they became more fiercely competitive. They fought for bargain supplies of crude oil, for freight cars, for skilled hands, and above all for sales. Even at the beginning of 1866 the list of Cleveland refineries—a list lengthened by twenty more firms before the year ended—was ominously long.[25]

Alexander, Scofield & Co.	Lambkins & Langdon
Backus, Williams & Co.	Marshall, Barkwell & Co.
G. H. Bierce & Co.	Morehouse, Meriam & Co.
Burton & Douglas	J. H. Miller
A. M. Burke & Co.	Outhwaite, Shurmer & Co.
Clark, Shurmer & Co.	Wm. Poole & Co.
Corning, Hooper & Co.	Brewster, Pelton & Co.
Critchley, Fawcett & Co.	H. Potter & Bros.
Clark, Bros. & Co.	Rockefeller & Andrews
Chandler & Reed	Wm. Rockefeller & Co.
W. J. Guild	Raynolds, Bishop & Co.
Gardner, Myers & Co.	Major, Smith & Co.
Hussey, McBride & Co.	Henry C. Smith & Co.
Hanna, Doherty & Co.	Smith & Lee
J. B. Huston & Co.	Short, Niel & Co.
	J. W. Turnbull & Co.

[23]The price-statistics in Boyle, *The Derrick's Handbook*, 783, are sufficiently reliable.
[24]Cleveland *Leader*, July 2, 1867.
[25]Annual Report, Cleveland Board of Trade, 1866; City Directory.

Many of these were tiny establishments. *The Leader* enumerated a number of refineries which employed but three to eleven men each.[26] It required no prophet to foresee that the weaker firms would soon find the competitive pace too hot. Strong establishments like Rockefeller's two plants, Hussey, McBride & Company, and Alexander, Scofield would leave the rest behind to be devoured by the wolves of bankruptcy. So long as the boom lasted all was well—but how long would it last?

The sun of high prices brought out an equally lush growth of tender shoots in other cities. Eastern Long Island had an increasing number of refineries. The Pittsburgh *Chronicle* for November 9, 1865, enumerated no fewer than eighty plants operating in that city. Refineries had sprung up in Boston, New Haven, Jersey City, Baltimore, Buffalo, and Erie. The Regions of course contained many; William Wright, who carefully inspected them in the spring of 1865, found about thirty, and numerous others were soon added. The two largest were still the Downer works, covering half a dozen acres, employing nearly two hundred men, and capable of producing 1800 barrels a week, and the great Humboldt Refinery. Downer, a pioneer in coal-oil refining before Drake struck oil, had quickly recognized the importance of petroleum for expanding the kerosene trade. Boldly taking his principal experts and a number of skilled workmen with him, he had invaded Pennsylvania in 1861 and built the nucleus of the town of Corry, strategically situated just north of the petroleum fields at the crossing of two railroads,[27] and the nearest railroad point to Titusville and the first wells. His brick buildings, erected at an initial cost of $125,000, were fireproof and admirably arranged. The Humboldt refinery at Plummer was almost equally extensive. The owners, well-educated Germans conversant with chemistry, had built their plant in the richest part of the original oil fields, close to the Tarr farm. At first they had no railroad facilities, and for several years were compelled to team their products to the Allegheny River or the nearest railhead; but a line was soon built from Cherry Run. They owned twenty stills, with a capacity of a thousand barrels of kerosene a week; they produced paraffin, benzine, and even aniline dyes; and they set up their own

[26]See its series of articles, Jan. 4–20, 1866.

[27]The Philadelphia & Erie, and the Atlantic & Great Western; Giddens, *Birth of the Oil Industry*, 92.

sawmills and cooper shops. Much of their product went to Europe, where they had excellent connections. Their buildings were scattered over twenty-five acres to lessen the fire hazard. Every visitor commented on their luxurious offices, where hardwood floors, marble mantels and statuary, fine furniture and carpets, created one elegant spot in the mud and disorder of the oil country.[28]

The Warren Brothers' refinery at Plummer, with sixteen stills capable of producing 900 barrels a week, had distinguished itself by an early resort to the piping of refined oil—a much more difficult matter than piping crude. Wright found that a powerful Worthington pump forced the refined product to the summit of a two-hundred-foot ridge east of the works, whence it flowed by gravity to the Allegheny. The four or five Titusville refineries, and the score that were scattered along Oil Creek, were all small. Some had shut down when Wright visited them, overproduction and the heavy government tax having wiped out all profits. A year later several remained idle. Refining capacity, as the number and size of the nation's refineries increased, distinctly exceeded even the boom demand, and establishments could no longer be operated without a careful regard for efficiency and economy.

Overproduction, overproduction!—this was to be the curse of both the well owners and refiners for years to come. Among refiners one great basic cause of overproduction was the smallness of the capital required to set up a plant. Most readers of Lloyd and Tarbell later thought of the industry as involving heavy investments. But essentially the process was merely one of cooking combined with purification by a few chemicals; some vats, stills, and pipes sufficed. Any man with $10,000 could establish a small refinery, any one with $50,000 a large one. Alexander, Scofield had founded their Great Western refinery with $7000; A. M. Burke & Company began business in 1865 with $15,000, and in a few months were turning out more than 300 barrels a week; the Star Oil Works, built the same year for $27,000, had within a few months a capacity of 1200 barrels a week.[29] The bait in this boom period of rapid price fluctua-

[28]The Humboldt works are described in William Wright, *The Oil Regions of Pennsylvania*, 201, 202.

[29]Cleveland *Leader*, Jan. 12, 1866. A contemporary authority, Thomas A. Sale, says (*The Wonder of the Nineteenth Century*, 40) that in 1860 a very efficient refinery could be erected in the Regions for $1500, and one able to keep pace with the richest well for $4000.

tions was the fact that a single lucky turn might double the capital of a small adventurer. This drew men by dozens into the business. Some, caught by an unlucky turn, were crushed, but they were replaced by newcomers.[30]

For years the cost of becoming a refiner, with all the dignities and hopes of that position, remained about as low as the cost a generation later of setting up a well-equipped garage or good jewelry store. In 1875 one of Rockefeller's competitors in Cleveland, the firm of Scofield, Shurmer & Teagle, built for $65,000 a refinery which had an annual capacity of 180,000 barrels of crude oil, and which made $40,000 the first year.[31] In 1888 an expert testified before a Federal Committee that a refinery using 3000 barrels of crude oil weekly could be built in good order for from $30,000 to $50,000.[32] Just after the Civil War, equipment had cost more, but on the other hand the process had been simpler and cheaper. The industry was fatally easy to enter. An early Cleveland refiner, Manuel Halle, said of conditions in the late sixties:[33]

The business was running along haphazard, up today and down tomorrow. . . . Many men were failing as the market jumped up and down. In those days if you saw a big black cloud of smoke in the sky, it meant that somebody's oil refinery was burning; that so much oil was being destroyed, and therefore the price of refined oil might jump from fifteen or sixteen cents a gallon to eighteen or nineteen. I remember when Scofield and I were overstocked with oil that had cost us dear and the price of crude had fallen very low—refined, of course, dropped with it. I started west to try to get rid of our refined at a decent price. At Kalamazoo I got a telegram from my partner—Dean's refinery had burned down; we were saved. That telegram stopped me and brought me home. So much refined oil was burned that the price of all that was left went up.

Already the refineries of the United States were falling into distinct groups, and regional rivalry accentuated the fierce competition of individual firms. The seaboard establishments of New York, Philadelphia, and Baltimore all felt a powerful group interest; so did the Oil Regions refineries; so did the Pittsburgh refineries; and so did the Cleveland refineries. No economic reason existed for cen-

---

[30]Rockefeller, *Random Reminiscences,* 81. "All sorts of people went into it: the butcher, the baker, and the candlestick-maker began to refine oil."
[31]Ida M. Tarbell, *History of the Standard Oil Company,* I, 165 ff.
[32]*House of Representatives Trust Investigation,* 1888, 149.
[33]Inglis, Conversations with various citizens of Cleveland, 1917.

tralizing the industry at one point. With the requisite capital, skill, and care, a refinery could be run profitably at any place furnishing cheap fuel, cheap transportation, and a market. But reasons did exist why one district, the Cleveland area, was destined to draw ahead of the three others and within a decade establish its primacy.

At the outset, the Oil Regions refineries had seemed to hold a clear advantage. Adjacent to the wells, they saved large sums upon transport of the crude oil, though this was partly offset by the high freights on machinery, coal, and chemicals from outside, and by the difficulties which many of them encountered in getting their refined oil to river or railroad. The owners could take immediate advantage of every turn of the market in purchasing crude oil, while they often gained special favors through their personal acquaintance with managers at the wells. But they faced two tremendous handicaps. For one, costs of real estate, fuel, labor, and other necessities were half again as high, sometimes twice as high, as at other points. Until the oil boom ended and a more orderly régime obtained, these costs would continue exorbitant. For another, the centers of production in the Region shifted rapidly and unpredictably, tending to strand various refineries. When in the late seventies the principal production passed to the Bradford field, far northeast of the original Regions, the works about Titusville and Oil City rapidly lost all hope of large supplies. Meanwhile the local shifts were sufficient to keep the Corry, Plummer, Oil City and Titusville operators anxious.

By 1865, as William Wright states, Pittsburgh appeared to many the best point for refining, and already boasted of receiving half of all the crude oil produced.[34] It possessed an abundant labor force; coal at the lowest prices; large banking and credit facilities; a direct railroad to the heart of the Regions; and cheap transportation by the Allegheny River. Oil could be floated down this stream for much less than the cost of freight by rail. And Pittsburgh had also, to the superficial eye, a favorable position with respect to the three great markets; it could ship refined oil to Philadelphia for the Eastern and export trades, could send it down the Ohio for the Western trade, and could reach the South by combined river and rail facilities. Pittsburghers looked forward exultantly to extending their leadership. They unquestionably possessed marked advantages

[34]William Wright, *The Oil Regions of Pennsylvania*, 204, 205.

over Philadelphia and New York refiners, who paid high freight rates on the long haul of crude oil and were distant from the inland markets. They also held an advantage over the Erie refiners, who were no nearer the sources of supply, had less labor and capital, and possessed no river facilities. Erie and Buffalo, in fact, simply failed to grow as refining centers.

Yet though few men saw it in 1866, Cleveland was not only a formidable competitor of the Regions and Pittsburgh, but possessed weapons that were destined to prove decisive. So far were some Clevelanders from seeing this that in the middle sixties they actually established refineries in the Regions. But Cleveland had more abundant labor and capital than Pittsburgh, for it was a larger, faster-growing city; it had cheap Mahoning Valley coal; being within one hundred and fifty miles of the first oil fields, it was less handicapped in obtaining crude-oil supplies than Philadelphia and New York. It was closer to the really rich Western market for refined oil than Pittsburgh. All this was cogently set forth by the Cleveland Board of Trade in 1866:[35]

It has been supposed that Cleveland could not compete successfully with Pittsburgh, which has hitherto been the greatest oil-refining point, and that we could not expect to secure so large a proportion of the export trade, while it is conceded that Cleveland now possesses and can securely hold the entire western trade. Now the facts in the case are these:

1. The average cost of crude oil during the past year has been no higher in Cleveland than at Pittsburgh, notwithstanding we have had only one main outlet from the oil regions, viz., the Atlantic & Great Western Railway. We may therefore conclude that we may have the same basis of price in future, and more especially as it is now probable that we shall have one, if not two, additional and competing routes to the oil regions.

2. The costs of manufacturing, such as labor, coal, chemicals, and cooperage, taken together, are as cheap here as they can be at Pittsburgh. Two large acid manufactories have been established here, chiefly to supply this trade with sulphuric acid. Ironworks have also been started for the manufacture of iron hoops, while the cooper shops have kept pace with the demand for barrels.

3. It has been sufficiently demonstrated that our transportation lines can make a fair profit on carrying refined oil from Cleveland to New York at the same, or even a less rate than that charged by the Pennsylvania Railroad to its legitimate export market, Philadelphia, although at the present time by a combination the freights are 15 per cent higher.

[35]Annual Report, 1866.

4. We have a decided advantage in selling our oil in the New York market, which has ruled in advance of the Philadelphia market on an average of one to two cents per gallon during the entire year 1866.

From the foregoing facts it will readily be seen that Cleveland possesses the natural advantages for becoming the greatest oil-refining point in the United States, a position which she will speedily take if our Railroad and Lake transportation men will adopt a liberal policy as to freights and establish a low and uniform rate to the Seaboard which will enable us, at all times, to compete with Pittsburgh.

If the railroads would take a liberal attitude!—and they did. For Cleveland soon had two trunk-line railroads and the Erie Canal, while Pittsburgh was left at the mercy of one line, the grasping Pennsylvania Railroad. On this fact above all others turned the fate of the oil empire.

IV

All too soon the great oil boom gave way to depression. The Regions were the first to feel the blow. The development of a petroleum industry in Canada and Europe, the expiration of Young's British patents for manufacturing kerosene from shale, the operations of eastern speculators, and above all, sheer overproduction, resulted in 1866–67 in a calamitous price fall for crude oil. Hundreds of small wells were shut down, and drilling stopped on thousands more; the whole area was covered with abandoned derricks.[36] So great was the outcry that Congress hurriedly repealed the tax on crude oil. Yet the root of the trouble was not reached, for new "strikes" swelled the general output. Perhaps the word depression is misleading, and it would be more accurate to say that the Oil Regions were half-boom and half-broke. In some areas immense new floods of oil were pouring forth. Lucky men were becoming millionaires, and a fever of hope excited thousands. Over other districts brooded a midnight gloom. From Oil City to Tidioute only one well in fifty yielded any oil, hundreds of houses were tenantless, whole villages were deserted, and advertisements of sheriff's sales filled the newspapers.

The depression swiftly spread to the refining industry. The historian of the Oil Region says that there "scores of small refineries

[36]See the vivid description of this blighting depression in Giddens, *Birth of the Oil Industry,* 153 ff.

began shutting down." In 1867 and still more in 1868 cobwebs gathered on dozens of refinery doors in Cleveland and Pittsburgh. The price of refined oil had fallen as heavily as that of crude; the average per gallon in New York in 1867–68 was 28 and 29 cents.[37] Small establishments, inefficiently managed, winked out all over the country. Rockefeller, ceaselessly busy, radiating vitality as he managed two great refineries with abundant resources and every appliance for economy, had more reason for confidence than most men. "There was never a year in the business that we didn't get ahead, didn't accumulate," he remarked later. "That could be said of hardly another firm." But even he was worried.

[37]Patrick C. Boyle, ed., *The Derrick's Handbook of Petroleum*, 783.

XI

Wife and Home

THE year 1864 was far the busiest that Rockefeller had yet known. He had two businesses to manage, both exacting, profitable, and expansive; he was the real head of the family, his father's long absences placing more and more responsibility upon him; he was becoming one of the pillars of the Erie Street Baptist Church; and in midsummer he married his high-school classmate, the lovely Laura Celestia Spelman. At twenty-five, one of the best-established and most respected young men of the city, he was making his own fireside.

This was a year of nation-shaking battles: of Cold Harbor and Spottsylvania, of Farragut at Mobile, of the March to the Sea. The war spirit rose high in the Western Reserve, and every private pursuit —business, pleasure, instruction, travel, courtship—was carried on under the shadow of the conflict. Crowds gathered in the Public Square to cheer bulletins of victory, or to read in silent anguish the long lists of dead and wounded. Trains puffing into the station hard by discharged a steady stream of men invalided home; wearing bandages, hobbling on crutches, borne on dirty stretchers. In every ward this summer men rang doorbells and handed inside pledges to be signed, devoting the population to "rigid economy of living" and abstinence from all imported luxuries. The whole city felt the shock when news came that two of its gallant young captains, W. W. Hutchinson and J. T. Philpot, had fallen in battle almost simultaneously. Their bodies were brought back, carried through streets draped in mourning, and given a moving funeral together in the First Baptist Church, which Rockefeller may well have witnessed. With a different kind of emotion, the city celebrated the Fourth by wildly cheering a great procession of discharged veterans, to whom it served a civic banquet that evening.

This was a Presidential year too; and Cleveland watched with apathetic interest when four hundred Radical Republicans, meeting to nominate Frémont for President, gave the town its first national convention. The loyal citizens showed scant enthusiasm for the Wade-Davis Manifesto denouncing Lincoln's Reconstruction policy, a document of which Ohio's senior senator was joint author. A· little later large crowds, Rockefeller doubtless among them, applauded Salmon P. Chase and other leaders who spoke for Lincoln's re-election.[1]

With a brother at the front, Rockefeller followed the war with anxious interest. His account book mentions early in 1862 an expenditure of $25 covering "two large maps one for M. B. Clark and one for self"; and while these may have been for business, they were more probably war maps. Clark & Rockefeller received a steady flow of market telegrams with which, when important battles were being fought, military news was often mingled. Political developments likely to affect the markets were also telegraphed in. "Our office became a great rallying-place," said Rockefeller many years later. "We were all deeply interested. Men used to drop in often; and we followed the war keenly, reading the latest dispatches and studying the maps, just as we do nowadays."[2]

But another interest had been coming into his life. As an ill-paid clerk and struggling new commission merchant he had possessed neither time nor inclination for young women. But as his position improved he began calling on Laura, or as her friends then called her, Cettie Spelman. The Spelmans were Congregationalists, but Cleveland was a small city, and they had many opportunities of meeting. Their sustained acquaintance, according to Rockefeller, began about 1862. "My brother and I used to go out to ride on horses," he recalled, "and we came to know she was living on the Heights. I first knew of her presence in the city evidently before we went there to ride, ostensibly to see the boys and men enlisting and training for the war. Soon thereafter, I learned that they [her family] had moved into the city, from across the Cuyahoga Valley;

---

[1]Files of the Cleveland *Leader;* Cleveland *Plain-Dealer.*
[2]Inglis, Conversations with Rockefeller, 1917.

then I called upon her there in Perry Street, then upon Euclid Avenue, then on Huron Street. . . . The first call was presumably on some such occasion as New Year's, when the young men made as many as sixty or seventy calls."[3] John was impressed by her father, for Harvey Spelman was a man of character and experience, who had ranged from New England to Iowa, and had managed many business ventures. Apparently the family also welcomed John. We are told that as the friendship progressed they liked him none the less because he sometimes arrived in the muddy top boots in which he had splashed about the refinery yard until a late hour.

Laura Celestia had been twenty-four on September 9, 1863. Her photographs show her a girl of very uncommon prettiness, as her friends have testified to her very unusual poise and charm. She had heavy chestnut hair, a clear olive complexion, a pleasant, expressive mouth, a firm chin, and dark brown eyes whose sparkle was enhanced by her arching eyebrows. The many photographs the Spelmans had taken testify to their pride in her and her sister Lucy. One daguerreotype in particular, apparently made in Albany, shows her not long before her marriage; she is demure in black silk, velvet-trimmed, with white lace collar and wristlets, but her face shows animation and humor as well as strength. She was a spirited girl, much more vivacious than John, better read and more widely travelled than he. Yet in some ways they were alike, for she had much his own combination of seriousness, humor, and determined force. Her sister Lucy has aptly characterized her: "She was full of mirth and cheer, yet always gentle and rather inclined to be grave and reserved. She was gentle and lovely and loyal to her friends. Her generosity was a sort of sheath for her resolute character and indomitable will, which could not be shaken. She was naturally religious and most punctilious about the observance of her duties at church and Sunday school. . . . She was very quiet in her movements and speech. She was very cordial. . . . There was persuasion in her touch as she laid her fingers ever so gently on your arm."[4]

We are fortunate in having an early group of letters by Laura Celestia. They were written in 1858–62 inclusive from the Oread

[3]Rockefeller thus wrote in reply to my inquiries in 1936. Soldiers drilled in large numbers at Camp Cleveland.
[4]Inglis, Conversation with Miss Spelman, 1917.

School in Worcester, Mass.—as good a finishing school as the country then had—and from Cleveland to Mrs. Hawley, a former music teacher in Iowa. They reveal warmth of heart, intellectual seriousness, and natural good sense. She sends Mrs. Hawley "as much love as this letter can possibly hold." She finds the headmistress of the stately Oread School disappointingly cold and severe —"She fully comes up to any ideas of 'Miss Prim' I have ever formed"; and she agrees with Lucy that she would "prefer some heart, and a little less education." She likes the East less than the Iowa prairies because the Yankees "are not so genial and open, frank and warmhearted, as the Westerners." She writes of "fun and frolic" with the other girls, some of it stolen "after the retiring bell has rung and the lights are extinguished," but all the better for that—"the attendant risks only inspire us with courage and zeal."[5]

This spontaneous warmth modified Laura Celestia's more sedate qualities, for she had a sharp ethical bent and, as her sister said later, was essentially a religieuse. Christianity and the church were vital concerns in her life, and she was animated by a strong sense of duty. Out of school she worked hard at the piano, practising three hours a day, and adding voice-exercises; for music was her principal amusement, as painting was Lucy's. When she became friendly with John, who had not forgotten his lessons, they sometimes played duets together. She read standard novels and poetry. In Cleveland she writes Mrs. Hawley of her attendance upon public lectures, hearing Henry Ward Beecher, Bayard Taylor, Ralph Waldo Emerson (whom John also heard),[6] and Wendell Phillips. Once she lamented that in the United States "the desperate struggle to obtain the 'almighty dollar' usurps the place of all other thoughts, and leaves little desire for the improvement of the mind," while she often regretted the lack of opportunity to hear much really good music.[7] Her range of recreations was limited by the strict ideas she had drawn from home and from church. When Mrs. Hawley told how young people in Iowa went to dances, Laura Celestia deplored the fact that they "are engaged in so unworthy and sinful an object."[8]

[5]MS Letters of the Misses Spelman, Rockefeller Papers.
[6]Rockefeller entered in his account book Jan. 9, 1863, an expenditure of fifty cents for a ticket, five days before Emerson appeared under the auspices of the Cleveland Library Association. Cleveland *Leader,* Jan. 14, 15, 1863.
[7]MS Letters, p. 84.   [8]*Ibid.,* p. 85.

The theatre was likewise under the ban. She had been in the habit of writing some letters on Sunday, but after listening to a sermon on the proper employment of the day came home determined not to commit that particular error again.[9]

This sedateness and these rather strict ideas as to amusements were to influence Rockefeller's home. Till late in life she would not countenance the theatre. "I would not wish my children to be players, and I cannot encourage an institution which makes players out of the children of other people," she said. It was the old Puritan attitude which went back to Cromwell and Jeremy Collier, and which long led New England and Western towns to frown upon plays unless called "moving tableaux." But she came to enjoy seeing young people dance; while friends have testified that she was never critical of others, detested censoriousness, and showed good-humored tolerance for more latitudinarian views than her own.

In the spirit of Laura Celestia's graduation essay, "I Can Paddle My Own Canoe," the sisters had looked forward to forming classes in music and art, or teaching school. In the spring of 1856, the year after Cettie's graduation from high school, they applied for positions in the city system. Their letter was addressed March 8 to Samuel H. Mather, secretary of the Cleveland board of education:

Sir:
We desire to engage in teaching, and would respectfully solicit situations in your city schools at the commencement of the spring term. Please present our application to your Committee on Teachers.
                              Yours with respect
                                    Celestia Spelman
                                    Lucy Spelman

Returning from Worcester in May, 1859, Celestia had unsuccessfully tried to form music classes, while Lucy began teaching in the city schools. That autumn Celestia was substituting for Lucy. She found a permanent place on January 1, 1860, in the Hudson Street School, of which L. B. Eaton, later a distinguished Union officer— she and other teachers bought him a sword, sash, and overcoat when he went away to war[10]—was principal, and she did not relinquish this position until she married.

Tradition in Worcester later had it that Rockefeller corresponded

[9]*Ibid.*, p. 48.   [10]Cleveland *Leader*, Nov. 25, 1861.

with Miss Spelman while she studied in the castellated stone building of the Oread School, and former classmates even testified to the salutation and ending of the "tender missives."[11] Rockefeller has denied this local myth, which is belied by Celestia's letters to Mrs. Hawley as well. In these she evinces no concern with marriage. She writes with amusement of some Iowa friends who succumb to the contagion of matrimony. "It is an exceedingly fortunate thing, I think, that we were not there." Back in Cleveland, she still disclaimed in 1860 any anxiety to obtain a husband. "A gentleman told me not long ago, that he was in no particular hurry to have me get married, but he hoped that in the multitude of my thoughts I would not forget the subject. Perhaps I speak with too much assurance when I say, there are enough days coming. Father and mother are in no hurry to get rid of me."[12] On June 23, 1862, she wrote: "I am school-teaching yet, and expect to be always, I have said, but I guess I do not exactly mean it." She was then busy, in the intervals of teaching, with a singing class, her Congregational church choir, other musical organizations, and Sunday school work.[13]

The two did not become engaged until March, 1864, and then said little to their friends about it. Both reached the decision to marry only after careful deliberation. Miss Spelman liked teaching and liked independence; "I shall not stop until I find something better to do," she had declared in 1862, "for as to being idle I cannot." Rockefeller had been deeply engrossed in his two businesses. By 1864 he had a large income and a considerable sum of money saved. But if both acted deliberately, they showed no lack of deep and happy feeling. All of Rockefeller's emotional relations were intensive rather than expansive, and this was the most intense of his life. Far more than that of most powerful and prominent men, his life was destined to center in his home, and his interests outside of money-making and money-giving were to be bound up in family and church.

The marriage ceremony was performed in the Spelman residence at 58 Huron Street on September 8, 1864, by Doctor Samuel Wolcott, the bride's Congregational pastor, with the Reverend S. B. Page,

[11]Worcester *Evening Post,* July 1, 1922.
[12]MS Letters of the Misses Spelman, Rockefeller Papers.
[13]Inglis, Conversation with Miss Spelman, 1917.

minister of the Erie Street Baptist Church, assisting.[14] Rockefeller gave a dinner that day for his employees, at which twenty-six men sat down together. He did not attend himself: "I had more important business on hand," he chuckled when asked about it seventy years afterward. The head of the cooperage shop records that as he left the works the day previous he paused on the stairs and called back to Andrews: "Sam, keep them all at work. Keep them all busy. But don't ask anybody to do anything for nothing."[15] The couple took a wedding trip to Niagara Falls, Montreal, and Quebec, and down through New England, stopping at Boston, Worcester, Fairfield, Conn., and New York City. At Worcester, Celestia showed her husband the Oread School and her favorite walks.[16] Returning to Cleveland, they boarded for a time with Rockefeller's parents, and then moved into a house next door at 29 Cheshire Street.[17] Mrs. Rockefeller was essentially a homemaker. While she took a keen interest in her husband's business labors, she never had an active share in them, and, realizing their complexity, seldom gave him any advice.

II

By 1867 the William Avery Rockefeller family had struck firm roots into the soil of Cleveland and was expanding in numbers. The children were now all grown men and women, and Lucy and William married before John did. Lucy had become the wife of Pierson D. Briggs, to whom, before the end of 1866, she had borne three children, two dying in infancy. William, just a month and a half before John's wedding, was married in Fairfield, Conn., to Almira Geraldine Gooddell—called "Mira"—who gave birth to their first son in 1865. John's first child, named Elizabeth and always called Bessie, was born August 23, 1866. Frank had come back from the war, attended business school, and in 1866–67 found employ-

[14]Rockefeller himself so entered in the family Bible (H. & E. Phinney's Stereotype Edition, Cooperstown, 1834).

[15]Inglis, Notes of Conversation in 1917 with Andrew Stein, who began work in Rockefeller's coopershop in July, 1864. Perhaps it was to him and not Sam Andrews that Rockefeller gave this admonition. He told how Rockefeller himself used to push a wheelbarrow with three barrels on it.

[16]Worcester *Evening Post*, July 1, 1922.

[17]Cleveland Directories. Rockefeller told Mr. W. O. Inglis in 1917 that they lived for six months with his parents.

ment as a bookkeeper with Clark & Sanford, Maurice Clark's commission firm. He and Mary Ann still lived with their mother at 33 Cheshire Street, the house which John had built; but Frank was to marry Helen Scofield in the fall of 1870, and Mary Ann to marry William C. Rudd two years later.[18]

"Doctor" Rockefeller returned regularly, as in earlier years, from his long trips afield. Apparently these were now confined largely to the trans-Mississippi West; but it must be said that little can be learned of the colorful doctor during these years. His absences appear to have grown longer. Eliza received a sufficiency of money from him, for he was prosperous. She also had money of her own, for when her father died in 1858 he had left her a small annuity. John D. Rockefeller's second private ledger (that following the famous Ledger A) shows that he assisted in the final settlement of Grandfather Davison's estate, two pages being given to a list of assets and liabilities. By arrangement with the other heirs, Eliza on April 26, 1865, took over the little trust fund, amounting to $1872.31, from which she had been paid. John witnessed his mother's signature, "Elizabeth" and not "Eliza," and safeguarded the money for her.[19]

As we have said, he had already become the real head of the family. At twenty-five he was moderately wealthy, and steadily growing wealthier. His business connections were more and more important. An advertisement of 1865 shows that he was one of seven directors of the Weikel Run & McElhinney Oil Company, a producing concern which owned a large tract of land in Venango County. Its president was A. B. Stone, and its vice-president the banker, Dan P. Eels, while the directors included W. C. Scofield, a refiner, and Henry Chisholm, before mentioned as prominent in iron manufacture.[20] In 1866 we find Rockefeller a director of the State Fire Insurance Company. Late in 1868 he was elected a director of the new Ohio National Bank, capitalized at $1,000,000—Robert Hanna being its president. As he gathered dignity with years and success, he made a grave and imposing appearance on the streets of Cleveland. He

[18]Entries in the Rockefeller family Bible cover all these marriages.
[19]Rockefeller Papers.
[20]See the notice of the McElhenny Oil Company in the advertising pages of J. H. A. Bone, *Petroleum and Petroleum Wells* (1865). I am indebted to Miss Ida M. Tarbell for this item, which contradicts the frequent statements that Rockefeller never engaged in oil production.

dressed carefully—frock coat, pin-striped trousers, silk hat, polished black shoes. His face, still smooth-shaven, had taken on firmer lines. His figure, always well proportioned, had become more powerful. When he spoke it was with deliberate authority; the piercing, thoughtful gaze of his blue eyes carried a greater self-confidence. The whole family, from his mother down to Mary Ann, leaned upon him—even rash, adventurous Frank.

He had no doubt obtained Frank his position with Clark & Sanford. When a little later, in the spring of 1868, Frank joined a former partner of William's to launch a new commission firm, David & Rockefeller, John probably helped finance him. As soon as feasible John took William into partnership; their relations in work and play had always been close, and now he was to assist his brother to wealth and power. Eliza let him manage all her small business affairs and assume other burdens, her trust in him becoming touchingly complete. He has related how proudly he came home one day in these early years to tell her that his firm had made $4000 on a single large contract. She believed that this strong son of hers could do anything. John D. Rockefeller, Jr., recalls how years later, when she fell seriously ill, she fretted and worried, unable to sleep, until her first-born boy could arrive. He came, took her hand, and said: "It will be all right, Mother." She was instantly serene and confident again, for John had never once failed her.

The life of John and Celestia Rockefeller was busy and happy. Mrs. Rockefeller gave up her Congregational church, an easy step because of her long previous absences, and became a Baptist. Their social contacts were therefore chiefly with members of the Erie Street congregation. Doctor S. B. Page, minister throughout the war —"a sterling man," said Rockefeller[21]—was succeeded early in 1867 by Doctor Samuel W. Duncan, a young cleric whose eight-year pastorate brought him close to the family. "How we loved him, how he loved us, how he loved the cause!" Rockefeller once remarked. Before Page left he had a two-hour talk with John, as they drove through the streets of Cleveland, on the question whether the young man was giving enough. "I think the Doctor was satisfied," Rockefeller said later.[22] We shall see that Doctor Duncan's

[21]*Euclid Avenue Baptist Church Fiftieth Anniversary*, 31.
[22]*Idem*, 32.

pressure upon him for giving ultimately had its part in the founding of the University of Chicago. As president of the board of trustees, superintendent of the Sunday school, and principal donor, Rockefeller was becoming almost as powerful in the affairs of the church as the minister himself.

We have a full, or nearly full, record of Rockefeller's gifts in these years—a record that constantly grew longer and more varied. It shows that in the last two months of 1855, after he had got his first job but before he had been paid a cent, he gave the church, the Five Points Mission, and other objects a total of $2.77. In 1856 his total donations increased to $19.31. In 1857 they went up, so far as the record shows, to $28.37. By this time they included home and foreign missions, a Ragged School, various churches, the Baptist State Convention, and the Y. M. C. A. In 1858 the total grew to $43.85, and in 1859 to $72.22. One item this last year was a gift to a Negro of Cincinnati "to buy his wife." In 1860 his gifts aggregated $107.35, while in 1861 they rose sharply to $259.97. A Negro church and a fund for the purchase of a slave figured in this first war-year roster. In 1862 the total donations reached $283.06, one item being for a Jewish missionary, and in 1863 it was slightly larger, $292.03. During the war he gave to a Catholic orphanage, a colored mute and blind society, an industrial school, and a Swedish mission in Illinois. In 1864 his gifts suddenly swelled to $671.86, and then his growing wealth was reflected in still larger amounts:

> In 1865, a total of $1012.35
> In 1866, a total of $1320.43
> In 1867, evidently a poor business year, a total of $669.14
> In 1868, by way of amends, a total of $3675.39
> In 1869, doing still better, a total of $5489.62

He had not waited to grow rich before he began giving. It is to be noted that save for one year, his gifts constantly grew larger, and that by the later sixties he was giving some considerable lump sums —$558.42 to Denison University, for example. In his early giving, as later in life, he freely crossed lines of creed, nationality, and color.[23]

At that date the superintendency of the Sunday school was a

[23]I am indebted to Mr. John D. Rockefeller, Jr., for a careful compilation of his father's gifts, made from old account books.

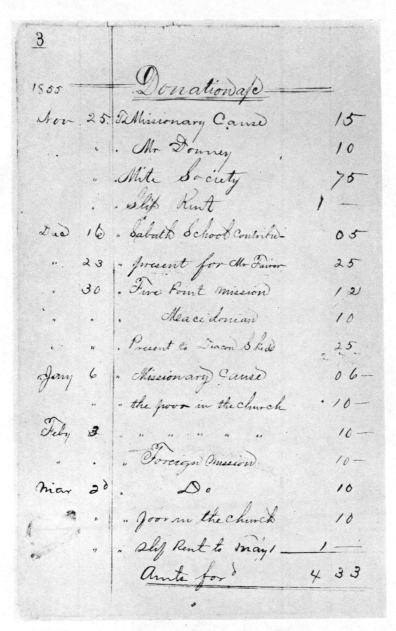

1855		*Donations*	
Nov	25	To Missionary Cause	15
"	"	" Mr Downey	10
"	"	" Mite Society	75
"	"	" Slip Rent	1 —
Dec	16	" Sabath School Contribu-	05
"	23	" present for Mr Fairer	25
"	30	" Five Point Mission	1 2
"	"	" Macedonian	10
"	"	" Present to Deacon Shed	25
Jany	6	" Missionary Cause	0 6 —
"	"	" the poor in the church	10 —
Feby	3	" " " " " "	10 —
"	"	" Foreign Mission	10 —
Mar	2d	" Do	10
"	"	" poor in the church	10
"	"	" Slip Rent to May 1	1 —
		Amts ford	4 3 3

A page of Ledger *A*.

Gifts made by Rockefeller in the first months
in which he was employed.

Lucy Spelman and Laura Celestia Spelman.

Laura, shown in a more smiling mood than her sister, became Mrs. John D. Rockefeller.

position of greater importance than any one is likely now to realize. A fervent Sunday school movement was under way in the Middle West. Few figures in Cleveland were more honored than the founder of the pioneer Sunday school there, Elisha Taylor, who died in 1862 at the age of seventy-five. A Sunday School Union had been formed in the city, and Rockefeller and the banker T. P. Handy, its president, were prominent at the monthly meetings; meetings which in war years drew delegates from thirty schools with more than five thousand pupils. Union concerts were frequently given at the different churches. An annual State convention brought together hundreds of enthusiastic leaders, for more than a fourth of the young people of Ohio were enrolled. The position of superintendent was second only to the minister's in influence and usefulness. Mrs. Rockefeller first took a Bible class for young women, and then became head of the "infant department," while she and her husband both taught for a time at a mission organized by the Judson Society.

They had other altruistic labors as well. Rockefeller was an officer of the Western Seamen's Friend Society, in which the bankers T. P. Handy and Dan P. Eells were vice-president and auditor respectively; while Mrs. Rockefeller was one of the committee which organized the Y. W. C. A. in the city. Both were active in the temperance movement.[24]

At home Rockefeller was an attentive, considerate husband and father. His sister-in-law, Lucy Spelman, who presently gave up her teaching and came to live with them, recalled that in these early years of marriage he was always willing to shoulder his wife's cares, perform small household duties, and, no matter how tired at night, walk the floor with the baby girl, Bessie. "He was patience itself. I never heard him complain. He never failed in this, no matter how hard he had been driven or how tired he might be." His children have testified that they never once saw him lose his temper or show petulance; that whenever anything went wrong his habit was simply to give calm consideration to means of setting it right.

Some letters survive which give us glimpses of the family life in these years. In 1867 Rockefeller intended to take his wife and baby

[24]See Cleveland *Leader,* May 14, 1862, etc., for the Sunday school movement; June 11, 1866, etc., for the Seamen's Friend Society.

to New York for Christmas. Her parents were there, and so were William Rockefeller and his wife, while he had business to transact. When it became impossible for Mrs. Rockefeller to go, he left hurriedly just before Christmas. He missed his train, which sped on its way to disaster. Having caught another, he immediately telegraphed back: "Thank God I am unharmed—the six-forty train I missed had bad accident." Then he wrote:[25]

> No. 181 Pearl Street,
> New York, Dec. 20th, 1867
>
> My Dear Wife
>   I arrived last eve at four O'C and after doing some shopping to replace my stock Clothing and Toilet articles, called on Will & Mira & spent the night very pleasantly. The Christmas presents were burned with the Valice and Umbrella. Our friends appreciate them as though recd and join in expressions of *gratitude* that I did not *remain* in the car with the Baggage. I do (and did when I learned that the first train left) regard the thing as the *Providence of God*. I will not by letter rehearse particulars of the Accident, but hope to Vivavoce, as early as Wednesday next. Your folks all well, I expect to spend the night with them. You no doubt recd my telegram sent at 6 P.M. 18th from Ongola. It was *well* that a good work kept you and Bessie at home. We certainly should have been in the burned car as it was the only one that went that we could have entered at the time we should have arrived at the station.—I am thankful, thankful, thankful.
>
> Kiss the darling Baby.
>   Truly
>   Jno.

Another visit to New York the next spring produced a longer letter. Rockefeller was now taking the leading rôle in the construction of a new church building on Euclid Avenue, while he and his family were moving into a new home on that street.

> 82 Adams St. Brooklyn
> Apr. 19th '68
>
> Dear Laura
>   This is the first attempt at Sunday letter writing I have any recollection of for many years. Your mother loaned me the pen with which I am writing & she is rocking in her little chair, while your father on the lounge and Lute (Lucy) in her room are enjoying their Sunday afternoon sleep.
>   Your Father secured very desirable rooms yesterday & with Mother & Lute is rejoicing in prospect of a change; he is unsettled as to future business but not nearly as despondent as when with us—the remainder of the

[25]Rockefeller Papers.

trio are well and cheerful. We attended the "Rev. Bartletts" church this A.M. & afterwards made an examination of the building & lecture room, also Sunday school room Pastors Study—the whole cost of which was 35 or $40,000 & built in the time of high prices from 62 to 65, it has a stone front and will seat one thousand persons. I am *decided* we want our Lecture room & Sunday school room above ground, & if our means are not sufficient to build elegantly and accomplish this, then let it be plain, as the comforts & convenience are worth more to our Church than the elegance, though I would like this also.

I expected a letter from Mr. Chisholm advising me where I could meet Mr. Stephens, the owner of the Euclid St. lot & am disappointed in not receiving a word from him. I wish he would telegraph me immediately & I will try & see the party & make the purchase at once. My preference is decidedly in favor of this lot. I forgot to mention, that the Organ & Choir are back of the Pulpit and elevate about, say ten or twelve feet, and this suits me exactly.

I expect to go with Will & Mira tomorrow eve to Fairfield & Bridgeport that is if they can "gow," & on my return will spend some time examining Churches in N.Y. & Brooklyn, as I may not have another opportunity before we must decide on our plans. . . .

Monday morn 12 O'C

Yours 17th at hand. We cannot decide on the Gas Fixtures until my return. I fear they are not good enough. If we can afford it I want our house *well* furnished. You better engage the men to whiten the walls (select the *best* man & make *best* bargain you can). I want you a splendid business woman & this *may be* more business than you covet.

This Bacheldor life I am *disgusted* with & want to return your bed & board & will at earliest moment. I have Mr. Chisholms letter & if I happen to see Stephens will figure on the Euclid St. lot.

Your loving husband   J_{NO}

We have no more letters until the last weeks of 1871, when Rockefeller was again in New York. By this time a third baby, Alta, had arrived. The father wrote from the St. Nicholas Hotel on lower Broadway, the great resort for Middle Westerners, to express regret for being absent at Thanksgiving:[26]

My Dear Wife: St. Nicholas Nov. 30 '71

Yours of last Saturday *thankfully* received. I telegraphed you today at Cheshire and [am] sorry sorry sorry we could not all have been together.

[26]*Ibid.* Alta Rockefeller was born April 12, 1871. An earlier daughter, Alice, had died at the age of thirteen months. Chronology prepared by Lucy Spelman, Rockefeller Papers.

I have been more than busy all the time—though am feeling well and hopeful, yet of course there are many matters to harmonize requiring patient labor and effort—

I stayed with your people last night—and came to St. N this morn then to dinner with Will and now back again to spend the evening on business. I cannot enter into details before my return and cannot at the moment tell when can return but probably in very few days, though may then have to come back quite soon.

Will telegraph you when I leave. I think it not unlikely we will spend more time here than formerly. . . .

I feel more and more like arranging to have my family move around with me. Will is anxious [for us] to have a house here together.

Mira & Children well. I can understand how *you* must be very lonely and feel myself as I just told Mr. Devereux like a wandering Jew.

It makes me cross to think of Sylvester [a servant] and we will try and improve our condition as soon as I can give it attention. I ran down from Mr. Watsons room to write this and now go to him and then home. A man who suceeds in life must sometimes go against the current and in hearing of Mrs. Dr. Treadwell whose husband went west without seeing her in the employ of the Govt expecting to stay *all winter*—I thank God my family have a home and a protector—at their head and to a *man* it is worth working for.

Many kisses to you and our children.   Truly J<small>NO.</small>

Next day he sent a short note from the Pearl Street office, saying that he had hopes of starting for home on the morrow. "I dreamed last night of the girl Celestia Spelman and awoke to realize she was my 'Laura.'" But he did not get back. December 15 found him still writing from New York. He was thankful to hear from Laura; he was taking good care of himself, eating two meals daily and not overworking; and he hoped that she was equally cautious. "I really fear, from your letter, you are doing too much work & taking too much anxiety. I am not going to scold, nor continue complaining lest I lose my influence. I would give *anything* to be quietly at home until Monday next without a soul *outside* knowing it. Oh! for a *home* dinner good cream & the quiet & peace of our own table. I bought Bessie a big stick [of] candy last night & will try to get it home without breaking—gave Emma [Will's daughter] one and she was *delighted*. She thinks a great deal of her Uncle Jno." He added that he was anxious to hear about a church suit then pending, and sympathized with Henry Chisholm in some troubles with a church carpenter. "I shall be disappointed not to be present at next social—but am resolved to take a philosophical view and save my flesh." He signed the letter "Yours lovingly Yohon."

A month later he was staying at Will's residence, 117 West 47th Street, and writing under date of Sunday evening, January 13, 1872. A new baby was now expected.[27]

My Beloved Wife
Last eve I recd yours of 6th 8th and 10th and they afforded me much pleasure. It is now nearly 10 O'c I am just in from Church and to be up for a 6:30 breakfast in the morn and off to Philad—where I will remain say two or three days— If your husband *does* show any evidence of improvement or growth he is indebted to his wife, whose influence would uniformly aid in improving elevating & ennobling—how much I am indebted, but how can I duly estimate a silent steady influence for good in the midst of so much evil. How happy I should have been to be at home today—but I seem to shrink from the responsibility of the Superintendency, I feel unworthy and fear lest with many other things upon me I may not be the best one for the place.

I stayed in Brooklyn last night and this morn heard Reverend Pentecost on "Revival" it was an extemporaneous effort and good. He is pastor of Hanson Place B. Church and I think a promising young man. This eve Dr. Armitage gave us a sermon to Young Women.

You write long letters, I fear you weary yourself thereby, don't do so. A short letter from you is worth much more than a long one from me.

Old Mrs. Gribble remarked on New Year's day how much comfort Harriet had been to her, and also that she *didn't want her* when she came into the world thought she had enough before,—how do we know but in old age we may be left to lean on the one, we hoped would delay in coming some time yet. Dont allow any misgivings—we will together make the most of our experiences and try for all the good and happiness that can come from our united life and never hug a Ghost while we are spared to one another.

Mira not very well tonight—all the rest well and join me in love.
                                        Affectionately yours
                                                    JNO

The ensuing letters contain equally warm protestations of affection and homesickness. "How much I would give for wings to reach you tonight," he wrote from the Pearl Street office on January 20. "Tell Bessie I would fly down [the] chimney. . . . I feel more than ever thankful for a true and loving wife, why shouldent a man be

[27]*Ibid.*

stimulated to *efforts?* The world is full of Sham, Flattery, and Deception, the *home* is a haven of rest and freedom." On the 24th he scribbled a similar note from the St. Nicholas. "I shall go off the handle if I do not reach home Saturday night but if I do I wish could be relieved of duties and responsibilities Sunday and get a good rest and a quiet day with you and the children. Am feeling better today and taking the best of care of myself. Allow me to inform you that when I come here again to stay two weeks *you* are coming too." Next day he had to notify her of further delays. "I feel like a caged Lion and would roar if it would do any good." But he consoled himself with the thought that his labor was for his family. "It is pleasant though to me that my family have all the comforts of home, and that we have been so prospered and placed in *independent* circumstances. It seems a fabulous dream but I assure you it is a solid and very comforting fact."

Mrs. Rockefeller's letters are like his in spirit, if better in orthography and less hurried in style. It has been snowing heavily in Cleveland; little Bessie's cold is abating; Mrs. Spelman has gone back to New York, taking a lower berth in the four-ten train; she has called on Mrs. Eyears; the accident to Mrs. Chisholm will mar her appearance for life; Sam Andrews and his wife came in and stayed an hour—"I told them I thought they were sent to relieve my loneliness"; she was taking Mrs. Duncan to a funeral in her carriage—so ran her budget of news. But above all, she is lonely for her husband.[28]

When Rockefeller later remarked that he was "all business" during this period, he meant that he was all business in his office hours. Yet the phrase has been taken literally by those who overlook the generous time and energy he gave his family and church. The problems of the latter alone undoubtedly cost him many hours of toil every month. When the time came in 1868 for the new church building on Euclid Avenue, he made arrangements for selling the Erie Street property, complete save for bell and organ, to the German Evangelical Church, which paid $13,000 for it. He negotiated for the Euclid Avenue lot; he supervised the new building plans. The minutes of the church trustees for September 21, 1868, show the entry: "Moved by Bro. Rockefeller that the Euclid Avenue front

[28]Letters of Jan. 16, Jan. 23, 1872; Rockefeller Papers.

Laura Celestia Spelman and John D. Rockefeller.
Photographs taken not long before they became engaged.

Rockefeller and his wife on top of Mt. Washington on their wedding trip.
Rockefeller wears the tall silk hat; his wife the gray jacket.

and Huntington Street side of the new church building be built of stone"—these being the two walls exposed to public view. Meanwhile, he continued to give to a wide list of charities.

Nor while "all business," did he work with health-wrecking intensity. As soon as he had his own home he used it for rest. "Ever since I was married," he said in 1917, "I have made it a practice to lie down in the afternoon and take a brief nap. I find that I can do more work that way. . . . As a rule I have had a daily nap, sometimes two, ever since I was a young man."[29] In this period nearly all well-to-do American families kept a horse and carriage, and most men of means enjoyed fast driving. It was a favorite recreation of President Grant at Long Beach; the California millionaire, Ralston, drove pell-mell from his San Francisco office to his Burlingame home; Henry Cabot Lodge, as he tells us in *Early Memories,* saw the leading men of State Street and Beacon Street sweep in cohorts along the Boston-Jamaica speedway. New Yorkers used to watch Commodore Vanderbilt, his white hair and keen blue eyes contrasting with his ruddy cheeks, as he raced August Belmont in Central Park. In these days before the automobile and golf-links, driving took their place. William Avery Rockefeller had taught all three of his sons to love horses, and John had learned to drive at the age of eight. As soon as he had any money to spare—even in 1857, as his account book shows—he occasionally hired a riding-horse from some livery stable. In 1859 he bought a brown saddle-mare from Isaiah Reynolds; by the time of his marriage he owned a carriage and pair. As he said later, he turned to horses "for recreation—to study them, drive them, exercise them in the open air."[30] At first he purchased "good ordinary road horses," but a little later he placed more value upon speed, and raced other Clevelanders on Euclid Avenue with zest.

While Cleveland offered frequent dramatic performances, and Shakespeare was played by competent stock companies, he never cared for the theatre. He belonged to the Union Club and often lunched there, but never visited it at night. "I was happy in my own home life," he explained in reviewing these years. "When I was not working at my own business there were other duties which kept me occupied; so that when I came home at the end of the day

[29]Inglis, Conversations with Rockefeller.   [30]*Idem.*

I was not eager to go out again. My family would rather have me at home—even if I were snoring in an easy chair—than going out for the evening and certainly I preferred to stay at home. Club life did not appeal to me. . . . I had no need of that. I was meeting all the people I needed to meet in my day's work."[31] He might have added that business gave him all the adventure that he needed. Such a life, satisfying to him and well-balanced within its limits, does not support the picture sometimes drawn of a man warped and repressed, starved intellectually and emotionally, and coldly concentrated upon money-making.

Yet his bearing did have a quality of aloofness, and his temperament a restraint and reticence, which make it easy to understand how a hostile impression became fixed in the minds of many observers. Men who knew nothing of his interest in church and home found something remote, calculating, and frigid in him. It was this quality of withdrawal which had led blunt-tongued Deacon Sked to tell him that he liked William better; which had made James Clark profanely hostile. His own brother, Frank, found it antipathetic, though in his headlong, careless way he probably chafed still more under John's precision and efficiency. From an early date we find Clevelanders who saw only the business side of Rockefeller telling stories which present him as a cold-blooded, inexorable money-making machine. "Always got the best of a bargain," Miss Tarbell reports old oil men saying, and wincing as they said it. One man asserted that the only time he ever saw Rockefeller show enthusiasm was when a report came from Oil Creek that his buyer had obtained a cargo of oil at a bargain price. "He bounded from his chair with a shout of joy, danced up and down, hugged me, threw up his hat, acted so like a madman that I have never forgotten it."[32] A similar story quotes his exclamation after another lucky stroke: "I'm bound to be rich, bound to be rich, *bound* to be rich!" Neither tale rings quite true; Rockefeller later emphatically denied

---

[31]*Idem.*

[32]Ida M. Tarbell, *History of the Standard Oil Company,* I, 43. Rockefeller was never explosive or outwardly emotional. In a conversation with Mr. Inglis in December, 1920, he took up Miss Tarbell's story of these exclamations, and denied her account emphatically and *in toto.* He would have been no more likely to indulge in such unguarded utterances than taciturn old Charles Lockhart of Pittsburgh, he said; and he pointed out that Miss Tarbell offered no authority.

the first; and if true they show but one aspect of the man. But they are proof that many people disliked him. He was not made to be likeable except by those who knew him well, and to the world at large he remained unlikeable to his later years.

Though he keenly realized the distrust and even hostility which his personality inspired in many observers, he always protested that this was unjust. "I have had the name of being cold, reserved, distant —a sort of remote, impersonal Cause," he said once in old age, "not the usual companionable human being. The fact is that no man takes a deeper or more friendly interest in his fellow humans than I." But it should be said again that he intensely distrusted any display of emotion. It should also be said that he never made any strong effort to break through the chilly aura his personality cast about him; he never made any such advances as Woodrow Wilson's to the Indianapolis crowd—"call me Woody." He was content to remain in character. Indeed, he made reticence, even secretiveness, a consistent policy, steadily impressing upon his business subordinates that "silence is golden," and schooling his family in the same uncommunicativeness. In business he was wont to mature his plans completely, to ponder and test them carefully, before he divulged them; in conference he was the last to speak. His personal decisions were never announced until the eleventh hour, for he felt that silence was wisdom, that a deed is best revealed like Minerva, fullborn. He even took a certain pleasure in the inscrutable, and in later years would smilingly recite a bit of doggerel:

> A wise old owl sat on an oak;
> The more he saw the less he spoke;
> The less he spoke the more he heard;
> Why can't we be like that old bird?

From the beginning those who knew him best and worked with him most closely uttered many protests of trust and affection, and denied that his taciturnity hid any sinister quality; that it was anything but a quaintly amusing trait. Yet the habitual inscrutability of Rockefeller, so often followed by unexpected and irresistible action, was to be one of the principal causes of the tremendous hostility which he ultimately aroused. His gestures of self-revelation in the days of his retirement came too late to have much effect in softening the picture of him which millions had formed.

III

Rockefeller by the time of his marriage had fully developed his business principles and his characteristic method of conducting affairs. This method, to define it briefly, was founded upon a union of precision with imagination. Inside his establishment, faultless order, rigid economy, a complete mastery of details, must be established; but in its relations with other establishments and with the general world of business, bold enterprise should be given full play. In part this method was the result of his fifteen years of observation and training, his nearly ten years of actual business practice; in larger part it was the natural outgrowth of his own traits. In studying these traits it is difficult not to refer a certain dualism in the man to his ancestry—to the shrewd, cautious, precise Davisons on his mother's side, and to the bold, enterprising, farsighted Avery-Rockefeller line on his father's. While any such reference is hazardous, it is certain that he had the dual traits here implied. He had precision; the precision of a bookkeeper, a carefully drilled office-manager. He also had imagination and thrust; the imagination of a born entrepreneur. He proposed to use them together, for he believed that no necessary conflict existed between imagination and exactness. In his business management he had shown that he would tolerate no haste, no rashness, no wastefulness; but in his treatment of Maurice Clark he had proved that he would tolerate no plodder's slowness. His union of precision and imagination was unusual in American affairs. The country had plenty of cautious, meticulous, old-fashioned businessmen with bookkeeper souls, who never made a mistake, but who lacked foresight and daring. It had also, as was natural in a land of vast natural wealth and constant speculative opportunities, plenty of bold, dashing adventurers who took long chances, but who wanted precision and solidity. Rockefeller combined the best traits of the two types in a way that amounted to business genius, and he placed behind them an extraordinary degree of personal force and energy.

His mind was now fixed in pattern. It was a curious mind, of a type seldom encountered in any field, and especially in business; a type that might seem better suited to a metaphysician than a captain of industry. It was ratiocinative, analytical, and deep-probing; its primary quality was its subtlety, its mastery of intricate combinations of force. Among a crowd of financiers, manufacturers, and railroad presidents who relied on "hunches" and shouldered their way forward by a burly combativeness, he always maintained an isolated place; for he detested the speculative temper, the use of instinct rather than cold reason, the tendency to plunge. Disliking "hunches," he insisted on looking at every problem in the chill, clear light of logic, and on dissecting it until every element was crystal-clear in his mind. He had the intellect of a great chess-player. Over the bewildering board of industry he brooded until every piece, in all their possible combinations, stood clear in his mind; until he had foreseen every move his opponents could make, and provided against every contingency; until his own course was perfectly plain to him. Then he touched his piece—and it was instantly clear that he had made the shrewdest possible move, and that the rest of the game would be played out according to his plan.

His subsequent partner, John D. Archbold, once summed up his genius in a few sentences. "You ask me what makes Rockefeller the unquestioned leader in our group. Well, it is simple. In business we all try to look ahead as far as possible. Some of us think we are pretty able. But Rockefeller always sees a little further ahead than any of us—and then he sees around the corner!"

His character was now also becoming fixed; a character marked not by elevation, but by strength and harmony. It was precisely the kind of character that fortified and amplified his business gifts. Patience and imperturbability were important ingredients of his nature. He admitted in old age that as a very young man he had been irascible; "I had a bad temper—I think it might be called an ugly temper when too far provoked." But he saw that irritability did not pay and gradually conquered it. His incessant vigilance, minute observations of details, careful forethought, and good judgment supported his precision in affairs. A keen ambition, a desire to outstrip rivals and become rich and powerful, supported his imagination. He could plan an edifice large and strong without neglecting a brick or beam that might later prove weak. He possessed still other qualities which chimed with those just enumerated: persistency, industry, quiet humor, an innate dislike for all excess, a sharp condemnation of the various forms of immorality which his church denounced. In his relations with others he was self-contained, and reserved. But as his business grew he knew how to hold the reins of authority tightly yet easily, and to make himself respected and liked by the men he directed. In those close to him over a long period of years the sense of loyalty and respect was transmuted into a feeling of positive devotion.

Certainly he concentrated upon business with an intensity, and planned his policies, with a care, an assiduity, and a vision that few men have ever matched. And certainly also he recognized the necessity of uniting caution as to details with audacity as to the large plan in his operations. It was a deliberately planned union. "It has always been my rule in business to make everything count," he once said. "To make everything count something. I never go into an enterprise unless I feel sure it is coming out all right. For instance, a promising scheme may be proposed to me. It may not altogether satisfy and is rejected. My brother Will would probably go into it and make $10,000. Another equally promising scheme comes along. He goes into that and loses $10,000. The result is he hasn't made any advancement in these two ventures and is actually losing time. Meantime in some surer enterprise I have made, say, $5000 in the same time the other fellow has made and lost twice as much. But mine counts and his doesn't. I believe the only way to succeed is to keep getting ahead all the time."[33]

It would have been difficult to find in America a spirit which contrasted more sharply with that of the oil producers and the more speculative refiners against whom he was soon to be pitted. The spirit which pervaded the Oil Regions was one of insouciant adventure, rash gambling, and ill-restrained lawlessness. While crimes of violence were few, sharpers and rogues abounded, goldbricking the gullible by thousands and selling worthless stock or dry wells for as much as they could get. A Pittsburgh citizen papered his bedroom with stock certificates which had originally cost him $53,000. Landbrokers hung about the Venango County towns like vultures, men in long-tailed black coats who accosted the stranger with an unctuous "Do you wish some first-rate oil territory, sir?" or "I'd like to sell you a quarter interest in a fifty-barrel well." Fake demonstrations were arranged, in which a well pumped up oil that was constantly resupplied by an underground pipe connected with the tank into which it was discharged. The output of wells was shamelessly exag-

[33]Inglis, Conversations with Rockefeller.

gerated; "smart" devices for a hurried sale were innumerable. And then at times a supposedly barren area really would yield a fortune to its purchaser, for no man could tell where oil might appear. The boom oil towns like Pithole roared and flared like Sacramento mining-camps or Transvaal diamond-pits. As J. J. McLaurin, long editor of the Oil City *Derrick*, put it:[34]

Lawless, reckless, wicked communities sprang up. The close of the war flooded the region with paper currency and bold adventurers. Leadville or Cheyenne at its zenith was a camp-meeting compared with Pithole, Petroleum Centre, or Babylon. Men and women of every degree of decency and degradation huddled as closely as the pigtailed Celestials in Chinatown. Millions of dollars were lost in bogus stock-companies. American history records no other such era of riotous extravagance. The millionaire and the beggar of today might change places tomorrow. Blind chance and consummate rascality were equally potent.

Still more antithetical to John D. Rockefeller's habits was the general atmosphere of prodigality, makeshift, and waste that enveloped the Regions. He knew the value of pennies, but nobody counted them in the Oil Regions any more than in the California gold-fields. At first there seemed no time for pennies, and original necessity became ultimate habit. The rule among well-owners was to buy what they needed —coal, barrels, horses, wagons, machinery—at the prices asked; the oil would repay it all. The rule at first was also to handle the oil in a hurry—to pump in a hurry, build storage facilities in a hurry, transport and sell in a hurry; and meanwhile not to worry about leakage or accidents—about oil spilled at the well, barrels bounced from the wagons, rafts wrecked. Throughout the Regions most stores, houses, hotels, roads, tanks, and even railways were haphazardly built. If an erection would serve it was good enough. The new railways were so dangerous that passengers on the line running along the Allegheny River called their route "The Valley of the Shadow of Death."

As the oil traffic grew larger and capital became more important, the Regions naturally abandoned or bettered many of their wasteful and hazardous ways. Ingenious inventors like Van Syckle, shrewd organizers like Henry Harley, aggressive builders of refineries like Downer and Abbott, emerged. But the tradition of carelessness continued to color many aspects of life. Men rose to wealth and then sank

[34]*Sketches in Crude Oil*, 393.

again to ruin. Doctor M. C. Egbert, to name one of many, became a millionaire, lost everything, and years later appeared in Cleveland, a harmless megalomaniac, begging a million dollars of Rockefeller at the Baptist Church door. Abbott, for all his shrewdness and solidity, overreached himself, lost his fortune, and began at the bottom again as a book peddler. Harley, who had been a partner of Jim Fisk for a time, got into jail, where his wife, a woman of culture, took up her abode with him. S. C. T. Dodd, who often spent a pleasant social hour with them in their prison, writes: "When I came to New York I found him there, ready to borrow a dollar from whoever would lend it to him, but even then he would never go a block in the city without a cab. Although he had no doubt pawned his real diamonds, he was still resplendent with diamonds of paste."[35] Fraud, dry wells, and fire became after a few years less important sources of loss than the rapid fluctuations in prices, and when oil exchanges were established these fluctuations supported a new form of gambling. Solid gold vanished into thin air as quotations dropped; the oil gave and the oil took away.

One fatal weakness of many oil men was their inability to adjust themselves to a falling price level. Oil oscillated violently from the outset, but for several years a downward dip was always followed by a rise. Some producers could not see that the *general* tendency, as production swelled, was downward; they could not forget twenty-dollar oil when they were getting five, or five-dollar oil when they were getting one.[36] They felt that they had a right to a high price, even if their own overproduction prevented it. Often by operating with care and economy they could have made a fair profit at the very prices they denounced, but they were incapable of economy. They scorned patience and demanded miracles. Miss Tarbell frankly admits this in her work on the Standard Oil Company, though her sympathies were wholly with the producers. Furthermore, many Regions men regarded themselves as a chosen people, with a natural right to the lion's share of profits in the industry. Did they not dwell in the region which gave the oil? Their habit of calling the rest of the country "the States" indicated this somewhat arrogant self-absorption. They regarded refining as properly a part of their own

[35]Dodd, *Memoirs,* 28.

[36]Doctor Giddens entitles chapter nine of his *Birth of the Oil Industry* "The Speculative Boom, 1864–65"; and chapter twelve, "The Depression Years."

heritage, a business which it was rather artificial and reprehensible to take outside the Regions. And in any event, they thought of refiners as a quasi-parasitic group, who deserved to get little out of oil. A large organization of well-owners was soon to propose restricting the profits of refining to one tenth of a cent a gallon!

In the first years after he broke with the Clarks, Rockefeller spent much time in the Oil Regions, for with his experience as commission merchant he naturally assumed the work of buyer. He made Franklin his headquarters, with a shipping office near the Erie station.[37] Here he boarded sometimes at the Exchange Hotel, sometimes with a Mrs. Sarah Mayes, who has testified that he was "very gentlemanly in every respect and exceedingly simple in his habits." Various traditions of him remain there: how at rush moments he helped roll barrels into the freight cars; how he often ordered bread and milk for supper; how he tried to have nine barrels put on to every wagon hauling his oil, against the haulage company's rule that only eight be taken; how he often paid a newsboy a dime for a five-cent copy of *The Derrick*.[38] Franklin is at the junction of French Creek and the Allegheny. At that time much oil was rafted down the river to Pittsburgh, and was stored in French Creek while the owners awaited the best moment. Late one Saturday night, according to Mrs. Mayes, a heavy freshet on the creek imperilled the oil moored there, and all her roomers but one hurried out and worked all day Sunday to try to save it. The exception was Rockefeller. He donned his Sunday suit, and joined a group of Baptists who worshipped in Hanna's Hall. "And strange as it may seem, his was the only oil that was saved." We may doubt that Providence intervened to save the Baptist oil, but there is no doubt whatever that Rockefeller would not have violated the Sabbath.

Rockefeller saw much of the waste, speculative temper, and arrogance of the Oil Regions and did not like them. He saw much, similarly, of the carelessness and prodigality of the first refiners in

[37]Miss Ida M. Tarbell kindly gave me some material upon Rockefeller in Franklin, and Mr. M. M. Lutton of that city collected much information for me.

[38]Edward P. Watson, the former newsboy, who furnished his recollections to me in March, 1939, recalled that Rockefeller "was tall, nice-looking, and wore a gray suit." Elizabeth Watson, whose father was agent of the Philadelphia Oil Company, told of the attempt to put on the extra barrel. He would have paid for the extra barrel, but he would not have paid ten cents for a nickel paper.

Cleveland and elsewhere, who made money hand over fist in the flush war years, but by 1868 felt the iron grip of competition and price-contraction. There was no common ground for the spirit of these two groups and the spirit which possessed Rockefeller. At first he merely deplored the waste and slackness of much of the industry; it seemed no concern of his. But as his business grew and his power with it, he saw that the losses resulting from overdevelopment, price-cutting, and extravagance injured the disciplined and efficient units only less than those which were crazily managed. Upon this fact he began to brood. Within a few years his peculiar genius, his combination of economy, precision, imagination, and boldness, was to clash with the wasteful, impetuous, domineering producers who believed that the kingdom of oil was theirs by right of discovery, and with the refiners who, having invested $10,000 or $25,000 in a plant, thought they ought to make 50 per cent indefinitely.

IV

The finest thoroughfare in Cleveland and one of the most beautiful streets in America was Euclid Avenue; once a buffalo and Indian trail and later a muddy country road, by 1868 it was the center of what wealth and fashion the city could exhibit. Fine elms arched the wide avenue all the way from Erie Street downtown to Case Avenue on the east. The stone or brick houses, nearly all imposing, were built far back from the roadway, each surrounded by spacious lawns and well-kept flower beds. From their porches the spumy edge and sparkling bosom of Lake Erie could be glimpsed through the trees to the north. Here, from the Presidency of Lincoln to that of Theodore Roosevelt, dwelt nearly all the great figures of the city—the bankers, railroad leaders, iron and coal magnates, and manufacturers. Here lived Amasa Stone, principal builder of the Lake Shore; Stillman Witt, the banker, and his son-in-law, Dan P. Eells; Henry Chisholm, the iron-master, his house once considered the finest in the city; and Henry B. Payne, first representative and later senator, whom Tilden selected for his successor in the leadership of the Democratic Party. Here John Hay resided after marrying Amasa Stone's daughter, and here he wrote *The Breadwinners*.[39]

[39]See Miss Ella Grant Wilson's interesting if chaotic volume, *Famous Old Euclid Avenue*. The street is described in Hay's *The Breadwinners* and in the anonymous answer to it, *The Money-Makers*.

It was an outward token of Rockefeller's increasing prosperity and importance that in 1868 he bought the large house at what was then 424 Euclid Avenue, near the present East Fortieth Street. To be sure, in that year the situation was far out toward the easterly outskirts of town; Amasa Stone's house stood at what is now East Thirteenth, T. P. Handy's at East Nineteenth, Henry B. Payne's at East Twenty-First, and that of the shipping owner, Rufus K. Winslow, at East Twenty-Fourth. Moreover, his residence was on the south or less fashionable side of Euclid. People on the north side were facetiously termed "nabobs" and those on the south "bobs." Nevertheless, the house belonged to what was soon called "millionaires' row," and if not pretentious it was at least large and handsome. Then recently completed, it was perfectly 1860 in style; a two-story rectangular building of brick, with mansard roof, high arched windows, a square portico in front, and a hexagonal porch with five stone pillars on each side. Like all houses on the avenue, it had a beautiful lawn and fine trees. The grounds occupied almost half of one of the large Cleveland blocks; they paralleled Case Avenue to the east, while they extended all the way from Euclid on the north to Prospect Street on the south. At the back Rockefeller shortly built a very large two-story carriage-house and stables, with ample room on the second floor for hay and grain. The house lay perhaps eighty feet from Euclid Avenue, while the stables were at the very rear close against Prospect.[40]

Inside, the house was well-lighted, commodious, and cheerful. Double doors at the front led to a small entryway, which opened into a large central hall, almost ten feet wide, running nearly the full length of the house. Halfway down this hall broad stairs rose to the second floor. On the right as one entered downstairs was the parlor, a room perhaps fifteen by twenty feet, high-ceiled, and lighted by both front and side windows. Its light mahogany woodwork harmonized with walls and ceiling of chocolate-colored plaster. The side wall was broken by a white marble fireplace and mantel, surmounted by a high gilt-framed mirror. On the left of the hall was the music-

[40]I examined the house, now demolished, in 1936. The stone stables, which old Clevelanders say cost more than the house, still stand and were used in 1939 as a night-club. Lucy Spelman told Mr. W. O. Inglis in 1917: "A very large brick house stood next door to this house. It was in the way, and Mr. Rockefeller moved it away to another street and set it on new foundations, where it was as good as ever. This was a marvelous undertaking; but then he was always undertaking marvelous things."

room, the largest in the house. It also had mahogany woodwork, a ceiling and walls of chocolate-colored plaster, and a white marble mantelpiece. Back of these front rooms were the plain dining-room on one side, a bedroom on the other, and a large kitchen; while the servants' quarters filled the rear of the main structure. On the second floor were four chambers of varying sizes, two with fireplaces; the attic offered storage space. It was a large house, but before many years passed there were four children—and then Rockefeller had means to live in a large way.

More attractive than the house were the grounds. A gardener was hired; beautiful shrubbery and noble trees lent retirement, while the fine lawn was broken by carefully kept flower beds. It was such grounds which gave the length and breadth of the Euclid Avenue district a parklike look hardly to be matched in America. With flowers Rockefeller was never expert, but he delighted in creating green effects with trees and bushes.

Here he entertained fellow churchmen and other friends. Here Henry M. Flagler, Sam Andrews, his brother Will and he sat up late over knotty business problems. Every weekday morning his horses champed at the side door until he sprang into the seat and took the reins; every Sunday Mrs. Rockefeller and he drove off sedately to Sunday school and church. He knew nearly everybody along the full stretch of Euclid Avenue, and they knew him. His life was not yet filled with the tension that began to come in 1871. He was busy, but not distracted; he was not yet plunged into bitter economic war, not yet widely hated. He might well be called a happy man.

BOOK TWO

THE MAKING OF THE GREAT TRUST

XII

Built on Oil—and Rebates

THE cool, determined young Rockefeller could not be accused of failure to act rapidly and vigorously. In 1865 he had bought out the Clarks, taken his brother into partnership, helped organize a second company, and built a new refinery. In 1866 he had sent his brother to take charge of a New York agency and formed a third company there. The year 1867 found him at twenty-eight, taking Henry M. Flagler into partnership, and incorporating the new firm of Rockefeller, Andrews & Flagler, which represented a combination of the two pre-existing companies in Ohio. Meanwhile, he was using all his profits and borrowing large sums in addition for a swift expansion of the two refineries, their subsidiary works, and his transportation and marketing facilities.

So steadily did he plow all his resources back into the business that a curious legend soon grew up. John Moody a generation later pictured him as a man who "insisted that every possible cent be reinvested. 'Take out what you've got to have to live on, but leave the rest in,' he kept urging his partners. 'Don't buy new clothes and fast horses; let your wife wear her last year's bonnet. You can't find any place where money will earn what it does here.'"[1] This is absurd. Rockefeller himself bought fast horses and a large house on Euclid Avenue, while there were plenty of new bonnets. But it is true that he labored for a rapid and efficient expansion of his enterprise.

He did this because he saw that in the recklessly competitive oil industry size offered the one means of minimizing the grave and

---

[1]John Moody, *The Masters of Capital*, p. 53. This statement first appeared in the series "The Masters of Capital in America" in *McClure's*, March, 1911, by John Moody and George Kibbe Turner.

constant risks. The bigger the refinery and the ampler its reserves, the less it was at the mercy of sudden, unpredictable fluctuations. The small man might be wiped out by a sudden price-slump; but the largest establishments could be sure of economical buying and effective selling, of savings in maufacture, and of capital adequate to meet a series of mishaps. Looking ahead, he foresaw that if new oil basins were opened and the industry grew to ever-larger size, only companies with great financial resources could hope to command the field. Firms which distributed their profits in dividends would have to give way in the end to corporations which had steadily strengthened themselves. The depression which struck the oil industry in 1867 and grew worse in 1868–70 reinforced these conclusions.

It was fortunate for Rockefeller that his business prestige, his many friendships, and the growing value of the refining industry to the city made it easy to obtain banking support. We have already said something of the first two assets. As for the third, the annual volumes of the Board of Trade indicate how warm a pride Cleveland took in its fast-expanding oil business. Rapid advances were chronicled every year. The report for 1868, for example, boasted that the amount of crude oil received had surged upward from 220,000 barrels in 1865 to 956,500 three years later. In the same period the refined oil shipped out of the city had leaped from 154,000 barrels to 776,400. Pittsburgh, still in the lead, had received in 1868 about 300,000 more barrels of crude oil than Cleveland; but the lake city was catching up.[2] Every one knew that in spite of falling prices and widespread gloom among oil men the world demand was advancing. In the three years just named American shipments of refined oil abroad more than trebled. Since between three and four million dollars were now invested in the city's refining business, Cleveland bankers were willing to encourage so important a local industry—particularly when they could lend to a man as able and reliable as Rockefeller.

And Rockefeller was eager to borrow. He was determined to achieve leadership in both the domestic and home markets. In 1867 his and William's names appeared together in the New York directory, thereafter his trips east were frequent, and his plans grew larger. Walking in Cleveland one day with H. S. Davis, president of the Y. M. C. A., he was talking of them when a leading banker drove

[2] Reports, Cleveland Board of Trade, 1866–1868.

down the street. Drawing up at the curb, the banker hailed the two young men and demanded:

"Mr. Rockefeller, do you think you could use $50,000?"

This was a windfall indeed, but Rockefeller gazed dubiously at the financier, and seemed to be giving the question judicious consideration. Finally he replied:

"Wel-l-l, Dan, can you give me twenty-four hours to think it over?"[3] Inwardly he burned with anxiety for the money.

Next day he took the loan, which might have been lost by precipitate eagerness.

II

But he needed permanently invested capital, not loans—for he disliked dependence on banks—and he wanted able partners. Rockefeller's instincts as to men seldom erred. When soon after William went east he brought Henry M. Flagler into active and Stephen V. Harkness into silent partnership, he knew that they would contribute brains, experience, and money. Their entry into the business marked the beginnings of that oligarchy of petroleum magnates who were to build up huge fortunes in conjunction with Rockefeller, and play important rôles in the history of American philanthropy. Rockefeller had his office running smoothly—a subordinate says it had "the certainty of a perfect mechanism"[4]—but he wanted more aggressiveness, power, and drive.

Flagler, whose name was ultimately to be written large upon the oil industry, Southern railroad-building, and the development of Florida, was nine and a half years older than Rockefeller. Born at Hopewell, N. Y., near Canandaigua, on January 2, 1830, the son of a $400-a-year Presbyterian minister, he attended school till he was fourteen. "At that age," he wrote later, "I concluded that my father and sister needed the lean pay which my father received for preaching. So I left home and walked nine miles to Medina, carrying a carpetbag in my hand."[5] He went west by the Erie Canal and a lake boat. A series of Algeresque adventures followed. He had a few coppers, a French coin, and a nickel when he landed in Republic, Ohio—

[3]Inglis, Notes of Conversation with Henry Davis.

[4]Charles J. Woodbury, *Saturday Evening Post*, Oct. 21, 1911. Woodbury entered the office in 1879, but his remarks would apply to the earlier period.

[5]N. Y. *Tribune*, Dec. 23, 1906; interview with Flagler.

and the five-franc piece he kept until the day of his death. Employed in a country store at $5 a month and board, he learned some elementary business lessons. "There was a keg at the foot of the cellar steps which was filled with brandy from a larger vessel. Three classes of people were in that region in separate communities—English, German, and Pennsylvania Dutch. Out of that little keg we sold one kind of brandy to the English at $4 a gallon, another kind to the Germans at $1.50 a gallon, and still another kind to the Pennsylvania Dutch for what we could get." Later he worked at Fostoria, Ohio, and other places; "I was contented but not satisfied."[6] Managing to save a little money, he finally went to the fast-growing town of Bellevue, not far from Toledo, to set up a grain commission business. He prospered, and on November 9, 1853, married Mary Harkness, niece of a leading citizen, Stephen V. Harkness.

This marriage was a turning-point in Flagler's career. Harkness owned a distillery at Monroeville, in the Huron River Valley a few miles south of Bellevue, in which Flagler became interested for a time. Senator John Sherman, chairman of the Committee on Finance, was a friend of Harkness, and soon after the outbreak of the Civil War is said to have warned him that a heavy excise tax would be placed on whiskey. This may not be true. Harkness could readily foresee it for himself. At any rate, he collected large stocks of untaxed liquor which he subsequently sold at a high profit, emerging from the war a rich man. The year 1866 found him living in Cleveland, one of its wealthiest citizens—buying real estate in East Cleveland, setting up a company to manufacture "iron-clad" roofing, paint, and mastic,[7] and carrying on other business ventures. Meanwhile Flagler, after accumulating about $50,000 in the grain and produce business, had gone to the salt-mining and lumbering town of Saginaw, Mich., where he sunk salt-wells and disposed of the product through the firm of Flagler & York. In that industry, marked by chaotic overproduction and cutthroat competition, he at first did well. But with the advent of peace in 1865 salt prices crashed, and he not only lost all his capital but went some $40,000 or $50,000 in debt. For a time he engaged in barrel-manufacturing as a partial resource. Then, about the end of 1865, he came to Cleveland to recoup his fortunes.

In this effort Flagler was given financial assistance, for which he

[6]*Ibid.*　　　　　　[7]Cleveland *Leader,* Dec. 27, 1867.

proudly paid the ruling rate of 10 per cent a year, by Harkness and other relatives. For a time he had desk space in Rockefeller's offices on the second floor of the Sexton Building, overlooking the Cuyahoga; and when Rockefeller moved into larger quarters in the Case Block on the northeastern corner of the Public Square, Flagler went to the same building. He sold barrels to Rockefeller and other oil refiners; he dealt in grain again; and he also tried to market a patent horseshoe. The city directory for 1866–67 shows that he was associated with Clark & Sanford, commission merchants, and he soon bought them out. Within a short time he was once more prosperous.

Indeed, Flagler made a forcible impression upon the business community. He presented a distinguished appearance; not tall, but erect and alert, with glossy black hair, heavy black mustache, snapping dark eyes, and an air of magnetism and energy. Whereas Rockefeller had a slow, deliberate power, Flagler radiated a brisk vitality. Like Rockefeller, he felt a passion for wealth—he, too, was "bound to be rich." He had a powerful imagination, and his quick step and rapid movements showed his bold temperament. Having passed through a harsh school of experience, he had been trained to a certain ruthlessness. Critics said later that although a religious man, he was hard, quick to seize an advantage, and not always scrupulous or absolutely law-abiding. He was determined to march straight through business disorder to his goal. But he had a flair for large projects, and late in life, when captivated by his vision of a magnificently remade Florida, showed that he could devote his wealth to constructive and in part altruistic objects of the first magnitude.[8]

The acquaintance between Rockefeller and Flagler was of long standing, for they had known each other in Bellevue when Rockefeller was a mere youth buying grain for his commission house and Flagler a newly married grain merchant. "I sent him a good many carloads of wheat," Flagler said later. In their ambitious temper, their taste for expansion, and their shrewdness, they were thoroughly congenial. Close association in the Sexton Building made them warm

[8] I have generously been given much information upon Flagler by Mr. Wallace Goldsmith, author of an unpublished biography of him. See also *In Memoriam Henry M. Flagler*, 1830–1913, a 53-page brochure containing reminiscences by friends and newspaper articles. The N. Y. *Sun*, Feb. 23, 1885, republished an article from the St. Louis *Globe-Democrat* which stated Harkness's investment at $60,000. I have been unable to obtain any exact information from the Harkness family or the Flagler estate.

friends. Henry would drop into John's room and talk of business, while frequently they walked home together. It was not difficult to interest the adventurous Flagler, said by Cleveland gossip to have made $50,000 or $60,000 in a fortunate grain speculation at just this time, in the rich possibilities of oil, and then to enlist the wealthy Stephen V. Harkness. The grain-dealer, "full of vim and push," as Rockefeller said later,[9] knew how to convert his uncle-in-law. They agreed to establish a new company to operate the largest refining organization in Cleveland.

The result was the formation early in 1867 of Rockefeller, Andrews & Flagler. Just what Harkness invested we do not know—estimates vary from $60,000 to $90,000. He remained a silent partner. The size of Flagler's investment is equally indeterminable. This new money was immediately used in plant expansion. As early as April, Cleveland newspapers refer to Rockefeller, Andrews & Flagler. The new partner pooled his imagination, energy, and will-power with Rockefeller's gifts, and from beginning to end the two thought and acted in perfect harmony. Theirs was a friendship founded on business, which Flagler used to say was better than a business founded on friendship. In his *Random Reminiscences* Rockefeller pays Flagler a warmer tribute than any of his other early associates. He writes:[10]

For years and years this early partner and I worked shoulder to shoulder; our desks were in the same room. We both lived on Euclid Avenue, a few rods apart. We met and walked to the office together, walked home to luncheon, back again after luncheon, and home again at night. On these walks, when we were away from the office interruptions, we did our thinking, talking, and planning together. Mr. Flagler drew practically all our contracts. He has always had the faculty of being able to clearly express the intent and purpose of a contract so well and accurately that there could be no misunderstanding, and his contracts were fair to both sides. I can remember his saying often that when you go into an arrangement you must measure up the rights and proprieties of both sides with the same yardstick, and this was the way Henry M. Flagler did . . .

Another thing about Mr. Flagler for which I think he deserves great credit was that in the early days he insisted that, when a refinery was to be put up, it should be different from the flimsy shacks which it was then the custom to build. Everyone was so afraid that the oil would disappear and that the money expended in buildings would be a loss that the mean-

[9]*Cf.* Rockefeller, *Random Reminiscences*, 11.   [10]Pp. 12–15.

est and cheapest buildings were erected for use as refineries. This was the sort of thing Mr. Flagler objected to. While he had to admit that it was possible the oil supply might fail and that the risks of the trade were great, he always believed that if we went into the oil business at all, we should do the work as well as we knew how; that we should have the very best facilities; that everything should be solid and substantial; and that nothing should be left undone to produce the finest results.

There can be no question that Flagler was for nearly a decade— until John D. Archbold joined the group—Rockefeller's strongest associate.

The new investments permitted a growth which quickly carried Rockefeller, Andrews & Flagler into undisputed pre-eminence not only in Cleveland, but in the United States and the world. Their two plants on Kingsbury Run became larger than any in Pittsburgh, even Charles Lockhart's or O. F. Waring's; larger than any in the Regions, even the Ludovici Brothers' or Downer's; larger than any in Philadelphia, even William G. Warden's; larger than any near New York, even Jabez A. Bostwick's. Their capacity when Flagler came in was apparently slightly more than five hundred barrels of refined oil a day. By 1869, according to Rockefeller and others, it was not less than 1500 barrels a day, and one Cleveland banker put it at 3000 barrels of crude oil. An indication of the growing scope of the business is furnished by two items in the Cleveland *Leader* in 1868. One, in May, recorded that Rockefeller, Andrews & Flagler had lost $5000 in a fire that consumed some transfer-platforms at Oil City. Another, in September, stated that the firm had contracted with C. P. Born for the manufacture of 300,000 five-gallon oil-cans to be used in shipping refined oil to Europe. William was getting the export orders!

III

In short, the clear-headed, resolute young man who had gone into refining in 1863 and gained control of his company in 1865, was by 1868 head of the largest oil manufactory in the world. This growth in size was important in itself, for it made possible great economies in buying, manufacturing, and selling. But it was more important as the basis for achieving a notable reduction in transportation costs, a decisive step in Rockefeller's rise not merely to leadership, but domination. After that achievement, his business became the Aaron's rod which swallowed up all the other rods.

This step was the arrangement of a comprehensive and profitable system of railroad rebates, and the cementing of a virtual alliance between Rockefeller and the Lake Shore-New York Central system. The rebate arrangement was of a kind already common in the relations of industry and the railroads, but it was pushed to an uncommon point. Transportation at this period, to quote an accepted authority,[11] "was regarded by both railroads and shippers as a matter of bargain and sale, the shrewdest shipper securing the lowest rates, and the cleverest freight solicitor the largest traffic." One of Flagler's first acts after joining the firm was to take over the negotiation of freight rates. He found the fast-growing business in a favorable position for obtaining rate concessions.

Three important railroads had hastened to throw tracks into the Oil Regions, untouched by any line when Drake sunk his first wells. The oil traffic was too rich to be neglected, for according to *The United States Railroad and Mining Register* it had a product-value of fully $20,000,000 in 1864. The Atlantic & Great Western forwarded more than 530,000 barrels in 1863, and more than 675,000 barrels in 1864, on which, according to Sir Morton Peto, it charged not less than eight cents a ton-mile.[12] The other two lines which invaded the field were the Pennsylvania and the Lake Shore & Michigan Southern.

We have seen that by 1868 the Atlantic & Great Western, entering the Oil Regions at two points, had built a line from Corry on the north to Titusville, and another from Meadville on the northwest to Franklin. The Lake Shore had a line running from Cleveland to Jamestown, Pa., which it was fast pushing eastward to Oil City. The Pennsylvania controlled the Allegheny Valley Railroad, which followed the river in a shallow crescent from Pittsburgh north to Franklin; while it dominated another road in the northern part of the State, the Philadelphia & Erie, which by a tributary line traversed the entire "valley of petroleum" from Corry through Titusville to Franklin. All three railroads fought hard for the traffic and made large profits from oil. The Atlantic & Great Western boasted that in 1864

[11]Logan Grant McPherson, *Railroad Freight Rates in Relation to the Industry and Commerce of the United States.*
[12]Sir Morton Peto, *The Resources and Prospects of America.*

the petroleum revenues of its Cleveland office alone averaged $1200 a day. The Allegheny Valley Railroad in 1865 received $600,000 from oil freights, and $300,000 more from trade connected with oil—that is, coal, machinery, and drilling materials. To swell the oil traffic on its Philadelphia & Erie branch, the Pennsylvania in 1865 helped organize a fast-freight line, of which we shall hear more, called the Empire Transportation Company.[13]

By 1868 trunk-line competition was spirited, and a battle of giants for both the crude-oil and refined-oil traffic was beginning. The Pennsylvania, already a powerful system, was presided over by J. Edgar Thomson, a shrewd organizer at whose side stood the brilliant vice-president, Thomas A. Scott, who had made so strong a record as Assistant Secretary of War under Lincoln.[14] The New York Central was in the hands of Cornelius Vanderbilt, the dominant railroad genius of the country, who had just completely integrated the lines connecting New York City and Buffalo. He looked forward to an early annexation of the Lake Shore, more than 500 miles in length, as part of a through road from the Atlantic to Chicago.[15] The winter of 1867–68 witnessed the spectacularly shocking "Erie War" between Vanderbilt and the Daniel Drew-Jay Gould forces for control of the Erie Railroad. The latter won, and in the fall of 1868 the unscrupulous Gould was elected president of the Erie. He at once absorbed the Atlantic & Great Western as part of his trunk-line, which thus reached Cleveland.[16] The struggle of these three great systems over the rich quarry of the oil traffic was destined in the next few years to arouse nationwide attention; and it created a situation in which Cleveland and John D. Rockefeller could reach out for high stakes in the refining industry.

The firm of Rockefeller, Andrews & Flagler could obviously ship refined oil east either by the Erie or the Lake Shore-New York Central route, while in summer it could use the waterways. Flagler in

[13]It is possible to follow the growth of the Oil Region lines accurately by comparing the successive annual reports of Pennsylvania's Department of the Interior, 1865–1870.

[14]Mr. S. R. Kamm, of Haddon Heights, N. J., who is preparing a doctoral dissertation upon Thomas A. Scott at the University of Pennsylvania, has kindly given me much information upon him.

[15]John Moody, *The Railroad Builders*, pp. 33, 34.

[16]H. S. Mott, *The Story of Erie*, contains a special chapter on the checkered history of the Atlantic & Great Western.

1867 began bargaining. He found that an ambitious young veteran, General James H. Devereux, had just become vice-president and general manager of the Lake Shore Railroad, and was eager to make a record. Devereux hoped to obtain a large oil traffic, for the Lake Shore was just completing its Jamestown & Franklin branch into the very heart of the Oil Regions. Up to this year nearly all crude oil had come into Cleveland by way of the Atlantic & Great Western, but the energetic general meant to change that. Since it was important to be on good terms with the largest refiners, we can imagine him shaking hands eagerly with Flagler.[17]

Unquestionably it was Flagler and not Rockefeller who undertook the negotiations, for late in life he said as much. Speaking of rebates, he remarked: "A lot of rubbish has been printed on that subject, too. Mr. Rockefeller is charged with inventing the plan by which the Standard secretly got advantages over its competitors in the matter of freights. Now the truth is that I, and not Mr. Rockefeller, was in charge of the transportation department of our business. I remember when the Standard received its first rebate. I went home in great delight. I had won a great victory, I thought. A year later I discovered that other refiners received similar favors."[18] He believed that Tom Scott of the Pennsylvania had introduced rebating, but this is more than dubious.

An agreement on crude-oil shipments was easily reached. Such oil was carried from the Regions to Cleveland at a cent a gallon or 42 cents a barrel. Flagler pointed out that his firm was already much the largest in Cleveland; that its business was invaluable, for it moved both the greatest body of crude oil west and the greatest body of refined oil east; and that both parts of its traffic were growing fast. Rockefeller and he could promise shipments sufficiently large and regular to enable the Lake Shore to effect important economies. As a matter of fact, 42 cents a barrel was excessive. Cleveland was already taking nearly a million barrels of crude oil from the Regions, and in 1870 would take more than two millions; in view of these quantities, rates might well be cut. Undoubtedly other Cleveland refineries had received rebates prior to this time. Rockefeller, like Flagler, has ex-

[17]See the affidavit of Devereux in the suit of the Standard Oil Company against Wm. C. Scofield and others in the Court of Common Pleas, Cuyahoga County, Ohio, in 1880, printed in Tarbell, *Standard Oil Company*, I, 277–279.
[18]Interview, N. Y. *Tribune,* Dec. 23, 1906.

plicitly stated that this was true—that such concessions antedated even his entry into refining.[19] "Rebates and drawbacks were a common practice ... for many years preceding and many years following this period; that is, the period before 1862 and long after." While this perhaps fixes the practice earlier in petroleum history than it actually occurred, it had become a fairly old story soon after the war.

In any event, Rockefeller, Andrews & Flagler obtained their rebate in 1867. Though the amount has never been disclosed, it seems to have been not less than fifteen cents a barrel. The Atlantic & Great Western doubtless matched it. Rockefeller records that from this time the New York Central-Lake Shore system and the Erie-Atlantic & Great Western system "regarded us as their allies in the freight-competition."[20] Several years later the head of Alexander, Scofield & Co. told a committee of the Federal House that, rendered suspicious by the prosperity of Rockefeller, Andrews & Flagler, he had gone in 1868 or 1869 to the offices of the Atlantic & Great Western. He said: "You are giving others better rates than you are us. We cannot compete if you do that." The agent did not deny the charge, but offered a compensating rebate. Alexander, Scofield & Co. were to pay the full rate, send in their railroad vouchers every month, and be refunded fifteen cents a barrel on crude oil. W. H. Doane, a shipper of crude oil who served Rockefeller and other refineries, made complaint and obtained a ten-cent rebate—apparently not his first.[21]

It would be interesting to know how many other Cleveland refineries obtained rebates on crude oil, with the precise dates and sums. Probably the smallest shippers got nothing, and paid the published rates. It is also probable that Rockefeller, Andrews & Flagler received a higher allowance than nearly any one else. According to the code of the time they, with the great power to make demands, would have been foolish had they not exacted it. It was commonly believed in Cleveland that in 1868–70 they also received a rebate on shipments of refined oil, but Flagler, when later examined under

[19]Inglis, Conversations with Rockefeller.   [20]*Idem.*
[21]Testimony of Messrs. Alexander and Doane, Committee of Commerce of the Federal House of Representatives, April, 1872. Rockefeller, commenting on this, said (Inglis, Conversations) that Alexander was "an ignorant Englishman, with more than the usual amount of conceit," who became jealous. Doane was a good friend of Rockefeller, and his testimony was "not intended at all to be adverse or prejudicial to the Standard Oil Company."

oath, declared they had obtained "None whatever." Precise evidence has disappeared along with the railroad books and refinery records. Secrecy was a vital element in rebate-granting. The railroads took care to keep their concessions secret from other roads or other shippers, while the manufacturer held his rates secret from all competitors. "Neither railroad nor shipper," remarks McPherson, "knew what concessions were obtained from other railroads by other shippers." Of course Rockefeller and Flagler had means of guessing at the rebates to other refiners, just as these refiners could guess at the favors accorded to Rockefeller.

But what of the ethics of this special advantage which Rockefeller, Andrews & Flagler had gained? How widespread was the practice of rebating, and how was it regarded by businessmen at the time? Miss Tarbell says that the theory was "generally held then, as now, though not so definitely crystallized into law, that the railroad being a common carrier had no right to discriminate between its patrons."[22] John T. Flynn takes an opposing view. After pointing out that Rockefeller "did not invent the rebate," he states that the principle that the railroad has no right to make discriminatory rates is of more recent birth. "This idea had practically no public support in the sixties. The roads were in the possession of men who believed they had a right to run them to suit themselves. ... The railroads were in a state of perpetual warfare with each other. The managers were attempting to build their roads and the territory through which they ran. In this competition they made all sorts of concessions to large shippers. And it is quite certain that when Rockefeller and Flagler went to Stone for a rebate they believed they were acting not only within their rights but in accordance with the permissible stratagems of the game."[23]

This is an issue which lies at the very root of any judgment upon Rockefeller's business methods. Elucidation of the subject is also important to an understanding of transportation itself. Curiously enough, neither Miss Tarbell nor Mr. Flynn uses the most authoritative evidence upon the place of rebates in business in 1867–70.

[22]Tarbell, *Standard Oil Company*, I, 49.
[23]Flynn, *God's Gold*, 137. As Doctor Edwin F. Gay stated to me, rebating was long an almost universal practice in America. It was the child of intense railroad competition and was little known in England only because competition was slight there.

IV

In 1867 the railroad committee of the Ohio Senate made a highly illuminating investigation of railroad rate-practices. Its reports demonstrated that rate-reductions—rebates, drawbacks, special rates— were widely prevalent. Numerous instances of rebating in a variety of industries were cited, and it was shown that the grant of preferences to favored communities, companies, and persons was particularly common in the coal trade. Many railroad officers defended these practices. Though the committee condemned them, it clearly did not know what remedy could be applied. They were the result, it pointed out, of a bitter competition between rival roads, in which the lines "seemed to have been in some measure helpless and in part reckless." These contests were ruinous, being marked by an amount of confusion, trickery, distrust, and empiricism "found in no other branch of business"; but the committee did not know how to reach their root. It condemned fast-freight lines, and recommended that all rate-schedules be published. As a result of the inquiry, a bill was drafted which required publication of charges, forbade all deviation from the open rates, prohibited rebates of any kind, declared railroads to be common carriers, and created a Railroad Commissioner with powers of investigation and enforcement. After passing the Senate, it was defeated in the House. Such legislation was impracticable without concurrent action by neighboring States; for if Ohio forbade special rates and Pennsylvania did not, Ohio railroads and cities would suffer while Pennsylvania railroads and cities gained important advantages.[24]

This inquiry was immediately followed by a similar investigation of the Pennsylvania Senate into "alleged extortionate charges" by the railroads of the Keystone State. Public hearings began May 14, 1867, and after seven sessions in various cities, closed on November 8. Scores of witnesses, whose sworn evidence fills 238 closely printed pages,[25] testified to rate discriminations, rebates, and drawbacks. The

[24]*Report of Railroad Committee, Ohio Senate Journal,* 1867; see Cleveland *Leader,* Feb. 4, 7, 25, 1867, on the report and bill.

[25]*Testimony Before the General Judiciary Committee of the Senate of Pennsylvania Relative to Alleged Extortionate Charges upon the Freight and Passengers by the Railroad Corporations of the Commonwealth* (1868). Hereafter cited as *Pennsylvania Senate Inquiry.*

inquiry had been provoked by widespread and long-continued public complaint of these evils, which had brought many shippers to the point of desperation. A specimen petition against abuses by the Pennsylvania Railroad, submitted in 1866, read as follows:[26]

> The *special* rates of this company are a discrimination of a more evil character than the regular freight list is. *They are a delusion and a snare.* As, if a man erects works on their line, under the influence of them the company hold him in their inexorable grasp from that moment; as, if he raises his voice or his vote against the company, they can stop his *special* rates, or offer lower rates to his rival in business, and crush him. If the special rates were *legalized,* as we understand it was projected by the company to do, on a sliding scale—(so) that a man shipping one thousand tons should have a low rate, and ten thousand a still lower rate, and one hundred thousand the lowest—we aver that they would be opposed to the principles of a free government that advocates the greatest good to the greatest number; that they would build up a privileged class and would allow no fair and free development of the resources of the State of Pennsylvania.

The witnesses made little complaint that the average level of rates was too high; but they offered universal and frantic complaint that rates were uneven, discriminatory, and shot through with favoritism and privilege. All of the abuses that provoked the Interstate Commerce Act of 1887, the Elkins Act of 1903, and the Hepburn Act of 1906—that furnished a battleground for defenders and attackers of the railroads during a long generation—appear full-blown in these grievances of the embattled Pennsylvania shippers in 1866–68. Not one is missing. The long-and-short-haul discrimination; the charging of far higher rates at non-competitive than at competitive points; the semi-secret "special rate" to large shippers; the wholly secret rebate to specially favored shippers; the secret drawback, or end-of-the-month refund to a shipper—all are described in detail.

The unfair rate discrimination between different cities need not longer detain us, for they have no application to individual or group rebates and drawbacks. A large miller of Duncannon, Pa., 234 miles east of Pittsburgh on the main Pittsburgh-Philadelphia line, testified that the Pennsylvania Railroad charged him the same sum to haul Western wheat this 234 miles that they charged Philadelphia millers

[26]*Pennsylvania Senate Inquiry,* 7.

for hauling it 355 miles from Pittsburgh. He then had to pay the regular Duncannon-Philadelphia charge on flour to the latter city. Obviously he could not compete with the Philadelphia mills. Several Pittsburgh oil refiners complained that they suffered by this same discrimination between cities. The Pennsylvania Railroad charged precisely the same amount to haul crude oil from Oil City to Philadelphia, 441 miles, as to haul crude oil from Pittsburgh to Philadelphia, only 355 miles. In other words, the railroad gave Oil City shippers the advantage of free transportation for 86 miles.[27] Nor was this all. Pittsburgh refiners bought their crude oil in the Regions, paying freight down the valley; they refined it in Pittsburgh; and then when they shipped to Philadelphia, they found that the Pennsylvania charged five cents a barrel more on refined oil than on crude, though refined oil was cleaner and less liable to loss by fire! Pittsburgh men also testified that in 1866–67 the Erie and New York Central charged only 45 cents a hundredweight on refined oil from Cleveland to New York, while the Pennsylvania charged 50 cents a hundredweight from Pittsburgh to Philadelphia.[28] In short, Pittsburgh refiners were at a cruel disadvantage in competing with Oil City, Philadelphia, and Cleveland.

But the most important testimony related to various forms of rebates: that is, to "special rates" allowed to rather large groups; to rebates proper, given secretly to individuals at the times they shipped; and to drawbacks, which were secret refunds allowed at the end of the month. Numerous men offered evidence as to the "special rates" granted to large shippers, especially on the Pennsylvania. The Harrisburg freight-agent admitted that in shipments of iron west or east, "all the prominent parties have special rates." He further declared that "as a general thing it [the low rate] is not confined," but that "there may have been instances" where one man alone got it. Moreover, he testified that nobody could find out about the special rates except by inquiry. A shipper living at Port Royal, Pa., gave evidence that special rates were frequent.[29]

The rebate proper, unlike the special rate, was given the individual and not the group. It varied from shipper to shipper, according to his power and his demands. Henry McCormick, a prominent Harris-

[27]*Ibid.*, 167, 168.   [28]*Idem*, 167, 168.   [29]*Idem*, 19.

burg ironmaster, testified frankly to his own acceptance of rebates. He simply could not do business without them, and saw no impropriety in them:[30]

In shipping small quantities along the road, our rates are made to conform to the public toll-sheets. In selling nails or pig-iron in large quantities, we find it impossible to compete with others at toll-sheet rates, to any point at any distance from our works. There don't seem to be any system about it; I have been shipping various articles for ten or twelve years, and the rates seem to be entirely arbitrary, and every man seems to make a special or private bargain with the general freight agent at Philadelphia, Mr. Houston. For instance, I have an inquiry for nails at points in the West or Northwest, and if we were to figure according to the rates given us by the officials of the company, here, it would be entirely out of the question to compete with others. To fix the price of any commodities at points at any distance, we must have a special rate given us by the general agent in Philadelphia; we cannot live by the sheet rates. Those rates seem to be arbitrary.

In short, rate-making on the Pennsylvania and other lines was a chaos. The "special rate" was fairly uniform for large shippers, though each man had to be alert to find out its existence. The individual rebate was not uniform but arbitrary. The drawback was still more secret and capricious. S. K. Hoxsie, a retired builder, pungently described it:[31]

The Pennsylvania company have in their office a very important book which it will be necessary to have examined; it is called in their accounts, drawbacks, and the object of this book is twofold; one object is to favor certain shippers over their road—certain corporations or individuals—and the other is to swell the gross receipts of the road to the satisfaction of the stockholders. The discrimination is much larger than any one, perhaps, outside of their immediate circle, knows anything about. The freight paid by certain parties, for instance, appears to be $7.20 a ton for coal; that is credited, of course, to the gross earnings of the road; that swells up the gross receipts, say for 1866, to $16,717,289.20; that makes it very satisfactory to the stockholders; it also enables parties whom they wish to favor to keep down competition in coal and lumber. Then that same party goes monthly into the treasurer's office and receives what is called a drawback, secretly—an overcharge, as they term it—the effect [of which] is to satisfy the stockholders on the one side, and prevent competition on the other.

[30]*Idem*, 33.   [31]*Idem*, 37, 38.

Mr. Hoxsie presented evidence that this drawback system went back at least as far as 1862. The following exchange shows that Rockefeller was doubtless correct in asserting that rebates were well known in oil long before he obtained them in 1867:[32]

Q.—Have you any idea of the percentage of that drawback?
A.—It is impossible to tell; I hold in my hand here from their [the Pennsylvania Railroad's] office, some copies of the drawbacks; they commence at number one, I think, each year, and so run up through the year; I have here number 3865, for the year 1862; on twelve of these drawbacks the company paid out $30,000.

Indeed, we know from other sources that rebating by the anthracite railroads of Pennsylvania had begun at least as early as 1856. In that year the competition between mine-operators in the Schuylkill Valley, operators in the Lackawanna field, and operators in the middle anthracite region, had reached a fierce intensity. These three coal areas were served respectively by the Philadelphia & Reading Railroad, the Delaware, Lackawanna & Western Railroad, and the Lehigh Valley Railroad. Each operating group turned to a supporting railroad for aid. It is recorded that, faced with ruin from the bitter competition of their rivals, the Schuylkill operators in May, 1856, compelled the Philadelphia & Reading officials to grant them a heavy rebate as a means of continuing in business.[33]

The mass of testimony taken by the committee showed that while the Pennsylvania Railroad was the worst offender, all lines carried on similar practices. Various witnesses accused the Lackawanna, the Lehigh Valley, and others, as well as the canal companies. One railroad official said defiantly: "We have special rates for large shippers; if the trade legitimately belongs to us, we charge full rates—that is, if there is no competition for it; if there is competition for it, we give drawbacks."[34]

In short, this report demonstrates that immediately after the war the system of rebates and drawbacks flourished luxuriantly in Pennsylvania, yielding enormous but uneven profits to certain interests, and heavy losses to others. It shows that rebates had been counted in thousands on the Pennsylvania Railroad alone as early as 1862. It

[32]*Idem*, 44.
[33]Jules I. Bogen, *The Anthracite Railroads: A Study in American Railroad Enterprise*, 50, 51.
[34]*Pennsylvania Senate Inquiry*, 44.

indicates that railroads granted and large shippers accepted such rebates as a matter of course; that since rates were arbitrary, with no accepted business code or public authority to govern them, in sheer self-protection everybody had to get the best rate he could. The ironmaster McCormick deplored the situation, saying that he thought it would benefit both railroads and shippers "if a regular tariff were prepared, on equitable principles, over the whole State." Tom Scott and other railroad officers, though full of denials and excuses, likewise evinced a certain queasiness. But nobody indicated any expectation of early reform. Indeed, nobody knew just how reforms could be instituted. The report of the Pennsylvania committee was firm in condemning all rebates. Without heat, it pointed out that although the motives of the railroad managers were doubtless often commendable, all preferences were wrong, and as common carriers the lines had "no right to show partiality among their customers." If any preference were necessary to foster a particular branch of industry, it should be granted by the legislature. But nothing was done to effect any essential modification of law, custom, or corporate practice. The legislature, after disclosing how widespread and indeed general the rate discriminations were, allowed them to continue. As a matter of fact, the fierce competition of the transportation companies in this period of rapid growth made them unescapable, and nobody paid any attention to the Mrs. Partington reproofs of the investigators.[35]

Indeed, in dealing with the long-and-short-haul discrimination, the Pennsylvania committee stated flatly that it was not prepared to recommend legislation "which might result in driving the whole of this through trade out of the State to rival lines." That is, it *was* prepared to approve any rate discriminations which favored Pennsylvania as against New York or Maryland! And meanwhile the same attitude was being taken in other States. Some had statutes which forbade discrimination; some did not. Ohio had various rate laws, one of which, dating back to 1852, forbade any railroad to charge more than three cents a mile for carrying passengers, or five cents a ton-mile for carrying freight over distances of thirty miles or more. Beginning in 1867, it also had a Commissioner of Railroads and Telegraphs to help enforce these laws. But the Commissioner re-

[35]*Report of the Judiciary Committee of the Senate of Pennsylvania on Extortionate Charges*, 1868, 7 ff.

ported in 1870 that strict enforcement would drive some lines into bankruptcy. The maximum-fare law was "entirely disregarded." Of freight charges he remarked: "This is a more fruitful source of complaint than any other subject attempted to be regulated by statute. There is not a railroad operated in the State, either under special charter or the general law, upon which the law regulating rates is not, in some way, violated nearly every time a regular passenger, freight, or mixed train passes over it."[36]

The rebate was destined to continue flourishing until the Elkins Act of 1903, effectively enforced by President Theodore Roosevelt, extirpated it.[37] For forty years it was to be a potent and unescapable factor in American business. When Robert M. La Follette became governor of Wisconsin, he had special investigators examine the books of the railroads, and found that they had paid $7,000,000 in rebates between 1897 and 1903 in his State alone.[38] Paul Morton of the Santa Fé Railroad declared in 1903 that there was not a city of a hundred thousand people in the United States in which he could not point to one or more fortunes founded upon railway rebates. From beginning to end these multiform rebates, favoring large shippers as they did, were a powerful ally of consolidation in industry. They were one of the principal factors in promoting the growth of great American cities, and in concentrating industry in these cities in ever larger units.[39]

If rebates existed on the Pennsylvania railroads in 1862–67, we may be sure they existed on the Ohio roads. Indeed, a committee of the United States Senate declared in 1865 of the nation as a whole: "The effect of the prevailing policy of railroad managers is, by an elaborate system of secret special rates, rebates, drawbacks, and concessions, to enrich favorite shippers, and prevent free competition

[36]Annual Report, Ohio Commissioner of Railroads and Telegraphs, 1870, pp. 6–8. See the Report of the same commissioner, 1867, p. 23, for a typical instance of rate discrimination, and the justification offered by a railroad official.

[37]Officers of the Erie, New York Central and other railroads tell me that applications for rebates are still frequent, and are met by sending the applicant a brief excerpt from Federal laws on the subject. In 1939 the Pennsylvania Railroad was fined for granting certain rebates.

[38]Ray Stannard Baker, "The Railroads on Trial," *McClure's Magazine,* Vol. 26 (1926), 13; *Congressional Record,* XL, 5699 (La Follette's speech), April 23, 1906.

[39]John Burton Phillips, *Social and Industrial Effects of Railroad Ratemaking,* University of Colorado Studies, III, No. 4.

in many lines of trade." It must be remembered that the extremely rapid growth of railways between 1850 and the panic of 1873 had placed their business upon an improvised, hastily arranged, and largely experimental footing. Their managers had to grapple hastily and blindly with complex problems of financing, rate-making, and competition. Only by a process of trial and error could they learn how to regulate charges with some uniformity; and for years the freight toll-sheets had scarcely a speaking acquaintance with logic, consistency, or ethics. The public attitude toward the railroads meanwhile oscillated violently between extremes of love and hate. New and fast-growing communities needed roads so badly that they recklessly issued bonds and made other concessions to obtain them; and down to 1871 the nation itself ladled out far too generous land grants. At the same time, the discontent of the Western farmers with rates which they thought extortionately high was helping to breed the Granger movement. Railroad managers were alternately caressed and assailed, flattered and denounced.[40]

Most new industries pass through a reckless, disorderly phase; railroading was still new; and most railway managers looked strictly at the day-to-day interests of their roads. They sought in every possible way to build up freight receipts, and when two or more tapped the same territory competition was bitter. "In those days," says McPherson, "there was never enough business to satisfy all of them."[41] Hence they made whatever reductions seemed necessary to gain or hold shippers, and paid commissions to anybody through whose influence traffic could be obtained. Prominent citizens took such commissions; a class of irresponsible agents sprang up who made a living by them. The rigors of competition by rebates, secret rates, sudden cuts, and commission-granting could be moderated only by Federal law or concerted action on the part of railroad heads, and for neither was the time ripe.

As railroads grew in length, rebates increased in importance. In 1869, the New York Central, gaining full control of the Lake Shore,

[40]"The attitude of our public authorities toward the railroads has been very much like that of an injudicious parent toward a wayward child—alternately giving him liberty which he was certain to abuse, and making rules which were so strict that they could not be permanently enforced." A. T. Hadley, "American Railroad Legislation," *Harper's Magazine*, LXXV (1887), 141 ff.

[41]McPherson, *Railroad Freight Rates*.

furnished through service to Chicago; in the same year the Pennsylvania acquired the Pittsburgh, Fort Wayne & Chicago, thus offering parallel facilities; the Erie had already reached St. Louis through the Atlantic & Great Western and other connections; and the Baltimore & Ohio was extended to Chicago in 1874. The building up of these great competitive systems lifted rebating from a relatively local to a national status. Its effect upon business became nationwide and revolutionary; and in no field was it to be more revolutionary than in oil.

v

John D. Rockefeller always intimated that the competitive advantage his company obtained through rebates was negligible. "I do not think the Rockefeller firms got better rebates than the others," he said in 1917.[42] He stated that his firm's larger, more regular shipments, with other benefits which their size and efficiency conferred upon the railroads, "should have entitled them to more consideration than the smaller and less regular shippers." He pointed out that "each shipper made the best bargain that he could," and that "it isn't for a moment to be supposed that any intelligent businessman would make shipments without making an effort to get rates —such efforts as he would use, in buying goods, to make the best possible arrangements." But he commented upon the ignorance of every shipper about his comparative standing: "Whether or not he was doing better than his competitor was only a matter of conjecture."

Indeed, Rockefeller repeatedly expressed the belief that small shippers—taking the situation over long periods—obtained as good rebates as any; and that considering the advantages which the large manufacturers offered the roads, "the favored shippers were the small shippers." This was unfounded, as we shall later demonstrate. What we know of the years 1867–70 indicates that Rockefeller, Andrews & Flagler vigorously pushed their opportunities for preferential treatments, and that they secured better rebates than many of their Cleveland competitors for the simple reason that they could bargain with greater power.

But they did have other sources of strength. Rockefeller could

[42]Inglis, Conversations with Rockefeller.

justly assert later that his partners and he were better organizers, administrators, and technicians than the other Cleveland refiners. In evidence, he pointed to their careful bookkeeping; to the superior business sagacity which Flagler and he displayed; and to the undisputed primacy of Andrews as a plant-manager. Unquestionably they had ampler and better-planned facilities, commanded greater capital, and operated with more energy and precision than any other refinery in existence. With larger resources and production came increasing opportunities for economy, increasing progress in efficiency.

The cooperage plant had developed in step with the company's growth. It was in 1867 or 1868 that Rockefeller and his partners first began buying tracts of white-oak timber and seasoning part of their own staves. They bought their own hoop-iron, and installed machines for barrel-making. They thus cut the cost of the finished barrel from the $2.50–$3.50 rate usually charged to about half those figures; and the barrels, strongly hooped, tightly glued, and painted blue, were exceptionally good. In charge of the cooperage plant they placed a remarkably shrewd young veteran from one of the Cleveland regiments, Ambrose McGregor, whose father had made barrels in East Cleveland.[43] They manufactured their own sulphuric acid, and devised means for recovering it after use. The refineries by 1868 possessed a complete drayage service—twenty wagons which did the hauling cheaply, and which in slack periods were even hired out to competitors. They had their own warehouses in New York and their own lighters on the Hudson and East Rivers. They were among the first to ship by tank cars—as yet only big wooden tubs mounted in pairs on flatcars—and in this economical form of shipment kept ahead of other companies. In 1869 they owned 78 cars.

Another form of economy open to the Standard, but not to its small rivals, is indicated by the report of the Cleveland Board of Trade for 1867. This states:

The large refineries are now provided with immense reservoirs for storing both crude and refined oils until they are wanted for manufacture or for shipment. The great bulk of crude oil is now brought from the Oil Regions to our refineries in tanks, two of which are placed upon one platform car. This mode of transportation is a decided improvement upon

[43]I have had much valuable information upon Ambrose McGregor from his nephew, Mr. W. H. Kendall of Cleveland.

the old way of shipping in barrels. These tanks are estimated to contain about 82 barrels for the use of smaller works. By decision of the Commissioner of Internal Revenue refined petroleum is not taxed until drawn from the reservoirs for sale or shipping.

It is evident that a huge establishment like the Standard could draw off crude oil from tank cars direct into "immense reservoirs." But the small refiners had to draw it off into barrels.

Month by month Rockefeller, Andrews & Flagler increased their profits from by-products of petroleum. The mere volume of oil which they now handled gave them a tremendous advantage in this field. A small company would have negligible amounts of by-product material, too trifling for use. Rockefeller's refineries, on the other hand, had ample quantities for manufacture or sale. They also commanded the trained workmen, the expensive equipment, and the marketing arrangements requisite to make a profit from the residual matter left after distilling kerosene, while small companies did not. The Board of Trade report for 1867 says, apropos of the demand that had arisen by 1867 for petroleum lubricants:

The sale of "still bottoms" or residuum, as lubricating oils, soon brought all petroleum lubricators into discredit. At first all the refiners of petroleum burning oil dealt also in "lubricating oil," in order simply to make a market for their residuum. Experience, however, has proved it to be unprofitable, both to themselves and their customers. The proper preparation of lubricating oils is now made a distinct department of business, and as a result, the popularity of petroleum lubricators is rapidly increasing. The manufacture from residuum of a light colored oil, free from odor and paraffine, and when properly prepared, nearly equal to lard oil in value, but costing less than half as much, is doing much toward relieving the refiner from forcing the sale of a waste product, and the machinist from getting poor oil.

One Cleveland refiner of early days, Frank Arter, has recorded how he slipped out at night to let his gasolene, for which the market was not yet developed, run into the Cuyahoga River. The inflammable liquid was dangerous to keep about—and also dangerous to put into a navigable stream. "Tugboat men would throw overboard a shovelful of hot coals," he recalled, "to 'start a fire on the water and have some fun,' as the gasolene and offal blazed up. Many a refiner was summoned to the police court and scolded for letting out the gasolene . . . though we always had some cock-and-bull story about an accident to account for it."[44] For many years the popular name for gasolene was "gas-house naphtha," for much of what was saved was sold to gas manufacturers.[45]

Rockefeller, Andrews & Flagler never threw away gasolene, or anything else. They employed some of the residuum for fuel, and at a later date also for paving. They manufactured benzine, paraffin, and petrolatum (later called vaseline). They shipped naphtha to gas-plants and other consumers. They doubtless sold lubricating oil in 1867–68, for Rockefeller & Andrews had advertised some in 1865. But as we have seen, this was becoming a specialty; and after 1868 they apparently sold part of the materials to manufacturers who dealt solely in that product, while they traded part for kerosene which the lubricating-oil manufacturers did not want—this was their arrangement with the Backus Company in the early seventies. But whatever their precise methods of utilizing the various by-products of kerosene, they sought to make the most of them and had the reputation of doing so.

All this was part of Rockefeller's policy of ceaseless enterprise, ceaseless vigilance, ceaseless economy. He imposed his own precision and foresight upon his lieutenants and workmen. Several years later, when the Standard was buying out other firms, some competitors were amazed and wryly amused by the thoroughness of its methods. They found that nothing was guessed at, nothing left uncounted or unmeasured. The precision was a ritual, important in itself as well as in relation to profit and loss; just as discipline is a ritual in any superb army, fostered for itself as well as for winning battles. Rockefeller found men who responded to this alert spirit and who felt his own pride in it.

From this period survives a pocket memorandum book, dated "1869," which he used.[46] At first glance it seems a mere jumble of jottings, intelligible only to the writer—names, fragmentary statistics, phrases, occasionally complete sentences. Evidently he carried it with him about the works, about town, and on business trips, and later referred to it for planning and checking. But while nothing of great scope or importance can be gleaned from its pages, it suggests the temper and habits of the man. It shows that he was study-

[44]Inglis, Conversation with Frank Arter.
[45]Doctor W. M. Burton to the author, June 8, 1939.
[46]In the Rockefeller Papers.

John D. Rockefeller and William Rockefeller in youth and middle age.
The two photographs on the left are of John; the two on the right of William.

Early office buildings used by Rockefeller in Cleveland.

The upper left shows the office of Rockefeller & Andrews on the Cuyahoga River. The upper right shows the Standard Oil Building on Euclid Avenue, the second home of the Standard Oil Company. The company's offices in the early seventies were in the second floor of the building in the Cushing block shown in the lower left. The lower right shows the Case Building, in which Rockefeller, Andrews & Flagler had quarters.

ing all aspects of his business, small and large, with remarkable absorption and close attention to detail. Once more it must be emphasized that, like Wellington, he believed that genius was mastery of detail.

Some entries have value in showing the methods used by the firm. For example, we find the notation: "Tank cars in use Sepr 1/69 Doan Westlake 50 Payne 42 Shurmer 15 Scofield 30 Hanna 12 Critchely 12 Hussey 15: 216 (the total) R A & F 74 Added say Sept 20th 4." This offers some indication of the relative strength of the important Cleveland refiners. It does not necessarily measure their size, as a large firm might be content with shipments in barrels, while a small one might be energetic in using the new cars. However, it shows Rockefeller, Andrews & Flagler owning more than half again as many cars as their best-equipped rival. And of equal importance, it proves how closely Rockefeller was watching the activities of the other Cleveland refiners.

Some indication of the size of the cooperage shop is afforded by an entry of August 24, 1869: "Not over 10,000 good barrels on hand and coopers must work *more*." Another entry on barrels, undated, shows sharp attention to details and the instinct to associate these with results in the large: "Barrels in sheds cost 12 to 15¢ to repair. 6 mo storage & 6 mo Int. 10¢. Chgs to bbl houses 1⅜¢—some of the H.S. barrels were in *very bad* condition and never were fixed of any account." And again: "James says both Barrel houses on hill settling for want of foundation." Still other entries manifest a hawk-like eye for small matters. "Don't leave oil in pipes leading from tanks to stills"; 4955.84 coal Received in Septem was it all used in that mo"; "Take into account, in settlement with James, the Lumber used in making all boxes."

From various entries it is evident that the company manufactured paraffin in quantity, but apparently sold it to Samuel Downer for marketing. Downer from the first had made paraffin a specialty and possessed the advantage of an established reputation. One item reads, "Don't put Downer brand on paraffin." Another, "If Downer don't come by 28th run all paraffin (light) together." The Rockefeller was exploring steps toward still greater efficiency, and took the initiative in suggestions for manufacture, is revealed in another jotting upon paraffin: "Run one still full of the light paraffin (1st run Gregor?) why not dump some of it in the Crude Refining Tank. 13¢ paraffin is 520 say 550 for 42 crude and will probably yield 8¢ more."[47]

The total results of the operations, the broad aspects, of company policy, were always in his mind. "Aug. 1869," he notes: "How many vessels loaded this week?" This indicates a vigorous traffic by lake, and a keen concern with shipments. Again, his mind is upon supply. "Must get oil delivered faster to Oil City," he writes in an undated memorandum. "Some 60 B. G. cars only go up creek daily and 20 of these are coal and merchandise." One entry shows, though in vague fashion, that he was pondering another mode of transportation: "9000$ Pipe Line." Several jottings suggest his concern with freight rates: "Condition Erie and Central"; "Argument with Erie low prices Oils transportation."

Altogether, these varied jottings adumbrate a young Rockefeller —only thirty the summer of 1869—familiar with every corner of his organization, tireless in watching operations, and indefatigable in exploring new opportunities. They suggest also a sense of mastery, a power of command, natural in one who had risen brilliantly to large opportunities. They yield some impression of the velocity of a business fast becoming one of the most important in Cleveland. As yet most conservative manufacturers regarded refining as precarious, and many declared flatly that it had no future. Rockefeller was proving that system, method, and enterprise could divest it of speculative elements. Mary K. Tibbetts of Cleveland told long afterward of the enthusiasm he showed in his Pennsylvania journeys to obtain shipments of crude oil. He had an old suit that he took along for roughing it in the muddy fields. "When he came back he would always have great tales to tell, and his eyes would snap as he would speak of his desires to succeed."[48]

Nevertheless, the rebates were indispensable. In smooth times they added to profits. In periods of crisis they could be used against competitors, as we shall see, with absolutely crushing effect. It was the union of rebates with the advantages of economy, system, and foresight which explains the swift rise of Rockefeller's organization. Neither element can be ignored.

[47]Rockefeller spelled paraffin "paraphine."
[48]Cleveland *Plain Dealer,* July 13, 1905.

VI

Upon profits our evidence is clear, though lacking in specific detail. Rockefeller later said emphatically that they made money every year; "we made large profits from the beginning, but we kept them in the business." Various facts support this statement. In 1869 alone, $60,000 was spent on plant improvements as distinguished from expansion. *The Leader* tells us that the gross receipts of four Cleveland refineries in the three months ending September 30, 1869, were $2,433,669; and Rockefeller's was probably as large as the other three combined.[49] President Dan P. Eells of the Commercial National Bank of Cleveland sent on September 20, 1869, to the National Bank of Commerce of New York a letter which gives an illuminating appraisal of Rockefeller, Andrews & Flagler by their bankers. Eells had long taken a deep interest in the oil industry, and had been a partner in Hussey, McBride. He remarks that Rockefeller, "through all the changes of his firm . . . has kept his account in this bank"; and he pays a high tribute to his depositor.[50]

"I have never known him to equivocate or in any particular to misrepresent the facts about his business, and I do not recall a single instance in which his obligations have not been promptly met on the day they were due, or in which his paper has suffered dishonor. . . . His transactions with us have at times been very large, amounting in the aggregate to a number of millions, and we have sometimes had his paper to the amount of $250,000 at one time." Eells went on to describe the strength of the company. "The present firm employs in its business a capital of about $1,000,000, of which $360,-000 has been invested in their refinery and real estate, and the balance, say $600,000, is used by them in carrying on their business. Their indebtedness does not exceed $150,000 at the present time, and at certain seasons of the year they owe nothing and have a large surplus of funds. They have a manufacturing capacity of nearly 3000 barrels of crude oil per day."

This letter may have painted too brightly the position and prospects of the company, for Eells was anxious to have the Bank of

---

[49]Cleveland *Leader*, Oct. 22, 1869.

[50]A copy of this letter is in the Rockefeller Papers. Eells had been elected president of the Commercial National Bank on Dec. 7, 1868, after the death of the former, head, W. A. Otis. Cleveland *Leader*, Dec. 10, 1868.

Commerce assist in financing it. The daily capacity in 1869 is supposed to have been 1500 barrels of refined oil, which would have required considerably less than 3000 barrels of crude. Incidentally, the New York institution declined to serve Rockefeller, Andrews & Flagler; from Wall Street the oil industry still looked dangerous. However, Eells's letter is of value as the frank opinion of an important Clevelander, who had every opportunity to know the facts, upon the strength of the Rockefeller interests at an important point in their history. What it says of the high working capital, $600,000, and the low debt, wiped out at certain seasons, is noteworthy. It is also of significance in the emphasis it places upon Rockefeller's pre-eminent position in the organization. Eells endows the firm with all the characteristics of the "senior partner," as he terms him. The company indeed manifested a remarkable unity of spirit. Part of this spirit lay in the precision and foresight of which we have spoken. A very important part of it, not to be underrated, lay in the youthful zest and enthusiasm of the members. The two Rockefellers were young in years, energy, and spirit. Flagler and Andrews, though considerably older, were also relatively young, and their character made them share the zest and optimism of their associates.

It was Flagler who, next to John D. Rockefeller, counted for most in Cleveland. Samuel Andrews, ruddy, portly, and genial, looking more and more like the John Bull he was, attended exclusively to the technical work. "He had nothing whatever to do with the office affairs, or the oil freighting business," said Rockefeller years later in commenting on the situation, "and would not have had as much knowledge about these questions as the clerks in our office."[51] But Flagler and Rockefeller, lunching at the Union Club together, walking home together at night, agreed on every policy. The latter has recorded that they never quarrelled but once, and then "only for a moment." Rockefeller found Flagler "always an inspiration to me. He was always on the active side of every question, and to his wonderful energy is due much of the rapid progress of the company in early days." That they labored so harmoniously can be explained by the fact that Flagler, while positive and eager, was always constructive. Arguing that the firm must have faith that oil production would last and grow, he stood for the most solid and comprehensive

[51]So Mr. Rockefeller wrote in reply to a query from me in 1936.

facilities. "His courage in acting up to his beliefs," wrote Rockefeller, "laid strong foundations for later years."[52]

As we have said, some observers thought Rockefeller self-seeking and even avaricious. The truth is that he was interested most of all in power, in progress, in playing a leader's part in the great American game of business. The frame of affairs had been ready-made for him, as for most men, and in that frame his object was to distinguish himself by superlative achievement. He knew that he had great abilities, and meant to use them. It was the achievement, not the money, that counted most, and it is evident that earnest as he was, he did not take the game of business too seriously. The two Rockefellers, Flagler, and Andrews had lighthearted moments, and sometimes made an enjoyable sport of their incessant labors. "We were all boys together, having a lot of fun as we worked hard every day," said Rockefeller in 1918. He told of a code word in their telegrams —"Amelia." This, he explained, meant "Everything is lovely and the goose hangs high." The word re-creates not a little of the spirit of the firm in 1869. "We were often borrowing in those days," said Rockefeller, "and if my brother was far away and knew I was having a hard time trying to raise some money, I would cheer him up, if I succeeded, by telegraphing him the one word, 'Amelia'!"

Steady progress in the petroleum industry, so new, so violently competitive, so heavily affected by crude-oil supply, changes in market-demand, and the caprice of railroads, so much a bone of contention among Pittsburgh, the Regions, Philadelphia, New York, and Cleveland, demanded youthful optimism and courage. Rockefeller, Andrews & Flagler never lacked daring. They never looked back—always ahead. As 1870 opened, they were about to undertake the most momentous step that Rockefeller had thus far made.

[52]Rockefeller, *Random Reminiscences*, 15.
[53]Inglis, Conversations with Rockefeller.

XIII

The Birth of Standard Oil

HE years 1869–71 witnessed a series of political events in
Europe and America which have more than a symbolic
significance to students of economic history. At home
these were the first years of the Grant Administration,
conducted by a hard-jawed man who had done more than any one
save Lincoln to maintain the unity of the United States, and whose
Reconstruction policy was directed toward completing that unification. In Canada they brought the triumph of confederation and the
full emergence of the Dominion. In Europe they saw the dramatic
unification of Italy and Germany. The idea of consolidation in
political affairs was conquering the idea of separatism at the same
time that consolidation in economic affairs was creating trunk-line
railroads out of petty separate systems, centralizing much of the
meat packing in Chicago and of flour milling in Minneapolis, and
erecting ever-greater factories, banks, and insurance companies. Nor
was it a mere coincidence that sovereign states and business units
followed parallel paths. To a large extent the same forces—improvements in transportation and communication, the accumulation of
capital, the growth of a wider vision—operated in both fields.

In the petroleum industry these three years were marked by a
continuance of the general depression resulting from heavy production and falling prices; by a sudden striking transfer of leadership
in refining from Pittsburgh to Cleveland; and by the formation
of the Standard Oil Company, under Rockefeller's guidance—very
much the largest corporation the industry had yet seen. The two
latter events accomplished a veritable revolution in the fast-growing
and fast-changing manufacture of oil. It ceased to be a business in

which several centers held a fair parity, and a considerable number of refiners might claim almost equal ranking. It became an industry in which one city stalked far and away in the lead, and one huge company dominated the business of that city. These developments have a complex industrial background, and they offer some particularly interesting relations with railroad history.

II

When in 1869 oil men celebrated the tenth anniversary of Drake's discovery—Drake himself, ageing and infirm, was now in dire poverty[1]—they could boast that never in American history had an industry grown so rapidly. In 1859 the production of crude oil in the United States had been authoritatively stated at two thousand barrels; ten years later it was nearly four and a quarter million barrels, and in 1870 well over five and a half millions. The manufacture of refined oil in America naturally kept pace with these figures; for all the crude petroleum was utilized, roughly at the ratio of three gallons of kerosene for four of raw oil. Since prospecting continued with amazing success, and new and deeper wells were constantly being driven, it was certain the flow would go on increasing. At ever lower and lower prices the demand seemed insatiable. Cheap oil for the lamps of the world was in fact a crying need of civilization. Most people unthinkingly suppose that because tallow candles were a poor illuminant they must have been inexpensive. The truth is that they and whale oil alike were so costly that only well-to-do people had kept their homes lighted evening after evening, while all over the globe workingmen, peasants, farmers and clerks went to bed early to save costs. The refined oil exports of the United States almost touched 100,000,000 gallons in 1868, and in 1870 exceeded 140,000,000 gallons. This gain in quantity meant a sharp fall in prices, and the low charges were a blessing to all mankind.

But not to the oil industry. What the historian of the Oil Regions calls "the years of depression"[2] continued down to the Panic of 1873 for most producers and refiners alike. In the spring of 1868 the

---

[1]Subscriptions were being circulated in 1870–71 for his benefit, with poor results; letter of Henry Purdon, Titusville *Morning Herald*, Feb. 9, 1871.
[2]Giddens, *The Birth of the Oil Industry*, 153 ff.

Titusville *Herald* printed a list of twenty-seven bankrupt oil companies whose assets had been sold to satisfy their creditors.[3] The price of crude oil bobbed up and down as production fluctuated and dealers along the valley felt bullish or bearish; but the general tendency was toward a decline. By September, anxious well owners were discussing the formation of an association to protect their interests. This movement grew, and on February 1, 1869, when markets were reported unfavorable and prices weakening, a producers' meeting at Oil City appointed an organizing committee. Twelve days later a new gathering at Titusville formed the Petroleum Producers' Association of Pennsylvania, with George K. Anderson as president. Just what this body could do was uncertain.[4] It promptly took up arms against a proposed State tax on crude oil, it collected statistics, and it conducted patent litigation; but the real cause of the depression lay in too many wells, and this was difficult to reach.

As the year 1869 wore on conditions improved, and at its close the press reported fair profits for many producers.[5] But prices grew worse again in 1870, dropping in June to about $4 a barrel. In desperation, on the 29th of that month a new meeting of producers at Oil City resolved to stop the drill for three months, and appointed a committee to canvass the possibilities and report at the next meeting of the Petroleum Producers' Association.[6] Next day the Oil City *Derrick* printed a report which its editor has summarized in one eloquent sentence: "More wildcatting in progress than at any time since the discovery of oil." It was simply impossible to stop the drill, and the Association itself reported 152 new wells completed in August, with 288 more being bored! The flow this summer broke all records. Chiefly for this reason, though partly because of the Franco-Prussian War and other factors, prices of crude oil fell to low levels, and in December stood at $3.25 to $3.50 a barrel. Some producers, holding especially rich wells, always did well, but many

[3]Titusville *Herald,* April 29, 1868.

[4]Boyle, *Derrick's Handbook,* 102.

[5]Speculative combinations in Pittsburgh and the Oil Regions, and in particular a great end-of-the-year "bull ring," affected the prices of oil. This ring, which held up the movement of cars between Oil City and Pittsburgh, caused much hard feeling and many lawsuits. Pittsburgh *Commercial,* Jan. 31, Feb. 6, 1872.

[6]Boyle, *Derrick's Handbook,* 132.

small men were ruined whenever the market fell into a prolonged slump. Oil production was still half boom, half broke.

As Rockefeller well knew, the depression in the refining industry was more general. The basic conditions of the business had swiftly changed, and the days of broad margins, when a series of lucky strokes might make any reckless plunger rich, were gone forever. The year 1868, which witnessed a brief but severe trade recession all over the country, brought up many ill-financed refineries with a jerk. Meanwhile, a consistent long-term price trend was wiping out all chance of easy profits, so that only the largest and most efficient plants could long survive. Clear proof of this is furnished by the annual reports of the boards of trade in the principal refining cities. All tell the same story of a grimly narrowing margin between the charges that a refiner paid for crude oil and the price he received for kerosene. The figures of the Chamber of Commerce of the State of New York are typical and conclusive.[7]

Year	Price of Crude per Gallon	Price of Standard White Refined	Refiners' Margin
1865	38.37 cents	58.87 cents	19.50 cents
1866	25.78	42.45	16.67
1867	17.43	28.41	10.98
1868	19.66	29.52	9.86
1869	23.25	32.73	9.48
1870	18.45	26.35	7.90

Any one with a few stills and vats might make money when he could sell a gallon of refined oil for twenty cents more than a gallon of crude cost him; four gallons of crude oil, as we have said, making about three gallons of kerosene. But when the margin sank to ten cents a gallon, refiners with inefficient works and little capital began to scent bankruptcy. And when it fell below eight cents, weaker establishments from New York to Cleveland trembled on the precipitous edge of ruin. It was because he perceived the significance of this fast-narrowing margin that Rockefeller had strenuously strengthened his works. He had done it in the nick of time. Indeed, a future executive of the Standard Oil, Charles M. Higgins, who joined it as an

[7] *Annual Reports,* 1865–71. These contain an intelligent annual section on petroleum. In interpreting these figures it should be recalled that it took approximately one and a third barrels of crude petroleum to make a barrel of illuminant; often more.

office boy in 1872 and talked with older employees, gained the impression that the years 1867–68 had witnessed a crisis for even Rockefeller, in which the Harkness-Flagler investments had proved indispensable. Although Rockefeller declared that his firm made profits every year, there may be some truth in this; and perilous indeed was the position of little refineries which had never expanded and possessed no reserves.

The refining industry was now feeling the results of that reckless invasion by a host of ill-equipped men which the high profits of the war and immediate postwar years had naturally caused. It was not merely overgrown—it was bloated. In 1870 the capacity was three times as great as the demand warranted.[8] It was in precisely the same position as the silver-mining industry in the eighties, or the soft-coal industry in the decade after the World War. Some excess capacity was inevitable and proper, for even the best works did not expect to run at full capacity the whole year; but there was far too much. It led to frantic price-slashing by hard-pressed and panicky refiners whenever times became gloomy, and such slashes injured manufacturers, both great and small.

In refining as in production the depression had been somewhat alleviated in 1869, but next year it became more crushing than ever. This was not because of any lack of world demand. Though the Franco-Prussian War gave a temporary check to the export trade, shipments abroad for the year rose, as we have seen, very sharply. The great difficulty was that prices remained lamentably low—lower than ever before. The table above shows that the average quotation for good kerosene in New York in 1870 was less than half what it had been five years earlier, and less than four fifths what it had been the previous year. Nor was there any temporary and artificial reason to explain this. Too many wells, too many refineries, a glut in both raw and manufactured oil—that was the chief reason, and it threatened to be permanent unless some remedy were applied.

"The business of refining, taking the year altogether," stated the Chamber of Commerce of the State of New York at the close of 1870, "has been unremunerative, refiners hardly getting a new dollar

[8] See the *Reports of the Chamber of Commerce of the State of New York* and the *Cleveland Board of Trade,* 1870.

for an old one." Had it not been for the reduction in costs through large-scale operations and improved processes, it added, no refiner could have continued in business. The situation grew worse as 1871 advanced. Early that year the market was affected by a number of speculative combinations and rings formed in the Oil Regions to advance the price of crude oil. These groups raised the cost of raw materials so sharply that many Pittsburgh refineries shut down. The plight of Cleveland was even worse. The middle of March found trade practically at a standstill, with not more than one tenth of the refinery capacity in use. According to a Cleveland observer quoted in the Pittsburgh *Gazette*,[9] "this result can easily be traced to the unreasonable and unscrupulous policy of the petroleum producers. No one knew better than they that there was no demand for margin which would warrant refiners in paying the ruling price for crude; yet they would not concede in the least, but by a series of 'corners' and other gambling arrangements, have run up and held up the price of crude. . . ." Pittsburgh and Cleveland writers pointed out that while the producers had organized a strong association, the refiners possessed no such protection.

"Dull"—"dull"—"dull"—so, month after month, ran the market reports which Rockefeller scanned. Conditions had seemed tragic to small refiners when the average margin between crude and refined oil was driven below eight cents a gallon. But in 1871, according to the Chamber of Commerce of the State of New York, it fell to 6.15 cents a gallon. While high ocean freights were a factor, keeping export prices down, sheer overproduction was the main difficulty. Refineries in the Oil Regions suffered along with those in the cities. The Pittsburgh *Gazette* early in the fall published a letter from an irate Titusville manufacturer. He wrote:[10] "Refined is so low that refiners cannot run their works. Many have suspended because they cannot pay the price for crude and sell it at the price that refined has been so long. Taking present prices as a basis, refineries cannot make even cost of their stock. . . . Are they willing that the shippers shall make their 33 per cent, and they make their percentages in losses, as many refiners have been doing for the last year?"

[9]See the Cleveland *Review*, quoted in Pittsburgh *Gazette*, March 17, 1871.
[10]Pittsburgh *Gazette*, Oct. 5, 1871.

So much for the depression; but what of the sudden rise of Cleveland to primacy over her rival Pittsburgh, a development which Rockefeller watched with exultation?

III

For a few years after Drake's discovery, the Oil Regions had seemed the best place for refiners. Men there looked rejoicingly at the tanks and smokestacks of Downer, the Ludovici Brothers, and Van Syckel outlined against the green hills.[11] Then Pittsburgh had temporarily taken the lead. It was easy to ship crude oil down the Allegheny River, particularly after Jacob J. Vandergrift of Pittsburgh, owner of the steamer *Red Fox,* showed how easily a string of barges could be pulled by one boat. A branch of the Pennsylvania Railroad arched from Pittsburgh northward into the heart of the oil fields; and the Pennsylvania, as General Devereux of the rival Lake Shore Railroad bitterly remarked, long asserted a "patent right" to oil transportation. Moreover, the first main expansion of the oil fields was southward, toward Pittsburgh. In time hustling wildcatters drove their shafts close to the corporate boundary. The smoky rumbling city offered abundant labor, fuel, and chemicals. For a few years Pittsburghers surveyed the scene with lordly arrogance. We have seen that the first postwar spurt produced seventy refineries, and in 1867 a conservative count gave them fifty-eight, with a capacity of 37,000 barrels of refined oil weekly.[12] Then, to their amazement, Cleveland swiftly and surely forged ahead, until just as Rockefeller formed his Standard Oil Company in 1870, the Ohio city easily took the lead. How did this happen?

The principal reason for Pittsburgh's loss of ground lay in the gross unfairness with which the Pennsylvania began to treat the city. This railroad was just springing into greatness. Begun as a line from Harrisburg to Pittsburgh, it had not been linked with Philadelphia till the summer of 1858, when the first through train clattered between the eastern and western metropolis of the State, carrying the first smoking car ever built. J. Edgar Thomson, a quiet, determined

[11]See Titusville *Morning Herald,* April 15, 1871, for description of the Van Syckel refinery.
[12]George S. Davison, "The Petroleum Industry," *Greater Pittsburgh,* VIII, No. 48 (March 26, 1927).

builder, interested in solid, constructive achievement, built up the system until within a decade it owned nearly a thousand miles in Pennsylvania alone, and controlled a branch northward through New York to Lake Erie. Then in 1869, as his master accomplishment, he acquired the Pittsburgh, Fort Wayne & Chicago, giving the railroad a continuous line from Delaware Bay to Lake Michigan. After this acquisition, a slowly-forming indifference toward Pittsburgh interests became sharply crystallized, and the steel city definitely ceased to be a terminal and became a way station. Until 1867 the Pennsylvania management had dealt generously with Pittsburgh refiners and other manufacturers, but it now ceased to do so. Within a few years western Pennsylvania was seething with resentment against the railroad.

Why the indifference to Pittsburgh refiners? For one reason, the Pennsylvania wished to haul the main body of crude oil not a short distance to Pittsburgh, but a long distance to Philadelphia and New York. It was not the branch line running north from Pittsburgh into the Oil Regions which interested the arbitrary and ambitious Tom Scott, who was in charge of the Pennsylvania's traffic arrangements. Instead, it was the branch line running northwest from tidewater, the Philadelphia & Erie, which had opened its tracks into Oil City and Pithole in 1866. For another reason, the Pennsylvania's main line through Pittsburgh from the west had all the freight it could carry anyhow, without adding oil shipments. Officers of the road were ready to make low through rates from Chicago and other distant points at Pittsburgh's expense. For Pittsburgh had to ship east by the Pennsylvania anyway—it possessed no other adequate outlet; while the Pennsylvania had to fight with the other trunk lines for the rich grain traffic of the Mississippi Valley. This attitude created a situation from which Rockefeller and other Cleveland refiners profited enormously. For while the Pennsylvania showed a cavalier disregard for oil shipments in and out of Pittsburgh, the Erie and the New York Central-Lake Shore system did their utmost to develop the Cleveland oil traffic.

Incensed Pittsburghers, appearing before the State Senate Committee in 1867, described the readiness of the railroad to favor Mississippi Valley freights as against their own, and emphasized the growing unfairness of the line to the local oil industry. We have quoted a witness who complained that refined oil was carried as cheaply from Oil City to Philadelphia as from Pittsburgh, 114 miles nearer. This man, chairman of the railroad committee of the Pittsburgh Petroleum Association, burst out vehemently:[13] "We complain that they rob us of our natural position, and that those at Cleveland get their oil carried cheaper than we do." In August, 1867, he declared, refined oil shipments from Pittsburgh had reached 88,000 barrels. "At that time the Pennsylvania Railroad lowered their rate to about the proportion it should be, compared with other roads. The other roads immediately lowered their rates, and the Pennsylvania Central remained the same, and the great proportion of the works in Pittsburgh had to shut down. Our route was relatively the longest route to the seaboard." These August shipments were much the greatest in Pittsburgh history, not more than 50,000 barrels having been shipped in any other month. He added: "Our great trouble has been that they take it [oil] from Oil City to Philadelphia or New York as cheap as from here. If they had carried at the same rate per mile, or even one-half as cheap as half the other roads, we could have run and done a business."

Another Pittsburgh witness, H. M. Long, offered a still more resentful comparison between his city as Cinderella and Cleveland as the favored princess. His establishment brought crude oil from Oil City, refined it, and shipped the product to Philadelphia:[14] "Our principal trouble," he said, "has been the rate established by the Pennsylvania Railroad during the last year. The rate from Cleveland, our chief competitor, to New York, was 45 cents per hundredweight, whilst on the Pennsylvania Railroad, from here to Philadelphia, was 50 cents per hundredweight. . . . It is evident that the advantage against us has driven trade from Pittsburgh to a great extent. Oil was cheaper in Cleveland than we can make it here and ship it to Philadelphia, thus cutting off one third to one half the business in Pittsburgh. . . . I believe Pittsburgh could make and ship 100,000 barrels every month in the year. By the course the railroad pursues, we cannot ship more than half that amount." And he added: "An officer of the road said to one of our committee that they didn't care whether they carried any oil from Oil City [to Pittsburgh]; they preferred carrying it over the Philadelphia & Erie."

[13]*Pennsylvania Senate Committee Hearing,* 166, 167. [14]*Ibid.,* 167, 168.

Indeed, for an entire generation after the Civil War Pittsburgh was treated with outrageous insolence by the Pennsylvania Railroad, secure in its monopolistic position. Though the city grew into a tremendous creator of freight, its other industries suffered nearly or quite as much as the oil refiners. Flour manufacturers actually loaded their product on boats, sent it to Cincinnati, a "competitive point," reloaded it on freight trains, and sent it to New York through Pittsburgh again. Steel was treated as harshly. Midway in the nineties the Carnegie interests became so enraged by the Pennsylvania's overcharges that they commenced building a railroad of their own to seaboard.[15] A State investigation after the violent railroad strike of 1877 showed that the Pennsylvania had kept many thousands of workmen unemployed and half-starving in Pittsburgh by maintaining freight rates, without real justification, at levels which made it impossible to operate the glass, steel, and other industries for the export trade.

By 1870 both New York and Pittsburgh were complaining that Cleveland had captured the lion's share of the refining business. Cleveland listened to their outcries with complacent exultation. In November, 1869, *The Leader* gaily reprinted certain charges by the Pittsburgh *Dispatch*. This newspaper grumbled that although Cleveland was decidedly farther from Oil City than Pittsburgh was, it paid only the same freight charges on crude oil; it paid no transshipment charges, as Pittsburgh did to get oil across the river; and it actually shipped refined oil to the seaboard for ten cents a barrel less than Pittsburgh. Furthermore, Cleveland was permitted by the New York Central and Erie systems to use 43-gallon barrels for crude oil, while the Pennsylvania restricted Pittsburgh to 42-gallon barrels. Altogether, lamented *The Dispatch,* Cleveland held a clear advantage of forty cents a barrel. "All of which is true as gospel," gleefully exclaimed *The Leader*. "And to this may be added the fact that its [Cleveland's] oil is shipped from this port direct to England, which is the great mart for petroleum, without the expense of railroad freights to the seaboard. Considering all these advantages, it appears demonstrated beyond all possible doubt that Cleveland far excels Pittsburgh as a point for oil refining!"

In similar fashion, *The Leader* on October 27, 1870, quoted a com-

[15]Burton J. Hendrick, *Life of Andrew Carnegie*, II, 24–33.

plaint of the New York *Commercial Bulletin* that Cleveland, by playing one railroad against another, received "special rates"; and that these enabled her, in spite of being one hundred and fifty miles west of the Regions, to "control the prices of oil in the New York markets" and "seriously threaten the permanence of the refining business in that city." Again *The Leader* enthusiastically agreed. "From this it is found that Cleveland conquers by the very magnitude of her operations. The enormous daily shipments made in oil to and from this city enable the Cleveland dealers to secure such advantageous rates of freight that they easily distance the limited operators of New York, even with the disadvantage of three hundred miles further transportation."

These newspaper statements are corroborated by the annual volumes of the Cleveland Board of Trade. The report for 1869 jubilantly asserted that the city that year received more than 1,120,000 barrels of crude oil, and shipped about 925 barrels of refined; thus clearly outdistancing Pittsburgh, which stood in second place. "Cleveland now holds the leading position among the manufacturers of Petroleum," boasted the Board of Trade, "with a very reasonable prospect of holding that rank for some time to come. Each year has seen greater consolidation of capital, greater energy and success in prosecuting the business, and, notwithstanding some disastrous fires, a stronger determination to establish an immovable reputation for the quantity and quality of this most important product. The total capital invested in this business is not less than four millions of dollars, and the total product of the year would not fall short of fifteen millions." The report went on:

The facilities for shipping Petroleum by Lake and by Rail have been largely increased and systematized. Extensive docks, with sheds to protect the barrels, have been built upon the River, while the Lake Shore and Columbus Railroads have built a large and substantial depot where all oil to be forwarded by these roads is received, stored, and shipped. From 40,000 to 50,000 barrels of oil were shipped monthly from this depot, while the River docks furnished full cargoes to the vessels intended for Atlantic ports or for Europe, by way of the Welland Canal. Of course fifteen millions of dollars, the estimated value of manufactured petroleum, is but a part of the real value of this branch of business. Some 800,000 barrels were needed, and for them a vast amount of staves, increasing yearly, until thirty millions were reecived with hoops and heading in proportion, and hoop iron not less than 4000 tons. A very large number of workmen were directly or indirectly employed in the petroleum business.

Rockefeller helped supply statistics to the Board of Trade. The census of 1870 seems at first blush at variance with these assertions, for its figures credit Pittsburgh (Allegheny County) with twenty refineries employing 330 men and manufacturing $6,950,000 worth of "refined coal oil," while they give Cleveland (Cuyahoga County) only sixteen refineries, employing 209 men, and manufacturing $4,283,000 worth of oil. But the census of manufactures was scandalously inadequate, as Director Francis A. Walker himself pointed out, and but little reliance can be placed upon it. Moreover, it referred principally to 1869 (the year June 1, 1869 to May 31, 1870), and by the close of 1870 the situation had materially altered. Cleveland actually had nearly twice the sixteen refineries credited to it. The census credited Philadelphia with only fifteen refineries and a "coal oil" production worth but $1,404,000, and New York (Kings and Queens Counties) with only nine refineries and a production of $2,090,000. It gave the Oil Regions (Crawford and Venango Counties) a total of thirty-two refineries, but most of them were very small; they employed 243 men, and their product was worth $5,349,-000.[16] The fact was that Cleveland stood first in 1870, with Pittsburgh rather uneasily leading the Regions for second place.

So much for the basic elements of the situation: the rapid growth of the refining industry as a whole, overproduction and overcompetition, fast-dropping prices, the rise first of Pittsburgh to primacy over the Oil Regions and then of Cleveland to ascendancy over Pittsburgh. Rockefeller realized that kerosene manufacturing was becoming an industry in which only large establishments had any certainty of survival. The year 1869 was the last in which a firm of poor facilities and inadequate capital reserves stood even a gambler's chance of making money. This was because prices rose slightly. "More money has been made from petroleum during the past year," declared

[16]The Census Report clearly omitted a large number of refineries in both Cleveland and Pittsburgh; sixteen and twenty are absurdly low numbers. According to J. T. Henry, *The Early and Later History of Petroleum* (1873), in 1872 the refining capacity of Cleveland was 12,732 barrels; of New York, 9790; of the Oil Regions, 9231; of Pittsburgh, 6090; of Philadelphia, 2061; Baltimore, 1098; Boston, 3500; Erie, 1168, and other points 901.

The Leader in retrospect, "than during any year when excitement was keenest." But the clouds thickened again in 1870–71, and only extensive works like Rockefeller's could make a real profit. Such establishments could wait until prices were low to buy their crude; could hold the refined oil till prices were high; could make use of new devices like the cylinder refining still patented in 1866, improved tank cars and better loading methods; and could manufacture their own supplies.

IV

By 1870 the time had come for Rockefeller and his partners to embark on broader seas. Revenues for the previous year had been large; the credit of the firm was second to none in Cleveland; and its prospects were brighter than those of any other refining organization in the country. Scouring Manhattan from his Pearl Street office, William Rockefeller was selling large quantities of oil in New England and to European buyers. Men who had learned something of the profits of Rockefeller, Andrews & Flagler were anxious to participate in the business. One was William's brother-in-law, O. B. Jennings of New York. Another was Benjamin Brewster, a comparatively young man with an adventurous record; he had gone to California in 1849, remained there until after the Civil War, then entered railroading, and had become vice-president of the Omaha Railroad.[17] He possessed Cleveland connections. "These men had money," writes Rockefeller, "and we soon found ourselves able to raise a million dollars as more money was needed." But Rockefeller did not wish to add partners in a random, careless way which might jeopardize his and Flagler's control. He resolved to replace the firm of Rockefeller, Andrews & Flagler with a joint-stock corporation.

Such corporations, though by this time important in manufacturing as well as banking and transportation, were still less numerous than partnerships, and in many communities were sufficiently a novelty to be objects of suspicion. Their enemies charged that they gave a few men control of such large bodies of capital that they constituted a long step toward monopoly. A more rational accusation was that the directors of corporations founded upon a wide distribution of

[17]House Trust Investigation, Fiftieth Congress, 1st Session, No. 3112, p. 365.

stock were more irresponsible and heartless than the old-fashioned firms of a few members. In 1863 a large shareholder in textile enterprises in Lowell, Mass., had published a furious exposé of stock manipulators. He declared that a small clique of New England financiers had gained control of numerous corporations in that district; that they had collected proxies from the general body of ignorant or careless stockholders; that then, holding the annual company meetings in small rooms, they pushed through their machine programs without discussion; and that twelve or fifteen rich Yankees, who thus dominated numerous businesses, manipulated their securities shamelessly, and gave high salaries and fat contracts to insiders. While other men had to behave themselves, he wrote, "only the managers of our Manufacturing Corporations can outrage right and common decency." The history of the Erie Railroad under Drew and Gould, of the Crédit Mobilier under Oakes Ames, of the Freedmen's Savings Bank, and of various other concerns in the Grant period showed how villainously large corporations might be perverted or exploited. Meanwhile, the oil-producing industry, like Western mining, was honeycombed with a special kind of corporate dishonesty—with fly-by-night companies selling vast quantities of worthless stock to gullible people.

But the corporation which Rockefeller planned late in 1869, however fiercely it was to be assailed in future years as a grasping monopoly, was never once to be charged with unfairness toward investors. The small group which controlled it, in which Rockefeller always stood paramount, was destined to act with a resolute and single-minded attention to the benefit of stockholders. This group did not intend to sell shares to the general public, and never contemplated for an instant the stock-manipulating methods of Jay Gould or stock-watering devices of the elder Morgan. Incorporation was planned to facilitate the entrance of new capital as desired, and at the same time maintain the two Rockefellers and Flagler as controlling heads.

The change took place January 10, 1870. On that day the Standard Oil Company of Ohio replaced Rockefeller, Andrews & Flagler. The corporation name was taken from the Standard Works which the Rockefellers had erected near the older plant in 1866. A few days later the directors elected John D. Rockefeller president, William

The Standard Oil Company

Know all men by these presents that we John D Rockefeller, Henry M Flagler, Samuel Andrews and Stephen V Harkness of Cleveland Cuyahoga County Ohio, and William Rockefeller of the City County and State of New York have associated ourselves together under the provisions of the Act of the Legislature of the State of Ohio entitled an Act to provide for the creation and regulation of incorporated Companies in the State of Ohio passed May 1st 1852 and the Acts Supplementary thereto passed April 8th 1856 and the Act to amend the last named Act passed February 14th 1861 and other Laws of the State of Ohio applicable thereto for the purpose of forming a body corporate for manufacturing Petroleum and dealing in Petroleum and its products under the corporate name of The Standard Oil Company —

And we do certify that the purpose for which said body corporate is formed is the manufacture of Petroleum and to deal in Petroleum and its products —

That the Capital Stock necessary for said Company and the amount agreed on as comprising the Capital Stock is the Sum of One million Dollars —

That the amount of each Share of Capital Stock is One hundred Dollars —

That the name of the place where said Manufacturing establishment shall be located for doing business is Cleveland City Cuyahoga County State of Ohio

(over)

Facsimile of the Articles of Incorporation

That the name and Style by which said Manufacturing establishment shall be known is The Standard Oil Company

Cleveland Ohio January 10th 1870

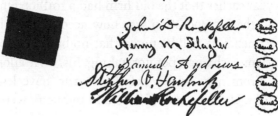

John D Rockefeller   (Seal)
Henry M Flagler   (Seal)
Samuel Andrews   (Seal)
Stephen V Harkness   (Seal)
William Rockefeller   (Seal)

The State of Ohio
Cuyahoga County ss }

At Cleveland in said county this 10th day of January 1870 personally appeared before me the undersigned a Justice of the Peace in and for said county John D Rockefeller Henry M Flagler Samuel Andrews Stephen V Harkness and William Rockefeller Signers and Sealers of the foregoing instrument and acknowledged the Signing Sealing and execution thereof to be their free act and deed —

In witness Whereof I have hereunto set my name officially at Cleveland in said County this 10th day of January A D 1870

Fred'k A. Brand
Justice of the Peace

The State of Ohio,
Cuyahoga County, ss.

I, FREDERICK S. SMITH, Clerk of the Court of Common Pleas, a Court of Record, of Cuyahoga County, aforesaid, do hereby certify that Fred'k A. Brand before whom the annexed Acknowledgement was taken, was, at its date, a Justice of the Peace, in and for said County, duly authorized by the laws of Ohio to take the same, and that I am well acquainted with his handwriting, and believe his signature thereto is genuine.

In Testimony Whereof, I hereunto subscribe my name and affix the seal of said Court at Cleveland, this 10th day of January A. D. 1870

Frederick S. Smith, Clerk.

Deputy Clerk.

of the Standard Oil, 1870

Rockefeller vice-president, Flagler secretary, and Andrews superintendent.[18] The capital was $1,000,000, divided into ten thousand shares of $100 each. This was clearly much less than the assets and working funds. President Eells of the Commercial National Bank had stated a year earlier that the old firm had a million employed in its business; and the incorporation was now accompanied by substantial new investments. It will be noted that no banking house assisted in the flotation, each incorporator taking his own allotment and paying for it. From now on Rockefeller was to have less and less to do with banks. Unnecessary expense and publicity were, as always thereafter, avoided.

In this new corporation John D. Rockefeller took 2667 shares, representing not only his old part in the business, but a new investment. Stephen V. Harkness subscribed for 1334 shares, worth at par almost twice his supposed original investment. Flagler, Andrews, and William Rockefeller took 1,333 shares apiece, and the firm of Rockefeller, Andrews & Flagler 1000 shares.[19] Thus the little group of three active partners and one silent partner which had owned the old business held nine tenths of the stock in the new corporation. The remaining one tenth, or 1000 shares, was taken by the before-mentioned O. B. Jennings. Property owned by Rockefeller, Andrews & Flagler was estimated at $400,000; good will and operating capital made up the remainder. But, as we have said, $1,000,000 represented a decided undervaluation of the holdings, tangible and intangible, of the Standard Oil Company. It held (according to John D. Archbold's subsequent estimate) one tenth of the petroleum business of the country. It owned sixty acres in Cleveland, two great refineries, a huge barrel-making plant, lake facilities, a fleet of tank cars, sidings and warehouses in the Oil Regions, timberlands for staves, warehouses and tanks in the New York area, and lighters in New York harbor.

However, the most important feature of the change was the new form which it gave the Rockefeller-Flagler interests, making for both greater flexibility and greater expansibility. Unquestionably this form had been carefully considered by the partners in relation to a definite

[18]Cleveland *Leader,* Jan. 18, 1870.

[19]Walter F. Taylor, MS History of the Standard Oil Company, 13. Mr. Taylor's history was based on the minute book of the Standard Oil Company and on legal records, and was carefully scanned by John D. Rockefeller and others prominent in the organization.

program; for their acts soon proved that the corporation had been launched with specific ends in view.

As for Rockefeller, he passed with this new organization from leadership in a local partnership to leadership in a great corporation destined within fifteen years to achieve almost complete control of one of the major industries of America, and to throw a network of marketing agencies around the globe. The expansion which he had begun when he brought William Rockefeller, Flagler, and Harkness to his side was to be carried forward by a series of headlong strides. The story of these bold steps is of absorbing interest. To be sure, his creation of the Standard Oil Company does not mean that he clearly foresaw its future. "None of us ever dreamed of the magnitude of what proved to be the later expansion," he said forty years later.[20] And later still, in a musing mood: "Who would ever have thought that it would grow to such a size!"[21] But he knew that the company had potentialities of expansion limited only by the petroleum industry itself, and as he pondered upon the difficulties and losses caused by excessive competition, he meant to make the most of these possibilities.

v

The most exigent problem facing the Standard Oil Company was not one of supplies, processes, or markets—those had all been solved; it was the company's relation with the railroads. That relation was sufficient, in the chaotic and unregulated rate situation of the day, to make or break any company. It had been a source of constant worry to Rockefeller and Flagler ever since the latter made his rebating arrangements in 1867.

That Rockefeller himself gave personal attention to the subject we know from one of his few surviving letters of this period, written to his wife under date of April 19, 1868. He was in New York with Will. "We were sent for by Mr. Vanderbilt yesterday at twelve o'clock," he related,[22] "but did not go. He is anxious to get our business & said he thought he could meet us on the terms. We send our Card by the messenger, that Van might know where to find our offices, & later in the day, at the St. Nicholas, saw the card in the hand of Amasa Stone,

---

[20]Inglis, *Conversations with Rockefeller.*
[21]Mr. Harold V. Milligan to the author, May 11, 1937.
[22]*Rockefeller Papers.*

Jr., who is figuring with Van for the business. I made a proposition to draw 100,000 barrels & Mr. Stone desired to meet with Van last eve at Manhattan Club rooms & Will engaged to meet them at 9 o'clock. We talked *business* to Amasa & guess he thinks we are rather prompt young men." Both the independent spirit of young John D. Rockefeller, who made the great Commodore Vanderbilt come to him, and the importance of the traffic he was able to deliver, are evident from this passage. Amasa Stone, Jr., was the son of the railroad builder and banker who this year became president of the Lake Shore. The revenue from 100,000 barrels of freight meant much to the Lake Shore-New York Central system.

In 1869 a furious rate war had broken out among the trunk-line railroads connecting the Atlantic Coast and the Middle West. The three great systems, the Erie, the New York Central, and the Pennsylvania, began fighting over Western trade like three lions over a kill. Late that summer, rates on shipments from Chicago to New York dropped to preposterously low levels. This rate war promptly involved the rich oil freights of western Pennsylvania as well as the agricultural products of the prairie States; for all three lines kept an anxious eye upon their feeders reaching into the heart of the Oil Regions. General Devereux later termed the contest one of the most desperate he had ever seen. "Such rates and arrangements were made by the Pennsylvania Railroad," he swore,[23] "that it was publicly proclaimed in the public prints of Oil City, Titusville, and other places that Cleveland was to be wiped out as a refining center as with a sponge." Refining was to be restricted to points served by the Pennsylvania. Already numerous refiners in the Oil Regions hated Cleveland for its rapid progress. They thought of it, far outside the State boundaries, as somehow having less title to an oil business than the Regions, Pittsburgh, or Philadelphia; and along with many members of the Petroleum Producers' Association, they were eager to push the sponge—to destroy the Cleveland industry.

Most Cleveland refiners were temporarily panic-stricken. They rushed to the Lake Shore offices, and doubtless also to the Atlantic & Great Western; they talked of giving up business forthwith, or removing to points in the Oil Regions. This was largely a bluff to win

[23]Affidavit, Standard Oil Company vs. William C. Scofield and Others, Court of Common Pleas, Cuyahoga County, Ohio.

rate concessions. But Alexander, Scofield & Co. did establish a branch refinery at Petroleum Center. Rockefeller, Andrews & Flagler alone kept a stiff upper lip—or so Devereux averred. Obtaining the Lake Shore's pledge that it "could and would handle oil as cheaply as the Pennsylvania," they promptly "proposed to stand their ground at Cleveland and fight it out on that line." Naturally the Lake Shore was determined to keep its oil traffic, and met the Pennsylvania with such rates for all Cleveland refineries that they felt encouraged to hold fast.

Then in 1870 a new and fiercer rate conflict opened between the Erie, New York Central, and Pennsylvania. Commodore Vanderbilt and a party visited Ohio in May to explore the possibilities of a new through connection for the New York Central between Cleveland and Cincinnati, while groups of directors for two other railroads toured the West. New timetables that month revealed a spectacular competition in speed, both the Pennsylvania and New York Central running thirty-hour expresses between New York and Chicago. In mid-June the struggle between Gould and Vanderbilt over freights brought charges down by one half to three fourths. A very pleasant controversy for the people of the West, exclaimed the Cleveland *Leader*. "It is truly a noble and Christian form of revenge, and even the sires of the Central Stock Ring and the Erie Opera may be forgiven if the two roads will keep on doing this sort of thing indefinitely." When the Erie slashed its rates on livestock from Buffalo to New York, Vanderbilt replied by cutting his charge to a dollar a car! On learning this the redoubtable "Jim" Fisk embarked heavily in the livestock trade, buying whole yards full of cattle, shipping them over the Central to New York, and selling them at a handsome profit. It was said that Vanderbilt "swore horribly" when he heard of this stratagem. For a time, as *The Railroad Gazette* commented, the corporations seemed bent on utterly ruining each other.[24]

And while the summer days of 1870 thus found the trunk lines fighting for the grain trade and oil trade, Rockefeller and all other refiners were hard pressed by falling prices, their margins even lower than in 1868. It was a season of general belt-tightening. The threat of the Pennsylvania and its Oil Regions allies to erase Cleveland as with a sponge still stood. Every manufacturer was reaching for what-

[24]*Commercial and Financial Chronicle*, XI (1870), 236, 273.

ever advantages he could get. Rockefeller and Flagler, with the increased facilities of their new million-dollar company, were in a stronger position than any competitor. This was the year in which shipments of crude oil to Cleveland made their astounding growth from roughly one and a quarter million barrels to roughly two million barrels, a leap for which the Standard was largely responsible. Soon after the incorporation of Standard Oil, Rockefeller and Flagler determined to ask for better rates.

Flagler went to Devereux with a proposal which had almost revolutionary implications. He informed the Lake Shore that the Standard Oil would guarantee steady shipments the year around. In the five warm months Rockefeller, Andrews & Flagler had made considerable use of the lake and canal,[25] but now they were willing to restrict their summer shipments to the railroads; and they were also prepared to ship in astounding quantities. "You want both regular trade and a large volume," said Flagler in effect. "We will give you both. We will guarantee shipment by rail throughout the year, and will send sixty carloads of oil every day whether business is good or bad." In return the Standard asked for a heavy rebate.

All Cleveland refiners at this time paid a freight charge of forty cents a barrel on crude oil from the Regions; but most of the larger firms—and probably all—received some rebate or drawback from the official rate of $2 a barrel from Cleveland to New York. Two besides the Standard Oil later admitted taking such rebates, in terms indicating that the practice was general though secret. Flagler now asked for a total two-way rate of $1.65 instead of $2.40—35 cents on crude oil to Cleveland and $1.30 on refined oil to the seaboard. At least Devereux subsequently testified under oath that this was what he asked. Other refiners asserted that what Flagler proposed and got was a two-way rate of $1.15—25 cents on crude oil, and 90 cents on refined; but they were disposed to exaggerate the Standard's advantages.[26]

Devereux found that Flagler's proposed contract would be profit-

[25]"Formerly we shipped by lake and canal," said Rockefeller in 1917. "We had the capital and could do that. The others had not the capital and could not let the oil remain so long in transit by lake and canal; it took twice as long that way—I should think you might use the general statement that it would take a great deal longer, much longer." Inglis, Notes.

[26]Affidavit, The Standard Oil Company vs. William C. Scofield and Others, Court of Common Pleas, Cuyahoga County, Ohio.

able to the Lake Shore. He later explained that until then, the average round trip for cars from Cleveland to New York had taken thirty days; and that to move an average of sixty carloads of oil daily would therefore have required 1800 cars if shipments were irregularly mixed with other freight cars, as had been the practice. But with absolutely regular and uniform shipments every day the round trip could be made in ten days, and the number of cars required would be only 600. This would demand an investment of only $300,000 in rolling-stock, as against an investment of $900,000 for 1800 cars. The Lake Shore thus stood to save the interest on $600,000, together with handling costs, repair costs, and depreciation costs on 1200 cars, by the factors of quantity and regularity. Devereux concluded that Flagler's proposal "offered to the railroad company a larger measure of profit than could or would come from any business to be carried on under the old arrangements. . . . The proposition of Mr. Flagler was therefore accepted, and in the affiant's judgment this was the turning point which secured to Cleveland a considerable portion of the export traffic." He added that the Lake Shore's expectations of larger profits were pre-eminently justified.[27] Doubtless *The Leader* was aware of this general arrangement when it boasted this fall that Cleveland "conquers by the very magnitude of her operations."

No sooner did competitors of the Standard Oil in Cleveland hear rumors of this coup than they hurried to the Lake Shore to demand similar concessions. George O. Baslington of the new refining firm of Hanna, Baslington & Co. (headed by Mark Hanna's brother, Howard M. Hanna) later testified that Devereux was polite but firm. He smilingly promised to give precisely the same rebate to any other firm that could ship the same quantity. Discontent, apprehension, and resentment filled the breasts of the Standard's rivals in Cleveland.[28]

Though, as General Devereux told the story, the Standard Oil applied for the new rates and worked out the new plan of shipment, it is altogether likely the Lake Shore took more than a receptive attitude —that it invited proposals. Most treatments of oil rebates have emphasized the Standard's ability to play the Erie against the Lake Shore, and vice versa. It is true that it could and did use this advan-

[27]*Ibid.*

[28]But Devereux testified that when he explained the reasons for the large rebate, both Hanna and Baslington "recognized its propriety."

tage. But it is evident that a still more important factor lay in the eagerness of both the Lake Shore and the Erie to obtain an advantage over their great rival to the southward, the Pennsylvania. They regarded the Cleveland refiners as allies in this, just as the Pennsylvania regarded the Oil Regions and Philadelphia refiners as allies; they were anxious to develop manufacturing in Cleveland, just as the Pennsylvania was anxious to develop it in the Regions and on the Delaware. There can be no question that the Pennsylvania gave rebates to its favored refineries, some directly, and some through its affiliated fast-freight line, the Empire Transportation Company. It was a struggle of giants, this railroad battle; a struggle not only of system against system, but of city against city and section against section. The Standard Oil and the other Cleveland refineries which obtained rebates from the two "northern" trunk lines were not taskmasters making harsh exactions. The Erie and Lake Shore looked upon them rather as associates and co-workers, and we may be sure that Vanderbilt and Amasa Stone regarded Devereux's contract with deep satisfaction.

The report of the Cleveland Board of Trade for 1870 offered a clear indication of this tacit partnership between refiners and carriers. It remarked:

The Petroleum business has continued to increase, and has become better organized and much enlarged in capacity and conveniences for receiving and handling the crude material. In addition to the receipts by the Atlantic & Great Western Railway, heretofore and still the chief source of supply, the Lake Shore Railway has opened a connection with the Oil Regions of Pennsylvania by which a large supply is being obtained to meet the ever-increasing demand. Great improvements have been made in the manner of carrying and transferring and storing crude oil. Extensive arrangements have been made to supply Refiners with the different qualities of oil they need. The consolidation of capital and the erection of larger and safer reservoirs, as well as the improvements in manufacture suggested by experience and stimulated by competition and success have established the Petroleum business upon a safe basis and made it one of the leading branches of manufacture.

The receipts of crude oil from all sources for the year have been over two millions of barrels, showing an increase of 878,000 barrels over 1869. The great bulk of the refined oil was disposed of in this country and Europe. Nearly one and a half million of barrels were shipped; by lake, 75,000 barrels; by rail, 1,388,000; by canal, 600.

VI

And what, once more, of the ethics of this rebating? It favored one city against another, and Pittsburghers denounced it as deeply immoral; it favored one manufacturer against another, and we may be sure that Rockefeller's Cleveland rivals, though themselves rebate-takers when possible, regarded it as wicked. But it was what Rockefeller termed "the railroads' way of doing business," and general sentiment was slow to crystallize on the subject.[29]

The public, as we have said, regarded railroads with mixed feelings. It was pleased by their rapid growth (much too rapid between the Civil War and the panic), and the rapid consolidation of many small lines into grandiose systems. "One fact must be accepted to begin with," wrote Charles Francis Adams, Jr., in 1871, "the railroad system has burst through the State limits. . . . Capital does not recognize the territorial divisions of a common country; nominally it may evade them, but practically it destroys them." Even while New Yorkers denounced Jay Gould's and Cornelius Vanderbilt's practices, they took pride in the huge physical properties which these men tied together. Americans in general were proud of locomotives swinging thousands of miles across the continent; of through trains running from Boston to Chicago, from Omaha to San Francisco; of sleeping-cars finished in oak and walnut, with velvet seats and ceilings frescoed in gold and green; of patent brakes and steel rails. When in 1868 the Baltimore & Ohio united a series of roads under one management, providing a through highway from New York to Washington and the Ohio River cities, the Philadelphia *Public Ledger* hailed its achievement as "long needed." The public was tired of changing cars and of rebilling freight over half a dozen roads; and it praised the men who, though sometimes careless of the means, built up mighty unifications. If this meant concentrated economic power, let the power come.

Yet at precisely the same time there arose in the land a frantic protest against railroad abuses. This era of growth and enthusiasm

[29]"There was a great demoralization of freight traffic," said Rockefeller in 1917. "It is hard for anyone to look back from this day and get a clear picture of how great that demoralization was, with the trunk lines bidding against one another, and all the shippers trying to get the most advantageous rates." Inglis, Conversations with Rockefeller.

was also an era of grievances, criticism, and stern legislative curbs. Construction itself was often accompanied by blackmail; lines projected from city to city would demand heavy tribute from every intervening town, threatening to pass around any that refused to subscribe. The exceptional town that refused to pay was ruthlessly starved while its rivals flourished. Promoters lined their pockets, again, at the expense of investors. They used predatory construction companies like the Crédit Mobilier; they watered stock shamelessly and then hoisted their charges to pay dividends; or they followed Drew and Gould in manipulating railroad credit for Wall Street speculation. Railway corruptionists, waxing impudent at the State capitals and in Washington, and poisoning even the courts of justice, aroused widespread indignation. Above all, outcries arose regarding the rates. Shippers complained that charges were too high; still more vehemently, they complained that they were discriminatory. It is sometimes stated that railroad managers become conscious of their formidable power to make or ruin men, industries, and cities, and levied tribute accordingly.[30] But it would be truer to say that most of the discriminations grew out of a fierce struggle for freights.

The result of all this conflict of feeling and interest was that while railroad regulation made its entry into American government at the beginning of the seventies, it was an uneven, confused, and halting entry; some States acting energetically while others did nothing, and the national government stood inert. Massachusetts led the way to State supervision by her act of 1869 establishing a commission. This body, of which Charles Francis Adams, Jr., was the first chairman, was given broad powers of investigation and recommendation, but was left to depend upon public opinion for the enforcement of its findings. It was simply a lens by which the otherwise scattered rays of public sentiment could be brought to a focus. The Northwest showed a more militant spirit. In that region many charges were clearly exorbitant; the agricultural interest rightly looked upon moderate and uniform rates as a matter of life and death; and after the Grange began its swift growth in 1867, the farmers gradually gained control of many legislatures. Illinois and Minnesota passed the first "Granger Laws" in 1871. By this legislation they boldly fixed

[30]See the editorial of the N. Y. *Nation,* April 6, 1871, on the revolt of the merchants against the tyranny of the railroads.

maximum freight rates and passenger fares, and forbade discriminations; while Illinois also established a commission to supervise the
railroads and to assist in enforcing the laws for their regulation. The
demand for similar "Granger" laws spread like a prairie fire from the
Wabash to the Rockies. Within a few years drastic statutes had been
put on the statute books of Iowa, Wisconsin, Missouri, Kansas, and
Nebraska, those of Iowa and Wisconsin being particularly detailed
and severe in their prescription of rates. Cases contesting these laws
were soon brought up to the Supreme Court, which in 1876 fully upheld the right of the States to regulate railroads or any other business
affected with a public interest.

Though no Eastern State save Massachusetts as yet took action, the
existing railroad rate practices in many came under a withering fire.
Five hundred New York merchants signed a petition against the
Hudson River roads on March 27, 1871, protesting that rates were
oppressively high, that they were irregular and discriminatory, and
that as soon as canal competition ceased in winter the "exactions"
promptly mounted. Though Ohio passed no "Granger" law, its legislature in the spring of 1872 made pro-rata charges on freights man-
datory within the State—a blow at discriminations and high local
charges. The long-and-short-haul discrimination in particular seemed
outrageously unjust to nearly all second- and third-class cities on
through routes. Cleveland, Pittsburgh, and Cincinnati complained
that their freight rates to San Francisco were higher than New York's.
They even asserted that they could ship to San Francisco by way of
New York and save money! On the other hand, cities like Buffalo and
Rochester complained that farm products and even manufactures
shipped from Chicago on through trains could reach the seaboard
more cheaply than their own goods. They complained also of high
local rates. "The West has the benefit of low charges, while the East
suffers," grumbled the New York *Commercial Advertiser* on March
2, 1871. "The West is built up at our expense."

The idea that railways and warehouses were affected with a public
interest and hence subject to regulation was widely asserted years before the Supreme Court upheld it in Munn vs. Illinois and Peik vs.
Chicago & Northwestern. It was adopted in conservative as well as
radical circles. Even railroad stockholders often supported it, for it
gave them a certain sense of security in their investments. The New

York *Commercial Advertiser,* a journal highly friendly to business, remarked in October, 1869: "Railroad corporations sought franchises from the State on the ground that the railroad was a public highway. On this ground they exercised the right of 'eminent domain.' Now, having used their public charter as a means of gaining a privilege, they begin to claim that they are private corporations, and, as such, exempt from legislative interference." Later that year the same paper exclaimed, apropos of the Erie: "Right of way is granted, sections of land given, and the State credit guaranteed to enable these public carriers to build up their roads, and when fairly in operation they practise the most barefaced swindles on the public." Plainly it believed in the *right* of regulation as much as Governor John M. Palmer of Illinois, who declared a year later that railroads were "public highways" and were "subject to the right of the State to adopt and enforce such regulations as will protect the public from arbitrary exactions and unjust discriminations." So did Charles Francis Adams, Jr., who called the roads lessees of the public. And so did the Boston *Advertiser,* which announced that railroads were "semi-public corporations," and that the right of the State to "fix a maximum rate of tolls and charges" needed no argument.

Yet in other quarters this right, as exercised in the Granger laws, was vehemently denied. Railroad officials early adopted the attitude that these acts were confiscatory, that they took property without due process of law, and that they ought not to be obeyed. A long letter written by President Mitchell of the Chicago, Milwaukee & St. Paul to the governor of Wisconsin on April 28, 1874, stated this position emphatically. And throughout the East the expediency of drastic regulatory laws was widely and vehemently denied. Most observers agreed with E. L. Godkin, that they would discourage investment, impair service, and do shippers more harm than good. The history of the "Granger" laws bore out this view, for as time passed they were repealed or left in innocuous desuetude.

Both the New York *Commercial Advertiser* and *Scientific American* strongly advocated free competition, and more of it, to lessen the rate abuses. Various experts, including Charles Francis Adams, Jr., and his colleagues on the Massachusetts Commission, proposed a competitive test between government-owned and privately-owned roads. Peter Cooper believed that the government should have built and operated the Pacific railroad. In the fall of 1867 an agitation was begun for a Federal freight railway between the Atlantic and the Mississippi, and a great Cooper Union meeting in New York endorsed the idea. Yet the railroads soon proved that unlimited competition offered as many evils as drastic governmental interference. Such competition gave an all too precarious benefit to shippers; it did all too permanent an injury to investors; and it proved the very mother of rebating. Stability is a primary desideratum in railroad rates, for fluctuating and uncertain rates injure trade; and all stability was lost when competing lines began slashing their charges. As early as 1870 the three trunk lines connecting Omaha and Chicago, the Northwestern, the Rock Island, and the Burlington, found it imperative to end their cutthroat rivalry and form a pool; and that same year there was talk of an association or pool of the Erie, Pennsylvania, and New York Central, which *The Railroad Gazette* thought might possess "decided advantages" for everybody.

All in all, the railroad rate problem throughout the seventies seemed baffling to most Americans. Rates had to be high enough to yield a fair profit, but they must not be too high lest they injure industries and agriculture. They had to possess certain stability, for if the grain rate from Chicago to the seaboard fluctuated by ten cents a bushel within sixty days, many Chicago and New York dealers would go bankrupt. Yet they must have a certain elasticity to compensate the railroads for a reduced volume of business or for higher working costs. To frame tariffs which met all these conditions, in a new, experimental, and till 1873 fast-growing industry, was exceedingly difficult; and it was not less difficult when the nation passed from boom to depression and many railroads went bankrupt. It is not strange that we find an English expert writing some years later that rates were fixed arbitrarily by men who knew little of them:[31]

A railroad tariff, as a rule, includes from 20,000 to 30,000 items, for there must be a rate for each class of freight from every point on the system to every other. The managers and higher officials, of course, cannot look after details, and the work must be performed by clerks, often under the influence of advice given by local agents, who are ignorant of the cost price of transportation, and of the profits that have to be made, and merely look at their commission, or may try to steal a march upon the local agents of rival lines. . . . Nearly all of them [rates] vary constantly.

[31]S. F. Van Oss, *American Railroads as Investments*, 88.

I have often asked local clerks about rates, for the sake of making an experiment, and I usually found they had to look at amendments, or amendments to amendments, or amendments in the third, fourth, and fifth generation before they could tell me what I wanted to know.

Rapidly a public sentiment was to arise that would outlaw rebating, albeit ineffectively. But Rockefeller himself never outgrew the feeling that in so far as it compensated "eveners" of traffic it was right and proper. "So much of the clamor against rebates and drawbacks," he said in 1917, "came from people who knew nothing about business. Who can buy beef the cheapest?—the housewife for her family, the steward for a club or hotel, or the commissary for an army? These people would make no difference between wholesale and retail. Who can handle merchandise more cheaply, those who handle it in bulk, or those who handle it in small lots? Who is entitled to better rebates from a railroad, those who give it for transportation 5000 barrels a day, or those who give 500 barrels—or 50 barrels?"[32]

VII

The year 1871 drew toward a close amid gloomy conditions for all branches of the oil industry. The producers, with a rich new field about Parkers' Landing pouring out a fresh river of oil, felt as keenly as ever the effect of low prices. Refiners in general were in the same plight. The trunk-line railroads, having cut their rates below profitable levels, were now experiencing the harsh effects of their indiscretion. When *The Railroad Gazette* commented on the Pennsylvania's annual report for 1870, it exclaimed over the weak showing of the principal oil feeder, the Philadelphia & Erie. "The business is chiefly a through and mineral traffic, and it has had to compete with the Erie Railway, which last year kept the rates extravagantly low for a large part of the year." Operating expenses alone had eaten up 82 per cent of the road's earnings. Meanwhile the Erie was faring even worse. Gould had leased the Atlantic & Great Western for twelve years beginning in 1868, and this would have proved a sound acquisition had the oil traffic remained valuable. But in the fiscal year 1869–70 the road lost $386,000 on the lease; the following year, $694,000. Midway in 1871 the Erie threw up the lease, and the line was sold on October 2, 1871, to George B. McClellan and others. As for the Lake Shore,

[32]Inglis, Conversations with Rockefeller.

one of its chief officers, Peter H. Watson, subsequently testified that it had done little or no better.

Upon astute leaders among the producers, the refiners, and the railroad managers the same question pressed with growing force. What could be done to lessen the reckless competition and constant price-slashing, to stabilize the charges for goods and services at a profitable level? Rockefeller thought more deeply upon the subject than any other man, and looked farther ahead.

XIV

The South Improvement Scheme

As THE year 1871 opened, Rockefeller realized that Cleveland's primacy in the refining trade, now recognized by all, could not be held without strenuous effort. Early this year the New York *Commercial Bulletin,* remarking that Cleveland and Pittsburgh refined half of America's oil, and that the former fixed the prices for all refining centers, predicted that New York would soon dislodge her. The Cleveland *Leader* disagreed. "We see no reason to apprehend that Cleveland is likely to lose the commanding position as an oil market to which it has attained," it declared. But by midsummer the New York press had better reason for its hopes. The Pennsylvania Railroad, acquiring control of lines across New Jersey, had suddenly made New York its Eastern terminus;[1] and news leaked out that it had offered the Long Island refiners such heavy rebates that they could undersell their Cleveland rivals. Tom Scott's intention was to build up a great freight business in oil between the Regions, Philadelphia, and New York, and to thrust Pittsburgh and Cleveland to one side. "Fortunately for us," asserted the *Leader,* "the Erie managers have a keen eye on Mr. Scott, and we may rely upon them to so adapt their oil rates to the market that Cleveland refining interests will not seriously suffer."

In Pittsburgh, meanwhile, the refiners had plucked up hope from two new developments. One was the completion late in 1870 of the Connellsville Railroad, connecting Pittsburgh with the Baltimore & Ohio Railroad at Cumberland, Md., and affording some prospect of

[1]For the Pennsylvania's lease of the United Canal and Railroad Companies of New Jersey, see Wheaton J. Lane, *From Indian Trail to Iron Horse,* 276–277, 318–319.

an escape from the throttling tyranny of the Pennsylvania. Its construction was accompanied by a series of conferences between Pittsburgh refiners and President Garrett of the B. & O.[2] The other was the introduction in the legislature early in 1870 of a "free pipe-line bill," which would enable men to condemn land, lay a pipe line to the city, and bring in crude oil more cheaply than by rail or steamboat.[3] After it passed the House the powerful influence of the Pennsylvania crushed it in the Senate, but Pittsburghers hoped for better luck later on.

But while the refining centers carried on their struggle, Rockefeller and other leaders realized that they had a common problem in the depression. To him this was far more exigent and menacing than the question whether one city or another should hold first place. Times grew worse than ever in the second half of 1871. Everywhere small refineries were going bankrupt. A writer in the Titusville *Herald* for November 8 remarked that "at present rates the loss to the refiner, on the average, is seventy-five cents per barrel," and that most refineries throughout the country had closed or were preparing to do so. He called for an organization to stop "the spasmodic fluctuation in prices and ruinous shutting down of large and expensive works."[4] Refiners could then refuse to buy, contract, deliver, or sell "except at a standard margin of profit." The Pittsburgh *Gazette,* chronicling the stoppage of many works in that city, remarked that "to use a common phrase among oil dealers, the bottom has fallen almost completely out of the market."[5] Its only consolation was that other centers were suffering as badly. "Private and re-

---

[2]The Pittsburgh *Chronicle,* May 23, 1872, says that at a meeting between local refiners and G. R. Blanchard, general freight agent of the Baltimore & Ohio, Blanchard expatiated on the benefits to be reaped when the Connellsville line was completed. "Baltimore would then be thirty miles nearer by railroad and tidewater to the oil region than New York or Philadelphia, and would consequently be the natural point for export. He said that every possible facility would be given to the trade, when the road was finished, for the shipment of oil via Baltimore." See the Titusville *Herald,* Sept. 22, 1871, for the Oil Regions' attitude.

[3]William Brough, president of the Petroleum Producers' Association, appealed in the Titusville *Herald,* April 1, 1871, for all "who are interested in the cheap transportation of oil," to petition for passage of the bill. A formidable delegation of producers and Pittsburgh refiners visited Harrisburg. Titusville *Herald,* April 8, 1871.

[4]*Cf.* Pittsburgh *Gazette,* Nov. 10, 1871.   [5]*Idem,* Nov. 24, 1871.

liable advices from Cleveland report the oil business as being in a very unsatisfactory condition there; it is said to be worse than it has been for several years. . . ."[6]

Fifty years later Rockefeller vividly remembered the effects of the dropping prices, disappearing margin of profit, and constant fluctuations and uncertainty. Every one was suffering, he told W. O. Inglis. "A panic had been on for a considerable time in the oil-refining business, resulting in loss to nearly all refiners"; and most of his rivals faced "impending ruin."[7] In an earlier statement, a letter of 1888 to S. C. T. Dodd, he wrote that he had been reviewing the situation in 1871 with his brother Frank; and they agreed that "more than three fourths of the oil refiners of the country did a losing business" that year. One prominent Clevelander, Alexander of Alexander, Scofield & Co., offered his interest in his firm to Frank at ten cents on the dollar.[8] We have other evidence that at least half the refining industry in Cleveland was on the verge of destruction while the plants in Pittsburgh were in an equally precarious position. The Pittsburgh *Commercial* for January 13, 1872, spoke of the demoralized condition of the oil markets for months past, and the intense anxiety of many manufacturers. A few weeks later it summed up the history of the preceding year in a pithy paragraph.[9] While large quantities of crude oil were being shipped abroad for refining, at home the refinery capacity was "already equal to three times the average production." In consequence, "there has heretofore existed a ruinous competition between the refineries, by which all parties have lost money. The entire petroleum business has been a losing one for the past year, not only for refiners and producers, but for the railroad companies who have transported the oil, the only parties who have profited by the situation being the foreign consumers."

According to orthodox economic theory, the situation was perfectly natural, and the overbalanced industry would soon right itself. Since any one with a few thousand dollars could go into the business, production had inevitably become inflated. Free competition was forcing prices below the cost of production. When this happened, the most inefficient manufacturers would become discouraged and suspend operations. Supplies would then be reduced and prices

[6]*Idem*, Aug. 23, 1871.   [7]Inglis, Conversations with Rockefeller.
[8]Rockefeller to S. C. T. Dodd, July 14; 1888; Rockefeller Papers.
[9]*Cf.* Pittsburgh *Gazette*, Jan.–Feb., 1871.

would rise. A constant movement in and out of production was a salient feature of the old style classical economy. It was true that it caused a great deal of human suffering; but according to Manchester theory, it made for enterprise, efficiency, and the welfare of the greatest number.

But Rockefeller had no trust in theoretical economics; he believed that the situation was not proper, and that the industry could not right itself. The theory of free competition worked well enough when an industry was restricted to a large number of small firms. But it ceased to work when a number of great establishments, like his own, entered the field. For when competition drove prices below production costs, these establishments could not resort to a temporary shut-down. Their overhead costs, the interest on investment, the charges for maintenance, continued. These were so heavy that bankruptcy loomed ahead if they were not alleviated. Hence the establishment was forced to carry on even at a loss, selling at low rates to cover *part* of its expenses. This period of cut-rate selling, of ruinous competition, of low wages and long hours, might be protracted for years, and then end in general bankruptcy. Thousands would be ruined, tens of thousands thrown out of work. Then the whole cycle would perhaps repeat itself. Rockefeller's practical approach showed that he believed that industry was outgrowing the old theories, and that the one solution was combination; the great units must combine, or their huge investment values would be wiped out.

His refining company was the strongest in America, and he had no anxiety as to his personal future, for his other holdings were considerable. "You know we are independently rich outside of investments in oil," he wrote his wife in 1872. Yet he knew that mere drifting would never do. In his intense, hardheaded way, trying to peer far ahead, he pondered the future of the industry and discussed it with his partners. Other men were searching for a way out. The result was the emergence of two plans, the first that of a Pennsylvania group famous as the South Improvement Scheme, and the second that of Rockefeller and Flagler.

II

The idea of organizing the various branches of the oil industry to check overproduction and ruthless competition was far from new.

Pennsylvania had heard of recurrent schemes for years. As early as the fall of 1866 oil producers in the Regions had discussed a combination "for the purpose of attempting to make better terms with the refiners in the price of the crude market." A year later jobbers there debated the formation of an Oil Buyers' Association, with a million dollars' capital, to build storage tanks and hold oil when necessary for higher prices. "Rings" of oil dealers shortly became common.[10] In 1868–69 the refiners of Oil City, Titusville, and other points in the Regions formed a league, and after signing an agreement with the producers and getting new low rates from the Pennsylvania Railroad, made their famous boast that they would wipe out Cleveland as with a sponge. We have seen that the Petroleum Producers' Association came into existence in 1869, and that a year later, under the spur of falling prices, its members passed a futile resolution to stop drilling for three months. Some of them urged a close and continuous restriction of production. At the same time, C. V. Culver, a prominent banker influential with oil-well owners, sent word to Rockefeller that the associated producers would like to make an agreement with the Standard Oil by which it would refine oil for them at a commission of one tenth of a cent a gallon—the Standard and other Cleveland men to furnish the refineries! His proposal, coming on the heels of the threat to wipe out Cleveland, aroused Rockefeller's indignation. "Information of this kind was of good assistance to us . . . as indicating what we might expect if we were subject to the control of producers as such," he remarked later,[11] "and that if the refining interest was to be protected, it must secure protection by a concerted action among the refiners."

The refiners had never yet gone so far toward union as the oil producers. To be sure, they had taken steps as early as 1868 to im-

[10]See Giddens, *The Birth of the Oil Industry*, 182 ff. for these speculative combinations against which Rockefeller later waged relentless war. The Pittsburgh *Commercial*, Jan. 31, 1872, gives the details of one of many suits which grew out of "the famous bull ring" of 1869.

[11]Inglis, Conversations with Rockefeller. The Titusville *Herald* of Nov. 8, 1871, issued an extraordinary appeal for a refiners' combination. "As a class, refiners have not looked so much to their own interests as producers—they have no Refiners' Association similar to the Producers' Association. If refineries refused to either buy, contract, deliver, or sell, except at a standard margin of profit, the whole matter would regulate itself, and the spasmodic fluctuations in prices and ruinous shutting down of large and expensive works would not occur so often." Rockefeller would have said a hearty amen!

prove the quality of their products, holding a National Petroleum convention in March of that year in Pittsburgh, and in December of the next year in New York. Their main objects were to prevent the marketing of poor and dangerous kerosene, for the frequent explosions injured business, and to protect the industry against unjust taxation. The Cleveland *Leader* early in 1870 published a list of refiners in various cities who had agreed to meet certain standards in manufacturing oil. Twelve Cleveland firms, including the Standard, had signed, and Flagler served on one of the committees appointed to protect the quality of oil.[12] But the conventions never attempted to deal with output or prices, and never led to a real trade association.

A hesitant effort was made in 1869 to organize the refiners of Cleveland. On a bright June day they took their families for a picnic at Rocky River, where the men held a meeting. Some photographs of that gathering survive, and show on the porch of a summer hotel a group of keen-faced, strong-jawed men, most of them surprisingly young, and handsomely dressed, attractive women. "The question of organizing the oil interest into something of the nature of a board of trade was seriously discussed," reported the *Leader*. As a result, the Association of Cleveland Refiners was shortly set up, a tentative step toward union against the refiners of other cities and the producers of the Oil Regions. But little was done, and though the Standard was a member, neither Rockefeller nor any associate became an officer. In this, as in the National Refiners' Association that grew out of the petroleum conventions, Maurice and James Clark were prominent.[13]

For Rockefeller and Flagler these feeble attempts at union doubtless had an educational value. They demonstrated the impossibility of proceeding through a loose association of all refiners, weak and strong. The Pittsburgh and New York meetings also provided opportunities for an acquaintance with prominent competitors there and in Philadelphia, which was soon to be valuable to the Standard.

It is clear that Rockefeller felt increasingly distrustful of the Oil Regions men. Their hostility toward Cleveland was outspoken; their

[12]Cleveland *Leader*, Feb. 11, 1870.

[13]Cleveland *Leader*, *passim*. See Rolland H. Maybee, *Railroad Competition and the Oil Trade, 1855–1873*, 218 ff., on these gatherings. A Petroleum Board had been organized in Cleveland in 1866; Cleveland *Leader*, Sept. 11, 1866.

various attempts to unite against that city might yet be successful. And what if the producers of the Regions formed a really effective alliance with the refiners there?—perhaps with those of New York as well? Supported by the Pennsylvania, they could arbitrarily limit the crude oil sent to Cleveland, and ruin the Ohio industry. As late as 1917 Rockefeller's resentful apprehensions of that period were still fresh in his mind. "Was not the Pennsylvania Railroad, with its ally the Empire Transportation Company, trying to eliminate Cleveland as a refining center, and did not the Oil City and Titusville papers boast that this could be done?"[14]

Rockefeller also saw that the constant losses of the refiners made some form of combination inevitable, and that if it were not led from Cleveland, it would be led from Pennsylvania or New York. But why not from Cleveland? Since Flagler's new contract with the Lake Shore, the Standard had become by far the most powerful refining organization in the world. A company which could ship fifty carloads of refined oil a day—fully 3000 barrels, a fifth or sixth of all the refined oil then produced—was in a position to exert tremendous force. As Rockefeller discussed the subject with Flagler, his ideas rapidly crystallized. His observation of the facts of any business situation was always searching and complete, and his deductions were always penetrating and farsighted. He soon made up his mind as to the true solution of the problem—a solution much simpler, more direct, and, as the event proved, much more effective than that proposed by the railroad managers.

What was it? His plan called for a consolidation of all oil-refining firms and corporations into one great organization, which should eliminate most of the excess capacity and stop the price cutting. He knew that a mere association was useless and that no pool could long be held together; but he thought that with the Standard as nucleus, an immensely powerful merger could be built up. "The idea was mine," he said long afterward. "That has been conceded on all hands; but I don't want to put it in an offensive way. The idea was persisted in, too, in spite of the opposition of some who became faint-hearted at the magnitude of the undertaking, as it constantly assumed larger proportions."[15]

As Rockefeller did not commit his plan to paper, no documentary

[14]Inglis, Conversations with Rockefeller.   [15]*Idem.*

evidence of its formulation in 1871 exists. Some writers have therefore assumed that he had no plan prior to the appearance of the South Improvement Company, and have stated that this represented an idea which he or Flagler took to the railroads. But Rockefeller and Flagler always denied any part of the authorship of the South Improvement Company, and the facts support this denial. The former made an emphatic disclaimer in 1917. "It was not our idea," he categorically told William O. Inglis. "We had an idea of our own." He described how the formation of the Refiners' Association led him and Flagler to discuss the problem of "protecting the industry." Out of their talks soon emerged his own project. "We were gathering information which confirmed us in the idea that to enlarge our own Standard Oil of Ohio and actually take into partnership with us the refining interest would accomplish the protection to the oil industry as a whole, both producing and refining, which had not been accomplished by any of the efforts previously resorted to, including the effort to control production—to restrict production —of crude oil for the betterment of prices."[16]

During 1871 Rockefeller and Flagler were busy preparing to carry out "our plan." They enjoyed the confidence of the best Cleveland bankers. Truman P. Handy, long an admirer of Rockefeller, was the dominant figure in the Merchants' National Bank.[17] Both Dan P. Eells, president of the Commercial National Bank, and his father-in-law, Stillman Witt, a director of the Second National Bank, felt certain of Rockefeller's genius for business. So did Amasa Stone, Jr., connected with the Second National. Before the end of 1871 all these men were persuaded to support the scheme for enlarging the Standard Oil by a series of mergers. We know this because they took stock—Amasa Stone, Jr., 500 shares; Stillman Witt, 500; O. B. Jennings, 500; T. P. Handy, 400; and Benjamin Brewster, 250. These five new participants appeared as stockholders when on January 1, 1872, the Standard petitioned for an increased capitalization; they were already in it![18] The raising of the capital to $2,500,000 was an

[16]*Idem.*

[17]See sketch of Handy's career, Cleveland *Leader,* May 17, 1882, on the occasion of a banquet given him at the Union Club.

[18]Taylor, MS History of the Standard Oil Company. The stockholders' list on January 1, 1872, is worth giving in full. It runs: John D. Rockefeller, 2015 shares; William Rockefeller, 1459; H. M. Flagler, 1459; S. V. Harkness, 1458; Samuel Andrews, 1458; Amasa Stone, Jr., 500; Stillman, W. H. (represented

indispensable step if the Standard was to become an all-embracing organization, the core of a great merger. Rockefeller never made his preparations hastily, though when they were completed he could move with devastating swiftness. His activities in Cleveland late in 1871 indicate that the greater Standard Oil had been fully planned before the South Improvement Company was presented to him, and that he and Flagler felt confident of uniting nearly all the city's refineries in one huge corporation.

They of course decided to deal with Cleveland first. Once masters of refining there, they would be ready to treat successively or simultaneously with New York, Philadelphia, and Pittsburgh. They discussed the trade outlook frequently with their Cleveland rivals, and may have been suggesting a merger. They had doubtless felt out sentiment in other cities. But on November 30, 1871, Rockefeller first heard in New York of the South Improvement scheme. As a letter to his wife next day shows, he instantly realized that the powerful railroad backing it enjoyed must give it precedence over his own: "I wrote last night from the St. Nicholas and after writing saw Mr. Watson with Will arriving home about 11:30—There is a *new* view of the question just introduced & I don't know how it may turn though am hopeful—indeed the project *grows on me.*"[19]

The man who brought him the project was Peter H. Watson, then prominent in the Lake Shore-New York Central system.[20] As Rockefeller felt it 'grow on him' a new chapter in petroleum history was opening.

III

The genesis of this scheme is particularly interesting. By 1871 the railroads of the United States had done a good deal of experimenting with that form of combination called the pool. A group of roads serving the same district would agree to maintain rates at a fixed

by Amasa Stone, Jr.), 500; O. B. Jennings, 500; T. P. Handy, 400; Benjamin Brewster, 250. Mr. Charles T. White has kindly given me a similar list compiled from various Standard Oil records. Rockefeller said later that he was emphasizing the importance of large cash reserves "to ballast the manufacturing interest"; *U. S. vs. Standard Oil,* XVI, 3067.

[19]Rockefeller Papers.

[20]For material on P. H. Watson, patent attorney, Assistant Secretary of War, railroad administrator, and Democratic politician, see my *Abram S. Hewitt, With Some Account of Peter Cooper,* 202 ff.

level, and divide the revenues on a prearranged scale. But it was difficult to apply the railroad pool to such a situation as existed in the hauling of oil freights. Here the railroads were tied to highly competitive interests—the Erie and Lake Shore to the Cleveland refiners; the Pennsylvania to the Oil Regions refiners. The three principal oil carriers, the Erie, the Lake Shore-New York Central, and the Pennsylvania, could easily have agreed to split their petroleum traffic or its revenues into three parts, charging rates profitable to all. But could they maintain the agreement? The Pittsburgh or Regions refiners might begin fiercely undercutting the Cleveland refiners; and to keep Cleveland solvent the Erie would then have to make special rates for the Western plant. To ensure stability for railroad rates, some stabilization of the refining industry would also have to be effected.

In studying this situation—and the frantic rate wars of 1870 and 1871 made railroad leaders study it furiously—the managers were much influenced by recent events in the anthracite field. Here during the Civil War profitable contracts and rising prices had brought about a hectic development of new mines. When peace came, a bitter competition for the suddenly limited market set in. Operators in the various districts slashed prices recklessly. Inevitably the five coal-carrying railroads—the Reading, the Lehigh Valley, the Delaware & Hudson, the Lackawanna, and the New Jersey Central—were drawn into the conflict.[21] When coal operators along the Lackawanna, for example, cut their prices sharply in 1867, the Lehigh Valley had to reduce its freight rates to permit Lehigh mine owners to keep on competing. A continuance of this bitter competitive struggle would have ruined the operators and railways alike. But by 1871 a simple solution was being found.

Nearly all the conditions in the anthracite fields were favorable to the establishment of a monopoly: a limited source of supply, a limited number of coal carriers, and a rapid disappearance of the weaker companies under competitive pressure. Between 1868 and 1874 Pennsylvania laws offered no obstacle to the joint ownership of coalpits and railroad facilities. The carriers therefore took rapid steps to acquire the greater part of the fields by purchasing mines and coal acreage, for this seemed the only certain means of gaining

[21]S. F. Van Oss, *American Railroads as Investments*, 289 ff.

an ample and regular coal business. Most of the few independent operators who survived were induced to sign long-term contracts with the railroads for carriage of their coal. In this way, by the close of 1871, seven great corporations had obtained almost complete control of the anthracite supply: the five railroads just named, the Lehigh Coal & Navigation Company, and the Pennsylvania Coal Company. Having thus stamped out overproduction and price-cutting, the roads by informal agreement established profitable freight rates. In 1873 they went a step further, and, defying popular resentment, formed a pool to make their control of prices and freight rates complete.[22]

The managers of the Pennsylvania, Erie, and New York Central saw in 1871 that their problem in the Oil Regions of western Pennsylvania had a close resemblance to the problem which President Franklin B. Gowen of the Reading and President Asa Packer of the Lehigh had faced in the anthracite domain of the eastern counties. They perceived, that is, that the fates of oil refiners and oil carriers were bound up together; chaos, price-cutting, and ruin for the one meant chaos, rate-cutting, and ruin for the other. The railroads could not buy up the enormously costly and fast-expanding oil fields, but they could help the stronger refiners to organize and so bring the situation under control. At the same time, they could arrange among themselves for restoring freight rates to a profitable level and dividing the proceeds. It was a clear perception of these facts, with certain other elements, which gave birth to the South Improvement Company.

What were the other elements? Several, as Rockefeller knew at the time, were exceptionally interesting. By 1871 the Pennsylvania Railroad had carried through an expansion which elated J. Edgar Thomson and gave his energetic second-in-command, Tom Scott, roseate dreams of grandeur. It had secured a permanent entry into New York City on the east and Chicago on the west, and had signed contracts with lines beyond the Mississippi which promised a large new volume of western freight. It had bought the Camden & Amboy Railroad, the Philadelphia & Trenton, the Delaware & Raritan Canal, and the property of the New Jersey Railroad & Transporta-

[22]Bogen, *The Anthracite Railroads: A Study in Combination*, covers the subject.

tion Company. "Henceforth," prophesied the Cleveland *Leader* on May 1, 1871, "the Pennsylvania Central will own New Jersey as absolutely as it has hitherto owned Pennsylvania." Vice-President Scott, restless and ambitious, "the grand Coryphœus of Pennsylvania railroadism," was eager also to dominate a network of western and southern lines; for he was already president of the Union Pacific, and was soon to be elected head of the Texas & Pacific. His power seemed tremendous. Wendell Phillips caustically remarked that as he trailed his garments across the country, the members of twenty legislatures rustled like dry leaves in a winter's wind behind him.[23]

At this very time, moreover, the Pennsylvania Legislature, responding to pressure from Tom Scott and other representatives of special interests, was chartering a number of corporations with very extraordinary powers. As yet the holding company had virtually no existence in America. State courts generally accepted the common law principle that no corporation had a right to own stock in another corporation save by specific legislative enactment. Various States, including New York and Ohio, even forbade such holdings by statute.[24] But in the boom years 1868–72 the legislators at Harrisburg went on a splurge. By special enactments they gave more than forty corporations charters which conferred extremely broad powers, including the right to hold the stock of any other company whether in or out of the State. One, the Pennsylvania Company, is still a major element in the Pennsylvania Railroad system, and is perhaps our first specimen of a pure holding company. Indeed, it was created partly to enable the Pennsylvania to take over the New Jersey lines. Another, the Reading Company, became a basic element in the Reading Railroad system. Another was the Southern Securities Corporation, a $5,000,000 company in which Tom Scott was the principal agent, and the chief object of which was supposedly to buy control of various Southern railroads. Still another was the National Improvement Company, which, as one newspaper sarcastically remarked, out-mobilized in its vague powers the Crédit Mobiliers of

[23]The late Charles J. Barney, who became a clerk in Jay Cooke's offices in 1867 and later married his daughter, gave me interesting impressions of Tom Scott. He was a man of stalwart physique, and till lamed by a paralytic stroke, of fine bearing and impressive manner. Mr. Barney was struck by his florid face, imperious air, and look of shrewdness and power. He affected a felt hat of ten-gallon dimensions.

[24]See article on Holding Companies, *Encyclopædia of the Social Sciences*.

both France and America. And finally, one was the ever-memorable South Improvement Company.

This South Improvement Company was created by the Pennsylvania Legislature in the spring of 1870, with Tom Scott's private secretary and two of Scott's friends as incorporators.[25] No immediate use was made of it, and its charter was for sale in the fall of 1871 to the highest bidder. The principal value of this charter has often been misstated. It lay to some extent in the mere breadth of the powers conferred—powers "to construct and operate any work or works, public or private, designed to include, increase, facilitate, or develop trade, travel, or the transportation of freight, livestock, passengers, or any traffic by land or water, from or to any part of the United States." Far more largely, however, it lay in the authority given the company to hold the stocks of other corporations, quite outside the bounds of the State; an authority possessed by few companies in America at this time. The promoters of the South Improvement scheme for controlling oil refining and oil transportation quietly bought the charter, completing the purchase January 2, 1872. They immediately sold a group of insiders 1100 shares at $100 a share, 20 per cent thereon being paid into the treasury.

And who were the original promoters? The idea that Rockefeller and Flagler were the principal figures is quite baseless. In its inception this was primarily a railroad plan; Tom Scott stood in the background, and the 1100 shares sold on January 2 were taken exclusively by Peter H. Watson and a group of Philadelphia and Pittsburgh refiners. No Cleveland man was on the original list.[26]

Upon the origins of the South Improvement plan we have a wide variety of testimony. The report of the Chamber of Commerce of the State of New York for 1872 remarks of petroleum: "The past year has been fruitful of schemes to manage and control the trade in this important article of commerce. First the Southern Improvement Company took the field, we believe, *in some railroad interest. . . .*" Some years later the editor of the Oil City *Derrick*

[25]The private secretary was R. D. Barclay; the two other "tools of T. A. Scott" were S. S. Moon and J. A. Fowler. See *The Road,* II, 178 (July 15, 1876).

[26]See William G. Warden's testimony before the Congressional Committee of 1872 in *A History of the Rise and Fall of the South Improvement Company,* 30–41; *cf.* Leonard W. Bacon, *History of the South Improvement Company,* 34, 35, a thoroughgoing defense of the company.

testified that the scheme had "its origin, as a matter of fact, *with the railroad interests* rather than with the oil interests."[27] Rockefeller asserted in 1908 that the first active promoters were some Philadelphia and Pittsburgh refiners "in connection with Mr. Scott, and perhaps one or two officials in his freight department."[28] Later he said more emphatically to W. O. Inglis: "It was a Tom Scott scheme —Tom Scott's and some of the Philadelphia and Pittsburgh people."[29] For this we have also the evidence of Orville T. Waring, Pittsburgh refiner, who said:[30]

We went into that scheme on the suggestion of Thomas A. Scott, the [vice] president of the Pennsylvania Railroad Company. It was he who originated the plan. I remember when it was first suggested to us, a committee of oil refiners at a conference in Philadelphia in which we were trying to find some way out of our troubles. We oil men were not making money. The railroads were not making any money out of the oil business. We were groping around for a way out. We were having conferences every little while with the railroad heads.

Now I'm not sure whether it was Mr. Scott in person or his assistant who made the original suggestion. . . . One of them said: "Why don't you try this plan?"—and he outlined the general idea. . . . We had not much faith in the proposition because it seemed too drastic. But we were in a bad situation and ready to try almost anything that seemed possible; so we went in.

Finally, we have the statement of Joseph Seep, at this time connected with the New York refiner Jabez A. Bostwick. He later declared that the South Improvement scheme was not Rockefeller's at all; that "P. H. Watson, W. G. Warden, and a lot of Philadelphia and Pittsburgh refiners and the *Pennsylvania Railroad people* were the originators and promoters of that."[31] And the New York *World,* in a well-informed article of March 16, 1872, declared that Tom Scott had devised the South Improvement Company "to clutch the oil region, and, if possible, to crush out all competition there." Altogether, the evidence seems conclusive that it was the vice-president of the Pennsylvania Railroad, distressed by the heavy losses of his oil-feeder the Philadelphia & Erie, who broached the

[27]*Hearings Before the United States Industrial Commission (1899)*, 421.
[28]*United States vs. Standard Oil Company.*
[29]Inglis, Conversations with Rockefeller.
[30]Inglis, Conversation with Waring.
[31]Undated newspaper interview.

plan. The Pennsylvania had made the arrangements with Oil Regions refiners in 1868 which threatened to wipe out the Cleveland refining business "as with a sponge." Scott took his new plan to Peter H. Watson of the Lake Shore and to Philadelphia and Pittsburgh refiners. This evidence overthrows Miss Tarbell's story that the plan originated with "certain Pennsylvania refiners" but was most actively pushed by "Mr. Rockefeller and Mr. Watson and their associates." It overthrows the theory of John T. Flynn that "the scheme adopted has all the earmarks of Flagler's mind and experience."[32] He points out that Flagler had once engaged in the salt industry at Saginaw, Mich., and was doubtless familiar with the fact that in March, 1871, a combination of Saginaw salt-manufacturers had joined with Ohio River and New York producers in a great selling-pool. But Flagler's experience with salt now lay far in the past, while all businessmen of the time had numerous other pools and loose combinations before them. The work of the anthracite railroads in stamping out destructive competition was more pertinent to the oil situation than was the simple and still experimental salt pool.

The statements of Flagler and Rockefeller that other men were prime movers in the South Improvement scheme, and that they themselves entered it with many doubts,[33] were never questioned by their associates. They never apologized for their part in the South Improvement Company, but they did say that they had always believed that it would be difficult to operate successfully. Rockefeller, having seen "a fatal lack of cohesiveness" in previous associations of refiners, doubted whether the new plan contained sufficient cement. Flagler agreed with him. "We did not believe in it," he declared. To both Flagler and Rockefeller their own plan was the only one likely to succeed. "It was apparent to the leaders of the Standard Oil Company," said Rockefeller in a conversation long afterward, "that one common ownership, with the simple ideas

[32]Tarbell, *Standard Oil Company*, I, 55 ff.; Flynn, *God's Gold*, 152, 153.

[33]Flagler said (*House Trust Investigation, Fiftieth Congress, 1st Session*, No. 3113, pp. 289, 290): "Neither of the Messrs. Rockefeller, Colonel Payne, nor myself, nor anyone connected with the Standard Oil Company, ever had any confidence in or regard for the scheme known as the South Improvement Company." Rockefeller said (*U. S. vs. Standard Oil*, XVI, 3069, 3070), "We did not share their views as to the plan. We so frankly stated to them, and more than once."

which controlled the Standard Oil Company, was the only really feasible thing."

Why, then, did the South Improvement idea "begin to grow" on Rockefeller that November night in New York? For one reason, the average price of refined oil that month in New York touched one of the lowest levels in its history, 22.33 cents a gallon; something must be done, and done quickly. For another, Rockefeller's plan for one great company would require the support of men in other cities; and this being so, the leading refiners of Pittsburgh and Philadelphia must not be antagonized. Tom Scott and Watson had not found enthusiastic co-workers in Warden of Philadelphia and Waring of Pittsburgh. In other words, here were the Pennsylvania refiners bringing the Standard a cooperative plan, supported by two great railroads, on a silver platter. Possibly the South Improvement scheme would work, and if it did not, a loyal attempt by Rockefeller and Flagler to carry it out would gain the good will of the others.

Rockefeller phrased his position crisply years later: "We acceded to it because he [Tom Scott] and the Philadelphia and Pittsburgh men, we hoped, would be helpful to us ultimately. We were willing to go with them as far as the plan could be used; so that when it failed, we would be in a position to say, 'Now try our plan.' Thus we would be in a much better position to get their co-operation than if we had said 'No' from the start."

IV

An outline of the scheme will make clear both its strength and weakness.[34] It was essentially a plan to unite the oil-carrying railroads in a pool; to unite the refiners in an association, the South Improvement Company; and to tie the two elements together by agreements which would stop destructive price-cutting and restore freight charges to a profitable level. The railroads were to divide

[34]A defense of the South Improvement Company is presented in advertisements published widely in the American press just after its demise, and reproduced in *United States vs. Standard Oil*, pp. 2618–2624. The N. Y. *Commercial and Shipping List*, March 2, 1872, presented the scheme as primarily a railroad pool. "An immense and overshadowing combination," it said, "has been entered into by the several lines of railroad communicating with the Oil Regions, to control the whole refining and carrying trade, and force up the rates for transportation some 55 to 65 per cent above the previous schedules."

the oil-freights by a prearranged scale; the refiners were to act as
eveners, insuring each road its proper share of the business from
consigners; and in return the refiners were to get rate concessions
which would wipe out all recalcitrant competitors. The authors also
had a hazy notion of bringing the producers into the general combination. They said later that had their company not been ready-
named, they would have called it "The American Cooperative Refining Company."

The first refineries enlisted in the South Improvement Company
were five: Lockhart, Waring & Warden in Pittsburgh, Warden,
Frew & Co. in Philadelphia, the Atlantic Refining Co. in Philadelphia, Jabez A. Bostwick in New York, and the Standard Oil in
Cleveland. The 1100 shares originally issued soon became 2000,
representing a capital of $200,000. Peter H. Watson of Ashtabula
took 100—the only railroad shareholder. The other twelve stockholders, with their shares, were as follows:

William Frew, Pittsburgh,	10	W. G. Warden, Philadelphia,	475
W. P. Logan, Philadelphia,	10	H. M. Flagler, Cleveland,	180
John P. Logan, Philadelphia,	10	O. H. Payne, Cleveland,	180
Charles Lockhart, Pittsburgh,	10	William Rockefeller, Cleveland,	180
Richard S. Waring, Pittsburgh,	10	John D. Rockefeller, Cleveland,	180
O. T. Waring, Pittsburgh,	475	Jabez A. Bostwick, New York,	180

The intention was that these five strong companies, in the four
principal refining cities, should unite by purchase, merger, or alliance with the other refineries of their respective centers. Purchase
or merger was favored. They asserted that if certain strong firms
had been willing to come in, they would have been admitted as
separate units. "It was decided to include within our company every
refinery we could possibly get," Warden testified before a House
Committee this year.[35] Rockefeller wrote his wife on March 15
that he hoped "to get at least a good fraction of the N. Y. Refiners
to join." But there is no proof that some brutal squeezing was not
contemplated. Peter H. Watson was elected president, and Warden
secretary. It will be noted that no city held a controlling interest,
and that Watson's presidency would protect the railroads.

At the first meeting on January 2, 1872, the stockholders agreed

[35]His testimony was given on March 30, 1872. See *Rise and Fall of the South
Improvement Company,* 30-41.

that no refiner who accepted their basic principles should be shut out. As Rockefeller said later, "the doors were open." Meanwhile, the arrangement with the railroads was being perfected. On January 18, 1872, the contract with the Pennsylvania was signed, followed by similar contracts with the New York Central and Erie. The South Improvement Company agreed to ship 45 per cent of all its oil over the Pennsylvania, 27.5 per cent over the Erie, and 27.5 per cent over the New York Central system; to keep careful records; and to furnish adequate tank facilities. Tom Scott and Watson helped arrange for the signatures of William H. Vanderbilt, vice-president of the New York Central; H. F. Clark, president of the Lake Shore; J. Edgar Thomson, president of the Pennsylvania; Jay Gould, president of the Erie; and George B. McClellan, head of the Atlantic & Great Western.

The South Improvement Company also agreed to establish much higher rates for oil shipments.[36] The freight charge on crude oil from the Regions to Cleveland was to be fixed at 80 cents a barrel instead of the previous 40, and Pittsburgh was to pay the same. The rate on refined oil from either Cleveland or Pittsburgh to New York was to remain at $2 a barrel. The open rate on crude from the Regions to Philadelphia was fixed at $2.41; to New York, $2.56; to Boston, $2.71. But so far as members of the South Improvement Company went, these rates were fictitious, for they were to get large rebates. In return for dividing shipments fairly and laboring to end the ruinous price-cutting in oil, Cleveland and Pittsburgh members were to receive rebates of 40 cents on shipments of crude from the Regions. They were to be given 50 cents on shipments of refined oil from either city to New York. The New York and Philadelphia

[36]For the South Improvement contracts, see *Rise and Fall of the South Improvement Company*, 27 ff. The question of the precise freight rates before and after the contracts is complex and obscure, for no such thing as a standard, uniform, unchanging freight rate existed. Rates were raised on Feb. 26 and again on March 4. Charges for bulk shipments and shipments in barrels differed slightly. These increases kindled a flame of indignation. The Titusville *Herald* grumbled even before the increase of Feb. 26 that the rate-extortions of railroad combinations had burdened the Regions since their infancy, and that by far the largest share of profits on oil had gone to the railroads. The Cleveland *Herald* called the increase of March 4 "wholesale robbery." It would appear that many shipments of crude oil between the Regions and Cleveland —perhaps most—had been made at 35 cents a barrel; and the rise to 80 cents seemed preposterous.

members were to get large rebates on crude from the Regions—$1.06 deducted from rates of $2.56 and $2.41 respectively. They would not need rebates on refined oil, since they exported it or sold it to local jobbers and dealers. The original plan was to put the schedules into effect March 1.

In short, the new open rates, applicable to all companies outside the South Improvement organization, were outrageously high. Cleveland refiners had been paying 40 cents a barrel on crude oil from the Regions; now those outside the South Improvement Company would pay 80. The Standard, under Flagler's agreement with the Lake Shore, had been paying $1.65 a barrel for oil carried from the Regions to Cleveland, and then (when refined) from Cleveland to New York. Now the open rate on such two-way shipments would be $2.80. Open rates to and from other points were similarly raised. But the rebates granted to members of the South Improvement Company ran from 40 to 50 per cent on crude, and 25 to 50 per cent on refined oil. These would assure them high profits while their rivals were rapidly pushed into bankruptcy. Taken alone, without other factors, they would guarantee a swift rise of the South Improvement Company to monopoly—if the plan worked out as designed. That monopoly was precisely what the railroads wanted. For the new rates between the railroads and the South Improvement Company, even after the deduction of rebates, were materially higher than those previously collected. For example, the Standard had paid $1.65 on round-trip oil shipments; now it would pay $1.90 a barrel, or 35 cents more.

We have said that the rebates alone would have crushed all competition, but they did not stand alone. To them was added a shocking new device, the drawback on competitors' shipments. By their railroad contracts, members of the South Improvement Company were allowed on each barrel shipped by an outsider a sum equal to the ordinary rebate. Bostwick of New York, for example, not only received a rebate of $1.06 on every barrel of crude which he brought from Titusville to New York; he got another $1.06 for every barrel which a New York competitor, paying the full rate of $2.56, brought from the Regions! The Standard Oil not only got the 40-cent rebate on crude from the Regions; it got 40 cents for every barrel brought to Cleveland by a competitor—that competitor paying 80. Of all devices for the extinction of competition, this was the cruellest and most deadly yet conceived by any group of American industrialists.

The contracts also provided that each railroad should make out waybills for all petroleum or petroleum products transported over any part of its lines, these stating the name of the shipper and consignee, place of shipment and destination, and amount and quality of product shipped; and that every day these waybills should be sent to the South Improvement Company. Thus members of the combination would be given full information about every detail of their competitors' business. Moreover, the South Improvement Company was to have access to all railroad books. This was obviously a means of enforcing the payment of the drawbacks as well as rebates; a means of making doubly sure that no independent refiners could long survive.

The drastic character of these devices, the ruthlessness of the machinery for crushing all competition, pointed to the object the organizers had in view. They meant to make it utterly impossible to stay out of the South Improvement Company. Who could afford to do so? "It never entered my head that the refiners would not all be brought in," Warden told a committee of the Federal House of Representatives in 1872. If they were all brought in, what injustice would be done? Nobody would then suffer; all would gain the benefits. The authors of the scheme could argue that a less drastic machinery for enforcing combination would leave many refiners hesitant. They would remain outside, the old struggle would continue, and the chaos in the industry would be perpetuated. According to this view, the most ruthless course would be the most merciful. This argument is specious, for compulsion of such a brutal kind was indefensible. Nevertheless, if the organizers of the South Improvement Company had made it clear that they intended to let all outsiders enter on a perfectly fair basis, keeping their identity if they liked, and finding their financial interests perfectly protected, the plea might have had some plausibility. Unfortunately, they did not make this clear. It is far from certain that some members did not wish to use this ruthless machinery to enrich themselves.

Then, too, what of the producers? What treatment were they to receive from this powerful new combination of railroads and refiners? Later, in a formal public statement, the South Improvement Company asserted that it meant to invite the producers to participate. The company admitted that some members consented to this reluctantly. Warden, testifying in 1872, said that several were hostile to any union with the well-owners. "I took the ground personally against forming a combination," he confessed, "inasmuch as the interests of the producers were in one sense antagonistic to ours, one as the seller and the other as the buyer. We held in argument that the producers were abundantly able to take care of their own branch of the business if they took care of the quantity produced." (A large if!) But Tom Scott and President Potts of the Empire Transportation Company felt that exclusion of the producers would invite failure. "You can't succeed unless the producers are taken care of," Scott insisted. Warden testified that the others had assented, and Watson corroborated him, producing for the House Committee a pencil draft of an agreement which the refiners had intended to submit to the producers. He believed that it had been drawn up in December, 1871, some weeks before the contracts between the railroads and the South Improvement Company were signed.[37]

The company's alleged intention to admit the producers should have been far firmer, and far more promptly and clearly stated to Oil Regions leaders. The well-owners were a vigilant and irritable body, keenly awake to their own interests. The draft agreement which Watson exhibited was fair enough. It specified that the producers were to limit the flow from the wells, and in return the South Improvement Company was to pay not less than a stated minimum price for crude oil, to be fixed each year by a joint committee. It was to take the oil, store it if necessary, and for all stored oil pay a deposit of three quarters of its value, with interest. Profits from sales were to be equitably divided.

But this draft agreement had not been shown to any producers when the Oil Regions first became aware of the South Improvement scheme. Company leaders asserted later that it would have been submitted had their plans gone according to schedule. Their first task, they said, was to organize the refiners, and as soon as this was done, they meant to approach the producers. The well-owners in

[37]See Watson's testimony in *Rise and Fall of the South Improvement Company*, 76–96; reproduced in Tarbell, *History of the Standard Oil Company*, I, 309 ff.

later years always doubted whether the South Improvement Company had any intention of dealing with them fairly, saying it meant to dictate, not co-operate. However this may be, the event proved that Scott, Watson, Warden, and Rockefeller should have moved to organize the refiners and producers simultaneously, not successively. For when the producers discovered the combination of refiners and railroads, their rage and excitement made them deaf to anything that Watson and his associates had to say.

This excitement precipitated a series of dramatic events, and left the South Improvement Company facing immediate extinction and eternal ignominy.

v

Though years later Rockefeller protested that he had gone into the South Improvement scheme as a second-best plan, a *pis aller* which promised moderate benefits rather than complete success, his hesitation quickly gave way to wholehearted espousal. He was never Laodicean. His letters to his wife prove that he threw himself into the enterprise with tremendous zeal.

The first requisite was to make sure that all three railroads would accept the plan. On December 15 Rockefeller wrote from New York: "Our negotiations are chiefly through Watson and there is much waiting and consequently a good chance for rest—he saw Commodore Vanderbilt last night and succeed(ed) *admirably*—So that now we count surely on Clark, him & W. H. Vanderbilt." That is, they counted on the three principal officers of the New York Central and Lake Shore. The sentence indicates that Watson had taken up the plan on his own initiative, and had to convert his superiors, Vanderbilt of the Central and Clark of the Lake Shore. Rockefeller also wrote that he had received a telegram that Flagler could come "tonight or tomorrow morn if wanted," and added: "I answd. not before Monday or Tuesday."

Meanwhile Tom Scott, whose electric brain first conceived the plan, had met no difficulty in converting other officers of the Pennsylvania, the first road to close its contract with the South Improvement Company. On January 20, 1872, Rockefeller again wrote his wife from New York: "We got our contract from Scott O.K. *19th* yesterday and feel *well* over it—are hopeful will soon have balance (of) the signatures." The New York Central and Erie were tardier. On January 24 Rockefeller wrote: "We are progressing and the contracts are being drawn." The following day he announced: "We have fully agreed with Mr. Vanderbilt to come into the So. I. Co. as also Mr. Bostwick, some progress every day but these men (Gould, Harley & others) are *selfish* and cant ask enough, and it is very trying."[38]

To the end Rockefeller played a leading part in the negotiations. This was natural, for he was the leading refiner of the country. "I had insisted on going tonight or tomorrow *but our men would not hear of it,*" he wrote January 25. "They are nervous and lean on me—It requires the patience of Job—I am very much disappointed that my hands seem tied & I can neither go nor bring you." With Watson, Scott, and Warden, he was fighting hard and doing his utmost for the organization.

His mention of Bostwick shows that the projectors were signing refiners as well as railroad executives. Indeed, the comment of January 20, when Scott sent him the Pennsylvania's contract—"are hopeful. will soon have balance the signatures"—suggests that a general drive was being made. The idea was that every refiner should be given stock in the company in proportion to his interests. Rockefeller's letters show that he oscillated between Pittsburgh and New York, with stops in Philadelphia. On January 24 his old employer Hewitt appeared in New York—"seems anxious but I could not give him information"—and on the 25th Rockefeller wrote his wife: "I telegraphed Scofield to come at time I telegraphed you as it seemed quite evident I could not get away this week."[39] Scofield and Hewitt were partners in Alexander, Scofield & Co., and Rockefeller's words indicate that they had already been approached with plans for a merger, and were weighing the step.

During January and early February many other refiners were asked to throw in their fortunes with the South Improvement Company. All were bound by a written pledge to absolute secrecy. Two prominent refiners of the Oil Regions, J. J. Vandergrift and John D. Archbold, were solicited to enter and refused. So did H. H. Rogers of the newly-organized Charles Pratt & Co., of New York, and many others. But the leaders were not discouraged. They hoped

[38]Rockefeller Papers.   [39]Rockefeller to his wife; Rockefeller Papers.

that economic pressure, the crushing force of their rebate and draw-back contracts, would reduce these men to a humble attitude and bring them knocking at the door. Aware of the power they would be able to exert, they resolutely proceeded with their organization.

VI

A secret known to a score of people is no secret at all. By the end of January, 1872, when the Erie and New York Central had signed the South Improvement contracts, more than a score of people knew about them. Railway presidents had to consult their principal subordinates; the promoters had to buttonhole refiners, who talked with their friends. The middle of February found rumors floating about the Regions of a formidable combination between the railroads and leading refiners. On February 21 the Cleveland *Plain Dealer* published a warning paragraph upon "a gigantic 'little game' " of monopolizing refiners and the oil-carrying railroads. The Petroleum Center *Record* next morning showed more definite knowledge. Mentioning reports of a "gigantic combination among certain railroads and refiners to control the purchase and shipment of crude and refined oil from this region," it denounced such "robbing and swindling," and threatened immediate reprisals. A day later the Oil City *Derrick* adopted a still more belligerent tone. It declared that "a torpedo is filling for the scheme" and would blow it sky-high.[40]

It was on February 25 that the fear and resentment of the Oil Regions finally burst in a terrific storm. That day an officer of the Jamestown & Franklin branch of the Lake Shore became confused, and put the new rates into effect on the oil-carrying business. The firm of Lombard, Ayres & Co. in New York learned of them, and telegraphed its buyer in the Oil Regions, Josiah Lombard. "Oil rate prohibitive," ran the message. "What is the matter?" Lombard was astounded to find that the charge for carrying crude oil from Warren to New York had shot up from 87 cents to $2.14. He and others soon learned that rates on crude and refined oil between all points

[40]Early comment was vague. As late as February 26, the Pittsburgh *Gazette* remarked that "notwithstanding there has been a good deal of inquiry made in regard to the matter, as yet but little seems to be known definitely about it. It is rumored that a number of Cleveland refiners have or are about to dispose of their works to this company, or 'ring' as it is termed. . . ."

had similarly risen. They were aghast. The news of Fort Sumter had not produced more excitement in western Pennsylvania.

Streets and hotel lobbies in the Oil Regions towns immediately filled with angry, gesticulating men. Refiners pledged to secrecy forgot their promises and told all they knew, so that within a few hours the most carefully guarded details were public property. The producers learned that Watson was president of the combination; that Lockhart, Waring, Warden, Bostwick, and Rockefeller were in it. They learned that the three oil-carrying railroads had signed contracts with the combination which, if forcible action were not taken, would ruin all independent refiners, or drive them into the "ring" on any terms the monopoly wished to make. It is not strange that the two-fisted fighters of the Regions prepared to struggle to the bitter end.[41]

On the night of February 27 three thousand wrathful men from all over the Regions gathered in the Titusville Opera House. Well-owners, refiners, oil-brokers, shopkeepers, bankers, all trooped in. They bore banners with defiant slogans: "No Compromise!" "Down With the Conspirators!" "Don't Give Up the Ship!" Denunciatory speeches were received with deafening cheers. Leading refiners were wildly applauded as they described the oath of secrecy, the base proposals made to them, and their indignant rejection of the conspiracy. The interested railroad presidents had been interrogated by telegraph, and had not had time to agree upon their answers. The chairman read a telegram from George B. McClellan, president of the Atlantic & Great Western:

Neither the Atlantic & Great Western, nor any of its officers, are interested in the South Improvement Company. Of course the policy of the road is to accommodate the petroleum interest.

Applause was checked by violent hisses from a little group whose leader sprang forward waving another telegram. It was from Jay Gould, president of the Erie:

Contract with South Improvement Company signed by George B. McClellan, president of the Atlantic & Great Western Railroad. I only signed it after it was signed by all the other parties.

The meeting rocked with jeers and derisive laughter. Its members

[41] I have used files of Oil Regions newspapers in the Carnegie Institute at Pittsburgh, the Drake Museum at Titusville, and elsewhere.

took heart from the evidence that one railroad system was ready to desert the scheme instantly—was in fact crawling out of it with timid equivocations.[42]

But this gathering was only the first wave sent up by the tide of fury that had seized the Regions. The meeting had more violence than effectiveness, for it did little beyond passing resolutions which excoriated the railroads, the combination, and the legislative charter. What was needed was an organization, and organizations are created by a few leaders, not by mass-meetings. The gathering adjourned to meet at Oil City two days later. In the interim a half-dozen vigorous men were hard at work laying plans. The Titusville *Herald,* in language typical of the whole Oil Regions press, declaimed:[43]

The South Improvement Company also claim that they are organized for the protection of refiners. For their protection against whom, or against what? is the question. . . . Astounding as it may appear, it is for the protection of Cleveland, Pittsburgh, and New York against the city of Titusville and Oil Creek, which is the only natural refining point in the country. It may not be generally known that our refiners in this city have for years had to contend against drawbacks granted by railroad companies to some of the largest refining houses in Cleveland and Pittsburgh, and that notwithstanding this they are languishing and do not pay, while Titusville refiners have been flourishing, and have always made a respectable margin of profit. This fact is patent to every refiner engaged in the oil business, and now these refiners are endeavoring to combine to wipe Titusville and Oil City refiners out of existence.

On March 1 crowds moved in a black stream through the streets of Oil City to a gathering at Love's Opera House as large and passionate as that held in Titusville. This time the leaders organized a real army from the furious mob, and planned its campaign. The Petroleum Producers' Association already existed. It was now revitalized and given new and aggressive leadership. A board of directors was appointed which included William M. Irish, John D. Archbold, J. J. Vandergrift, A. P. Bennett, and H. H. Cummings, refiners, with H. T. Beers, William Hasson, E. G. Patterson, W. L. Lay, and

[42]Descriptions of the excitement are to be found in the Oil Regions correspondence of the N. Y. *Evening Post* and the N. Y. *Sun* in March, 1872; see particularly *The Sun's* article of March 6, "Crushing the Oil Ring."
[43]See article in the Titusville *Herald,* Feb. 26, 1872, "The Great Conspiracy," and similar articles in succeeding issues. Probably no Oil Regions refinery was making a better profit than the Standard; many plants were losing.

F. W. Mitchell, producers. A series of rousing speeches was delivered. One producer declared that the South Improvement Company was well named—it improved on the South by enslaving white men. Others derided it as the "Cleveland and Pittsburgh Relief Association." John D. Archbold, a short, smooth-faced, boyish-looking refiner of Titusville, one of the youngest yet most dynamic of the Oil Regions leaders, made an eloquent appeal for union "against the common enemy." He was followed by another young man distinguished by his handsome bearing, resourcefulness, and love of battle—Lewis Emery, Jr., destined to be a lifelong enemy of Rockefeller. Emery urged that producers and refiners of the Regions at once combine to restrict production and to control marketing. He recommended three immediate steps: (1) That all producers shut off one third of their capacity; (2) that no torpedoes or other artificial aids to production be used; and (3) that no new wells be commenced for thirty days. These proposals, embodied in a resolution, were immediately carried.

Even the mighty Tom Scott was now retreating. On March 2 he telegraphed an Oil Regions representative: "On my return last evening I received your message. Our lines will not do anything which will interfere with the mutual and relative interests of producers and shippers. There is more money invested now than can be made to pay fairly, consequently additional capital will be a useless sacrifice."

The reinvigorated Producers' Association was given a new name, the Petroleum Producers' Union, and its leaders planned to extend it over the entire oil-bearing area, enlisting every producer. Members were pledged to start no new wells for two months, to stop work on Sundays, and above all, to sell no crude oil to any representative of the South Improvement Company, but only to Oil Creek refiners and to such others as opposed the combination. The Oil City *Derrick,* edited by C. E. Bishop, published a "black list" of promoters of the South Improvement Company, and kept it standing in a box at its "masthead" day after day. To these promoters no true son of the Regions would ship oil. Within a few days 112 producers had signed what the *Derrick's Handbook* later called a "shut-down pledge"—the agreement, as urged by Emery, to cut off one third of production. Feeling continued to mount, and any producer who did business with Warden, Waring, Logan, Bostwick, or Rockefeller, or any man who pumped oil on Sunday, risked his property and even his life.[44]

The Petroleum Producers' Union thus prepared to fight monopoly with monopoly. If it could extend its sway over most wells in the Regions, it would control the supply of crude oil which every South Improvement refiner must have, and starve the "anaconda" to death.

VII

Seldom has an economic organization been greeted with a wilder uproar of attack than that which now raged about the South Improvement Company. For weeks almost the whole body of oil-producers abandoned business and surged from town to town denouncing the combination. Their assault was posited squarely on moral grounds. The "Forty Thieves," the "Monster," the "Octopus," the "Ring," the "Gigantic Railroad Monopoly"—so men called the company; its members were "conspirators" and "robbers." This judgment was later accepted by a long series of writers. Even Gilbert H. Montague, defender of the Standard Oil Company, writes that the South Improvement scheme "has never since had an apologist." What, then, of Rockefeller and Flagler? How did they defend an organization which they entered so vigorously and aggressively?

Combinations to reduce or abolish competition were of course no novelty in 1870, and whenever competition had been economically destructive, were not clearly condemned by public opinion. The railway pools had been praised by many shippers as well as investors, for sharp fluctuations in rates were more ruinous to shippers than high schedules. A well-known pool in cordage manufacturing had been formed in 1860. The Michigan salt pool was too weak to be effective, but for a time it promised benefits to consumers (in improving the quality of salt and regularizing prices) as well as manufacturers. The oil-producers, now so bitter in denouncing monopoly, had not long since attempted to form one themselves! Combination was constantly cropping out in new fields. The New York *Times*

[44]But the Pittsburgh *Gazette* stated March 12, 1872: "We are reliably informed that many of the largest producers refuse to enter into any combination, but aver that they will remain unentrammeled, will conduct their business in their own way, and will sell their product to who ever will pay the most money, regardless of the South Improvement Company or any other company."

for January 21, 1872, for example, called attention to a monopolistic organization planned by manufacturers of manila paper. If this oil combination were really inclusive—a trade association embracing every one, not a mere ring of greedy insiders—then much could be said for it; and apparently Rockefeller so regarded it.

Nor was the use of rebates and drawbacks a novelty, or in any general degree condemned by public opinion. We have traced it as far back as 1856, and seen that it was so widespread as to provoke a legislative investigation in Pennsylvania in 1867. No evidence exists that Rockefeller received rebates any earlier than dozens of other refiners. Indeed, Henry Ohlen, an oil broker fiercely antagonistic to the South Improvement scheme, spoke in March, 1872, of six years of drawbacks or rebates. "We would raise a howl and get a drawback," he said, "when Cleveland would come in again and get a higher one."[45] This statement places the origin of oil rebates at least as far back as 1866. As Rockefeller later said, the refiners who assailed rebates were usually those who had not been successful in obtaining them. He often told how Samuel Downer, first of the great refiners, remarked to Flagler in New York, where both were seeking railroad concessions: "Flagler, I am opposed to the whole scheme of rebates and drawbacks—without I'm in it!"[46]

It was therefore easy for Rockefeller and Flagler to find arguments for resorting to combination at a time when—though they were avowedly making money—unrestricted competition was ruining many refiners and threatened universal disaster. There was every prospect in January, 1872, that production for the year would break all records. It actually did so, rising above six million barrels. There was every prospect that prices would remain at levels which meant sheer bankruptcy. Crude oil sold in New York in January at $12\frac{3}{4}$ to $13\frac{1}{2}$ cents a gallon; refined oil at $22\frac{3}{4}$ to $23\frac{1}{2}$ cents. The refiners of Cleveland, Pittsburgh, and Philadelphia saw nothing but losses and sheriff's sales in the immediate past, nothing but despair in the immediate future. Their leaders had quite as good reason to attempt combination as the leaders in Western and Southern railways, in salt and cordage manufacture, and in anthracite production. It was also easy for Flagler and Rockefeller to find arguments to

[45]*Rise and Fall of the South Improvement Company.*
[46]Rockefeller, *Random Reminiscences,* 112.

justify accepting moderate rebates. General business sentiment of the time would have justified them even in the bargain they made with the Lake Shore in 1870. The rebate was roughly analogous to what we call today a quantity discount, and even a housewife thinks it natural that ten-cent bars of soap should sell three for a quarter.

But the savage and destructive drawbacks envisaged by the South Improvement contracts are another matter. The favored refiners were to be given such a crushing advantage over all competitors as to assure the complete ruin of the latter. To make ruin doubly certain and rapid, these competitors were to be subject to secret as well as open exactions. Can this be defended?

The answer is that it was utterly indefensible. It was one of the great errors of Rockefeller's career that he hurriedly aligned himself with an arrangement so repugnant to public sentiment then and afterward. This cruel feature of the South Improvement Company fixed a most unfortunate stigma upon his and Flagler's names. Something, to be sure, can be said in extenuation. The "Tom Scott scheme" had been sprung upon the refiners unexpectedly, and adopted in haste to meet an exigent crisis. Its worst devices were probably intended not to ruin competitors, but to bring them within the combination—to coerce, and not to crush. Here was an industry in which overproduction, chaotic marketing, and price-slashing were producing ruinous effects. A little group of refiners and railroad heads were organizing to stop all this. They knew well that they could not *persuade* everybody to join, that they would need a club. Would it not be well to brandish a cudgel so massive that its mere exhibition would frighten every refiner within the organization? Once more we may recall Warden's testimony in 1872: "It never entered my head that the refiners would not all be brought in."

But such excuses fall far short of covering the ground. We may grant that the South Improvement Company was later grossly misrepresented. Various writers have tried to produce an impression that the oil business was thriving up to the time the company was launched, when actually it was disorganized, half-ruined, and filled with apprehension.[47] These writers have asserted that the com-

---

[47]These roseate pictures are drawn by Henry Demarest Lloyd in *Wealth Against Commonwealth*, and, with much less exaggeration, by Ida M. Tarbell in *History of the Standard Oil Company*, I.

pany was planned by Rockefeller, when actually it originated elsewhere. They have represented the company as devised, in a selfish and arrogant spirit, for the enrichment of a little group of insiders, when at least its *professed* intention was to combine the competitors, not crush them, and to bring the whole body of refiners together upon a new basis of prosperity. But when all this is said, the great fact remains that its brutally aggressive rebate-contracts were quite outside the pale of business ethics, even in that loose period. They ran counter to the essential spirit of freedom and democracy in American enterprise.

Indefensible was the verdict of impartial observers then; indefensible must be the verdict now. Yet having said this, we must point out that Rockefeller sincerely persuaded himself that the South Improvement scheme was just. His letters show that he had discussed his plans carefully with his wife and kept her fully informed. This alone goes far to prove that he was convinced he was following a proper course, for Mrs. Rockefeller was a highly religious woman with stern moral standards. His letters from New York also show that he was indignant over the attacks showered upon him. "It is easy to write newspaper articles but we have other business," he exclaimed on March 15. "We will do right and not be nervous or troubled about what the papers say, by and by when all are through possibly we may briefly respond (though it is not our policy) and leave future events in the business to demonstrate our intentions and plans were just & warranted. I want to act perfectly conscientiously and fearlessly in the matter and feel confident of good results. Sorry it seems best not to go at once to you and our dear children but duty to this matter seems imperatively to demand my stay here few days longer and I am hopeful can get at least a good fraction of the N. Y. Refiners to join at an early day." Two days later he wrote in the same vein:[48]

We do not allow the newspaper articles to trouble us, knowing by whom written and the influences that induce them. Your F(ather) thinks we are quite right in making no answer. My health has been splendid—and I am yet decided to persevere—it may take weeks and months yet to succeed but the Union of our American Refineries is worth much labor and patient effort—and that I will give and at the same time not let it chafe and annoy me. I was never more thankful for good health. . . .

[48]Rockefeller Papers.

And again on March 21:

I am still persevering and hopeful, remember *our* side have not yet been in the papers. We know a *few* things the people generally may not, at all events we know our own intentions, and that they are *right* and *only* so—but please say *nothing* only you know your husband will stand by and *stick* to the right. (It may be the best thing to have the public feel we are defeated in order to allay the excitement but we will not decide that yet.) I have hopeful indications (this is a game of chess not chequors). I desire to be remembered to my friends who inquire after me.

And still again on March 23:

We had meeting in our office with three Producers (part of the R.R. Committee) and these meetings bring us into better relations all the time. I go with Will, Bostwick & others to Continental (Hotel) Phild. & expect to return here next day (tomorrow) late at night. I assure you it is not my pleasure to remain all this time but a stern sense of duty to this cause. I haven't any idea giving up ship or letting go my hold, though I feel pleasantly even towards those who have misused me, and will try and not allow all this *noise* and bluster to cause me to yield any vital point. Already we could compromise, by giving up our freight contracts, the Producers recognizing we *ought* to *unite,* as Refiners for protection, but the fact is we *did* not contemplate swindling the public in *it* and it is not the business of the public to change our private contracts. I cannot write you in detail. I am now *hurrying* to go.

These letters show the stubborn unemotionalism and intellectual imperturbability so characteristic of the man. The excitement of the Oil Regions did not move him, for he despised excitement. The idea expressed by the Regions men did not impress him, for he believed his own idea far superior. What he did not realize yet was that behind this idea of free competition lay the massive and immovable convictions of the American people. But even if he had realized it he probably would not have wavered. He had considered his steps in advance. It was in the spirit of this consideration, and not merely to rationalize his own conduct, that he exclaimed in 1917:[49] "I had our plan clearly in mind. It was right. I knew it as a matter of conscience. It was right between me and my God. If I had to do it tomorrow I would do it again in the same way—do it a hundred times."

But we must return to the battle between the South Improvement Company and the outraged Oil Regions, now nearing its climax.

[49]Inglis, Conversations with Rockefeller.

XV

War, Open and Understood

SUPERFICIALLY, this battle between the South Improvement Company and the Oil Regions was simply a struggle of two regional groups for the major profits of the petroleum industry. Actually its significance went much deeper. In essentials it was a contest between heavily capitalized industry, seeking concentration and organization, and the individualistic small businessman; between a new economic order and the old. The conditions of the oil domain had changed. Refining was fast becoming an industry of big units which found chaotic price-slashing by small competitors intolerable, while oil production was still a field for adventurous men of moderate resources. There was a natural affinity between the large refiners and the railroads, while most well-owners displayed basically the same spirit as the Grangers. Many of the former, thirsting for stability, were ready to found a great monopoly; the latter, devoted to free enterprise, were quick to call in the State to dispel any threat to the competitive régime in their industry.

The Regions men shrewdly perceived the paramount importance of public opinion, and their principal efforts were exerted to enlist it. They not only united to control the supply of crude oil and starve the "monster" to death; they not only appointed a committee to demand that the Pennsylvania Legislature annul the South Improvement charter, and sent another to Washington to request a Congressional investigation; they not only prepared a ninety-three-foot petition asking the State to legalize "free" pipe-lines. Over and above all this, they held more meetings, they filled the press with denunciations, and they took steps to prepare a history of the battle against the nefarious organization, and to scatter 30,000 copies throughout the nation, "to the end that enemies of freedom of trade may be known and shunned by all honest men."[1] Finally, they enrolled a thousand men to move instantly upon Harrisburg should a mass demonstration seem expedient.

In short, it was a battle on three fronts—to crush the South Improvement Company by cutting off its oil supply, to destroy its legal basis by taking away its charter, and to array public sentiment in iron hostility against it. The leaders included prominent producers, refiners, and editors, of whom the first group naturally were the most prominent. Their dominant figure was Captain William Hasson, whom the meeting at Oil City elected president of the Petroleum Producers' Association. A stocky, belligerent little man, Hasson had been brought up in the Oil Regions, and owned a number of profitable wells. A little more than a year previous he had been prominent in an attempted "beer squeeze" planned in Titusville to break Jabez A. Bostwick and other buyers; but Bostwick and some associates, gaining control of the car supply, had unexpectedly smashed the corner and turned the tables on him. Resentment over this reverse perhaps played a part in his fiery efforts to stir up opposition. With him were ranged such wealthy producers as John L. Mitchell, B. B. Campbell, John Fertig, Foster W. Mitchell, Edwin E. Clapp, and D. S. Criswell.[2] Among the group were two men of whom we shall hear more—William M. Irish, who subsequently joined the Standard and whose son became president of the Atlantic Refining Company,[3] and E. G. Patterson, destined in a few years to play the rôle of Benedict Arnold in the struggle between the Regions and Standard.

Although the vast majority of the producers were men of moderate means, taken as a body they held tremendous wealth. During the past two years the large well-owners had fared better than most refiners. Hasson, Fertig, and the Mitchells were probably as rich as Rockefeller, while still others brought both substantial fortunes and the hope of large future gains to their battle with the South Improvement Company. They have usually been pictured as an impoverished and

[1] Ida M. Tarbell, *Standard Oil Company*, I, 72. The record was duly published under the title of *A History of the Rise and Fall of the South Improvement Company*.

[2] For material on Fertig, see J. J. McLaurin, *Sketches in Crude Oil*, 119; on the Mitchells, p. 146; on Hasson, p. 153; on Criswell, p. 149; on Clapp, p. 176. See also Boyle, *Derrick's Handbook*, biographical section.

[3] Mr. Irish has kindly given me much information.

struggling band, oppressed by a league of plutocrats, and battling disinterestedly for a great principle. But most of them were men of some property, while a few were rich; and like Warden, Lockhart, Frew, and Rockefeller, who also declared they were fighting for a great principle, their moral objects were strictly subordinate to personal profit. Fundamentally, everybody engaged was fighting for money and power.

At least two of the Oil Regions refiners were men of conspicuous ability. Captain Jacob Jay Vandergrift, famous as steamboat captain and pipe-line organizer, had indignantly rejected the overtures of Watson and thrown in his lot with the Regions men. Still abler was the young Titusville refiner, John D. Archbold. Only twenty-four, slight, short, and boyish-looking, he had nevertheless made a powerful impression when he spoke at the Oil City meeting. With dramatic vigor he told how, when summoned by Watson to New York, sworn to secrecy, and asked to join in establishing a monopoly, he had scornfully refused the proposal. He had warned Watson: "If you think the people of this region will quietly submit to a tax of five million dollars a year, from this or any other corporation, you very much mistake their character!"[4] Archbold's dynamic traits would have arrested attention anywhere. The son of an impecunious Baptist minister, he had come to the Oil Regions from Salem, O., as a spindling lad of sixteen. Finding work with William H. Abbott of Titusville, he had learned every department of the oil business, for Abbott was a producer, refiner, oil-broker, and pipe-line operator all at once. When in 1869 Abbott's ill-financed company collapsed, the twenty-one-year-old Archbold struck out boldly. Adding to his savings $800 borrowed from one of Abbott's dump workers, he became a partner in the refining firm of Porter, Moreland & Company. His energy, shrewdness, and popularity were important factors in building up this new business. There was something wonderfully infectious in his debonair manner, quick smile, and friendly wit. He delighted in every type of jollity; he was manager of the Titusville baseball nine, a lover of fast horses, a tireless poker-player, and at times a convivial drinker. By 1872 Porter, Moreland were refining 25,000 barrels of oil a month, more than any other firm in Titusville. The alert, audacious, and highly temperamental young man was already the principal force

[4] See Archbold's statement in Titusville *Herald*, March 4, 1872.

in this company, and was plainly to be reckoned with in all petroleum affairs.[5]

Sometime in 1871 Rockefeller, visiting Titusville to buy crude oil, registered at a hotel. He looked at the other names on the page. Just above his own he read, in a bold hand, "John D. Archbold, $4 a bbl." It was the young refiner's trade-mark, his method of proclaiming the price which he believed oil ought to bring; and Rockefeller was impressed by this touch of advertising genius. Decades later the irrepressible Archbold, harder and more aggressive, but still debonair and fun-loving, was to succeed Rockefeller as president of the Standard Oil Company. But for the present the two men were opponents. At the Oil City meeting Archbold urged the producers to form a fighting alliance with the refiners of the Regions. The latter, he said, stood ready to appoint a committee to arrange for joint measures. "They trust that the good result of this great agitation will be to center the whole refining business in this, its natural location, the producers' region." He and Vandergrift assured the producers that if they withheld crude oil from the South Improvement refiners, they would still find an ample market in the plants of their own district and in allied refineries outside.

The press of the Regions played an important part in the battle, for its editorials and articles were copied far and wide. Two editors were particularly effective. One was N. M. Allen of the Titusville *Courier,* a refiner as well as journalist; a slender, alert man with watchful dark eyes, whose heavy mustaches and dangling sideburns gave him the aspect of a stage villain.[6] Equally aggressive was C. E. Bishop, editor of the Oil City *Derrick,* who prided himself on his command of satire, and a sledgehammer invective. He is credited with inventing the terms "octopus" and "anaconda" for the combination, and he it was who placed the "black list" of guilty refiners and railroads in a staring box.

II

On March 5, a third mass meeting at Franklin, Pa., carried forward the enthusiastic campaign of the Regions against monopoly; and

[5]Austin L. Moore, *Life of John D. Archbold, passim.*

[6]John J. McLaurin, *Sketches in Crude Oil,* 312, 313. The editor-in-chief of *The Courier* in 1872 was Colonel T. J. Henry, who the next year published *The Early and Later History of Petroleum.* The owners were Major W. W. Bloss, H. C. Bloss, and J. H. Cogswell.

again the hall was jammed by delegations from all over the valley. Amid howls of applause men held up a gigantic cartoon. It showed Watson being tossed by a bull whose tail he vainly tried to grasp, Jay Gould and General McClellan calling each other liars, and the scared refiners of Cleveland, Pittsburgh, and Philadelphia hustling for cover. Producers and refiners of the Regions were depicted as gleeful spectators, shouting "No oil for the ring!" This caricature breathed the spirit of jubilant triumph which possessed the gathering. They were winning and they knew it. After adjournment, special committees for organizing the district labored night and day, and had their reports ready at a fourth meeting in Oil City on the 8th. Here the final plans for stopping all shipments of oil to the enemy were adopted with enthusiasm.

By this time aid had been assured from important allies. New York dealers and refiners had dispatched cheering messages, and promised to send on a delegation. Boston and Erie men expressed their sympathy.[7] Buffalo businessmen had telegraphed the first Oil City gathering: "Hope your meeting will devise speedy means to bring oil to the lake shore."[8] They immediately promised a low freight rate of sixty cents a barrel on all crude oil routed through their city to New York, and held out the hope that they could raise large sums for a railroad running direct to the Regions. Indeed, a deputation of about fifty Buffalonians, headed by Mayor Bush, soon hurried to Oil City to pledge a million dollars to the enterprise.

But particularly heartening to the Oil Regions was the support offered by New York refiners. This group telegraphed on March 8 that they were organizing an association to fight alongside the embattled Regions men, and three days later sent up a special committee to lay plans for joint resistance. This delegation, frock-coated and silk-hatted, marched to the train behind a handsome young man who was destined to play a great part in Rockefeller's career and in American business history—Henry H. Rogers. Only thirty-two, a native of Fairhaven, Mass., he had operated a refinery on Oil Creek for a time, and then had gone to Long Island in 1868 to join the refiner Charles Pratt. His chiselled features, urbane and polished air, careful dress,

---

[7] Boyle, *Derrick's Handbook*, 171. The best summary account of the four meetings is in the Titusville correspondence of the N. Y. *World*, July 9, 1872.
[8] N. Y. *Journal of Commerce*, March 2, 1872.

and magnetic personality made him a distinguished figure in any gathering; he could grace a drawing-room or dominate a business meeting with equal skill. But this polished exterior covered a gamester's recklessness and a total lack of scruple in financial affairs.[9] He was now really the dominant figure in the Pratt Manufacturing Company, which with a ten-still refinery on Long Island, tanks holding 23,000 barrels, and special facilities for exporting, was making "Pratt's Astral" famous throughout Europe.[10] He was able to assure the Regions men that Bostwick of the South Improvement Company was weak compared with his New York rivals, and that a union of the Long Island refiners and the Regions interests would be invincible.[11]

The leaders of the opposition naturally did not pause to examine the South Improvement plan in detail, or to listen to whatever arguments might be offered in its behalf. Watson made a desperate effort to gain a hearing, for he had a wide reputation, political and financial, and knew well that his public character was involved. In particular, he wrote a series of indignant letters to a prominent producer, Foster W. Mitchell, expostulating and explaining. Watson had distinct personal grievances, an oil tank which he owned at Franklin having been broached, while he had received an anonymous threat of damage to

[9] No biography of Rogers is yet available; see, besides the sketch in the *Dictionary of American Biography,* the incisive characterization in Thomas W. Lawson, *Frenzied Finance,* Ch. 3. An effort by the author in 1936–37, several times renewed, to gain access to Rogers' papers, was met by information from an attorney connected with the estate that the business papers were being destroyed.

[10] See the description of Pratt's works in *The Scientific American,* May 18, 1872; they were at Williamsburg (East Brooklyn).

[11] See the interview with Rogers in the N. Y. *Herald,* March 17, 1872. The South Improvement Company played its cards badly in New York. A meeting of dealers and refiners (the New York Petroleum Association) on March 10 called upon the South Improvement Company to "present in writing a proposal for consolidation." It declined, the officers instead inviting individual refiners "to meet representatives of the company." This looked like an effort to cajole or bludgeon the New York refiners into line one by one, and the invitation was indignantly rejected by the group acting as a whole. N. Y. *Times, Tribune,* March 11, 12, 1872. At a second meeting of the Petroleum Association on the 11th, Charles Pratt declared that the South Improvement Company was made up of Westerners, that the interests of New York refiners were alien to those of Pittsburgh and Cleveland men, and that open competition would be best for the trade. He offered several resolutions which were quickly adopted. One attacked "any system of railroad transportation rebates in freights or carrying charges"; another pledged the New York refiners to support competition as "the only sound and permanent base" for the oil business. N. Y. *Times, Herald,* March 11, N. Y. *World,* March 12, 1872.

the Jamestown & Franklin branch of the Lake Shore.[12] In his first letter, dated March 4, he recalled that he had talked with Mitchell in New York and had made it clear that the well-owners were not to be left out of the protective scheme. "On meeting you here on your return from the South, I explained to you very briefly that the whole plan of the South Improvement Company was founded upon the expectation of co-operation with the oil producers to maintain a good price for crude oil. . . . I stated to you in the strongest terms the desire of the South Improvement to enter into an arrangement for a series of years with the producers, whereby good prices for crude oil at the wells and fair and reasonable rates of transportation would at all times be assured. The desire still exists."

He begged his friend to urge the appointment of a producers' committee to confer with the South Improvement Company and arrange a plan of co-operation. But this plea fell upon deaf ears. When Mitchell presented it at the Franklin mass meeting, the majority received it with epithets and shouts of "No." "We are lowering our dignity to treat with Watson!" shouted one producer. "He has set a trap for us!" cried another. Watson appeared before the New York dealers and refiners on the 11th, and made a cool explanation of the origin and plans of the company, confessing the railroads' initiative. But when Mitchell tried to induce him to speak before a meeting in the Oil Regions, he wisely declined. "A mass meeting is not a deliberative body," he wrote. He would meet the producers at any point favorable to calm investigation, but not in the atmosphere of excitement that filled the Allegheny Valley. Of course the producers rejected any such suggestion. Why treat when they were winning?

For winning they were. When the deputation under H. H. Rogers reached the Regions, the crude-oil blockade was almost completely effective. The tanks of the Standard Oil and other members of the South Improvement Company would soon be running dry.

III

Though he felt none of Watson's agony, Rockefeller experienced a deep chagrin as he watched this sudden storm. The swiftness with which it burst had dismayed him and Flagler. They had hoped that

[12]Watson's letters are given in Leonard W. Bacon, *The South Improvement Company.*

the pledge of secrecy would prove far more effective. If all their arrangements, including the treaty with the producers, could have been perfected before the public gained any knowledge of the plan, this tempest might have been avoided. At the outset Rockefeller barred his door to reporters. Cleveland newspapers had to obtain what news they could from the resentful Flagler, who pooh-poohed the first mass meeting at Titusville as the work of "a few soreheads."[13] But when the second and third meetings proved that the Regions were in arms, when it appeared that New York, Buffalo, and Erie were uniting with the valley, and when the flow of crude oil to the Standard dried up to a trickle, even Flagler could not make light of the opposition. He soon ceased to talk at all, for Rockefeller still advised silence.

Any convulsion in the Oil Regions was sure to be news to Americans, for that district, in color, sensationalism, and general human interest, was in 1870 much what the California gold-diggings had been in 1850. The press of the whole country took a keen interest in this economic war in Northwestern Pennsylvania. Papers from Boston to Omaha were devoting columns, half amusedly, half indignantly, to the subject. For obvious reasons, they gave most of their space and still more of their sympathy to the Regions. In New York *The Sun, Tribune, Times,* and *Commercial Advertiser* either denounced the new combination openly, or criticized it by implication, while in Boston *The Advertiser* and in Philadelphia *The Public Ledger* took the same ground.[14] They regarded the producers as a valiant band of individualists fighting for the sacred cause of free competition. If the industry were sick and half-ruined, they declared, the remedy lay not in monopoly but in time, patience, and still more competition.

At this period public opinion was decidedly nervous over the darker possibilities of monopoly. The exposure of the Tweed Ring in New York, with which Jim Fisk and Jay Gould of the Erie were involved, and the Crédit Mobilier scandal, had caused many to associate indus-

---

[13]Cleveland *Plain Dealer,* March 5, 1872.

[14]I have examined files. The N. Y. *Sun's* news article, March 6, 1872, spoke of the Company as "one of the most gigantic and villainous schemes ever known"; the *Evening Post's* editorial of March 11 was headed, "Monopoly Not Authorized by Congress." The N. Y. *World,* itself antagonistic, quoted on March 2 a long denunciatory article from the Boston *Advertiser* entitled "What the Combination Means—How It Works—Its Consequences."

trial combinations with political "rings" and to feel a stern hostility to both. Moreover, ordinary shippers were eying the railroad pools with increasing suspicion. The salt, cordage, and other combinations had called forth protests from injured manufacturers and awakened fears of extortionate prices. Editors, legislators, and plain citizens, while still consciously ignorant of the economic issue involved and wary of attacking really powerful interests, were ready to turn sharply upon any combination which seemed both wicked and vulnerable. The South Improvement Company, comprehending three great railroads and the principal refining interests, was the most extensive combination yet formed. Its rebate scheme seemed impudent robbery. It was also the first large combination to be opposed in its own field by powerful foes, and was plainly fated to meet an early death. With Behemoth already brought to its knees, a thousand men hastened to pour arrows into its hide. The company thus became for millions of Americans, as for many years it remained, a symbol of monopolistic aggression upon human liberty.

Flagler, Warden, and Tom Scott were slow to perceive the depth of the passions they had aroused, and Rockefeller did not completely grasp it until decades had passed and several books had dealt with the subject. He failed to realize how unfortunate were the circumstances under which he had first appeared before the general public. But fifty years later, looking back upon these exciting months, he saw what he had lost. He explained that throughout his early business career he had followed a fixed principle of reticence.[15] "I determined that it was useless to waste energy on denials and disputes with jealous or disappointed people. I persuaded our partners to keep silence too. The more we progressed yet kept on gaining success and keeping silent, the more we were abused." In another connection he remarked, "Our silence encouraged the wildest romancers to spread wild tales about us."[16] But with the perspective of half a century he comprehended the damaging results of his taciturnity in 1872, and exclaimed:

"I shall never cease to regret that at that time we never called in the reporters."

Every writer on the subject—Henry Demarest Lloyd, Gilbert H. Montague, Ida M. Tarbell, Mark Sullivan, John T. Flynn—has treated the South Improvement Company as substantially without defenders

[15]Inglis, Conversations with Rockefeller.　　　　[16]*Idem.*

except in its own ranks. But this is an error. It had convinced champions, particularly among the editors of Pittsburgh and Cleveland: men who believed that it would furnish a remedy for conditions that had grown intolerable.

Even the New York *Times* of March 10 gave space to a long news article which outlined the case for the South Improvement Company with considerable sympathy. The writer asserted that it had never aimed at absolute monopoly, that it held out a promise of beneficial stabilization, and that the opposition was inspired by small refiners who had not been made "generals and major-generals in the concern." Nine days later *The Sun* published an illuminating interview with the pipe-line pioneer, Henry Harley, who said that he emphatically believed in the scheme. "The only mistake the company has made is that it did not conciliate the producing interests, which are not fairly represented in the company."[17] In Philadelphia *The Commercial List and Price Current* defended the company and assailed the producers for an intolerance which it compared with "the lawless Ku Klux Klan." Meanwhile, several Pittsburgh papers supplied a belligerent defense of the new scheme. *The Chronicle* published an interview with a refiner who declared that the combination was an effort "to revive the trade, to remove the ruinous competition existing, and to place the business on a firm and permanent basis."[18] The opposition he ascribed to one unnamed man who, after he had "made every effort to become a director of the company, and failed," had travelled throughout the Oil Regions to stir up enmity. The Pittsburgh *Gazette* came out as a vigorous champion of the combination. On March 8 it appended an editorial note to a long news dispatch upon the uproar. Watson, it remarked, was one of the ablest attorneys of Ohio, who had done Lincoln invaluable service, and was primarily responsible for the consolidation of the Lake Shore and New York Central. "From our knowledge of his antecedents and character we deem him incapable of engaging in any enterprise of questionable propriety. When the present agitation shall have had time to quiet down, and reason shall take the place which riot has usurped, we feel satisfied that the ends and purposes of the South

[17]N. Y. *Sun*, March 19, 1872.
[18]Quoted in Cleveland *Plain Dealer*, March 5, 1872; probably Waring, who would have been much more likely to speak than the tight-lipped Scotchman, Lockhart.

Improvement Company will be hailed as beneficial and praise-worthy." *The Gazette* continued to express this view.

The Pittsburgh *Commercial,* particularly concerned with industry, was even more outspoken. It deplored the "artificial" excitement in the Regions. It suggested that the Titusville and Oil City refiners had been maneuvering for a similar arrangement with the railroads as against Pittsburgh and Cleveland, and were enraged at being fore-stalled. Why did they not make an honest inquiry before flying into a passion? They would find out that some form of combination was imperative:[19]

Through our utter want of system we are literally throwing away our great advantage, giving Europe the benefit of our vast oil deposits for a mere song, whilst she would be glad to take it at twice the figures we charge her.

The causes of this state of things are, first, the chronic strife between the competing railroads, creating unhealthy fluctuations in the value of oil; second, the facilities for and disposition to make it an article of specu-lation; third, the excessive refining capacity of the country, leading to a constant underselling of the manufactured article, thus placing us at the mercy of the foreign buyer, and steadily hammering down the value of the raw material, until an illuminator which has no equal in the world is sold in Europe at one-half the price that would gladly be paid for it. . . . Today crude petroleum is selling at the wells at three and a half dollars per barrel, when it should steadily command five, and the refined article is selling in New York and Philadelphia at twenty-two cents per gallon, when it would be cheap at thirty or thirty-five.

Now what is the remedy for this state of things? The first thing to be done is to bring the railroads to a mutual understanding and a permanency in the charge for transportation, on a paying basis for themselves. Second, a union of the refining interests of the country, so that fair, uniform, and equitable prices can be secured; and third, a hearty cooperation on the part of the producing interests.

The South Improvement Company, declared *The Commercial,* would do as much for the oil industry as the existing iron and glass associations had done for price stabilization in those commodities. Till the very end the editor, feeling that the city's interests were gravely threatened by the Regions, defended the combination. But even he was significantly silent about the drawback upon competi-tive shipments.

[19]*The Commercial* printed numerous arguments Feb. 26–March 10. On March 2 it declared that if the Regions calmly investigated the Company, "they will find it a friend and not an enemy."

As for Cleveland, the South Improvement Company found a valiant defender there in *The Leader*. Its editorial on February 24 was vehement in tone:[20]

The league is a natural and,. as the world goes, a legitimate reply to the desperate attempt recently made by Titusville and Oil City to break down and swallow up the refining interests of Cleveland. Not content with the profit of producing and thereby controlling the crude market, the ambitious giants of the oil country felt that they must freeze out the Cleveland and Pittsburgh refiners, and play the whole game themselves. For eighteen months past the producers have carried a high hand, and Cleveland and Pittsburgh, who had invested their millions in the refining business, and would not be forced to the wall, were forced to dance as the men of the Creek might choose to fiddle. In locking horns with Pittsburgh and Cleveland, the Titusville men have found themselves pitted against ample capital, strong determination, and business ability of the highest order. They have made the fight, they drove the refiners to the necessity of combined action, and if the result leaves the Titusville plotters high and dry, they have themselves mainly to blame. We are not now discussing the moral aspects of business combinations of any kind, but simply stating the causes which have led to the consummation of which our oil country friends complain. For ourselves, it would be impossible not to admire the rare ability displayed by the refiners of this city in making Cleveland, in spite of all geographical disadvantages, the leading refining center of the world, fighting the combined hosts of Pittsburgh, New York, Tom Scott, and Erie, from year to year, always winning every point and wringing a heavy profit from a contest in which their opponents were pocketing constant losses.

Other emphatic editorials followed, and *The Leader* expressed hope that the producers would quiet down to await a fuller revelation of the purposes of the South Improvement Company. It explained just why the Regions now faced a seemingly hostile combination. The daily production of crude oil was 17,000 barrels; the total refining capacity of the country was 46,000 barrels; and the refiners' competition for this crude oil supply had placed them at the mercy of producers. The latter had taken a cruel advantage of this situation—and hence the combination. Its purpose was neither destruction nor exorbitant profits, but simply to bring refining capacity into a proper relationship with production:[21]

In carrying out this purpose the South Improvement Company has proceeded in a conspicuously fair and liberal manner. With the fullest

[20]Cleveland *Leader*, Feb. 24, 26, 1872.   [21]*Idem*, Feb. 27, 1872.

knowledge of all the facts in the case, we predict that when the producers and refiners of the oil regions understand the matter thoroughly and listen to the propositions that will be made to them, their hasty indignation and their apprehensions of injustice and exorbitance will be at once dismissed. If the oil business is to be made permanent and profitable to those engaged in it, it must be conducted not as a competitive speculation, but, like other legitimate business, in strict accordance with the laws of supply and demand. It is the good fortune of Cleveland that in the new arrangement her refining interests have been fairly and equitably protected. Cleveland will receive her fair share of crude petroleum; so will Pittsburgh, and likewise Titusville, and "The Creek," if they act sensibly and give up their purpose of monopolizing everything. No one has been wronged or cheated, and we predict that sixty days hence the entire petroleum interest of this country will be more satisfactory and prosperous than ever before.

The Leader continued to argue that "this great oil fight is simply the struggle of six men for a cake that three can eat,"[22] and to predict that when the Regions really understood the objectives of the company their fury would subside.

In the Cleveland *Herald* appeared the most notable protest by a Cleveland refiner, a long letter by Fred M. Backus, manufacturer of lubricants. While he had not yet been asked to sell out to the Standard, he was accurately informed as to the contracts signed by the South Improvement Company. The resulting advance in freights, he wrote, had already cost one firm $2000. He admitted that the situation prior to the formation of the new combine had been disastrous. Refining had been grossly overexpanded, the railroads were losing money, the refiners were facing bankruptcy, and the special interests of Cleveland were in danger of total ruin. But, he argued, the remedy was worse than the disease, for it was immoral—it involved enriching the strong at the expense of the weak. It was worse also because, if successful, it placed illimitable power in the hands of a small group. They might by a word wipe out Cleveland as a refining center, and transfer the whole industry to Pittsburgh or New York; they might take arrogant steps that would rob the consumer and destroy large business groups.[23]

[22]*Idem*, March 5, 1872.

[23]Cleveland *Herald*, March 2, March 6, 1872. Backus's letter is given in full in Tarbell, *Standard Oil Company*, I, 85–88. He states that the freight increases had gone directly to swell the profits of the new combination; but the combination was not in working order, and this was not true. It never received any rate-payments from the railroads.

The third important Cleveland newspaper, *The Plain Dealer,* tried to give a fair hearing to the South Improvement group. A reporter early in March made inquiries among leading refiners of the city. He stated that "some of the gentlemen called for were absent from their offices, some were absorbed in business, others were not thoroughly posted, and still others considered it not best to divulge all they knew just at this time." But he concluded that "if the unanimous verdict of these gentlemen interviewed be just, if what they say be true, then Cleveland has nothing to fear, but much to hope from the South Improvement Company."[24] However, a later editorial, "The March of Monopoly," denounced combinations in general as instruments by which "the many are plucked and robbed with no more compunction of conscience than the highwayman feels when stripping his victim," and pointed to the South Improvement Company as the latest monopolistic effort. The editor concluded that this company "is, like all great monopolies, thoroughly bad in spirit, and grounded in selfishness and injustice. If it dies it will have few mourners."[25]

IV

Before mid-April the destruction of the South Improvement scheme was rapidly completed. The Pennsylvania Legislature astonished everybody by passing a "free pipe-line bill," giving the right of eminent domain to pipe-companies. It had been repeatedly petitioned to do so since 1866, but the influence of the Pennsylvania Railroad had always blocked action. Unfortunately, the new law was restricted to the eight oil-producing counties, excluding Allegheny, in which Pittsburgh lies. The Cleveland *Leader* chuckled over this clever device for preserving railroad control of oil transportation.[26] By March 20 it was certain that Congress would investigate the South Improvement Company, and every one knew that Congress would be hostile. A bill to repeal the South Improvement charter was being pushed through the Legislature, and neither the railroads nor the Pittsburgh refiners dared to offer much opposition. Early in April it became law. The Pennsylvania Railroad was particularly frightened, for Tom Scott feared that the special charter of the Pennsylvania Company, so vital to its expansion, might also come under attack.

[24]March 5, 1872. *The Plain Dealer* was Democratic.
[25]Cleveland *Plain Dealer*, March 25, 1872.   [26]March 15, 1872.

But neither laws nor investigations were needed to finish the rout of the South Improvement group. The stoppage of oil shipments alone would have ruined the scheme. Day after day and week after week the producers, who had divided their territory into sixteen tightly policed districts, maintained their embargo against the South Improvement refiners. It was almost as dangerous for a Regions man to be suspected of traffic with the enemy as it had been for a Northerner to be suspected of copperheadism and treason ten years earlier. One incident out of a hundred will illustrate the intense feeling which pervaded the valley. A special meeting of the Titusville Oil Exchange was summoned to deal with Daniel O'Day, Joseph Seep, and others accused of being tools of the South Improvement Company. O'Day, a burly, energetic, rough-spoken Irishman who had been working for Bostwick, but who did not yet know that his employer had joined the combination, denied any connection. Indignant producers surrounded him, yelling, gesticulating, and threatening him with physical violence. They also menaced Seep, a lovable German-American who had been employed by Bostwick for a dozen years, and who had risen from a sick-bed to go to the meeting on crutches. Facing the infuriated men, both feared for their lives. But as Seep said later, "little John D. Archbold, his boyish face aglow, rose out of that meeting of angry, bearded, husky men, and in his manly voice protested against the proceedings, saying that we should not be held responsible for the views or doings of our employers."[27] This quieted the assemblage. However, when reports spread that John Mawhinney of Titusville had sold 5000 barrels of crude to the South Improvement Company, another excited gathering denounced his act as angrily as if it had been arson or robbery.[28] Many producers rejected tempting offers from the oil-hungry refiners. F. S. Tarbell, father of Ida M.

[27]Moore, *Life of John D. Archbold*, 82, 83.
[28]Cleveland *Leader*, March 16, 1872. For a time grave fears existed in Cleveland and Pittsburgh that a combination of Regions men and the New York Petroleum Association would try to freeze out the Western cities. At this time the production of crude stood at about 17,000 barrels a day. The capacity of the New York refineries, Regions refineries, and other units outside Cleveland and Pittsburgh was fully 18,000 barrels a day. Why should not these establishments take the entire output, leaving Cleveland and Pittsburgh to utter ruin? When H. H. Rogers returned from Titusville on March 16, he gave out an interview which some interpreted as a summons to the Oil Regions and New York to take complete control of the refining industry; N. Y. *Herald*, March 17, 1872. What had thus begun as a battle against one monopoly would thus end as a

Tarbell, proudly refused a contract for his whole year's output at $4.50 a barrel.

The railroads were naturally the first to surrender, for they had most to fear from public antagonism and the threat of legislative action. When a committee of twelve independents, three from New York, and nine from the Regions, called on Tom Scott in Philadelphia on March 18 to ask the Pennsylvania to cancel its contract, it found him full of apologies and explanations. He said he had supposed that Rockefeller, Warden, Waring, Bostwick, and their companions represented the petroleum trade; but now that the Pennsylvania Railroad knew they did not, it would be glad to make similar contracts with the committee of twelve who did represent it! The committee declined this kind favor. On March 19 they called on the New York Central authorities. Commodore Vanderbilt expressed sympathy, told them how much he hated monopoly, and blamed the contracts on his son. "I told Billy not to have anything to do with that scheme," he remarked. He also read a letter from the South Improvement Company offering to compromise its differences with the Regions, and to co-operate with all producers and refiners there. Apparently the New York Central and other railroads would have been glad to work out such a compromise, and made repeated efforts to do so. But the committee of twelve told Commodore Vanderbilt that they would never treat with the South Improvement Company or any member of it.[29]

By March 25 all the railroads involved in the South Improvement contracts were willing to repudiate them, and a meeting for that purpose was called at the Erie offices in New York. Besides the committee

---

contest to establish another. The Cleveland *Plain Dealer* had already (March 11) sounded a note of warning to the local industry. "The oil fight," it said in a news article, "has been reduced to a battle of monopolies for supremacy." If these suspicions had any validity, the South Improvement Company was the less objectionable combination of the two. It professedly looked to a *general* union rather than one between two districts.

Regions papers waxed arrogant in the extreme. The Titusville *Courier* (quoted in Cleveland *Plain Dealer,* March 12, 1872) pronounced Cleveland and Pittsburgh thoroughly unsuited to the oil-refining industry. "How many cents on a dollar of the cost is a refinery situated in Cleveland worth for refining oil for export? NARY RED. What are refineries worth situated in Pittsburgh? Ask the Philadelphia commission men; they own them. *Where is the proper place to refine oil?* At Oil Creek, New York and Philadelphia."

[29]Tarbell, *Standard Oil Company,* I, 91.

of twelve, representatives of the Erie, New York Central, Pennsylvania, Lake Shore, and Atlantic & Great Western were present. President Clark of the Lake Shore presided. No South Improvement men had been invited. But Rockefeller and Peter H. Watson, eager to gain a final hearing, appeared. The scene was the ornate Grand Opera House on Eighth Avenue where "Jim" Fisk had so flamboyantly pursued art, moneymaking, and pleasure. When the two men knocked at the door, they were refused admittance. "We want nothing to do with you!" protested the oil producers. But President Clark intervened with strong feeling. He insisted that they must not shut out "my lifelong friend, Watson." The latter actually pushed inside the room, while Rockefeller paced the corridor. But Watson's reception was so hostile that he soon emerged, red-faced and flustered. The newspapers reported that as he and Rockefeller walked away they both looked "pretty blue."[30] And well they might—for they had no sooner gone than the railroads agreed to drop the South Improvement contract forever, and make a new one with the independents.

In this abandonment of their recent allies the railroads showed the coolest indifference. Under the new contract, all rates were to be public and equal. Representatives of the five roads agreed that the transportation of oil should be upon "a basis of perfect equality to all shippers, producers, and refiners, and that no rebates, drawbacks, or other arrangements of any character shall be made or allowed. . . ." On refined oil all shippers, whether in the Oil Regions, Pittsburgh, or Cleveland, were to pay $1.65 a barrel to Boston, $1.50 to New York, and $1.35 to Philadelphia. Crude oil was to be hauled from the Regions to Boston for $1.50 a barrel, to New York for $1.35, to Philadelphia and Baltimore for $1.20, and to Cleveland and Pittsburgh for fifty cents. Nor should any increase or decrease be put into effect without at least ninety days' notice to the Producers' Union. The railroads, still anxious to find some means of "evening" traffic, had made an effort to persuade the independents to accept a contract resembling that of the South Improvement Company, and to ship as much oil. The New York Central and Lake Shore in particular had stood out for this arrangement. But the committee of twelve refused to listen. They insisted that exclusive contracts and special favors should be outlawed in the carrying of oil; they had fought for a great principle,

[30]N. Y. *Tribune,* N. Y. *Times,* March 26, 1872.

and they were not going to prove traitors to it now that their battle was won.[31]

Beyond question both the Oil Regions men and the New York refiners believed that open and equal rates would give tnem a conclusive advantage over Cleveland and Pittsburgh. Cleveland and Pittsburgh refiners now paid precisely the same rate on oil to Atlantic Coast points that the Regions refiners did. That is, Rockefeller in Cleveland, and Waring in Pittsburgh, paid $1.50 a barrel to New York; Porter, Moreland & Company at Titusville paid just the same. But Archbold, Vandergrift, Irish, and other Regions refiners had the advantage of being next door to the wells. While Rockefeller and Waring, under the new contract, paid fifty cents a barrel to get their crude oil to Cleveland and Pittsburgh, the Regions men paid little or nothing. As for New York, it held unique advantages for reaching the export market. The Regions and their Long Island allies were therefore jubilant. They believed that the destruction of this nefarious combine would restore free competition for an indefinite period—that the railroads would think twice before entering into such a conspiracy again; and meanwhile, they expected to gain a clear lead over Cleveland and Pittsburgh.

Yet the Cleveland *Leader* still expressed confidence in the future. It asserted that the city's refiners, with an advantage of twenty cents a barrel in cooperage costs and other savings, would prosper even under the new schedules. Cleveland was nearest to the Western markets, it possessed low-priced chemicals, and every summer gave it cheap water facilities to the East.[32] All this was perhaps whistling to keep up courage. But *The Leader* might have added that Cleveland possessed one advantage worth more than cheap barrels or competitive lines of transportation. It possessed the skill, courage, unsleeping enterprise, and penetrating resourcefulness of John D. Rockefeller, who had not been astonished in the least by the shipwreck of the South Improvement Company—in which he had never wholeheartedly believed—and who had never wavered in his determination to push forward steadily with "our plan."

[31]The contract was published in the N. Y. *Sun,* March 26, in a long article, "The Close of the Oil War," while next day the *Evening Post* made "a few additions"; it is given in Tarbell, *Standard Oil Company,* I, 327, 328.

[32]Cleveland *Leader,* March 30, 1872.

v

The crude-oil embargo was not relaxed until the Producers' Union had gained explicit assurances that the old contracts were not being secretly maintained. This embargo had brought the Cleveland industry almost to a standstill. In the last two months of 1872 the Standard Oil had employed from 500 to 1200 men, according to weekly variations in business; on March 27 it employed seventy. This was admitted by Samuel Andrews at a Cleveland meeting called to discuss the unemployment and poverty caused by the "oil war." Even after the new railroad contract of March 25 and the repeal of the South Improvement charter, the Oil Regions remained deeply suspicious of the South Improvement group.

Early in April news that an Oil City firm had sold some 20,000 barrels of crude oil to the Standard produced a wild outburst of indignation. The firm was showered with abusive letters and telegrams; a large New York refiner annulled all contracts with it; the Producers' Union expelled it from membership, and the Oil Exchange passed a resolution of censure. A few days later news that another dealer was preparing to ship 5000 barrels to the Standard resulted in a mob. It refused to let the cars be moved, and but for an armed guard, would have destroyed the oil. Yet by this time a marked division of opinion was appearing. Many producers and brokers, restive under the losses of the embargo, were eager to resume business relations with their old customers. Since the objects of the embargo had been attained, why not abolish it? The question was debated at another great Oil City meeting.

Before this meeting, on April 4, the head of the Producers' Union telegraphed the five railroads demanding an "official notice" that the South Improvement contracts had been cancelled. "Please answer at once," he concluded, "as we fear violence and destruction of property." The railroads assured him that the contracts no longer existed. A similar inquiry went to Rockefeller, who replied on April 8 that the Standard Oil "holds no contract with the railroad companies or any of them, or with the South Improvement Company." He added a resentful sentence: "I state unqualifiedly that reports circulated in the Oil Region, and elsewhere, that this company, or any member of it, threatened to depress oil, are false." Thus when the meeting took place, its officers held evidence that nothing need be feared—for the moment—from secret rates. The committee of twelve reported a complete victory, and its statement that the time had arrived for trading with all buyers on equal terms was hailed with delight.

The oil war thus officially ended. The South Improvement Company had been crushed, and the producers felt that a grim and fearful monster had been destroyed. Monopoly had been taught a lesson that it would not soon forget. Or would it?—some were not so certain. What were John D. Rockefeller's reflections at this moment?

He felt then, as he continued to feel all his life, that the South Improvement Company had been egregiously misunderstood. He believed that its great aim had been to unite all the refiners for stabilizing prices and "evening" freights, and not to crush anybody. Its panoply of rebates and drawbacks, a terrific weapon, was intended for threatening the independents, not crushing them; the mace would be waved before reluctant firms, but except in extreme instances would not be brought down upon anybody's skull. Years afterward he was questioned about this weapon. He answered, in effect, that the combination had never been allowed to show just how it meant to use it. "There never was a shipment made or a rebate or drawback collected under this South Improvement plan. It is on the plane of the story of the Negro who complained to the court that his wife was asking a dollar of him every day, and the judge asked him what she did with all that money. The Negro answered: 'I dunno, Jedge. I ain't give her none yit.' "[33] As for the well-owners, Rockefeller always declared that a fair contract with them had been intended.

Immediately after the collapse of the South Improvement Company, its members published in the principal journals of the Oil Regions, Pittsburgh, and Cleveland a detailed explanation of its purposes. This declared that only one side of the dispute had really been heard, and asked for a calm consideration of their case. Their purpose, they asserted, had been to end ruinous competition, to compel foreign countries (which purchased more than four fifths of the product) to pay six to eight millions a year additional for American oil, and to obtain a larger reward for oil-producers, railroads, and refiners alike. The existing refineries had a capacity of fully 35,000 barrels of crude oil daily, when only 16,000 to 17,000 were required, and constant

[33]Inglis, Conversations with Rockefeller.

price-slashing had prevented even those which were most favorably situated from making a profit. The railroads were hauling oil at a loss. More and more crude oil was being exported to build up the refineries of Europe. The plan was to unite all the refineries in a general stock company, in which each would benefit according to the value of the property put in; and leaders of the combination had expected to reach a fair agreement with the producers. "It was understood that . . . the producing interest should be fully protected about somewhat as follows: 'We were to have a manufacturing profit of 50 cents per barrel when crude was down to and below $4 a barrel, and $1 per barrel when it was up to and above $5 per barrel.'" This fact—or alleged fact—had not been brought out before! Finally, the advertisement predicted that some stabilizing mechanism akin to that envisaged by the South Improvement Company would yet be created. "We believe yet that some such course as we proposed to adopt will be found necessary to save our refining interests from great loss and destruction, and to save our country millions of dollars."[34]

It was a declaration that although one battle had been fought and lost, the campaign would still go on.

VI

At this point we may well pause to sum up certain conclusions regarding this famous combination and its dramatic history:

(1) Although at a later date assailants of the company liked to pretend that the oil industry was in a delightfully happy and prosperous state when the company was organized, much evidence exists that in 1872 it was overexpanded, disorganized, and in great part on the verge of ruin.

(2) The railroads, which had been particularly pained by their losses on oil traffic at a time of disastrous rate-wars, which had in Tom Scott and Peter H. Watson astute and sleepless organizers, and one of which, the Pennsylvania, knew well the usefulness of holding-company charters, first devised the general scheme for the South Improvement Company; and Warden of Philadelphia and Waring of Pittsburgh seconded them, Rockefeller then taking it up.[35]

[34]This advertisement is reprinted in *U. S. vs. The Standard Oil Company* (1908), pp. 2618–2634.

[35]Watson told the New York refiners on March 11 that the railroads had become desperate over their heavy losses; that conferences of railway officers had

(3) From the railroad standpoint, it was essentially a plan for a refiners' pool to "even" traffic. In return for seeing that the Pennsylvania Railroad got 45 per cent of the traffic, the Erie 27.5 per cent, and the New York Central 27.5 per cent, and for furnishing facilities for storing, loading, and shipping oil, the refiners were to get drawbacks on both their own shipments and those of other shippers. Similarly, a little later (in 1875) the Chicago-New York trunk lines gave a Western group that undertook the "evening" of livestock shipments an allowance of $15 a carload *by whomsoever shipped.*

(4) From the standpoint of the Standard and other pool refiners, the combination was (if we accept their statements) a device to *compel* all refiners to enter one organization, willy-nilly, for their own benefit; for those who stayed out would face ruin. Thus, overcompetition would be abolished, ruin averted, and profits assured.

(5) From the standpoint of producers and independent refiners, it was a scheme to force every one to bow to a selfish ring of Cleveland, Pittsburgh, and Philadelphia monopolists, who would hold a tyrannous whip over all other interests.

(6) From the standpoint of the general public, it was a plan to create a dangerous monopoly in what had become a necessity of life. The plea that the combination would eliminate the cheap, dangerous "benzoin oil" widely sold, and substitute really good oil at a more reasonable price than cautious Americans were paying for special "high-test" oils, was not believed.

(7) Our own verdict must be that while something can be said in defense of a refiners' pool to stabilize oil-prices and "even" oil-shipments, this particular scheme was defective and dangerous. Planned with excessive haste, it took inadequate account of well-owners and consumers. Its weapon against stubborn independents belonged not to legitimate commercial warfare but to industrial frightfulness. Its sponsors never furnished proof that they intended a general industrial association rather than a small ring. We must

been held; and that "they had placed it in the hands of Mr. Watson to make a general compromise of the various interests of the railroads." N. Y. *World,* March 12, 1872. He had gone to see the principal refiners and buyers of oil; "and after a consultation, terminating in a general conversation, it originated into the South Improvement Company." This indicates that Tom Scott originated the idea of using the South Improvement charter for a great combination to "even" the oil traffic; that he asked Watson to draw up a detailed plan; and that Watson took this plan to the equally desperate refiners.

add that while Rockefeller's adherence to it for tactical reasons can readily be understood, his participation was highly unfortunate for his business reputation. In the Regions especially it left a black mark of discredit and suspicion against his name.

But while this chapter of errors had been drawing to a close, on another and more important field Rockefeller had been winning a spectacular victory. Out of the ashes of one type of combination, another and more formidable type, embodied in an enlarged Standard Oil Company, was arising like a phœnix.

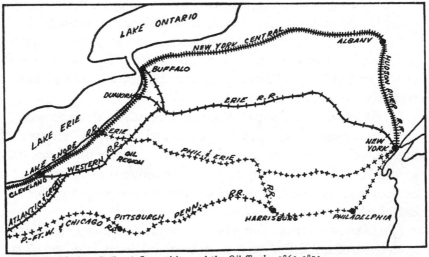

From R. H. Maybee, *Railroad Competition and the Oil Trade, 1865–1873.*

Early Trunk Lines Tapping the Oil Regions

The Atlantic & Great Western was in general closely allied with the Erie; the Philadelphia & Erie was a branch of the Pennsylvania

XVI

The Conquest of Cleveland

WHILE this battle over the South Improvement Company was being lost, Rockefeller's attention was in great part elsewhere—in the grimy manufacturing section of Cleveland, where chimneys smoked, drays clattered over the muddy streets, and tugboats hooted and puffed in the yellow Cuyahoga. He had never lost sight of what he and Flagler called "our plan" for consolidating most of the country's refineries into one gigantic organization. While the Oil Regions boiled with hostility to the "anaconda," he was fighting upon two fronts. Half of his time he labored in New York and Philadelphia to build up the new company; the other half found him at home, completing the consolidation of the Cleveland refineries with the Standard Oil. From the Lake Shore station, carpetbag in hand, the clean-cut, alert young manufacturer would hurry over to the public square and climb the stairs to the second-floor offices which the Standard had taken in the Cushing Block. Big arched windows looked out on the square; the clatter of horse-cars, carts, and buggies rose from the roughly paved street, while the whistles of shipping and grinding of railroad-cars drifted in from the lake front. So fast had the company grown that the quarters were jammed with desks and employees. Here he would talk with Flagler, Harkness, and Andrews; then catching up his silk hat, he would sally out to meet bankers and fellow oil-men. When the smoke of battle blew away, "our plan" had been pushed a long stage toward ultimate success; and the story of how it was done constitutes one of the most dramatic chapters of Rockefeller's life.[1]

[1]Rockefeller's letters indicate that he was in the East in late November, 1871, remaining until after Dec. 15; in Cleveland over the holidays, returning east about Jan. 5; that he spent nearly all of January in the East; late January, most or all of February, and early March in Cleveland; and was back in New York for a short visit by March 11. Rockefeller Papers.

II

One chill December morning in 1871, Rockefeller sent a message asking Colonel Oliver H. Payne, of Clark, Payne & Co., the Standard's strongest Cleveland competitor, to attend a conference that afternoon at a Cleveland bank. He had important proposals to make with which the bank was conversant. This was doubtless the Second National, whose officers, Stillman Witt and Amasa Stone, now controlled a thousand shares of the Standard Oil. Probably Payne was aware that Rockefeller wished to arrange a merger. His firm, which included Maurice and James Clark, and in which the wealthy Hussey family had an interest, had lately been losing money.

This conference marked the beginning of Rockefeller's effort to purchase or coalesce with his local competitors, an effort equally in harmony with "our plan" and with the South Improvement scheme. He had planned his strategy with characteristic foresight. Clark, Payne & Co., had on Walworth Run one of the largest refineries in the West, with its own cooperage shops. A less farsighted leader than Rockefeller would have approached the weak refineries first. That course would have meant initial success, increasingly difficult battles, and final failure. "What we did was to take the largest concerns first," remarked Rockefeller years later.[2] Had Clark, Payne & Co., with the support of the Payne and Hussey millions and of the Merchants' National Bank, in which James Clark was a director, taken a hostile attitude, the hope of a great consolidation would have vanished. But once they joined the Standard Oil, the merger would be locally irresistible.

Moreover, Colonel Payne's personal prestige was invaluable; for he was a sharply individual scion of an important family, already making an impression of dignity, austerity, and power in both Cleveland and New York. His father was Henry B. Payne, Cleveland's most aristocratic leader, an able, cultivated, and earnest man, who, after making a fortune as lawyer, manufacturer, and president of the Cleveland & Columbus Railroad, had gone into politics, becoming congressman and a Democratic leader of national repute. De-

---

[2]Inglis, Conversations with Rockefeller. Rockefeller testified in 1908 that John Huntington was associated with Clark, Payne; *U. S. vs. Standard Oil,* XVI, 3064.

spite prejudiced statements to the contrary, the elder Payne was a man of principle and integrity. Next to Leonard Case and Amasa Stone, he was considered the richest figure in the Western Reserve. He had married a daughter of Nathan Perry, beloved pioneer merchant of the city. Young Payne was a patrician and knew it; just Rockefeller's age, he had been with him in Cleveland High School, but had quickly moved into different circles. From Phillips Andover he had gone to Yale, where he was a close friend of William C. Whitney and William Graham Sumner; then into the army as one of Ohio's most efficient colonels; and then into iron and oil. He was well-read, high-minded, and ambitious, very different from the rough-and-tumble businessmen about him, and yet so able that he had already made a distinct success. Since he showed an austere preference for his own social circle some thought him haughty, and Flagler called him "kin of God." Though he and Rockefeller were almost strangers, Payne had enough hard sense to welcome the advances of the president of the Standard Oil.[3]

An agreement was soon reached. Rockefeller did not need to point out the necessity of ending the blind, slashing competition of too many wasteful refineries. He did not need to urge that the principal refineries must pool their resources and institute greater economies if they were to face the threat of the Oil Regions and New York. Payne knew all this. What Rockefeller did was to explain how the merger could be effected.[4] The Standard Oil would increase its capitalization, the Clark, Payne establishment would be appraised, the owners would become partners, and they would be given Standard Oil stock in proportion to the value of their property and good will. It was intended that Payne should take an active part in the Standard management, and the Clarks should not.

It is clear that Payne never hesitated. He had watched the steady growth of Rockefeller's organization; he knew how remarkable were Rockefeller's and Flagler's abilities, how important their alliance with strong Cleveland banks, how efficient their works, and how valuable their marketing arrangements. He was familiar with Flagler's con-

[3] I have derived information on Payne from his niece, Mrs. Leonard Elmhirst, and a partly completed biography of his brother-in-law, William C. Whitney, by Mr. Mark Hirsch.

[4] Rockefeller gave Mr. W. O. Inglis a full account of this interview; Inglis, Conversations.

tract with the Lake Shore Railroad. The Standard Oil was still making money, and its offer presented a happy road out of a dark situation. Rockefeller has recorded his reply:

"Your idea strikes me favorably. I shall consult with my partners and let you know their view as soon as possible."

His associates quickly agreed to the merger. Their land, buildings, and other assets were valued, and in the first days of 1872 the transaction was completed. As we have noted, the stock of the Standard Oil was increased from 10,000 shares with a par value of $1,000,000 to 25,000 shares with a par value of $2,500,000. Of the increase, 4000 shares were offered to existing stockholders, while the executive committee were empowered to use the other 11,000 "in paying for certain refinery properties in Cleveland and elsewhere that had been offered to the company." It was by a similar increase of stock that the Western Union Telegraph Company, one of the trail blazers toward monopoly, had bought out some of its principal competitors.[5] The Clark, Payne establishment was appraised at $400,000, and the partners received shares having a par value of that amount. In later years Rockefeller spoke with gratification of Payne's alacrity. "You can see that the Cleveland refiners had reached a period of stress when I had that meeting with Colonel Payne. He accepted my proposition at once and said, 'Let us get the appraisers in and see what the plant is worth.' "[6]

Two other properties were immediately added. One was the Long Island refinery of Jabez A. Bostwick & Co., successors of Bostwick, Tilford, a firm which also owned tugs and important terminal facilities; the other a small refinery owned by Joseph Stanley in Cleveland. By these mergers the Standard gained absolute dominance in Cleveland, and a strong foothold in New York. It had been the greatest refining corporation in the world; now it was many times over the greatest, and one of the most important manufactories in America. These first mergers took place, be it noted, before the South Improvement uproar began; fear of the South Improvement scheme had nothing to do with Clark's or Stanley's consent.

The expansion involved a small increase in the list of Standard

---

[5]See *38–93 N. Y. 162; Williams vs. Western Union,* for the principal legal case arising out of the Western Union mergers.
[6]Inglis, Conversations with Rockefeller.

stockholders, but at the same time Rockefeller decidedly enhanced his own share of stock by purchasing a considerable part of the new issue. The situation just before and just after the mergers is indicated by the following lists:[7]

Stockholders Jan. 1, 1872		Disposition of 15,000 New Shares After Jan. 1, 1872	
John D. Rockefeller	2,015 shares	Existing stockholders, pro rata	4,000
William Rockefeller	1,459 shares	Clark, Payne & Co.	4,000
H. M. Flagler	1,459 shares	John D. Rockefeller	3,000
Samuel Andrews	1,458 shares	H. M. Flagler	1,400
S. V. Harkness	1,458 shares	John D. Rockefeller as agent	
Amasa Stone, Jr.	500 shares	for company	1,200
Stillman Witt	500 shares	Jabez A. Bostwick	700
O. B. Jennings	500 shares	J. Stanley	200
T. P. Handy	400 shares	P. H. Watson	500
Benjamin Brewster	250 shares		
		Total	15,000
Total	10,000 shares		

In brief, Rockefeller in 1871 held a little more than one fifth of the stock of the Standard Oil, capitalized at a million dollars. Early the next year he raised his holdings to 5821 shares, or considerably more than one fifth of the increased capitalization of two and a half million dollars. In addition, he held 1200 shares as agent, to be used on behalf of the company in new merger negotiations. Clark, Payne & Co. had been well paid, while Bostwick and Stanley had gotten $90,000 in shares; but the original Standard Oil partners—the two Rockefellers, Flagler, Andrews, and Harkness—still retained firm control with much more than half of the stock.

Having acquired his most formidable Cleveland rival, Rockefeller turned confidently to deal with the others. He and his partners were supported by the railroads and at least three of the principal Cleveland banks, the Second National, Commercial National, and Merchants' National. He proceeded to make the same proposals to every refinery. They should pool their resources with the Standard, give up their identity, and accept stock or cash for their property. The heavy losses that nearly every one had incurred during 1870–71 made

[7]Taylor, MS History of the Standard Oil Company, 18, 19, based on the minutes of the stockholders' meeting Jan. 1, 1872. Mr. Charles White of the Standard Oil Company has shown me similar figures.

the situation favorable to his plans. We have already noted his emphatic statement that four fifths of the refiners in the country in the long run failed, that at this time their situation was deplorable, and that their anxiety was feverish. He later told W. O. Inglis:

"At this juncture what happened? That which had never happened before in the competitive struggle. The strongest competitor turned to them (those in peril) with the confidence which it showed in its propositions and said: 'We will take your burdens. We will utilize your ability; we will give you representation; we will all unite together and build a substantial structure on the basis of co-operation. We know your condition. Notwithstanding that, you shall have representation according to the value of property or any contribution of service which you can render to this united effort.'"

Alexander, Scofield & Co. ranked next in size to Clark, Payne & Co., with a capacity of nearly 1000 barrels a day. This firm and Alexander, Hewitt & Co. were negotiating with Rockefeller late in January, 1872. They at once decided to merge with the Standard. Before spring of 1872, all but five of the twenty-six Cleveland refineries had taken similar action. Most of them sold out for cash; a few took Standard Oil stock. In less than three months from Rockefeller's meeting with Colonel Payne, the Standard Oil interests had achieved a practical monopoly of production in the principal refining center of the country. They controlled a capacity of not less than 10,000 barrels of refined oil a day.[8]

III

Two versions exist of this extraordinary achievement—versions in sharp conflict with each other. One is the story told by men like Alexander of Alexander, Scofield & Co., George Baslington of Hanna, Baslington & Co., and Frank Rockefeller. The other is the story of John D. Rockefeller, supported by some of his partners and employees.

[8]Devereux, according to Charles H. Tucker, at the beginning of 1872 credited the Standard Oil alone with shipping 5000 barrels a day (W. O. Inglis, Conversation with Tucker). Hanna, Baslington & Co. were credited by Hanna with a like amount (*Standard Oil Co. vs. William C. Scofield, Court of Common Pleas, Cuyahoga County, Ohio*). Clark, Payne & Co., and Alexander Scofield & Co. must each have produced as much or more. The seventeen others would have brought the total acquisition to at least 5000 barrels daily.

The first account pictures the Cleveland refiners as with few exceptions reluctant to sell. To be sure, they were not making money; Baslington, whose refinery was as strong as almost any, admitted in an affidavit half a dozen years later that his firm had earned no profits between July, 1870, and February, 1872.[9] But he and others implied that most refiners wished to keep their businesses in expectation of better times.

The reasons they gave for surrendering to the Standard were two. First, Rockefeller and Flagler told them of the South Improvement Company, and they learned enough of its railroad arrangement to feel that competition would be impossible. As they grasped the rebate provisions of the South Improvement contracts, they fell into a panic. In the second place, they declared that the Standard leaders definitely threatened them with ruin if they resisted. They consulted with railroad officers and bankers, who were largely allied with the Standard. They became convinced that even if the South Improvement Company failed, the Standard, made doubly powerful by the Clark, Payne merger, would soon drive them into bankruptcy.

Part of this testimony is practically contemporaneous with the extinction of the Cleveland independents. W. H. Doane told a subcommittee of the House Committee on Commerce in the spring of 1872:[10] "The refineries were all bought up by the Standard Oil works; they were forced to sell; the railroads had put up the rates and it scared them. Men came to me and told me they could not continue their business; they became frightened and disposed of their property." As a matter of fact, the advance in rates was quickly rescinded and the extra charge refunded.[11] "There was a pressure brought to bear upon my mind, and upon almost all citizens of

[9]*Standard Oil Co. vs. William C. Scofield, Court of Common Pleas, Cuyahoga County, Ohio.*

[10]*Rise and Fall of the South Improvement Company,* 45.

[11]So Peter H. Watson, declaring the sudden announcement of the advance a blunder, told the House Committee on Commerce. According to the N. Y. *World* of April 20, 1872: "He said freights were advanced about March 1 through a mistake of railroad managers, particularly those of the New York Central and Michigan Southern, and not by order of the South Improvement Company. The New York lines afterward refunded extra charges to shippers. He further testified the laws of New York forbade railroad combinations to raise freights; but the opinion was legally expressed that this company could contract separately with each road and thereby evade the laws."

Cleveland engaged in the oil business, to the effect that unless we went into the South Improvement Company we were virtually killed as refiners; that if we did not sell out we should be crushed out." His partner Hewitt was told that they would be destroyed if they did not enter the combination. "We sold at a sacrifice, and we were obliged to. . . . It was stated that they had a contract with the railroads by which they could run us into the ground if they pleased. After learning what the arrangements were I felt as if, rather than fight such a monopoly, I would withdraw from the business, even at a sacrifice." But he added that all his information came from Hewitt, for he himself had never talked with any member of the South Improvement Company.

Hewitt told the Hepburn Committee in 1879 that the threats came not from Rockefeller but from the New York Central and Lake Shore. Having learned that the South Improvement Company had seized control of oil transportation from the West to the seaboard, he called in New York on W. H. Vanderbilt and Peter H. Watson. Vanderbilt was noncommittal. But Watson remarked ominously: "You better sell—you better get clear—better sell out— no help for it." Hewitt and his partners decided to do so. While appraisals were being made, Rockefeller advised him to refuse cash and take Standard Oil stock, which would suffice to maintain his family "for all time." When asked why, Rockefeller answered: "I have ways of making money that you know nothing of." Hewitt did take the stock, but later became uneasy, and to the lasting regret of his children, sold it. He got $20,000 for an interest which, had he kept it, would have made him a millionaire.

Robert Hanna testified that he was approached by Rockefeller and Flagler, who asked him to sell his property. "But we don't want to sell," Hanna expostulated. As he recalled it, Rockefeller used threatening language: "You can never make any more money, in my judgment. You can't compete with the Standard. We have all the large refineries now. If you refuse to sell, it will end in your being crushed."[12] When Hanna and his partner Baslington hurried to the Lake Shore office and made alarmed inquiries, the railroad earnestly counselled them to yield. They took the advice. As for Frank Rockefeller, he told a Congressional committee in 1876 that

[12]Tarbell, *Standard Oil Company*, I, 66, 67.

Flagler and John D. Rockefeller had threatened his refining firm (he was then associated with Alexander, Scofield) with extinction. "If you don't sell your property," they told him, "it will be valueless, because we have got advantages with the railroads."

All these Cleveland refiners declared that the Standard paid them much less than the true value of their properties. Alexander alleged that his company received $65,000 for a refinery which they thought worth $150,000,[13] and Hewitt roughly corroborated this, saying that the price paid was about one half the invested value. Hanna asserted that he sold his works for "truly and really less than one half of what they were worth," while Baslington said that they had received $45,000 for a plant which had cost $76,000.[14] Beyond question these men were sincere, and the editorial comment already quoted from *The Plain Dealer* shows that a good many Cleveland oil-men were talking of sales under duress and at unfair prices.

Years after the event Frank A. Arter told of his sale in more tolerant terms. He had been encouraged by Robert Hanna, a banker as well as refiner, to go into the business. His $12,000 plant was tiny and inefficient, and his losses grew heavier and heavier. When he complained to Peter H. Watson of the Erie's charges, Watson told him he would get the same rates as the big refiners if he shipped as much oil, and Arter thought this fair. Finally, he saw Ambrose McGregor about selling, for he knew McGregor and Flagler and thought highly of their business integrity. The Standard then arranged to buy:[15]

It was a hard blow when the appraiser valued my plant at only $3000. It had cost me $12,000, and I was carrying a debt of $25,000; but what could I do? When conditions were so bad in the oil business that a small refiner could not make money, his plant was worth only what it would fetch as material—old material. So I sold out for $3000. I had my choice

[13]Alexander's testimony is vague and confused. "We had spent over $50,000 on our works during the past year, which was nearly all that we received. We had paid out $60,000 or $70,000 before that; we considered our works at their cash value worth 75 per cent of their cost. According to our valuation our establishment was worth $150,000, and we sold it for about $65,000, which was about 40 or 45 per cent of its value." The first sentence here suggests that he may not have discriminated between maintenance costs and capital investment. *Rise and Fall of the South Improvement Company.*

[14]See the affidavit of George O. Baslington in Tarbell, *Standard Oil Company,* I, 290, 291.

[15]Inglis, Conversation with Arter.

—to take cash for my business, or stock in the Standard Oil Company at the market price. Mr. McGregor advised me to take the stock, and I relied on his judgment, and I asked Mr. Rockefeller, and he told me to take the stock.

I remember talking with Mr. Rockefeller and Mr. Flager after I had sold out, and asking them whether I had better take cash or stock for my $3000. I said, "I put myself in your hands, and I'll be guided by your judgment." They both spoke at once: "If you will take that stock and hold it, some day you will get back the full price you asked for your refinery." I had faith in them, and I held on to my stock, though it was a hard job to carry it along with a debt of $25,000. That $3000 of Standard Oil stock in time made me a good deal of money. . . .

Within ten years, in fact, Arter's stock was worth a small fortune. His son James remarked in 1917 that "far from feeling that we were oppressed by the Standard Oil Company or Mr. Rockefeller, we have always felt that we were obliged to them, greatly obliged."

Rockefeller's story of these critical two months is unquestionably just as sincere as Hewitt's or Hanna's. However, it is a much later version, a story first told nearly forty years afterward. He flatly denied that his competitors had been unwilling to sell. Many of them, he recalled, had shown a positive eagerness to get rid of their businesses. But whether they wished to sell or not, the long depression had left them in such a predicament that a merger with the Standard was obviously the best policy. If Colonel Payne had been losing money, what then of the weaker firms? They had been losing far more disastrously, and should have been "still more ready and willing to unite their interests with the stronger concerns for the protection of all." Rockefeller testified in 1908 that though he owned "the model refinery of the industry" and had an excellent credit-rating, such Cleveland capitalists as J. H. Wade about 1870 refused to invest any money with him; it seemed too risky. For needed capital he had to go to New York—where fortunately interest rates were lower than in Ohio.

As proof of the dire straits of his rivals, he cited the admissions of his old employer Hewitt. "I had a personal conversation with Mr. Hewitt, and he said to me, 'Yes, John: I want to go in with you, but I can't because we have lost money, and my interest in the business I can't get stock for, because I am indebted to the firm on account of the losses we have sustained." The before-mentioned

Joseph Stanley, a tall, powerful Yorkshireman who had once been a brick-maker, was asked to promise not to re-enter the business. He said with feeling: "Maister Rockefeller, if the good Lord will forgive me this time I'll never go into it again!"[16] Later on, when the Standard Oil sued Scofield, Shurmer & Co., for re-engaging in refining after promising not to do so, Stanley saw Scofield outside the courtroom in Cleveland and denounced him with fierce epithets.

To the end of his life Rockefeller maintained that the whole Cleveland refining industry was on the brink of bankruptcy when the Standard began absorbing its competitors. Commenting on Miss Tarbell's statement that the independent oil interests of the city collapsed in the first three months of 1872, he exclaimed: "They didn't collapse! They had collapsed before! That's the reason they were so glad to combine their interest with ours, or take the money we offered as an alternative." And referring to a statement by Hewitt that "we were all kind of paralyzed" by the South Improvement Company, he cried:

"They were 'paralyzed'! What paralyzed them? The competition that came before that—the ruinous competition! The South Improvement contract? Never a barrel of oil was hauled under it. What harm did it do them?"[17]

Rockefeller also denied that he had ever made any threat whatever of "crushing" a rival firm if it did not come in. The South Improvement Company was not used as a weapon in the negotiations he asserted. "I did not say anything to those people about the South Improvement Company at all." And on another occasion he remarked: "They didn't—any of these Cleveland refiners—go into the South Improvement Company. They were never asked to go into the South Improvement Company. They were asked to go into the Standard Oil Company." Of course, as the Standard Oil was a member of the South Improvement Company until the latter blew up, this was essentially the same thing. But he made a sweeping denial, so far as he himself was concerned, of what Alexander, Robert Hanna, and Frank Rockefeller had said of the use of menaces.

"That is absolutely false!" he told William O. Inglis in 1917.[18]

[16]Inglis, Conversations with Rockefeller. See also Rockefeller's testimony of 1908 in U. S. vs. Standard Oil, XVI, 3053 ff.
[17]Idem.   [18]Idem.

"And no man was told that by me or any of our representatives. That statement is an absolute lie." Such a course, he asserted, would have been bad business. "How could our company succeed if its members had been forced to join it and were working under the lash?" More than that, he added, it would have been repugnant to his whole nature. "Do you think it possible, from what you know about me and what you see about me, that I would have been so foolish as to start out with such a prophecy to men with whom I expected to start in business, thus incurring their ill-will, their hatred, at the inception of the business?" And again: "I think you know enough of me to know that 'crushing' or compulsion is no part of my scheme of organization. In all the history of the world men have never made a success of a concern into which they have been forced or driven."

What then was the Standard's attitude, as recalled by Rockefeller? He described it repeatedly. He had gone to his rivals with a frank, moderate statement that *every one* faced ruin.

"What I did say in these cases," he explained, was this: " 'We are here at a disadvantage. Something should be done for our mutual protection. We think it is a good scheme. Think it over. We would be glad to consider it with you if you are so inclined.' " Some competitors, he admitted, did not regard his proposals favorably. "With these our relations continued, entirely pleasantly, until at length, one by one of their own volition they were pleased . . . to join their interest with ours." A former Methodist minister in Cleveland named Mix, who had set up a weak and antiquated plant, was offered a fair price though he was utterly unimportant. He refused, but soon repented. Being offered the usual choice of cash or stock, he took the latter, and though he died before the transfer was completed, it made his daughters wealthy.

Finally, Rockefeller could hardly find words of sufficient strength to characterize the injustice of the charge that the Standard had forced competitors to sell for inadequate prices.[19] He pointed out that it was easy for men to exaggerate the value of their properties —that few of his rivals had up-to-date refineries. "Improvements had come which had made them unprofitable," he said. Moreover, the overcrowding of the industry had compelled all refineries to

[19]*Idem.*

operate on part time and thus reduced their value. "An oil refinery can be used only for the purpose of refining oil, and when the capacity of oil refineries was several times as much as was needed for the oil produced, and when the competition in oil refining had resulted in a loss, then oil refineries, in the nature of the case, were of little or no value." Alexander's complaints about selling for two fifths of the investment he pronounced particularly disingenuous. The fact was that Alexander had not sold his interest to the Standard Oil at all, but to his own partners. These partners, including Hewitt, then sold to the Standard: and the price paid, according to Rockefeller's recollection, "was perfectly satisfactory to the gentlemen."[20]

Indeed, in his later years he believed that the Standard Oil had overpaid the firms which sold out, appraising their assets too generously. "Much of it was old junk, fit only for the scrap heap." Most of the works, ill-constructed and inefficient, "were not worth in cash what we paid for them." After taking them over, the Standard was forced to shut them down and pay high rentals on the land they occupied. Moreover, in getting rid of their weak and antiquated plants, the sellers had the advantage of exchanging frozen assets for liquid capital; for even if they took Standard Oil stock instead of cash, the former was readily marketable at good prices. "At no time was the stock which they took worth less in the market than the price at which they took it. This stock could be used as collateral for borrowing money in the banks. But the old refining properties for which this stock was given could not be used to borrow money on." Altogether, he believed that his company, appearing at this bitter crisis and saving men from the bankruptcy court, had been the salvation of many Clevelanders. "The Standard was an angel of mercy, reaching down from the sky, and saying: 'Get into the ark. Put in your old junk. We'll take all the risks!'" But, he added, "I never talked that way. It has never been my habit at all"—which was true.[21]

There seems particular reason to believe that the firm of Alexander, Scofield & Co. was in much more serious straits than Alexander would later admit. It had suffered from a number of fires. In the fall of 1868 it sustained a loss of $25,000 from a conflagration, and the following March had two employees killed in an explo-

---

[20]*Idem.* [21]*Idem.*

sion.[22] On June 8, 1871, it lost $20,000, partly covered by insurance, in another fire.[23] On May 18 of that year its entire refinery at Petroleum Center in the Oil Regions burned. The company shut down this branch of the business in September because it was not paying expenses.[24] Incidentally, Doane had been the victim of a $40,000 fire in 1870.[25] With business so depressed in that and the following year, these losses must have hurt both firms seriously.

And one of the most detailed records of negotiation between an independent and the Standard in 1872—indeed, the only really detailed account—lends support to Rockefeller's story. It was furnished in 1921 by Charles H. Tucker, the only surviving partner of Hanna, Baslington & Co. Tucker was secretary and treasurer of this firm, and had also been secretary and treasurer of the Cleveland Refiners' Association in 1870. Taking part in the bargaining, he later represented his firm in the appraisal of the property.

Tucker states that Hanna, as president of the company, received a letter from Rockefeller early in 1872 proposing a merger. Busy with his banking interests, Hanna told Baslington and Tucker to go over and "hear what they have to say." The two men breasted the icy winds of the public square and climbed the echoing stairs of the big stone Cushing Block. Passing a huddle of desks and clerks, they entered a sunny second-floor room, at one end of which was a fireplace surmounted by a fine marble mantel, with a blaze snapping on the hearth. Rockefeller and Flagler greeted them cordially.[26]

As he opened the question of the merger, Rockefeller held a clay pipe in his hand. He explained that he never used tobacco, but that having a sore throat, he had been told that smoking mullein leaves would give him relief. After some general remarks upon the desperate situation of the refining industry, he stopped talking, tamped down his mullein leaves, lit his pipe, and began puffing.

"As he did this," relates Tucker, "Mr. Flagler spoke up, explaining that they believed we would find it profitable to come in with them because they had better ways of refining oil and doing business generally on a big scale. He thought it would be to our advantage—

[22]Inglis, Conversation with Charles H. Tucker.
[23]Cleveland *Leader*, Jan. 4, 1869, March 21, 1869.
[24]Boyle, *Derrick's Handbook*, 157.
[25]*Idem*, 127.   [26]Inglis, Conversation with Tucker.

and their advantage, too. We knew, of course, that other Cleveland refiners had joined them."

When Rockefeller put his pipe down Flagler stopped talking and let the dominant partner take up the argument; and when Rockefeller resumed his smoking, Flagler once more seized the floor. Clearly, the pipe played a definite part in the parley. Rockefeller argued in conciliatory vein, Flagler talked more bluntly. Finally, Rockefeller proposed that Hanna, Baslington & Co. and the Standard each appoint representatives to examine the Hanna properties and fix their value. Then the Standard would give capital stock for the full valuation, "or half stock and half cash . . . or all cash—we could fix that to suit ourselves."

Tucker and Baslington reported the interview to Hanna, who hastened to Devereux of the Lake Shore to inquire about oil rates. The polished general received him affably. "Will you give us the same freight rates you give those Standard people?" inquired Hanna. Devereux countered by asking, "How many barrels of oil do you ship?" Hanna answered, "One thousand." Actually this represented the top capacity of the plant, which both men knew hardly averaged daily shipments of five hundred barrels.

Devereux replied: "Mr. Hanna, do you expect that a shipper who gives us one thousand barrels a day can get as low a rate as a shipper who gives us five thousand barrels a day?"

"No," admitted Hanna, "I don't suppose he can."

And after he had repeated this conversation to Baslington and Tucker, Hanna concluded—as they had probably urged him to do: "You boys go over and close with them." In all this no word of threat appears. According to Tucker, Hanna made no complaint at this time that the Standard's rebate was unfair, and to Tucker's certain knowledge, Hanna never spoke to Rockefeller in person about the impending merger at all.

Tucker recalled that Rockefeller chose Ambrose McGregor as the representative of the Standard in the valuation of the Hanna, Baslington properties; and that the auburn-haired Scot was prodigiously thorough and meticulously fair. "Why, there wasn't a poker alongside a furnace that McGregor didn't examine and put it on the list. I remember thinking, 'Well, Ambrose has had a good business training.' He verified everything. We had 250 barrels of glue, with the gross and net weight marked plainly on each barrel, as well as the bill for the lot; but McGregor weighed every barrel and listed it. We had a lot of new fire hose that had never been off the reel . . . but McGregor unreeled it all and measured every foot of it. Oh, I didn't mind; that was good business." Tucker thought that the valuation was just. He was convinced also that neither Rockefeller nor Flagler had said anything in his presence—as was reported by Hanna or Baslington—about crushing the firm. "I never heard either [partner] make any complaint of being threatened that we would be crushed or anything like that. The only thing George Baslington and I said was that we regretted we did not take stock in the Standard Oil."

For the strong-willed Hanna prevailed upon his partners to take cash instead. Wishing them to join him in the wholesale grocery business, he declared that the stock would be risky. "Right there we made the mistake of our lives," Tucker said ruefully. After the purchase Rockefeller saw little of Hanna. But for many years he remained on cordial terms with both Baslington and Tucker, once presenting the former with a cane.

Rockefeller himself, puzzled in later years by these accusations that he had used threats, thought that the railroad officers might have been to blame. They were anxious to see the Standard Oil succeed. "It is fair to say that, taking what Peter H. Watson or General Devereux or some other railroad man may have said who was desirous of corralling all the oil business, they may have assumed that we were in with the railroads, and assumed that we said it, whether we did or not." He thought also that some of his accusers were prejudiced. Alexander, he pointed out, had testified upon transactions in which he had personally taken no part. Frank Rockefeller had given his evidence in 1876, when he was trying to sell his oil company, for he had entered refining again, and when he was on bad terms with his much abler, cooler, and richer brother. Naturally rash, headstrong, and impetuous, Frank differed too sharply in temperament from John to understand him, and felt increasingly jealous of his success. Periods of friendship and enmity alternated rapidly. In 1876, according to John, he was attempting, by making trouble for the Standard Oil, to force that company to pay him a handsome sum for his refining property. "He and others were up to such schemes all the time until they got their property sold out at the price they wanted." John declared categorically that Frank had never heard him threaten any one. "My statement would go for more, I think, than my brother Frank's. Poor Frank!"[27]

IV

It would be difficult to find two accounts of the same occurrence that, on the surface, are more contradictory. Yet it is not impossible to reach a conclusion on both of the main points in dispute—the question of threats, and that of the fairness of the prices.

The question whether threatening language was used involves a great deal of human psychology. We might acquit Rockefeller and his partners of any menacing statement whatever, and yet be sure that the independent refiners felt themselves very emphatically threatened with obliteration. What Rockefeller may have thought was a plea, an argument, or an explanation may have seemed to the men who faced him before that Cushing Block mantelpiece—men harassed by financial worries and harrowed by the knowledge that firms into which they had put so much pride and effort were close to extinction—a grim menace. We must note, again, that while the independents hesitated between surrender and resistance they naturally conferred with bankers, railroad heads, and Standard Oil of-

[27]Inglis, Conversations with Rockefeller. Frank had held an interest in one of the competing refineries purchased by the Standard in 1872. With the sales money and some additional funds from John, he had acquired control of a fleet of lake boats, and was helping transport whatever Standard shipments went east or west by the lake route. In this capacity he maintained a close relationship with the Standard, and had an office not far from their quarters. Fond of hunting, he would occasionally disappear for several days with his gun and dogs, leaving affairs to a subordinate. During one of these absences, the Standard received an order for a heavy emergency shipment by water, but found that the lake fleet was in no condition to take it, and that Frank's clerk was hopelessly inadequate to meet the crisis. After Frank returned, his older brother took up the matter with him. One of the men in the office, filing papers, heard them clash. "Frank," said John firmly, "this will have to stop. If you are going to attend to business, very well. If not, we shall have to make other arrangements." Frank replied heatedly. He had always resented John's success, disliked his strict ways, and believed that he had been "squeezed" in 1872. The talk threatened to become quarrelsome, and John asked: "What do you think your interest in those boats is worth? State your figure!" Frank named a sum. John suggested that he give the Standard an option for twenty-four hours, and this was agreed. The following day he presented Frank with a check for the specified amount. Charles M. Higgins to the author, 1936.

ficials, and that these now constituted a powerful triple alliance. Obviously, different men in the three groups may have used different language. The Standard Oil partners were probably tactful, for they were inviting the other refiners to become stockholders, and no corporation head desires to have a body of hostile shareholders. The bankers were probably suave. It appears that the railroad men employed the bluntest words. W. H. Doane, always a friend of Rockefeller, did not say that the Standard Oil had employed threats, but that the railroad rate-changes had "scared" the defendants. Alexander testified that "there was a pressure brought to bear upon my mind," but did not say whether by the Standard or the railroads—and pressure is a vague term. Hanna did state that Rockefeller told him, "If you refuse to sell it will end in your being crushed." But this may have been less a threat than a prophecy; by his own statement, Hanna was most impressed by what he heard at the railroad offices; and Tucker says that Hanna did not see Rockefeller at all.

The all-important fact, however, is that a grim threat was inherent in the situation. Once the Standard Oil had joined hands with the two principal railroads and three of the most powerful banks of Cleveland, its position was menacing enough to any rival. Once it had merged with Clark, Payne & Co., the very office-boys in the refining area must have seen that profitable competition with it would be impossible. With jeopardy so distinctly a basic element in the situation, menacing language would have been superfluous. Why use words when the situation spoke so eloquently for itself? Small refiners had only to look at the front of the Cushing Block to feel conscious of a mighty power resting behind those doors!

When it comes to the alleged underpayment of firms which surrendered to the Standard Oil, we may readily give greater weight to Rockefeller's denials than to the accusations. For one reason, the whole subsequent policy of the Standard Oil was to pay generously for properties taken over. We shall meet numerous illustrations of this fact in the pages to come. For another, he had every reason of policy to deal justly with prospective stockholders. And for a third, the complaints which have survived are neither numerous nor convincing; they are just the kind of grumblings that would have been heard anyway, no matter how much had been paid.

After two or three years of highly unprofitable business, in an overdeveloped industry in which equipment swiftly became obsolescent, what standard should be used to fix the value of a refinery? Should it be capitalized upon past earnings, or net investment, or reproduction costs? We do not know what basis McGregor and his associates used; presumably it represented a compromise between different views. We do know that long years afterward Flagler boasted that it was he who had devised the yardstick they used, and that it had been extremely fair. He told of a man who had been running a little refinery on the lake. "It was so small a refinery that I had never known it existed. I asked him if he wouldn't like to come in with us, and told him our plans. He said, 'Come and measure my property.' I valued his plant at $4700. He said he had had $2000, and had borrowed $2500: 'That must be a pretty good yardstick.' "[28] Of course a man like Arter, who had spent $12,000 upon a refinery, would think he deserved to get $12,000 out of it—even though his losses had plunged him $25,000 in debt, and his plant was worn out. Of course a man who had made 25 per cent in one good year would believe that his plant should be valued on that basis, forgetting the recent deficits. Had Rockefeller and McGregor accepted these views, they would have done a grievous wrong to all future investors in Standard Oil. History has delivered a plain verdict upon the ethics of J. P. Morgan's purchase of steel properties at inflated valuations for the United States Steel Corporation and his subsequent sale of watered stock to a confiding public.

Sellers like Tucker thought that the payment was adequate. No man failed and nobody was "ruined." Those who took Standard Oil stock in payment ultimately became wealthy, while those who took cash could use it in new investments. Of course, as soon as the Standard Oil completed its mergers and scrapped many small plants, the profits of refining in Cleveland became much surer and larger. Hanna, Baslington & Co., after signing the agreement to sell, were permitted to continue operating their refinery for several months as an independent unit. They naturally made a profit, and both expressed a naïve desire to cancel the sale—which Rockefeller and Flagler of course refused to permit. Hanna may have founded his allegations of inadequate payment upon these last few months

[28]*In Memoriam Henry Morrison Flagler*, 9.

of profits. Moreover, a man who is elated to take ten thousand dollars for a property soon begins to reflect morosely that he might have had fifteen, and to feel cheated. The verdict of Halle, a partner of Scofield's, is emphatic as to Rockefeller's justice:[29]

"He treated everybody fairly. When we sold out he gave us a fair price. Some refiners tried to impose on him and when they found they could not do it they abused him. I remember one man whose refinery was worth $6000, or at most $8000. His friends told him, 'Mr. Rockefeller ought to give you $100,000 for that.' Of course, Mr. Rockefeller refused to pay more than the refinery was worth, and the man . . . abused Mr. Rockefeller."

v

Thus was the Cleveland field conquered. There were exultant hearts in the Cushing Block; there was gloom in a dozen other offices; about the doors of the small refineries clustered sullen groups of workmen, uncertain of their future. Rockefeller at the age of thirty-five presided over the second largest industry in Cleveland, and one of the greatest industrial units in the world. The enlarged Standard Oil Company was soon employing 1600 men on a payroll of more than $20,000 a week. Its capacity of at least 10,000 barrels a day was more than the entire capacity of the Oil Regions (estimated this year at 9231 barrels), or the entire capacity of the New York area (9790 barrels), or the combined capacity of Pittsburgh, Philadelphia, and Baltimore (9249 barrels). It was master of approximately one fourth of the refining capacity of the United States, and master, it would be safe to say, of fully one third the *efficient* refining capacity. The South Improvement Company, by this date, had practically been destroyed. But the Standard Oil had taken a long and impressive step toward Rockefeller's goal of one great unified company. While his apprehensions as to the workability of the South Improvement Company, "Tom Scott's scheme," had been justified, his belief in the practicability of his own simpler but grander plan was fast being vindicated.

This conquest of Cleveland was accomplished, as Rockefeller preferred to have all his work done, with but the slightest and most casual public notice. During late February, all of March, and the

[29]Inglis, Conversation with Halle.

first fortnight of April the oil men of other cities and of the Regions, like the general public, kept their eyes riveted upon the clash and clamor of the South Improvement battle. But meanwhile, all unnoticed, Rockefeller was winning a conflict quite as important. He was proving that an absolute unification of refineries, not a mere loose alliance, could be effected in the most important refining center of the world. If there, why not in secondary centers like New York and Pittsburgh? And what more logical than to effect this consolidation through the Standard Oil Company, now so clearly preeminent on the continent? The second largest refining corporation in the country, Sone & Fleming of New York, had a daily capacity of only 1700 barrels, or less than one sixth of the Standard's output. By its acquisition of the Bostwick establishments, the Standard had gained a strong foothold in New York. Its quasi-alliance with Charles Lockhart in Pittsburgh and William G. Warden in Philadelphia outlasted the dissolution of the South Improvement Company. The uproar of the great battle over the South Improvement scheme slowly died away; and as it did so the refiners of the country at large realized, with a sense of shock, what a massive and irresistible corporation had arisen in Cleveland.

It is evident that the Standard officials did their utmost to keep the work of consolidation secret. On February 21 the Cleveland *Plain Dealer,* having heard rumors of what was happening, printed a two-line paragraph: "A gigantic 'little game' has been going on in oil circles in Cleveland to the effect that a single firm has bought up or got control of all the refineries in the city and proposes to monopolize the business, having allied itself with the oil-carrying railroads as well as a similar monopolizing firm in Pittsburgh. Rockefeller and Andrews of the Standard Oil Works are credited with being the shrewd operators in Cleveland." But readers desired more exact news. A *Plain Dealer* reporter therefore came to the Standard Oil offices, and asked Colonel Payne some direct questions.

"Do you suppose any one firm exists which can obtain control of all refineries here?" the new partner replied. "In this country a man wants to look after his own money, and no man or set of men can buy up all the refineries."

Of course Rockefeller and Flagler were then fast obtaining control of nearly all the local plants, and Payne's statement was evasive.

The reporter then began asking questions about the South Improvement Company which met with equally foggy answers. "Does the Cleveland combination have some connection with it?" he inquired.

"Do you suppose I would be fool enough to tell you?" Payne retorted with a laugh, and walked away.[30]

When the unification of the Cleveland industry was finally disclosed, the ablest producers of the Regions and most discerning refiners in other cities at once perceived what a terrible portent it offered. The aggrandized Standard Oil might well accomplish what the South Improvement Company had failed to do. Indeed, did it not represent all that had been strongest in the South Improvement alliance? A chorus of alarm broke forth. "The trade here," commented the New York *Bulletin* in mid-April, "regards the Standard Oil Company as simply taking the place of the South Improvement Company, and as being ready at any moment to make the same attempt to control the trade as its progenitor did." The Cleveland *Herald* spoke of "the South Improvement Company *alias* Standard Oil Company." The Oil City *Derrick* quoted Rockefeller as informing a prominent oil man of the town that the South Improvement Company could operate under the Standard Oil charter, and that within two months the men of the Regions would be glad to join him—a statement which sounds very unlike the reticent Rockefeller. Alarmist reports from New York dealers reached the Regions newspapers setting forth that the Standard Oil had simply stepped into the shoes of the South Improvement Company, and that it intended to force the price of crude oil on the creek down to two and a half cents a gallon! This was absurd, but it showed a shrewd perception of the strength of the gigantic corporation in Cleveland.

To be sure, the producers and independent refiners still had one seeming bulwark of safety. This was the solemn promise of the railroads, in their written contract of March 25, 1872, that they would permit "no rebates, drawbacks, or other arrangements" of any character that would afford any shipper the slightest discrimination in rates. But this was a fragile protection, a scrap of paper. Experienced oil men knew that the railroads would be quick to break such a pledge the moment it paid them to do so.

Yet it is to be noted that even after Rockefeller had swept the

[30]Flynn, *God's Gold*, 164.

board in Cleveland and was busy integrating his new facilities, not a few men predicted that his company would ultimately fail. He was a mere youth compared with most businessmen of the city, and to many his swift rise to power seemed half an accident. Some of the sagest businessmen believed that his enterprise was altogether too grandiose; that a permanent union of so many establishments was impossible, and would shortly fall to pieces. Hewitt, on first hearing of the plan to merge all the companies of the city, had remonstrated with his former clerk.

"John, it can't be done," he cried. "We've tried it on the lake shipping. They won't hold together. You'll find it a rope of sand."[31]

Others spoke of the scheme as "too scope-y."[32] Robert Hanna was positive in his predictions of failure. "Don't touch it," he warned his younger partners. "It has no future. The organization will fall by its own weight."[33]

These observers knew that analogous combinations in salt, anthracite, and other commodities had proved or were proving failures; they knew how hard it was to control American individualism; they believed that refining was still a risky business. "I call attention to the fact," said Rockefeller later, "that while Clark, Payne & Co. had in its membership representatives of two wealthy families, they were not willing to risk one dollar of their good money by taking stock in the Standard Oil Company and contributing 100 cents on the dollar for the same. They brought in only their refining business."[34] This could be said of the others.

Some of the pessimists, croaking like ravens on a withered bough, had discreditable reasons for wishing Rockefeller ill. Bitterly jealous of his success, and mortified by their own recent losses and blunders, they belittled him and hoped for his failure. Henry P. McIntosh, a clerk in Colonel Payne's office in 1872, has left us a vivid description of the behavior of James Clark, who as partner in Payne's refining firm had taken some of the 4000 shares allotted to Clark, Payne & Co. "Jim Clark used to come down to Colonel Payne's office every day about ten o'clock, in the morning," said McIntosh, "and sit around for an hour or two. . . . How he would curse John D. Rockefeller! He would say over and over again that the Standard

[31]Inglis, Conversations with Rockefeller.   [32]Flynn, *God's Gold*, 161.
[33]Inglis, Conversations with Rockefeller.   [34]*Idem.*

Oil Company would never make a success with 'that man' at the head of it. They were trying to do an impossible thing. . . . 'Damn Rockefeller,' he'd say. 'That Standard Company can't succeed. They'll bust, sure!'" Clark talked so much of selling and was so disruptive an element in the company that Colonel Payne soon offered to buy him out; and by obtaining a high straw bid, Clark got $112.50 a share—a total of $110,000. He thought he had done well. But when before many years passed the value of these shares rose into millions, his inveterate hostility toward Rockefeller grew deeper still.[35]

But Rockefeller felt sure of the future. The emergence of the Standard Oil as a corporation of unmatched efficiency and irresistible power was a result which he viewed with unalloyed satisfaction. He had taken absolutely decisive measures to end "ruinous competition" in one city; he could now move to end it elsewhere. He believed that, while serving the interests of his own firm, he had also labored to impart order and prosperity to the entire industry. "It was forced upon us," he said later of his spectacularly successful campaign for the consolidation of the industry in Cleveland. "We had to do it in self-defense. The oil business was in confusion and daily growing worse. Some one had to make a stand; some one with force, who could not only see the best way out of the difficulties, but would act at once. So we . . . went from one to another of our neighbors: 'Will you come in? What will you have?—stock or cash? Here you are, so much money or so many shares of stock in our concern.' The intelligent man saw that what we were doing was necessary if the business was to be saved from going to pieces." All refiners, he added, were given the same opportunity. Those who rejected it were left "to the mercy of time."[36]

VI

It was a decisive stride toward the consummation of his plan— and the other steps were to be taken with a swiftness characteristic of Rockefeller. But in one direction it may be doubted whether even

[35]*Idem.* According to Rockefeller, the men—Alexander, Hanna, and others —who took cash instead of stock later became furious to think of what they had missed. "They took the cash, and when the stock became many times increased in value, they blamed us for their own bad choice."
[36]*Idem.*

Rockefeller recognized its implications. He had not yet set up a monopoly, for strong competitive interests existed in other centers. He had not "crushed" any one, or done much more than time would soon have accomplished in Cleveland. Even without his intervention it would have been impossible for twenty-five or thirty refineries to continue operations there; within a few years the industry must have been reduced to three or four strong plants at most. The numerous little packing-houses of Chicago were being replaced at this very period by a few great establishments. Rockefeller simply speeded up the inevitable extinction of the weak refineries and brought forth one great corporation where there might have been several. He perhaps prevented a half-dozen Clevelanders like Robert Hanna from making moderate fortunes in oil, but he saved many men from the complete bankruptcy that must have come soon after the panic of 1873. Consumers were still well protected by competitive shipments from other centers; and indeed, they had suffered from the reckless competition of the past, which had flooded the market with cheap, unreliable, and dangerous oils. As yet there was no great quarrel between Rockefeller and public opinion.

But the quarrel was coming. He had set his foot—deliberately and determinedly—upon a path which led straight to monopoly, or something very near it. The majority of Americans in those days believed as fervently in the gospel of laissez-faire as in the gospel of Christianity. They put their faith in private enterprise and free competition. They were convinced that the stress of such competition enabled consumers to buy goods and services at the lowest price; that it compelled industry to take full advantage of new inventions and better techniques; that it destroyed extortionate and inefficient units, and brought about a survival of the fittest. They held that unrestricted competition released enterprise, stimulated ingenuity, and resulted in a maximum production at minimum prices, with the result that more workers were employed, and more consumers were supplied. On the one hand any State interference, beyond the protection of certain rights of property, was denounced; on the other hand, any encroachment upon the happy field of laissez-faire by the foul monster of monopoly was fiercely resisted. The American public, still shaped by a pioneering mould, strenuously exploiting the virgin wealth of the continent, and looking to Adam Smith for theory and Alexander Hamilton for practical doctrine, held to its simple faith as ultimate truth.

But as regards that faith Rockefeller was a heretic. He had seen enough of industry to know that unrestrained economic individualism did not always work. The theories might have fitted the early machine capitalism of the beginning of the century; they did not fit a system wherein the scale of production had vastly increased, wherein small businesses could not operate economically, and wherein overdevelopment meant waste, bankruptcy, and unemployment. He saw the ravages of excessively free competition in railroading. He saw that in various industries the growth of techniques (for example, the Bessemer process soon to revolutionize steel-manufacture) so enlarged the scale of production that the market afforded room for only a few establishments, and a host of small entrants would mean chaos. He saw that unbridled competition often inflated the costs of production, and that it increased in still greater degree the expense of distribution. He saw the human tragedies involved in the rapid mortality of small manufacturers and small traders. After the anxieties of 1868–71, he intended to organize his industry as completely as possible. He would be the leader upon a new road. He knew that this meant opposition and opprobrium. But it is unlikely that he realized how completely he was about to antagonize the basic convictions and dominant policies of the American people, how fierce would be the enmity he aroused.

XVII

The Tide Rolls On

WHATEVER we may think of John D. Rockefeller's vision, he was true to it. His imagination had shown him that if the amorphous, overdeveloped, wasteful refining industry, prolific of bankruptcies and ruin, could be unified and firmly controlled, it might become an efficient source of wealth to the small group which reorganized it; his instinct for practical method had discerned the one avenue by which such integration was possible. The terrific storm over the South Improvement Company did not divert him one inch; it simply confirmed his determination to fall back upon his own original plan, which he knew was far better than "Tom Scott's scheme." Silent amid the attacks of February and March, 1872, he was nevertheless keenly aware of the bitter hostility of most producers and independent refiners. But the invective of the Regions, the annulment of the South Improvement charter, and the submission of the railroads to a new rate-schedule which heavily penalized Cleveland, did not lead him to doubt his goal for an instant. While a few men encompass great achievements by sudden strokes of inspiration, many more accomplish them by tenacity of purpose and steadfast trust in their own aims. Rockefeller, with his clear grasp of a situation, his searching mind, and his cool resolution of purpose, conquered all impediments by a steady, relentless adaptation to circumstances. Walls of brass might be erected before him, but he would go through, or over, or under them.

As yet he was so little known to the public that for years to come his name seldom appeared in print, and when it did was often spelled Rockafellow or Rockafeller. Yet actually at thirty-four he was one of the leading business organizers of the nation. He had gained pre-eminence in his chosen field of industry earlier than most of his contemporaries. Andrew Carnegie, nearly four years older, was head of the Keystone Bridge Company, but he did not concentrate his energies upon steel and so begin his real career until in 1873 he began erecting the J. Edgar Thomson works near Pittsburgh. J. Pierpont Morgan, more than two years older than Rockefeller, has just formed Drexel, Morgan & Co., but it was not until 1873 that, dividing the flotation of a Treasury loan between his own syndicate and Jay Cooke's, he leaped to public prominence in finance. Philip D. Armour, seven years older, still lived in Milwaukee, and his grain-commission and pork-packing house of Armour & Co. was as yet little known. James J. Hill, one year older, was still an obscure agent for the St. Paul & Pacific Railroad, and his chief occupation was furnishing that weak line with fuel. In sheer ability, grasp of basic principles, and variety of experience Rockefeller equalled any of these men, while in singleness of aim and immovability of purpose he surpassed most of them. His manner already had the quiet force and air of mastery which, together with the quick penetration of his intellect, henceforth made him so impressive a figure.

A few significant anecdotes indicate his strength better than any business record. One story, told by Rockefeller himself, shows the young organizer crossing swords with the dominant figure in Cleveland business, Amasa Stone, whose fortune was estimated in 1872 at $6,000,000. A stout, powerfully built man with iron jaw and stern eyes, Stone had shown for years the autocratic and domineering traits which led a novelist of the day to present a savage portrait of him under the name of Aaron Grimstone. Everybody feared his arbitrary ways, harsh temper, and biting tongue. "Amasa Stone!" exclaimed one observer. "The richest man in Cleveland, and he'll have the smallest funeral!"—and in fact his life ended in a terrible tragedy.[1] He overrode his engineers, dictated an old-fashioned type of railroad-bridge at Ashtabula, and lived to see it collapse under a crowded passenger train. Some years later he committed suicide. At this time he viewed Rockefeller's fast-increasing power sourly.

[1]The novel portraying him is Henry F. Keenan's *The Moneymakers,* written in part as an answer to John Hay's *The Breadwinners.* For the tragedy, see *Dictionary of American Biography;* Tyler Dennett, *John Hay,* 101. Rockefeller repeated to W. O. Inglis the remark about the largest fortune and smallest funeral.

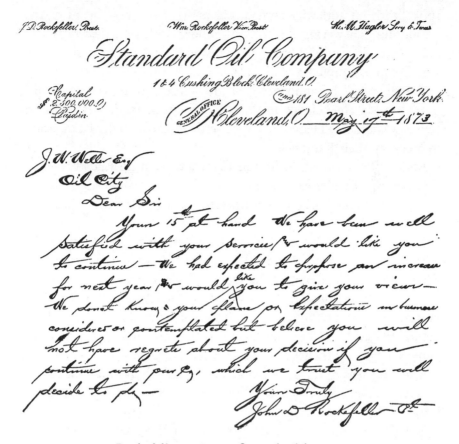

Rockefeller writes a firm of oil buyers

According to Rockefeller, at the critical moment in the spring of 1872 when the South Improvement Company had just broken up while the Standard Oil was gaining full control of the Cleveland industry, the Standard directors met in the second-story office in the Cushing Building. An important issue had arisen. Though he does not go into details, it probably concerned expansion. The directors—dictatorial Amasa Stone, the bankers Truman P. Handy and Stillman Witt, the kindly Harkness, the polished, formal Colonel Payne, and the two brilliant young men at the head of affairs, Rockefeller and Flagler—could not agree. Stone wished to take a cautious economical course. Rockefeller, tall, spare, a reddish mustache imperfectly masking the youthfulness of his face, might have seemed too quiet in manner to give battle to the rugged railroad-builder. But he spoke with an authority born of his mastery of every detail of the oil business, answering the railroad-builder with relentless facts and arguments. In vain did Stone raise his voice and hammer the table. Finally, he attempted a bold stroke.

"Gentlemen," he announced, "I am willing to arbitrate this dispute. Let Mr. Rockefeller and myself lay our views in detail before two stockholders—Henry B. Payne and Stillman Witt. I am ready to abide by their judgment."

Rockefeller assented. As he and Flagler walked up Euclid Avenue that evening, Flagler expressed uneasiness at his firmness in resisting the mighty Stone. "But he is mistaken," said Rockefeller with calm finality.[2]

Next day Stone, Rockefeller, and the two arbitrators met in the office with the large marble mantel. Stone made a vigorous argument. Then Rockefeller presented the facts and his logical deductions, expertly and irresistibly. He knew that while Witt and Payne had looked up to Stone as the leading figure of financial Cleveland long before they had heard of him, they had the best interests of the company at heart. As their questions revealed a growing conviction that Rockefeller was right, the irascible Stone played an unfair card:

"Gentlemen," he exclaimed, "remember who appointed you arbitrators!"

But Payne and Witt decided in Rockefeller's favor, and Stone thumped angrily downstairs into the street.[3]

Previous to this encounter, Stone had held an option to buy some of the new issue of Standard Oil stock. He carelessly allowed it to expire. Some weeks later he entered Rockefeller's office, and remarked that he had just sold some government securities and would like to purchase the additional stock. Rockefeller, who had no desire to see Stone's influence in the company extended, courteously told him that the option was void and that the company no longer wished to sell. At this Stone flared up so angrily that even Flagler was intimidated. He and Stone belonged to the same fashionable Presbyterian con-

[2]Inglis, Conversations with Rockefeller.
[3]Inglis, Conversation with Rockefeller, Sept. 5, 1917. Rockefeller indicates that age was clouding Stone's mind and temper. "That evening," said Rockefeller, "at a social meeting I happened to meet Mr. Chisholm . . . and told him what had happened. How he roared! There were many who truckled to Amasa Stone, but I never could see any reason for it."

gregation, and were frequently thrown together in Cleveland society. For example, when Stone entertained the Grand Duke Alexis of Russia in Cleveland in 1871, he had invited Flagler to the glittering party, but not Rockefeller. Flagler was in favor of placating the magnate by selling him the stock—but Rockefeller remained adamant. By this refusal, he said afterwards, "we probably saved two or three million dollars, based on the later value of the stock." In resentment, Stone shortly sold the five hundred shares he had previously acquired.[4]

While Stone was still angry, the Standard Oil suffered a spectacular fire at its Hunter's Point property in New York (July 30–31, 1872) which destroyed about $700,000 worth of property.[5] The Liverpool & London & Globe Co. refused to pay the insurance until it had made an investigation. Rockefeller, much worried, called on Harkness at his lumber office to say that the Standard might have to borrow some money in order to rebuild. "John, I'll give you all I've got," remarked Harkness sympathetically. ("That was the kind of man Stephen V. Harkness was," commented Rockefeller.) But the other officers preferred to go to a bank, and the question was laid before the directors of the Second National. Here Stone saw an opportunity. In his most caustic manner, he remarked that the condition of the Standard Oil ought to be critically scrutinized before any more money was loaned to it. This aroused Stillman Witt, one of the directors, who spoke across the table to his son-in-law Dan P. Eells, the president.

"Send for my strong box," he said defiantly. "We'll let them have anything they want."

According to Rockefeller, for once the combative Stone was silenced. A few days afterward the Standard Oil received a check for nearly $700,000 from the Liverpool & London & Globe, and no borrowing was necessary.[6]

[4]*Idem.*

[5]This fire is described at length in the N. Y. *Sun, World, Herald,* and *Tribune* of July 30 and 31, 1872. Some account of it will be found later in this work.

[6]Inglis, Notes. A slightly different version of this story appears in Rockefeller's *Random Reminiscences,* 18, 19; he retold it many times—for example, to the delegation of Cleveland citizens which called to do him honor in 1906 just after the "tainted money" uproar. In 1917, speaking to Mr. W. O. Inglis, he said that the bank in question was the United States Trust Company in New York, and that William Rockefeller, Amasa Stone, Stillman Witt, and Dan P. Eells were all directors. Some confusion with the Second National of Cleveland seems evident.

Possibly some details of these stories, told in Rockefeller's old age, are inaccurate. But they indicate that Stone tried to form a conservative group in the directorate, and that Rockefeller unhesitatingly put him in his place. Rockefeller speaks of overriding him on still another point—his ungenerous objection to continuing the salary of an officer of the Standard who was forced to go to Europe for his health.

II

The late spring and summer of 1872 found Rockefeller, Flagler, and Payne busier than ever before. They had acquired control of some twenty Cleveland refineries. Which parts of the plants and equipment should be saved, and which scrapped? What should be done with the officers, clerks, and workmen? A cardinal object of the mergers had been a reduction in the refining capacity of the city and the nation, but at just what point should the reduction halt? Patient exploration was required to ascertain which refineries would make effective units of the enlarged Standard, and how they could best be remodelled. It took time to find out which men would be useful as officers and which as subalterns.

The work of integration and reconstruction taxed all the energies of Rockefeller and his partners for eighteen months. We lack a detailed knowledge of what was done, for office records have vanished and the press paid little attention to the subject. But we know that by the end of 1873 patient, skilful effort had welded all the usable refining properties in Cleveland into one six-plant organization, by far the most efficient in the country. Most of the refineries were dismantled and sold. Some buildings were emptied and used as warehouses. In the works they kept, a good deal of amalgamation and remodelling took place. The original Standard Oil refineries were now called Plants No. 1 and No. 2; the additional plants, numbered 3, 4, 5, and 6, were modernized by adoption of the latest mechanical devices, improved in arrangement, and in part expanded. The old Hanna, Baslington refinery, now No. 6, was one of those retained and enlarged.[7] As part of the expansion, larger offices were badly

[7]Charles M. Higgins, who joined the Standard Oil in 1872, gave me a careful description of its works in interviews during March–April and October–November, 1936. He stated that all of the refinery-works numbered 1 to 6 were in active use in the fall of 1872. I have also gleaned information on the plants from Cleveland newspapers. The Standard Oil of Ohio still operates important works on the sites of Plants No. 1 and No. 2.

needed. In 1874 Rockefeller and Harkness therefore erected on downtown Euclid Avenue the Standard Oil building, a four-story brick-and-mortar structure, faced with stone, which had shops on its ground floor, and offices above. A central skylight lighted a large wooden stairway, no elevator being provided until later the height was increased to six stories. It was not a handsome or even imposing building, and each office was heated by a base-burner; but it provided space and convenience that had been sadly lacking in the Cushing Block.[8]

Meanwhile the heads of the Standard Oil were experimenting with better types of tank-cars—cylindrical wrought-iron tanks instead of wooden tubs; studying the acquisition of pipe-lines and tankage in the Oil Regions; and planning a large invasion of the by-product field. Up to this time the Standard had concentrated its energies upon kerosene and naphtha, selling most of the raw materials for by-products to other companies. It did not make even lubricating oil in any quantity, but turned the base for it over to Morehouse & Freeman, Fred M. Backus, and other manufacturers. Rockefeller believed that the Standard would now do well to produce lubricants, candles, paraffin, dyes, paints, and other materials, and that it could profitably set up its own plant to supply acid. While all this was done by degrees, expansion—bold, relentless expansion—remained the keynote of his policy. The capital came in part from banks, in still larger part from profits. "I urged that we put our earnings into developing the business, build for the future," said Rockefeller later.

Though at the time of the producers' boycott early in 1872 the working force had sunk to seventy men, the beginning of 1873 found it about 3000, and it continued growing.[9] Little if any permanent unemployment resulted from the consolidation of the Cleveland refineries. All the more efficient operators of the merged plants were taken over, often at increased wages. During the first period of reorganization, shifts in personnel, equipment, and even whole departments were frequent, and executives endured much resultant worry and confusion. Sam Andrews, stopping one afternoon at the main office, growled in his blunt English way: "I never know from one

[8]Description furnished me by Mr. James N. Fleming, Gates Mills, O., and other old residents of Cleveland.
[9]Charles M. Higgins to the author, Oct. 27, 1936. Cleveland newspapers contain corroborative material. On working conditions, hours, and wages at this period practically no facts are obtainable.

day to another where I can find a superintendent or a department!"
"Neither does the main office," he was told. "The business is growing too fast, too fast," grumbled Andrews.[10] Disturbed by the rapid
expansion, he was beginning to fear that his partners had become
reckless, while he wished more of the profits used for dividends. Yet
actually no changes were made without careful forethought, while
the revenues gave every partner a large personal income. The Standard's production in 1873 more than doubled that in 1872.

The men needed as managers were rapidly found, trained, and
imbued with the Standard's own *esprit de corps*. In Colonel Payne,
who possessed not only brains, energy, and social connections, but a
faith in the company which he later evinced by large purchases of
stock, Rockefeller obtained almost as valuable a lieutenant as Flagler. Andrews was sleepless in his oversight of the stills. As other
plant-operations expanded, the hard-working young Ambrose Mc-
Gregor gave them a shrewd surveillance that never failed, for his
eyes were as sharp as Rockefeller's. "If there was a worm-eaten stave
in a barrel anywhere in the yard," remarked a Standard officer long
afterward, "Ambrose would smell it out." Carefully selected by Rockefeller, a good many officers from what had been rival companies
joined the staff. Among them were Melville Hanna, brother of Mark
Hanna, formerly with Hanna, Baslington; John W. Fawcett, once
with Critchley & Fawcett; Horace A. Hutchins, recently a partner
in Westlake, Hutchins & Company; and George and Henry Lewis of
Clark, Shurmer & Co.[11] Hutchins, a brevet-colonel from Ohio, a fine-
looking man of chiselled, austere features, and a lover of travel and
society, became head of the domestic trade department. Various young
men hitherto unconnected with refining came in as clerks.

Rockefeller gave vigilant oversight even to the minor positions.
To one youth of twenty, D. E. Leslie, recommended by a friend, he
suggested that he request a two weeks' leave of absence from his employer, and find out whether he liked the job. "Then if you don't
fit here you won't lose anything," said Rockefeller, with a kindly
glance at the boy's slight figure. "Frankly, I don't think you are
strong enough for the desk you are asking." Leslie proved his

[10]Charles M. Higgins to the author, March 31, 1936.
[11]Charles M. Higgins to the author, April 7, 1936; other Cleveland sources.
Fawcett did not long remain with the Standard Oil. See the sketch of Hutchins
in D. R. Crum, ed., *Romance of American Petroleum and Gas*, 314, 315.

strength, and precisely six months later, Rockefeller called him into the inner office and gave him a check for $250. In time he was promoted to be travelling auditor. A Catholic, he had been told that Rockefeller would count his faith against him, but found this absurd: "All he wanted to know about a man was that he was honest and able."[12] Another bright young fellow who came in was William Cowan, son of a poor widow at whose Pacific Street boarding-house Ambrose McGregor had stayed. He became McGregor's assistant; Rockefeller took a warm personal interest in him, and when presently Samuel Andrews withdrew, Cowan helped McGregor assume charge of the works. "What a help he was to us; a loyal man, devoted, conscientious, and able!" exclaimed Rockefeller years after.[13]

Rockefeller was the very soul of the Standard Oil Company, his spirit permeating it from the center to its widest ramifications. While gifted with the imagination to conceive a grandiose plan and the steadfast courage to carry it through, for a time he still gave indefatigable attention to details. In this he was unlike Carnegie, who deputed as much labor as possible; he was like Harriman, whose quick eye caught every misplaced signal-post on his road and whose indelible brain memorized every item in his plans. In an industry full of romantic gamblers he sought unfriendly facts, and always based his calculations on hard realities. Nobody in American business was bolder, but even as he built his tower high he remained concerned with his foundations. He knew every ledger in the Standard offices, and would sometimes enter unexpectedly, displace a bookkeeper from his stool, and give expert scrutiny to the books. One accountant has described an incident. "All at once he stood by my side. With a polite 'Permit me,' he began turning page after page of one of the books. 'Very well kept—very, indeed,' he said. Then he stopped at a page and pointed out a mistake of entry: 'A little error here; you will correct it?' and he was gone. And I will take my oath that it was the only error in the book!"[14] Similarly, he knew every machine, vat, and pipe in the refineries. He knew every part of the cooperage shop, and every detail of shipping. He knew buying and selling, for he had directed both. He was familiar with the methods of

[12]W. O. Inglis, Conversation with D. E. Leslie.
[13]Inglis, Conversation with Rockefeller, August 14, 1918.
[14]Charles J. Woodbury, "Rockefeller and His Standard," *Saturday Evening Post,* Oct. 21, 1911.

by-product manufactories, the inside of railroad offices, the ways of jobbing and retailing. Sometimes, to speed a consignment to New York for export, he would leave his desk, go down to the tracks beside No. 1 or No. 2 works, and toil with the freight-handlers far into the night.

"I shall never forget how hungry I was in those days," he said later. "I stayed out of doors day and night; I ran up and down the tops of freight cars when necessary; I hurried up the boys. And we all worked together with a will and were happy when we telegraphed our New York connections that the cars were secured not only, but were loaded and on their way to New York."

Into his manner had grown the precision and power of the business he had built. Never aggressive, always serene, so quiet that to many he seemed sly, he was nevertheless determined and self-confident. Before taking action he planned his course in detail, and always spoke with superior knowledge and conviction. Just as Amasa Stone had given way before him, so Flagler, Harkness, and Payne, all older, seldom thought of questioning his decisions. They appreciated his superior insight, and his mastery of the intricate combinations of business. "They never treated me as a junior," he recalled years later, adding with characteristic understatement: "I had my own way a good deal."[15] Indeed, he radiated a force of personality which many found irresistible. "You never saw any one so confident as he was!" exclaimed one oil man in looking back on this period.

Another veteran, Thomas H. Wheeler, recalled a conference in Pittsburgh between Rockefeller and certain Oil Regions refiners, probably in 1872, the year Rockefeller became thirty-five. After the meeting a number of men, dining at the Monongahela House, began to talk of him. "I wonder how old he is?" inquired one. Various guesses were made, until a refiner named Warner spoke up.

"I've been watching him," he said. "He lets everybody else talk, while he sits back and says nothing. But he seems to remember everything, and when he does begin he puts everything in its proper place. He doesn't use many words, and he never crosses his tracks. I guess he is 140 years old—for he must have been 100 years old when he was born!"[16]

[15]Inglis, Conversations with Rockefeller.
[16]Inglis, Conversation with Thomas H. Wheeler.

As he took pains to obtain able lieutenants, so he took pains to hold them. His formula for producing a spirit of loyalty and efficiency included close personal scrutiny of the work done, a total avoidance of harsh rebukes or summary discharges, and cool praise whenever it was due. He made it clear to associates that he appreciated their brains. He was to make it equally plain, in the years at hand, that he was eager to acquire other good brains—those of John D. Archbold, William G. Warden, Charles Lockhart, and Charles Pratt. "I wanted able men with me," he declared years later. "I tried to make friends with these men. I admitted their ability and the value of their enterprise. I worked to convince them that it would be better for all to co-operate . . . and if I had not succeeded in getting their friendship the whole plan of the Standard Oil Company would have fallen to the ground. I admit that I tried to attract able men; and I have always had as little as possible to do with dull businessmen."[17] His clerks were drawn from his own Sunday school classes, or from youths recommended by trusted friends. His workmen were a picked body of sober, steady men. A remarkable unity pervaded the organization.

Employees often caught glimpses of the young president walking about, hands behind his back, quiet and unruffled, but seeing everything and showing a remarkable memory for names. A worker who was inspecting miscellaneous materials in the yard of the cooperage shop recalled his saying with a smile as he passed: "That's right—eternal vigilance!"[18] He realized the value of small savings in mass production. He hated waste, and, as Thomas H. Wheeler later testified, "he managed somehow to get everybody interested in saving, in cutting out a detail here and there of an unnecessary sort." Wheeler recalled that early in the seventies Rockefeller suggested lopping several inches off the overlap of the iron hoops that bound each oil-barrel. Experiments proved that this would not weaken the barrels, for the overlap had reached four or five inches. Execution of the idea saved thousands of dollars every year in iron hoop. On being reminded of this in 1918, Rockefeller exclaimed, "A fortune!"

A sharp impression of Rockefeller's early attention to details has

[17]Inglis, Conversations with Rockefeller. Rockefeller also treats his business associates in *Random Reminiscences,* 6 ff.
[18]Inglis, Conversation with John T. Sencabaugh.

been left to us by Charles M. Higgins, who as a mere lad went to the Standard Oil on September 9, 1872. Having first applied to Ambrose McGregor for a place, he was told to report to the cashier, Stewart McDonald, and to wait for an interview with Rockefeller. Higgins was all eagerness:[19]

I got downtown the next morning about 6:30, and waited around the front of the building until I could enter, and then waited in the inside office for Mr. Rockefeller, who came in about ten o'clock. I remember very clearly—as if it were yesterday—every detail of that interview.

Mr. Rockefeller came in with a calm air of dignity. He was immaculately dressed—he looked as if he had been turned out of a bandbox. He carried an umbrella and his gloves, and wore a high silk hat. He said, "Good morning, Mr. Vail; good morning, Mr. McDonald. Is everything going well this morning?" Mr. George I. Vail was the auditor.

McDonald soon followed him, and presently brought me word that I was to go in.

Mr. Rockefeller was seated at his desk; I can see him now as clearly as if I were looking at him. He was tall and rather slender, with a clear but pale complexion, and a mustache that was rather full and reddish-gold. He had plenty of hair then, of course. He looked at me with very piercing eyes. I remember that his cuffs were held with little black onyx links, each with the letter "R" cut into it. On his watchchain dangled a little black onyx charm, and this also bore the initial "R."

I had no idea that Mr. Rockefeller knew my family or anything about me, but apparently he had taken the trouble to learn not a little as to my background. He said, "Let's see, how old are you?" I replied that I was fifteen.

"You live at home with your parents, don't you?" he then inquired.

"I live with my mother," I answered, for my father was dead.

"Yes," he said, "I think I know your mother. Do you make good figures, Mr. Higgins?"

"I think they are pretty good."

"Well, here is a board"—and Mr. Rockefeller pointed to a portable blackboard sometimes used for posting oil quotations in the office. "Take the crayon and make some figures."

I did this. Finally he said, "That will do," and indicated that I was to be seated again.

"I think you are the boy we are looking for," he remarked. Then he touched a bell, and Horace Hutchins came in. He told Hutchins to take charge of me and instruct me in my work.

[19]Charles M. Higgins to the author, Oct. 27, 29, 1936. See also Mr. Higgins's pamphlet, "A Few Recollections" (1913).

Hutchins then had oversight of what was called the Western Department. He took me down to the general freight office of the Lake Shore & Michigan Southern Railroad, and presented me to Mr. Valliant, the General Freight Agent, whose name had to be signed to the bills of lading for the Royal Daylight Oil that we were at that time shipping from the Whiskey Island Oil-Sheds in Cleveland to Hunter's Point, New York.

I had to write in the numbers of the cars, and so on. These figures on the bill of lading went to New York, to William Rockefeller's office, and I understood why Mr. Rockefeller had asked about my capacity to make figures clearly.

Another employee, C. G. Taplin, afterward vice-president of the Standard Oil of Ohio, joined the organization in 1873. He had been a bookkeeper. Rockefeller could offer him only a position as bill-clerk, but promised that if his work was good, he would be advanced. On the last day of the year he was called into Rockefeller's office, commended for faithful service, and promoted to be bookkeeper.[20] Thus the president of the fast-growing company kept acquainted with even minor figures in its personnel.

III

But while thus attentive to his own business, Rockefeller continued to reflect earnestly upon the problems of the industry as a whole. He was anxious that the consolidation which the Standard had carried through in Cleveland should be extended to the whole industry; for he believed as fervently as ever that unification was essential if the oil business was to be spared recurring periods of chaos and prostration. "Our plan"—his and Flagler's—was intended to bring all or nearly all refiners into one huge company; but since the South Improvement debacle he was quite willing—indeed, he was eager—to enlist the newly organized producers as well. We find him therefore actively laboring, first, to interest the associated producers in his huge scheme for organizing the industry, and second, to do something more to convert the principal refiners of the East.

The producers believed that from their defeat of the South Improvement Company they had gained not only the destruction of that nefarious organization, but an explicit promise by the railroads, in the famous agreement of March 25, 1872, to charge fixed and pub-

[20]Inglis, Conversation with C. G. Taplin.

lic rates on oil, and to grant no rebates. But this agreement was not worth the paper on which it was written. Within a month the rates and the promise had been scrapped. The oil industry and railroads were back upon the old precarious basis of secret tariffs and special favors that had existed before the demands of the Producers' Union, and that had meant ruin to scores of refiners and producers.

Probably nobody acquainted with the basic conditions of railroading had expected the contract of March 25 to last. Next to the Western grain traffic, the oil freights were the richest prize within the grasp of the trunk-line railroads, a quarry for which their managers fought tooth and nail. The producers had just struck down a great eveners' pool intended to put an end to the ruthless railroad competition; they had failed to erect any substitute; and yet they seemed to think that the managers would keep the peace with one another! As a matter of fact, even if the managers had done so, local freight agents would have broken away and granted special rates to get special business. So long as no pooling arrangement or well-enforced Federal law existed to stabilize the situation, aggressive competition would breed reckless rebates. The contract was broken almost before its ink was dry, and apparently broken by every trunk line. George W. Blanchard, at this time general freight agent of the Erie, testified in 1879 that it had not lasted two weeks. Practically all the large refining companies throughout the East benefited by the new rates; they asked for favors, and they got them.

It is illuminating to trace the benefits received by the Standard Oil, though we must remember that other refiners took precisely the same course. Now that it was much the largest oil-shipper in the world, its leaders felt entitled to preferential treatment. With a capacity of ten thousand barrels of refined oil a day, it could furnish just the fixed, steady flow of freight which railroad heads most desired. The March 25th contract handicapped it severely, for it paid fifty cents a barrel more than its Regions competitors to bring crude oil to its refineries. To be sure, it found compensation in certain advantages—practical control of the Western trade, proximity to chemical plants, abundant labor supply, the command of a water route for refined oil in summer, and above all, the economy of its large-scale operations. But why not gain favorable freight rates as well? The agreement of March 25 provided that refiners in Cleveland, Pittsburgh, and the Regions, whether large or small, should all pay $1.50 a barrel on the oil they sent to New York. But Flagler at once went to the Lake Shore, applied for a reduction, and got it. The new contract, signed during April, 1872, provided that for the next seven months—till ice closed the water route—the Standard, for furnishing not less than four thousand barrels of oil a day or one hundred thousand a month, should get a special rate of $1.25 a barrel to New York.

The Lake Shore-New York Central line thus proved faithless to its agreement with the producers. It yielded to Standard Oil pressure, to the resentment expressed by Cleveland newspapers and businessmen, and to the threat that Cleveland would lay a pipe-line to bring crude oil from the Regions for a fraction of the railroad charge. (The Ohio Legislature hurriedly passed an act facilitating such a line.) But above all, the Lake Shore yielded because it knew that its rivals were slashing rates. Blanchard of the Erie declared in 1879 that he had seen proof that the Pennsylvania Railroad broke the March 25th agreement within two weeks by granting a large drawback to its great fast-freight subsidiary, the Empire Transportation Company, which served the Regions.[21] The Pennsylvania was probably the first contract-breaker, and Blanchard confessed that the Erie quickly followed suit. The grim war of the Producers' Association to abolish discriminatory rates thus achieved hardly even a momentary victory. This first rate-reduction to the Standard may have been indirect rather than direct—that is, it may have been what men later called a "smokeless rebate." Flagler, testifying in 1879, tried to produce that impression, saying that the railroad had paid a rebate for the use of terminals:[22]

Perhaps I can give it so you can understand it: we keep a separate account with each refinery, and if we spend $50,000 or $100,000 to create what we term terminal facilities, warehouses, loading facilities, etc., we make an arrangement whereby they pay us a fair compensation for the property that is created by our money. That consideration is credited to that investment and has nothing whatever to do with the freight. The refinery making the oil is charged with the rate of freight just as anybody else pays, and the compensation for the use of tank cars and terminal

[21] *Hepburn Committee Hearing* (*Special Committee on Railroads, New York Assembly*), *1879*, III, 3393 ff.

[22] Quoted from report of a committee appointed by the Ohio Legislature in 1879, by Tarbell, *Standard Oil Company*, II, 329–335.

facilities at the shipping and receiving ends of the line is given for the use of these ends. I will say that in the contracts we have made, the railroad companies have expressly reserved the right to give to other parties the same privileges if they furnish the same conveniences.

But the probability is that the $1.25 rate was not so much a rebate as a plain reduction, given almost simultaneously by all three roads —the Erie, Pennsylvania, and Lake Shore-New York Central systems —to a number of shippers.

Flagler's testimony of 1879, when carefully studied, reveals a number of other interesting facts. He declared under oath:[23]

I want to say what the facts are under the contract just read. You will remember that during seven months of the year we were to give them 4000 barrels of oil per day or 100,000 barrels per month, and the smallest of the shipments during those months was 108,000. We gave them during the rest of the time more oil and paid them the contract on it when we could have shipped by canal for forty cents less. On the first day of December, a competing line of railway (the Pennsylvania) lowered the rate to $1.05 a barrel. I went to Mr. Vanderbilt and told him that the rate should be maintained at the agreed price or else we would not have made the contract with him. I said to Mr. Vanderbilt that if he insisted on the fulfillment of the contract basis and exacted the payment of the contract price, it would result in our being compelled to close our refineries, for we could not afford to pay $1.25 when other people were paying only $1.05. I called his attention to the fact that during the season of canal navigation we had given the maximum shipments of oil, 180,000 barrels a month, and some in excess of it, and paid $1.25. I said, if you will reduce these rates to the rates made by the Pennsylvania Company, in my judgment thirty days will not elapse before they will be willing to restore their rates, and all we ask is to be put on a parity with other shippers.

After a moment's hesitation he asked if I thought he ought to stand all of this twenty cents. I told him that if he should stand any part of it he should stand it all. I said, it is a transportation fight and not a fight of manufacturers. When it comes to competition of the manufacturers we would take care of ourselves. I said that we would not have made this contract except on their assurance that the contract price of $1.25 was to be maintained. He said: "I will make your rate $1.05," and this was after we had done more than we had agreed to do under the contract. The next day we sold between 50,000 and 60,000 on the basis of $1.05 a barrel. Mr. Vanderbilt allowed that rate of payment for one month, and then said he would exact the contract price, $1.25. I said all right, and we shall ship just the amount of oil we are compelled to ship to fulfill our contract, and then

23 *Ibid.*

we shall stop. We paid him $1.25 for all over the month, and then we did not run a barrel of oil from the city of Cleveland more than that until the expiration of this contract for more than three months. That is the good the contract worked on us. You might consider it a baby act to plead the equities of the case, but we could not place our oil on the market and compete with other refineries.

From this evidence emerge some brilliant rays of light. We learn something of the size and prosperity of the enlarged Standard Oil; its shipments to New York alone (and it had a considerable Western and Southern trade) did not drop below 108,000 barrels a month in the summer of 1872, and rose at one time above 180,000, though this was the first summer of reorganization. We learn that the railroads had apparently all determined to maintain an "agreed price" of $1.25 a barrel to New York. We learn that as the rate-wars flared up again, the Pennsylvania within three months cut the charge from Pittsburgh to New York by twenty cents a barrel, and the Standard began to lose money. When the Lake Shore-New York Central system met this cut, the Standard sold 50,000 to 60,000 barrels of oil in one day. But when after a single month the Lake Shore-New York Central management reverted to the higher rate, the Standard again lost money. We learn that for half the year the Standard could have shipped its refined oil by way of the Great Lakes and Erie Canal, which were not included in the compact of March 25, for 85 cents a barrel. It did not do so because it had an agreement with the New York Central, while it also wished to place its oil in New York with the greatest possible dispatch.

Out of this rapid scrapping of the March 25th agreement later grew a charge of mendacity against Rockefeller and some railroad officers. According to the report of the Ohio legislative committee which investigated railroad discriminations in 1879, the new contract of the Standard began on April 1, 1872. But on April 4 President William Hasson of the Petroleum Producers' Union interrogated the railroad heads as to their contracts. Tom Scott, Horace Clark, W. H. Vanderbilt, and George B. McClellan sent immediate replies that they had no understanding with the Standard Oil or the South Improvement Company as to rates. "The only existing arrangement is with you," telegraphed McClellan. Were all four of these reputable railroad heads lying? Of course, the thought is absurd. On April 8

Rockefeller, in answer to a telegram from Hasson, replied that "this company holds no contract with the railroad companies or any of them." He was certainly telling the truth. Miss Tarbell remarks with evident suspicion that she cannot explain this discrepancy.[24] But a close inquiry suggests that there may be no discrepancy at all. The contract has long since disappeared, and the summary of its contents given by the committee reporter is brief and vague. This reporter speaks of it as calling for the $1.25 rate "From the first of April to the middle of November, 1872, about seven months." But from April 1 to November 15 is seven and a half months. The contract probably ran from April 15 to November 15, and was written after the telegrams by Scott, Clark, Vanderbilt, McClellan, and Rockefeller. Perhaps it was written after April 8, and made retroactive to April 1, or perhaps it ran from the *last* of April.

Clearly, the background of the refining industry during the latter half of 1872 was the old background of railroad wars, rate-cutting, and semi-secret rebates. The enlarged Standard Oil Company was in a strong position, but not so strong that it could not lose money, or could yet dictate to the railroads. Even its closest ally in past years, the Lake Shore, resisted some of its pleas. The effort of the Producers' Union to freeze the eastward rates on oil at $1.50 a barrel had given way immediately to the new "agreed price" of $1.25, but the Pittsburgh refiners had shortly forced a cut even in that. Many shippers, from the great Empire Transportation Company to small refiners like Adnah Neyhart of Tidioute, Pa., were getting rebates. Chaos was returning. The need for railroad stability was as imperative as ever.

IV

And the general situation of the industry called for organization. "We may now look for a revival of the petroleum trade, which has been in a comparatively stagnant condition for many weeks," trumpeted the New York *Commercial and Shipping List* just after the March agreement.[25] But the revival signally failed to appear.

As a new step to meet the need, various prominent refiners stepped forward in the spring of 1872 with a project for a pool of refiners to work in co-operation with the united producers. Their program,

[24]*Cf.* Tarbell, *Standard Oil Company*, I, 332–334.   [25]March 30, 1872.

called the "Pittsburgh Plan," was apparently devised by William G. Warden, Charles Lockhart, and other manufacturers of that city. It called for a loose but comprehensive organization of all American refiners, acting openly and with the aid of the well-owners to stabilize the industry. A central board was to be set up with broad powers. It was to control the buying of crude oil, determine just how much each plant should refine, and fix and maintain a price for the product; and it was also to negotiate uniform and public freight rates with the railroads. To safeguard the pool against secession, an arrangement was to be devised by which it should lease the member-refineries. Each participant would receive profits proportionate to the appraised value of his property, whether his refinery operated on full time, half time, or not at all.[26] Roughly similar pooling arrangements had already been tried with scant success in several industries. The Northern whiskey distillers, for example, had thus attempted in 1870–71 to cut down their production by three fifths. The refiners' plan was frankly tentative, its sponsors inviting amendments and professing readiness to accept a better arrangement if one could be devised. Though Rockefeller had no confidence in so loose and flimsy an association, he unquestionably believed that the attempt to make it work would have educative benefits.

As spring crept northward into the mountain valleys of Pennsylvania, the newspapers contained vague adumbrations of the scheme. The Pittsburgh *Gazette* of April 2, 1872, announced that some refiners who had been interested in the South Improvement Company would soon try to bring together a sufficient number of manufacturers to accomplish its main object, "namely, limiting the working interest of the present refining capacity of the country and at the same time securing for the diminished product more remunerative though perfectly legitimate figures." It added that "something will have to be done, the sooner the better," and that the authors of the plan wished to make an amicable agreement with the producers, assuring them of a fair price for crude oil. A special expedition of refiners was shortly organized to extend an olive branch to the lately embattled Regions. Early in May, Rockefeller and Flagler boarded a train for Pitts-

[26]In May, 1872, nearly all Pittsburgh, Cleveland, and Oil Regions newspapers published outlines of the Pittsburgh Plan. It is most conveniently found in the appendix to the first volume of Tarbell, *Standard Oil Company*, 336.

burgh. There they met Warden, Frew, and Waring, and the five men, silk-hatted and frock-coated, were soon journeying up the beautiful Allegheny Valley to Titusville.

They must have made a picturesque sight as, bags in hand, they swung off the puffing little train into the frowsy metropolis of the Regions—for Titusville deserved that appellation. The trees were shooting into full green, the dogwood was in bloom, the neat dooryards showed lilacs and peonies. The oil country, half boom and half broke as always, was showing its usual springtime flush of activity; the railroad-sidings lined with wooden tank cars and boxcars full of lumber, engine-parts, and pipes; the streets busy from dawn to dark; the lobby of the Mansion House crowded with expectorating dealers and speculators. Startled glances and black looks followed Rockefeller and his companions as they walked up the main thoroughfare, but they stepped boldly into the principal offices. They had come, they explained, to meet their recent opponents and ask for a general union, avoiding the objectionable features of the South Improvement Company, but aiming at stabilization. Naturally an odor of brimstone clung to their black broadcloth garments. The Petroleum Center *Record* of May 11, indignantly reporting their presence, expressed a hope that Regions men would "not allow themselves to be soft-soaped by the honeyed words of monopolists and conspirators."[27] Less than a week before a sub-committee of the House Commerce Committee had agreed to report that the South Improvement Company was one of the most gigantic and dastardly conspiracies ever attempted. Yet it must be remembered that Rockefeller had spent much time at Franklin, making numerous friends in the Regions, while the Standard Oil had taken a leading part the previous year in founding the Oil Exchange in Oil City, and had many adherents among oil dealers. Miss Tarbell goes too far when she describes the visit as a piece of sheer effrontery at which the Regions gasped, and pictures the envoys as a set of serpentine plotters who "slipped around, bland and smiling, from office to office, explaining, expostulating, mollifying."[28] While many suspicious men took this view, others regarded the visitors as sincerely interested in restoring the sick industry.

[27]Boyle, *Derrick's Handbook*, 179. The Pittsburgh *Gazette* said again on May 15: "That something must be done is evident, and the sooner the better."
[28]Tarbell, *Standard Oil Company*, I, 105.

A perceptible change of sentiment, in fact, had taken place in the Oil Regions since the agreement of March 25. For one reason, victory had brought a subsidence of bitterness. For another, many oil men had shrewdly perceived that the compact would not end their troubles. A *Sun* reporter asked a prominent New York refiner the day it was signed: "Do you suppose this agreement will hold any length of time?" "No, I don't," was the reply. "I think that ninety days from now war will break out again."

Leaders like J. J. Vandergrift and John D. Archbold knew that a sudden reformation of railroad rate practices would be unbelievable. These two bold spirits of the Regions, together with Charles Pratt and H. H. Rogers in New York, also realized that even if the railroads could have held Pittsburgh and Cleveland to the harsh agreement of March 25, refiners elsewhere would remain in a precarious situation. Cleveland had the water-routes east and west, the abundant labor supply, and the chemical plants which the *Leader* had long ago proclaimed as important advantages. Concentrated in one company, her industry enjoyed immense economies in purchasing, manufacturing, and selling. Pittsburgh, with cheap fuel, the Allegheny River for crude oil, and promised aid from the new branch of the Baltimore & Ohio, would also continue battling. The general overdevelopment of refining and the cutthroat competition would still ruin weak establishments and sap the vitality even of the strongest. South Improvement leaders had expatiated upon the folly of letting ninety firms struggle for a business which could give prosperity only to twenty. When May quotations in New York sank to 21¾ cents a gallon, as low a price as ever recorded,[29] refiners began to ponder these pleas anew. Everywhere the weak establishments were again facing a desperate competition.

It was natural for shrewd "independents" to question whether they had gained anything from the recent struggle, and to ask if the idea of co-operation did not deserve fuller investigation. Vandergrift and Rogers, Pratt and Archbold were now conspicuously willing to discuss the problems of the industry. And so, it must be added, were many well-owners, for overproduction again menaced the Regions.

[29]Boyle, *Derrick's Handbook*, 783. "The trade here regards the Standard Oil Company as simply taking the place of the South Improvement Company, and as being ready at any moment to make the same attempt to control the trade," said the N. Y. *Bulletin*, April 15, 1872.

A rich new field had been opened in Clarion County by the sinking in August, 1871, of the famous Gailey Well No. 1. The area about Parker's Landing had become the scene of another rush.[30] Land values soared upward. Speculators sunk wells by hundreds, and the flood of oil steadily grew. The total production in Pennsylvania rose from 5,277,000 barrels in 1871 to 6,504,000 in 1872, and to 9,850,000 in 1873.[31] As tanks overflowed and prices fell, the well-owners cast about more tolerantly for an escape from their troubles. Although the Producers' Union still existed, its powers were far from adequate to control the output. Many Regions men admitted that a broader stabilization of the industry was needed; and while they might distrust Rockefeller and Warden, while they might disapprove of some aspects of the "Pittsburgh Plan," they were ready to confer.

On May 15-16, 1872, public meetings were held in Titusville to discuss the scheme. Conservative producers were electrified when Archbold, Vandergrift, and several other leading refiners boldly espoused it. Although reiterating their hatred of the South Improvement Company, they deplored the chaos of the industry, and advocated immediate action to restore order and profits. The Pittsburgh Plan was open to all on equal terms; it included no discriminations or penalties; it was to be frank and fair in all its workings. It might prove weak, but it offered hope. "I am willing to do anything which will be of benefit to the trade," declared Archbold. "In whatever is the best plan, I am willing to co-operate."[32] Vandergrift and others expressed similar views.

But the opposition was sufficiently strong to carry the day. N. M. Allen of the Titusville *Courier* fiercely asserted that the Oil Regions refiners could never trust to "the integrity and honesty of others to take care of our interests in a joint-stock corporation."[33] Other speakers, after denouncing the visiting emissaries as "monopolists," reproached their adherents in the Regions as "deserters" and "ringsters." Feeling grew so bitter that fist-fights were barely avoided, and moderate men hesitated to speak. At one point Allen seized his hat and stamped out of the hall. The principal speakers presenting the Pittsburgh Plan were Flagler, William Frew, and O. T. Waring, Rocke-

[30]J. J. McLaurin, *Sketches in Crude Oil*, 205 ff.
[31]Figures of Chamber of Commerce of the State of New York, *Annual Reports;* those in Boyle, *Derrick's Handbook*, 805, are substantially the same.
[32]Moore, *Life of John D. Archbold*, 93.   [33]*Courier*, May 16, 17, 1872.

feller not being present; and they spoke well. But by sheer numbers they, Archbold, and Vandergrift were overborne. A majority believed that if the Pittsburgh Plan went through, men conspicuous in the South Improvement scheme would be dominant. Rockefeller and his Cleveland partners would possess the largest single percentage of interest in the pool, while Warden, Waring, Frew, and their friends would have substantial holdings. Acting together, they would almost certainly control the central board. Moreover, many feared that this new combination, despite its fair professions, would use the rebate to stamp out competitors. A reporter of the Oil City *Derrick* who asked one advocate of the Pittsburgh Plan what its supporters would do with any refiners who stubbornly stayed outside, received the quick reply: "Go through them." "How?" he asked. "By the co-operation of transportation," was the reply—that is, by rebates.

The two meetings at Titusville, therefore, ended in a flat refusal of most Oil Regions producers and refiners to co-operate in the Pittsburgh Plan. *"Sic semper tyrannis, sic transit gloria* South Improvement Company!" exulted the Oil City *Derrick*. It seemed to many a logical decision. The real strength of the Pittsburgh Plan must lie in a refiners' pool, in which the Cleveland and Pittsburgh proposers would be the ruling body; the confused, ever-changing multitude of producers, even if they acted loyally through their union, would be a subsidiary and not a co-ordinate element. Some of the largest refiners of the Regions, realizing that their isolated position would soon be untenable, heartily wished to enter the pool. But the great body of producers and smaller refiners instinctively drew back from a plan which would place them in an inferior position, and possibly under the power of men whom they thoroughly distrusted. Time showed that they would have done well to try to write full safeguards into the plan, and then accept it. But, headstrong, defiant, and elated by their recent victory, they stood adamant.

V

Yet Rockefeller, Warden, and the other promoters had accomplished much—perhaps nearly as much as they had hoped. They had won over the two ablest refiners in the Oil Regions, Archbold and Vandergrift, and two of the ablest men in New York, Pratt and

Rogers; and to Rockefeller especially these new allies were to mean much. They were now ready to face the hostile Regions. During June and July they pushed their pool steadily by correspondence and conferences. On August 5 the Pittsburgh *Gazette* announced that the plan "promises to be a success, and will soon, if not already, be in practical operation. It is said that all the refiners here, with two exceptions, have gone into it; that Cleveland, Philadelphia, and New York refiners are favorable to it, and there, as here, nearly if not all of them have connected themselves with it." *The Gazette* had no details, but stated that the new organization would be independent of all railroad companies, and that its sole object would be to protect the refining interest, menaced with bankruptcy by low prices. A few days later it remarked that although some refiners feared that the scheme was too big, and many conflicting interests had to be reconciled, progress was being made. On the 26th it reported that the National Refiners' Association, for such was its name, had been completed, and that it would begin to operate on September 1.[34]

This was the exciting summer of the Grant-Greeley campaign, and of the last refulgent months of the great post-war boom. The meeting which adopted the final plan for the National Refiners' Association was held in Cleveland, with oil men of the whole country represented and Rockefeller and Flagler much in evidence. Basically, the Association was a loose pool, dependent entirely upon voluntary co-operation, and bringing together four fifths of the nation's refining capacity. Nearly all the really large refiners had recognized the stern necessity for some such organization. While an outgrowth of the abortive South Improvement enterprise, it was a very mild outgrowth.[35] That scheme had represented a highly centralized refiners' pool planned with the railroads, and embracing a harshly coercive system of rebates as an essential feature; the new plan represented a decentralized pool standing independent of the railroads and avowing no railroad-rate features at all. The main objects and features were to be as follows:[36]

[34] *The Gazette* was profuse in its assertions that this refiners' pool could not hurt the producers. "The two interests are so closely allied together that when the one is in a flourishing condition the other will be similarly affected."

[35] This mildness is emphasized by a letter in the Titusville *Herald,* Aug. 8, 1872, signed by "A Member of the Proposed Refiners' Association."

[36] See Titusville correspondence of N. Y. *World,* Dec. 7, 1872.

First, a reduction of the refining capacity of the country by one half.

Second, the pledging of members not to sell at a lower price than that fixed by the Board of Directors upon information furnished by statistical agents, who were to collect data in regard to production, stocks, consumption, and other factors.

Third, the retention by each refiner of the privilege of buying his own oil at his own prices.

Fourth, an agreement not to sell "short," or to do business with any dealer who sold "short."

Fifth, a division of the refining business on the following basis: Cleveland, 25.25 per cent; Pittsburgh, 25.25 per cent; the Oil Regions, 18 per cent; New York, 16.75 per cent; and Philadelphia, 14.75 per cent.

The original Pittsburgh Plan had been heavily diluted, for the pool contained no leasing agreement, and no means of coercion. This refiners' pool was even weaker than certain pools already set up in other overexpanded and disorderly industries, such as salt-making and whiskey-distilling. It differed from the latter in two other important respects. While neither the salt-makers nor whiskey-distillers offered an enormous body of freight, the petroleum-refiners did, and three great Eastern railroads depended upon them for a substantial part of their revenues. While neither the salt-makers nor whiskey-distillers dealt with any special group of producers (the salt-makers owning their wells, while the distillers bought grain in a market existing chiefly for other uses), the petroleum-refiners stood vis-à-vis a large body of oil-producers. These two peculiar features made the petroleum-refiners' pool an object of especial and sensitive public interest. Only consumers, watching for price rises, were keenly interested in the salt and whiskey pools. But consumers, railroads, and producers were all vitally concerned in the oil-refiners' pool.

Whether the organization would long endure or prove really effective nobody could tell. Other pools had quickly dropped to pieces. In 1871 the dogged resistance of a single salt manufacturer, Duncan Stewart, had forced the hopeful Michigan Salt Association to suspend its operations. The distillers' pool produced, as its historian states, "no very decisive result." Rockefeller certainly entertained but slender hopes for the National Refiners' Association, which to him was simply another step toward his real goal of consolidation. Yet its mere formation had achieved two noteworthy results. It had brought the Standard Oil into close association with the leading refiners of Pittsburgh, led by Lockhart and Frew; the leading refiners of Philadelphia, led by Warden; and the leading refiner of New York, Charles Pratt. It had also dissolved the unnatural coalition of refiners and producers in the Oil Regions, and led the principal Regions refiners, including J. J. Vandergrift and John D. Archbold, into the new group. They were now united not with their geographical neighbors, but with their trade associates. The long-continued threat that the producers, by a close alliance with a few great refineries in the Oil Regions and New York, might make infinite trouble for the Cleveland and Pittsburgh refiners, and even "wipe them from the map as with a sponge," was completely and finally dispelled.

It is significant that Rockefeller was elected president of the Refiners' Association. This was a tribute to the force of his personality, his fame as an organizer, and his position as head of the largest refining company in the world. He had achieved the primacy in the industry that he was to hold for the next forty years. That rugged, versatile, and much-respected industrialist of the Regions, J. J. Vandergrift, now owner of the United Pipe Lines, the largest existing system, was honored with the vice-presidency. Charles Pratt of New York was treasurer. Thus the East, the West, and the oil districts were all represented. H. H. Rogers and Archbold, so recently implacable enemies of consolidation, now stood aligned with the movement. The tide of business concentration was rolling on. Within a few months after the shock of the South Improvement defeat, the outlook for a systematic organization and for rapid progress toward Rockefeller's and Flagler's goal of close unification had become unexpectedly bright.

XVIII

Rockefeller and the Producers

THE oil industry was unlike any other in American history in the explosive energy with which it had expanded. New fields were constantly opened, the number of men engaged in production rapidly increased, the flow of petroleum rose, and prices, with some fluctuations, fell. Perhaps the closest analogy in this period was furnished by the silver-mining industry, which was also expanding with such rapidity that it broke the world-price for the metal, the mine-owners then turning to the Federal Government for relief in the Bland-Allison Act of 1878. The various departments of the oil industry, unable to beg help from Washington, had to save themselves. Complete order would have required a union of practically all the well-owners to limit production, an equally effective union of practically all refiners, and a clear-cut division of oil-freights among the trunk-line railroads at stable rates. While the world was able to absorb almost unlimited quantities of oil, if the stocks were forced upon it too rapidly prices would collapse. In the same way, Western grain-growers were soon to find that while the world was hungry for breadstuffs, if the shipments became too heavy the prices would fall to ruinous levels.

Americans are familiar with the frantic efforts of the silver-producers to gain relief, culminating in the great free-silver battle of 1896. They are familiar with the more recent attempts of the Brazilian coffee-growers, Malaysian rubber-producers, and American wheat-raisers to protect themselves from gluts and bankruptcy. But the spasmodic effort of the Pennsylvania oil-producers in 1872–73 to cut down their output and restore prices has never been given the attention it deserved. One reason for this is that the fullest existing account, that of Ida M. Tarbell, mistakenly treats it as a defensive campaign against the Standard Oil and John D. Rockefeller, and so obscures its real meaning. It was primarily a desperate movement against overproduction and low prices. It actually received the assistance of Rockefeller and other enlightened refiners, not their opposition, for they were anxious to see order introduced into all branches of the industry. The reasons for its early breakdown were substantially identical with the reasons for the breakdown of the schemes for valorizing Brazilian coffee and Malaysian rubber, and of Hoover's device for aiding the wheat-farmers.

We may summarize this extraordinary chapter in our industrial history, if we wish, in a few sentences. The leaders of the oil-producers, frightened by unrestricted production and fast-dropping prices, formed an association to deal with the situation. It first agreed to stop new drilling for six months, and then to shut down existing wells for one month. But although sporadic violence was used to enforce these agreements, many lawless producers disregarded them, and the output of oil quickly rose to high levels again. Thereupon the leaders turned to a new plan, setting up a Petroleum Producers' Agency to buy and store surplus oil, holding it off the market until prices should recover. The Standard Oil and other powerful refiners supported the Agency, agreeing in the so-called Treaty of Titusville to buy all their oil from it, and to pay not less than $4 a barrel—so long as the producers held the output within certain bounds. But it shortly became evident that the producers could not keep it anywhere near these bounds, while a multitude of lawless well-owners began selling oil to refiners outside the treaty at less than $4 a barrel. The result was that the ill-financed agency scheme collapsed, the flow of oil became greater than ever, and the well-owners saw prices sink to a more distressing point than ever. Like the rubber-growers and coffee-producers, they had exhausted themselves in vain; their latter state was worse than their first.

But some parts of this remarkable story, which Rockefeller followed with the keenest concern, are worth relating in detail.

II

It was the terrific torrent of new oil loosed by the Clarion County discoveries which furnished the principal impulse toward a restrictive union of producers. The Regions leaders, having destroyed the South Improvement Company by their hastily formed Producers' Union, now realized that reckless overdrilling was an even greater enemy. The summer of 1872 saw prices go down, down, down under the weight of the green flood. Yet even while they fell, fresh diggers joined the rush. By August 24 nearly 350 new wells were being drilled![1] Production for the Regions as a whole rose from 12,000 barrels a day to 15,000, to 16,000, and to 17,000. In August, 1872, the average price paid for crude oil fell to $3.47½, or almost a dollar a barrel less than a year earlier. Even the blindest drillers perceived that the Regions could not continue swamping the market and escape a terrible penalty. The Titusville *Courier* asserted on August 26 that it was becoming impossible to move the huge output of oil from wells along Clarion River and Turkey Run, where tanks and pipe-line terminals were filled to overflowing. Some desperate producers, unable to obtain sufficient cars, were compelled to run their oil into the river. Yet men were still bidding for fresh sites, drills were thudding down at new spots every morning, and new wells were daily coming in, amid vast excitement, to add their hundreds of barrels to the glut. What could be done? The only answer was—Organize! That spring an association had placed an embargo on oil to the South Improvement monopolists. Now another must place a partial embargo on oil to the whole world.

The result was the formation late in August of a new Petroleum Producers' Association. *The Courier* hailed the emergency of this body joyously. It congratulated the producers on having "at last recognized the cause of the great reduction in crude oil," and determined to "apply the only true remedy to the great evil of overproduction" by a solemn compact to stop drilling for the next six months. "We heartily approve of this movement and are pleased to see so many of our producers, refiners, bankers, and citizens signing the pledge. To this committee we can only say, get the name of every resident, and we may then live to see oil reach five dollars per barrel." That this new organization did not imply any hostility to the National Refiners' Association is evident both from this statement and from an editorial in the Titusville *Herald* of August 30, 1872:

[1]According to Parker's Landing producers, Buffalo *Courier,* Aug. 24, 1872, wells under way numbered 347.

The producers and refiners show every indication of arriving at a speedy mutual understanding, or coalition, by means of which both crude and refined petroleum will eventually assume a standard value of between four and five dollars per barrel, and each interest will receive a fair and legitimate margin of profit. This has become a virtual necessity, as while the two great interests have been quarreling, the one bulling and the other bearing the market, the ring speculators have reached in and divided the spoils. There are more rich men in New York today who have realized princely fortunes out of oil corners and who have never produced or refined a barrel of oil in their lives, than there are in both branches of the legitimate business. There is now a tremendous upheaval going on among producers with a spirit of determination to organize into associations for their mutual self-protection. The refiners on their side have already almost completely perfected their organization. When two such bodies march in solid phalanx to defeat a common enemy, it certainly looks ominous. . . .

Captain William Hasson, so successful as head of the Petroleum Producers' Union, was naturally made president of the Association. A crusading spirit pervaded the organizers, who were determined to make this new body strong enough to protect the operators for years to come. To ensure fair prices literally every one must be enlisted, the men who pumped ten barrels a day as well as the men who pumped hundreds. Buoyant, self-confident, and ready-tongued, Hasson toured the fields, he and his deputies seeing that everybody received a pledge to drill no shaft, and to lease no lands for drilling by others, for six months beginning September 1, 1872. The theory was that this would prevent the sinking of about 500 wells, and that as the old wells fell off, production would decrease by from 3000 to 5000 barrels a day. With public sentiment and the press behind the movement, operators rich and poor fell into line. Each signer agreed to forfeit $2000 for every well he commenced, the money being collectible like any other debt, and to use all honorable means to prevent others from boring.[2] The pledge met a widespread acceptance everywhere but in the one area where acceptance was most important—the Clarion County field. Here many of the landowners were illiterate Pennsylvania-German farmers, narrow-minded, greedy, and stubborn. Some were so ignorant that when offered a royalty of one eighth of the product they rejected it as unfair, demanding one tenth, while others were so suspicious that they thought the pledge

[2]See N. Y. *World*, Sept. 3, 1872, "No More Oil Wells."

simply a scheme to rob them. For that matter, it was natural that holders of promising sites in a new field should think it unfair to be kept waiting while the existing producers grew fat upon their monopoly. Moreover, many speculators who had bought lands or options needed a quick return on their money and insisted on immediate drilling.

III

As it became evident that the stop-drilling agreement was neither effective nor equitable, the Producers' Association went on to close existing wells. We might rather say that it was forced to this step, for during August and early September production exceeded 18,000 barrels a day and was still rising. Titusville prices dropped in mid-September to $2.75 a barrel. Experts estimated that the district was then losing fully a dollar a barrel on the total output, or more than $500,000 a month; and though this was probably an exaggeration, we must remember that the cost of sinking a well averaged $5000, and that nearly all wells had to be pumped. The movement for a thirty-day shutdown rapidly gained ground. Unanimous action was finally taken at a meeting in Oil City, with every district represented, and at midnight on September 28 three fourths of the wells in the older areas were stopped.

Captain Hasson deserves most of the credit for the success of this new pledge.[3] When eloquence was of no avail, rough methods were used. The Titusville *Herald* for October 1 reported: "About 150 men forced the wells on Woods, Pierson, Stevenson, and other farms in the vicinity of Petroleum Center to stop today, but work has since started up. The crowd threatened the Central Company, but steps were taken to prevent the use of any further force." And on the same date the Pittsburgh *Gazette* declared that a feverish excitement reigned in the Regions.[4] "Everywhere the intensest feelings prevail over the movement made to suspend production. Dispatches from various districts generally show that the movement is universal, and there are probably not over fifty wells producing tonight. From

[3]N. Y. *World*, Sept. 30, 1872. Resolutions were adopted prohibiting the use of torpedoes for six months. "Advanced prices in the oil market are expected immediately," wrote *The World's* Titusville correspondent.

[4]Titusville dispatch. The same report appeared in the N. Y. *World*, Oct. 1, 1872.

some localities it is reported that violence has been resorted to in carrying out the measure. Well-rigs were burned and engines were destroyed by sledge-hammers, and oil tanks tapped."

Half a dozen wells were burned one night near Parker's Landing, while next day a mob of several hundred men headed by a brass band closed more than thirty shafts about Rouseville.[5] And at first these stern tactics promised results. As day after day a mere half-stream flowed from the lately superabundant regions, a Sabbath hush fell upon the land. The air, usually filled with dust and coal smoke, grew clear and sparkling. Long trains of empty cars stood on the sidings; teams champed idly in their stables. In every village crowds of laborers sympathetically discussed the shutdown. Ida M. Tarbell, then growing up in the Regions, long afterward described the pervasive quiet. "The crowded oil-farms where creaking walking-beams sawed the air from morning to night, where engines puffed, whistles screamed, great gas-jets flared, teams came and went, and men hurried to and fro, became suddenly silent and desolate, and this desolation had an ugliness all its own—something unparalleled in any other industry in the country. The awkward derricks, staring cheap shanties, big tanks with miles and miles of pipes running hither and thither, the oil-soaked ground, blackened and ruined trees, terrible roads—all of the common features of the oil-farm to which activity gave meaning and dignity—now became hideous in inactivity." Far outside the Regions, in Chicago and New York, businessmen read the news dispatches, and exclaimed over this unprecedented strike against overproduction and low prices. Abroad, in Liverpool and Berlin, it provoked the wonderment of every one interested in the oil trade.

However, the effort proved merely spasmodic. It was simply impossible to continue long this stoppage of a business employing 10,000 men and yielding many millions a month. The embargo had begun to be effective about September 20. Average daily production for September was cut to 16,561 barrels, against 18,816 the month

---

[5]See the N. Y. *World,* Oct. 9, 1872, for a description of this violence. It states: "The same sort of persuasion was brought to bear in other districts, and with signally successful effect on the suspension of oil wells. In some instances the well-owners were indignant beyond measure, and forcibly resisted the action of these men, but with no avail, and though the government was called on for assistance, no attention thus far has been paid to the call."

previous. In October it fell to 14,308 barrels. Then on October 28 the embargo was removed—and the next month production soared to 23,275 barrels, a new record! It remained above 22,000 barrels in December, while prices naturally sagged once more.[6]

It was evident that only a comprehensive, highly centralized, and permanent organization could control the glut in the market. Hasson and his associates had therefore already begun maturing a new plan, to which co-operative-minded producers everywhere looked hopefully. The leaders, seeking advice in numerous quarters, were deluged with suggestions, some wild, some helpful. One proposal is worth noting for the vengeful attitude toward the refiners which it revealed; a meeting of well-owners at St. Petersburg voted to urge foreign governments to place heavy tariffs on refined oil and admit crude oil duty-free, so that European refineries might be built up at the expense of American manufacturers.[7] The Pittsburgh *Commercial* greeted this with a warning growl. Of American crude oil, it remarked, 97 per cent was refined in the United States, and public opinion would insist upon the preservation of this great American industry.

Finally, late in October, 1872, Hasson presented the committee's new scheme. He proposed the formation of a new corporation of $1,000,000 capital, called the Petroleum Producers' Agency, the stock of which would be held only by actual producers or men for whom they vouched. It would purchase all available oil from the Producers' Association, paying not less than $5 a barrel. If the price could be maintained at $5 or more, the full amount would be paid at once; if not, the Agency would store the oil in tanks which it meant to build, paying partly in cash, partly in tank certificates. Whenever the Board of Directors deemed it advisable, they might establish refineries and take other steps to maintain a high price. They were also to determine the line at which production should be restrained, and when necessary were to adopt measures for the stoppage of drilling. Meanwhile they should constantly collect statistics as to wells, drilling, oil-production, and stocks on hand. In this way the committee hoped to control production and prices with an iron grip, to restrain

[6]*The United States Railroad and Mining Register,* Jan. 25, 1873, gives these figures. Stocks which went down to 759,630 barrels during the stop-drilling agreement, rose in December to 924,000 barrels, and kept rising.

[7]Boyle, *Derrick's Handbook,* 188.

the fast-growing and much-hated body of oil-speculators, and to offer a defiant front to the refiners. The Agency was to oppose all monopolies valiantly—all save its own![8]

For a time this scheme for co-operative storage and marketing seemed to promise success. Bankers of the Regions voted their support, and by October 24 about $200,000 in stock had been subscribed. Hasson called upon every one interested in production to invest. "Advise every employee to take at least one share of stock for himself, and one for his wife and each of his children," he exhorted the well-owners. When on November 6 a new producers' convention met at Oil City, with Colonel Thomas McDonough in the chair, confidence and unanimity prevailed. Next day the press announced: "Agency plan an entire success—over $1,000,000 subscribed to capital stock." Trustees and officers were elected, and December found the scheme apparently almost ready for operation. Consumers of oil began to take notice, for $5 a barrel was a high charge, and if the agency could establish a total monopoly, it might keep the price there. Public hostility was appearing in various quarters. "It is an attempt," warned the New York *Herald,* "to force oil to high prices for the public; the consumers are likely to take a hand in the matter and use their efforts to frustrate the design and intent of the shutdown movement by refusing to pay the high prices."[9] The Pittsburgh press was hostile. The New York *Commercial and Shipping List* declared the plan injudicious and "reasonably certain to react against the producers in the long run. The better way would have been to leave the matter to the law of supply and demand." And the report of the Chamber of Commerce of the State of New York for 1872 sharply condemned the Agency scheme, declaring that "the remedy is generally held to be worse than all the temporary evils growing out of overproduction."[10]

IV

Yet actually this portentous Producers' Agency was a giant with feet of clay. Supported enthusiastically by a majority of the large

[8]N. Y. *World,* Dec. 7, 1872, contains a full account by its Titusville correspondent.
[9]This statement was made while the movement was still gathering strength, Sept. 9, 1872.
[10]*Report,* 1872, Part II, 42.

and well-establshed producers, it was regarded with a jaundiced eye by small owners and new investors. The little producers, whose wells yielded them—like the Tipperary farmer's cow—just enough for a living, made up a great part of the population of the Regions. Traversing the glens and defiles of the Allegheny Valley, the traveller found many obscure men whose engines pumped from five to twenty barrels a day, and who sang the Dee miller's song about caring for nobody. They dreaded a monopolistic combination among their more wealthy and powerful brethren. If these big fellows established an agency able to raise or depress prices, they would be able to crush their associates at will, for by merely sending down quotations without warning they could extinguish producers who had no resources. The little men were aware that the Oil Regions, in their limited confines and their practical freedom from outside competition, strongly resembled the anthracite area of Pennsylvania; and they feared the fate of the small operators in the anthracite counties, whose holdings had been swallowed up by a few powerful corporations, and who had been reduced to economic serfdom. As for the recent investors, they felt it bitterly unfair that they should be deprived of the chances their predecessors had so blithely seized.[11]

Moreover, the number of wells was increasing too rapidly, both in the new Clarion field and in the Butler County area first opened in 1869, for any restraint. Far down the Allegheny River operators were now busy leasing land, sinking shafts, and founding new towns. Foxburg, a river hamlet in Clarion County, leaped into a small city; St. Petersburg, a rural post-office three miles from the river, soon had 3000 people; other boom towns sprang up, and all about them a forest of wells. The bold speculators who reaped wealth in these new fields snapped their fingers at the Agency. One firm, Lavens & Evans in Triangle City, had gained notoriety in the days of the non-drilling agreement by its manifesto: "Resolved, that we don't care a damn!" The oil country was irresistibly expanding, and the pioneers responsible for its growth were too individualistic to be bound by any pledges. For that matter, some of the older operators were equally recalcitrant—equally selfish, undisciplined, averse to look-

[11]These attitudes are described by the Titusville correspondent of the N. Y. *World,* Dec. 7, 1872. He writes of the Agency: "For combination, in this case, means monopoly in a truer sense than the word can have when applied to almost any other business combination."

ing ahead, and intent on quick gains. A revolt by a few lawless souls could break down whatever price the Agency might set, while at any moment a new oil discovery and a new rush would render any agreement worthless. When it grew evident in December that production in the Clarion, Butler, and Venango fields was breaking all records, the $5 price became preposterous, and the movement faced a certainty of failure.

But while the scheme still appeared hopeful, the Agency had received from Rockefeller and the Standard a remarkable offer of support. There was nothing strange about this, for from the outset intelligent refiners had welcomed the stabilizing influence of the Agency. The Titusville correspondent of the New York *World* testified that most manufacturers were "pleased" by the producers' agreement, declaring that "any action which will tend to establish a firm price for crude oil must be helpful to the trade."[12] Like the producers, they were at deadly feud with the speculators in the Regions who constantly manipulated the price of oil. Rockefeller favored a strong association of refiners, a strong association of producers, and some agreement or union between the two. No sooner had the Agency obtained its million dollars' capital than he ordered an Oil City agent of the Standard to buy 6000 barrels of crude from it at $4.75 a barrel, expressing the warmest good will for the new organization.

"It has been represented to us," he telegraphed,[13] "that if we would buy of the producers' agent at Oil City and pay $4.75 a barrel, they would maintain the price. We are willing to go further and buy only of the producers' agent, hence the order we have given you. See Hasson and others and let there be a fair understanding on this point. We will do all in our power to maintain prices, and continue to buy, provided our position is fully understood. We do this to convince producers of our sincerity, and to assist in establishing the market."

Appropriate action quickly followed. The Titusville *Courier* for November 11 announced: "The heavy purchases [yesterday] at Oil City were made by the Standard Oil Company of Cleveland, they,

[12]Quoted in *United States Railroad and Mining Gazette,* Dec. 21, 1872.
[13]Tarbell, *Standard Oil Company,* I, 120. Miss Tarbell mistakenly treats this as a Machiavellian scheme to break down the Agency by indirection.

with other leading refiners, asserting that they will buy no oil outside the Producers' Agency."

The first sentence of Rockefeller's telegram indicates that members of the Producers' Association had asked him to co-operate in price-maintenance, and to refrain from going to wildcat producers who offered bargains in oil. The fact was that many producers heartily believed in joint action with the refiners, and not a few panted eagerly for it. To be sure, Captain Hasson, Editor Allen of *The Courier,* and others who had fought the South Improvement scheme in March and the Pittsburgh Plan in May, still opposed any combination with their late enemies. They held that their organization must *dictate* the price rather than agree upon it with the refining interests, for in any union the refiners would soon gain the upper hand. *"Timeo Danaos et dona ferentes!"* exclaimed the belligerent Oil City *Derrick*. "Liberal translation: Mind your eye when the Cleveland refiners get generous!"[14] The editor believed that Rockefeller was merely offering a generous initial bid to wheedle the Producers' Agency into an agreement upon prices, and so break the well-owners' unity; once this was accomplished, he and other refiners would then turn about and smash the price. Hasson likewise argued that the producers should stand aloof from "foreign entanglements" until they had fully perfected and tested their own organization. Psychologically there was a certain justification for this attitude. The producers had never acted with real unity except under the spur of fear and anger, and a resolute antagonism toward refiners might seem the best basis for their new organization. But the majority took a saner view. They thought of the Producers' Association and Producers' Agency as bodies which should attempt not an absolute monopoly, but simply a general control of production. They could then tell the organized refiners: "We think the price ought to be such-and-such. If you will agree with us on that level, we can jointly maintain it against the irresponsible producers who are slashing prices. Let us act together."

It was evident when Rockefeller made his offer that co-operation alone offered a real chance of success; for if intransigent producers forced the refiners into open war, and into dealing with speculators and unorganized wells, the Agency would quickly be broken down.

[14]*Ibid.,* I, 122.

In trying to manage the runaway industry the Agency needed all the support it could find, for at best its outlook was dark. With meager capital and weak storage facilities, it faced the liability of a large and rapidly rising surplus of crude oil. By early November more than a million barrels of petroleum were in storage. The danger was that many producers would become discouraged and desert, while speculators would grow more defiant in sinking new wells. The expansive nature of the producing industry and the rough, untamable character of the Regions population were inimical to any ironclad union. It was expensive to keep drilling machinery idle; laborers clamored for work; and shoestring operators had to sink shafts and sell the oil for early returns. "The Oil Region was a mining camp," Rockefeller once disgustedly said.[15] Even historians who have written from the producers' point of view speak bitterly of their faults. Except in brief spasms of anxiety or rage, they displayed no more foresight than Far Western prospectors, while many of them never learned to show any real efficiency in managing their properties. "Nobody in the Oil Regions in 1872 looked with favor on economy," Miss Tarbell admits.[16] Many thought a return of 100 per cent a year only reasonable, and scorned wells yielding ten barrels a day, though at a profit of fifty cents a barrel this meant $1800 a year. As *The Derrick* said, their industry had been "born in a balloon going up, and spent all its early years in the sky." They threw money away by digging shafts in hopeless ground, by discarding costly tools which might easily have been mended, by running their offices slackly, and by speculating on the oil exchanges. They kept no books, sent telegrams instead of letters, and scorned those careful savings which Rockefeller regarded as the very foundation of business. Prudently administered, oil production ought to have yielded high returns at $3 a barrel, and the constant demand for $4 or $5 was a token of mismanagement.[17]

[15]Inglis, Conversations with Rockefeller. See his statement in *U. S. vs. Standard Oil*, XVI, 3071: "They had the characteristics of miners the world over."

[16]Tarbell, *Standard Oil Company*, I, 112, 113.

[17]So the Titusville correspondent of the N. Y. *World*, Dec. 7, 1872. The bankers carried large quantities of non-negotiable oil-paper. Many merchants feared that the Agency "promises to develop into a close monopoly which may eventually drive out of the country a large class of thrifty prompt-paying customers."

Rockefeller's offer of support by the Standard Oil was quickly followed by a similar proffer from the refiners' pool which he headed. The first days of December found oil men standing on the slushy street corners of Regions towns in eager discussion of a plan which had been hammered out to meet the objection that the refiners would naturally wish to keep the price of crude oil low while raising that of refined oil high. It was a plan, since guarantees were wanted, under which the price of crude oil would move up by a sliding scale whenever the price of refined oil advanced. Rockefeller played a leading part in the protracted meeting of representatives of the two interests soon held at the Fifth Avenue Hotel in New York to iron out their differences.[18] Tentative approval was given the plan by the producers' executive committee,[19] and men waited uneasily to learn if it would be made final. On December 23, the Producers' Council, sitting in Oil City, approved by an overwhelming vote the proposals made by the National Refiners' Association. General jubilation greeted the news. Yet despite the heavy majority against him, Hasson had fought to the end, with a bitter persistence which did much to sow dissension among the operators. He and *The Derrick* predicted that the "Treaty of Titusville," as the agreement was called, would fail with calamitous results, and their dark prophecies fed a defeatist spirit.[20]

v

This was unfortunate, for the "Treaty of Titusville" was decidedly more favorable to producers than any previous plan. It provided that the Petroleum Producers' Association should sell crude oil exclusively to the Refiners' Association, while the latter organization should buy

[18]This meeting was greeted by the N. Y. *Evening Post,* Dec. 10, with an editorial on "New Conspiracies Against Trade," denouncing "these combinations and corners."

[19]Boyle, *Derrick's Handbook,* 198.

[20]N. Y. *World, Herald,* Dec. 24, 1872. The Titusville *Herald,* Jan. 6, 1873, said of President Hasson: "He not merely opposed it [the plan] but took advantage of his official position to endeavor to kill it by the most scathing and unjust attacks, even after it had passed." It called him a traitor, declaring: "As a monied speculator, it is believed that his interest was in diametrical opposition to the success of any movement that would bring high-priced oil. It is specifically charged that for the sake of purchasing cheap oil and holding it for a rise, it was in the interests of himself and friends to sow the seeds of discord and faction and dissolve the whole organization again into chaos."

crude oil exclusively from the former; each body to take in all the willing members of its branch of the industry. The refiners pledged themselves to buy from the Association daily, for the next sixty days, 15,000 barrels of crude oil or such other quantity as the markets of the world might require, to be determined from time to time by a joint committee. The price of oil so purchased was to be $5 a barrel, of which $4 was to be paid unconditionally upon delivery. The remainder was to be paid conditionally. That is, whenever refined oil in New York was 26 cents a gallon or less, nothing above $4 was to be paid; but for every cent of advance upon kerosene, 25 cents a barrel was to be added to the price of crude, until the prices reached 30 cents a gallon and $5 a barrel respectively. The Refiners' Association might discontinue the arrangement at any time by giving ten days' notice in writing, and the Producers' Association might discontinue it after the expiration of sixty days by similar notice.[21]

It was understood that the producers should keep their output at or near 15,000 barrels a day, this part of the agreement, at the well-owners' request, being merely oral, but no less binding. The refiners further agreed that Sections I and III of the agreement of March 25, forbidding rebates or special arrangements with the railroads, should remain in force. Evidently they had no difficulty in reconciling this new pledge with their existing business arrangements, which is further proof that the rate-changes made by the Erie, Pennsylvania, and Lake Shore since March 25 were not so much rebates as open and general reductions.[22]

"It now remains to be seen," commented the New York *World,* "whether the new expedient—an alliance between the producers and refiners for the purpose of making arbitrary figures at which petroleum shall be sold to merchants—will meet with success."[23] During late December the news was ominous. The Boston refiners, who had not joined the National Refiners' Association and detested the new compact, announced that they would get all the crude oil they wanted from independent producers. The Pittsburgh *Gazette* re-

[21]A full exposition is in the N. Y. *Evening Post,* Dec. 21, 1872. See also Titusville *Courier,* Dec. 12, 1872.

[22]Questioned in old age, Rockefeller said that the refiners were merely agreeing not to seek rebates in connection with their dealings with producers—*i.e.,* upon crude oil. Inglis, Conversations with Rockefeller.

[23]N. Y. *World,* Dec. 24, 1872.

ported that many well-owners were uneasy." While they are very anxious that something should be done to place the trade on a better and more substantial basis, they are apprehensive that in the cooperative project refiners might be enabled in some way to take advantage of them; hence they want to drop it and take up something else. The latest suggestion is to run the wells but twelve hours out of the twenty-four . . .; this might do, but like all their projects attempted already, it is open to objections. The great trouble among the producers is a want of unanimity of sentiment—it seems impossible to get them all to come into a movement." This report was dated December 15. Two days later a panic seized the crude-oil market, prices falling precipitously. Shippers for the export trade, announced the New York *Commercial and Shipping List,* regarded the combination as unnatural, arbitrary, and unjust, were predicting its early downfall, and meanwhile were curtailing their purchases. Even after final ratification of the plan, the market remained weak. The current price was so far below the $4 quotation set as a base that, by emergency action, $3.25 was agreed upon instead!

As the agreement went into effect the Standard Oil dutifully ordered 50,000 barrels at $3.25. But the utter lack of discipline among producers was fast becoming evident. Though the Producers' Council had immediately recommended that no new shafts be drilled till July 1, 1873,[24] the oil seekers' hopes of a rise in prices caused them to shake off all controls upon output; and heedless of the fact that $3.25 could be paid only if the flow were kept somewhere near 15,000 barrels a day, they sank new wells more furiously than ever. Whereas winter ice and snow usually slowed up production, the first two months of 1873 found the average daily output approaching 22,000 barrels. As the glut increased and export buyers still hesitated, many impatient well-owners became pressed for cash, and began selling oil to speculators for $3, $2.50, and even $2 a barrel. The inexorable march of disaster in the Regions was chronicled in long news stories.

When January opened, the Pittsburgh *Gazette* reported that some producers were selling oil for as little as $2.60 a barrel, and that nobody knew how to restrain them. On January 4 the New York *Shipping and Commercial List* pointed out that exports of petroleum in 1872 had fallen below·the previous year, and attributed the decline

[24]Boyle, *Derrick's Handbook,* 199.

to "the insane and hopeless effort to control the price of the article through the agency of cliques and combinations." Brokers, it added, were buying large quantities of oil from independent producers at cut rates. "For several days," declared another journal on the 9th, "there have been signs of a total breakup of the co-operative combination between producers and consumers, and a general financial crash in the Oil Regions. A speculative ring has been formed to break up the Producers' Association, and several prominent producers, notably Hasson, president of the Association, and Parker, of Parker's Landing, have refused to be bound by the articles of agreement." William Parker, a malcontent member of the executive committee, had in fact sold 5000 barrels of oil at a cut price on the very first day of the agreement. News of his action had spread through the oil markets and been telegraphed to Europe, creating widespread distrust. Quotations had naturally dropped to $2.50 and less.[25]

And the end came swiftly. On January 15 the discouraged Producers' Council met in Titusville with Hasson in the chair. Culver made an informal report for the executive committee. He had just come back from a meeting with the Refiners' Association in New York, where he and other Regions leaders had reluctantly confessed that they could not hold the producers under control. His statement effectually disposes of Miss Tarbell's contention that it was Rockefeller who broke up the producers' organization. The Titusville *Herald* of January 16 quotes him as saying that Rockefeller and other refining leaders were deeply disappointed:

Mr. Culver then read the correspondence of the committee by telegraph with the refiners, to prove that they had acted in good faith. He said, further, "everything that has passed, and all my connection with the refiners, convinces me that they proposed standing up to their agreement in good faith ... and I believe they are the most honorable set of businessmen I ever met. They are men whom I would personally be willing to trust under any circumstances, and I further believe that if the producers showed any indication of being able to control themselves, these men would be willing to take the balance of the oil [Cleveland had taken about half its allotment; Pittsburgh none], even if the open price was down to $1 a barrel. I was shown in New York a telegram from the second district to Mr. Rockefeller, offering to sell 5000 barrels at $2.25. Mr. Rockefeller re-

[25]The Pittsburgh *Gazette*, N. Y. *Shipping and Commercial List*, Cleveland *Leader*, and Titusville and Oil City newspapers for January, 1873, cover fully the unrestrained production and price-slashing in the Regions.

plied that he had made the arrangement in good faith, and he would abide by it. Mr. Warden also telegraphed to his agents who offered oil at open rates not to buy a barrel of oil outside the arrangement."

Culver added that "we are ourselves at fault." When a member asked if Parker's sale of oil at a cut rate had not violated the contract, his reply was emphatic: "Mr. Culver said if a refiner had been found out in such a transaction, he thought doubtless we would have considered the contract broken." Another member laid the calamity to "treachery in our own ranks." It was shown at this meeting that more than 300 new wells were being drilled in the lower districts, one man having started 16. On Culver's motion, the Council voted that since the contract with the Refiners' Association had never really gone into effect, it "is hereby declared inoperative and void."

The project failed because the individualistic well-owners could no more be organized for production-control than the Dakota wheat-growers or Far Eastern rubber-planters a generation later. Rockefeller attended several meetings of producers who were trying to discipline renegades. "I remember particularly," he said later,[26] "one man who was caught exceeding his allotment. He was brought up and questioned. He was an old man and he chewed tobacco. When he was asked why he had broken his pledge he chewed hard and replied, 'Well, I thought it would be a fair commercial transaction!' Most of the men who produced oil were like that; they violated their covenants." Miss Tarbell, led sadly astray by her Regions bias, places the blame for the failure chiefly upon Rockefeller, but partly upon an overproduction that she treats as purely automatic. "It seemed as if Nature, outraged that her generosity should be so manipulated as to benefit a few, had opened her veins to flood the earth with oil." Upon this Rockefeller made the drily adequate remark: "It is to be remembered that Nature would not have opened her veins if the producers had not compelled her to do so."[27] All press comment of the time agrees that the breakdown of the Treaty of Titusville, completed by the middle of January, was due to disunion and treason among the producers—and the production figures are additional proof of where the fault lay. *The Derrick* acridly commented that the pledge to drill no wells until July 1 had merely tended to increase the development by selfish well-owners eager to take advantage of

---

[26]Inglis, Conversations with Rockefeller.   [27]*Idem.*

the idleness of others, and it hailed the breakup with exultation.[28] Rockefeller and other refiners had done their part. But the lawless elements in the producing association had proved too strong for the loose organization built to combat them.[29]

VI

The well-owners were back to the disorganized conditions of 1871. Upon this sad footing, moreover, they were to remain for years, for their failure to act in concert had completely wrecked their own morale. The Butler and Clarion fields continued to pour out more and more oil. "Verily," exclaimed the New York *Commercial and Shipping List* in February,[30] "our friends the producers of petroleum in Pennsylvania are to be pitied. It really seems as if Providence had ordained that their efforts to enhance the value of their staple should be defeated." And in June it lamented that "the unheard-of price" to which petroleum had fallen "seems to us to have no parallel in the history of any article of merchandise of equal consumption." In 1874 production reached the new record of 10,810,000 barrels, while in 1875 came the discovery of the great Bradford field, which proved so rich that in 1880 it alone produced about 22,000,000 barrels. The veins of Nature had been opened indeed! The truth is that the failure of the Producers' Association was inevitable. The oil fields were growing too rapidly, and too many centrifugal forces were at work. No matter how hard Culver and his aides might have struggled, no matter how loyally Rockefeller and his associates might have assisted them, the effort would still have broken down. Oil production was never controlled in the United States until the Federal Government undertook the task— and then not for long.

In vain did *The Derrick* insist that a six months' suspension of all production would still rescue the industry. In vain did various leaders call for a new stoppage of drilling. As the price of crude oil sank lower, operators drove their engines all the harder to produce enough oil for an income. The significance of this spectacle was not

[28]Boyle, *Derrick's Handbook,* 201.
[29]Miss Tarbell's account of this episode in *Standard Oil Company,* I, 124, 125, seems to me profoundly misleading. The producers' plan was ruined not by Rockefeller but by treacherous producers.
[30]Feb. 12, 1873.

lost upon men like John D. Archbold and J. J. Vandergrift. While they hesitated for two years more to throw in their fortunes with the Standard Oil, the penalty which the producers paid for failing to unite undoubtedly made a powerful impression upon them.

Meanwhile the National Refiners' Association was also failing to meet the hopes of its founders. This loose pool, setting quotas for member-plants and fixing prices, lacked the strength to make its authority respected. Some members refined more oil than their allotments, while others cut the price of their product. And even without internal disloyalty, enough refiners remained outside the association to render overproduction and price-slashing a menace. These independents, manufacturing all they pleased and shaving prices at will, profited by any stability which the Association established—they got a free ride. Membership became a penalty rather than an advantage, and various participants, thinking enviously of these refiners who stole the icing from the cake, longed to be released. The slight but alarming slump in exports, with shipments declining from 132,000,000 gallons in 1871 to 118,000,000 in 1872, also injured the Association.

Rockefeller, who had feared precisely this result, was quick to perceive the tokens of impending breakdown. "It was apparent to me early after the organization of the Refiners' Association," he said years later, "that among so many men untrained in business there were many who could not be relied upon to aid in solving a problem so difficult as the reformation which my associates and I sought to bring about in this industry. But it was deemed desirable to continue patiently the study of these same people . . . to confirm or disprove the impressions early formed of their unreliability. We proved that the producers' and refiners' associations were ropes of sand."[31] As disobedience to the decrees of the Association increased, its uselessness became obvious to all. At a meeting in Saratoga on June 24, 1873, it was dissolved.[32]

Once more Rockefeller and Flagler had joined with other leading refiners in trying to give the industry a partial degree of organization, and once more they retired from the field in apparent defeat. They had effected no such dramatic extension of their business as

[31]Inglis, Conversations with Rockefeller.
[32]Moore, *Life of John D. Archbold,* 100.

by the conquest of Cleveland early in 1872, but for this they were not yet ready. They were still busy consolidating their recent gains, and the Standard's earnings for 1872, materially in excess of $1,000,-000, were almost wholly turned back into the business for extension and modernization of equipment. But the heads of the Standard could nevertheless reckon up certain gains from their latest experiment—gains important even though not at all tangible. For one, they felt a new assurance as to the proper line of development. It was consolidation or nothing. They had proved to themselves and to others that they could place no reliance upon a mere pool—that the industry required a far closer, stronger type of organization if it were to gain stability, and the original plan of Rockefeller and Flagler for a single great company presented the only hope. And a second gain lay in an increasing knowledge of the competitors—their talents, capacities, outlook—matched by a corresponding appreciation on the part of their rivals of the strength and efficiency of the Standard Oil.

XIX

Leviathan

As ROCKEFELLER and Flagler sauntered up Euclid Avenue on summer evenings in 1873, discussing the state of the oil industry, they were undoubtedly possessed by mixed emotions. Outwardly, the prospects of both producers and refiners seemed dark. Attempts to unite for the control of competition had broken down, and the price of crude and refined petroleum alike was falling disastrously. During June the well owners cursed to see crude oil selling at $2 a barrel, while gloomy refiners found it hard to obtain 18 cents a gallon. Yet this was but a beginning. Such rich new strikes were made this summer that production at times ran above thirty thousand barrels a day, crude oil prices touched a low point of $1.02 in August, and before Christmas quotations stood at the ruinous level of 83 cents a barrel. These bargain rates led numerous refiners to introduce apparatus for burning oil under their stills. Rockefeller must have read the editorial which the Cleveland *Leader* devoted one hot August day to the overproduction. "The problem is what to do with it all. Tanks, barrels, cars, and markets are full to overflowing, and the prices are away down. . . . The supply of petroleum has for two years past largely exceeded the demand."[1]

For the heads of the Standard Oil, however, the clouds had a silver lining. While they were being hurt by the depression, their rivals suffered a great deal more. Not only were the refiners as a group in a happier position than the producers, but of all refiners the Standard Oil was now in the most favorable situation. The company had demonstrated in two ways the benefits of consolidation; for one, it had reduced the total amount of refining in Cleveland,

[1]Cleveland *Leader*, Aug. 27, 1873.

433

and for another, it had placed its manufacturing upon a much more efficient foundation.

The Standard's own shipments increased heavily during 1873, for it more than doubled the production of the previous year. But Rockefeller had consistently maintained that the absorptions in Cleveland would constitute a step toward reducing the excessive refining capacity of the nation; and statistics show how rapidly he actually lopped off the inefficient margin of the city's industry. In January, 1872, Cleveland had been the greatest buyer of crude oil in the world. But in June, after the Standard's consolidations it bought only 117,300 barrels of crude oil as against New York's 190,000, and stood but little in advance of Pittsburgh, which bought 111,652 barrels. Throughout the remainder of 1872 Cleveland usually kept in third place. Totals for the year showed that shipments of crude oil to New York had increased over 1871 by about 400,000 barrels, and to Philadelphia by about 300,000, while those to Cleveland had decreased by 650,000![2] While the producers' embargo against the South Improvement Company accounted for part of this, the wiping out of wasteful plants by the Standard Oil was responsible for much more.

A profit was now being made on the whole Cleveland output of refined oil, while New York and Pittsburgh were losing money on a wide marginal production.[3]

II

But as soon as the Standard reorganized its Cleveland holdings, it proceeded to carry forward that process of expansion on which Rockefeller and Flagler had set their hearts. The company invaded other cities, extending its enterprises all the way from New York to Louisville, it began to acquire pipe lines, and it looked more energetically abroad. It is easy to find evidence in all this of Rockefeller's grasp and foresight. Expansion, he said later, meant economy. By 1879 "we had taken steps of progress that our rivals could not take. They had not the means to build pipe lines, bulk ships, tank wagons; they couldn't have their agents all over the country; couldn't

[2] *Annual Reports* of the Chamber of Commerce of the State of New York; Boston Board of Trade.

[3] We have no exact figures for total net earnings in 1872 and 1873, but they were larger.

manufacture their own acid, bungs, wicks, lamps, do their own cooperage—so many other things; it ramified indefinitely. They couldn't have their purchasing agents as we did, taking advantage of large buying."

When Constance Fenimore Woolson visited Cleveland to record her impressions of the city in *Harper's Magazine,* she was taken to the newly renovated Standard plants. What impressed her was the speed with which enormous quantities of green oil were turned first into "rainbow water" and then a dozen products. "Beneath the reservoirs were rows of blue barrels," she wrote. " 'Click!' went the automatic faucet, showing that a barrel was full."[4] Not only had operations been speeded up, but relations with jobbers and other middlemen had been strengthened, closer attention was being given to quality, and marketing facilities were being extended both East and West. Most of the oil was shipped in barrels, though for the Far West and foreign markets two five-gallon cans in a wooden case—the cans later so familiar from China to Peru—were already employed. This "case oil" brought five or six cents more a gallon. The Standard barrels were now recognized everywhere on sight. Double-glued, bound with six hoops, and painted a bright blue, they commanded respect throughout America, while the "Royal Daylight" brand on them was familiar over half of Europe. The cooperage yards of the company, well out on Cleveland's Broadway, held gigantic piles of oak staves and heads. On Whiskey Island, where the Cuyahoga emptied into Lake Erie, the Standard had built a huge warehouse. It owned tugs and barges, and bringing the bright blue barrels filled with oil down the river from the refineries, swept them by conveyors from the boats to the landing-platform of the warehouse, whence they were placed aboard steam-ships bound for all Great Lakes and St. Lawrence ports. The speed with which the oil was handled amazed beholders.

After the unexpected drop in 1872, exports of refined oil and naphtha rose again in 1873 to almost five and a half million barrels, and the company took shrewd measures to increase its share of the trade. These two years witnessed a spectacular development of its facilities in New York harbor. Rockefeller's success early in 1872 in bringing Jabez A. Bostwick into the company was important

[4]"Round by Propeller" in *Harper's Magazine,* XLV (1872), 572 ff.

chiefly for his overseas marketing. Bostwick & Co., successors of Bostwick & Tilford, owned a refinery on Long Island, but their principal business had been buying refined oil from Cleveland and other points and selling it abroad.[5] They were an export marketing agency—probably the largest in the field. Having leased the Weehawken Oil Docks from the Erie Railroad in 1872, they were managing them and the connected tanks and warehouses. All these facilities and their fleet of tugs and barges in New York harbor passed into the control of the Standard.

But this was not all. The Standard Oil had already built up extensive warehouses and transfer facilities at Hunter's Point on the Brooklyn side of the East River, roughly opposite Thirty-fourth Street. Here also stood one of the oldest and largest refineries in the New York area, operated by the Long Island Oil Co., which had been organized in 1862 and now had a capital of $200,000. In May, 1872, it was purchased by the Standard, which thus gained a large consolidated property at a strategic point.[6] William P. Wardwell and the family of Josiah Macy, the principal owners of the Long Island Company, became stockholders in and officers of the Standard. Macy, a Quaker, united piety and business astuteness in a way that pleased Rockefeller, who once remarked: "I think a real Quaker is a fine type of man." It was at Hunter's Point that there occurred this summer the tremendous fire already mentioned. All downtown New York was covered for hours with a pall of smoke; half the fire-fighting apparatus of the city was called out, and some accounts estimated the loss at a million. Three canal boats, a steamer, and two sailing ships loaded or loading with oil, four large tanks, warehouses, sheds, and about 25,000 barrels of kerosene, together with the refinery, were destroyed.[7] But the facilities were soon more than replaced.

Then in January, 1873, Rockefeller made an even more important acquisition—the Devoe Manufacturing Company, which with a capital of $500,000 operated extensive Long Island works, specializ-

[5]Crum, ed., *Romance of American Petroleum and Gas,* 283; Boyle, *Derrick's Handbook,* 918. Bostwick was born in Delhi, N. Y.

[6]Taylor, MS History of the Standard Oil Company, 20. The owners of the Long Island Company were paid 350 shares of Standard Oil stock and $25,000 in cash.

[7]N. Y. *Sun, Evening Post,* July 30, 31, 1872.

ing in the export of "case oil," for which it made its own cans. Its refinery facilities were invaluable. It is significant that aid was lent the Standard in financing this Devoe purchase by Charles Pratt of the Pratt Manufacturing Co., who had long been a partner of Devoe's but had broken away to organize his own refinery. Less than a year earlier he had been one of the Standard's fiercest antagonists! Then he had joined the Refiners' Association, and now he and his partner H. H. Rogers, though maintaining their business independence, entered into a quasi-alliance with Rockefeller. It was evident that they had seen a light—that mutual confidence had been established between them and the Standard Oil, and that the alliance might soon become a complete union.

These steps were indispensable to give the Standard national and international greatness. For obvious reasons, the refining industry still seemed to be gravitating toward the Atlantic seaboard. While Cleveland was the best point for supplying the Western market,[8] the export trade was far richer, and until the opening of the great Ohio and Indiana oil fields, the Atlantic cities were therefore to hold a position of quite clear vantage. Although Rockefeller's consolidations had saved Cleveland as a refining center, he knew that New York and Philadelphia were much better situated to command world commerce. By the close of 1873 he had obtained an important share of New York's manufacturing capacity, and had gained a secure basis for a great export trade, which William Rockefeller could rapidly expand. The Standard Oil was soon to extend these New York holdings, and then to advance upon Philadelphia and Baltimore.

Meanwhile, the company had begun to undertake certain entirely new activities: those of systematic oil purchasing, of local distribution West and South, and of pipe line transportation. The fact must be emphasized that until 1873 the Standard Oil had remained almost purely a manufacturing corporation. It owned no oil-producing territory. It had its buyers in the Regions, but for supplies of crude

[8]Rockefeller testified in *United States vs. Standard Oil of New Jersey,* Vol. 16, 3508 (Nov. 18, 1908): "Cleveland as a distributing point for the oil was, I should say, without doubt the best to secure the domestic trade. There were transportation facilities by the railroads leading from Cleveland into the West, different railroads; and we always had trade which we could supply by the Lakes as well, reaching up into all the large northwestern territory."

petroleum it depended in large part upon such prosperous firms as Neyhart & Grandin, Abbott & Harley, and Vandergrift & Forman. As for its selling organization, that had been concerned only with wholesale shipments and not with retailing. The domestic marketing of refined oil in 1872 was still controlled by a multitude of special houses, large and small. Several firms had gained national prominence as jobbers and retailers, notably the Waters, Pierce Oil Co. in St. Louis and Chess, Carley & Co. in Louisville, but most of the distributors operated locally. The Standard Oil was often embarrassed by its lack of authority over this complex intermediate structure of middlemen. Some of them speculated in oil, disturbing the market; many threw large quantities of cheap, dangerous kerosene upon the market in competition with Standard products. Both the sale of poor oil and the wastefulness of the distributing system irked the methodical Rockefeller.

The obvious remedy lay in systematic expansion into the new field, and as a first step the Standard Oil in 1873 suddenly acquired control of Chess, Carley. This firm owned a Louisville refinery, which might become important if the flow of the West Virginia and Kentucky wells increased; but its wholesale and retail distributing business was more valuable. "The purchase undoubtedly represented the Standard's intention to corral the distributing field," said a company officer later.[9] He added that F. D. Carley embraced the opportunity of union eagerly. "When the Standard proposed a merger, he said, 'Sure, sure, come on down.' John D. Rockefeller loved a man with initiative and the spirit of co-operation. That's why they waltzed around the hall with Carley; their arms were about him all the time when he came to Cleveland." The combination opened up for Standard Oil products a lucrative Southern territory, in which Chess, Carley rapidly increased their operations. This device of maintaining intact a company which had already proved its efficiency soon became a settled Standard policy.

Steps were also taken to systematize the purchasing of crude oil. When Bostwick & Co. were bought out, they agreed to carry on the business with the name of the old corporation, but under the direction and for the account of the Standard, which was to furnish the cash capital required—save that Bostwick might employ $250,000

[9]Charles M. Higgins to the author, March 23, 1936.

of his own, on which he was guaranteed 7 per cent and commissions.[10] He possessed two extremely capable agents in the oil districts, Joseph Seep and Daniel O'Day. Bostwick & Co. thus became the principal buyer and shipper of crude oil for the Standard, and "Joe" Seep was soon handling orders that ran into many millions monthly.

III

In acquiring control of its own pipe lines the Standard entered a highly competitive field. As yet, and for several years to come, all such lines were merely local. They connected little groups of wells in the Pennsylvania fields with the nearest railroad, and that was all. But they were sufficiently effective to have driven most teamsters out of existence, and year by year they were being linked together in longer and more important systems, like that of Abbott & Harley's Allegheny Transportation Co.[11] The method of operation was simple. The well owner, after tubing a successful shaft, flowed or pumped the oil into a tank which might hold as little as 250 barrels or as much as 2500, according to the capacity of the well. The tank was measured to ascertain its capacity, and marked for each quarter-inch of height. The pipe line company connected a two-inch or three-inch pipe to the tank, with a stopcock, and when the tank was ready to run they gauged it, drained a quantity into their own central line or storage tanks, and then regauged it to find how many barrels of oil remained. The well owner was given a certificate for the quantity taken out, which could be bought and sold. As the years went by pipe line owners, refiners, and oil dealers built larger and larger tanks for storage, until some structures in the Regions held 30,000 barrels or more. Most local pipe lines were laid on the surface, but when trunk lines came into existence they were placed underground.

By the end of 1876 the total length of the pipe lines in the Oil Regions was estimated by a good authority at 2082 miles, operated

[10]Besides the guarantee on the $250,000 investment, Bostwick & Co. were paid 822 shares of Standard Oil stock and $58.82 in cash. Taylor, MS. History of the Standard Oil, 21.

[11]This, formed 1867, was the first great pipe-line company. J. T. Henry, *The Early and Later History of Petroleum,* 527 ff.; Giddens, *Birth of the Oil Industry,* 147.

by thirty-five or forty companies.[12] Only six companies owned more than a hundred miles of pipe each, while a number operated but two, three, or five miles. The whole tank capacity of the Regions at this time was placed by another authority at about 6,400,000 barrels, but this was probably an exaggeration. The network as a whole might even at this date, fifteen years after Drake's discovery, be regarded as rudimentary. Within the next decade it was to be extended with amazing rapidity, great trunk lines being laid to carry crude oil from the Regions east to Philadelphia and New York, south to Baltimore, west to Cleveland, and north to Buffalo—but that time was not yet. In 1872 no pipe line company commanded much capital. Profits were little or nothing. Nominally thirty cents a barrel was charged for transporting oil, whether for half a mile or twenty miles, but actually competition often drove the rate down to five cents.

Rockefeller and his associates, who vividly remembered how completely, at the crisis of the South Improvement war, they had been deprived of crude oil by the producers, realized that the pipe lines offered another potential source of interference with their designs. Suppose they fell into the hands of some determined opponent? One of the railroads, or an ambitious fast-freight line like the Empire Transportation Company, might rapidly absorb them. A pipe line monopoly would be far more dangerous than a producer's monopoly, for it would rest in fewer hands and be open to a more unscrupulous manipulation. The obvious safeguard for the Standard Oil lay in the purchase of a number of lines, with their storage tanks. Indeed, why not set up a Standard Oil system which would help to assure a steady supply of crude, and in time lower the cost of transporting it? The genial but ruthless Daniel O'Day had a special knowledge of transportation. His abounding energy and two-fisted fighting qualities made him precisely the man for erecting a great pipe line fabric, and the Standard Oil, through Bostwick as its new partner, turned to him.[13]

[12]Cf. S. F. Peckham, *Production, Technology, and Use of Petroleum and Its Products,* House Misc. Docs., 47th Cong., 2d Sess., Pt. 10. O'Day told his own story in the *House Trust Investigation* of 1888, 50th Cong., 1st Sess., 266 ff.
[13]See the eulogistic sketch of O'Day in Boyle, *Derrick's Handbook,* 920–927. I have talked with numerous New Yorkers and Regions men who knew him, and who agree upon his fine personal but excessively hard business traits.

O'Day had passed through a harsh school of experience. Born in County Clare but brought to America as a small child, he had grown up in Cattaraugus County, N. Y. At fifteen he had abandoned his father's farm for the freight yards of Buffalo, and working there throughout the Civil War years had thoroughly mastered freight handling. At twenty-one, in 1865, he went to Titusville, and soon joined the Empire Transportation Company, then newly organized as a fast-freight feeder of the Pennsylvania Railroad. His chief duties were the movement of cars and solicitation of freight. He found that the post-war oil boom had thrown service into a state of chaos; all the shippers wanted transportation at the same time, and the car shortage became frightful. O'Day introduced system and order, and met all demands promptly. After leaving the Empire, he was hired by Bostwick & Tilford in 1870 to handle their large oil shipments from the Regions. This firm had a close alliance with the Erie, monopolizing most of its oil business. Soon after joining its employ, O'Day was summoned to New York by Jay Gould, president of the Erie; for Gould believed that the Empire Transportation Company and its protector the Pennsylvania Railroad were getting altogether too much of the oil traffic, and wished O'Day to intervene. The tall, broad-shouldered young man, taking charge despite the hostility of the general manager, went to work with immediate success, and practically living on the rails for a month, diverted much of the current oil freight to the Erie lines. During the South Improvement war, he and Joseph Seep remained inflexibly loyal to Bostwick. Denounced by mass meetings, threatened with mob violence, subjected to every cajolery and blandishment, they refused to yield an inch, and their iron nerve finally extorted an unwilling admiration. Bostwick had strongly recommended O'Day to Rockefeller as the right man to build up the company's pipe line system.

It was high time for the Standard to act. In the summer of 1873 the newspapers announced the sale of the Union Pipe Line to the Empire Transportation Company, already owner of the Mutual Line, two of the longest systems in the Regions thus being suddenly consolidated. This coup gave Joseph D. Potts's fast-freight company, so closely associated with the powerful Pennsylvania Railroad, more than a hundred miles of continuous pipe line, tankage facilities approximating 100,000 barrels, and 600 oil cars. Moreover, during the next few months the Union Line rapidly pushed its pipes forward into the Butler County field. It was plain that Potts, the astute, persistent, and intensely ambitious head of the Empire, intended to expand his network aggressively, and to make certain of a lion's share of the crude oil freight business. In 1875 he built a line to Olean, N. Y., and by the end of 1876 his various systems aggregated 680 miles of pipe and boasted more than 1,300,000 barrels of storage capacity. He was fast becoming a formidable threat!

At Rockefeller's instance, Bostwick commissioned O'Day to build a pipe line from Emlenton to the new Clarion County oil fields, and by the fall of 1873 the energetic Irishman had put down about eighty miles. This property was shortly consolidated with other lines under the name of the American Transfer Company; and O'Day continued his building until in September, 1874, he opened a line from Turkey City in the Clarion field to Oil City, with but one pumping station en route. During 1875 the enterprising young fellow, hearing of explorations for oil in the Bradford area to the northeast, also ran a pipe line into that new area. Laboring at first under Bostwick's supervision, both Joseph Seep and O'Day became widely renowned as agents of the Standard in buying crude oil and piping it. Every one in the Regions knew them, and much as the Standard came to be hated there, every one respected them.

For "Joe" Seep the feeling was more than respect, for he was a lovable personality.[14] Born in Hanover, Germany, he had been brought to America at the age of eleven. His father died of cholera, and the lad, compelled to help support his mother, learned the cigar-making trade, toiling at it throughout his teens. At twenty-one he went to Lexington, Ky., where Jabez A. Bostwick employed him in the grain and hemp business, the beginning of a lifelong connection. When Bostwick went into oil, Seep followed him, and settled down in Titusville in 1869 as Bostwick's agent. Ruddy, bald-headed, full-bearded—looking strangely like later portraits of Charles Dickens—he was as genial and paternal as O'Day was brisk and aggressive. The kindly, jolly German and the rough and rollicking Irishman, both Catholics, maintained a friendly rivalry in the size of their families, Seep finally taking the lead with eleven children! Both had a genius for making friends, and though O'Day made bitter foes too, Seep's

[14]See the sketch in Boyle, *Derrick's Handbook*, 930, 931.

admirers became as the sands of the sea. Thirty years after his death, his modesty, honesty, and generosity, for his personal charities were inexhaustible, kept his memory fragrant throughout the Regions. "I don't think he ever had an enemy," one veteran oil man has testified. "Seep did more for the poor in Oil City than any other man."[15]

But the Standard, more and more disturbed by the activities of the Empire Transportation Company, was not satisfied merely with what lines O'Day constructed. Rockefeller cast an envious eye on the largest of the old pipe line companies, Vandergrift & Forman, and was one of the first to learn that J. J. Vandergrift, hard hit by the collapse in oil prices, needed capital. Both William H. Vanderbilt and Amasa Stone heard it also, and were eager to buy a controlling interest for the New York Central. In 1873 a somewhat complicated transaction was carried through. The Standard Oil, by paying $233,-333.33 in cash, and contributing a fractional interest it already held in one line, gained a one third share in the Vandergrift & Forman pipes. Vanderbilt and Stone each took one sixth interest in the system. The remaining third was kept by Vandergrift and George V. Forman. Renamed the United Pipe Lines, the system became one of the two cornerstones of the Standard's pipe line network.[16] The other cornerstone, the American Transfer Company, was soon completely owned by the Standard Oil, which on November 15, 1874, paid $200,000 to Rockefeller, Bostwick, Josiah Macy, Jr., and A. J. Pouch for it. At the close of 1876 the two systems comprised about 400 miles, and had a tankage capacity of nearly 1,400,000 barrels. Rockefeller had thus completely safeguarded the Standard against a pipe line monopoly formed by the Empire or any other group. Indeed, he was already dreaming of his own pipe line monopoly.

IV

The depression of 1873–78, which fell with ruinous force upon so many businesses, did the petroleum industry less harm than others, and the Standard Oil itself some indirect benefit. Kerosene was now regarded throughout Europe and America, and even in much of Asia, as a necessity, not a luxury; and the price was so low that the poorest family felt able to afford it. The panic broke September 18,

[15]So Charles M. Higgins told me Oct. 15, 1936.
[16]Taylor, MS History of the Standard Oil Company, 23.

when the sudden collapse of the powerful banking house of Jay Cooke & Company appalled the financial world. Banks closed their doors; stocks came down with a crash; mills and factories swung their gates shut, unemployment became general, and breadlines soon formed in all the great cities. The country dropped into the trough of a long and merciless depression, from the misery of which it did not escape until 1878.

At first petroleum fell to low prices. Crude oil sagged late in 1873 to nearly 80 cents a barrel, and despite a partial recovery, still averaged only $1.33 early in 1874; while refined oil, which had brought an average of 26 cents a gallon in 1872, sold after the panic for just 13 cents. During six months of 1874 crude oil averaged only a dollar a barrel or less, and for a considerable period in 1875 the average price was about 90 cents.[17] But this was due far more largely to overproduction than to the depression. Indeed, the price of crude recovered amazingly in much of 1876–77, while the depression was still at its worst—largely because production then fell below world demand. In these two years producers reaped golden profits, and, along with agricultural products, the trade brought a great deal of much-needed gold from Europe to America.

Moreover, the disastrously low prices of 1873 and 1875 had their brighter side for Rockefeller in helping him promote that policy of consolidation which he had long pictured as the one rock of hope for the industry. Faced with constant losses, the well owners seemed helpless, but the refiners had been most perseveringly and eloquently assured by the Standard Oil that salvation lay within their grasp. Whenever Rockefeller met men like Pratt, Lockhart, and Warden, he renewed his argument that the refiners still possessed a capacity crazily out of proportion to the market, that two efforts at a mere pool, the South Improvement Company and the National Refiners' Association, had now effected nothing, and that complete unification offered the only true road to prosperity. Even the doubters listened to him now.

Meanwhile, the railroads, hard hit by the depression and the rate wars, were struggling to sustain their petroleum traffic. Two of them especially courted the Standard Oil. The New York Central-Lake

[17]Boyle, *Derrick's Handbook,* 713. In July, 1875, the price of crude fell to 70 cents.

Shore system had actually entered into partnership with it in acquiring a pipe line to compete with the Empire-Pennsylvania system; and the Erie now also joined hands with it in a spectacular way. The overthrow of the old rate agreement of March 25, 1872, had led to a general restoration of rebating, and every oil shipper of consequence received some favor. Archbold and Vandergrift, so prominent during the South Improvement struggle in insisting that all rebates must be abolished, had been quick to obtain concessions. Adnah Neyhart, an oil jobber who had also been conspicuous in opposing the South Improvement scheme, collected $7000 in rebates from the Erie in the single month of September, 1872.[18]

When the Standard's contract with the New York Central expired on or about April 1, 1873, it apparently made another with that road more satisfactory in character. Whatever this new arrangement was, it increased the sharp dissatisfaction which Erie men felt over the oil traffic situation. In handling both crude and refined, the Erie was being pushed steadily to the wall by the Pennsylvania and the New York Central-Lake Shore systems. The Pennsylvania monopolized the Pittsburgh trade, and controlled the most direct outlets from the Regions to the seaboard, while the New York Central had gained most of the Standard's shipments. Although Jay Gould's deadly grip had been loosed and the presidency was assumed in July, 1872, by the able Peter H. Watson, oil receipts had shown little improvement. In the latter half of 1872 the Erie was carrying only about 53,000 barrels of petroleum a month, while the Pennsylvania had about 300,000 barrels, and the New York Central almost all the Cleveland traffic.

Watson and Blanchard grew alarmed. When Blanchard made inquiries, he learned from Adnah Neyhart that the March 25 agreement had been violated by all roads and all large shippers. He was told, in fact, that it had been exploded in part by the action of the Producers' Union itself! The Erie then plunged into the general game of rate-cutting, giving Neyhart such large rebates that he collected $188,000 for the year; and in March, 1873, it made an agreement with the Oil Regions refiners which it hoped would bring it nearly all their shipments from Titusville, Oil City, and other centers to New York. But its cuts were promptly met by the Empire Transportation Company,

[18]Blanchard's testimony is in *Report of the Hepburn Committee* (*Special Committee on Railroads, New York Assembly, 1879*), III, 3393-3395.

which seduced the Regions establishments back to the old allegiance. Their shipments again began passing in Empire cars over the Pennsylvania tracks. "We are left," Blanchard plaintively testified, "with but one small shipper of refined oil, Mr. G. Heye, whose consignments were small, and to retain even this small business, against similar solicitations by our rivals, we were compelled to make his rate $1.10 in November, 1873. . . ."[19] Since the Erie could do little to regain the business of the Oil Regions refineries, it turned to the Standard Oil.

In June, 1873, General Devereux, formerly of the Lake Shore, became president of the Atlantic & Great Western, the Erie's affiliate reaching down into the oil fields; and he naturally took a good many of the Lake Shore's secrets with him. Within a few months he and Blanchard called at the Standard Oil offices to make a vigorous protest. The New York Central and the Pennsylvania, they pointed out, were getting a hoggishly unfair share of the oil trade. The Erie was transporting only one seventh of the petroleum—indeed, final figures for 1873 showed that it carried only 762,000 out of very nearly five million barrels of oil. They asked the Standard for more.

"Give us a share equal to the Central's," they urged.

While Rockefeller and Flagler were willing to arrange for a more equal division, they raised an objection with respect to terminal facilities. Ever since the acquisition of the Long Island Oil Co., they pointed out, their main eastern terminal had been at Hunter's Point on the East River. There they had had refineries, a cooperage plant, great wharves and warehouses, and a trained force of men for transferring oil from both cars and boats. The New York Central delivered all shipments to Hunter's Point without additional charge. The Standard could draw refined oil from tank cars there and barrel it for sale at home or abroad, could inspect whatever oil arrived in barrels, making necessary repairs, and could transfer crude oil to the refinery tanks. The Erie had an oil terminal at Weehawken, N. J., where its own force barrelled refined oil from the tank cars, inspected ready-barrelled oil, and performed other operations. But it served all shippers alike, and charged a considerable fee. Devereux and Blanchard had assumed that the Standard would pay these transfer fees, but Rockefeller declined to do so.

[19]*Ibid*, 3395.

"We do transfer work cheaply at Hunter's Point because we are expert oil men," he argued. "We pay nobody an extra profit, and cannot and ought not to pay you. If you will deliver our oil at Hunter's Point and let us attend to the transfer business, all right. But we wish to keep the transfer in our own hands. We cannot pay the Erie at Weehawken a profit on all that work, for we have our own facilities in another part of New York harbor. It is not part of your business as a carrier anyhow. It is ours."

While this was reasonable, the Erie could not throw its expensive transfer plant into an already heavy list of bad investments. Blanchard and Devereux quickly devised a solution. They suggested that the Standard lease the Weehawken yard, and take over the whole business of cooperage, repairs, and transfer, both for itself and other shippers. Paying so much a barrel for use of the terminal, it could collect the usual fees from other refiners, jobbers, and oil-commission men. An elaborate agreement was shortly worked out. The Erie guaranteed the Standard Oil as low a rate on refined oil as any made by the New York Central, while the Standard gave a written promise that no other road or roads should receive more than half its shipments to the East. Doubtless it also furnished informal promises of good will for the Erie, which after the outrageous looting by Gould and Fisk needed business friendship.

This fresh acquisition by the Standard Oil marked another important step toward a monopoly of the oil business. The company enlarged its terminal facilities by a yard which was exceptionally convenient for routing oil to New England or the South, and simultaneously gained a full acquaintance with all competitive shipments over the Erie. No refiner served by that line could now do business without its knowledge, and without submitting to the fees it charged for terminal service. But not too much should be made of these last facts. Most plants in the Regions now shipped over the Pennsylvania Railroad-Empire Transportation Company system. Moreover, no evidence exists that the Standard Oil did ask excessive fees—it was never seriously charged with doing so. To be sure, the arrangement later brought the Standard under heavy criticism. Some opponents accused it of proposing the lease, though Blanchard's statement that the railroad did so is conclusive. Others deemed the scheme primarily a new, audacious, and Machiavellian device for gaining information about the shipments of competitors. As a matter of fact, such leasing was not new at all; in 1870 Bostwick & Tilford, as New York refiners and oil buyers, had operated the Erie's oil terminal under a similar arrangement.[20] Nor was knowledge of competitive shipments over the Erie valuable; they had shrunk to a low point. The important gains were simply the new facilities, the new freight rates, and the general alliance. Bostwick, familiar with the Weehawken terminal, gave expert aid in knitting it into the Standard's system.

The agreement between the Standard and the Erie was formally signed on April 20, 1874. Thereafter the Standard Oil apparently sent about half its shipments of refined oil eastward by the Erie, and the other half by the Lake Shore-New York Central System. With both roads it was on the best of terms; it shared an oil terminal with one, a pipe line with the other. It tended to unite more and more closely with them in a defensive alliance against the Empire Transportation Company, under the smooth and subtle Joseph D. Potts, and the Pennsylvania Railroad, under the aggressive Tom Scott.

And meanwhile Rockefeller had executed another remarkable coup by the purchase in January, 1874, of the large Imperial Refinery near Oil City owned by J. J. Vandergrift, G. V. Forman, John Pitcairn, Jr., and other Regions men. The Standard paid for it in cash, and business was continued under the name of the Imperial Refining Company, with Vandergrift as president. The Regions had thus been directly invaded! Such a foothold in enemy territory was worth much, for the refinery had a capacity of 15,000 barrels a week, and was one of the most efficient in the oil country. But the experience of the burly, round-headed, bull-necked Vandergrift, a man of infinite resource, was worth much more. The president of numerous companies, most of them flourishing, this bluff river skipper had proved himself a born organizer. He was not to end his days with the Standard Oil, for banking and the iron business in Pittsburgh ultimately called to him. But for several years he was a powerful ally, and the mere news that a man of such enterprise and ability had gone over to Rockefeller staggered the company's opponents.[21]

[20]Taylor, MS History of the Standard Oil Company, 8.
[21]See J. J. McLaurin, *Sketches in Crude Oil*, 274-276; Boyle, *Derrick's Handbook*, 643-650. Vandergrift founded the steel and iron town of Vandergrift, Pa., where he refused to allow any liquor-selling. A biography of this remarkable figure is much needed.

The Standard Oil had now completed an imposing structure. It owned practically all the refineries in Cleveland save a few lubricating plants. It was far on the way toward ownership of the strongest network of pipe lines and largest body of oil tanks in the Regions. It held large properties in New York—the busy oil terminals at Hunter's Point and Weehawken, the bustling refineries of the Long Island Company and Devoe Company, the tugs, barges, and refining works of Bostwick, a great array of lighters, barges, and miscellaneous property. It had entered the field of oil buying with new efficiency through Bostwick & Company, and had begun to set up its own marketing machinery through Chess, Carley & Co. The pipe lines directed by Daniel O'Day assured it of a continuous supply of crude oil. Through its ownership of refineries at widely separated and strategic points—Cleveland, New York, Louisville, and Oil City—it was measurably independent of railroad wars and combinations. It had the best barrel-making shops in America, with the incomparable McGregor in charge. It made its own acids. Its unrivalled facilities in New York harbor and the export organization built up by William Rockefeller enabled it to compete efficiently for the European trade. In its expansion it had constantly acquired not only materials, but men and brains. It was one of the soundest and strongest industrial organizations in the world, making money even in years of depression, and growing steadily and inexorably.

Even in 1874 the Standard Oil Company was Leviathan.

v

Each year had brought some new vindication of Rockefeller's business foresight. "It seemed as if he saw years ahead," remarked one of his associates at this time. "In 1872 he seemed to see right through the years to 1892, and planned for what he believed would happen then." Not least among the evidences of his self-confidence and acumen was the assiduity with which he increased his stockholdings in this constantly growing property. From the outset he had held by far the largest single block. In 1873 this amounted to between 3500 and 4500 shares; in 1875 the total amount was 4549. Stephen V. Harkness with 2500, Payne with 2425, and Flagler with 2042 shares were then the next largest stockholders. From that time forward Rockefeller added rapidly to his holdings, until in 1882 he had acquired

9500 shares. "I was a regular dumping ground for stock," he remarked once of this period.[22] While the nominal value of shares in 1875 was only $100 each, the real value was constantly rising. In 1874, to judge from various company transactions, it was not less than $300.[23] One of the large American fortunes was beginning to appear.

During the later months of 1873 an event was impending which bore an important relation to this growing fortune. The Euclid Avenue household was expecting an addition. On January 24, 1874, a fourth child joined the three daughters who already made a lively family. This time it was a son—the male heir for which both husband and wife had hoped. He was named John D. Rockefeller, Jr.

The father was inexpressibly happy. On the morning his son was born he burst into the office to tell his associates the news, and Flagler and Payne affectionately put their arms about him, while the room rang with their congratulations, and tears of joy stood in his eyes.[24]

[22]Inglis, Conversations with Rockefeller; Taylor, MS History of the Standard Oil Company, 26 ff.
[23]Taylor, MS History of the Standard Oil Company, 27. *Cf.* Rockefeller's testimony in *U. S. vs. Standard Oil Company,* XVI, 3082.
[24]Charles M. Higgins described the scene to me Oct. 27, 1936.

XX

The Crucial Twelvemonth: 1874–1875

EVEN while Leviathan grew powerful, even while he dominated Lake Erie with his head and lashed the waters of New York Bay with his tail, many other fish disported themselves bravely in oily seas. The refining industry remained badly overcrowded. Our fullest list of plants for 1873, manifestly incomplete, gives the country more than one hundred, with a daily capacity of 47,000 barrels of crude oil. Since the production of crude oil this year but slightly exceeded 27,000 barrels a day, Sundays included, some of which was shipped abroad, it is evident that the existing works had a capacity fully double the utmost requirements. Refining was still done on a considerable scale in Boston, Baltimore, Portland, and Erie. A round dozen refineries were being operated in Philadelphia, with a capacity of 2000 barrels daily. And scattered through various towns in the Oil Regions—Oil City, Petroleum Center, Rouseville, Miller Farm, Tidioute—were numerous small plants, most of them struggling hard to turn out a few hundred barrels a day or even a week.[1]

But the four principal centers, in the order named, were Cleveland, New York, Pittsburgh, and Titusville; and one of these four plainly stood apart from the others. In Cleveland six refineries, all owned by the Standard Oil, were credited with a capacity of 12,500 barrels daily, and undoubtedly operated more nearly at full time than any others. Fifteen refineries in New York had a capacity of 10,000 barrels daily; in Pittsburgh twenty-two refineries had a capacity of 6500 barrels daily; and in Titusville eleven refineries had a capacity of 4800 barrels. We know that operations in Cleveland were now confined

[1]Boyle, *Derrick's Handbook of Petroleum*, 780.

451

substantially to two plants, so that the average plant capacity there was 6350 barrels a day. In contrast with this, the average plant capacity in New York was 666 barrels a day; in Titusville 436 barrels a day; and in Pittsburgh a little less than 300 barrels. This meant that New York, Titusville, and Pittsburgh had a few large and prosperous plants, and many small works, each refining from 50 to 200 barrels a day in a hand-to-mouth way. Hard times were descending on the country, the depression after 1873 destroying confidence, making money tight, and throwing markets into chaos. It was clear that an industry so overcrowded must undergo drastic changes, and that the owners of small plants were the men likely to get hurt. In the next six years of depression the weakest manufactories were of course ruthlessly liquidated in nearly all fields of American activity.

If refining was being overdone, so was oil production. The failure of the Petroleum Producers' Association had left the gates wide open to unlimited drilling and pumping. During 1872 men had thought the flow of oil a veritable torrent at 6,539,000 barrels; but in 1873 it rose by nearly half again as much, falling but little short of ten million barrels. Conservative producers watched this flood with a feeling of despair.[2] Prices of course went down and down. At the beginning of October spot crude was selling at Parker's Landing for 85 and 90 cents a barrel. *The National Oil Journal,* commenting on the "suicidal" production and the low price, remarked that the cause lay in an alliance of greedy land-owners with still more greedy producers, the former urging the latter to sink wells everywhere. On October 10, 1873, one hundred and fifty wells were reported drilling in the Millerstown district. By the middle of November the question of a shutdown was again being vigorously discussed. Pittsburgh speculators had tanked half a million barrels of oil, which they were holding for better times; but when would the better times come? December 1 found oil selling at Parker's Landing for 70 cents a barrel, and the new year brought important discoveries in Butler County and Armstrong County.[3]

[2] Producers later petitioning Governor Hartranft spoke of "the overproduction of 1873–75 and the consequent almost entire destruction of petroleum values." *House Trust Investigation, 1888, 50th Cong., 1 Sess.; Report 3112,* p. 351–365; hereafter cited simply as *House Trust Investigation, 1888.*

[3] *The United States Railroad and Mining Register,* April 18, 1874, contains an article by John P. Zane to prove that only 2,100,000 barrels of oil were stored or tanked. Other estimates ran up to 2,500,000.

Two scenes in the oil regions of Pennsylvania.

Above: The Titusville Oil Exchange, July 18, 1883. *Below:* Early tank cars
with horizontal metal tanks.

Rockefeller in England.

Two scenes on the Isle of Wight, that on the right showing Mrs. Rockefeller and their daughter Alta.

Altogether, with a record-breaking production of nearly ten million barrels in 1873 and more than that in 1874, with a refinery capacity of about twenty million barrels, with crude oil sinking to 50 cents in the Millerstown field during 1874, and with refined oil proportionately low, the petroleum industry could not be called in a healthy condition. Of course the railroads were carrying increased freights. About three fourths of the refined oil was exported. But the railroads were far from a happy family. Peter H. Watson, now president of the Erie, and Tom Scott, now head of the Pennsylvania (for J. Edgar Thomson died early in 1874), were both eager for the lion's share of the trade; while the New York Central and the Baltimore & Ohio hoped to add to their own haulings. As general traffic declined after the panic, oil became more important. Everywhere—among producers, among refiners, among railroad heads—a feeling existed that more organization was required.

II

It was the hard-hit well-owners who moved first. "Producers are still hopeful and doing their best to sustain prices," reported the Pittsburgh *Gazette* on March 9, 1874, "but everything appears to be against them, and the market is slowly but steadily going back in spite of their best and strongest efforts to prevent it." Frantic leaders were encouraging speculators to buy oil and store it, and urging well-owners to put their output into tanks instead of selling. "It seems that the bull ring in the producing region are resolved to put up crude regardless of refined," grumbled *The Gazette* a few weeks later.[4] April brought another definite movement to stop the drill and shut down the pump. Hopeful producers thought that, since development was in fewer hands than before, and not so many small interests had to be controlled, the outlook for success was bright. With Butler County men in the lead, a plan for a ninety-day stoppage enlisted the support of many large owners, while the little fellows were simply ignored. The Regions press cheered the leaders on. "These operators have only to go ahead like sensible men in this arrangement," declared the Titusville *Courier*,[5] "and by the large advance in the price of oil which will inevitably follow, they can realize handsome fortunes out

[4]March 31, 1874.   [5]Quoted in Pittsburgh *Gazette*, April 17, 1874.

of the stocks which they already hold." A meeting at Petrolia on April 21 displayed marked enthusiasm. By the end of that month boring had been stopped at 130 sites, and owners of twenty-seven drill-rigs had promised to do nothing till the expiration of the three months. Prices had risen sharply.

But alas for the producers! This movement proved even more abortive than those which had preceded it. From the outset it was an object of suspicion to many hard-headed oil men. They pointed out that it was fostered in the main by well-established producers who had large stocks on hand and who would realize handsome profits by an increase in prices. Was it fair to ask other men, who had no oil stored in tanks, to cease drilling simply to let those with accumulated reserves get out at a high profit? "It is a trick of Venango millionaires," said many;[6] or as Wesley Chambers, a well-known producer of Oil City, put it in a letter to the Titusville *Herald,*[7] "it is a conspiracy, directly intended for somebody to cheat somebody else, which will result—as such movements always do—in a few profiting by the loss of the many, the fruits of conspiracy." By hundreds, these dissenters emphatically refused to sign.[8] Meanwhile, the Standard Oil, which had not accumulated such large stocks at low prices as the Pittsburgh refiners, was accused of bearing the market by suddenly refusing to purchase.[9] This may have been true. Speculators and exporters who had an interest in cheap oil also took a hand. The result was that on May 15, a new meeting of oil producers at Titusville unanimously adopted a resolution releasing everybody from the ninety-day pledge.

"We can all go to hell together," one disgusted man telegraphed his friends at home. At once the drilling of hundreds of wells recommenced. Among various post-mortem explanations of the rapid collapse of the movement, that given by an unnamed producer in the Pittsburgh *Gazette* is the most illuminating. He described the contest as a desperate four-week fight "between the oil producers on the one

[6]Pittsburgh *Gazette,* April 20, 1874.

[7]April 21, 1874.

[8]Another consideration was stated by the producer Thomas W. Phillips in 1888: "Owing to the fluid nature of this commodity, the oil in one tract of land may be extracted by wells upon an adjoining property. One owner, therefore, cannot stop producing while his neighbor continues." *House Trust Investigation, 1888,* p. 111.

[9]Pittsburgh *Gazette,* May 6, 1874.

side as bulls, and a large refining company assisted by a number of petroleum exporters as bears." The bears tried to curb the rising market by selling oil for future delivery at low prices. "It is also said a number of exporters in the interest of the bears took themselves off to the Dutchland across the sea, and are now pouring into the ears of our German cousins the gloomiest kind of stories of 'enormous' production of oil in the Butler regions of Pennsylvania. The effect of these greasy ambassadors is manifest—Berlin, Antwerp, Stettin, and other foreign importers have withdrawn orders for the present." The bears were also aided by "the large quantity of oil in the hands of tankers, bought last winter when oil was cheap. These people sold oil on the market every day until they were unloaded."[10]

It is evident that the ethics of a combination of oil producers to restrict output (*i.e.,* competition) and raise prices does not differ in the slightest from the ethics of a combination of mine-operators, factory-owners, or refinery-heads for the same object. At a later date Miss Tarbell pictured the recurrent failure of the producers to unite as due to the machinations of the refiners. Of course it was due primarily to the producers' numbers and rampant individualism. Some well-owners, including Wesley Chambers, accused the Standard Oil of being wickedly behind this new combination; others of being wickedly against it! The Titusville *Herald* for April 20 struck the nail on the head in its review of six years of attempted union. "Combinations and 'movements' were initiated time and again to ward off the impending era of 'cheap oil.' Many and imposing names, many and powerful interests, nursed them into existence. . . . Why did they fail? How was *The Herald* denounced for expressing a doubt as to the practicability of the Culver scheme for a Producers' Union! But did not time justify our prediction? And what has become of the Refiners' Combination? Of the joint Producers' and Refiners' Combination? And why did they all fail? Was it not from a want of mutual confidence and a conflict of interest inherent in the nature of the case? Who made the money out of the Producers' Combination during its gestation? Was it the producers as a class, or a few individuals who had set themselves up as leaders? Were not those who were resoluting most loudly indoors to 'hold on' and 'pull together' secretly giving their brokers orders to sell?"

[10]*Idem,* May 17, 1874.

The well-owners suffering from overproduction had no government to help them; no Herbert Hoover to give them a compact like the Jacksonville Agreement in the soft-coal industry, and no Franklin D. Roosevelt to set up an agency like the A.A.A. They could only take their medicine, and bitter it proved. On November 19, 1874, 47½ cents a barrel was offered for crude oil at the Millerstown pool. Oil was literally cheaper than water, for many people had to pay 50 cents a barrel for hauling water for domestic use.[11]

III

It was now the turn of the railroads and refiners to make fresh attempts at organization; and they succeeded a good deal better.

The year 1874 found the railroads in an unhappy mood. It opened with a fresh rate battle between the Baltimore & Ohio and the Pennsylvania, the former cutting its through rates to the Mississippi by about one third, and arranging for a fast-freight service from Baltimore westward on this basis. Pittsburgh immediately became a center of this war. No sooner did the Baltimore & Ohio reach that city by the Connellsville line than President Garrett began slashing rates on all Pittsburgh freight, while he sent agents on to Cleveland and Chicago to drum up trade. "Just fancy," remarked the Cleveland *Leader* this spring, "it costs only $10.50 to visit the capital by this new route!" All the competing roads had to cut their fares between Chicago and the Atlantic.

Moreover, other causes of dissension quickly arose. We have described the compact between the Erie Railroad and Standard Oil in April, 1874, which gave the former an increased oil traffic, and the latter low rates and the Weehawken oil terminal. This naturally excited the resentment of the Pennsylvania and the New York Central. Vanderbilt's lines lost a great part of their Cleveland oil freights, while Tom Scott's fears were deeply stirred; for the Pennsylvania had always dreaded that the lion's share of the oil business would go to the Erie. At the same time, railroad heads complained that the new Erie rates were too low to permit a profit, and set a bad example. The competition for oil traffic, so costly just before the South Improvement war, had been broken by only a brief truce. Now, early in 1874,

[11]N. Y. *Tribune,* Feb. 6, 1875; Boyle, *Derrick's Handbook,* 237.

it was raging as implacably as ever, and the press agreed that it was likely to precipitate another general rate war.[12]

What could be done to prevent such a disaster? Early in July the heads of all the principal Eastern lines met at the Windsor Hotel in New York. Discussing the terrific fall in revenues since the panic, they agreed that harmony was indispensable, and that they must adopt a standard freight tariff, to be accepted by all the roads and maintained without any alteration whatever. Several of them also vigorously denounced the fast-freight lines, and called for their abolition. They declared that in the districts where one fast-freight line, by virtue of its railroad contracts, held a practical monopoly of some classes of freight, it made excessive charges, and that the companies were guilty of other malpractices. These complaints alarmed Joseph D. Potts, head of the Empire Transportation Company, for this fast-freight line had long been under fire from a large group of the Pennsylvania's stockholders.[13] Another meeting of railroad officers quickly followed at Long Branch, and still another at Saratoga.[14] At both, representatives of the Pennsylvania and New York Central argued that the Erie, since its agreement with the Standard, was crowded beyond its carrying capacity.[15] All the roads asserted that freight and passenger rates were too low and must be raised. While naturally little was revealed to the public on this point, word soon leaked out that another rate-arrangement was contemplated. "At Saratoga it was reported," said the New York *Tribune* of August 3, "that the object was to appoint a commissioner, who shall fix the rates on all through traffic on the trunk lines, each line agreeing (as heretofore in these combinations) to adhere strictly to such rates." The financial

[12]The Baltimore & Ohio gained access to Chicago early this year (1874), and was in a position to offer stiff competition to the other trunk lines. Its head, John W. Garrett, a wealthy Baltimorean who had assumed control soon after the panic of 1857, believed in aggressive expansion. "He seemed to be almost an Aladdin of railroad management," writes John Moody (*The Railroad Builders*, 101). Blame for the rate war of 1874–75 between the Pennsylvania and B. & O. is difficult to apportion. The Pennsylvania refused to carry B. & O. cars over its track to New York at any figure whatever; the B. & O. retaliated by using every weapon within reach. The B. & O. had nearly as much power in the Maryland legislature as the Pennsylvania exercised at Harrisburg. Van Oss, *American Railroads as Investments*, 273.

[13]"Parasitical," said the Pittsburgh *Gazette*, Sept. 3, 1874.

[14]On these railroad meetings see the N. Y. *Tribune*, July 11, July 20, July 31, Aug. 3, 4, 1874; *Railroad Gazette*, Aug. 8, 1874.

[15]Pittsburgh *Gazette*, July 31, 1875.

editor of *The Tribune* predicted that any such compact would soon be violated.[16] But the railroads were in a predicament which made action simply imperative. They signed a number of rate-agreements, of which that on oil alone concerns us.

In enforcing this agreement it was necessary to have the co-operation of the principal refiners, and the intermediary between the railroads and oil men was Potts of the Empire. While his fast-freight line was essentially an adjunct of the Pennsylvania Railroad, it served other railroads as well, and held a nominally independent position. Potts was a man of commanding personality and striking ability.[17] A member of an old Pennsylvania family, he had been trained as a civil engineer, and before the Civil War had become superintendent of the western division of the Pennsylvania Railroad. In 1861 the State made him head of its department of transportation and telegraphs, with the rank of lieutenant-colonel, and the next year he became military superintendent of the Western Transportation Company. When later in the war the Pennsylvania Railroad leased the Philadelphia & Erie, Potts was appointed general manager. Then in 1865 he was detached to organize and manage the Empire Transportation Company; and he had been so brilliantly successful that he was an outstanding figure in the railroad world of the seventies.

Potts, uneasy lest a general rate-war break out, and equally uneasy lest the attack on the fast-freight lines become dangerous, urged a clear agreement among the three great oil-carrying railroads and the principal refiners. With his long, solemn face, grave voice, and earnest manner, he was extremely persuasive. According to Rockefeller, his first convert was William G. Warden, who explained what was contemplated to a little group of refiners which also met in Saratoga this summer of 1874. In some way a plan was hammered out to which both trunk lines and a large body of refiners subscribed.

This agreement embodied three main features. First, it provided for an equitable division of oil traffic among the Pennsylvania, Erie, and New York Central, the first-named getting approximately one half, and the other two a quarter each. The Standard and other leading refiners were to act as "eveners." In the second place, it called for an advance in freight rates. But it was the third feature of the

[16]Aug. 3, 1875.
[17]Potts gave a sketch of his career in *House Trust Investigation, 1888,* pp. 257 ff. In 1937 I received much information from his son William M. Potts.

compact which proved most arresting; for this decreed that the whole of the Oil Regions should be treated as a single station, and that a uniform rate should be established from this station to the Eastern ports *by way of all refining points*. For example, the charge for transporting enough crude to make a barrel of refined oil from the pipe lines to a Cleveland refinery, or Pittsburgh refinery, or Titusville refinery, and then for taking the barrel of refined oil from any of these places to New York, was made precisely the same as the charge for transporting the same amount of crude directly from the Oil Regions to a Philadelphia or New York refinery.

The effect of this, obviously, was to place all refining points on precisely the same level as regarded transportation costs. The Cleveland or Pittsburgh refiner could put a barrel of oil on the wharf in Philadelphia or New York for shipment to Europe just as cheaply, so far as freight charges went, as his rivals in the Oil Regions or the coastal ports; though obviously his combined crude-and-refined haulage was much longer. This constituted an extension of the "group rate" plan then familiar in railroad practice, and applied, for example, in hauling the coal traffic from the anthracite regions to the seaboard, and from some Southern fruit-growing areas to the North.

The system by which this equalization was effected was simple. To establish "equality," the Pittsburgh and Cleveland refiners were to receive a rebate covering the entire cost of hauling their supply of crude oil from the Oil Regions to the refineries. Cleveland firms had apparently been paying 35 cents a barrel to get their crude oil brought from the Regions to the refinery door. Now these charges were simply abolished. Rates on refined oil were similarly "equalized." It was arranged that the rates should be made uniform at $1.85 a barrel from every inland refining point—whether Titusville, Erie, Pittsburgh, or Cleveland—to Philadelphia and Baltimore, and $2 to New York. By these changes the railroad giant roughly seized the industry, and at one blow destroyed the advantage in short-haul transportation which the Regions refineries had enjoyed over the Pittsburgh and Cleveland works. The changes likewise wiped out the transportation advantages of the New York and Philadelphia refineries. These coastal plants made but one haul, fetching the crude oil east; Cleveland had two hauls to make, first west, then east; and yet the charge was the same! To the Regions refiners the change seemed especially outrageous.

While losing their old advantage of position, they were still weighed down by all their handicaps of poor labor supply, high fuel costs, higher charges for chemicals, and inadequate barrel works. They had weak terminal facilities in New York, while those of the Standard Oil were superb. Under the name of "equality," they were being relegated to a desperately unequal position. New York and Philadelphia might remain the peers of Cleveland, but the Regions seemed doomed as a refining center.[18]

As to the authorship of this third feature of the compact, very little doubt can exist. The Standard Oil and its allies were almost certainly responsible for it. Colonel Potts, William H. Vanderbilt, Tom Scott, and Hugh J. Jewett, the Erie's latest head, had proposed that the refiners should help them divide the oil traffic at fair freight rates. Very well, Rockefeller and his associates had replied; we will help apportion the freights among the railroads if you will reward us by giving equality to all refining points. Officers of the Standard Oil had even talked of removing their refineries to the Oil Regions if their proposals were not accepted, a threat which the Erie and New York Central could not for a moment regard with indifference.

By now the Standard was so powerful that when it called the tune, nearly all refiners had to dance. The Saratoga meeting of oil men this summer resulted, as we shall see, in a marked expansion of the Standard organization. The equalization plan at once received the cordial endorsement of Warden and other leading Philadelphia refiners. It found substantial support in New York, where the Standard Oil not only controlled several leading plants, but now enjoyed the distinct good will of Charles Pratt and H. H. Rogers. The principal Pittsburgh firms had excellent reason to support it whether allied with the Standard Oil or not, and as we shall see, alliances were fast being formed there. Even in the Oil Regions adherents came forward, for J. J. Vandergrift had become a member of Rockefeller's organization, while John D. Archbold stood on the verge of joining it.

As for the railroads, they had every reason to stand loyally behind

[18]This railroad arrangement was described by various witnesses in *House Trust Investigation, 1888.* For a contemporaneous view see the Pittsburgh *Commercial*, Sept. 19, 1874. The scheme was by no means wholly unprecedented. The "group rate" system was an adjustment intended to abate the fierce competition between railroads; see Montague, *The Standard Oil Company* 16–19.

the scheme. The new uniform rates on refined oil were decidedly higher than the old, and at once made oil-hauling really profitable. Moreover, the promise of the Standard Oil and its associated "eveners" to do the utmost to maintain the agreed division of traffic between the three lines was invaluable. The roads knew that while their pledges to one another never held for long, those of the Standard were absolutely dependable.[19]

IV

The railroads having stabilized their position, the principal pipe lines in the Oil Regions immediately took steps to do the same. A heavy network of these lines crisscrossed the fields. Enterprise had run wild, a grossly excessive amount of pipe had been laid, competition had become sharp and relentless, and rates had been cut until losses were terrific. The owners felt that the situation had grown intolerable, and later declared as much in the preamble which justified their agreement. This set forth that "the pipe lines owned and controlled by the parties hereto have a joint capacity for transportation more than twice as great as the total volume of petroleum produced in the district traversed." It pointed out that "the separate and discordant relations now prevailing among the parties hereto lead to a needless multiplication of extensions, branches, and other matters involving heavy cost." And it asserted that the competition "also leads to the offering of open or secret inducements of an illegimate nature, such as rebates, special rates, (and) selling oil for less than its cost and full pipeage rates."

A movement to restrict competition, in fact, was just as inevitable among pipe owners as among producers, railroads, and refiners. Henry Harley, the eccentric pioneer builder of pipe lines, now practically a bankrupt, was apparently the moving spirit.[20] Probably four fifths of the pipe line mileage of the Oil Regions entered into this pooling compact signed on September 4, 1874; as Rockefeller later stated, only a few short lines were omitted. The agreement

[19]See Potts's testimony in *House Trust Investigation, 1888*, p. 264. He admitted that the railroads had never been able to keep promises to each other. He conceded that the Standard Oil remedied this, but thought the remedy too drastic.

[20]The best source for this pipe line agreement is the *Hepburn Committee Report, 1879*, III, 343 ff.

called for strict maintenance of a rate of 30 cents a barrel for piping. Each line was to keep 8 cents a barrel for itself, and hand the remaining 22 cents over to the pool. A central committee was to apportion expenses, and at stated periods divide profits among the members. The Standard controlled a little over one third of the system; and its pipes, managed under the names of the United and the American Transfer lines, were to receive 36.5 per cent of the net revenue.

The plan for the pool included an arrangement with the railroads. To help maintain the agreement, they consented to collect from the shipper 22 cents a barrel, above other charges, upon all crude oil delivered to them by the lines.[21] To the inside companies maintaining the 30-cent charge they refunded this 22 cents, but to the lines outside the pool they made no refund. The logic of this discrimination was simple. An independent pipe line might try to undercut the pool lines by charging a shipper only 20 cents, or even 10 cents—for pipe line history had been a record of savage undercutting. But now the rate-slasher would be checkmated. Even if the shipper got his oil at a 10-cent charge for piping, he would pay the extra 22 cents, or a total of 32, without hope of refund, and be the loser by 2 cents a barrel. He would do better to patronize the pool.

This was a shrewd plan for stabilizing the business of the pipe lines at a profitable level, and also a shrewd scheme for giving the pool a monopoly. No line could stand out against the arrangement unless it transported oil for less than 8 cents a barrel, a preposterous figure. The pool consisted of the Union Pipe-Line, a subsidiary of Potts's Empire Transportation Company; the Pennsylvania Transportation Company, still operated by Henry Harley, but in a very shaky condition; the old Vandergrift & Forman pipe lines, which the Standard had renamed the United Pipe-Lines; the older Standard property, the American Transfer Company; and a long list of minor lines —the Grant, Karns, Relief, Antwerp, and others. The railroads were glad to assist in harmonizing the hitherto quarrelsome pipe lines, for if the pool was effective each road would be protected against any sudden undercutting by a rival road allied with a pipe company. The Erie need no longer fear rate-slashing by a combination of the Pennsylvania Railroad, Empire Transportation Company, and Union Pipe-Line; and the Pennsylvania need not dread similar slashes by

[21]Tarbell, *Standard Oil Company,* I, 140.

a combination of the New York Central and United Pipe Lines.

By the end of September, 1874, the railroads had accepted the proposals of refiners and pipe lines, and the three were ready to act together. If the new arrangement proved successful, it meant the doom of both the independent refiners and independent pipe lines in the Regions; they must either surrender or die. That the arrangement was just or fair no believer in free competition could grant. The strongest were combining against the weak, and intended to trample them underfoot. But the men who made this arrangement were not believers in free competition. On the contrary, they were convinced that it had led refiners and pipe lines to the brink of ruin, and must be replaced by a less chaotic and incalculable system. We must keep in mind the gloomy background of the oil industry in 1874; the grisly depression, the heavy overproduction of crude oil, the excess of refining capacity, the abysmal prices, the pipe line wars, the constant threat of railroad dog-fights, the consciousness of Pittsburgh refiners that the selfish policy of the Pennsylvania Railroad was pushing them steadily nearer bankruptcy. If the new plan could be maintained, it would accomplish even more in the direction of stabilization and assured profits than the South Improvement Company had attempted.

And this plan, in the oil-manufacturing industry, would inure above all to the benefit of the Cleveland (and to a lesser extent Pittsburgh) refineries.

v

Rumors had for some time been running through western Pennsylvania that an advance in freight rates was imminent. The existing rate schedule for the Regions was fairly satisfactory to refiners there, though testimony as to their condition varies. In the summer of 1874 the Oil City *Derrick* reported that the large manufactories in Titusville and Oil City were prosperous, while the small ones at minor points were "jogging along pleasantly." The Pittsburgh *Gazette,* however, learned from an observer who toured the Regions in July that the outlook was discouraging to all engaged in the business. It reported again in August: "Everywhere throughout the Oil Regions are complaints heard of the stringency of money and extraordinary depression of business."[22] Apparently the Regions refineries made

[22]Aug. 26, 1874.

profits only because of the combination of low freight rates and extremely low crude oil—the overproduction this summer rendering various frantic well-owners almost ready to give petroleum away. If crude oil went up faster than the price of refined, or if freights were hoisted, profits would disappear. Reports that the railroad charges on refined oil ($1.35 to Philadelphia, $1.50 to New York, and $1.65 to Boston) would be raised therefore excited the keenest apprehension.

The blow fell in September. On the 9th the general freight agent of the New York Central, James H. Rutter, sent out a private circular announcing the plan, which by accident was published earlier than the railroads had intended.[23] It was dryly succinct. Rates on refined oil from Cleveland, Pittsburgh, Titusville, and other points in or adjacent to the Regions, it announced, would after October 1 be uniform; to Philadelphia and Baltimore, $1.85, to New York $2, and to Boston $2.10. On crude oil a new schedule from the Regions was fixed—$1.50 to New York, Philadelphia and Baltimore, and $1.75 to Boston. "From which" (it was stipulated) "shall be refunded twenty-two cents per barrel only on oil coming from pipes which maintain the agreed rate of pipeage." Rutter consolingly added: "You will observe that under this system the rate is even and fair to all parties, preventing one locality taking advantage of its neighbor by reason of some alleged or real facility it may possess. Oil refiners and shippers have asked the roads from time to time to make all rates even, and they would be satisfied. This scheme does it, and we trust will work satisfactorily to all."

In any other time than this period of grinding depression, the Oil Regions would have met the new arrangement with a storm of hostility. As it was, M. N. Allen, the fighting editor of the Titusville *Courier,* tried again to rally his neighbors. His journal vehemently denounced the new rates. He had no trouble in demonstrating that by "equalized" freight rates the Regions would lose their geographical advantage without gaining any compensation whatever. Equality! "If they will make the price of sulphuric acid $1\frac{1}{2}$ cents a pound, the same as it is in New York, instead of $2\frac{1}{2}$," he blazed; "If they will deliver caustic soda here free of freight from New York; if they will put paints and glues here at the same price

---

[23]The Rutter Circular is in *House Trust Investigation, 1888,* p. 363.

as these articles sell for in New York; if they will put staves and headings and hoops for barrels here at the same figures these articles cost in Cleveland . . . we will accept the new arrangement without complaint. . . . We submit to the railroad managers whether it is not right to charge for hauling goods in proportion to the distance hauled."[24]

The argument in this last sentence was irrefutable. In equity the railroads ought to charge less for hauling oil from the eleven Titusville refineries to New York than from Cleveland, some 140 miles farther west, to New York. A demand that the more obvious equities should not be disregarded in railroad rate-making was now being urged with increasing energy from Maine to California, and was to lead within thirteen years to the Interstate Commerce Act. But in 1874 "the railroads' method of doing business" by rebates, drawbacks, and other discriminations was still unshaken.

In its efforts to arouse the Regions, Allen's *Courier* was abetted by the Oil City *Derrick*. This journal pointed out that not the refiners alone, but the producers, were threatened. Ever since the South Improvement victory, it said, "the oilmen have been in a disorganized and disaffected state. Their interests have had no watchful eye to protect them. Their resources have been taken away one by one. The price of their product has declined until it has reached a mere nominal figure; and dissatisfaction, despondency, and listlessness brood over the entire region. In this state of affairs the enemies of the producers have made another bold stroke. Calculating upon the weakness of the oil men to gain them a victory, the railroads seek to impose a heavier load upon the region by an increase of freights. Arouse at once! Gather your forces immediately! Titusville's producers have sounded the first cry of organization; let our other towns follow her example."

It must be realized that there were still about twenty-five refineries in the Oil Regions, some of considerable size. It was a large manufacturing interest, and its welfare meant much to all residents of the area. The roster of independent Titusville refineries, as called this

[24]The Pittsburgh *Gazette* stated Sept. 18, 1874: "Our refiners are nearly, if not all, bitterly opposed to the uniform rate proposed by the Pennsylvania Railroad Company." It naïvely added: "Very likely, when the matter is explained to the proper officials of the corporation in question, different arrangements will be made."

autumn by *The Courier,* shows just how important was the local industry thus threatened with extinction:[25]

Firm	Daily Crude-Oil Capacity	Employees	Cost of Construction
Porter, Moreland & Co.	3,000	90	$500,000
Pickering & Chambers	900	30	80,000
Octave Oil Co.	400	25	75,000
Easterly & Davis	500	28	90,000
M. N. Allen	250	11	26,000
J. A. Scott & Co.	350	10	40,000
Bennett, Warner & Co.	1,200	65	175,000
R. H. Lee	350	13	30,000
Cadam & Donehue	150	9	20,000
J. W. Jackson	375	11	40,000
Total	7,475	292	$1,076,000

A great meeting of producers and refiners was called at Parker's Landing for October 2. Its chairman, A. N. Perine, declared its object to be the adoption of measures to save the oil business "from the unholy and illegal alliance" of railroad and pipe lines, which threatened to destroy the large and increasing business of the district. Allen made a characteristically fiery speech, and assurances were received that some Pittsburgh refiners sympathized with their associates in the Regions.

In vain, at this meeting, did S. D. Karns attempt to defend the pipe lines. Their pooling agreement was not intended to defraud the oil producers, he protested, but was simply an effort to obtain a fair compensation for transporting oil to the railroads. The convention passed resolutions denouncing the new railroad and pipe line rates; invited the chief independent pipe line, the Columbia Conduit Company, to extend its system; and provided for hiring lawyers to initiate a prosecution. The charge would be conspiracy; "the new Constitution of the State affords the producers ample grounds for redress," Allen assured his readers.[26] Subscriptions were circulated to obtain money to conduct the prosecution, arrangements were made to carry the anti-monopoly cry into the next elections, and a shutdown pledge was adopted on condition that enough signatures

[25]Oct. 1, 1874.   [26]Quoted in Pittsburgh *Gazette,* Oct. 8, 1874.

were obtained to make it effective. For a few days the Oil Regions presented a defiant mien. They would again show the transportation interests that they could not take one of the richest industrial areas of the nation by the throat!

Yet when the refiners and producers of western Pennsylvania calmly examined their weapons, they found themselves singularly helpless. An agreement among producers to cut off the flow of oil, as in the South Improvement fight, was impossible. Look at the overproduction, flooding the country with oil! Look at the great pipe lines and storage tanks now owned by the Standard and New York Central, the Empire and Pennsylvania! The number of producers had greatly increased, and many would do anything for money. The Pittsburgh *Gazette* had reported on July 20 that if it were not for the new tanks being hastily erected, oil would be worthless in many localities. It added on August 26 that throughout the Regions everything was gloom, hopelessness, and impotency. "Seventy-five cent crude is telling with fearful effect. . . . Yet reckless operators persist in flooding the market with a supply of petroleum greatly exceeding the world's requirements, and from the lower districts come reports of new wells starting and rigs multiplying with a rapidity perfectly inexplicable under the existing condition of affairs." The Oil City *Derrick* correctly said in September that the producers were "in a disorganized and disaffected state." Titusville refiners, sending a delegation to the Eastern railroad offices, obtained a few concessions, but they were trifling.[27]

As for conspiracy suits, they had a dubious basis in law and could be fought for years in the courts. The State government which would conduct them was largely controlled by the Pennsylvania Railroad and its allies.

VI

The one club that could be used against the three trunk lines was the development of the independent Baltimore & Ohio route from Pittsburgh to the seaboard, over which a thin trickle of oil already passed; and a spasmodic effort was at once made to give volume to the flow. The Oil Regions had been moving southward, and the railroad was to be connected with the "southern field" by the long new pipe line of the Columbia Conduit Company.

[27]Described in *The Railroad Gazette,* Oct. 10, 1874.

The Columbia Conduit Pipe Line was the creation of one of the most picturesque figures in Pittsburgh, Doctor David Hostetter, who had made a fortune by selling the nostrum called Hostetter's Bitters.[28] He had become interested in petroleum, and had bought wells in the rich new Butler County field. Resenting the excessive charges of the Pennsylvania Railroad for transporting crude oil, he decided to pipe it to Pittsburgh, where connections could be made with the Pittsburgh & Connellsville branch of the Baltimore & Ohio. Surveys for a three-inch line capable of carrying 3500 barrels a day were undertaken early in 1874. The laying of the pipe began at Millerstown, in the northern part of Butler County, in June. It was within reach, by other pipe lines, of much of the production of Venango and Clarion Counties.[29] Since the distance from Millerstown to Pittsburgh, as the crow flies, is less than forty miles, this was not a major engineering enterprise. From the outset Pittsburgh refiners were enthusiastic over the undertaking, while after the Rutter circular, leaders in the Oil Regions urged that it be given every support.

"Let the producers, traders, and refiners of the region join," exhorted the Oil City *Derrick*, "in doing all they can by word and act to encourage the Baltimore & Ohio Railroad to enter this region, through the Columbia Conduit Company's line or in any other way. With that road fairly connected with the region, and with a producers' and tankers' pipe line running through from Titusville to the Butler oil fields, we shall be in a position forever thereafter to command recognition of our rights from the grabbing combiners and to control our interests to a great advantage. This accomplished, there will be an end of combination, for the Baltimore & Ohio Railroad never joins in unholy alliances to make victims of its patrons. . . . Act at once and make the action decisive."

In Pittsburgh the press displayed equal fervor in supporting the line. *The Gazette* published articles to show that but for the tyranny of the Pennsylvania Railroad that city would be by far the greatest refining center of the Union. It had to bring its crude oil 60 miles, and ship its refined oil 350, a total of 410; Cleveland had to bring its crude oil 150 miles, and ship its refined 750, a total of 900; Titus-

---

[28]Elderly Pittsburghers describe this medicine as originally a mixture of whiskey and wormwood.
[29]Boyle, *Derrick's Handbook*, 226, 229.

ville had to bring its crude oil 85 miles (from Parker's Landing) and ship its refined 520, a total of 605. "Yet notwithstanding that Cleveland has more than twice the distance to overcome, its refineries furnish about two fifths (much more than Pittsburgh) of the entire exports of refined oil from the United States; and Titusville, having about a half more distance to overcome than Pittsburgh, its refineries furnish about one fifth of such exports, and both at prices with which Pittsburgh and Philadelphia cannot compete. And if you ask why, the only answer is because that great monopoly, the Pennsylvania Railroad, wilfully and wantonly drives the trade away from Pittsburgh and to a great extent from Philadelphia. . . ."[30] The editor declared that most Pittsburgh refiners were against the "equalization" agreement. They felt bitterly that Cleveland gained too much from it. If the Pennsylvania persisted in its unfair policy, they would be forced to find another route, the Baltimore & Ohio. And on October 3 *The Gazette* remarked threateningly: "Our refiners appear determined to fight this thing out, and the Pennsylvania Railroad . . . will soon realize this fact. . . . It is . . . the wish of all Pittsburghers who understand the matter that the refiners may be successful."

But the Columbia Conduit Company soon ran into heavy difficulties. In July it laid its pipes under a branch line of the Pennsylvania Railroad between Delano and Dilken Station in Butler County. Anticipating trouble, the builders did this at dead of night. Although the pipes could not possibly injure the roadbed, at four o'clock next morning a railroad gang dug them up and filled the excavation. The Conduit Company replaced them, and once more the Pennsylvania tore them out.[31] While a court fight began, Hostetter stubbornly pushed his line on down through Butler County to Allegheny County, in which lies Pittsburgh. Acquiring a right of way, he laid pipes to within a few miles of the city, where again he met a branch of the railroad. Here he bought the bed of a stream, Powers Run, which the tracks crossed by a culvert, and laid his pipes in the bed, asserting that the Pennsylvania merely held the right to span the stream. The railroad sent an armed force, tore up the pipes, and

[30]Pittsburgh *Gazette*, Sept. 3, 1874.
[31]N. Y. *Tribune*, Feb. 6, 1875, describes the struggle at Dilken Station. See the Pittsburgh *Gazette*, July 7, Sept. 5, 29, etc., 1874, for its later phases.

fortified the spot against all comers. When a large body of oil men, watching their opportunity, suddenly arrived and took possession, the Pennsylvania had thirty of them arrested for provoking a riot. It failed to send them to jail, but it did prevent the re-laying of the pipes.[32]

While the general public watched this conflict with keen sympathy for Hostetter, the anger of many Pittsburgh refiners knew no bounds. They were in a desperate temper. As *The Gazette* put it: "Upon the reduction in the cost of transportation, not only upon the raw article from the wells here but upon the product from here to the seaboard, depends the life and death of the trade, so far as Pittsburgh is concerned. If our refiners were dependent upon the Pennsylvania Railroad, in the present condition of affairs, they would be unable to do anything at all, and they would be forced to abandon their business and sell their refineries for old scrap iron. They have been receiving considerable crude by river within the past few days, and if navigation only continues for a week or so longer, they will have crude enough to last them until the Conduit Company are enabled to supply them."[33]

Alas for the Conduit Pipe Line! The railroad managed to hold Powers Run and to drag out the litigation. In the spring of 1875 Doctor Hostetter again used armed force, and again his pipes were ripped up. Disgusted with a venture in which he had now sunk about $400,000 without success, in May he leased his line for ten years to three courageous and energetic young men, Bryon D. Benson, Robert E. Hopkins, and David McKelvy.[34] All three were from Titusville, and all three were later to become famous in connection with the Tidewater Pipe Line. Inventive and pertinacious, they made a terminal at the Run, drained the oil into tank wagons holding

[32]No power to condemn a route existed. The producers petitioning Governor Hartranft in 1878 stated that "the Pennsylvania Railroad influence was strong enough to exclude Allegheny County from the operation of the [free pipe line] act, thus shutting out western Pennsylvania from Pittsburgh . . . the natural outlet of the oil region"; and that later efforts to pass a better free pipe law "have been defeated invariably by the opposition of the Pennsylvania Railroad." *House Trust Investigation, 1888*, p. 353.

[33]Dec. 7, 1874.

[34]This estimate of Hostetter's investment is given by Robert D. Benson in the pamphlet, *History of the Tidewater Companies*, 8. O'Day testified in *House Trust Investigation, 1888*, p. 267, that a three-inch pipe line cost about $3000 a mile.

1000 gallons each, carted it across the tracks, poured it into storage tanks, and re-piped it to Pittsburgh. The railroad tried to keep long trains of cars standing on the crossing, but the authorities soon stopped that. During the spring session of the legislature in 1875 efforts were made to pass a "free pipe-line bill," so that the Columbia Conduit Company could condemn a through route; but the Pennsylvania Railroad, aided by Colonel Potts of the Empire, nearly all the old pipe-line companies, and a part of the Pittsburgh refiners —no doubt that part now closely allied with the Standard—defeated these efforts.[35] New York and Philadelphia interests applauded the defeat, for they had no mind to see the enormous export oil trade diverted from their wharves to Baltimore. The Conduit Company still laboriously sent its cartloads of oil over the branch line of the selfish corporation.[36] Such Pittsburgh refiners as survived talked bitterly of removing to some other point, where they could find cheaper transportation facilities.

Still another attempt to circumvent the Pennsylvania and its allies ended abortively. On November 30, 1874, *The Gazette* announced that for the first time in months several barges had brought crude oil down the Allegheny River to Pittsburgh. Winter soon sealed the navigation, but early in April refiners again began buying large quantities for delivery by barge. The rates were much lower than those charged by the Pennsylvania's subsidiary, the Allegheny Valley Railroad, and an adequate stage of water could be counted upon for two thirds of the year.[37] Men proposed to bring the crude oil to Pittsburgh by barge; then to ship the refined oil down the Ohio River to Huntington, W. Va.; and thence to carry it by the Richmond & Chesapeake to Richmond. To such desperate expedients were the Pittsburgh manufacturers being driven! Poor though Baltimore was as a point of export, Richmond would be far poorer. Yet some hope was aroused by the plan, and the cry "On to Richmond!" was raised encouragingly.

Once more, however, malign influences were exerted to defeat the undertaking. Early in May the pipe lines which had recently

[35]N. Y. *Tribune*, Feb. 6, 1875. For Potts's lobbying, see *The Road*, April 1, 1875.

[36]Robert D. Benson, *History of the Tidewater Companies*, 8, says the tank-wagons carried 5000 gallons each across daily.

[37]Pittsburgh *Gazette*, April 8, 1875.

gone into the pooling agreement announced that they would refuse to deliver oil thereafter to barges. They gave no reason, but merely refused.[38] It was even reported, though erroneously, that all pipes between the storage tanks and the river had been ripped up. In vain did the refiners and barge owners rage; in vain did they deny that the pipe lines had any legal right to take such discriminatory action, and threaten lawsuits. The pipe-line companies, obviously acting in collusion with the Pennsylvania Railroad, sat tight. Neither threats nor pleas availed, and though Benson, McKelvy, and Hopkins maintained a small volume of oil shipments, Pittsburghers had to confess themselves checkmated once more.

With the Columbia Conduit Company half-blocked, with the free pipe-line bill defeated, and with the barges stopped, independent oil men of both Pittsburgh and the Regions lost heart. Overproduction and low prices had long since drained the pocketbooks of most producers. Every newspaper in the Allegheny Valley spoke of widespread financial prostration. When lawyers were consulted about a prosecution for conspiracy, they declared that the Attorney-General of Pennsylvania would have to bring action—and the Regions knew how little hope there was of that.[39] Apparently a species of fatalism took possession of many Regions men. They no longer believed that they could control the flood of oil which impoverished them by its very volume; they no longer thought it worth while to combat the railroads which choked them in iron arms. Some of the Regions refiners, too, had been half-hearted from the beginning. The new rates were higher, and the "equalization" principle was an outrage —yes; but in view of the rebates that Pittsburgh, Cleveland, and other outside refiners had previously obtained, were they not *comparatively* about as good rates as before? So Editor Allen himself had said at the meeting of October 2. The effort to wage war against the Rutter Circular arrangement collapsed in a general atmosphere of defeatism.

But the difficulties of Pittsburgh and the Oil Regions offered a

[38]For indignant comment, see Pittsburgh *Gazette,* May 10, 1875.
[39]For the movement in the Regions and the depression there see Boyle, *Derrick's Handbook,* 234, 236 ff.; Pittsburgh *Gazette,* Oct. 24, 1874, and later dates. *The Derrick's Handbook* for Nov. 22, 1874, says: "The sheriff is doing a good business in Butler County, and has the property of seven operators in the Millerstown field advertised for sale."

tide in the affairs of the Standard Oil which Rockefeller had seized with lightning swiftness and address.

VII

In all the debates on the Rutter Circular in the Regions, and all the attacks on the Pennsylvania Railroad in Pittsburgh, Rockefeller's name was scarcely mentioned. There was no reason why it should have been. The idea of an arrangement by the three trunk lines apparently originated with their presidents and Joseph D. Potts of the Empire. The idea of a pool of the pipe lines to maintain rates apparently originated with Henry Harley of the Pennsylvania Transportation Company. Rockefeller had no alliance with the Pennsylvania, no trust in its promises, and no liking for its unprincipled head, Tom Scott. Yet unquestionably at an early date he knew all that was being planned in the matter of the new rates—for it was his business to know everything that affected the oil industry, and nobody was more sleeplessly vigilant, more intimately informed. He was very close to the Erie and the New York Central, and he was in control of two pipe companies. Late in life he said he thought he had never taken part in the conferences that brought about "equal" railroad rates and the stable pipe-line charges. But somehow the schemes adopted seem to have a curious affinity with his subtle, far-seeing mind. Somehow these schemes operated with marvellous precision and effectiveness to promote that very consolidation of refining interests which he had in view.

There were shrewd observers who thought that more was going on than met the eye. The Pittsburgh *Gazette* remarked on October 10, 1874: "The stupendous folly of the railway companies in adding to the encumbrances already pressing heavily upon the petroleum interest, can be accounted for only on the supposition that there is hidden away from public inspection some great project which the railroads are aiding to establish." It was right. The great hidden project existed—and it was Rockefeller's project for a consolidated industry.

All the new agreements he thoroughly approved. The "equality" in freight charges seemed to him perfectly just. Questioned late in life, he emphasized the importance of an arrangement among the three rival trunk lines and the many rival pipe lines to avoid cut-throat rate wars, and also the selfishness of those interests in the Regions which thought that all refining should be confined to their valley. "The railroads had to consider the greatest good of the greatest number," he said. "They had to consider the fact that they could not get remunerative rates by regarding the attitude of only the comparatively small refining interest in one section, namely the Oil Regions, which would seem to the railroad people not nearly so important as to have a comprehensive scheme which woud recognize the capital invested in oil refining at various other points to the extent of many hundreds of thousands of dollars. And these refineries were necessary to be continued in order to refine the amount of oil which was being produced. They could not be ignored at the urgency of this small refining interest in the Oil Regions."[40] This quite misses the point. The railroads never worried much about the greatest good to the greatest number, and no danger existed that the Regions would stamp out all outside refineries—the stamping-shoe was on the other foot. But the statement makes it clear that Rockefeller thought highly of the "evening" plan embodied in the Rutter Circular!

And even if he attended no transportation conferences, he had been far from idle during these months. While the railroad presidents were sitting in New York, Long Branch, and Saratoga, and the pipe line heads were conferring in the Regions, he had been the dominant figure at a meeting of refiners in Saratoga. It is difficult to believe there was no connection between the three groups. It is difficult not to see in his plans the web which united them. For while the railroad and pipe-line plans had an improvised look, his own scheme was well matured; and the three arrangements worked together toward that magic formula for salvation in the refining industry which he had always championed—consolidation. We may be sure that when the National Refiners' Association broke down he was already full of plans to use that disaster to gain fresh successes. The very hallmark of his business genius was his ability to arm himself with new weapons in the catastrophe of old undertakings. He had given reluctant fellow refiners time to be educated

[40]Inglis, Conversations with Rockefeller.

in the doctrine of consolidation, and harsh experience had fully schooled them.[41]

As we have seen, early in 1874 the Standard Oil had bought one of the greatest refineries in the Regions, that of the Imperial Refining Company at Titusville, owned by J. J. Vandergrift and others. The money-payment for this property may have been largely a matter of bookkeeping, for at this time or soon afterward Vandergrift and his partner, John Pitcairn, Jr., acquired five hundred shares of Standard Oil stock.[42] By the time the Rutter Circular was issued, the Imperial refinery had been fully incorporated in the Standard organization.

Rockefeller's next step was to renew his approaches during the summer and fall of 1874 to the leading refiners of Pittsburgh, Philadelphia, and New York; that is, to William G. Warden of Philadelphia, Charles Lockhart, R. J. Waring, and William Frew of Pittsburgh, and Charles Pratt and H. H. Rogers of New York. Few details as to these *pourparlers* have been preserved. Miss Tarbell later stated that Rockefeller wrote to Warden, inviting him and Lockhart to the refiners' conference at Saratoga, and at this conference persuaded them to unite with the Standard.[43] When Rockefeller's attention was called to this statement, he denied it. Warden, he thought, had instigated the Saratoga meeting of refiners, and had brought to it Potts's proposal for an "evened" division of oil traffic among the three trunk lines. But it does not matter who called the meeting; Rockefeller was the great force behind it, and the great proponent of consolidation. Charles Lockhart in some reminiscences dictated late in life has given his version of what happened; a statement substantially accurate except that it abbreviates the time involved.[44]

In the summer of 1874 John D. Rockefeller, Henry M. Flagler, William G. Warden and myself met by agreement and spent one whole day trying to make some agreement to form a business connection which would be materially advantageous to all of us. We agreed to form a company to be

[41]Rockefeller later remarked: "It was necessary to form one organization under a common ownership if we were to succeed and stay alive. Here it was, the Standard Oil Company of Ohio, good for one hundred cents on the dollar!" Inglis, Conversations with Rockefeller.
[42]Taylor, MS History of the Standard Oil, 24, 27.
[43]Tarbell, *Standard Oil Company*, I, 146, 147.   [44]Lockhart Papers.

called the Standard Oil Company [*i.e.,* to merge with the Standard]. Rockefeller, Andrews and Flagler were to put in their refineries, barrel factories, stock of barrel staves, and so much money. Warden, Frew & Company and Lockhart & Frew were to put in the Atlantic, Crystal, Model, Brilliant, Nonpareil, and Standard, and all other refineries that they controlled, and so much money. We invited any other large refineries to join us on the same terms. In a few days Charles Pratt & Company joined us. We formed a stock company and any one who wanted to come in with us took stock and put their works in.

Rockefeller tells us that after the conference, Warden, Lockhart, and Waring, still hesitant, came to Cleveland, and conferred and investigated for several days before committing themselves to a union. Particulars of their visit have not been recorded. But we can imagine Rockefeller's carriage meeting them at the grimy little station on the lake front. In the drowsy heat of late summer, while cicadas shrilled in the elms and maples of the little city, Rockefeller and Flagler doubtless drove them about the finer streets and pointed out the mansions of the wealthiest Clevelanders. They would be taken over every inch of Plant No. 1 and Plant No. 2, and given a more cursory inspection of the other four. With a quiet flourish, in the office in the Standard Building which he had just handsomely refurnished in leather, Rockefeller would throw open to them the books of the company. It was easy to make an impression. Ever since 1872, he said later, these men had been "entirely neighborly and friendly," and had been "frequently in conference" with the Standard officials on various matters. He impatiently denied the suggestion that they ever received an ultimatum from the Standard. A coalition had been "under consideration for several years," and Lockhart and Warden had been urged to take their time in studying Rockefeller's organization. "They were taking years to observe its workings, as careful and prudent. businessmen, and . . . came to Cleveland of their own volition and consummated a negotiation transferring all their refining interests to the Standard Oil Company, and taking most responsible positions of administration of the companies they brought it."

Warden's son has testified that his father carefully inspected the Standard's books. He was astonished by the economies and profits which they revealed.[45] The Standard could sell oil far more cheaply

[45]Allen S. Warden to the author, March 11, 1937.

than he could make it. Rockefeller's insistence that the union was accomplished only after careful study, and with no undue pressure, is also confirmed by recorded statements of Henry L. Davis, at this time an officer of the Warden-Lockhart organization, and by Orville Waring.[46] All the circumstances support this version.

It was early in October, 1874, according to Rockefeller, that Warden, Lockhart, and Frew finally decided to join with the Standard. Their properties were then held by two companies, Warden, Frew & Co., and Lockhart, Frew & Co.[47] The owners were recompensed by a large block of Standard Oil stock, and all three leaders entered the Standard's service. Chief among the works acquired were those of the Atlantic Refining Co., which had an extensive plant just below Philadelphia on the Delaware,[48] and seven different establishments in Pittsburgh—the Nonpareil, the Brilliant, the National, the Lily, the Crystal, the Model, and the Standard. The largest Pittsburgh plant, the Brilliant, had a weekly capacity of some 13,000 barrels of refined oil, and the next in size, the Standard, of 7250. Two minor firms of Pittsburgh, Brooks, Ballantyne & Co., and Livingston & Brothers, seem to have been concerned as part owners of the surrendered property. By this single acquisition, the Standard Oil of Ohio became master of much more than half of the whole refining capacity of Pittsburgh, and much the largest plant in the Philadelphia area. But merger is a better word than acquisition. The legal details we shall describe elsewhere.

On October 14 Charles Pratt & Co. of New York followed suit by joining the Standard—Pratt bringing with him the brilliantly able H. H. Rogers.[49] Once more the financial arrangement gave the owners a large block of Standard Oil stock. Once more, too, the heads of the company joined the management of the Standard, contributing their brains and experience. The Pratt works, situated at Newtown, L. I., had long possessed an importance in the oil business

[46]Inglis, Conversations with Orville Waring and H. L. Davis.
[47]Inglis, Conversations with Rockefeller.
[48]The Minute Book of the Atlantic Refining Company, which I examined in 1936 at the company offices in Philadelphia, shows the sale took place Oct. 19, 1874.
[49]Ida M. Tarbell gives the date of the Pratt purchase as October 15; *Standard Oil Company*, I, 148. But Rockefeller said in old age: "Charles Pratt & Company were brought into the Standard Oil Company of Ohio after Messrs. Lockhart and Warden and their associates came in." Inglis, Conversations with Rockefeller. This must have meant shortly after October 19.

out of all proportion to their modest capital of $250,000, and their "Astral" brand had given business value to an imaginative word. "Astral showers covered the heavens," wrote the poet; Astral oil lighted the homes beneath.

Both transactions were kept entirely secret. At a bound the Standard Oil had placed itself in possession of the inner citadels of the refining industry in Pittsburgh and Philadelphia, and had added heavily to its New York possessions—and nobody outside the group immediately concerned knew it. This secrecy was later a ground for indignant and well-justified complaints by the Philadelphia and Pittsburgh independents. They declared that Warden, Lockhart, and Frew bore themselves like free refiners, listened attentively to the talk of opponents of the Standard, picked up their confidential plans, and then hastened to the Standard Oil offices! Even if there were few secrets to learn, the duplicity was reprehensible.

But the importance of these acquisitions to the consummation of Rockefeller's plan for one great oil-monopoly was enormous. Leviathan had become huger than ever, stretching its limbs across all the refining centers of the land; or to change the image, the commander of the Standard, like some Border chieftain bringing new clans into an alliance, had converted the most astute of his remaining competitors into partners and fellow fighters. An irresistible coalition had been created, and was ready to undertake further conquests.

In order to cover these mergers, the Standard Oil on March 10, 1875, increased its capital stock from $2,500,000 to $3,500,000. Of the additional ten thousand shares which it issued, 6250 went to Warden, Frew & Co. and Lockhart, Frew & Co., while 3125 were allotted to Charles Pratt & Co. That ever-ready investor, Stephen V. Harkness, paid for the remaining 625 shares. But the new corporate allies were expected, in return for their stock, to bring in some ready capital as well as plant-resources. Rockefeller said in old age that the Standard Oil had always informed the refiners to whom it proposed a merger that they need not contribute any money unless they desired. "And I believe that in only one instance was any concern willing to do so, and that was the case of Warden, Frew & Co. and Lockhart, Frew & Co." This is not quite accurate, for not only did these two firms provide $400,000 in part payment for their shares, but Pratt &

Five leaders of the Standard Oil.

Top: Joseph Seep and S. V. Harkness. *Center:* Charles M. Pratt.
Bottom: John D. Archbold and Charles Pratt.

Ambrose McGregor and William Rockefeller.

Co. furnished $250,000. It is evidence of the high profits that the Standard was making even in 1874 that Pratt & Co. paid not less than $265 each for shares with a nominal value of $100. As Walter F. Taylor of the Standard's legal staff significantly puts it in his manuscript history of the corporation, in 1872 Rockefeller, buying out the other Cleveland refiners, had paid them in cash or in Standard Oil stock *at par*. But two and a half years later, in taking over the new Pittsburgh, Philadelphia, and New York properties, "the Company gave less than $1,000,000 in par value of its stock for properties and cash having a value of fully $3,000,000."

A series of lesser acquisitions did much to complete the great central structure of the Standard. Late in 1874 or early in 1875 the firm of Porter, Moreland & Co., with which the irrepressible John D. Archbold was connected, sold its refinery at Titusville to Rockefeller and his associates. At the same time Bennett, Warner & Co., also of Titusville, sold out. These were respectively the second and third largest of the Titusville establishments, and had tank facilities for more than 200,000 barrels of crude oil.[50] But much more important than their facilities were the talents—mixed, we shall see, with sad faults—of Archbold, who was made head of a new corporation, the Acme Oil Co., formed to operate them. His conversion had taken some time. "Mr. Warden of Philadelphia worked with Mr. Archbold," later recalled John D. Rockefeller.[51] "They had been united in an enterprise in rivalry of the Standard Oil Company. It took Mr. Archbold more than a year to come around." He immediately became one of the most active officers in the Standard organization; and the faith which many small refining firms of the Regions placed in his brains and energy did much to bring them into the Standard Oil. In Titusville alone the Octave Oil Co., Pickering & Chambers, Teague Brothers, and Easterly & Davis all presently joined the combination.

Rockefeller and other leaders of the Standard Oil quickly realized that Archbold's keen, resourceful mind was invaluable in their councils—that he was far abler even than Vandergrift. "His enthusiasm, his energy, and his splendid power over men" Rockefeller later called marvellous. "I can never cease to wonder at his capacity for hard

---

[50]*House Trust Investigation, 1888*, 233.
[51]Inglis, Conversations with Rockefeller.

work." After his death Rockefeller told W. O. Inglis a revealing anecdote of his adventure with some "blackmailers"—that is, men who had started up a refining business in order to sell out to the Standard:

"What a man Mr. Archbold was! He was afraid of nothing. He went to Newark one day to meet alone three blackmailers who had made big demands on us under penalty of a lot of trouble if we did not comply. The three men, big fellows all and big blusterers, found Mr. Archbold in a hotel room waiting for them. He was a little man —physically—and there he was alone with the three big bullies. They threatened him and all of us with what they could do and would do if we did not meet their terms.

"When they stopped talking Mr. Archbold said, 'Is that all?' Then he went over to the fireplace and called up the chimney: 'Come down —and bring your notes with you!'

"The blackmailers waited long enough to see a man come down the chimney with a notebook in which he had written every word they said. They ran without another word."

While the Standard Oil was thus adding executives of power and vision to its staff, it dropped one of the original partners. "Sam" Andrews, a big, ruddy, kindly man with expressive eyes—"lovely eyes" one Standard lieutenant later called them—had not kept pace with his associates. Essentially a technician, he remained in charge of Plant No. 1 in Cleveland, but by 1874 Ambrose McGregor had risen above him as superintendent of all six plants in the city. Andrews possessed but a limited understanding of the Standard's business problems, and at the directors' meetings grumbled over Rockefeller's policy of turning most of the profits into plant-expansion rather than dividends. In the spring of 1874, greatly irritated by a decision to declare no dividend until fall, he threatened to sell his stock. It was reported that Rockefeller said to him:

"Sam, you don't seem to have faith in the way this company is operating. What will you take for your holdings?"

Without hesitation, Andrews rejoined: "I will take one million dollars."

"Let me have an option on it for twenty-four hours," suggested Rockefeller, "and we will discuss it tomorrow."

Next morning Rockefeller had a check ready, and Andrews accepted it. As Rockefeller said later, it would never have done to let so important a block of stock suddenly go on sale. "The company was young then. . . . Its credit had to be most carefully guarded. If the large amount of stock owned by Mr. Andrews had been thrown on the market and no buyer immediately appeared, the price might have fallen considerably. That might have affected our credit very unfavorably if we had sought to borrow money—and we were often borrowing in those days." The price seemed high to Andrews, and he boasted of the bargain he had driven. However, before many years the stock rose sharply. Andrews then became resentful, and spoke bitterly to his friends about having been cheated. In view of his earlier boasting, his remarks were not taken very seriously, but Warden heard of them during a visit to Cleveland, and carried the news to Rockefeller. The latter promptly sent word to Andrews that he would sell the stock back for what he had paid for it if Andrews felt that he had been mistreated. But the former partner, who had invested his money in government bonds, replied that he could not take up the offer. Nevertheless, he continued to feel aggrieved, later gave evidence to the Hepburn Committee which was damaging to the Standard, and talked abusively of Rockefeller. He had meanwhile built an enormous mansion on Euclid Avenue which was long called "Andrews' folly," and in which, according to a story still told in Cleveland, he hoped some day to entertain Queen Victoria. He died wealthy, but he might have been twenty times richer had he kept his interest in the company.[52] His son, a man of ability and character, became a traction magnate and as such was for some years Tom L. Johnson's principal opponent.

VIII

Although the empire which Rockefeller was creating was thus greatly and secretly enlarged, the spring of 1875 found it still far short of monopolistic power. A large number of independent refineries survived in New York, Pittsburgh, Erie, the Regions, and Baltimore. Good reasons existed for attempting to revive the pooling arrangement that had failed two years earlier, and Rockefeller under-

[52]Charles M. Higgins gave me this account, March 21, 1936, and I have found confirmation among elderly Clevelanders. Maurice Clark said of Andrews in the N. Y. *Herald,* Nov. 29, 1908: "Before selling he was sore at John. After selling he was sore at himself." Clark makes it clear that Andrews was fairly treated.

took the revival. The oil refiners' association was reborn, stronger than ever, in the Central Refiners' Association.

The first news that Rockefeller was promoting another pool leaked out to the world in March, 1874. A rumor that the refiners were organizing to raise the price of kerosene and corner the market caused the New York *Tribune* on the 25th to send a reporter down to the Standard Oil offices. William Rockefeller scoffed at the idea of a corner, but said that he was heartily in favor of an organization to protect oil capital and regulate prices, while H. H. Rogers let it be understood that he hoped for a speedy union of all refining interests to fix just and profitable rates. Four days later *The Tribune* was able to publish the supposed "articles of agreement" for this new pool.[53]

It was quickly evident that all but two of the New York refiners were ready to enter the new combination. It had the support of the secret partners of the Standard Oil in Philadelphia and Titusville. As for Pittsburgh, *The Gazette* of May 12 reported that "about five-eighths of the refining interest have gone into the combination, and the other refiners contemplate going into it." A meeting was held next day. "Some of our refiners still hesitate about going in," said *The Gazette,* "being apprehensive that it will not stick together long, that there are too many conflicting interests to harmonize." The hesitation continued a few days longer. Then on May 21 *The Gazette* declared that all but one or two of the local works had subscribed to the plan, and that for Pittsburgh the combination might be called perfect.[54]

It was an elaborate and ingenious pool, this Central Refiners' Association. All refiners were asked to join. They were to be grouped in five districts—Cleveland, New York, Pittsburgh, Oil Creek, and Philadelphia—and an Executive Committee of five was set up, one man for each district. Twenty-five thousand shares of stock were to be issued at twenty-five cents each (only $6250 worth in all), and divided among the five districts in proportion to their refining capacity. Cleveland got the most with 7175 shares, New York came next

[53]March 26, 29, 1875.

[54]The Pittsburgh *Gazette* stated June 2: "The combination movement is said to be consummated so far as Pittsburgh is concerned, that all the refiners have either gone into it or signified their intention of doing so, and there is no question that this has had considerable to do with stiffening up the market within the past few days."

with 5375, Pittsburgh was given 5125, Oil Creek received 4125, and Philadelphia stood last with 3200. Owners of refineries might subscribe to the stock in the proportion that their capacity bore to the whole capacity of their district, but not until they had signed such agreements and contracts as the Executive Board might prescribe. Absolute control was to be effected by an ingenious system of leases. Each owner was to lease his refinery to the Association for one year, and then to re-lease it from that body as a tenant-at-will, liable to be ousted without notice for any violation of the rules. The five directors were to apportion all refining among the various members, to control all purchases of crude oil and all sales of refined oil, to make all rate agreements with railroads and pipe lines, and to divide all profits. The president of the Association was John D. Rockefeller.[55]

Altogether, this Central Refiners' Association was a remarkably well-planned and promising organization. Just how successfully it worked, and what objects it achieved, we shall see in the pages to come. But its most remarkable feature was this: It was highly difficult to say precisely where the Standard Oil organization left off and the Central Refiners' Association began, and any company which entered the Central Refiners' Association and executed a lease somehow found itself inextricably entangled with the Standard Oil!

From first to last, a great deal of history had been made in this crowded twelvemonth of 1874–75. First the well-owners had tried to combine for curtailing production, and had failed. Then the three principal oil-carrying railroads had entered into a neat combination to divide traffic and raise rates, while the pipe lines had combined in an effective pool. Finally, the refiners had established a new pooling arrangement, the Central Association, which held out a distinct promise of success. It was evident that the idea of combination was in the air, for every element connected with the oil industry was attempting it. But the extraordinary fact was that each step toward combination, whether taken by railroads, pipe lines, or refiners, had contributed directly toward the growth and strength of the Standard Oil Company. It might have been accident. It might also have been the work of some tireless, subtle, and extraordinarily farsighted brain controlling the pieces on the board.

[55]See N. Y. *Tribune*, April 29, May 10, 15, 1875. See also S. C. T. Dodd's brief account in his *Combinations*.

XXI

Sweeping the Board

O N A warm summer day in 1876 two men sat in front of the great Corliss engine at the Centennial Exhibition in Philadelphia. They watched the immense flywheel sweep round and round unceasingly; and in harmony with it their conversation came round and round to the same point. Should they sell out to Rockefeller and the Standard Oil? The two men were William W. Harkness and his brother Norris, who had been refining oil in Philadelphia for half a dozen years. They had set up their manufactory only after carefully weighing all the factors of supply, markets, labor, and by-products. They had managed their business with close economy, constant attention to detail, and rigid avoidance of speculation. In some years they had made money, but in others they had found it impossible to sell except at a loss for five months out of the twelve. Of late, times had become harder. Sometimes the market had been low; sometimes they could not get cars for their crude oil when they needed it most.

"There is a good chance to get out," said Norris. "Warden, Frew & Company are willing to buy the plant. They will pay us as much as we have put into it." William and he debated the matter thoroughly. "Do you really think we had better sell?" demanded William. "Or shall we fight it out?"

"I think we had better sell," decided the brother. "We shall get our investment back, and that is better than a heavy loss later on."[1]

This scene, in its essentials, might have been duplicated forty times over during the years 1875–78, in offices in Baltimore and Titusville, New York and Pittsburgh, Marietta and Oil City.

[1]*House Trust Investigation, 1888*, pp. 223 ff.

II

Tweedledum and Tweedledee—such was the relationship between the Standard Oil Company and the Central Association of Refiners. Perhaps at the outset some real distinction existed. The Pittsburgh press reported in the spring of 1875 that refiners there had gone into the Association conditionally, retaining the right to buy crude oil and sell the product as they pleased, and to ship over any route they chose.[2] If this were true, they kept their identity and a certain measure of independence. But as time passed the company and the Association became more and more nearly the same entity under different names, an approach to the same goal of consolidation by slightly different roads. Miss Tarbell remarks that the Central Association was "a clever device" which "furnished the secret partners of Mr. Rockefeller a plausible proposition with which to approach the firms of which they wished to obtain control."[3] This is correct. While the Standard Oil men were seldom really at a loss for an approach to an outside establishment, they could go to a firm which objected to an outright merger, and propose that it enter the Association tentatively by a one-year lease. Such firms could thus be brought into the combination by two steps instead of one.

S. C. T. Dodd, later attorney for the Standard, in his book on trusts describes the two organizations as at first coterminous, and finally identical.[4] He remarks that the Central Association was "a union not of corporations but their stockholders." So was the Standard Oil combination, the heads of which held the stock of acquired companies as trustees. Companies in the Association "ceased to be competitive in the sense of striving to undersell each other." So did companies in the Standard organization. "They continued to be competitive in the sense that each strove to show . . . the best results in making the best products at low cost." So did the Standard companies. Finally, writes Dodd, "the combination of refiners above referred to . . . came to be known as the Standard."

It was in accordance with a careful plan that the Standard Oil of Ohio increased its capitalization from $2,500,000 to $3,500,000 in the

[2]Pittsburgh *Gazette,* May 12, 1875.
[3]Tarbell, *Standard Oil Company,* I, 149.
[4]S. C. T. Dodd, *Combinations.*

same month, March, 1875, that the formation of the Central Association was announced.[5] These steps were the two vital preliminaries to an attack along all fronts to bring in the remaining independents. The campaign was led in the various districts by the ablest lieutenants of the Standard, composing the executive committee of the Association. In Pittsburgh, Charles Lockhart incorporated the Standard Oil of that city, and began buying, merging with, or leasing the independent plants. In Philadelphia Warden was the leader, organizing his conquests under the Atlantic Refining Company. In New York and New England, Charles Pratt and H. H. Rogers took charge of a similar campaign. All along the Allegheny Valley, John D. Archbold served as field marshal, his Acme Oil Company swallowing up refinery after refinery. Planning and co-ordinating the whole effort, tirelessly busy and ceaselessly alert to every opening, Rockefeller acted as generalissimo.

Since the plans were laid with shrewdness, the timing was perfect, and the field commanders were men of rare talents, success came swiftly. The campaign was maintained until the Standard had practically swept the board. By 1879 Rockefeller had achieved the substantial monopoly of which he had long dreamed. He ruled the empire of oil as Napoleon ruled Europe after Austerlitz—and there was no Wellington on the horizon. The grand result was summed up by H. H. Rogers in 1879. Testifying before the Hepburn Committee, he declared that from 90 to 95 per cent of the refiners of the country were working with the Standard Oil, and that those not in harmony comprised "most everybody who has a private grievance."[6]

In Philadelphia the enthusiastic Warden succeeded in absorbing thirteen companies before the end of 1877. We know the names of a few owners—W. King & Company; Stewart, Matthews & Pennington; W. L. Elkins; N. W. Hawkins. His procedure was de-

---

[5]Taylor, MS History of the Standard Oil Company, 26.

[6]*Hepburn Committee Hearings*, III, 2615. Rogers explained why Pratt & Co. went into the Standard Oil combination: "The competition was always very sharp, and there was always somebody that was willing to sell goods for less than they cost, and that made the price for everything."

It was from this period that there dated an oft-told and doubtless apocryphal story of Rockefeller's statement at a meeting of the Standard Oil executives: "Gentlemen, our figures show that 93 per cent of the American refining industry is now in our hands. But let us not think of this 93 per cent. Let us concentrate our attention upon the remaining 7 per cent!"

scribed by Henry L. Davis, a refiner who became one of his officers, as simple. He and the independent refiner first agreed on terms,
the property was then appraised by representatives of the owner and
the Atlantic Refining Company, and payment was made in cash or
stock. Here and elsewhere, the rule was to exact of sellers an explicit
covenant that they would not re-engage in refining. A number of
former independents, such as Malcolm Lloyd (cousin of Henry
Demarest Lloyd) and Norris Harkness, became officers of the Atlantic. As this Philadelphia unit of the Standard grew, its profits increased. They had been considerable before it joined the Standard,
showing net returns in one year of $132,000 on a capitalization of
$400,000, but now they became magnificent.[7] Only two or three
competitors were left in the Philadelphia district.

In the New York area Pratt and Rogers were not so rapidly successful. In 1876 James Donald & Co. sold a half interest in their extensive Locust Hill refinery on Newtown Creek to the Standard, and
gave a lease of the remaining interest for five years. The works were
carried on for the Standard under Donald's name. Long before the
lease expired the remaining half-interest was purchased, but members of the old company left $100,000 in the business, and its name
was retained for some years. Not until the spring of 1879 were other
important purchases effected. On April 1 George F. Gregory sold a
three-quarters interest in his Vesta Oil Works in Brooklyn for
$75,000, the business being carried on by a new partnership bearing
Gregory's name. Archbold and Rogers acted as trustees for the Acme
Oil Co., the Standard unit which was the real purchaser, and within
a short time the outstanding one-fourth interest was also acquired.
On April 7 Wilson & Anderson sold to Archbold and Rogers, again
acting for the Acme, a three-quarters interest in the Greenpoint Oil
Works. Once more the two men executed a declaration of trust to the
Acme for their share. A similar arrangement was made in the acqui-
sition of the Washington Oil Works, also on Newtown Creek.[8] But
several fairly vigorous New York firms remained independent—
Denslow & Bush, Sone & Fleming, and most stubborn of all, Lombard, Ayres & Co.[9]

[7] Atlantic Refining Company; Minute Book.
[8] Taylor, MS History of the Standard Oil, 43 ff.
[9] *The Railway World,* June 7, 1877, lists these firms and also Andrews &
Morgan of Buffalo.

Until late in the seventies the Standard had no interests in New England. But in the spring of 1878 it acquired controlling shares in Pierce & Canterbury, in Stephen Jannay & Co., and in T. H. Whittemore, all conducting refineries in Boston. The purchaser in each instance was Charles Pratt & Co., which made out a declaration of trust in favor of the Standard. In precisely the same way a half-interest was obtained in the Portland Kerosene Oil Company, which carried on both a refining and marketing business in Portland.[10]

Meanwhile, in the Regions Archbold was quietly but inexorably buying out almost the last of the remaining independents. He himself had received 375 shares of Standard stock, worth more than $100,000, and a directorship. His own Porter, Moreland plant was rechristened Acme No. 1, and the Bennett, Warner plant became Acme No. 2. In 1876 the John Jackson Refinery and the Octave Oil Company plant in Titusville were bought and merged to make Acme No. 3. That same year the Easterly & Davis works in Titusville became Acme No. 4. By 1878 only one independent refinery of importance remained in the valley, the Keystone of Titusville. The Acme practically completed its conquest by buying this plant on June 20, 1879, Archbold making his elder brother Charles the manager. Thereafter the Acme and Imperial controlled the entire field. "They wiped out the whole of the independent element," bitterly remarked Lewis Emery, Jr.[11] Archbold phrased it more crisply and impudently when he later told an investigating committee that all the competitors "retired from the business gloriously."[12]

As to the prices paid in the Regions we have a few illuminating details. For one plant the Standard gave $150,000, but this was unique, the others fetching from a few hundreds to $40,000. "In the great majority of cases," writes Taylor, "the prices paid were very small."[13] Yet some sellers found that they had considerable amounts in hand, for tales of the bad investments which they made with the money became common in the Regions. Archbold assured the Hepburn Committee that in every bargain he enjoyed "the free will of the sellers," and paid "full value"—"I can state this from a knowledge that is as positive as can be, because I myself made all the trans-

[10]Taylor, MS History of the Standard Oil, 38, 44, 45.
[11]*House Trust Investigation, 1888*, p. 232.
[12]Commonwealth of Pennsylvania vs. Standard Oil **Company.**
[13]*Op. cit.,* 41.

actions." Even his critics admitted that complaints were but few and mild. A fairly typical transaction, perhaps, was the purchase of the Pickering Chambers & Co. refinery. T. P. Chambers rejected Archbold's original offer in the hope that he could pull through, but then as bankruptcy loomed up, he reconsidered and accepted. His first hostility to the Standard soon evaporated, and he concluded that he had benefited by the sale. "I always thought well of the bridge which carried me over," he later remarked.[14] In general, the men expressing the most bitterness were the tiny operators who insisted that their refineries would have flourished like Jonah's gourd and made them all rich had it not been for the chilling frost of the Standard.

Most interesting of all was the conquest of Pittsburgh, which had once aspired to lordship in refining. Its industry had never escaped from the constricting grip of the Pennsylvania Railroad. We have explained that this line did not care to haul much Pittsburgh oil east because it was interested in through traffic, and because its rails were busy almost to capacity anyway.[15] But it would not even take kerosene west on fair terms. Again and again in 1873 the Pittsburgh press complained that cars were not furnished to shippers, or were needlessly delayed after they started. Refined oil was nearly a month in reaching St. Louis, grumbled *The Gazette,* and orders were going to Cleveland in consequence.[16] Six months later it reiterated the complaint. "Thus far few Western orders have been received, and it is attributable to the fact that Cleveland has cheaper freight."[17] Another year passed, and the story was the same. "If the railroads would put freights on a basis that would enable our refineries to compete successfully with other points, they would have no difficulty in finding a market West and South for a good deal of their products, but as it stands we have little or no show for Western or Southern trade."[18] For refineries the sole means of escape from the Pennsylvania's mortal grip lay in shipment over the Connellsville branch of the Baltimore & Ohio, and this was of dubious utility.

August H. Tack, who entered refining in Pittsburgh in 1869, gave some testimony before the Federal investigators of trusts in 1888

[14]Moore, *Life of John D. Archbold,* 114.
[15]The Hepburn Investigation showed that in March, 1878, the rate on grain from Chicago to Pittsburgh was 25 cents a cwt., and from Chicago to New York 15 cents. William Larrabee, *The Railroad Question,* 146.
[16]Jan. 31, 1873.   [17]Aug. 20, 1873.   [18]Sept. 16, 1874.

which might have been paralleled by many others.[19] At the outset, believing that Pittsburgh had the cheapest labor, coal, barrels, and transportation facilities, he had felt a roseate certainty of success. He installed the latest machinery, and manufactured every product then known, including paraffin; he burned his residuum under the boilers; nothing was wasted. For three years he prospered, but what then? "We began to feel the squeeze in 1872, began to feel that the cords were drawing tight on us. Our prospects were looking pretty blue." With other hard-hit refiners, he looked about for remedies. The cruelly high rates of the Pennsylvania were clearly responsible. They began holding meetings, selecting delegations, and travelling to Philadelphia to plead with Tom Scott; "meeting after meeting and delegation after delegation." But they got nothing save excuses, denials, or evasions, and finally became hopeless. Meanwhile their losses, which according to Tack sometimes reached $2.75 or $3.00 a barrel, continued to mount. Facing imminent ruin, many of the refiners tried to retrieve their position by gambling on the oil market. They would buy large quantities of raw material before they were sure of a customer, or if prices seemed to be advancing, sell the refined oil before they bought the crude. Sometimes they made a small profit, but the final result of the year's labor was almost invariably a loss. In 1874 Tack, half heartbroken, found himself insolvent.

Reading his graphic testimony, we can understand how much sorrow and suffering were wrapped up in the statement made by the Pittsburgh *Gazette* on February 22, 1875, that "not over one-fourth of our refining capacity is now in operation. . . . Unless relief of some kind is afforded, the refining trade of Pittsburgh will, it is thought by some of our most sagacious operators, soon be a thing of the past. The case is becoming desperate." We can understand why the debate among refiners over joining the new Central Refiners' Association raged furiously that spring, and why feeling became bitter. Little more than half as much crude oil was shipped into the city during the first half of the year as in the similar period in 1873, or 1874. Nothing but faint hopes could be pinned to the Baltimore & Ohio, for Baltimore lacked good export equipment or connections. It is conceivable that Pittsburgh interests of great determination, skill, and financial resource could have helped the Columbia Conduit Company

[19]*House Trust Investigation, 1888*, pp. 212–222.

and the barges to bring in large quantities of crude oil, and could have developed Baltimore into a great export outlet for kerosene and naphtha. But the city's refiners did not possess sufficient force or ingenuity, and were rapidly weakened.

In their extremity, they surrendered one by one to the local branch of the great combination, Lockhart's Standard Oil of Pittsburgh. The directors of this company included Warden, William Frew, David Bushnell, and Henry M. Flagler. Many who sold out to it, as to the Acme and the Atlantic Companies, did not know that they were dealing with the Leviathan. The once-rich firm of Waring Brothers was among the first. They owned the great Vesta, Cosmos, and Star works, credited with a capacity of more than 20,000 barrels of crude oil a week.[20] At the beginning of 1875 they were struggling with heavy financial embarrassments, and a disastrous fire sealed their fate.[21] By the end of 1877, according to testimony which Frew gave two years later, the conquest of Pittsburgh was substantially complete, only a few small independents surviving. Here, as in the Regions and Philadelphia, some works were dismantled, some were combined, and some were kept running as before.[22]

And what were the terms of these sales, mergers, and leases in Pittsburgh, Philadelphia, and other cities? Were they generous or harsh, fair or unfair? It seems now impossible to answer these questions. When William Harkness testified in Washington, he indicated that the arrangement made with his company was amicable, and the purchase price adequate. Tack was not so enlightening. He declared that in 1874, with ruin from Pennsylvania's exactions staring him in the face, he had gone to Rockefeller. Their interview had been brief. "He said there was no hope for us at all. He remarked this—I cannot give the exact quotation—'There is no hope for us,' and probably he said, 'There is no hope for any of us'; but he says, 'The weakest must go first.'" When Tack's refinery, in which he had invested about $300,000, went bankrupt, his partners bought it at public sale, and later leased it to the Standard; but he did not say whether the figure seemed just or unjust.

Numerous independents later testified in successive government

[20]*House Trust Investigation, 1888*, p. 234.
[21]Pittsburgh *Gazette*, Jan. 9, 14, 1875.
[22]See George S. Davison, "The Petroleum Industry," *Greater Pittsburgh*, Vol. VIII, No. 48 (March 26, 1927).

investigations that during these years 1875–78 they had been forced to sell by unfair pressure of various kinds. They asserted that they could not get rates which enabled them to compete with Standard Oil refineries, that the pipe lines gave them poor oil, and that freight agents were dilatory in furnishing cars. They said that railroad officials discouraged them from competing. Above all, they declared that, when they finally sold, their properties had been undervalued.

But other witnesses—railroad officers, Standard executives, and former independents who had gone into the company—denied these allegations. Their testimony was similar to the defense made by the Standard leaders after the Cleveland acquisitions of 1872. They asserted that the independent refineries had really been tottering because of bad management and inadequate facilities, that some had actually obtained larger rebates than the Standard, and that their properties had been fairly appraised. Indeed, Standard officials argued that many of them had been lucky to sell out instead of going bankrupt. John D. Archbold always contended that as an independent he had received just as large rebates as the Standard obtained, while similar testimony was given by Malcolm Lloyd, and a little later by John L. McKinney. Lloyd vehemently asserted that he had merged with the Atlantic Refining Co. on his own initiative; that he went to their offices, made his own arrangements, and was treated generously in the terms of the sale. He soon formed a strong conviction that business in America would require ever greater capital. Even Rockefeller's enemies admitted that the acquisitions were made by persuasion whenever possible.[23]

Naturally, some of the sharpest criticism of the mergers was based upon the secrecy surrounding them. The failure of men like Warden, Lockhart, and Archbold to make it clear that they had become partners in the combination; their refusal to explain that such companies as the Acme and Atlantic were arms of the Standard organization; the retention of the old firm names for small refineries after they had been bought up lock, stock, and barrel—this looked like sheer deception. To be sure, a technical ground existed for denials of iden-

[23]Tarbell, *Standard Oil Company,* I, 154. Doctor Edwin F. Gay told me, Nov. 17, 1937, that he had conversed with McKinney. The latter told him that after merging his business with the Standard he went over the Standard's records to see what their rebates had been. To his surprise he found them less than his own.

tity with the Standard Oil of Ohio, for that company could not legally hold property outside the State. But the policy of concealing the Standard's acquisitions was one which Rockefeller deliberately formulated. He believed that changes were more effective when quietly made, and that they were no business of the general public; they might be the business of the oil trade, but then the news soon leaked out in trade circles. Even if deception occurred, he does not seem to have regarded it as reprehensible.[24] In this he was emphatically wrong, and he is not excused by the fact that a similar secrecy was widely practised by other business organizations of the day. The concealment of these purchases was one of the blots on his business record.

III

Meanwhile, the Standard was strengthening its hold upon the business of purchasing and shipping crude oil from the Regions. In February, 1875, Adnah Neyhart, the well-known shipper whose skill in getting rebates from the Erie we have described, died.[25] For some time he had been so ill that W. T. Scheide had carried on the business for him. As the Standard's consumption of oil increased, its buyers, led by Bostwick & Co., naturally took a larger and larger share of the trade; and it soon appeared that the Standard wished to eliminate the Neyhart organization completely. It was altogether too useful to independent refineries. Scheide told the Hepburn Committee in 1879 that he suspected Rockefeller of laboring personally to this end, because he frequently met him in the Erie offices. However this may be, good evidence does exist that the Standard was attempting to squeeze Neyhart out, and that it offered the Erie ample car-loadings at a freight rate which it promised to increase by five cents a barrel if the railroad would give it exclusive control over shipments in crude oil. At this time the information upon competitive shipments which the Standard gained through its lease of the Weehawken oil terminal

[24]Inglis, Conversations with Rockefeller. Rockefeller said: "It is also to be remembered that the Standard Oil Company was a corporation organized under the laws of the State of Ohio, with limitations as to the ownership of property, confined wholly or largely to the State of Ohio. The Standard Oil Company did not buy Charles Pratt & Company; Warden, Frew & Company; Lockhart & Frew, and others in the State of Pennsylvania and the State of New York."

[25]Boyle, *Derrick's Handbook,* 240.

may really have had a sinister usefulness. To its credit, the Erie refused the Standard's proposal and continued carrying oil for other shippers.[26]

But what worried Scheide just as much as the Standard's machinations were the shady business practices of certain independent refineries in New York. He found that these firms, expecting shortly to sell to the Standard, were using him to screw higher prices out of it. They would assure H. H. Rogers that since the good Scheide had promised them steady supplies of crude, they meant to continue running; and thus they "would go around bidding up the price of their works on the Standard Oil Company." At the same time, they would tell Scheide that Bostwick & Co. were offering them crude oil at lower prices than his. One such independent refinery actually made a contract to buy oil from Scheide, and then broke it for 1/128th of a cent a gallon! Evidently squeeze tactics were being used all around. Utterly disgusted, Scheide resolved to abandon the field, although the Erie urged him to hold on. Probably the settlement of Neyhart's estate helped to render a sale desirable. In the spring of 1875 he sold the shipping business to Charles Pratt & Co., joyously ignorant of the fact that this house had just become part of the Standard organization![27] At the same time, the Neyhart & Grandon pipe lines were incorporated in the Tidioute & Titusville Pipe-Lines, part of the stock of which was held by the Neyhart estate, and part by the Standard's subsidiary, the United Pipe-Lines.[28]

The Standard Oil thus disposed of one of its principal competitors in buying and selling crude oil, and materially increased its pipe-line mileage. These were valuable acquisitions. The refiners who had depended upon Neyhart for raw materials now had to come to the Standard for their supplies, and were thus placed in a cruelly dependent position. Only three years earlier, in 1872, the Standard had been deprived of crude oil by a hostile combination, and forced to take the terms offered it. Now it was not only safe against any such embargo, but was in a position in which it could at will cut off the flow of vital supplies to some of its few remaining competitors.

Several small independent pipe lines were picked up by the Standard during 1875–76. The time was soon ripe for a consolidation of its

[26]Scheide's testimony is in the *Hepburn Committee Hearings,* III, 2758 ff.
[27]*Idem.*   [28]Taylor, MS History of the Standard Oil Company, 31, 32.

entire network, and early in 1877 a new company under an old name, the United Pipe-Lines, was incorporated with a capital of $3,000,000. The properties of the American Transfer Company, the old United, and various lesser lines were merged in it. The Standard shortly acquired a heavy majority of the stock and exercised absolute control, though Amasa Stone and W. H. Vanderbilt held nearly a thousand shares each.[29] Only one strong pipe-line system remained as a rival, that of the Empire Transportation Company; and Potts and Tom Scott realized with deep alarm that this was practically surrounded, and in a highly vulnerable position.

IV

Thus the East was fairly conquered, and the Standard, after a series of brilliantly successful moves, reigned all but supreme in the territory of three great trunk-line railroads, the New York Central, Erie, and Pennsylvania. Only one more stroke was required to round out its domain.

A careful study of the map showed Rockefeller that his position was vulnerable in just one quarter. He possessed no hold whatever on the broad territory of a fourth trunk line, the Baltimore & Ohio; invincible on the west, north, and east, he had a southern flank which was badly exposed. Not a little oil was being produced in West Virginia, where the Marietta-Parkersburg area had been opened immediately after Drake's discovery, and had since maintained a steady flow.[30] Running roughly parallel with the other three trunk lines, the Baltimore & Ohio extended from Chesapeake Bay to St. Louis and Chicago. Already it carried to the seaboard the kerosene of numerous small refineries which had sprung up between Parkersburg and Wheeling on the Ohio. While their daily production was not impressive, it was sufficient to affect prices, and it might grow. Moreover, President Garrett was making a determined effort to divert a great part of the Pittsburgh output to Baltimore, and early in 1875 was meeting with real success. He had reached the smoky city at the head of the Ohio River by the Pittsburgh & Connellsville branch,

---

[29]*Idem*, 31.

[30]West Virginia wells produced daily between 500 and 600 barrels of oil usable for refining, with which for good results approximately an equal quantity of Pennsylvania oil had to be mixed. J. N. Camden to Rockefeller, Jan. 1, 1878; Camden Papers.

and had there formed an alliance with the Columbia Conduit Company, whose officers detested both the Pennsylvania Railroad and the Standard. This Columbia Conduit oil helped to nourish a number of Baltimore refineries, striving desperately to build up an export trade. Figures were laid before the alarmed Board of Trade in Philadelphia to show that in the first three weeks of 1875 that city's exports of oil had fallen, as compared with the same period in 1874, from 94,561 to 33,550 barrels, while Baltimore's exports had risen from 3315 to 37,331 barrels.[31] Thus far Garrett had shown a stern independence. He had refused to enter into any arrangement with the other trunk lines, had evinced a strong hostility toward the Standard combination, and had stood staunchly by the small refineries along his route.

To meet the alliance of Garrett and the Columbia Conduit, to make sure of his grip on Pittsburgh, and to protect himself from the guerrilla fire of the little Ohio River refineries, Rockefeller turned his attention southward. His plan of campaign, identical with that he had used so successfully elsewhere, was to enlist the strongest leader in the doubtful sector, and arrange a series of mergers. His choice fell upon Johnson Newlon Camden of Parkersburg, well known as a lawyer, Democratic politician, unsuccessful candidate for governor and senator, and head of a refining company. Camden was blunt, hardheaded, and sincere, with a talent for political and business manipulation.[32] When 1875 opened, his refinery was not doing well. It was necessary to mix Pennsylvania crude with his lighter West Virginia oils, and this was expensive; while the new railroad rates had driven him out of virtually all Eastern markets except Baltimore.[33] He knew that the Standard Oil was planning a huge consolidation which would dominate the industry. Its wealth and power had impressed him, he admired the capacity of its leaders, and he was ready to listen to Rockefeller's proposals. Indeed, one plausible story relates that he made the first advances. It is said that in the spring of 1875 he and his partners sat gloomily around their Parkersburg table, wondering how to stave off their creditors, and finally decided to plead bankruptcy; but before the papers could be signed Camden

[31]N. Y. *Tribune,* Feb. 6, 1875.
[32]Festus P. Summers, *Johnson Newlon Camden. A Study in Individualism,* 115–140.
[33]*Idem,* 168, 169.

disappeared. A few days later he turned up, flourishing a contract with the Standard Oil before his delighted associates.[34]

It is certain that Rockefeller and he met early in the spring of 1875, and concluded a far-reaching agreement. J. N. Camden & Co., under a pledge of secrecy, transferred their refinery to the Standard Oil for a certain amount of stock. They were to continue managing the plant, and in addition to work toward a goal which the agreement clearly defined—the consolidation of the refining industry in all the Baltimore & Ohio territory east of Cincinnati and south of Pittsburgh. While Camden and his partners promised to co-operate closely with the officers of the Standard, they were allowed a wide discretion in their methods. The first result of this compact was the appearance of a corporation called the Camden Consolidated Oil Co., with a capital of $200,000. Not even the alert officers of the Baltimore & Ohio realized that this new company cloaked a transfer to the Standard Oil. "Mr. Garrett . . . is coming out to see us tomorrow," Camden wrote Colonel Payne in May, 1875, adding humorously, "I suppose he will encourage us to keep up our oil business and fight the 'combination.' "[35] The next achievement, carried out in the summer of 1875, was the company's quiet absorption of three Parkersburg competitors. And the third result was the opening of negotiations with the Baltimore & Ohio for special rates and preferences!

These negotiations proved entirely successful. On July 21, 1875, Camden sent Colonel Payne the gratifying news that the Baltimore & Ohio had granted his company a rate on crude oil from Pennsylvania to Parkersburg, and on refined oil from Parkersburg to Baltimore, which would enable him to undersell the Pittsburgh independents in the Baltimore market. That is, the charges for routing oil to the sea through the Parkersburg refinery were to be less than for routing it to the sea through the independent Pittsburgh plants. The Baltimore & Ohio still hugged the delusion that the Camden Consolidated Oil stood outside the Standard combination, for it made its rate concessions on condition that Camden should take his Pennsylvania oil from the Columbia Conduit Company alone.[36] It is impossible to acquit the Standard of the most flagrant deception in this matter. The arrangement, effective in October, was of course a heavy new weapon against the much-afflicted independents of Pittsburgh.

[34]*Idem*, 172, 173.   [35]*Idem*, 175.   [36]*Idem*, 176–179.

Rendering their position more untenable than ever, it doubtless had a great deal to do with the final sales and leases to the Standard. And meanwhile, Camden was making plans to extinguish the remaining independents of Parkersburg and Marietta.

The correspondence between Camden and the heads of the Standard shows that they immediately adopted a weird cipher, took other elaborate precautions to maintain secrecy, and made all their arrangements with an eye to the grand strategy of the combination. Relations were established with a Baltimore & Ohio official named Guilford, who treacherously sent Camden confidential information. When he wrote some letters in the autumn of 1875 which showed that the railroad had become uneasy, and that Garrett was now suspicious that the Standard was "trying to kill off Pittsburgh refiners" and with them the oil business of the Baltimore & Ohio, Camden urged Rockefeller do something to allay their fears.[37] A few months later Camden wrote: "I have no ambition in oil outside of Morose [Standard Oil], I want to see it the success it should be, nothing more—and by holding Pittsburgh well in hand, Maslin [Camden Consolidated Oil] will become a favorite, as the youngest progeny ought to be."[38] Early in 1876 he suggested to Colonel Payne a new method for bringing the last stubborn Pittsburgh independents to book. Let the Standard corner the barrel supply![39]

There is a section of country extending from the Big Kanawha to the Big Sandy River, including Coal and Guyandotte Rivers, that contains an almost unlimited amount of stave timber and a present production of five or six million a year or perhaps more—these staves we don't need at Parkersburg and they go to Cin[cinnati] and Pittsburgh or find a market whenever they can, but usually go in the direction of Cin and are sold there at low prices, and whenever bbls. are in demand at Pittsbg. the Cin Cooperage establishments push into Pittsbg on coal Barges returning empty at a cost of 10 to 20 cents—and the Pittsbg stave dealers also go down to that section to buy cheap staves for Pittsbg but usually not to any great extent.

It seems to me that we can to a great extent control the *oil business* of Pittsburgh by controlling their supply of *staves & bbls.* Pittsbg's resources in that respect are very limited there is very little capital in the cooperage business there, and no supplies kept on hand. So that when an active

[37]Camden Papers, Nov. 20, 1875.
[38]*Idem,* Camden to Flagler, Jan. 3, 1876.
[39]*Idem,* Camden to Oliver H. Payne, Feb. 18, 1876.

demand springs up they can be had only at ruinously high prices—this has been the case in the past, and we can make it more so in the future.

Another strategic blow which Camden urged was the absorption of the well-known Cincinnati oil distributors, Alexander McDonald & Co. They were able and influential:[40]

I think that if it was desirable to do so, we could controll all the oil from this section through them, and this would generally give us controll of prices in Cin market, for instance, last winter when oil was worth from 27 to 34 cents, the little outside refiners begged McD to take their oil at from 5 to 6 cents less than the market, when it was our interest perhaps to have it out of the way. But it was *not* our interest while paying McD a cent a gallon to handle our oil to let him take in that oil, to displace the sale of that amount of oil for us, at a profit of $2 to $3 per bbl. to himself. And so at the present time if McD was acting for us he could serve our purpose well by buying up the cheap oil now pressing on his market at from 1 to 2 cents less than cost of production. . . .
Cincinnati as you know is the receptacle of all the outside "guerilla" oil that goes West, except a sprinkling at Indianapolis, and from that point effects more or less other markets. What I have written has looked to the manipulating and controlling that oil at the proper time to our advantage.

And a letter to Ambrose McGregor indicates that very direct and brutal pressure was sometimes used on stubborn independents:[41]

Yours 25th inst. recd. When last in New York I had an interview with Mr. Pratt in relation to the Paraffine Works in Baltimore. Our conclusion then was to try to make the parties sick and get them in shape for a satisfactory arrangement. I think that since that time the business has turned on their stomachs and they would like to make arrangements. I think they prefer selling the works to making any other arrangements, as I have been approached confidentially with a proposition to take an interest in their works.

In view of these and similar letters, it is not astonishing to learn that long before the end of 1877 substantially all of the Maryland refineries had fallen into the hands of the Standard. Camden began by negotiating for the purchase of G. West & Son, a Baltimore firm that not only manufactured kerosene but also marketed it on a large scale in the Maryland-Virginia area, including Washington.[42] An

[40]*Idem,* Camden to O. H. Payne, March 20, 1877.
[41]*Idem,* Camden to Ambrose McGregor, Oct. 1, 1878.
[42]Taylor, MS History of the Standard Oil Company, 37, 38.

agreement was drawn up providing that the West Refining Company should become the arm of the Standard in Baltimore, and should take steps, with full Standard support, to control the entire refining business of the city.[43] Camden offered to give $60,000 for the refinery, and pay salaries totalling $10,000 a year to West and his son. When they demanded $25,000 a year he dropped the negotiations, writing Flagler that he intended to stand firm until "they become very sick." Turning to the Merritt refinery, early in 1877 he completed its purchase. Other plants were bought out, and finally the Wests gave way. The result was the organization this year of the Baltimore United Oil Company, which swallowed up nine Maryland refineries almost at a gulp.[44] Camden was made head of the company, and W. C. West vice-president. Most of the stock was issued to Camden as a trustee representing the Standard Oil, while a small minority was divided among men who had owned plants in the city. Once more it is impossible to say whether the payments were fair or unfair.

In Parkersburg and Marietta the Camden Consolidated Oil Company meanwhile bought up whatever independent refineries it could, and squeezed out those which refused to sell. This was done by purchasing large quantities of the West Virginia and Ohio crude on which they depended, and holding it out of the market. The independents, who had not enough capital to bring in much oil from Pittsburgh, were at the mercy of the local supply. When this was shut off in the summer of 1876 many reluctantly yielded.[45] But they were in no mood to observe their agreements not to begin refining again, and some of them surreptitiously used their purchase money to set up new refineries. Camden wrote in August that he was disgusted with affairs in his area: "It is so full of debris, both of *men* and old refining traps, that it will be as hard to keep down as weeds in a garden. The object of the whole crew of broken-down oil men is to pension themselves upon us, and to take them all in would clean us out like grasshoppers." Yet he assured the Cleveland office that he realized that it wanted guerrilla warfare suppressed, "and [I] will protect your flank this fall in the most practicable way. . . ."[46]

It was no use, Camden decided, to try to buy out the independents

---

[43]Summers, *Camden*, 185, 186.
[44]*Idem*, 186, 187; N. Y. *World*, Dec. 15, 1877.
[45]*Idem*, 181.   [46]*Idem*, 181, 182.

as fast as they bobbed up. "Dozens that have been hanging on the ragged edge are trying to get something in which to boil oils," he informed Rockefeller in October.[47] The true way to control the situation was to place a viselike grip on the West Virginia supply of crude oil. He wrote Rockefeller in November: "It is very difficult for you to understand this section—the number of persons hovering around in a small producing territory, and the facility with which persons of small means can rig up a *mongrel* lubricating and refining business. . . . There is no use trying to buy it and provide for the horde here, so long as we are keeping up this margin. . . . My theory is that in order to control the refining interests here, we must control the production in some shape." This was done. In 1877 we find him writing Rockefeller jubilantly:[48]

We have closed arrangements with the producers of West Va., so far as it can be done through their representative committee. The agreement is all drawn up, and meetings are appointed for tomorrow and next day, in the producing regions, for ratification and signatures. . . . The committee feel sanguine that it will be entered into unanimously by the producers. . . . The unanimity with which the Producers seem to regard this idea favorably is producing quite a stir among the small outside interests here, and I think it will be the means of enabling us to close the purchase this week of an outside refinery that has given us more trouble than all the other.

Of course the Baltimore United and the Camden Consolidated worked in the closest harmony. The former took care of practically all the refining and marketing between Chesapeake Bay and the Carolina border. The latter bought nearly all the West Virginia oil, refined it, guarded against the emergence of "guerrilla refineries" along the southern frontier, and marketed oil in many of the Ohio Valley cities. In this last work, it naturally kept in close touch with Alexander McDonald & Co., which the Standard duly purchased as Camden had advised, and with that other important cog in the Standard machine, Chess, Carley of Louisville. New channels of sale were rapidly opened into the heart of the South.

And what of that brave triumvirate of young Pennsylvanians who had been managing the Columbia Conduit Company? They made a courageous fight. One by one the independent refineries to which

[47]*Idem*, 183.   [48]Camden Papers, no date; probably early in 1877.

they had shipped oil sold out. Even the Baltimore & Ohio was lured into co-operation with the Standard. But they hung grimly on, and found still another resource. Byron D. Benson, the resourceful leader, made a friend of Collis P. Huntington, the principal builder and owner of the Chesapeake & Ohio Railroad. The two men closed an arrangement by which that line would transport crude oil from Huntington on the Ohio to Newport News. Bulk barges were chartered, the oil was floated southwest down the Ohio several hundred miles, and then shipped east to the coast over Huntington's line! The trio made substantial profits from this roundabout traffic.

But in the fall of 1877 the Standard stopped this competition too. Bringing upon Doctor Hostetter a pressure which we shall later describe, Rockefeller bought the Conduit Company from him for the staggering sum of $1,050,000—an amount explained by the fact that the Conduit controlled at least three refineries. It is pleasant to record that Hostetter paid $250,000 of this to Benson, McKelvy, and Hopkins for surrendering their lease.[49]

V

Once more, as after the absorptions of 1872 in Cleveland, Rockefeller and his aides were busied day and night with reorganization. It had to be carried out now upon a nationwide scale, and with a careful weighing of sectional advantages. Large responsibilities were given to men experienced with business in each sector—to Lockhart in Pittsburgh, Warden in Philadelphia, Archbold in the Regions, Pratt in New York, Camden in West Virginia; but the principal burden had to be shouldered by Rockefeller, Flagler, and Payne. Meetings were constantly held in Cleveland at which difficult issues were threshed out. One observer has recorded how easily Rockefeller dominated them:[50]

I have seen Mr. Rockefeller often at a meeting of the heads of the different departments of the Company, listening carefully to each one and not saying a word. Perhaps he would stretch out on a lounge and say: "I am a little tired, but go right on, gentlemen, for I know you want to reach a decision." He might close his eyes now and then; but he never missed

[49]Robert D. Benson, *History of the Tidewater Companies,* 9; W. F. Taylor, MS History of the Standard Oil, 32. The three Pittsburgh refineries known to have been controlled by the Columbia Conduit Company were the American, Citizens', and Miller's; Pittsburgh *Gazette,* Aug. 20, 1877.

[50]Inglis, Notes.

a point. He would go away without saying a word but good-bye. But next day when he came down he had digested the whole proposition and worked out the answer—and he always worked out the right answer.

In Pittsburgh a majority of the refineries bought by the Standard were dismantled, and their machinery was hauled away to other manufactories. The largest of the plants kept running were the well-known Brilliant works, formerly owned by Lockhart, Frew & Co.; the Vesta and Cosmos works, once the property of Waring Brothers; the American works, previously owned by Holdship & Irwin; and the Citizens' refinery.[51] Some smaller plants need not be listed. Since in the spring of 1875, as we have seen, only a third of the capacity of the Pittsburgh refineries had been in operation, the dismantling did not mean that many employees were discharged. In fact, more work was probably given on steadier terms than before. In Philadelphia the Atlantic Refining Co. was vastly expanded, its smoke rolling out over the Delaware in huge volumes while several small plants of from 1500 to 2000 barrels capacity a week were shut down. In the Regions, Rockefeller and his partners decided to concentrate nearly all their refining at Titusville and Oil City, though they manufactured lubricating oil at Franklin. The result of this policy was the dismantling in 1876–78 of large numbers of small refineries in Crawford and Venango Counties. Most of them, it seems safe to say, would shortly have gone out of business anyway. A roster compiled years later for the House Committee investigating trusts[52] showed that their weekly capacity varied for the most part between 150 and 1000 barrels.

Beyond doubt the dismantling was in many instances a bitter personal tragedy. Men who had put years of ambition and toil into their works watched them torn down with quivering lips, and drew sleeves across their eyes as they heard the axes at work. They loved every vat, every pipe that was so roughly scrapped or carted away. Whole communities in the Regions angrily resented the wiping out of the little refineries along the Allegheny and its tributaries, refineries which had struggled stoutly to the last. When they disappeared some valleys lost all their vitality. Throughout the sixties the Regions had tried bravely to believe they would become one of America's great manufacturing centers; they had boasted at the height

[51]*House Trust Investigation, 1888*, pp. 138, 139.   [52]*Idem*, 232, 233.

of the boom that they had 250 plants,[53] and now their hopes had borne only Dead Sea fruit. In Pittsburgh, men told each other bitterly that the Waring Brothers' refineries had cost $800,000, and that they had fallen to the Standard Oil for less than a tenth of that sum. No doubt these figures were exaggerated, while a bankrupt and fire-gutted manufactory always fares badly; but the story awoke a fierce indignation. Writers who have taken the Regions' point of view have quite naturally emphasized the widespread bitterness, the underlying anger.[54]

Yet there had been many bankruptcies and much dismantling of plants before the Standard loomed up as a giant. The list of ruined Pennsylvania refineries which we have just mentioned includes fourteen in Erie alone that were liquidated before the end of 1870.[55] Most of the 250 Regions plants of boom days had guttered out before the Standard entered the scene. Rockefeller sincerely believed that more men would have been injured by a continuance of unrestricted competition than were hurt by his purchases and leases. He took credit to himself and his associates, somewhat too smugly, for the consideration they had shown local feeling. "We proved by our acts that we were not crushing anybody or running over anybody. We did not try to confine all the refining to Cleveland, which was one of the things we were accused of contemplating, but we agreed to the continuance of refining at Boston, Philadelphia, Pittsburgh, and at Marietta, O. Perhaps in some cases this was not reconcilable with the utmost economy of production; yet we felt that consideration was due to local conditions, not only to the actual economy in refining oil but to the many homes that had been established near various refineries, to the families that had become attached to the various communities."[56]

[53]So Lewis Emery, Jr., said in *House Trust Investigation, 1888,* p. 230. The statement is to be taken with great reserve. But if even two-thirds true, it shows how grossly the refining industry was overexpanded.

[54]Tarbell, *Standard Oil Company,* I, 160.

[55]These works, with the dates of their failure, were the Wertz, 1864; Witter & Co., 1866; Kennedy & Co., 1867; Hammond, 1867; Boyer, 1868; Downing and Douglass, 1868; Ely & Co., 1870; Farwell, 1867; Boyce & Tennant, 1866; Everett & Bissell, 1866; Bannister, 1865; Wright & Co., 1865; V. M. Thompson, 1866. Every refinery center had a similar list. *House Trust Investigation, 1888,* pp. 232, 233. The idea that "crushing out" began with the Standard is somewhat naïve.

[56]Inglis, MS Biography, 198.

While the refineries acquired in 1874–75 were being co-ordinated
and systematized, Rockefeller seems to have taken pains to visit most
of them and to make suggestions for improvements. In talking with
men like Warden, Archbold, or Pratt, he lost no opportunity to emphasize the fact that he was a partner rather than a leader. "Don't
say that *I* ought to do this or that," he would exclaim. *"We* ought
to do it. Never forget that we are partners; whatever is done is for
the general good of all of us." But everywhere he carried his penetrating eyes and questioning mind. At Long Island City he inspected
a building in which refined oil was being packed for shipment
abroad. One employee has told us what happened:[57]

He watched a machine for filling the tin cans. One dozen cans stood on
a wooden platform beneath a dozen pipes. A man pulled a lever, and
each pipe discharged exactly five gallons of kerosene into a can. Still on a
wooden carrier, the dozen cans were pushed along to another machine,
wherein twelve tops were swiftly clamped fast on the cans. Thence they
were pushed to the last machine, in which just enough solder to fasten
and seal the lid was dropped on each can.
Mr. Rockefeller listened in silence while an expert told all about the
various machines used to save labor and time and expense in the process.
At last Mr. Rockefeller asked:
"How many drops of solder do you use on each can?"
"Forty."
"Have you ever tried thirty-eight? No? Would you mind having some
sealed with thirty-eight and let me know?"
Six or seven per cent of these cans leaked. Then thirty-nine drops were
tried. None leaked. It was tried with one hundred, five hundred, a thou-
sand cans. None leaked. Thereafter every can was sealed with thirty-
nine drops.

Another story, doubtless authentic, tells how a memorandum was
sent from Rockefeller's office to one refinery reading approximately
as follows: "Your March inventory showed 10,750 bungs on hand.
The report for April shows 20,000 new bungs bought, 24,000 bungs

[57]Inglis, Conversation with Orville T. Waring, 1919. At a later date Henry
C. Folger, who corroborated this story, was asked how much the drop of solder
had saved annually in the early seventies. After elaborate calculations he answered: "Saved nearly $2500." Rockefeller said that it saved $2500 the first
year; and as the export business doubled, quadrupled, and sextupled, the saving
accumulated into a fund of hundreds of thousands of dollars. Inglis, MS Biography, 251.

used, and 6,000 bungs on hand. What became of the other 750 bungs?"

Rockefeller grasped the great truth that inefficiency and waste are a form of dishonesty, a theft of wealth from a fund that might be used for the general good.

VI

Not less important than the new physical properties of the Standard were the new officers, some of whom were soon to become nationally famous. Various of these men, all products of a fiercely competitive business struggle, had glaring faults. In the long run it would have been better for the Standard and for Rockefeller's contemporaneous fame had one, H. H. Rogers, never entered the organization. But the leaders of refining in Pittsburgh, Philadelphia, and New York, when combined with the Cleveland leaders, constituted probably the ablest single group of executives in the history of American business. Rockefeller rightly placed a higher appraisal upon the energy, experience, and acumen which he had welded into a single effective force than upon the properties which he and others had united; for money could replace the plants, but such brains and enterprise could never be bought.

Of the group, Charles Pratt was outwardly the least interesting and inspiring, the most colorless. This Massachusetts Yankee, forty-five years of age in the autumn of 1875, had pushed his way up to a respected place in New York business by the routine virtues of industry, integrity, shrewdness, and courage. He lacked imagination or daring, and Rockefeller later commented frankly upon his limitations;[58] he seemed plodding and slow. But that he was really no commonplace man his career demonstrated. As a young clerk in the paint business in New York he had saved his money until in 1854 he was able to furnish part of the capital needed for founding Devoe & Reynolds, a house dealing in paints and oils. Two years after the war he was strong enough to establish his own refining company. One of the first men to perceive the rich possibilities of the export trade in kerosene, he had so developed Pratt's "Astral" that the brand remained well-known in Europe, Asia, and Africa, for years to come. Pratt was a taciturn, sagacious, conservative executive, whose steady

[58]Rockefeller added: "Mr. Pratt had shown ability as a good merchandiser." Inglis, *Conversations with Rockefeller.*

eyes and strong jaw under a short chin-beard suggested the stability that he brought into the councils of the Standard. He expected and received a strong personal loyalty from his employees, and as the years went on the Standard organization in New York was sometimes worried by a "Pratt clique." Like his chief, he was a devout Baptist and a generous giver to many philanthropies.[59]

Henry H. Rogers, Pratt's partner, was far more virile, magnetic, and commanding—a man, indeed, of electric personality and inexhaustible energy. Save Rockefeller himself, no member of the Standard group was to make so great an impression upon the public; for he possessed an adventurous and speculative temperament, he went into many enterprises, and in a half-dozen fields he made a spectacular record. A year younger than Rockefeller, he had fought his way up from an impoverished boyhood in Fairhaven, Mass., had wandered to the Oil Regions, had taken to refining, and after some initial successes, had become a valued associate of Pratt's. He was immensely attractive, immensely dashing, and immensely indifferent to codes. His keen mind, witty bonhomie, and alert physical presence made an instant impression upon every observer. He had much the striking outward appearance of Flagler, and even more vitality. His dark hair showed less of a mane, but his mustaches were longer, thicker, and more histrionic; his eyes flashed with more vivacity; and his speech was more vehement and picturesque. The moment he entered a roomful of men, they awoke to a keener sense of life—and some of them were likely in the end to be the poorer for it! In aggressive enterprises of every kind he was a natural leader. And a leader he immediately became in the Standard, where he first supervised its oil-purchasing, then directed its pipe lines, and finally became chairman of its manufacturing committee.

"Kaleidoscopic" was the word that observers applied to Rogers, and to realize its aptness a man had only to watch his handsome head for an hour at any business meeting, public investigation, or banquet. At one moment he was genial, talkative, and altogether delightful; the next he was frigid, sarcastic, bitter, and jeering. He passed in an instant from democratic cordiality to freezing hauteur, from beguiling kindness to blazing anger or cutting harshness—and

[59]On Pratt, see McLaurin, *Sketches in Crude Oil,* 365; Crum, *Romance of American Petroleum and Gas,* 329; Boyle, *Derrick's Handbook,* 928, 929.

each mood was natural. Like some finished actor, he could transform his expression in the twinkle of an eye. Within a few sentences his voice would run the gamut of hatred, politeness, utter indifference, affability, and plaintiveness. Wall Street called him "Hell Hound" Rogers, yet Mark Twain could write in all sincerity that he was a saint on earth. He paid for Helen Keller's education. He was a patron of the arts, and loved to be the brilliant center of an intellectual circle. With appealing sentiment, he spent large sums in adorning the seacoast town where he had toiled as newsboy and grocery clerk. Friends who knew him at his New York house or Fairhaven estate found him a prince of entertainers and an unmatchable raconteur. But everyday business acquaintances knew him as exacting, unsympathetic, and sharp; while his enemies dreaded him as a scheming, relentless, and tyrannical foe.[60]

In the Pittsburgh-Philadelphia group Lockhart was perhaps the most arresting figure, a granite rock of caution, hard sense, and resolution. All the canniness of his native Scotland had been distilled into his veins; he was austere, reticent, and almost dour. Rockefeller later spoke with delight of a sagacity as evident as his Scots accent— "one of the most experienced, self-contained, and self-controlled men in business." Reaching America as a lad of sixteen in 1836, he had begun as porter in a business house, saving his money as carefully as Andrew Carnegie. He soon entered business for himself, prospered, and was a merchant of means when in 1852 he first saw "rock oil." He began buying and selling it, with Samuel Kier as an early customer. It is said that he was the first man, just after Drake sank his well, to ship crude oil to England. The refining companies which he helped to establish in Pittsburgh developed steadily and safely. Rugged, forceful, and alert, he was an older and more broadly trained Ambrose McGregor—and everybody in the Standard knew that McGregor was worth his weight in gold. Lockhart was the senior member of the Standard group. His partnership in the combination always gave Rockefeller a sense of security, for he would be the first to sound a warning if any flaws developed in the organization.[61]

[60]*Dictionary of American Biography.* I have talked with many men who knew Rogers.
[61]Inglis, Conversations with Lockhart's sons.

Warden, as Rockefeller later remarked, was "a very different type." A big, genial man, with abundant mustaches and winged sideburns which gave him something of the appearance of Chester A. Arthur, he was the most frank, exuberant, and sanguine of the Standard leaders. The wild hopes which he had pinned to the South Improvement Company were an indication of his native optimism. Six feet two inches tall and powerfully built, he was full of energy, his mind incessantly active, his enterprising spirit delighting in movement. He had shown his mettle in the so-called Pittsburgh riots of 1860. Buchanan's Secretary of War, Floyd, had ordered some cannon shipped south from the Pittsburgh arsenal; whereupon a citizens' uprising, led by young Warden on horseback, had taken the guns off the flatcars and brought them back. The bold action was natural, for he was a strong Abolitionist. Once during a strike in some collieries which he owned he coolly carried a pay-sack on his saddlebows through a mob of hostile men. There was something volatile in his temperament; he had a keen sense of humor and a hearty laugh, and became very popular in Philadelphia (whither he removed in 1870), but flared up quickly when angered. As Rockefeller remarked, "he was effusive. He would sit up till two in the morning writing me a long letter." Yet, unlike the pleasure-loving Rogers, he was devoted to labor, and his sons testify that he "never knew anything but work—he never took any recreation." Some time he did allot to the Presbyterian Church, some to Negro philanthropies, but none to play. His broad spirit and active temperament prompted him to many activities, so that in Philadelphia he is even better remembered as founder and head of the United Gas Improvement Company, a great public-utilities concern, and as an active reformer in city politics, than as a partner in the Standard Oil.[62]

Yet to the Standard he gave himself with whole-souled energy. When its principal offices were removed to New York he went there two days a week, catching the seven o'clock train and frequently not returning before eleven at night. Lockhart and he had complementary talents, the one all shrewd caution, the other all hopeful enterprise. Rockefeller always liked the creative quality of Warden's enthusiasm. "They were progressive," he said of the Warden-

[62]Much information was kindly furnished the author by Mr. Clarence Warden and Mr. William G. Warden, Jr., sons of William G. Warden.

Lockhart-Frew combination, "and no sooner had they come in with us than they, and especially Mr. Warden, were among the most prolific in suggestion and urgency for progressive steps involving larger and larger outlays of money which, in common with our other progressive steps, brought us great prosperity."[63]

Warden, like Rockefeller, believed in constant expansion. Under his supervision, the Atlantic Refining Company was built up into one of the most efficient units the Standard had. Within a few years he undertook to buy a well-equipped refinery which Stephen B. Elkins, P. A. B. Widener, and others had built just below Philadelphia. The Standard's officers made two alternative offers, both based on their ability to refine oil at an extremely low rate; but being suspicious of a "squeeze," the Elkins, Widener group refused to believe that illuminants could be made so cheaply. They were invited to look at the Atlantic's books. Emerging with sober faces, they remarked: "If we had known that you were operating at such figures, we would never have gone into the oil business in the beginning!" —and the deal went through.[64] Orville T. Waring, another of the Pittsburgh-Philadelphia group, was a thin, ascetic-looking man, but energetic and direct. He was only thirty-five when he joined the Standard in 1876; two years later Rockefeller asked him to develop the manufacture and marketing of lubricants—and his success in that field is a striking page in Standard history.[65]

Of the Oil Regions men, Archbold was by far the most important to the Standard. It would be pleasant to say something of that romantic figure, J. J. Vandergrift, who began life as cabin-boy on an Ohio River steamboat, and became one of the most versatile industrialists in Pennsylvania.[66] But he soon left the Standard, while Archbold went forward to become its leader. The pale, boyish young man in 1876 weighed scarcely more than 130 pounds, and in repose wore the look of a shy, quiet student. But he was seldom in repose. A dynamo of energy, confidence, and good nature, his tongue bubbling with a wit that could be friendly or sarcastic, devastatingly frank with friends and ready to overwhelm enemies by his audacious attack, he seemed at twenty-six the master of any situation. One of

[63]Inglis, Conversations with Rockefeller.
[64]Allen T. Warden told me this incident.
[65]Crum, *Romance of American Petroleum and Gas*, 302.
[66]For Vandergrift see Boyle, *Derrick's Handbook*, 643–650.

his admirers compared his flexibility with an elephant's trunk: "He could with equal facility pick a needle from a pin-cushion, or throw an anvil across a street."[67] Already this son of an Ohio minister, left unprotected at ten by his father's death, and a clerk in a general store at fourteen, had gained a remarkable experience. At sixteen he was working in the Oil Regions; at eighteen he was member of a firm dealing in crude oil; at twenty-one he and some other partners had built a large refinery at Titusville. He had spent some time in New York selling the product of his own and other refineries. He knew all about well drilling and pumping, about the crude-oil trade, about refining, and about marketing; and what was more important, he knew how to deal with men, to organize a business or group of businesses, and to gauge industrial trends.

This young Napoleon of the Regions, brought up in a harsh school and taught sharpness in a pushing, aggressive, get-rich-quick atmosphere, lacked Rockefeller's scrupulous desire to be fair to all men. Impatient of restraints, when under pressure he disregarded equity and shaved legality close. He, Rogers, and O'Day were to be responsible for most of that malign business reputation which the Standard rapidly acquired after 1875. But his experience and quick insight were invaluable to the company. Moreover, his effervescent good nature and almost miraculous ingenuity made him extremely useful, now that the heads of the Standard were a large group, in reconciling divergent points of view. He was an admirable conciliator. On points of policy Warden, in his hearty, sanguine way, often differed from Charles Pratt. The cautious, analytical Lockhart and the impetuous, speculative Rogers were frequently in disagreement. Of course, Rockefeller was the undisputed master of the group, but Archbold had a special gift for maintaining harmony among them.[68]

It was a remarkably varied, thoroughly trained, and able group which now directed the Standard. Carnegie liked to compare his partners with Napoleon's marshals, but the heads of the great oil combination were a more gifted body—and far more devoted to their chief. No such feud as that between Frick and Carnegie ever marred the harmony of Rockefeller's circle. For all his deep reserve, Rockefeller had the talent to create a binding *esprit de corps*. About the

[67]Moore, *Life of John D. Archbold, passim.*
[68]*Idem;* see article in *Dictionary of American Biography.*

central group he built up a circle of lesser figures who also received a large responsibility. Daniel O'Day was one, and Joseph Seep another. Horace A. Hutchins of Cleveland, once an independent, who took charge of domestic marketing and held that position for thirty years, cannot be forgotten. Nor can Jabez A. Bostwick, who under Rogers supervised the buying of crude oil. He had spent some busy years in Covington and Lexington, Ky., as banker and trader, and showed a southern courtesy of manner, while as a devout Baptist he became known for his generous philanthropies. But he was a shrewd buyer on the oil exchanges, who did the Standard valuable service until in 1887 he turned to railroad management.[69]

Some distinct liabilities as well as gains were involved in this expansion of personnel. The Standard Oil combination had become a great oligarchy, with interests and leaders scattered all over the eastern map. Rockefeller was not a dictator in the organization, but simply *primus inter pares* in the Executive Committee that ruled it, the principal planner and co-ordinator. The burden now laid upon him was terrific, for he had to master and watch all parts of the great structure. After 1875 he spent nearly as much time in New York as in Cleveland. He would race through a morning's work in the Standard Block, catch the noon train, and wake up next morning as the Palisades gave way to the dingy, sprawling purlieus of Manhattan. Then, hurrying down to the comfortable Pearl Street offices that William had fitted up, he would begin a crowded series of conferences with the other leaders. They reached their decisions only after discussion, argument, and sometimes a heated clash of wills. Several of the men taken into the Standard group were hard, ruthless fighters, with impulses that looked only to business success and ignored the social good. They wished to make the Standard a hard and ruthless organization, and in accepting their brains, Rockefeller had also to accept their faith.

VII

It must not be supposed that this banyanlike growth of the Standard, the spreading of a whole tropic forest from one stem, took place without constant railroad support. The assistance lent it by the trunk lines is one of the most significant parts of the story.

[69]Boyle, *Derrick's Handbook*, 918.

The great co-ordinating and "equalizing" agreement embodied in the Rutter circular of 1874, itself so favorable to the Standard, could obviously not exist very long without infringement. In the following spring, as we have seen, the Pennsylvania reduced rates on refined oil slightly to Pittsburgh shippers—apparently a step to meet the menace of the Baltimore & Ohio.[70] The cut was too small to satisfy the Baltimore refiners, but it did indicate that the Pennsylvania had withdrawn from the Saratoga rate agreement. Tom Scott exchanged angry messages with the heads of the Baltimore & Ohio, and a letter of his published February 17, 1875, threatened a war to the death. President Garrett was a demagogue, wrote Scott, and the Pennsylvania Railroad defied him. It would improve its lines from New York to Baltimore and Washington, and if necessary cut its rates. "There shall be no inconvenience whatever to the public by reason of your effort to destroy the railroad property of any other parties. . . . It will be the duty and interest of the [Pennsylvania] Company to give to Baltimore a line in every respect equal both as to rates and facilities to any that the Baltimore & Ohio may be able to offer."[71]

Meanwhile, the Erie management suddenly accused the Pennsylvania of granting secret rebates to the Empire Transportation Company.[72] This charge was undoubtedly true, for the Empire was nothing more nor less than a subsidiary of the Pennsylvania. At this date, as for years past, it conducted all the oil transportation passing over the Pennsylvania's tracks except the Pittsburgh haulage. It of course carried that part of the Standard's oil freight which had been allocated to the Pennsylvania under the Saratoga agreement. If the Pennsylvania's rate-cut at Pittsburgh had begun the abrogation of the Saratoga arrangement, this secret rebate to the Empire finished it. As we have said before, any railroad compact which lasted more than six months was a miracle.

The Erie at once concluded a new agreement with the Standard, dated March 1, 1875, which slightly reduced the latter's freight bill. Once more the Standard agreed, as in the spring of 1874, to ship one half of its refined oil over the Erie; and in return the Erie gave the Standard a 10 per cent rebate on whatever open tariff rates should be

[70]Pittsburgh *Gazette*, Feb. 4–27, 1875; the cut was effective March 1.
[71]Pittsburgh *Gazette*, Feb. 17, 1875.
[72]Blanchard's testimony on the break-up of the pipe pool is in the *Hepburn Committee Hearings*, III, 3445 ff.

decreed by the trunk-line roads. Blanchard was determined to keep the Erie in its favored place. He knew that the Standard's oil traffic was becoming richer than ever, though he and other Erie officials were not yet aware of any of the recent acquisitions save that of Charles Pratt & Company.

Of course it was impossible to keep such a rate arrangement wholly secret. The Pennsylvania and New York Central were as quick to suspect the Erie of granting covert favors to the Standard as Blanchard had been to suspect Tom Scott of covert favors to the Empire. For this and other reasons a demand at once arose for another general arrangement among the trunk lines. About the middle of July representatives of the Erie, Pennsylvania, Central, and Baltimore & Ohio —all four roads this time—met at Long Branch. Their deliberations came to nothing, and later that month they met again in New York. It was shown that the Erie, despite its considerable facilities for handling petroleum, was crowded beyond its carrying capacity, and had to ship some of the oil which it accepted over other roads; it was getting more than its due share![73] The final result was an arrangement for a more equitable division of oil traffic, with the Standard Oil acting as "evener." Vice-President Cassatt of the Pennsylvania later testified that under this agreement his line hauled about 51 per cent of the entire oil traffic to the Atlantic seaboard, the Erie and Central about 20 per cent each, and the Baltimore & Ohio about 9 per cent.[74]

In return for its services as "evener," which really involved much trouble and expense, the railroads granted the Standard a moderate rebate, or commission. The Erie and doubtless the New York Central had already done so; but this was the first contract of the Pennsylvania with the company.[75] The concession aroused the ire of Joseph D. Potts. Up to this time the Pennsylvania's favors had been reserved for his Empire Line; moreover, he had ambitions of his own to play the part of "evener." His anger smouldered, and three years later he described the occurrence with pungent sarcasm:[76]

The rebate was a modest one, as was its recipient. Yet the railway Casandras prophesied from it a multitude of evils—a gradual destruction

[73]Pittsburgh *Gazette*, July 31, 1875.
[74]*House Trust Investigation, 1888*, p. 199.
[75]*Idem*, 196.   [76]Tarbell, *Standard Oil Company*, I, 152.

of all other refiners and a gradual absorption of their property by the favorite, who, with this additional armament, would rapidly progress toward a control of all cars, all pipes, all production, and finally of the roads themselves. Their prophecies met but little faith or consideration. The Standard leaders themselves were especially active in discouraging any such radical purpose. Their little rebate was enough for them. Everybody else would prosper, as would shortly be seen. They needed no more refineries; they already had more than they could employ—why should they hunger after greater burdens? It was the railroads they chiefly cared for, and next in their affections stood the one hundred rival refineries.

But the agreement among the railroads was precarious. They glared at each other suspiciously, and prepared for new rate wars. The centennial year, in fact, was to be celebrated by the bitterest railroad conflict of the period, with charges cut to the bone on all commodities.[77]

In the atmosphere of distrust which enveloped transportation during 1875, the pipe lines hastened to ally themselves with railroad protectors. The agreement among these lines had broken down along with the rest of the Saratoga compact. Now the Columbia Conduit Company cemented its attachment to the Baltimore & Ohio. The Empire Transportation Company on November 4, 1875, signed an elaborate new contract with the Pennsylvania.[78] It agreed to extend its pipe line to Olean, N. Y., to build more tanks, and to continue giving all its through oil traffic to the Pennsylvania; while in return it was guaranteed special rates, and a rebate of three cents a hundredweight for "terminal expenses." The United Pipe-Line Company, owned by the Standard, made a counter-alliance with the Erie and New York Central. By a new agreement it gave each road half its crude-oil deliveries, and guaranteed the Erie 27 per cent of all the oil freights in the Regions (this being the proportion the Erie had received under the Rutter Circular); and for this it received from both Erie and Central a rebate of 10 per cent upon all shipments. Most of the small pipe lines had by this time been absorbed by the three major systems. Those that survived took rapid steps to align themselves with one of them. It did not need much discernment to see what a battle royal would soon be raging between at least two

[77]Gilbert H. Montague, *The Standard Oil Company*, 51, 52.
[78]Copy in *House Trust Investigation, 1888*, pp. 210–212.

of the systems—the Empire-Pennsylvania alliance on one side, the Standard-Erie-Central alliance on the other.

While the truce lasted, the Standard of course used its rebates as an additional weapon to bring the independent refineries to its terms. Considerable testimony to this effect was given in public investigations of the next few years. Its possession of these rebates also enabled it to keep some would-be refiners out of the business. William W. Harkness, for example, testified that in 1878 he wished to re-enter the industry:[79]

We selected a hundred acres, with probably a thousand feet on the Schuylkill River, in Philadelphia, a little farther south than the one we had experimented on, and we knew exactly what we needed better than we did when we went there. We systematized all our accounts and knew where the weak points were. I was in love with the business. I selected a site near three railroads and the river. I took a run across the water . . . I came back refreshed and ready for work, and had the plans and specifications and estimates ready for a refinery that would handle 10,000 barrels of oil a day, right on this hundred acres of land. I believed the time had arrived when the Pennsylvania Railroad would see their true interest as common carriers and the interest of their stockholders and the business interest of the city of Philadelphia, and I took . . . the estimates themselves, and I called on Mr. Roberts [vice-president of the Pennsylvania] . . . I told him I wanted to build a refinery of 10,000 barrels a day. I was almost on my knees begging him to allow me to do that. He said, "What is it you want?" I said, "I simply called to be put upon an equality with everybody else, all the shippers, and especially the Standard Oil Company." I said, "I want you to agree with me that you will give me transportation of crude oil as low as you give it to the Standard Oil Company or anybody else for ten years, and then I will give you a written assurance that I will do this refining of 10,000 barrels a day for ten years". . . .

He said he would not go into any such agreement, and I saw Mr. Cassatt. He said, in his frank way, "That is not practicable, and you know the reason why."

The Standard could have answered such testimony with an argument which (if we grant its premises) was perfectly logical. After a vast outlay of labor and money its heads had organized an entire industry, and had stabilized its prices at a profitable level. Any man with a small sum of money, $50,000 or $75,000, could set up a refinery. Was he to have the free benefit of the stabilization so laboriously

[79]*House Trust Investigation, 1888,* pp. 224-226.

effected by Rockefeller and his aides? Were a hundred like him to be allowed to come in and disorganize the industry again? And the Standard seems not to have used the rebate to eliminate existing competitors brutally when a gentler course was possible; its practice was to buy or lease by amicable arrangement.

Take, for example, its relations with the Cleveland firm of Scofield, Shurmer & Teagle. The first two members of the group had been bought out by the Standard during the great consolidation of 1872 in Cleveland. It was agreed that the partners were not to reengage in refining for a fixed term of years. Nevertheless, in 1875 the two united with Teagle and built a $65,000 refinery with a yearly capacity of 180,000 barrels of crude oil. Prices in 1875–76 were good, and in its first year the firm made $40,000. But they felt unjustly treated by the railroads, and in the spring of 1876 sued the Lake Shore for "unlawful and unjust discrimination, partialities, and preferences," enabling the Standard to obtain "to a great extent" the monopoly of the Cleveland oil trade. Though Rockefeller in later years spoke indignantly of the firm as contract-breakers, he made no effort to crush them. Instead, he quietly made a leasing arrangement of a type then not uncommon in Standard practice. Scofield, Shurmer & Teagle were to operate the refinery, limiting themselves to 85,000 barrels a year; the Standard was to furnish $10,000 in ready money for alterations, obtain for the plant the same rebates that the Standard units in Cleveland enjoyed, and guarantee the firm $35,000 profit a year. Further profits up to $70,000 were to go to the Standard, and above that figure were to be equally divided. This guarantee, giving Scofield, Shurmer & Teagle an assurance of more than 50 per cent a year on their investment, could hardly be called ungenerous treatment!

VIII

It is clear that in bringing to success his grand plan of combination, Rockefeller had been much befriended by fortune. He had been aided by the chronic overproduction of crude oil, and the consequent inability of the Regions men to unite at critical moments; by the jealous rivalry of the trunk-line railroads; by the perverse hostility of the Pennsylvania toward Pittsburgh interests; by the labors of Colonel Potts, Henry Harley, and others to avert more rate wars among the railroads and pipe lines; and above all, by the intolerably savage competition among refiners. All this had created a confused, unhappy situation in which the compact power of the Cleveland industry, gathering ally after ally, had been exerted with telling effect. But it must be said that Rockefeller and his aides had moved their pieces on the board with amazing coolness, dexterity, and vision. After the South Improvement affair they had never faltered, but by swift and brilliant tactics had rushed upon their objective and conquered it. Above all, Rockefeller had shown wisdom in constantly wooing the ablest refiners by an explanation of the practical merits of his plan. Men like Warden, Archbold, Lockhart, and Pratt, all too well versed in the dizzy fluctuations, unforeseen crises, ruthless competition, and dismaying losses of the business, saw that the Standard was stable and prosperous. This was partly because its size commanded discriminatory advantages, but more largely because of the economies wrought by large-scale operations, internal efficiency, and shrewd leadership. These men finally accepted consolidation as a Gibraltar rising out of stormy seas.

Writers of a later generation tended to explain the rapid conquests of the Standard by a single word—rebates. It is plain that this was an oversimplification of a complex series of events. The crude idea that the Standard simply used rebates to club competitors into selling or merging has little relation to the facts. In old age Rockefeller declared that none of the new members joined the Standard because of its ability to obtain rate discriminations. Without accepting this sweeping statement, we must grant that most independents had themselves taken rebates. Testimony before the Hepburn Committee showed that the contract which Porter, Moreland had made with the Erie in 1873 had been just as favorable as the Standard's contract with the Lake Shore; yet Archbold soon gave up this Erie contract for an even better one with a branch of the Pennsylvania. Archbold explained his conversion to the Standard plan by saying that he became convinced that competition was obsolescent in many industrial fields, and that the future belonged to concentration. Others would have echoed him. Of course, there can be no doubt that coercion, and very rough coercion at that, was sometimes used in forcing the smaller independents to sell out. If the testimony of aggrieved refiners did not prove the fact, the passages quoted from Camden's letters would. A troublesome "outsider" was likely to encounter difficulty with his flow of crude oil, his barrel supply, or his orders for cars; he was undercut in the market, or found that his distributing agency had gone over to the Standard. But here again the story was more complex than writers of the next generation indicated.

Difficult problems lowered just ahead of Rockefeller. Could the gigantic organism he had created really breathe, move, and continue growing?—would it have a mobility and strength proportionate to its size, or would it prove clumsy and vulnerable? As 1877 opened, a violent attack by the strongest corporation in America, the Pennsylvania Railroad, was about to begin. To that brief titanic battle we shall turn next. But a far greater struggle lay beyond. Rockefeller knew that his combination was a challenge to the deepest convictions held by the American people upon their economic life, and that it could not be many years before that challenge would be angrily caught up.

XXII

A Battle of Giants

ON A chill January day in 1877, two men stood over a table in a richly furnished office in Philadelphia, scrutinizing a contract which lay thereon. One, tall, white-haired, clean-shaven, with a look of power in his stalwart figure and of imperious determination on his handsome ruddy face, was obviously a born leader. The other, of moderate height, sparely built, with a long, narrow face and long upper lip, seemed a quiet, unostentatious man, but he had a shrewd eye. The first was Tom Scott, president of the Pennsylvania Railroad, ruler in most years of the Pennsylvania legislature, and master of immense interests in the West and South. He moved with a slight limp, for he had suffered a paralytic stroke, but his natural force was unabated. The other, with the sober Quakerish aspect, was Joseph D. Potts of the Empire Transportation Company. Both fully realized the significance of the contract before them. It was essentially a declaration of war against the Standard Oil. In form an agreement between the Pennsylvania Railroad and the Empire, it began:[1]

First: The second party [Empire] agrees to enlarge its control of petroleum refineries, partly by investing its own capital in constructing refineries at or near the Eastern termini of lines controlled by the first party [the Pennsylvania] in which it will have a majority and controlling interest (as it has already in one existing refinery) and partly by contracting with other domestic refineries on the Eastern Seaboard and with foreign refineries or their representatives to supply them with crude petroleum at the seaboard and by contracting with them to furnish transportation for the petroleum they require.

[1] I was shown the original contract by Mr. Biklé, head of the legal department of the Pennsylvania Railroad.

The ensuing clauses provided that all petroleum obtained by the Empire through this control of certain refineries should be hauled by the Pennsylvania to its Atlantic terminals at rates not higher than those charged to similar shippers, "after deduction of any and all rebate or commission or other form of allowance made to any other party"; that the Pennsylvania should not pay any of the costs of the refineries; and that it should have the right to buy these refineries at their exact value, without allowance for good will, whenever it might elect to purchase the other properties of the Empire. Still another clause showed that a battle with the Standard Oil was distinctly anticipated:

Fifth: If because of action of other transporters or refining organizations the Pennsylvania Railroad Company reduces in any month the petroleum rates below the net rate on petroleum and products received in December, 1876, the second party agrees to use all the profits of its said refining interests in any such month which may be necessary for making up and paying to the Pennsylvania Railroad the amount of such reductions. This obligation shall only apply to petroleum transported by the second party under its contract of March 29, 1876, and only to the share of the said net rates due to the Pennsylvania Railroad, the Philadelphia & Erie, Western Pennsylvania, and Northern Central Railroad [branches of the Pennsylvania]. . . .

In brief, Colonel Potts's fast-freight line was going into the refining business on a large scale, and the Pennsylvania proposed to support it by drastic rate-cutting. The story behind this extraordinary move has been told us by Potts himself. He states that as the Standard Oil combination rapidly augmented its strength during 1876, he and his associates in the Empire Company had taken counsel together with growing alarm. "We reached the conclusion that there were three great divisions in the petroleum business—the production, the carriage of it, and the preparation of it for the market. If any one party controlled absolutely any one of these divisions, they practically would have a very fair show of controlling the others."[2]

This was a logical conclusion, and as Potts realized, very disturbing to the Empire. A great monopolistic organization with headquarters in Rockefeller's office in Cleveland could divert most of the Empire's oil traffic, if it pleased, to the Erie or New York Central.

[2]*House Trust Investigation, 1888*, pp. 259, 260.

The Standard, controlling all the principal refineries of Pittsburgh and the Regions, might even close them down. Since it was fast establishing itself in Baltimore, it could also at will use the Baltimore & Ohio against the Empire and Pennsylvania Railroad. Could Potts's line really afford to remain inactive while Rockefeller carried his expansion to full success?

II

By this time the Empire was itself a great power. When Potts first organized it in 1865 under the auspices of the Pennsylvania, the primary object had been to open a through freight line from the Middle West to New York and Philadelphia by way of Erie, Pa.[3] But the new company had quickly developed from a subsidiary of the Philadelphia & Erie, one of the Pennsylvania's leased lines, into a main feeder for the whole Pennsylvania system. This exceptional growth was traceable largely to Potts's energy and ability. Gradually, most of the fast-freight lines either merged with the express companies or sold out to the railroads. But the Empire remained a semi-independent corporation, valuable to the Pennsylvania because at Erie and other points it diverted to that line freight which would otherwise have gone to New York over the "northern routes." Pennsylvania officials owned much of its stock, and the Pennsylvania held a contract which enabled it to buy out the Empire on due notice whenever it pleased. Potts always tried to emphasize the autonomous character of the Empire, and it is true that it served a large number of roads which paid it the current fees for use of its rolling stock and warehouses, and commissions on whatever freight it brought them.[4] But it was really a partner and subsidiary of the Pennsylvania. The latter prompted it in many of its steps, such as the extension of its pipe lines to Olean;[5] and the oil-carrying agreement

[3] *The Road*, II, 193, 194. This well-edited weekly publication, extremely hostile to Tom Scott and the Pennsylvania, contains a wealth of information upon the operations of the railroad. It amounted to an early muckraking publication.

[4] *House Trust Investigation, 1888*, p. 258.

[5] J. Edgar Thomson wrote Colonel Potts Feb. 24, 1871: "The Pennsylvania Railroad desire you to put one or more lines of pipe from Garland on the Philadelphia & Erie Railroad to points in the oil-producing regions." He also demanded a pipe line from the new "East Sands region" to Emlenton. Legal archives, Pennsylvania Railroad.

which the two companies made in 1871 provided that they should divide the revenues in the proportion of one fourth to the Empire and three fourths to the Pennsylvania.[6]

The Empire devoted itself chiefly to special kinds of traffic which the Pennsylvania obtained largely through its agency. It controlled two lines of passenger and freight steamships on the Great Lakes, some twenty vessels in all; and through these fleets it gave the Pennsylvania a satisfactory slice of the important lake-and-rail trade, including large amounts of grain.[7] By means of its tank cars and rapidly growing pipe lines it also did a huge petroleum business, handling most of the oil sent to Philadelphia, and a large part of that going to Baltimore and New York. In 1876 it owned nearly 5000 cars, had contracts or business arrangements with more than 30,000 miles of railroad, and from gross earnings of about $11,000,000 a year, paid 10 per cent dividends on its $4,000,000 capital.[8] The Empire tank cars, some 1500 in number, were familiar to travellers for their bright verdant hue—they were called "the Green Line." Made of heavy wrought-iron cylinders with manhole, expansion dome, and valves, the older type holding 3600 gallons and the newer 4500, they were admirably suited to their work.[9]

In addition, the Empire owned about 520 miles of pipe, representing an investment of more than a million dollars. Great receiving tanks, the largest of 20,000 barrels' capacity, were placed at advantageous points on these lines. Some pretty engineering problems had been solved by the company's engineers—on one fourteen-mile line the pumps overcame an elevation of nearly a thousand feet. The Empire's oil terminal on New York Bay was at Communipaw. Here it had a tract of ten acres with a half mile of water frontage, warehouses capable of holding 50,000 barrels of refined oil, enormous tanks for crude, ample railroad facilities on the Central of New Jersey, and every appliance for pumping crude oil into bulk-boats. In

[6]This contract, which the legal department of the Pennsylvania Railroad allowed me to examine, called for charges of $6.60 for each long ton (2200 pounds) of oil shipped from any point on the Oil Creek and Allegheny River Railroad to Philadelphia.

[7]*Railroad Gazette,* Nov. 9, 1877.

[8]*Annual Reports;* for early profits see *Railroad Gazette,* Jan. 30, 1875.

[9]See Potts's unsigned pamphlet, *Theory and Practice of the American System of Through Fast Freight Transportation as Illustrated in the Operations of the Empire Transportation Company* (1876).

addition, it boasted of workshops, repair shops, and cooperage shops. The Empire provided all the soliciting agents for oil sent over the Pennsylvania system. In fact, it cared for every part of the railroad's oil business except the actual moving of the cars, and the oil traffic into and out of Pittsburgh, which the Pennsylvania managed as part of its local freighting there.[10]

In handling oil, the Empire-Pennsylvania alliance possessed important advantages over other railroads. The facilities of the "northern lines" were manifestly inferior. The New York Central route from the Regions was nearly twice as long as the Empire's, and involved at least one transfer.[11] At its terminal on the west side of Manhattan the Central had neither warehouses nor tanks, so that the moment the oil arrived it had to be lightered around the Battery to the Long Island refineries, or placed on ships. The Central owned no tank cars, most of the three hundred which it used belonging to the Standard. As for the Erie, its line from the Regions to New York was also much longer than the Pennsylvania's, it had few tank cars, and its Weehawken oil terminal, now in the hands of the Standard, was inferior to the Empire's. It is not strange that Tom Scott thought the Empire an invaluable ally, nor that when Potts was asked about its returns, he replied, "The average was very profitable."[12]

After a decade of uninterrupted growth, the Empire was nationally known and respected. Its heads had steadily anticipated new demands in freight-movement; its staff was prompt, efficient, and courteous. Men who shipped by it could rest assured that their goods would be placed in excellent cars and moved safely and expeditiously. The company owned large general terminals in Erie, Philadelphia, and Baltimore, while in New York it controlled three piers on the North River. Its tugs and car-floats on the Atlantic bays, its propellers and steamboats on the Great Lakes, were among the best of their kind. Potts had established soliciting agents in more than a hundred cities, reaching as far west as St. Paul and Omaha.[13] Occupying this strong position, the Empire seemed to have great capacity for growth, and it is evident that Potts was looking toward a

---

[10]*Ibid.; House Trust Investigation, 1888*, pp. 175, 176 (Cassatt's testimony in the State action against the Pennsylvania, 1879).

[11]*Railway World*, June 9, 1877.

[12]*House Trust Investigation, 1888*, p. 261.

[13]*United States Railroad and Mining Register*, March 22, 1873.

future which would extend its power, giving it a more independent status. He could not forget the important rôle he had played in 1874 in arranging an agreement for uniform rates among three of the trunk lines.

When Rockefeller visited the Centennial Exhibition in 1876, he must have gone to the Empire Transportation Building to examine its models of Great Lakes steamships, oil-refining plants, pipe-line transportation, and port terminals. He could not have overlooked a profusely illustrated pamphlet here given away, dealing with the theory and practice of fast-freight lines as exemplified by the Empire. Colonel Potts revealed his ambitions with alarming frankness. After a glowing description of his company's achievements, he predicted that "fast-freight organization" might soon become a grand national regulator of traffic. As yet, he wrote, fast-freight lines had not shown what they could do in securing a fair division of traffic among competing railroads. But when their adaptation to this function was fully recognized, they could perform a great service. "Unless prevented by an uninstructed public sentiment, or unwise individualism among railway managers, they will obliterate competition of the foolish and destructive sort, and the need for secret rates, and unjust distinctions between competitive and non-competitive localities; secure stability in rates, and all of the beneficial effects of consolidation, freed from many of the disadvantages."[14]

This was surely overweening ambition. Coming from the head of a Pennsylvania subsidiary, it was certain to excite suspicion and resentment. There can be no question that Potts was a man of admirable character and high intentions as well as of great energy and intelligence.[15] Modest and unostentatious, living in a $12,000 house, plainly furnished, in West Philadelphia; kindly and benevolent; fond of society, especially young people; markedly religious and thoroughly familiar with the Bible, yet in lighter hours full of humor and fun, he was widely respected. He worked hard and long; like Rockefeller, "he was always a great man to plan far ahead." The testimony he later gave in the House investigation of trusts showed a meticulous fairness, a conscientious desire to do other men justice, that is unusual and appealing. To be sure, his business methods were

[14]*Theory and Practice of the American System of Fast Freight Transportation,* etc., 45.

[15]Mr. William M. Potts gave me information upon his father, April 10, 1938.

those of the day, and he eagerly accepted rebates. General Manager Blanchard of the Erie attributed the action of that road in breaking up the pipe-line agreement to Potts's adroitness in getting special rates and other concessions, all quite secretly. "The agreement which gave it [the Empire] these growing advantages," he declared, "was properly annulled."[16] In behalf of the Empire, Potts promised rebates to oil shippers, and in 1879 was co-defendant with the Pennsylvania in a suit which one large shipper, Henry C. Ohlen, brought for damages because a rebating contract was not kept.[17] But his probity was never really questioned. His principal fault was simply an inordinate ambition, which he seemed to support by an excessive amount of shrewdness and contrivance, amounting to wiliness. Rockefeller thought him crafty and greedy for power.

"A shrewd, oily man, as smooth as oil," said Rockefeller later. "He was well understood, even by his own coterie of associates in the Pennsylvania Railroad Company with sufficient power to allow him to carry on his preferential scheme for the Empire Line. But he carried it too far, and the public would not stand it, and the competing companies would not be hoodwinked by any of this scheming of the Pennsylvania Railroad or any of its subsidiaries. And the effort of Colonel Potts to make it appear that he was the great Moses failed, utterly failed."[18]

III

When Potts decided to cross swords with the Standard combination, his first step was to acquire the important Sone & Fleming refinery on Newtown Creek, Long Island. His second, late in 1876 or early in 1877, was to begin erecting a new refinery on the Schuylkill River in Philadelphia, just beside the Atlantic Refining Company plant of the Standard combination. His son William M. Potts helped boss the construction of this establishment, which was hurried to completion and made its first run of oil in the summer of 1877. Sone & Fleming operated it, and Sone frequently came over from New York during its erection. Potts's third step was to begin a still larger refinery at Bergen Point, close beside his Communipaw oil

---

[16]Blanchard's statement is in *Hepburn Committee Investigation*, III, 3445 ff.
[17]Ohlen published a pamphlet on the subject.
[18]Inglis, *Conversations with Rockefeller*.

terminal. Meanwhile, he concluded an alliance with various independent refineries—the Germania works in Pittsburgh; the Andrews & Morgan works in Buffalo; the Denslow & Bush and Lombard, Ayres works in New York; and others. He did not expect to eliminate the Standard Oil, but to stop its march toward monopoly and reduce it to its proper status. He was confident of victory.

Both Potts and Scott had entered upon this new course deliberately. For some time independent refiners who wished to resist the Standard had been bringing the Empire definite proposals. Would it not buy an interest in their plants and extend them its protection? To accept these offers, as Potts himself confessed in 1888, meant taking the Empire down an absolutely untried road. "Our business was transportation and not anything else," he testified. If his company acquired refineries, a fast-freight agency would in effect become its own customer and would compete against other customers—no very ethical procedure. But how else could he check the growing power of the Standard?—how else give his line an assurance of adequate oil freights? He reached the conclusion that self-protection required his company to fight the Standard's steady absorption of refineries by absorbing some for itself; by making a "nucleus," as he termed it, for a refining business on whose freights he could count. He was actuated also, no doubt, by a deep-seated personal hostility to the heads of the Standard Oil. Ambitious himself, he regarded them as grasping and arrogant, while he had been touched by the piteous pleas of some of the small refineries, cowering before the lion. The breakup of the "Rutter circular" agreement during 1875 had left an aftermath of bitter feeling between Potts and the Rockefeller group, which had found various expressions. He could not forgive the Standard for its new activities as an "evener" for the trunk lines—for intruding on a reserve that he thought belonged to the Empire.[19]

But if Potts was actuated by direct motives, Tom Scott was not. The Pennsylvania was the largest freight carrier in the world and the most powerful business corporation in America, with net earnings in 1875 of $25,000,000;[20] and its head had long been distinguished by his absolutist tendencies and aspirations for grandeur. Though no longer president of the Union Pacific, he was still in

[19]This may be read between the lines in Potts's testimony, *House Trust Investigation, 1888*, 257–265.
[20]*Report, Philadelphia Board of Trade*, 1876, p. 89.

control of the Texas & Pacific, and still dreamed of making the Pennsylvania part of a gigantic transcontinental system. At one time his salaries from his various offices amounted to $200,000, then a tremendous sum, and he was rapidly piling up a fortune of many millions.[21] He had—it was said—political ambitions. Nothing less than primacy for his railroad in every field would content him. He had bought great tracts of anthracite lands in Pennsylvania for the Pennsylvania, one strip in the Lehigh Valley alone containing not less than a hundred million tons of coal.[22] When he encouraged Potts to go into refining, we may be sure that visions of dominating or at least half-dominating the petroleum industry danced seductively before his eyes. The Pennsylvania-Empire alliance, with its tangle of pipe lines, its host of friends among the producers, the country's largest fleet of tank cars, the most direct line from Regions to coast, the best oil terminals, could wield mighty weapons. Why should it not strike for first place? If it could gather the strongest of the hardpressed independent refineries under its control, it might utterly break up the Standard combination and erect its own system instead. Scott doubtless hoped to take a long step in this direction before the Standard awoke to its peril.

In short, Colonel Potts wished to limit the power of the Standard, and strengthen his Empire Line for the great rôle of arbiter and evener of traffic that he had in mind; Scott probably wished to smash the Standard, and create an oil empire of his own in its place.

But Rockefeller was not to be taken by surprise. While it is uncertain just when he, Flagler, and the other Standard captains first learned of the new activities of the Empire, it was at an early date. The Cleveland group had always regarded the Pennsylvania with mingled distrust and admiration. Rockefeller respected the abilities of Scott, whom he called "a daring, dare-devil, bold and courageous man," and had worked with him in South Improvement days. But Flagler and he had always kept a vigilant eye upon the Pennsylvania's concessions to their Oil Regions rivals. They were aware in 1875 of Potts's hostility, and were well posted the next year, thanks to his pamphlet, upon his grandiose ambitions. Late in 1876 H. H. Rogers in New York and Warden in Philadelphia reported that their

[21]See obituary in Harrisburg *Independent,* May 21, 1861.
[22]*Railroad Gazette,* Sept. 26, 1874.

acquisition of refineries was being checked by the Empire's support of independents. Within a short time they also reported its part-ownership of Sone & Fleming, and its plans for constructing a refinery in Philadelphia.

Rockefeller instantly grasped the significance of all this, and his action was as swift as his perception. In the past he had always been patient and persuasive, anxious to settle disputes by agreement rather than battle. Then his opponents had always been weaker individually than he. No doubt Scott and Potts believed that, now faced by so powerful an enemy, the Standard would be readier than ever to delay and parley. It is evidence of Rockefeller's business genius that instead he showed himself swift, bold, and uncompromising. He knew that victory depended upon immediate and crushing action.

First he went directly to Scott and Vice-President A. J. Cassatt with an ultimatum. He told them that he knew all about the Empire's activities. "The Pennsylvania and its subsidiary the Empire," he said in effect, "are carriers. The Empire has no business whatever in the field of refining. Such competition is unfair. We ask for its immediate withdrawal." He did not need to remind Scott that about 65 per cent of all the oil carried by the Pennsylvania came from the Standard combination.

Some of Potts's defenders have remarked that he and Scott could have retorted: "The Standard has no business in the field of transportation, yet it owns pipe lines."[23] But that would have been no real answer, and Potts knew it. The Standard had never gone into railroading, and the Empire had no more business refining oil than the Standard would have had running a railroad. The pipe lines were a special and peculiar industry, lying in a no-man's land between producing and railway transportation. Of course the Standard interests had an abstract right to acquire a railroad, as Henry Ford later did, and the Pennsylvania-Empire alliance had an abstract right to acquire refineries, as various roads had already acquired anthracite mines. But in either event the two interests would have become deadly rivals. Rockefeller's point was precisely that—the Empire's new departure had made it a direct rival of the Standard.

Before he made his demand upon Scott, Rockefeller had ascer-

---

[23]*Cf.* Tarbell, *Standard Oil Company,* I, 183, 184; Flynn, *God's Gold,* 193, 194.

tained that the New York Central and the Erie felt the same indignant hostility that he did. Indeed, President Jewett of the Erie later testified that his road would have fought the Empire even if the Standard Oil had not been disposed to do so. "Whether the Standard Oil Company was afraid of the Empire Line as a refiner I have no means of knowing," he told the Hepburn Committee in 1879.[24] "I never propounded the question. We were opposed to permitting the Empire Line, a creature of the Pennsylvania Railroad, to be building refineries, to become the owners of pipe lines leading into the oil fields and leading to the coast, without a contest." Jewett and William H. Vanderbilt conferred, and at once cemented an alliance. They too remonstrated with Scott and Cassatt; and when they did so, the Standard energetically renewed its representations. For a time, under this barrage of expostulation, Cassatt wavered. He even talked with Potts about getting the Empire Line to lease its refineries to the Standard, or sell them to third parties.[25]

Potts indignantly refused. "Rather than do that, we would have you buy our property and close out our contract with you," he exclaimed. He exhorted the officers of the Pennsylvania to stand by him. There is no evidence that Tom Scott wavered at all. If he did, he was kept in line by Potts's eloquent appeals, and by his own belief in the power of the Pennsylvania and Empire. After all, the Standard group—the Central Association—was a newly cemented league of more than a dozen leaders, some recently jealous of each other; the New York Central and Erie were rather competitors than allies. How could this relatively loose combination withstand the attack that the compact organization of the Pennsylvania and Empire was launching? Scott stood firm, and the Empire pushed its refining activities with accelerated vigor. Financial circles talked of Boston and Philadelphia interests which would furnish a backing of millions for the railroad in this battle.[26]

But the Pennsylvania underestimated both the unity and the resources of its opponents. The New York Central and the Erie were absolutely one, as Blanchard later declared, in feeling that the Empire

[24]*Hepburn's Committee Hearings*, II, 1466.
[25]Cassatt's story may be found in *House Trust Investigation, 1888*, pp. 174-207.
[26]*Railway World*, June 9, 1877. It was said that Union Pacific interests and certain Regions interests had been enlisted.

had been receiving unwarranted concessions, and in their determination to halt its progress before it became invincible. Their association with the Standard, moreover, was now very close. They depended almost entirely upon it for refined oil, and very largely for crude oil; it had kept its promise to divide its shipments evenly between them; it was dependable, and to them at least it was fair. As for Rockefeller and his associates, they saw that they must fight to the finish, for the Pennsylvania was threatening the basic purpose of their combination. Financially, they were well armed for the contest. The Standard had maintained its profits even in the darkest years, and the great price rise of the latter half of 1876 had added heavily to its cash resources. To be sure, considerable sums had been spent in effecting mergers with independent plants, but with his usual foresight, Rockefeller had prepared for such an emergency. As he said later, the Standard had "not only accumulated cash reserves in each day, each month, each year from its organization, which was some years back of 1870; but in addition to this, it was constantly holding out inducements to capitalists to add their capital. It was forehanded."[27] For that matter, most of the losses would come out of the allied railroads; it would be primarily a war of freight rates, and the object of the combination would be to bring the Pennsylvania to terms.

IV

The moment Tom Scott made it clear that he would support Potts —in March, 1877—Rockefeller cancelled the contract of 1875 with the Pennsylvania. Then he struck hard. He cut the price of kerosene in all markets reached by the Empire. He rushed the construction of 600 new tank cars, which the "northern lines" hastened to place upon trucks. Standard buyers bid actively for crude oil. The Erie and New York Central cut their freight rates; the Pennsylvania retaliated, and the "northern lines" cut again. Rockefeller temporarily closed down his Pittsburgh refineries and speeded up his Cleveland plants to their full capacity, so that he need not ship a drop over the Pennsylvania. Then, when he had arranged for shipments of refined oil eastward over the Baltimore & Ohio, he opened the Pittsburgh plants

[27]Inglis, Conversations with Rockefeller.

again.[28] His sellers were active in every export market trying to close the field to the Empire refineries. They were equally active in all the domestic markets.

Potts and Tom Scott, for their part, filled the Oil Regions with buyers trying to corner all the crude oil possible, and supplied the resulting stocks to all independents. The prices paid for this oil were of little consequence—the idea was to get it at all costs. At the same time, the Pennsylvania moved oil to New York for a song or for nothing at all. The experience of Henry G. Ohlen subsequently became famous. He was an independent refiner who signed a contract with the Empire on April 2, 1877, by which it agreed to carry his crude oil from the Regions to Communipaw at rates as low as those given to any other shipper whatever. Cassatt later testified that the charge for transporting Ohlen's oil amounted to eight cents a barrel less than nothing!

As the struggle became intense, the Empire made frenzied efforts to organize the producers as its allies, and to increase the output of its own and the independent refineries. In the first attempt it met but indifferent success. Potts persuaded a number of the leading Regions men, led by Benjamin B. Campbell of Pittsburgh and E. G. Patterson of Titusville, two of the largest shippers, to accept a three-year contract for sending all their oil over the Empire and Pennsylvania at low competitive rates, and to make an effort to get other producers to sign it.[29] Thus they would strike down this Standard Oil monster! As we have said, Potts was popular in the Regions, while his agreement was generous in its terms. His campaign, if successful, would have starved the Standard Oil refineries of crude oil in 1877 just as concerted action had starved them in 1872. But Campbell and his other allies made slow progress. It was much more difficult to organize the Regions now than it had been five years earlier, for the oil fields had grown far broader. In addition, while sentiment was generally favorable to the Empire, there were powerful dissenters; Archbold, Vandergrift, O'Day, Seep, and other prominent men were now enlisted in the Standard organization, and they exerted their influence in its behalf. Finally, many Regions men suspiciously recalled Tom Scott's connection with the South Improvement scheme.

[28]Pittsburgh *Gazette*, May 7, 1877.
[29]See testimony of B. B. Campbell, *House Trust Investigation, 1888*, pp. 134, 135.

After all, this was essentially a war between two of their former enemies, and they were slow to take sides.

Nor did the output of the refineries controlled by or allied with the Empire ever reach impressive proportions. At first some predictions ran high, and even in June a New York correspondent of the Pittsburgh *Chronicle* writing from what purported to be a full knowledge of Potts's resources, gave an extremely roseate statement. His estimate of the capacity of the plants under the Empire ægis reached a total of 50,000 barrels weekly. But of this 20,000 barrels represented simply a prediction for the still unfinished plant at Bergen Point, while in other respects the figures were plainly exaggerated. Potts later gave conclusive testimony on the subject: "The extreme limit was 4000 barrels a day only."[30] This was a bagatelle compared with the huge output of the Standard combination.

As the weeks passed it became clear that the war was injuring the Empire and Pennsylvania far more than it hurt the Standard group. The latter had no difficulty in obtaining ample supplies of crude oil from the Regions. Many producers, when offered high prices by the Empire buyers, would coolly go to the Standard agents and ask for a higher bid. Colonel Potts strenuously added to his pipe-line mileage in the Regions, but the Standard augmented its own system too. All the refined oil from the Standard plants was shipped over the Erie, New York Central, and Baltimore & Ohio, and shipped at extremely low rates; for as the Pennsylvania cut its charges, the Standard insisted that the other lines keep pace. At no time were the members of Rockefeller's combination severely pinched. They had to sell at low prices, but then they manufactured economically, and their resources were more than equal to the temporary deficits. The revenues of the Pennsylvania, however, were hard hit. It depended far more upon oil freights than did the Erie and New York Central; and while it received much of its usual volume of crude oil, the consignments of refined fell precipitously in March, and remained almost negligible thereafter. Philadelphia exporters reeled under the blow to their trade. As *The Railroad Gazette* stated in September, that city lost heavily while New York and Baltimore profited.[31]

The movement of petroleum during the summer was unparalleled in extent, and its channels showed strange dislocations. During

[30]*House Trust Investigation, 1888,* p. 260.   [31]Sept. 14, 1877.

June and July the share of New York in the total shipments of crude oil was very nearly twice what it had been the previous year, while Philadelphia's part fell to less than one third the old level. As for refined oil, in the first eight months of 1877 New York exported very nearly three fourths of all that was sent out of the county, while Philadelphia exported only one eighth. This represented a tremendous gain for New York, and a disastrously heavy reduction for Philadelphia. Baltimore, meanwhile, fully held the gains made since the opening of the Columbia Conduit pipe line.[32] It was said in various newspapers that the freights on refined oil paid by the Standard to the Pennsylvania during 1876 had aggregated about $6,000,000.[33] This may be an exaggeration, but certainly the railroad was being deprived of a very large sum. A State investigator subsequently declared that in three months it lost more than a million dollars.[34]

Nevertheless, the battle might have raged a long time had not exterior circumstances combined at this moment to weaken the Pennsylvania. It was dependent in such a contest upon its credit; the Standard was not. While the Standard had accumulated cash reserves, the railroad had constantly paid out its profits in high dividends upon outrageously watered stock. The Pennsylvania was therefore in a vulnerable position if anything shook its public standing, and in 1877 fate dealt it two heavy blows.

The first was not unexpected. We have seen that in March, almost simultaneously with the opening of the oil war, the bitter rate struggle of the Eastern trunk lines broke out again. Amid a vociferous exchange of accusations of bad faith, charges were slashed right and left. The guilt for this conflict is difficult to apportion. William H. Vanderbilt declared that the New York Central would carry on the war until its opponents were prostrated. A brief truce early in April was followed by more rate cutting. On May 10 the heads of the various lines—Scott, Jewett, Vanderbilt, and Newell of the Lake

[32]*Railroad Gazette,* Sept. 21, 1877. For the first eight months of 1876 the petroleum exports in gallons were: from New York, 89,500,000; from Philadelphia, 42,250,000; from Baltimore, 26,500,000. In the first eight months of 1877 they were: from New York, 167,000,000; from Philadelphia, 28,000,000; from Baltimore, 26,500,000.

[33]The Pittsburgh *Gazette,* May 7, 1877, gives this figure.

[34]This was M. W. Acheson, attorney for the Commonwealth of Pennsylvania in its suit in 1879 against the Pennsylvania Railroad; quoted in *House Trust Investigation, 1888,* p. 155.

Shore—met at the Brevoort House in New York, and agreed that as of July 1, all the trunk lines would pool their westbound traffic. But until that date open war continued to rage. The railroads advertised passenger fares from New York to Chicago at $15, and from Cleveland to Boston at $6.50. Losses became enormous. During the early seventies the Pennsylvania had declared a 10 per cent dividend annually, and even in the depression years 1875 and 1876 had paid 8 per cent. But on May 1, 1877, it reduced the quarterly dividend to a 6 per cent level, and early the next month its stock was selling at 28½. Even after July 1, rumors of an imminent renewal of railroad hostilities were constantly breaking into the press.

Then in midsummer the country was suddenly swept by the great railroad strike of 1877. The story of this violent and justified uprising of underpaid and overworked labor has often been told. Every one knows how rioting began along the Baltimore & Ohio on July 18; how it spread through western Pennsylvania and into upper New York; how governors ordered out militia, and President Hayes at their request used Federal troops to restore order; how dozens of men were killed and millions in property were destroyed. One city, Pittsburgh, was ruled for a night and a day by an angry populace. The Pennsylvania Railroad was more fiercely hated than any other line in the East. Tom Scott's dictatorial interferences with the State government were notorious. His labor policy was callous; not only had the road reduced wages a total of 20 per cent since the depression began, but it had recently doubled the number of freight cars in a train, thus causing a large number of discharges. In Pittsburgh it was especially detested for the unfair rate practices which had kept industries in that city impoverished, and had resulted in widespread unemployment and distress. The disturbance there assumed the character of a convulsive popular revolt against the railroad. Not only trainmen but a host of other workers and small shopkeepers joined in the attack upon stations, shops, and rolling stock. So intense was their fury that the police were helpless, and a force of State militia thrown in on the afternoon of Saturday, July 21, was quickly driven to shelter.

These militiamen, after pouring several volleys of musketry into the crowds, killing about twenty-five persons and wounding many more, were forced at nightfall into the machine shops and roundhouse. A grim siege, lighted up by blazing buildings, at once commenced. Because of the blockade which had begun two days earlier, the yards and the sidings which extended eastward for three or four miles were crowded with freight cars. Some contained merchandise; some were loaded with oil, coke, and coal. While part of the mob raged about the buildings in which the troops had taken refuge, others set fire to the cars. Within a short time lurid flames lighted up huge bodies of black smoke rolling skywards. The fire department promptly turned out, but the attackers refused to let them extinguish the conflagration. They said they were determined to destroy the railroad's property, but would do no harm to that belonging to private citizens, and they kept their word. When a lumberpile belonging to a businessman caught fire, they turned in and helped to save it. But the oil cars in the yards went up in flames. Cars of blazing coke were pushed down the tracks and against the roundhouse, where the troops were trying to reply to volley after volley that was poured in at the windows—for the crowds had broken into the gunshops. The position of the worn-out, smoke-suffocated soldiers became untenable. Marching out in a compact body, they retreated under a hail of missiles and bullets across the Allegheny River.

When the Pittsburgh uprising ended, more than a hundred locomotives and nearly fifteen hundred passenger and freight cars had been destroyed. In addition, roundhouses, machine and car shops, warehouses, stations, and office buildings had been gutted. The loss in disturbance of traffic might be counted in millions; the loss in good will in tens of millions. In due time the Pennsylvania made claims upon Allegheny County for $4,100,000, which were later settled for $2,765,891. Meanwhile, it had to bear the whole burden of the loss. The day after the rioting, it made an emergency call upon Drexel, Morgan & Company for a large loan—men said $600,000 or $700,000.[35] All the East knew of the triple strain imposed upon its finances by the rate wars, the battle with the Standard combination, and the riots. It passed its dividends in August and November, and its stock fell to 27.[36]

The credit of the railroad—and upon its credit Potts and Scott had chiefly relied—had been given a terrific shock.

[35]E. P. Fabber to John W. Garrett, N. Y., Sept. 25, 1877; Garrett Papers.
[36]For financial record see Philadelphia *Public Ledger,* Nov. 1, 1877.

v

While the Pennsylvania was passing its August dividend and borrowing money to replace its burned rolling stock, the oil war continued its merciless course. It was a war which the Standard could maintain for years, but which the railroad was now anxious to terminate. Scott and Cassatt realized that no vital interest of the Pennsylvania was bound up in this conflict; for the Standard combination it was a life-and-death conflict, but not for them. Their capitulation to Rockefeller would bring a loss of prestige, but prestige meant little in dollars and cents. If only a reasonable settlement could be made, the disappearance of the Empire Line would do no lasting harm to the railroad. It would merely place the Pennsylvania upon an equal footing with the other trunk lines.

From the beginning one great element of weakness in the Empire's position had lain in its peculiar relation to the Pennsylvania. However strong it might seem, it was the creation of the railroad, its policy was subordinate to that of the Pennsylvania, and by double-riveted contracts all its assets were subject to purchase, without allowance for good will, at the option of the road. While Potts was an able man, Tom Scott was much stronger, and had a vein of ruthlessness which Potts lacked. He could easily take the whip-hand. Moreover, Scott was keenly aware that an important group among the Pennsylvania's stockholders had always looked upon the Empire with suspicion, and that they would now ask why it had been allowed to drag the railroad into trouble.

Many stockholders regarded this fast-freight line as an anachronism that was being perpetuated for a few selfish beneficiaries. What was it, they asked, but an agency to manage the most profitable freight business and divert the profits thereon to favored hands? These critics had angrily insinuated that the stock of the Empire was largely held by high officials of the Pennsylvania, who thus lined their own pockets at the expense of the parent corporation. As early as May, 1866, at a meeting of heads of the four Eastern trunk lines, President Garrett of the Baltimore & Ohio had offered a resolution condemning all such agencies as costly and corrupting, and calling for their extinction.[37] This resolution was defeated by a single vote of Tom Scott; but inside the Pennsylvania organization, year after year, the same demand was heard. In 1872, for example, a former director, Joseph Hulme, rose at the stockholders' annual meeting to denounce "the policy of farming out the privileges of the road to fast-freight lines" and palace-car companies.[38] He declared that the cream of the freight business went to them, "and the cream of the profit of course goes to their own stockholders." The next year complaints of such vigor arose that Tom Scott had to reply to them by a public address.[39] In 1874 a committee of stockholders responded to further attacks by a still more elaborate defense,[40] but even this group showed a certain uneasiness, and the criticism continued to mount.[41] Some newspapers called the Empire a "parasite." Rockefeller later asserted that it had transferred part of the Pennsylvania's earnings into the bank accounts of "a favored coterie," and that by 1877 Potts was "overshooting the mark" by piling up profits for a closely owned subsidiary "to such an extent that the scandal of the doings of the Empire Line could no longer be risked."[42]

Tom Scott and Cassatt quickly saw that the storm demanded a reefing of sail, and as early as August, Cassatt made two trips to Cleveland to negotiate with Rockefeller, Flagler, and Warden. These approaches were satisfactory. The Standard leaders, who were not inclined to exact harsh terms, then came to Philadelphia, where at the St. George Hotel early in September they carried on discussions with Tom Scott directly. They wisely agreed with him upon a plan by which the Pennsylvania stood not to lose a cent—by which, indeed, since a new pool of the oil traffic of the four railroads was devised, it would gain.

"They insisted," Cassatt testified later, "that the first condition of their coming back on our line . . . must be that the Empire Trans-

[37]*Proceedings of the Railway Meeting Held at the St. Nicholas Hotel, N. Y., May 22, 23, 1866.* Garrett later wrote a letter, published in this pamphlet, in which he stated that the fast-freight lines were "a costly and vicious element in connection with railway interests."

[38]Philadelphia *Public Ledger,* Feb. 21, 1872.

[39]*United States Railroad and Mining Register,* March 22, 1873.

[40]See the pamphlet, *Report of the Investigating Committee of the Pennsylvania Railroad, 1874,* especially pp. 123, 124.

[41]H. H. Schotter, *Growth and Development of the Pennsylvania Railroad,* 153, 154.

[42]Inglis, Conversations with Rockefeller.

portation Company . . . must cease the refining of oil in competition with them." When the Empire was notified of this demand, it took a defiant position. Potts believed that if the fight were only maintained he and the Pennsylvania could win it. The Empire continued to show a profit, at least on paper, and he felt confident that victory would soon be in sight. When Tom Scott made it clear that he wanted peace, Potts obstinately declared that he would never haul down the flag; the Pennsylvania would have to exercise its option and buy him out if it wanted to surrender. Evidently there was a bitter quarrel between him and Tom Scott, for to the end of his days he believed that Scott had acted in a cowardly, treacherous fashion, and had quite unnecessarily played him false.[43] But the Standard leaders held Scott and Cassatt to their decision.

"Very well, if it is necessary to buy the Empire out," they told the Pennsylvania heads, "then between us we shall buy it out."

Rockefeller's first proposal was that the Standard combination should take over the refineries, and the Pennsylvania should buy the cars and pipe lines. But Scott and Cassatt objected that pipe lines were outside their proper field. The Standard then agreed to take the refineries, pipe lines, oil terminals, and harbor tugboats and barges, while the Pennsylvania took most of the rolling stock. On September 17 the railroad directors formally approved the purchase. The chagrined Potts always believed that the Standard must have bribed some of the directors, though he admitted that the riots might have frightened them. Newspaper reports of the sale, appearing September 19, created a profound stir. The Philadelphia *Record* correctly remarked that the oil business was by far the most important element involved. "In order to get these pipe lines in hand it has been necessary to cook up the purchase of the Transportation Company, and that is all the milk contained in that cocoanut."

Colonel Potts had no legal ground for resistance or even complaint. The Pennsylvania had created his company, and by its contract possessed a clear right to destroy it. On the witness stand a little later, Cassatt was asked whether the railroad had given formal notice of its intention to purchase the property. "No, sir," he replied,

[43]William M. Potts to the author, April 10, 1938. Colonel Potts believed Scott quite unprincipled. He told his son that in 1861 he had seen Scott the day after he was appointed Assistant Secretary of War. "I congratulate you, Scott," he said. "Yes," said Scott "this place in worth $100,000 a year to me."

"it was not a matter of notice; it was a matter of arrangement between us—a matter of negotiation." He might far better have said that it was a matter of compulsion.

Rockefeller has piquantly described the scene at the St. George Hotel when the negotiations there closed. A number of Standard and Pennsylvania officials had assembled, but Tom Scott was late. "I can see him now, with his big soft hat, marching into the room in that little hotel to meet us; not to sweep us away as he had always done, but coming in with a smile, walking right up to the cannon's mouth. 'Well, boys, what will we do?' Then he sat down and signed the papers."[44]

And he has also described how all the funds required were raised by himself and his brother William, both making "superhuman exertions." None of the money came from Lockhart, Pratt, Warden, or the other partners. William obtained all he could in New York, and then John set out to get the rest in Cleveland. He climbed into his old buggy, and driving from bank to bank, asked at each for the president. " 'I must have all you've got!' I said. 'I need it all! It's all right! Give me what you have! I must catch the noon train.' That's how we bought it."[45]

It was apparently necessary for the two Rockefellers to raise about $3,400,000 all told. Naturally enough, John D. Rockefeller later spoke as if the Empire had driven a hard bargain, while Potts believed that the owners of his company had been underpaid;[46] but various journals referred to the transaction as fair to both sides. By the final agreement, the Standard paid $1,094,805.56 for the Empire's pipe lines, $501,652.78 for its refining properties, $900,000 for its share in the Oil Tank Car Trust, and $900,000 more for personal property and certain settlements with outside refiners. These assets were of course nominally transferred to various individuals, not to the Standard Oil of Ohio. American business history up to this time had shown few purchases of such magnitude. But whenever an acquisition opened up the prospect of great earning power, Rockefeller did not haggle over payment; and the Empire had become the one formidable barrier to the Standard's control of the refining industry.

[44]Inglis, Conversations with Rockefeller.
[45]*Idem.*
[46]William M. Potts to the author, April 10, 1938; Inglis, Conversations with Rockefeller.

It was Potts who was vanquished, even though he retired from the field with his pockets full. The magnificent future which he had planned for his fast-freight line melted into thin air; his place as a great leader in railroading was gone forever. Some years of successful business activity remained to him, while his fine personal qualities were recognized in 1886 by election as a trustee of the University of Pennsylvania; but he was no longer a power in American transportation.

And he took his defeat hard. On October 17 he presided over a final meeting of the Empire's stockholders, at which a report was read showing that up to the last the net earnings of the company had sufficed to pay its reduced dividend rate. He recalled in eloquent words the brilliant history of the Empire system, and expatiated upon the strength which it had maintained until the last. "We hold the field still, and but for Tom Scott's desertion would have been able to fight on," was the implication of his statements. However, the only course open was compliance with the Pennsylvania's demands, and the stockholders duly ratified the sale. That same night a varied group of executives met in Potts's office in Girard Street. Tom Scott and A. J. Cassatt were there; William Rockefeller and Henry M. Flagler; and several other men connected with the Empire, the Pennsylvania, and the Standard Oil. The final papers were signed and the transfer was completed. Tom Scott handed a certified check to the treasurer of the Empire. Colonel Potts, his composure unbroken, bowed every one out. But then, it is said, he seated himself at his desk, buried his head in his outstretched arms, and wept.[47]

VI

The magnitude of the victory won by the Standard immediately became evident. As *The Railroad Gazette* remarked, it had greatly improved its position. "Now all the appliances which enabled the Empire Transportation Company to rival the Standard Company

---

[47]The meeting is described by Cassatt in *House Trust Investigation, 1888,* p. 179. The statement as to Potts's tears is in Flynn, *God's Gold,* p. 197. But William M. Potts denies the statement, saying that his father was of far too stoic a temper ever to weep. According to the N. Y. *World,* Oct. 18, 1877, only $2,500,000 was paid over at this time. This may be true; the N. Y. *Tribune,* Jan. 18, 1878, says that the Empire's pipe lines were not bought in October, but merely leased by the United Pipe-Lines with the privilege of purchase, the payment of "about $1,100,000" finally being made in Philadelphia on Jan. 16.

go to strengthen the latter."[48] In business as in other departments of life, to him that hath shall be given. The Standard, already holding almost complete control of pipe lines and refining, was now able to make it complete.

The defeat of the Empire and the imminent completion of a rival Standard pipe line to Pittsburgh brought Doctor Hostetter, controlling the Columbia Conduit properties, to Rockefeller's office with an offer to sell. Some bargaining ensued—the bargaining in which Rockefeller used his command of mental arithmetic to save $32,000. This new acquisition gave the Standard combination about three fourths of all the pipe-line properties of the nation. We have seen that early this year the Standard group had incorporated the United Pipe-Lines to bind together its holdings. Before the year ended Rockefeller and his associates had increased the capitalization of the company to $5,000,000, and included the former Empire pipes, the Hostetter pipes, and the new Pittsburgh line in the security for its stocks and bonds. At the same time, the management of the various lines was also centralized.[49]

To many independent refiners, the sale of the Empire naturally seemed the handwriting on the wall. They had looked to this company or the Columbia Conduit line for support against the Standard, and now they were helpless. Archbold and H. H. Rogers found the work of buying up the remaining competitors in Pennsylvania much easier. They were assisted by reports which became rife immediately after the downfall of the Empire that the Standard combination was requiring the several trunk lines to pay it a "royalty" of fifty cents a barrel on all crude oil shipped from the Regions, whether this went to Standard refineries or to "outside" refineries. Though Tom Scott denied this, the substance of the report was credited by many careful observers.[50] *The Railroad Gazette* remarked that as the Standard owned nearly all the pipe lines, and as the railways paid the pipe-line charges out of the sums they collected for freight, the Standard might easily demand such a "royalty" and then neatly conceal it as a pipe-line charge.[51] These reports did not lessen the readiness of wavering independents to hoist the white flag.

[48]Nov. 9, 1877.
[49]Taylor, MS History of the Standard Oil Company, 31, 32.
[50]N. Y. *World,* Oct. 25, 26, 1877.   [51]Nov. 9, 1877.

As a matter of fact, the destruction of the Empire was accompanied by the formation, as part of the general peace treaty, of the before-mentioned railroad pool. This time all four trunk lines participated, for the imminent sale of the Columbia Conduit line, its principal oil feeder, made the Baltimore & Ohio willing to join the Erie, the New York Central, and the Pennsylvania. All four were thoroughly sick of their rate wars. In this year 1877, indeed, they united in an epochal pooling arrangement on all west-bound traffic from New York. As for oil, the railroads and the Standard agreed that 63 per cent of the shipments to the coast, both crude and refined, was to go to New York, and 37 per cent to Philadelphia and Baltimore. Of the whole amount carried to these three ports, the Pennsylvania was to take 47 per cent; the Erie and New York Central 21 per cent each; and the Baltimore & Ohio 11 per cent. It was necessary to have an "evener," and the Standard combination naturally acted in that capacity. It agreed not only to divide the shipments as arranged, but to guarantee certain quantities of its own oil; to the Pennsylvania, for example, not less than two million barrels a year. For its services it received a commission initially fixed at 10 per cent on all its own shipments *and whatever other freights it might control.* No such commission was to be paid any other shipper unless he furnished the railroads an equally profitable volume of oil.[52]

Flagler was later at great pains to explain that the work of an "evener" actually justified some payment.[53] The Standard agreed to see that each road got its proper percentage, a matter of real labor. At the end of every month the railroads sent in a statement of the number of barrels they had shipped. It was incumbent upon the "evener" the following month to ship over any road which had received less than its due percentage an amount that would repair the deficit. This meant, as Flagler testified, much costly office work; it meant that the Standard combination sometimes had to run refineries at certain points where they were unprofitable, and to close down or reduce refineries at other points which showed a profit. It

[52]This pool was described by Cassatt in the State suit against the Pennsylvania in 1879, and his testimony is reprinted verbatim in the *House Trust Investigation, 1888,* pp. 183 ff. It is significant that the date on which the Standard and the Pennsylvania Railroad entered into this pooling agreement was Oct. 17 —the day of the Empire transfer.

[53]Flagler's defense is in *House Trust Investigation, 1888,* pp. 774, 775.

meant satisfying the little branches, like the Dunkirk & Allegheny Valley, as well as the main trunk lines. It meant the steady continuance of a large volume of business at periods when the Standard might have preferred to run its plants slackly.

Then, too, the Standard combination agreed to deliver the oil at points, so far as practicable, where the railroads would have short hauls, and to make the proportion of crude to refined as large as possible, for the railroads earned greater profits on crude. It gave the railroads the use of its terminals. It promised the Pennsylvania that it would refine as much oil as it could in Philadelphia. Finally, it assumed all the risk of loss by fire in transit, which would otherwise have fallen upon the railroads. Altogether, the services of an "evener" were important, and in helping to prevent costly railroad wars the "evening" system did American business at large no little benefit. According to Flagler, the Standard carried out its contract faithfully, and divided the traffic as had been arranged. Yet he declared that the Pennsylvania soon broke faith, and paid to other shippers a rebate precisely equal to the Standard's 10 per cent commission!

In principle, the scheme was by no means unprecedented. It was identical with that by which livestock shipments eastward from Chicago had now been apportioned for several years. The roads carrying cattle and hogs had selected leading shippers to divide the freight according to an agreed plan, and paid them handsomely in "commissions."[54] The real trouble with the situation was that for about two years the railroads granted the Standard other heavy rebates, and these in conjunction with the evener's "commission" made an altogether exorbitant sum. John Moody states that the general Standard rebate for these years was 68½ cents. Lewis Emery, Jr., later presented evidence, founded on court testimony, to show that on refined oil from Cleveland, Pittsburgh, and Titusville in seventeen months of 1877–79 the independents paid $1.44½ a barrel, and the Standard only 80 cents. This was a crushing and intolerable difference. The Standard not only had a giant's strength, but was using it with the tyranny of a giant.[55]

And equally indefensible were the payments which Daniel O'Day,

[54]*Railroad Gazette*, Nov. 1, 1878.
[55]Moody, *The Truth About the Trusts*, 118; *House Trust Investigation, 1888*, pp. 241 ff.

general manager of the Standard's American Transfer Company, exacted from the New York Central, Erie, and Pennsylvania. O'Day was practically in charge of all Standard pipes. He got the business for the lines and moved the oil. On February 15, 1878, he wrote Cassatt that for some months the American Transfer Company had been receiving from the Erie and New York Central certain sums, in no instance less than twenty cents a barrel, on every barrel of crude they carried—whether sent by the Standard organization, or by its competitors. He demanded that the Pennsylvania begin paying, as of February 1, twenty cents a barrel on all the crude-oil shipments it handled. Cassatt made an investigation. He was shown receipted bills proving that the Erie had paid twenty or thirty cents a barrel, and the New York Central thirty-five cents. Thereupon he ordered his comptroller to pay the American Transfer Company twenty cents a barrel upon all crude oil shipped *by any party* during the next three months.

This was in effect a revival of the brutal South Improvement scheme of levying a tax upon competitive shipments. To be sure, the Standard's officers later presented a partial defense. Flagler testified that the American Transfer Company pipe line had really been built in the interests of the New York Central. That railroad had no tracks south of Titusville, and the American Transfer Company, buying and collecting oil in the lower fields, pumped it up to the railhead. In other words, it acted as an agent for the New York Central, and he argued that the thirty-five cents a barrel was only a decent return for its labors. When the pipe line increased its business, the Erie also used it as agent on the same basis.[56] As for the charge to the Pennsylvania, O'Day's letter to Cassatt shows that this stood on a somewhat different basis. On November 30, 1877, the American Transfer Company completed a great thirty-mile pipe line between the southern oil belt and Pittsburgh, paralleling and rivalling the Columbia Conduit line. This enabled the refineries of the Standard Oil Company in Pittsburgh to receive their oil direct from the wells. The new line and the purchase of the Columbia Conduit, which together cost an enormous sum, made the Standard substantially

[56]O'Day's letter is in *Commonwealth of Pennsylvania vs. Pennsylvania Rr. Co., Appendix,* 734–736; more conveniently in Tarbell, *Standard Oil Company,* I, 374, 375. Flagler's defense is in *House Trust Investigation, 1888,* pp. 777, 778.

independent, in feeding its Pittsburgh plants, of the Allegheny Valley branch of the Pennsylvania. Nevertheless, in accordance with its rôle as "evener," the Standard protected this branch road, seeing that it got its full proportion of the oil traffic going to Pittsburgh, and got it at a profitable freight rate. It was for this service that O'Day asked twenty cents a barrel upon all the crude oil the Pennsylvania carried.

Such was the defense offered by the Standard's spokesmen. It was a weak and limping argument. The Standard might well have been justified in asking certain commissions on crude oil brought to the railhead by its own pipes. But the placing of a similar levy upon the crude oil shipped by its competitors was indefensible. One of the darkest pages in the Standard's history is that which records this crushing combination of rebates and commissions during the years 1877–79; a combination which explains the rapid surrender of nearly all surviving independents. To put it bluntly, the Standard's policy in these two years savored of the code of Robert MacGregor, better known as Rob Roy:

> The good old rule, the simple plan
> That they should take who have the power
> And they should keep who can.

When the public learned of such levies, it never regarded them but in one light—as a flagrant injustice; and when the law could reach them, they were instantly and completely abolished. No biographer of Rockefeller can ever excuse his consent to these harsh exactions.

XXIII

The Regions Challenge Rockefeller

THE centennial year witnessed the first striking demonstration of the power of the Standard Oil combination to deal with petroleum prices. Since the Jay Cooke failure the nation had of course been in the grip of a cruel depression, of which the oil industry ·had borne its full share. One expert, in reviewing 1875, declared that the twelvemonth had brought "absolute ruin" to many who had invested in oil lands and oil production. The average price of crude oil had remained that year at the mournful level of about $1.25 a barrel, while refined standard white in New York had established the lowest average mark (12.99 cents a gallon) in history. Lugubrious faces had filled the Regions, and in midsummer half-starving laborers had talked of applying the torch to the vast quantities of oil tanked in the Allegheny Valley, and thus wiping out the glut to force a revival of prices. The Cleveland *Leader* had called this madness: "If the producers cannot restrain their greed sufficiently to check the lavish production that has kept the market utterly swamped for two or three years, nothing can cure their difficulties."[1]

But in 1876 the story was different. That year the Standard combination staged a spectacular campaign against speculators in depression. When it opened, many exporters were predicting that Europe had become so used to thirteen-cent kerosene that it would never pay more. But meanwhile, wrote the expert for the New York Chamber of Commerce in reviewing the year, "an element was at work which eventually developed into an irresistible power—a power

[1]See *Report of the Chamber of Commerce of the State of New York*, 1875-76, pp. 57, 60, 61; Cleveland *Leader*, Aug. 7, 1875.

which has thus far proved a blessing to the trade on this side of the Atlantic, putting money into the pockets of refiners and producers, smoothing out the lines of care and anxiety, and making the waste places to blossom and fructify." The Standard was intervening against artificially cheap oil. Its heads knew that manipulators had been busy. During the three previous years, prices of both refined and crude oil had always been lower in the last six months than in the spring. European speculators, expecting a recurrence of this drop, had gone largely "short" of oil for the fall and winter of 1876. But in July the market for kerosene turned sharply up by two and a half cents a gallon, in August it rose two cents more, and September found it up almost another six cents! December brought a marked additional advance, the New York price then being 29.26 cents as against 14.02 of January. In brief, the "combination" had practically doubled the price of kerosene during the half of the year in which the bears had expected it to drop. No wonder that the New York expert wrote in a vein of exultation:[2]

The year has been an important one to the trade everywhere; decidedly advantageous to nearly all parties interested in this country, and disastrous only to the reckless speculators of the large centers in Germany and England. For the prosperity which has been showered upon it here—horse, foot, and dragoon—great credit is due to the boldness and wisdom of the gentlemen composing the "combination," who, while enriching themselves, have unavoidably benefited "outsiders." Whether the success which attended their manipulations during the past year will continue to smile upon them during 1877 remains to be seen. As the spring opens there will be a large increase in the refining capacity—several new refineries being now on the way nearly to completion, considerable additions having been made to several of the old ones, while some very important leases which kept others under control will expire within a few weeks; all these elements introducing fresh competition. How they can all be managed successfully will soon be a knotty problem, if it does not already vex the minds of the gentlemen composing the "combination."

During the year the consumption has materially increased in almost every portion of the world—on the Continent of Europe about ten per centum, while the domestic trade is estimated to have increased from ten to fifteen per centum.

[2]For the data on prices I depend on Patrick C. Boyle, ed., *Derrick's Handbook*, 703 ff., and the *Reports of the Chamber of Commerce of the State of New York*. The quotation here given is from the *Report* for 1876–77.

Since oil prices were always a complex matter, increased demand and other automatic factors doubtless played an important part in the price-rise. And unhappily for producers and refiners, it proved impossible to sustain it. Speculators could be caught short once—but not again. The chronic oversupply and overcompetition again made themselves felt. In 1877 prices went down once more. Refined oil brought an average price in New York of 24 cents a gallon in January; in July it had sunk to 13⅜; and in November it stood at 13¼. Crude oil showed the same course. In January the average price a barrel was $3.53; in July it was $2.20⅜; and in November it was $1.91⅜. The old discontent and fear seized upon producers. Though at depressed prices the powerful Standard combination could still make money, many well-owners were being forced into bankruptcy.

And while they were thus dismayed by the fall in prices, they saw with alarm that the Standard Oil was defeating its last strong antagonist, the one transportation company which had dared to face it. The moment the Empire capitulated a wave of resentment and fear swept across the Regions. *Rockefeller now controlled all the pipe lines; that is, all connections with the world market.* The feelings of that district were not unlike the feelings of Western Europe when Hitler's Reich struck down Poland. While the producers felt no love for the Pennsylvania Railroad, they trusted the Standard still less, and they were aghast at the prospect that Rockefeller might become the single omnipotent buyer of crude oil. They hated the idea of a dictator, and they particularly hated the Standard in that rôle, for they accused it of keeping crude-oil prices below their proper level. Men told each other that when kerosene sold for 14⅝ cents a gallon, as it did in October, crude oil ought to bring more than $2.25 a barrel. At once a movement for a new organization of producers gained impetus. Secret lodges were hurriedly formed, each enlisting the important well-owners of a particular community. Their avowed object was to protect the industry against unfriendly legislation, to improve its transportation facilities, and to correct "abuses and pernicious practices detrimental to the producing business."

In November, 1877, a general convention dubbed the "Petroleum Parliament" met in Titusville; 172 delegates in all, purporting to represent some two thousand well-owners and property worth hundreds of millions. Groups of stern-visaged men, roughly dressed but prosperous-looking, moved along the wooden sidewalks and clustered in front of the Universalist Church. An air of purposefulness hung over each earnestly talking lot. Though there was no secret as to their aims, they glanced suspiciously at strangers. The leaders included Benjamin B. Campbell, recently so busy in trying to rally the well-owners on the side of the Empire; E. G. Patterson, who had assisted him; D. S. Criswell, known for his intense hatred of the Standard; and young Lewis Emery, Jr., distinguished by his combativeness and ingenuity. Their sessions in the church were long and animated.

In effect, this "Petroleum Parliament" represented a new uprising of the Regions men against the Standard Oil combination. Producers looked to it with a passionate hope they had not evinced since the crisis of 1872. While the sessions were secret, it was soon learned that two leading proposals had been brought forward. One was for a renewal of the union between the producers and independent refiners —though it was obvious that this offered but slender possibilities, for the independents were now a ragged handful fighting in the last ditch. The other was for building a great pipe line to break down the carrying monopoly which the Standard had now achieved.[3]

It was clear that the alliance of the Standard with the trunk-line railroads, dependent on its services as "evener," could not be smashed. But the pipe line seemed to present a method of defying both the railroads and Rockefeller. The fertile-minded Lewis Emery, Jr., had already organized the Equitable Petroleum Company, whose stockholders included some two hundred producers in the new Bradford field. He proposed to gather oil from all over this northern area by branch pipe lines, and to lay a trunk pipe line to connect with the Erie Canal at Buffalo. His company had already begun to obtain a right of way and collect funds. Another proposal, more sweeping in character, was presented to the "Parliament" by the Seaboard Pipeline Company, controlled by Benson, McKelvy, and Hopkins of Columbia Conduit fame. General Herman Haupt had surveyed a

[3]This meeting was held Nov. 21-23, 1877, and is reported in the Titusville *Herald,* and Oil City *Derrick* that week. See *A History of the Organization, Purposes, and Transactions of the General Council of the Petroleum Producers' Unions, and of the Suits and Prosecutions Instituted by it, from 1878 to 1880* (pp. 690). This history was drawn up by a committee appointed by the Council. The body was popularly called the "Grand Council."

route for this company from Brady's Bend on the Allegheny River southeastward across the mountains to Baltimore, 235 miles. Thus far crude oil had never been pumped over any line which combined long distances with high altitudes; but the sturdy trio at the head of the Seaboard believed that the feat was practicable. Their proposed line would give direct access to the coast, and encourage independent refining in and near Baltimore.

At a second meeting on December 11, the "Parliament," or more properly Grand Council of the Petroleum Producers' Union, was swelled by a delegation of West Virginia producers. The market for crude oil had fallen early that month to $1.84, and the temper of the members was sterner than ever. Again a variety of suggestions were brought forward. Although the sessions remained secret, the Oil City *Derrick* reported that the delegates discussed a rapid tightening of the Union organization; the leasing of oil lands to prevent them from being immediately exploited; and a new effort to stop the drill. Some members believed that a compromise between the Union and the Standard might be worked out; and West Virginia producers suggested that it be based upon a sliding scale, so that whenever the price of refined oil went up, that of crude should rise in proportion. But the majority were for open war. This second meeting offered encouragement both to Lewis Emery's proposed pipe line and the longer venture of Benson, McKelvy, and Hopkins, while it urged that the work of organizing the producers be energetically pushed.

The Council also took steps to draft a free pipe-line bill, permitting condemnation of a right of way, which it hoped would be passed by the legislatures of New York, Pennsylvania, and Maryland; and a new bill for the Federal regulation of interstate commerce, flatly prohibiting all discriminatory rates.

II

Unfortunately, the angry producers meanwhile did nothing effective to check the avalanche of unwanted oil. From a record-breaking production in 1877 they moved recklessly to another and far greater in 1878, and still another in 1879. The first year, thirteen and a third million barrels; the second, fifteen and a third million; the third, almost twenty million—so ran the American output. Consumption could not keep pace. It is roughly accurate to say that in 1878 the daily production was 45,000 barrels and daily consumption 35,000; and what could be done with the extra 10,000 barrels that piled up every day in storage somewhere?

The principal new source of petroleum was the rich Bradford field in McKean County, northeast of the original oil area. The village of Bradford had contained but six hundred people when in September, 1875, a prospector sank a well which yielded nearly two hundred barrels a day. At once thousands flocked to the district. It proved lacking in spectacular gushers, but amazingly prolific in small, steady wells, and its area rapidly widened. Within a few years sixteen thousand shafts had been sunk, and Bradford had become a rich and populous city. Iron tanks studded the neighboring hills, narrow-gauge railways encircled the valleys, and pipe lines webbed out in all directions. One producer, whose company in a single year netted 50 per cent, later remarked that he could lay out wells "like rows of corn, and every well would be a success," while another declared that sinking a tube was "a dead sure thing."[4] By lucky strikes here Lewis Emery, Jr., laid the foundation of his fortune. At the same time new discoveries were being made elsewhere in northwestern Pennsylvania, bringing in such lesser Pitholes as Sunset City, which was born in 1876. Wells were pouring out their slow, green streams of wealth in the Cattaraugus area in New York, in Ontario, in West Virginia, and in southeastern Ohio. But the center of attention remained the Bradford golconda, which by midsummer of 1878 was yielding 18,000 barrels a day. The figures for this single district are eloquent:[5]

1876	384,000 barrels	1879	14,017,000 barrels
1877	1,346,000	1880	21,107,000
1878	6,180,000	1881	24,582,000

This was far too abrupt a rise, and in 1878 the petroleum expert of the Chamber of Commerce of the State of New York assailed the producers savagely. They were threatening ruin to the oil business—"persistently forcing the yield beyond all former experience and hope" of a sound market. They had shown "a recklessness that could only reap disappointment and misfortune." Prices sank until the

[4]*House Trust Investigation, 1888,* pp. 39, 43.   [5]*Idem,* 54.

average for both crude and refined oil was lower in 1878 than in any year since the war. The best rate paid for crude at the wells during January was $1.64 a barrel, and for refined in New York 12¾ cents a gallon. By October a barrel of crude could be bought in the Regions for less than 80 cents, and its drop had carried refined down to 8¼ cents a gallon. The latter price is evidence that the Standard by no means possessed absolute control of the kerosene market, which was governed in great part by consumers' demand, stored supplies, speculation, and Russian competition.

The surplus of petroleum created an appallingly difficult problem of transportation and tankage. Long before the end of the eighties the crude oil held in storage reached nearly forty million barrels. If the excess supply had been well distributed over western Pennsylvania it would not have been so burdensome, but most of it was concentrated in the Bradford field. Iron tank cars were expensive, and the railroads had built only what seemed absolutely necessary. When the flow of petroleum burst its banks, there were not enough to go around. Every producer shrieked for transportation, and could not comprehend why cars were not available. Inevitably, many Regions men blamed the Standard Oil, which was acting as "evener," for the shortage.

The tankage problem was equally difficult. The pipe lines, now nearly all Standard property, had long since adopted the rule of reaching every important well and providing storage for oil that could not be immediately sold. They ran the petroleum into tank-farms and gave the owners certificates. But in 1878, when the market was saturated, the steady torrent poured out by the Bradford field proved quite unmanageable. With much oil flowing into the ground and creeks, Rockefeller and his partners did their utmost to provide new tanks. On that point friends and foes later agreed. Bostwick and O'Day hurriedly drew up plans, ran trainloads of material into the field, and kept their gangs hustling day and night. "One of the greatest constructive feats the country has ever seen was put through in the years 1878, 1879, and 1880 in the Bradford oil field by the Standard interests," admits Miss Tarbell.[6] "It was a wonderful illustration of the surpassing intelligence, energy, and courage with which the Standard attacks its problems." While on Christmas Day, 1877, only

[6]Tarbell, *Standard Oil Company*, I, 216.

200,000 barrels of tankage existed in the Bradford area, the beginning of April found more than 1,000,000 ready. By 1886 the Standard Oil Company had provided storage in the Regions for nearly 36,000,000 barrels!

But temporarily the pinch was severe, and it produced agony and conflict. In vain did officers of the Standard's pipe-line system implore the producers to stop drilling. In vain did they notify their patrons on December 28, 1877, that the daily run of oil in the Regions exceeded shipments by 22,000 barrels, and that storage facilities were already overtaxed. Production continued to rise, and to create frightful confusion. Since the producers would not shut in their wells, and the collecting tanks simply could not hold all the oil, most of it had to go to market as fast as the overtaxed railroads could provide cars. The Standard, now purchasing and refining about nine tenths of the petroleum used, had its own problems of tankage and shipment. Reluctant to buy and store large quantities of oil while the markets kept sagging, it was anxious to see production checked. Many producers, eager to get their oil off their hands, began selling it at a discount below market prices. That is, in return for the relief of immediate shipment they would take less than the current quotation; and much of this cheap oil went to rivals of the Standard.

Within ten days after the warning of December 28, the Standard pipe lines took a drastic step. It had theretofore been the custom, whenever the receiving tanks of the pipe lines became full, to compel producers to sell their oil before having it run from the wells. This "immediate shipment oil" was supposedly sent out of the country direct in cars. Thrown on the market at forced sale, it brought less than "certificate" or tanked oil. The Standard now announced that it would not run more than one fourth of any man's production into tanks, and would accept the rest only on an "immediate shipment" basis. This meant forced sales at discounts ranging from two to twenty-five cents a barrel. Ample precedent existed for this order, for the pipe lines had issued similar notices in periods of excessive production in 1872 and 1874. They were intended to discourage production, and to encourage the building of tanks. But the orders obviously had another result. They cheapened the price of oil to buyers —and in 1878 this meant primarily the Standard. Men anxious to get "immediate shipment" for their oil began hunting buyers nervously, and J. A. Bostwick & Co., the Standard purchasers, could obtain crude oil at bargain rates.[7]

Viewed broadly, the so-called immediate shipment order was a device which penalized well-owners for overproduction, and stimulated them to cut down the flow or help provide means of storage, but which at the same time gave the Standard cheaper oil. Standard men naturally justified it for its disciplinary effects. They pointed out that even before it was issued many producers were selling to independent refiners at a discount for immediate removal. But the producers naturally thought the Standard was taking a vicious advantage of their plight—that it was using the excuse of disciplinary action to fill its coffers. "If the pipe-line companies can run oil for Bostwick," said one, "they can run oil for everybody at current prices." And the hard-pressed well-owners had still another grievance. Their eagerness to get rid of their surplus brought them in crowds to the offices of Bostwick and the United Pipe-Lines, which adjoined each other in Bradford. It was necessary to form the impatient producers in lines, sometimes of a hundred men, and admit them one by one. To the sturdy individualists of the Regions standing in line was a gross indignity.

A new meeting of the Grand Council in the first days of 1878 brought a veritable torrent of denunciatory speeches against the Standard. The well-owners were not willing to stop drilling, but they were ready to stand by hundreds in the Bradford public square and applaud inflammatory attacks on Rockefeller. Some orators urged the crowds to storm the pipe lines, burn the pumping-stations, and tear up the pipes. But the sober majority realized that this would hardly help to speed up the shipment of oil![8]

The producers' anger was given a special edge by the well-known fact that the great Standard combination was still making a profit. Indeed, the Standard found a silver lining in the depressed price-levels because they enabled it to undersell the Russian refineries throughout Central Europe, and even in St. Petersburg. "With the present low prices of the American production," declared the New York *Commercial Advertiser,* "there can be no fear of the United

[7]Philadelphia *Press,* Aug. 2, 1879, describes this competitive bidding.

[8]Much valuable material on the "immediate shipment" struggle is given in the before-mentioned *History . . . of the Petroleum Producers' Unions.* B. B. Campbell's version is in the *House Trust Investigation,* 1888, p. 129 ff.

States losing much of the European trade."[9] Well-owners who knew that the Standard was prospering while they were going bankrupt felt that somehow the United Pipe-Lines might have dealt with the situation more generously. And indeed, perhaps it might. No one can now say. The situation was so complex that it is quite impossible today to pronounce on its real equities; and even if an impartial commission had tried to sift the matter at first-hand in 1878 it might have been baffled. It is possible that the motives of the Standard in the "immediate shipment" order were mixed; that Bostwick wanted not only to discourage production, but to get his oil at a discount. Yet there is even less doubt that the main cause of the producers' losses lay in their own greed, haste, and disunion.

Impartial observers scoffed at the common complaint that the Standard was "bearing" the market. "The chief cause of the low price is overproduction," said the Pittsburgh *Gazette* in June.[10] "The main cause of the difficulty is overproduction," echoed William J. Ives of the New York Petroleum Exchange in July.[11] Figures showing that at the end of 1878 more than 4,300,000 barrels of oil were in storage spoke for themselves.

The Standard always protested that it had sought to deal with an overwhelming situation in the best way it could. Charles Pratt declared that the crisis was all the producers' fault. "We have large refineries under which fires have not been built in months. We have urged the producers to diminish production, but in vain."[12] Rockefeller later asserted that only the frantic exertions of the United Pipe-Lines had saved the Regions from a worse calamity. "Had it not been for the interposition of the Standard Oil interests in building tankage, making pipe lines, and otherwise providing for this surplus of oil which came gushing from the earth these producers, many of whom had no working capital, would have seen their oil go into the ground."[13] He pointed out that the Standard was compelled to hold its own oil in the tanks while it ran the "immediate shipment" oil

[9]Jan. 16, 1878.   [10]June 3, 1878.   [11]N. Y. *Tribune,* July 15, 1878.
[12]N. Y. *Tribune,* July 22, 1878. The United Pipe-Lines really maintained a semi-autonomous position. Its *active* directors (Rockefeller never attended a meeting) were Regions men with producing interests. Its manager was admitted by the Regions press to have a sympathetic understanding of local problems.
[13]Inglis, Conversations with Rockefeller.

of others. He further pointed out that the "immediate shipment" price was not fixed arbitrarily by the Standard, but was dictated by the bids which thousands of buyers, chiefly speculators, offered for certificate oil and discount oil. These buyers were constantly trying to anticipate the market. He argued that Bostwick paid a reasonable price, sufficiently high that men who got it showed no great eagerness to build tanks. He thought that the principal outcry came from a clamorous minority of soreheads, not from "the great multitude of able, sensible, practical producers."

"Men like spoiled children" was Rockefeller's characterization of the complainants; men "who made very bad exhibitions of themselves at times when they couldn't have their own way."[14] This was the natural verdict of a great pioneer in business concentration upon some of the most aggressive exponents of individualism in the world. The rugged producers had many virtues, but they were not of a kind to appeal to the nation's leading apostle of industrial discipline. The logic used by these producers, said Rockefeller, ran somewhat like this: "We have disregarded all advice, and produced oil in excess of the means of storing and shipping it. We have not built storage of our own. How dare you refuse to take all we produce? Why do you not pay us the high prices of 1876, without regard to the fact that the glut has depressed every market?" Rockefeller thought that if the Standard had obtained a profit from the discount on "immediate shipment" oil, it was no more than a just return upon its emergency construction of hundreds of miles of new pipes, and millions of barrels of tankage in the Bradford district.[15] On this complex problem in accountancy no judgment is now possible.

III

Fortunately for the producers, their best leaders were interested in constructive action. These men saw that if they could drive pipe lines to the ocean and the Erie Canal, they would at once relieve the terrific pressure upon existing arteries of oil transportation, and take a long step toward making the Regions independent of the Standard. The Grand Council in January, 1878, decided to support both Emery's Equitable line to Buffalo and the Brady's Bend–Baltimore

---

[14]*Idem.*   [15]*Idem.*

line. Subscriptions for the latter were circulated among the producers present, while two representatives of the Council were appointed to the board of directors.[16] The press meanwhile announced that Herman Haupt had almost completed the purchase of a right of way from the oil fields to Curtis Creek, a few miles from Baltimore, where he had bought three hundred acres as a site for a great independent refinery and barrel-plant. The pipe line was expected to bring down two million barrels of oil a year.[17] If free pipe-line bills could be carried through the New York and Pennsylvania legislatures, both companies seemed assured of an early success.

A tremendous battle forthwith developed in Harrisburg and Albany. In Pennsylvania monster petitions supported the bill, while Regions interests lobbied earnestly. The Pennsylvania Railroad instantly registered its opposition. The Philadelphia Commercial Exchange, after two public hearings, did the same. These hearings were marked by a spirited debate between a committee of producers on one side and a group of railroad men and Standard representatives on the other; and before final action was taken, the producers offered to amend the bill so that Philadelphia would become the terminus of the southern pipe line instead of Baltimore![18] The Pittsburgh Chamber of Commerce also prepared a hostile memorial, but when the Regions threatened to boycott Pittsburgh merchants, hastily withdrew it.[19] In New York the western counties supported the bill, but it was bitterly opposed by the railroads, the Standard, and various commercial interests of New York City. The New York Central and Erie declared that the carriage of oil tended to reduce the cost of transporting other commodities, and that if they lost this oil freight they would have to increase the charges on other goods.[20] Editorially, the New York *Commercial Advertiser* summed up the main objection in one sentence: "The tendency of the oil pipe-scheme would be to bring the crude oil to the seaboard, where it could be shipped in vessels specially constructed for the purpose and taken to other countries,

[16]N. Y. *Tribune,* Jan. 10, 1878.

[17]Baltimore *American,* Jan. 3, 1878; N. Y. *Tribune,* Jan. 4, 1878.

[18]N. Y. *Tribune,* Jan. 22, 25, 29, 1878.

[19]"The feeling here is very generally against the Seaboard line"; Pittsburgh *Gazette,* Jan. 21, 1878. But *The Gazette* had stated on Jan. 7 that the "outside" refineries in Pittsburgh were heartily in favor of the line.

[20]*Railroad Gazette,* April 19, 1878.

where it would be refined, thus ruining the refining business in the United States."

In Pennsylvania the opposition won a direct victory, while in New York it was indirectly successful. A delegation of prominent Philadelphians, representing important business interests, visited Harrisburg to assist the railroad and Standard Oil lobbyists,[21] and the free pipe-line bill was easily killed in the Senate, 27-19. In Albany the adversaries of the measure raised a constitutional objection. They declared that the right of condemning a route could not be granted save for a recognized public necessity, and that in this instance it would simply enrich a group of speculators—Pennsylvanians at that! Advocates replied that in principle there was no difference between granting the right to an oil line and granting it to a railway, and that reduction in the freight charges on oil from a dollar or more a barrel to ten cents would benefit millions. In April the bill passed and was sent to Governor Lucius Robinson. He let it become law without his signature, announcing that while he believed it unconstitutional, the courts ought to pass upon it.[22] Obviously, this meant that any attempt to condemn land for a pipe line would lead to a prolonged legal battle, with the chances much against the builders.

In this contest over free pipe-line legislation our sympathy must go to the producers. They were on the side of progress, while the railroads, the Standard Oil, and the seaboard merchants were trying to hold back the hands of the clock. *The Railroad Gazette,* recognizing the fact, rebuked the railroads sharply for laboring to delay an improvement which must attain success within a few years anyway.[23] Had the legislation become effective in 1878, the grievous congestion in the Bradford and Clarion County fields might have been remedied far more quickly than it was, and the defeat of the effort resulted in unnecessary losses to hard-pressed producers. Of course the railroads and the Standard had a perfect right to oppose the bills, and human nature being what it is, could hardly have been expected to do otherwise. The railroads preserved for a time their freights from crude oil, while the United Pipe-Lines maintained their practical monopoly of piping facilities for an additional year—and even

[21]N. Y. *Tribune,* Jan. 31, 1878.
[22]Charles Z. Lincoln, ed., *Messages From the Governors,* X, 241–247.
[23]Feb. 15, 1878.

then it was but slightly broken. Perhaps a long independent pipe line built in 1878 to Baltimore or Philadelphia would really have resulted in the export of much crude oil to build up foreign refineries; but the greater likelihood is that it would simply have promoted some independent plants in the terminal city.

However, Lewis Emery, Jr., was not easily daunted. For short distances he could dispense with the right of eminent domain. He extended his pipes from the Bradford field to Frisbie's Station on the Buffalo & McKean Railroad, whence the oil was shipped by rail to Buffalo, and there pumped from tank cars into canal boats for New York. The first cargo, five boatloads of nearly two million gallons, came down the Hudson on August 7, 1878. Independent refiners, who had been paying $1.15 and $1.40 a barrel for transporting crude oil from Bradford and Parker's Landing respectively, and who knew that the Standard was shipping for much less,[24] had joined hands with Emery to make the feat possible. It was hailed in the New York *Tribune* by a glowing news story:[25]

The oil-producers and the dealers of this city who have started this enterprise have a fleet of twenty oil-boats, and they expect to bring to this city by canal with their present facilities a daily average of 60,000 gallons of oil; and if the investment is a success, they promise to increase their facilities next year. The purchase and alteration of the present fleet of boats, building the necessary railroad extension to the works, and the pipe-lines, have already cost nearly $500,000, and it is estimated that twice that amount will be expended during the next year. The time occupied by the trip is expected to take twenty days. . . .

H. C. Ohlen . . . said yesterday: "We have been forced into this movement by the discriminating freight tariffs on petroleum by the trunk lines. At present they are moving oil under an apportionment agreement, and when dealers and producers desired to engage tank cars to be filled through the pipes of the United Company, the railroad agents threw every obstacle into the way. We simply demanded equal rates with other operators in proportion to the gross amount of oil shipped, which were refused. . . . The cost of transporting from the wells to New York by rail is $1.15 a barrel, and it is estimated that it will not cost half as much by canal and rail.

Unfortunately, Emery and Ohlen did not foresee certain impediments. One was the extent to which the Standard controlled the

[24]N. Y. *Tribune,* Nov. 23, 1878.   [25]*Idem,* Aug. 8, 1878.

New York refineries. Though Emery had allied himself with two large plants, not enough independents were left to take a third of the oil he proposed to send down, and it would require time to build up new establishments. Another obstacle was offered by the railroads. Hardly had he made his first shipments when they advertised sweeping rate cuts. Bradford-New York charges were reduced to 80 cents; and Emery had to pay between 40 and 50 cents for railroad haulage between Frisbie's and Buffalo alone. Worst of all, of course, winter sealed up his canal route. It is not strange that his associates, instead of putting more money into the enterprise, became interested in salvaging what they had invested! Within a short time he sold his pipe line to Benson, Hopkins, and McKelvy. This trio, who looked southward for an outlet, were just perfecting their organization under the new name of the Tidewater Pipe-Line Company. Their plans for a route to the seaboard could not be carried out overnight, and meanwhile the producers remained helpless.

Thwarted in these ways, and suffering from further increases in production, the well-owners showed an incandescent hostility to the trust. When the muddy roads dried in February and March, the Standard built so much pipeage and tankage that this, with a stronger market demand, temporarily lessened the immediate-shipment difficulty. But early in April the United Pipe-Lines warned the Regions that another terrible glut, the tanks running over, would—unless drilling were checked—occur by June. The prophecy was correct. Frenzied producers sent down hundreds of new wells in April, hundreds more in May, hundreds again in June and July. Despite strenuous tank-building, all the containers brimmed over. The United Pipe-Lines had to renew its immediate-shipment order; and a wave of the fiercest anger again swept the oil fields. Three fourths of the well-owners were convinced that the Standard had them by the throat, and was using its control of pipe lines, tanks, and railroads for the grossest extortion. In vain did directors of the United, nearly all Regions men, protest that they were doing their utmost to provide relief. In vain did even an anti-Standard paper like the Bradford *Era* assure its readers on May 14 that the Standard was not to blame—"the truth is producers must bear this responsibility themselves." In vain did it add: "Credit should be given to the pipe-company for the manner in which it has exerted itself to keep pace with the rapidly increasing production in this district." The producers had a genuine grievance in the Standard's efforts to impede the Equitable Pipe-Line, which ran even to bringing pressure on pipe manufacturers to withhold supplies. They had another genuine grievance in some unjust details of the system by which the Standard used privately owned tanks as part of its general storage facilities. They refused to believe that the car shortage was real, or the immediate shipment order justified.

By summer the indignation was so intense that numerous observers feared rioting. In June President Campbell of the Producers' Union, after studying the situation in the Parker's Landing district, uttered a vehement protest. He declared that he had never before heard of a car shortage there, yet a deficiency in transportation was now chronic. He called upon the Allegheny Valley branch of the Pennsylvania for an explanation. Its officers asserted they could not obtain cars from the Pennsylvania's main line. But that was no excuse, snorted Campbell; the preceding fall the railroad had carried 50,000 to 60,000 barrels of oil day after day. On his way home from Parker's Landing his train passed hundreds of empty tank cars bound for favored destinations in the Bradford field, and he believed they were being used for "immediate shipment" oil sent at low prices to the Standard refineries.[26]

Independent refiners shared this resentment, and some interesting testimony as to car discrimination was later given by W. H. Nicholson, an agent of H. C. Ohlen. He declared that in May, 1878, he had 10,000 barrels of oil in the United tanks, but could not get cars to transport it. Telegraphing the Erie, he obtained an order for a hundred cars, and took it to Daniel O'Day. But O'Day refused to pipe the oil from the tanks to the cars.[27] "I have an order from the Erie officials," expostulated Nicholson. "That makes no difference," O'Day replied. "I cannot load cars except on an order from Pratt"—and he did not. It is unquestionably true that the Erie, which one Regions paper called "the most subservient bedfellow of the Standard," was tied by a special car-supply agreement with Charles Pratt. "The Erie has always recognized only one shipper," Joseph Seep explained to a

[26]House Trust Investigation, 1888, pp. 131, 132.
[27]Investigation by the secretary of internal affairs of the Commonwealth of Pennsylvania.

reporter.[28] "First, Gould, Fisk, Harley, and their associates. Second, Bostwick & Tilford. Third, Adnah Neyhart, who sold out to Charles Pratt & Co. The Erie not having been able to build a sufficient number of cars themselves, Pratt & Co. have built cars which they own and are running on the Erie, of course at their own convenience."

But both the railroads and the United Pipe-Lines loudly protested that they were doing their best. Years later Rockefeller commented acridly upon Campbell's statement that men had never before heard of a car shortage in normal areas. "I think this really laughable,"[29] he said. "I may say for myself that I heard of little else than the scarcity of cars from the time I went into the business. We were on our knees to the railroad companies to build cars. We thought it a godsend when the New York Central agreed to build one thousand cars, and we bound ourselves by a contract to the steady use of them."

The producers' side of this quarrel is amply given in Ida M. Tarbell's pages; that of the United Pipe-Lines may be found in a long statement published in various Regions newspapers on November 20–21, 1878. The truth undoubtedly lies between the two. While the main cause of friction lay in the well-owners' egregious overproduction, some aspects of the Standard's management of its facilities were open to criticism. The United Pipe-Lines soon modified their contracts for controlling privately owned tankage. They also rescinded the "immediate shipment" order—Regions men said because of their justifiable clamor, Standard men because of a lessening of the glut. But the important fact was the intense hostility which the well-owners were developing against the Standard. They believed that an arrogant tyranny held them by the throats. The Producers' Union had issued an address on July 14th in which it proposed a great pool for oil, and numerous meetings were held to discuss the project, which ultimately came to nothing.[30] Meanwhile, other meetings, notably one in Oil City on August 26, bitterly denounced the rail-

[28]See Seep's frank interview in N. Y. *Herald,* Sept. 5, 1878.
[29]Inglis, Conversations with Rockefeller.
[30]It was proposed that the Producers' Union take all crude oil, issuing certificates to the owners, and hold it off the market until the central agency thought the demand justified a sale; N. Y. *Tribune,* July 15, 1878. The numerous meetings culminated Aug. 24, in a mass meeting which overflowed the Adelphi Theatre in Bradford, the object being to obtain signatures to a contract to sell oil only through the Producers' Union; N. Y. *Herald,* Aug. 24, 1878.

road rebates that were being paid to the Standard through the American Transfer Company.

At the same time, they resolved to turn to the State Government for redress. It had acted to destroy a monopoly in 1872; why not again in 1878?

IV

Few episodes in our business history are more dramatic than this appeal of the embattled men of the Oil Regions to the executive and courts of Pennsylvania. It had three aspects: a request that the Governor and Attorney-General bring *quo warranto* proceedings against the United Pipe-Lines to compel it to perform its duties as a common carrier; a call for suits in the State supreme court to enjoin the Pennsylvania Railroad, the lines of the Erie and New York Central in Pennsylvania, and the Standard Oil against discriminating in favor of any shipper either in freight rates or car distribution; and ultimately, an indictment of the principal officers of the Standard Oil for criminal conspiracy. Two of these three attacks failed. The *quo warranto* proceedings against the United Pipe-Lines broke down. The criminal indictment of Rockefeller and his partners was a vindictive blunder which injured rather than aided the producers. But the injunction proceedings elicited some startling evidence, aroused public opinion, and resulted in important concessions by both the Standard and the railroads.

We need say little of the *quo warranto* proceedings. The Producers' Union laid their grievances before Governor Hartranft, who was so much impressed by the description of the tremendous power of the Standard combination that he demanded: "How has all this been produced?"[31] At his suggestion, the Regions men drew up a long memorial which reviewed the checkered history of the oil industry since 1872; while they also called for an extra session of the legislature—a mere gesture.[32] The Attorney-General asked for a writ of *quo warranto* against the United Pipe-Lines, and Judge Charles E. Taylor granted it, with the result that a series of hearings shortly began. In these the Regions men made no progress. They were answered by a demurrer and faced endless delays. The proceedings

[31]N. Y. *Sun,* Nov. 23, 1878.
[32]*House Trust Investigation,* 1888, p. 170.

were a Pope's bull against the comet, declared N. M. Allen. Prominent oil men therefore filed with the secretary of internal affairs, William McCandless, formal charges that the United Pipe-Lines, the railroads, and the Standard had fixed discriminatory rates upon freight. As deputy for the secretary, Judge Atwell held a series of hearings, which elicited much indignant testimony. But after studying it, the secretary reported on October 17, 1878, that the allegations had "not been substantiated in any way that demanded action." This report threw the Oil Regions into a new fury of resentment. In various towns McCandless was hanged in effigy. At Bradford the figure dangling from the rope was cut down with ceremony, and men took from its pocket a check for $20,000 signed by Rockefeller and endorsed by the Pennsylvania Railroad—an absurd libel.[33]

The uproar in the Regions was now attracting national attention. Many newspapers carried long articles. The New York *Sun,* giving six columns to the subject, declared that western Pennsylvania had narrowly escaped a mob uprising to seize railroads and pipe lines, and to burn the Standard refineries. One producer had told *The Sun* that "four thousand men were ready to shoulder their muskets."[34] Meanwhile, the Attorney-General had filed bills in equity against the Pennsylvania, the Atlantic & Great Western, the Lake Shore, and the United Pipe-Lines, charging an unlawful combination to control the entire oil industry and a refusal to offer proper transportation facilities. He asked for injunctions.[35] Tom Scott immediately exploded in a public letter to his stockholders, denying the accusations *in toto,* and hinting that politics lay back of the Attorney-General's course.[36]

Public hearings on these suits began early in 1879 under J. B. Sweitzer as master examiner, and from the producer's point of view proved extraordinarily successful. A. J. Cassatt and other reluctant railroad officers were brought upon the witness stand, as were John D. Archbold, William Frew, Charles Lockhart, J. J. Vandergrift,

[33]I have used the Titusville *Herald,* Bradford *Era,* and New York newspapers for August–December, 1878, on this legal war. The appeal of the producers to Governor Hartranft, filling many columns, is printed in *The Era* of Sept. 4, 5, 1878. A good report of testimony before Judge Atwell in Titusville may be found in the Titusville *Herald,* Sept. 21, 1878.

[34]Nov. 13, 1878.

[35]Bradford *Era,* N. Y. *Tribune,* Oct. 8, 1878.

[36]*Annual Cyclopædia,* 1880, p. 618.

and others connected with the Standard Oil. B. B. Campbell and his associates recited the Regions' grievances at length. The whole story of the special rates established just after the downfall of the Empire came out, and made a profound public impression. The revelations of the size and power of the Standard combination, of the functions it had assumed as an "evener" of railroad traffic, and of the heavy drawbacks, rebates, and special concessions granted by the railroads, excited astonishment and indignation. Particularly telling was Cassatt's testimony on March 4. He had never been a friend of the Standard Oil. After relating the story of the Empire struggle with evident animus, he described the Pennsylvania's payment to the American Transfer Company first of 20 and later of 22½ cents a barrel on all crude oil brought to the railroad, whether it came through O'Day's pipes or not. He characterized this payment as a "commission," and defended it as proper; but his statement was far feebler than that made later by Flagler. As the State's attorney easily showed, the payment was not really a commission. O'Day had collected the fee on large shipments by independent refiners like Ohlen and Lombard, who had brought their oil to the road without any urging by the Standard officials.

Much of the testimony appeared at length in the press, and all of it was later published as a State document.[37] It is safe to say that many people who knew that rebating was the general rule were staggered by the scope of the favors given to the Standard since the fall of 1877. As we have seen, Cassatt testified that "outside" shippers who sent refined oil from Titusville or Pittsburgh to New York paid $1.44½ a barrel, while the Standard paid only 80 cents. Already *The Railroad Gazette* had expressed a significant opinion. Familiar with the "evener" contracts of 1875 and 1877, its editor remarked that the Standard was collecting roughly fifty cents a barrel on crude-oil shipments for the work and risk of effecting a railroad pool. It had not been expected or intended that the Standard should add this amount to its profits, but that it should cut the price of refined oil and so secure a larger and larger share of the business.[38] This it had done,

---

[37]*Commonwealth of Pennsylvania vs. The Pennsylvania Railroad, etc.* The suits were brought against each corporation separately.

[38]According to the *Annual Cyclopædia,* 1878, p. 682, the whole body of oil shipments in 1878 amounted to 13,000,000 barrels. The established rate of shipment was $1.50 a barrel, which should have given the railroads $18,500,-

establishing a very powerful combination. While the railroads cared nothing about promoting a monopoly, they had been helpless to resist the Standard. For some time it had been delivering in New York upon two railroads about 400 carloads of petroleum daily, besides large quantities upon a third; and imagine its power if, in the absence of any contract, it had been free to throw this immense volume of oil at will from one railroad to another! Moreover, the railroads had gladly assented to the arrangement because it was very profitable to them. Before the formulation of this "evening" agreement, "traffic was not secure and rates were a great part of the time unremunerative," while now the roads were making money from oil freights. But, continued *The Railroad Gazette,* in a remarkable pronouncement on the ethics of railroad discrimination——[39]

But in this matter, as in all others, the railroads owe a duty to the community as well as to themselves. And if they at once protect the interests of their stockholders and carry at reasonable rates, they will still be liable to condemnation if they make any unjust discriminations among shippers. And in deciding what is "unjust" in the matter of discriminations, the safety of the community, the freedom of industry, demand that there should be a severe interpretation, and that generally allowances of any kind should be prohibited, which it is not in the power of all in the same kind of business to secure, or which are not in proportion to the cost of the thing or service for which the allowance is made. . . .

But the most unjust of all discriminations are probably those founded on some actual advantage offered by the shipper, for which he secures a disproportionately large allowance. One manufacturer has a siding and loads the cars himself; a competitor carts his goods to the station and leaves them for the company to load. In such a case . . . an allowance may be . . . made so great as to work great injustice against the other shipper. . . . The common carrier should offer all his customers what are practically equal terms—terms which it is possible for them to fulfill. And, we are sure, he will have to do this sooner or later.

Contracts may be made now in practical violation of this principle— in years past we fear that a vast number of such contracts have been made—which yet come within the letter of the law; but we may rest assured that they will not remain within the letter of the law. No com-

---

ooo. Actually they received only $5,000,000, the other $13,500,000 being diverted to the Standard Oil. On this statement it is to be noted (1) that the established rates were $1.15 and $1.40, subject to certain discounts to everybody; (2) that the Standard probably paid more than double $5,000,000; and (3) that some of its saving went into the cheapening of refined oil.

[39]Nov. 1, 1878.

munity, fully understanding the facts, will permanently endure any such power in carriers or any other organizations as will make it possible at their will to destroy the business of whole classes of people.

This was sound doctrine and, as time proved, sound prophecy. A large number of Eastern newspapers expressed similar opinions. And meanwhile the railroads and Standard Oil were under heavy fire in two other States. In New York the Hepburn Investigation began in the fall of 1878 and furnished the newspapers with sensational material, while in Ohio a legislative inquiry was opened. It proved short-lived, but before it was ended various independent refiners of Ohio had told their stories, and H. M. Flagler had been examined as to the Standard's rebates. The cumulative effect of all this upon public sentiment was great, and the railroads and the Standard Oil realized it. Multitudes became convinced that the Standard Oil combination, now convicted of exacting a drawback upon other men's shipments of crude oil as well as its own—shipments which in the case of Ohlen alone amounted to about 30,000 barrels during two months of 1878—was essentially a revival of that South Improvement scheme which had excited such general indignation. The demand for effective railroad regulation was immensely strengthened.

The Grand Council of the Producers' Union was so heartened by the first result of its injunction suits that it determined upon a rash step. What would these suits accomplish? Beyond arousing public opinion, they would merely bring the issuance of restraining orders. What was needed, the Council believed, was exemplary punishment of the Standard officials on the charge of criminal conspiracy. Campbell and his associates actually had dreams of seeing Rockefeller, Flagler, Archbold, and others behind the bars. Though some of the saner members, like E. G. Patterson, strenuously opposed the plan for a criminal indictment, a majority of the Council took their stand with the bellicose Campbell.

On April 29, 1879, the grand jury of Clarion County indicted nine Standard Oil officials: John D. Rockefeller, William Rockefeller, Bostwick, O'Day, Warden, Lockhart, Flagler, Vandergrift, and the cashier of the American Transfer Company, George Girty.[40] The

[40]N. Y. *Times*, Philadelphia *Press*, April 30, 1879.

producers omitted railroad officials from the indictment, for they saw that they could not prove conspiracy on the part of Tom Scott and Cassatt, and they believed that the Pennsylvania Railroad was in reality unsympathetic with the Standard. Eight counts were included in the indictment. They alleged an attempt to achieve a monopoly of buying and selling petroleum; an attempt to oppress and injure the producers; a conspiracy to prevent others from engaging in refining; a combination to prevent the Pennsylvania Railroad and its branches from obtaining their natural oil traffic; a conspiracy to extort unreasonable commissions and rebates from various railroads; and an effort to control by fraudulent devices the market price of crude and refined oil. The grand jury gave the defendants no preliminary hearing, nor were any of them present when the indictment was found.

The Standard was thus arraigned on charges gravely inimical to its reputation, and which if sustained might lead to criminal sentences for several officers. Four of the indicted men were Pennsylvanians. They were arrested and gave bail. The others were not residents of the State and did not answer the charges. Governor Henry M. Hoyt was urged to request their extradition from Ohio and New York;[41] and when he finally refused to take action, another angry outburst came from the producers, who did not fail to charge that he had been bribed just like McCandless before him! The governor vigorously defended his course, asserting that the producers had first asked for a requisition, then had changed their minds and requested that it should not be made, and finally had renewed their demand. All this, he concluded, was connected with some bargaining under way between the producers and the Standard. "Finding that the highest process of the commonwealth was being used simply as a leverage for and against the parties to these negotiations," he remarked, "I deemed it my duty . . . to suspend action on the requisition."[42] The bargaining, as we shall see, was actually going on. Nevertheless, a letter which Tom Scott, then

[41]Philadelphia *Press*, June 28, 1879.
[42]G. E. Reed, ed., *Pennsylvania Archives, Fourth Series (Papers of the Governors)*, IX, 777. Hoyt was a graduate of Williams College who after admission to the bar became a colonel in the Civil War. Succeeding J. F. Hartranft, he was governor 1879–83.

abroad for his health, had sent to Senator Don Cameron from Antwerp on November 21, 1878, indicates that Hoyt may not have been unresponsive to corporation influences:[43]

It has occurred to me that it would be wise for you to see the newly-elected Governor Hoyt and have a clear understanding with him to say nothing whatever on the oil question in his message but let the whole matter now in court to remain there for its adjudication, and also see that he gets a good decent Attorney-General, a man whom you can always confer with on any important subject.

Gov. will have time between this and the first of January and before the inauguration to give these matters a little attention, and to get things in good shape, so that these conflicting issues may be kept out of your way and all your friends during the incoming administration at least.

I shall be glad to hear from you as soon as you have had an opportunity of having a conference and proper adjustment of the question.

The fact that the producers had committed a tactical error in forcing the indictments for conspiracy was soon clear as noonday. Proceedings in the injunction suits were still under way, and certain Standard officials immediately seized upon the conspiracy indictment as a reason for not testifying in them. On May 14, 1879, President Vandergrift of the United Pipe-Lines and General Manager O'Day were to appear and face questions which, on advice of counsel, they had earlier refused to answer. They now protested to the Attorney-General that any answers would be used against them in the criminal action, and requested a postponement until after the conspiracy trial. It was necessary to grant their plea. Then ensued a series of delays in the criminal case. Lewis G. Cassidy, counsel for the defendants, applied for a writ removing the proceedings from the Clarion County court to the supreme court. The prosecution, according to Cassidy,[44] was in the hands of Congressman George A. Jenks, who was a brother of the presiding judge before whom the case was to be tried. Moreover, a hostile press had whipped up so much sentiment against the defendants in Clarion County that a fair trial there was impossible.

This plea for a change of venue caused a series of delays. Early in January, 1880, after full argument, it was ordered that the trial should take place in the supreme court; but one of the seven judges

[43]Tom Scott Papers; given me by courtesy of Mr. S. R. Kamm.
[44]Philadelphia *Press*, Jan. 5, 1880.

was ill, and the case could not come up until he was in his seat.[45] All this automatically postponed the testimony of Vandergrift and O'Day in the injunction suit! The producers had played their cards badly.

v

But while these legal proceedings dragged on, various Regions men had been trying to effect a compromise between the producers and the Standard Oil. Rockefeller always preferred persuasion to force, and from the time that the "Petroleum Parliament" launched the new attack, he had been conspicuously brandishing a palm-branch. Indeed, he had made a definite offer in a letter to President Vandergrift of the United Pipe-Lines as early as March 19, 1878. He wrote:[46]

We are *now* prepared, to enter into a contract, to refine all the petroleum that can be sold in the markets of the world, at a low price for refining. Prices of refined oil for export to be made by a joint committee of producers and refiners, and the profits, to be determined by these prices, divided equitably between both parties. This joint interest to have the lowest net rates obtainable from the railroads. If your judgment approves, you may consult some of the producers on this question.

This would probably require the United Pipe-Lines to make the contracts and act as the clearing-house for both parties.

Nor was this Rockefeller's only conciliatory proposal. According to the New York *Tribune* of July 22, 1878, the Standard had assured the producers that if they would reduce the daily production to about 35,000 barrels, it would contract to take that amount for a year at $2 a barrel—the current price being about $1. On April 25, 1879, Rockefeller wrote a producer named Almon Raney of his readiness to strike hands with the Producers' Union and assure them steady profits if only they would restrict production. "It is true," he declared, "that the Standard Oil Company recently proposed a union

[45]S. C. T. Dodd writes in his *Memoirs:* "The local excitement was so great that a fair trial was impossible and we had the case moved into the Supreme Court of the State, a rather unprecedented proceeding, but under the circumstances clearly legal and right. The Supreme Court was charged with corruption in consequence of this movement. . . ."

[46]Tarbell, *Standard Oil Company*, I, 249, 250, misdates this letter, attributing it to the fall of 1878; actually it was written before the injunction suits began. Rockefeller Papers.

with the Producers on what we regarded a very reasonable basis, and we are advised the Producers' Council voted adversely. We are yet willing to make a fair arrangement, and think it would be of very great value to the producing interests, but of course it is not in our power to say whether an arrangement will be made."[47]

Into the complicated negotiations which followed it is not necessary to go. We need only say that after much wrangling among the Regions men, and after the passage of time had permitted a strong peace party to grow up there, an agreement with the Standard was reached. It gradually became evident to the well-owners that they were too weak to defeat the combination. Their various attacks in the courts might damage its prestige, but they could not overthrow it. Meanwhile, the appalling overproduction of oil in the Bradford field continued to exercise a paralyzing effect.[48] In June, 1879, petroleum fell below 70 cents a barrel, and a meeting of producers in Bradford to consider the subject voted the weird motion: "Whereas, the shortest way to $2 oil is through 25-cent oil, therefore be it resolved that we favor the pushing of the drill as rapidly and diligently as possible, until the goal of 25-cent oil is reached."[49] This was folly run mad. The Producers' Union gradually lost strength, and as many lodges became inactive, its funds ran low. Under these gloomy circumstances B. B. Campbell, who was the principal figure in the discussions with Rockefeller, brought before a meeting of the Grand Council on February 18, 1880, a set of terms which he reluctantly urged accepting.

In principle, this Compromise of 1880 obtained much from the Standard—with one exception almost all that the producers had fought for. It was a brief document, and boiled down to its essentials amounted to this:[50]

First: The Standard Oil combination agreed to make no opposition to the entire abrogation of the system of rebates, drawbacks, and secret rates of freight in the transportation of oil on the railroads.

Second: The Standard and its affiliates agreed not to accept any rebates which the railroad companies were not at liberty to give to other shippers, and to make no objection to full publicity for freight-rates.

[47]Rockefeller Papers.   [48]Philadelphia *Press*, July 23, 1879.
[49]Boyle, *Derrick's Handbook*, 314.
[50]N. Y. *Tribune*, Feb. 20, 1880. The contract is given in full in the *History of the Petroleum Producers' Union*, 41–44.

Third: The Standard combination agreed that the United Pipe-Lines should make no discrimination between or against their patrons, that rates of pipcage should be reasonable and uniform, and that they should not be advanced without thirty days' notice. They agreed also that so far as possible, there should be no difference in the price of petroleum between one district and another, except such as might be based upon differences in quality. The United Pipe-Lines were to make every reasonable effort to transport, store, and deliver all oil tendered to them, so long as the production did not exceed an average of 65,000 barrels a day during fifteen consecutive days. Even if the production exceeded that amount and the capacity of the pipe lines, the United agreed not to buy any so-called immediate shipment oil at a discount, provided it was not sold at discount rates to others.

Fourth: The Standard combination agreed to give certificates for all oil taken into the custody of the pipe lines, and to permit trading in these certificates as if they were equivalent to the oil itself; subject only to the 65,000-barrel-a-day stipulation.

This pledged the Standard to reform the practices of its pipe lines, and safeguarded the producers against any abuse of "immediate shipment" orders. It offered a gesture in the implied condemnation of rebates and drawbacks. But the second article was obviously inadequate. The Standard promised not to accept any rebates which the railroads were not "at liberty" to give to other shippers! This left the responsibility up to the railroads. Would they, after extending special favors to the Standard, exercise their "liberty" to give them to others? Campbell and his friends had sounded the railroads, and the best promise they could exact was that the Standard's petroleum rates should be made known to its rivals upon request. The railroads promised also not to discriminate in the allocation of cars. They and the Standard had yielded some ground, but rate discrimination had been preserved. This was the bitter fact which the Grand Council had to swallow.

In return for the Standard's concessions, the suits against the railroads, the Standard, and Rockefeller and his associates were dismissed.[51] The expenses of the litigation to the Union, some $40,000, were defrayed by the Standard—the gesture of a very rich body to a very poor one.

Rate discrimination had come to be the very symbol of what the

[51]Motions for this purpose were duly made by the Attorney-General; Philadelphia *Public Ledger, Press,* Feb. 16, 17, 1880.

producers opposed. That they had gained much by the agreement was almost forgotten in their quick and humiliating recognition of what they had failed to gain. Campbell sat with bowed head, the tears coursing down his cheeks, as his associates in the Grand Council denounced the weakness of the bargain which he had laid before them. But they knew he had worked like a man possessed, and had achieved all that was possible. By a close vote they accepted the report.[52] They had the grace to thank him for his hard labor. But they took exception to the provisions regarding rates, and in a resolution adopted separately they proclaimed: "We aver that the contest is not over and our objects are not attained . . . that the system of freight discrimination by common carriers is absolutely wrong in principle, and tends to the fostering of dangerous monopolies; and that it is the duty of the government, by legislation and executive action, to protect the people from their growing and dangerous power."

Seven years later, in the Interstate Commerce Act, they were to see a first installment of their demands substantially met. Meanwhile, they were to suffer less than before from the old abuses. The American public had been deeply impressed by the testimony in the Pennsylvania injunction suits and the New York and Ohio investigations, and Rockefeller realized it.[53] Officers and attorneys of the Standard later asserted that from this time forward it never took rebates. Other students of Standard Oil history have disagreed violently with them, and in essence are undoubtedly right, yet from this time forward the practice was indeed modified. The combination never again made so naked, unabashed, and exorbitant a use of its power to exact special railway privileges as it had done in the years 1877–79. To this extent the campaign waged by the Regions resulted in victory.

[52] N. Y. *Times*, Philadelphia *Press*, Feb. 19, 1880.

[53] As one evidence of this impression, see the report of Joseph Nimms, Jr., chief of the Pennsylvania Bureau of Statistics, Dec. 1, 1879, on the relations of railroads and public. He detailed the advantages enjoyed by the Standard, but intimated that they would not be continued much longer.

XXIV

The Pipe-Line Revolution

AT FOUR o'clock on the afternoon of May 28, 1879, a spectacular event in the history of the petroleum industry took place at Coryville, Pa., in the heart of the Bradford field. Hundreds of spectators had gathered about the tanks and pumping station of the Tidewater Pipe-Line Company, The officers formed a tense group inside the station. President Byron D. Benson stepped in front of a throbbing forty-horsepower Holly engine, and—with a hand that his small son distinctly saw tremble[1] —turned a valve. The chug and gurgle of oil being forced through six-inch pipes plainly reached the listening group. Knots of men began walking eastward along the glistening new wrought-iron line, keeping pace with the crude oil as it was carried over hill and dale toward the Olmsted pumping station some twenty-two miles away. Within an hour the flow was several miles distant, and only a few hardy mechanics and officers followed it into the twilight. At ten o'clock on the morning of May 30 it reached Olmsted, where new engines thrust it on over the mountainous, heavily wooded country to the east. Its destination was Williamsport, clear across the Allegheny range.

Rockefeller had built and consolidated his industrial domain largely through close attention to the problem of transportation. After his decisive war with the Empire and Pennsylvania, he apparently believed that his troubles in that sphere were ended; but if so, for once his foresight failed him. Despite the success of the Columbia Conduit Company and of his own line in pumping crude petroleum forty miles into Pittsburgh, he acted as if confident that oil transport would remain indefinitely in the hands of the rail-

[1]W. S. Benson, then the small son, so told me, May 14, 1938.

roads. The sudden emergence of a heavy trunk pipe line making direct railway connections with the seaboard took him by surprise, and threatened anew the practical monopoly which he had created.

The building of the Tidewater's 110-mile line ranked in some ways with the best engineering feats of the day—with the Hoosac Tunnel and Brooklyn Bridge.[2] The group responsible were the three enterprising Titusville men, Benson, McKelvy, and Hopkins, who had so successfully operated the Columbia Conduit system.[3] After the sale of the Conduit, they had used $125,000 to buy the Seaboard Pipe-Line Company, with its almost complete right of way from the Butler County field to Baltimore. But it was hard to raise capital to carry through this grandiose enterprise. Laying a pipe line of such size, equipped with pumping machinery, cost from $5500 to $6500 a mile.[4] Abandoning the scheme, they decided to build a much shorter line from the Bradford area to Williamsport, where they could join the Philadelphia & Reading Railroad, which was engaged in a bitter conflict with the Pennsylvania and wanted oil freights. The president of the Reading, the brilliantly erratic Franklin B. Gowen, had welcomed the project with open arms, and had induced his company to contribute $250,000 to the $625,000 capital of the pipe line, which was renamed the Tidewater.[5] Up to the last, betting was even on the oil exchanges that the line would prove a failure. The distance was about three times as great as any previously covered, the terrain was a rough and difficult mountain strip, and the six-inch pipe was heavier than any yet given extensive use. But if successful, the line would free the rich Bradford field from its complete dependence upon the railroads dominated by the Standard Oil.

[2]"The project of Doctor Hostetter in building thirty-five miles of three-inch pipe was larger in the minds of men in 1874 than the building today of a line from New York to San Francisco." *Short History of the Tidewater Pipe Line,* 45.

[3]In this group Benson was the bold planner, McKelvy furnished the legal mind and training, and Hopkins had practical engineering talent. Benson, who as a young man had been sheriff of Onondaga County, N. Y., carried an air of rugged strength. "He could go into a bank and when he came out he had what he wanted." W. S. Benson to the author, Dec. 22, 1938.

[4]*House Trust Investigation, 1888,* pp. 325, 326.

[5]Of the capital, $250,000 was furnished by the Reading, $250,000 by the incorporators, and $125,000 was represented by the right of way of the Seaboard Pipe-Line, never used. *Short History of the Tidewater,* 11.

Much of the success of the undertaking was attributable to its versatile engineer, Herman Haupt. A graduate of West Point in the same class as Meade, Haupt had been successively a professor of civil engineering, principal engineer and general superintendent of the main section of the Pennsylvania, and for five years chief engineer of the Hoosac Tunnel.[6] During the Civil War he made a memorable record as chief of the bureau of military railroads. In obtaining a road for the new pipe line he moved rapidly and stealthily. The Standard Oil boldly tried to thwart the plan by purchasing a right of way north and south across Pennsylvania in the supposed line of advance. Haupt as a ruse ran ostentatious surveys through many counties and in various directions, meanwhile quietly buying the rights he needed in areas unvisited by engineers. He always communicated with sellers through some third party, and always wrote to his agents in a secret cipher. He took extreme care in the preparation of legal papers and contracts, for he had to safeguard himself against injunctions and court attacks. A gap was finally found in what had at first seemed an impenetrable blockade. By a minute scrutiny of boundaries and titles in Lycoming County, the agents discovered a strip of unclaimed land sixteen feet wide between two farms—the bed of a creek, landholders owning to each bank—and acquired a patent for it from the State![7] The pipe was then laid along this strip. When Haupt's workers tried to cut through the Northern Central branch of the Pennsylvania Railroad by laying the pipe under a culvert, they met immediate resistance. A gang of section-hands hurried out before dawn, a locomotive was hitched to the pipe, and the smashed fragments were dragged out at 4 A.M. But an injunction stopped further interference, the pipe was relaid, and in 1940 it still ran through the culvert![8]

When, a week after pumping began, it was announced that the stream of crude oil had crossed the last ridge of the Alleghenies and was filling the great new tanks at Williamsport, every oil man with a spark of imagination felt a thrill. A new era had dawned. It was

[6]Cf. Frank A. Flower, ed., *Reminiscences of General Herman Haupt,* XXII–XXIX.

[7]*Short History of the Tidewater,* 31. Mr. W. S. Benson told me that the agent who found this unoccupied strip was "an old weasel" named B. F. Warren. Construction of the line began on Washington's birthday, 1879, and was completed just three months later.

[8]*Short History of the Tidewater,* 25, 26; W. S. Benson to the author.

evident that the railroads would soon cease to play an important part in carrying crude oil. At last, many believed, an escape had been found from the "oppression" of the Standard combination. And merely as a technological exploit, the work of Benson and Haupt was impressive. From Coryville to Williamsville the oil was raised more than 1900 feet, thence dropping by gravity 2100 feet to Williamsport. Two pumping stations did all the work. Several stretches of the line ran along mountainsides so steep that the heavy sections had to be let down the rocky slopes by cables. At first the pipes were not buried except where they crossed cultivated land. But when summer heat came, the engineers learned what expansion meant! Like a huge python, the line had thrust itself into the tops of high bushes, smashed down small trees fifteen feet from the original site, and coiled itself out across roadways, where horses reared in panic as they suddenly came upon the gleaming tube. The entire line was therefore buried, and the flow winter and summer became more equable. The pipe, which at first had a discharging capacity of 6000 barrels a day and soon much more, worked at a normal pressure of 400 pounds to the square inch. For adjustment to the rough country, it was made sufficiently flexible to permit a deflection of fifteen feet to a hundred. Tanks had been built at Williamsport holding 60,000 barrels, the Reading had spiked down a new half-mile siding, and a train of thirty cars could be filled in minutes rather than hours.[9]

By the middle of June more than 50,000 barrels had been pumped into Williamsport. The Reading had a fleet of 200 new tank cars waiting,[10] and its trains rapidly puffed into Chester, where a large independent refinery stood on Delaware Bay. On June 23 the first delivery of oil was made to Bayonne, 3500 barrels. Meanwhile work on an independent refinery at Williamsport, the Solar Oil works, was progressing so rapidly that its opening was set for the beginning of July. "The opponents of this pipe-line project are beginning to discover it is bound to be a grand success," declared a congratulatory article in the Philadelphia *Press*. "The managers have shown themselves to be quiet, methodical business men, who pursue their purposes steadily and with great determination. They evince no alarm at the threats just now reaching them of formidable movements be-

[9]Harrisburg *Independent*, April 11, Philadelphia *Press*, June 15, 1879.
[10]N. Y. *Tribune*, June 25, 1879.

ing started to cripple or wholly interrupt the workings of their lines."

But the most eloquent testimonial to the success of the new line lay in the quick mobilization of its opponents for resistance. The Pennsylvania on June 23 cut its charge from the lower fields to New York from $1.10 to 55 cents a barrel, and its charge on Bradford crude from 85 to 30 cents. The United Pipe-Lines simultaneously reduced the charge for local transfers from 20 cents to 5 cents a barrel! A relentless war of rates seemed about to begin.

For once Rockefeller was taken by surprise. He had been skeptical of the success of the undertaking. "We hear different rumors about the Tidewater Pipe Line," he wrote Camden on May 15, 1879.[11] "Rather doubt they will pump oil by the 25th inst., as has been published, and if they do, presume it will result in lower rates of freight, but am not a little skeptical about their doing it. They are quite likely to have some disappointments yet before consummating all their plans in that direction." But he was as quick as any one to grasp the significance of the achievement. A pipe line could penetrate where a railroad would not. It would cost far less to build. It could pump crude oil—few men yet thought of piping refined oil—over long distances much more cheaply. Haupt had calculated that while the cost of transportation from the Regions to the coast by rail had been 35 to 40 cents a barrel, by pipe line it would be only 16⅔ cents. When once pipe lines began carrying most of the crude petroleum, many of the advantages which the Standard combination had been deriving from discriminatory rates would be lost. Rockefeller must have regretted that he had not been the pioneer in this field, even though his position as "evener" and railroad favorite had made it almost indispensable for him to support the status quo.

The independent refineries rejoiced; for in its first year the Tidewater Pipe-Line carried 1,098,000 barrels of oil, and gave vigor and prosperity to several coastal plants.

II

But Rockefeller always moved rapidly and determinedly in such situations. He took immediate action to lay a system of trunk pipe lines for the Standard. He and O'Day planned one line from Brad-

[11]Rockefeller Papers.

ford to Bayonne, N. J., and three others to connect the Oil Regions with Cleveland, Buffalo, and Philadelphia—Pittsburgh already having its artery. His second step was to attempt an agreement with the Tidewater Company. When he offered to purchase Benson's interest for $300,000 and to give him employment at a good salary, he met a tart refusal.[12] Rockefeller then formally proposed to buy all the crude oil that the line could carry. "We will guarantee to take 10,000 barrels a day," he wrote, pointing out that this meant a capacity business for the pipes, with steady profits, and a like amount of freight for the Reading. But again his proposal was rejected.

At the same time, Rockefeller inexorably carried forward his plans for purchasing or arranging mergers with the last independent refineries in Philadelphia and New York—plans which if successful would deprive the Tidewater of its principal customers for crude oil. President Gowen later told how effective these activities were. "When this pipe-line was first constructed, it relied upon independent refineries to take its products," he said.[13] "One after another was bought up by the Standard Oil, and new refineries had to be constructed sufficient to take nearly all the products of the pipe-line." Paying high prices, the Standard shortly acquired Sone & Fleming, and all the other important refineries in the New York district save that of Lombard, Ayres, headed by the indomitable Josiah Lombard.

Meanwhile, all the old elements of opposition to Standard naturally rallied with elation about the new banner. Joseph D. Potts, burning with resentment over the destruction of the Empire, labored day and night to give the Tidewater-Reading alliance the benefit of his wisdom and experience.[14] The Tidewater men had no difficulty in finding experts to help them erect a refinery, the Ocean Oil Company Works, at Communipaw, the terminus of the Central of New Jersey; and this, with the Chester refinery and the Solar works at Williamsport, would afford a partial market.[15] During the first half of 1879 Gowen was striving hard to obtain the consent of British in-

[12]W. S. Benson to the author, May 14, 1938.
[13]Franklin B. Gowen, *Argument Before the Committee on Railroads of the House of Representatives of Pennsylvania Upon the Hulings Bill to Prevent Unjust Discrimination by Railroad Companies*, Feb. 13, 1877, p. 17.
[14]William M. Potts so told me Feb. 18, 1937.
[15]The Ocean Oil Company plant is sometimes spoken of as at Bayonne; the plant of the Chester Oil Company was really at Thurlow, Pa., just outside Chester. *Cf. Short History of the Tidewater*, 14.

vestors to a merger between the Reading and the Central of New Jersey, and though the Pennsylvania Railroad was bitterly antagonistic to this move for a new trunk line, he had high hopes of success.[16]

In Gowen, a combative Scotch-Irishman who was one of the first corporation lawyers in the country to rise to a high managerial position, the new combination had a leader of rare abilities. A year older than Rockefeller, he already possessed a wide experience. Beginning as practitioner of general law, he had become district attorney for Schuylkill County, then counsel for the Girard coal trusts and the Reading Railroad, and in 1869 president of the Reading. Under his aggressive sway the railroad had developed its facilities rapidly. He had been one of the leaders in the attempt by a few railways to form a practical monopoly of anthracite, and in buying coal lands for the Reading had formed the largest company for holding mineral areas thus far known in the United States. He had also been the shrewd and relentless commander of the campaign for breaking up the Molly Maguires, a secret labor organization in the anthracite fields which was in large part the natural product of oppression and injustice there. This dubious feat had given him national prominence. And unlike Jay Gould, Tom Scott, and other railway leaders who preferred working behind the scenes, Gowen liked to stand in the public eye. He enjoyed calling huge meetings of stockholders, inviting all the reporters, and delivering addresses of genuine eloquence on the problems of the Reading. His handsome presence, power of lucid exposition, and flashes of Whitefieldian fervor impressed every one. Yet the admiration which he evoked was mingled with distrust, for his belligerent and impetuous temper, his imagination, and his histrionic vein made him dangerous to friend as well as foe. "A wonderful man, but never quite dependable," was the summation of the financier E. T. Stotesbury.[17]

As Rockefeller knew, his ambitions almost rivalled those of Commodore Vanderbilt and Tom Scott. He wished to build up a great coal empire, and his Philadelphia & Reading Coal & Iron Company paid such exorbitant prices for land that by 1879 it and the railroad

[16]Rumor said that the Standard Oil began to make heavy purchases of Reading stock, but this is very improbable; N. Y. *Tribune,* June 9, 1879.
[17]Stotesbury to the author, April 24, 1938.

staggered under debts of almost $200,000,000. He was eager for oil freights. He wished not only to control the Central of New Jersey to the east, but to push a line to Port Allegheny on the northwest, and thus construct a system extending from the Atlantic to the Great Lakes. He planned an alliance with the Tidewater on the one side, the Baltimore & Ohio on the other. These were grand visions, and Gowen put a fierce tenacity into their realization.

When early in 1880 the Reading went into bankruptcy, and harsh accusations of fraud and extravagance were flung at him, he was not daunted for an instant. Contriving to be made one of the receivers, he kept control of the business management, and in 1882 was triumphantly re-elected president. Two views of the situation had developed. Conservative American and British investors, forming a strong party, wished to reorganize the Reading on the basis of estimated annual earnings of $8,000,000 a year. Gowen believed that the proper basis was $10,000,000 in annual earnings, a figure which would save the junior creditors and stockholders from loss. His sanguine policy was put into effect. In 1881 the railroad earned just over $10,000,000; in 1882, $10,600,000; and in 1883, $11,850,000—thus seeming to justify his policy. But graver troubles lay ahead. Reverses in the middle eighties again broke his hold on the railroad; and though he remained a successful lawyer, in 1889, this emotionally unstable leader ended his meteoric career by committing suicide in Washington. Rockefeller always respected Gowen's powers, and in later years paid tribute to him as "a very aggressive force," and an executive of "great ability."[18] What he needed was a cautious Lockhart or Pratt by his side, and Rockefeller always wished that the Standard might have enlisted his talents. "What a man Franklin Gowen might have been," he once mused, "if he had joined an organization like ours, surrounded by good men who would act like a balance-wheel for him!"[19]

In dealing with the Tidewater Rockefeller would, as usual, have preferred conciliation to coercion. He sent Flagler to confer with the railroad princes—Cassatt, Jewett, and William H. Vanderbilt—at Saratoga on June 5, 1879. These three men were for crushing the Tidewater by a swift attack. Following Rockefeller's directions, Flagler argued for compromise. "But we don't want you to make any

[18]Inglis, Conversations with Rockefeller.   [19]*Idem.*

alliance of a formal nature with the Tidewater," protested the rail-road heads, who believed that their only safety lay in destroying the pipe line. Flagler in reply pointed out that the fight would be stubborn and its outcome uncertain.

"I have never seen a contest of this kind begun but what there was an end to it," he said. "Now, we can make a satisfactory arrangement with the Tidewater and avoid this contest. It is not necessary for you to throw away any money. We are not seekers after low rates. . . . We would prefer not to have this contest; it is better that the Tidewater and Reading Railroad should be recognized." "But look at our investment," Jewett of the Erie protested. And the others chimed in: "We will never recognize them as carriers of oil."

In the end the Standard leaders—"like fools," Flagler remarked later—let the railroads cut their rates. "Very well, then, we will stick to you," he said.[20]

For the Pennsylvania, Erie, and New York Central the ensuing war was a disastrous contest, ending in a compromise which amounted to defeat. That summer they threw away a fortune in oil revenues. The first drastic cuts were quickly followed by others. Before July the open freight rate on crude oil from the Bradford district to Philadelphia and New York had fallen to twenty-five cents a barrel.[21] A little later it went to twenty cents, and in some instances fifteen. These slashes marked the beginning of the end of the vast rail traffic in crude petroleum, which for many years had kept thousands of cars continuously busy, and had often paid high profits. The Standard Oil of course gained rather than lost by the reduction in freight rates, which gave it cheaper raw materials. To be sure, it reduced its pipeage rates to five cents a barrel in the Regions, but then most of the oil it piped was bought by its own buyers for its own refineries.[22] Rockefeller had perceived that his company could keep in the background, and that if the Tidewater became sufficiently weakened, could step in to seize the fruits of victory. Altogether, it was the railroads which took practically all the risks. They acted

[20]Flagler reports this conversation in detail in *House Trust Investigation, 1888,* p. 783. Gowen asserted that the Standard Oil had urged the railroads to resist, but he had no knowledge of the facts and offered no evidence. Flagler's sworn assertion, which could and would have been contradicted by the railroad heads if incorrect, must be accepted. It is borne out by collateral evidence; and Rockefeller always preferred persuasion to force.

[21]*Railroad Gazette,* June 27, 1879.   [22]*N. Y. Tribune,* June 25, 1879.

foolishly, for the big pipe line had come to stay, and their rate-slashing could in the long run avail them nothing.

The well-informed *Railroad Gazette* remarked in August that the trunk lines were suffering heavily from their freight cuts. The agreement for the division of petroleum freights by fixed quotas, with the Standard acting as "evener," had of course gone by the boards along with the rate agreement, and the railroads were competing with one another for whatever consignments they could get.[23] Producers had not been helped by the reduction in freight rates, for Bradford crude was being quoted at seventy cents a barrel or less, touching the lowest prices yet known. At that level the wooden barrel was worth almost twice as much as its contents! Apparently the refiners were the principal beneficiaries. Early in November *The Railroad Gazette* announced that the railways, by then utterly sick of carrying crude oil at the abysmally low tariffs, would soon raise their charges. News that the Standard was about to lay a pipe line from the Regions to its refineries in Cleveland, thus cutting off an enormous traffic from the Erie and the New York Central, had apparently played a part in this change of attitude. The railroads were resigning themselves to the inevitable.[24]

President Jewett of the Erie and M. R. Smith, general freight manager of the Baltimore & Ohio, took the lead in demanding a rate advance. Correspondence between them was followed by a meeting at the Windsor Hotel in New York early in 1880, attended also by Vanderbilt and Tom Scott,[25] where a new agreement was discussed. The railroads shortly opened negotiations with Rockefeller and the heads of the Tidewater, and the result was a compromise satisfactory to all three parties. Its precise terms were not made public. But we know that early in June, 1880, the charge for carrying crude oil from the Regions was raised to 51 cents for New York traffic, and 38 cents for Philadelphia and Baltimore traffic.[26] We know also that the transportation world hailed the end of the rate war with relief.[27] The new tariffs gave the railroads, according to Haupt's figures, a slender profit, while they afforded large revenues to the Tidewater. Unquestionably the agreement represented a victory for the pipe

[23]*Railroad Gazette,* Aug. 15, 1879.
[24]*Idem,* Nov. 7, 1879.
[25]N. Y. *World,* Jan. 23, 1880.
[26]Boyle, *Derrick's Handbook,* 326.
[27]*Railroad Gazette,* Nov. 12, 1880.

line as against the railroads, and particularly for Benson and his ally Gowen as against Tom Scott and Cassatt.

III

The Standard Oil, in this breakdown of the old rate agreements, had lost its high rebate or commission as "evener"; but the strong public condemnation of these discriminations after the Pennsylvania injunction suits had made them practically untenable anyhow. In no other way had the Standard been hurt by the conflict. But Rockefeller knew that, looking to the future, it behooved him to act energetically to master the Tidewater. If the pipe line doubled and quadrupled its shipments, building up stronger and stronger "outside" refineries, good-by to his dream of a closely organized and perfectly controlled industry!

His object was not to attack the new line by destructive body blows, but to bring its heads to an agreement that would restrict its activities within harmless limits. He tried, first, to limit its energies by depriving it of outlets for crude oil; second, to weaken its independence by raising up a strong pro-Standard element inside the company; and third, to persuade Benson, McKelvy, and Hopkins to accede to a working arrangement with the Standard as just and reasonable. In this program he was aided by the weakness of the independent refineries, and the sea of troubles through which the Reading Railroad, the Tidewater's indispensable ally, had to buffet its way.

Rockefeller was able to write William G. Warden just before Christmas in 1881: "Our people are feeling pleasantly, and showing an interest in our work and plans most gratifying. Our outside competitors are unhappy, and we are of one mind in respect to a policy."[28] Better organization, the economies of mass purchasing and mass production, greater technical skill, and better facilities for retailing and export, all gave his gigantic creation a marked advantage over the independent plants. As it continued steadily to expand, the Tidewater men were kept in continual uneasiness over the fate of the last few "outside" refineries. As late as the summer of 1878, half a dozen such independents had survived in the New York area —Denslow & Bush, McGoey & King, W. & G. F. Gregory, Donald &

[28]Rockefeller Papers.

Company, Wilson & Anderson, and of course Lombard, Ayres.[29] But by the time the Tidewater pipes were fairly operating, only Lombard, Ayres remained.

And even Josiah Lombard was not ready to receive oil, for his establishment, situated on the Hudson at Sixty-sixth Street, had recently been condemned by the New York Central Railroad. He would have to build a new one. Could he stand alone in New York? And could the new plants at Communipaw and Chester long survive against the giant which now controlled fully 90 per cent of the nation's refining capacity?[30]

The refinery at Chester was hampered at every turn by the hostility of the Pennsylvania Railroad. In general, it expanded its product. But in the spring of 1882 it received some inland orders, and applied to the Pennsylvania for shipping facilities. The general freight agent informed the plant that he would grant it at a rate of $50 a tank car (not exceeding 100 barrels) from Chester to Washington. This was fifty cents a barrel for hauling oil 120 miles, or a good deal more than the Pennsylvania charged the Standard for hauling kerosene from Pittsburgh to Washington, about 350 miles![31] At about the same time the Pennsylvania sent the Chester refinery a significant note upon the carriage of its products westward. They would haul its kerosene from Chester to Lock Haven, Pa., for twenty-three cents a hundredweight (about $1 a barrel);[32] but "we cannot make a rate on the empty cars returning." On this Gowen made the pithy comment: "They will carry the oil. Oh, yes, they will make a proper charge for it, which is only three or four times higher than they charge the Standard Oil Company, but they will not permit the empty cars to come over the road in order to get the oil—'we will make no rates for the empty cars.' They must be taken on a wheelbarrow or by canal or by balloon."[33]

If the independent refineries which the Tidewater needed were in a precarious position, the Reading itself was a most uncertain support. Potentially it was a great railroad, its main line running

[29]*Hepburn Committee Hearings*, II, 1571 ff.   [30]*Idem*, IV, 3678.
[31]Franklin B. Gowen, *Argument Before the Committee on Railroads, ut supra.*
[32]A barrel of refined oil was generally estimated at 400 pounds, though it usually weighed more.
[33]Gowen, *ut supra.*

northwest from Philadelphia through Reading to Pottsville in the anthracite country, while it held branches to Harrisburg and Williamsport on one side, and to Bound Brook, N. J., on the other. The Bound Brook division was commonly regarded as the best piece of track in the country.[34] But ever since the railroad was founded in the thirties it had suffered from financial manipulation, while Gowen's lavish purchases of coal and iron mines had injured it. Heavily overcapitalized and debt-burdened, during the spring of 1880 it went into the receivership we have already mentioned.[35]

This was a severe blow to the Tidewater Pipe-Line. Gowen was harshly criticized for his reckless expenditure of scores of millions to acquire nearly one third of the anthracite lands then available for operation. It was said that one mine-owner with whom he was bargaining had mumbled something about $50,000. "Done!" exclaimed Gowen, who misunderstood him. "We'll pay you the $500,000 within a week!"[36] He also speculated in iron, buying rolling mills for the railroad at Pottsville and Danville. He had connived at the sale of bond issues upon what amounted to false representations, and the Philadelphia *Public Ledger* and New York *Tribune* accused him of outright frauds which merited a prison sentence. They declared that for years he had misrepresented the financial condition of the company, that he had paid stockholders some $15,700,000 of unearned dividends at the expense of debtors, and that he had helped conceal a floating debt of $7,000,000 from the directors. *The Tribune* denounced the management as "plunderers" guilty of "gigantic wrongs,"[37] while later writers have commented upon the weird combination of brilliancy with mendacity in Gowen's annual reports.[38] Soon after the receivers took charge they issued a statement

[34] Announcement of the lease of this Bound Brook section was formally made May 11, 1879; Philadelphia papers, May 15–19.

[35] The Federal Government had executed a lien on it for claims totalling about $500,000; N. Y. *World,* Jan. 27, 1880.

[36] E. T. Stotesbury to the author, April 24, 1938. See the *Commercial and Financial Chronicle,* May 29, 1880, on Gowen's reckless debt-making.

[37] N. Y. *Tribune,* July 6, 10, 12, Nov. 13, 1880, cover the subject; see especially the editorial on frauds, July 6.

[38] See the scathing account in S. F. Van Oss's careful work, *American Railroads as Investments,* 313 ff. He speaks especially of the report of 1874 as containing "false statements and false figures." Of Gowen's coal company he says that "there seems to have been no end to robbery, jobbery, and speculation on the part of officials." Some of the properties bought, however, later proved very profitable.

on the precise financial condition of the road which was highly damaging to its officers.

Conservative Philadelphians, headed by A. J. Drexel and John G. Bullitt, at once joined hands with the London financiers, McCalmont Brothers, to oust Gowen and temporarily succeeded, electing in January, 1881, another president in his stead. But Gowen rallied his own party of stockholders, and by pamphlets, newspaper articles, and speeches effectively appealed to the general public. In a tremendous three-hour address in the Philadelphia Academy of Music on April 23, 1881, he carried the war into hostile territory.[39] The Drexel-Bullitt group had attempted to get rid of him, he declared, so that in future the Reading might be operated in the interests of the Pennsylvania Railroad. And what would the Pennsylvania do with the property? Ruin it and betray the true interests of the State! He charged Tom Scott with bribing the City Council to defeat a bill granting legitimate transfer privileges to the Reading. He accused him of obtaining absolute control of a mile of the Junction Railroad in Philadelphia in 1879 by fraud, thus cutting the connection of the Reading with the South; and for the same object, with paying an outrageous price for the Philadelphia, Wilmington & Baltimore Railroad. No corporation in the country, he declared, followed such a dog-in-the-manger policy as the Pennsylvania.

Gowen also asserted that the oil traffic, on which the railroads ought to be making 10 per cent a year, had been ruined when the Pennsylvania tried to crush the Tidewater by carrying petroleum for the Standard 400 miles at fifteen cents a barrel. He estimated that during this rate war the Pennsylvania had lost 9 per cent on its original capital stock. In still another ringing speech in the same hall on June 16 he extended his indictment.[40] Tom·Scott, he declared, had sacrificed the interests of the city and State to his selfish whims. By devious maneuvers the Pennsylvania had diverted the oil and grain trade from Philadelphia to New York. In the previous year more than three times as much grain and nearly five times as much oil had been shipped to New York as to their own city. And as Scott had ruined Pittsburgh by his rate policy, so now he would ruin Philadelphia. He had notoriously bought up the Philadelphia & Erie merely in order to paralyze it, and he expected to treat the Reading

[39]Philadelphia *Press,* April 24, 1881.   [40]N. Y. *Tribune,* June 17, 1881.

in the same way. Reminding his hearers how the Pennsylvania for years had bought legislators like sheep, and that it was even accused of purchasing the higher judges, Gowen asked if the Reading stock-holders would surrender to such a corrupt corporation?

This violent assault upon the Pennsylvania diverted attention from more pertinent matters. It prevented any one from asking embarrassing questions about unprofitable mines, misleading balance-sheets, and the transfer of huge debt-items to the coal company's books to keep them out of the annual report. In 1882 Gowen was elected president again. He signalized his return to power by a brilliant stroke. In alliance with Garrett of the Baltimore & Ohio, he bought control of the Central Railroad of New Jersey from Jay Gould, announcing his coup in February. At last the Reading held a through track to New York Bay.[41]

Even yet, however, his road was beset by financial embarrassments which constantly threatened his position, and which in 1884 were to bring him toppling down again. He remained an harassed and uncertain ally of the Tidewater Company—which was suffering from varied and ceaseless difficulties in other fields.

IV

During 1881–82 the Tidewater pushed its pipe line forward to Tamanend in eastern Pennsylvania, on the Central of New Jersey;[42] and this required money. Credit difficulties immediately arose. President Benson, often hard pressed for cash, relied heavily upon the Second National Bank of Titusville, and when one director exerted all his influence to cut off loans, only the firmness of the head, Charles Hyde, averted serious trouble.[43] Even more alarming were the disputes which the Standard was accused of fomenting within the company's ranks, and which gave Rockefeller his opportunity to press for an agreement.

These grave dissensions among the Tidewater's stockholders arose in 1881–82. The original subscribers had been a homogeneous and apparently loyal group of Regions producers and shippers. They included four men of influence, however, who became dissatisfied with

[41]*Commercial and Financial Chronicle*, Feb. 18, 1882.
[42]*Short History of the Tidewater*, 29.
[43]W. S. Benson to the author, Oct. 12, 1938.

Benson's resolute antagonism to the Standard Oil, and who advocated a merger with that organization. The result was a bitter quarrel. The four dissenters were Hascal L. Taylor and John Satterfield, large-scale producers, who had sunk so many wells that at one time they were the principal oil sellers in the State; David Boyd Stewart, an ambitious, bright young man who had been secretary of the Columbia Conduit Company; and John L. McKinney, one of the most experienced and respected operators of the period. They held some $200,000 worth of stock. Taylor and Stewart had been among the original five who signed the Tidewater's organization papers. Naturally, the stand these four men took seemed to their associates sheer treason. Fierce charges were brought against three of them, the Tidewater officers publicly declaring that Satterfield was an unprincipled rascal, that Stewart was weak and extravagant, and that Taylor had "the morals of a medieval baron."[44] They were accused of taking Standard Oil bribes, and one of Benson's sons repeated that accusation to the author as late as 1938. They replied by angry counter-charges. Before long the company was divided into two warring camps.

One of the four men was manifestly upright, able, and sincere. No one ever seriously assailed McKinney, who had been reared in the Regions, had drilled his first well in 1861 at nineteen, had since been active all the way from Bradford to Parker's Landing, and was known the length and breadth of the oil fields for his manliness, shrewdness, and honesty.[45] He lived in Titusville, first next door to McKelvy, and then across the street from Benson, and was intimate with both.[46] Taylor and Satterfield were typical Regions speculators; they were after money with both hands, and often acted on the most selfish motives. But Taylor, contrary to Miss Tarbell's statement, was notoriously hostile to the Standard; she says his oil company had been sold "about this time" to the Standard, but actually that sale did not occur until eight years later![47] Possibly it is true that the Standard, through Archbold, Vandergrift, and Seep, had worked to

[44] *Short History of the Tidewater,* 12. Taylor and Satterfield both died in 1894.
[45] McLaurin, *Sketches in Crude Oil,* 237 ff.
[46] W. S. Benson to the author, May 4, 1938.
[47] Tarbell, *Standard Oil Company,* II, 19; the sale took place in 1890, not 1882.

enlist these men. But the Bradford *Era,* an anti-Standard paper which followed the contest closely, ridiculed this theory. The simple fact, it said, was that Taylor's Union Oil Company held $250,000 worth of stock in the line, and had demanded better representation in the management. It was no secret that he "has long been dissatisfied with the methods pursued by the head officials, claiming that the rights of the patrons of the line were not protected as they should be." All four men might well have been honestly convinced that the company should take a friendlier attitude toward the Standard. They were worried by the line's difficulties, they knew the strength of the trust, and they measured the danger ahead. Since the Tidewater had already made an agreement with the railroads, why not one with the Standard? While Benson, McKelvy, and Hopkins would feel a personal humiliation in any merger, the minority group had no pride at stake.

It must be remembered that the whole Allegheny Valley was now becoming divided into two angry camps—pro-Standard and anti-Standard. Enemies of the Standard accused its friends of dishonesty —they had been bought up! Men spat in disgust as they saw a Standard adherent pass. Women frightened their children by exclaiming: "Rockefeller will get you if you don't mind!" Knots in the grocery stores and taverns denounced any one who had gone over to the hated combination as men had denounced the Tories in 1776 or the Copperheads in 1863. Supporters of the Standard, on the other hand, accused its enemies of spiteful prejudice and mean envy. They told contemptuously of the Regions loafer who, stumbling over a rock, got up, rubbed his shins, and ejaculated: "Damn the Standard!" The fact was that both sides numbered men of sincerity and character, and that it would have been hard to choose between Vandergrift and Campbell, or between McKinney and Lewis Emery, on the score of honesty.

Yet it must be said that highly unfair weapons were used by the enemies of the Tidewater. Early in 1882 the company decided to borrow $2,000,000 to extend its lines. Benson made several trips to New York, on which he was shadowed by a mysterious spy, while the bankers upon whom he called received immediate warnings of his business incapacity. Finally, he reached a tentative agreement with George F. Baker of the First National Bank. At once hostile stockholders of the Tidewater assured Baker that the company was practically insolvent. Benson and Gowen succeeded in convincing him that these men were tools of the Standard and were trying to discredit the Tidewater so that Rockefeller could buy it at a low price. In October, 1882, a syndicate headed by Baker agreed to market $825,000 of 6 per cent bonds at 90, and $1,375,000 of loan certificates which not only paid interest but were entitled to the same dividends as the common stock—decidedly hard terms. Baker and James R. Keene between them bought nearly $500,000 of the loan certificates, eventually realizing enormous profits. But attacks on the credit of the company continued, and Gowen later declared that they gravely interfered with the flotation of its bonds in Europe.[48]

As part of these attacks, in September, 1882, the court of common pleas in Crawford County was suddenly asked to appoint a receiver for the Tidewater. The petitioner was none other than E. G. Patterson, who had been one of the stoutest opponents of the Standard until he quarrelled with his fellow producers on the conspiracy suit, when he had become bitterly hostile to some of them. Various circumstances had increased his resentment. For one thing, he had recently been employed to collect evidence in support of a claim which the State was making against the Standard for about $3,000,000 in unpaid taxes. After he had done much hard work, the State Auditor, on losing the case, refused to pay him the compensation he expected. Smarting under a new sense of injustice, he came into close relations with Archbold. Just what agreement they made is not known, but Patterson later admitted that Archbold had paid him a considerable sum, which seems to have been $7500, that out of this he bought fifty shares of Tidewater stock, and that he then applied for the receivership.[49] He alleged that the company had violated its charter by speculating in oil, that it was practically insolvent, and that he had been refused access to the books. This action by a prominent producer and recent arch-foe of the Standard caused a sensation. But on January 15, 1883, Judge Pierson Church in Meadville

[48]*Short History of the Tidewater, passim;* Gowen, *Argument Before the Committee on Railroads,* etc.

[49]Miss Tarbell says "some $20,000" (II, 18); but Gowen in his *Argument Before the Committee on Railroads,* etc., says $7500, and Governor Pattison in his special message to the Legislature, March 1, 1883, $7500. The fifty shares of stock would cost, at par, $5000. See *Derrick's Handbook,* 353, for some details; Titusville and Bradford newspapers, Sept. 16 ff.

dismissed the petition with a scathing condemnation of Patterson as a business blackmailer. Gowen, who argued the case, was able by a severe cross-examination to expose Patterson as a double-dealer, and to arouse a strong suspicion that he had been the tool of the Standard in an effort to ruin the Tidewater's credit—a suspicion that has never been dispelled.[50]

The next month the stubborn attempt of the minority group to wrest control of the company from its founders came to its dramatic climax. The Tidewater's annual meeting would normally have been held on January 17, 1883. This year the comptroller asked for a delay to enable him to complete a full financial statement for 1882. The management agreed, and McKelvy and two other officers arranged to open the meeting in Titusville, and then immediately adjourn it. But the minority group saw its opportunity. On the appointed day Taylor, Satterfield, McKinney, Stewart, E. G. Patterson, and others appeared in force and attempted to seize control. They mustered a large majority of the stockholders present, but not of the voting shares. By an irregular *viva voce* ballot, Satterfield was chosen chairman. McKelvy, taken by surprise but fortunately keeping his head, immediately executed the correct stroke, a motion to adjourn. He had enough proxies to carry it, but Chairman Satterfield arbitrarily declared the motion lost. When McKelvy appealed from the chair, the hostile block appointed tellers from their own ranks, who threw out his proxies. The meeting then elected Satterfield manager of the company and chairman of the board, with a slate of subordinate officers from his and Taylor's "crowd." The new secretary carried off the minute-book, in which he inserted a record of this highly irregular meeting.[51]

McKelvy took immediate precautions to hold possession of the company offices. These were on the second and third floors of the Ralston-Herrington Block in Titusville, and he barricaded the stairway with heavy planks, guarded by a colored giant named "Nigger" Wilson and other brawny recruits. The Taylor-Satterfield group was then compelled to defend its position in the courts—and it pos-

[50]Patterson vs. The Tidewater Company, Court of Common Pleas, Crawford County, Pa., Dec., 1882. A full and generally accurate history of Patterson's "treason" is given in the Philadelphia *Press*, Feb. 28, 1883.
[51]*Short History of the Tidewater*, 16, 17; W. S. Benson to the author, Oct. 12, 1938.

sessed no real defense. The Tidewater hired Bullitt & Dickson, perhaps the ablest attorneys of Philadelphia, to sue for an injunction against the fraudulent officers, and Gowen gladly assisted Samuel Dickson in arguing its case before Judge Church in Meadville. On March 16 the court issued a decision which not only sustained the old management of the Tidewater, but stigmatized the actions of the minority group as "farcical, fraudulent, and void." A telegram sped to the group anxiously waiting in Titusville—"Thank God, a just judge reigns in Crawford County." And on appeal, the State Supreme Court quickly sustained the judgment.[52]

The Tidewater management naturally accused Rockefeller of instigating the *coup* at the Titusville meeting, and he published a formal affidavit denying that he had played any part whatever in it. Doubtless this disclaimer was quite true. The Bradford *Era* declared that the Standard had nothing to do with the affair, which "is the legitimate outgrowth of a feud known to have existed in the inner circles of the corporation for years." Its correspondent in Titusville wrote that Taylor was highly unfriendly to the Standard. On the other hand, various people "whispered that Benson and his friends might not be entirely unwilling to have the octopus swallow the whole Tidewater system if the consideration were sufficiently liberal."[53] However, Patterson had clearly been used by the Standard. In the proceedings at Meadville James R. Keene, as one of the Tidewater managers, submitted an affidavit which made a marked impression upon public opinion. Part of it is worth quoting:[54]

From my first connection with the company it has been hampered and embarrassed in its business by the unscrupulous competition of the Standard Oil Company. When it first began to transport and deliver oil at tidewater, the refineries which bought and refined oil were one after another bought up by the Standard Oil or driven out of business by vexatious and oppressive annoyances. As one of the steps in this attempt to injure and destroy the Tidewater Pipe Company, they procured Elisha G. Patterson to institute a vexatious and dishonest litigation in the Court

[52]N. Y. *Tribune,* March 17, 1883; *Short History of the Tidewater,* 17, 18.
[53]See the Bradford *Era,* January 19, 20, 22, for a full history of the affair. "Public sentiment is considerably divided as to the merits of the struggle," it reported on the 19th, "but the opinion is gaining ground that the movement, at least as far as regards the new management, is rather against the Standard Oil Company, and in favor of strong capitalists outside."
[54]N. Y. *Times,* Feb. 21, 1883.

of Common Pleas of Crawford County. Patterson had been an original subscriber to the stock of the company, but had never paid his subscription. He was entirely insolvent and irresponsible, and one of the attorneys of the Standard Oil Company had bought up his debts, giving his own notes therefor, at fifty cents on the dollar. He obtained money from one of the officers of the Standard Oil on April 29, 1882, and on May 1, 1882, he paid his subscription and immediately began to collect materials for the filing of a bill in equity. He did in fact file a bill . . . and the officers of the Standard Oil Company took measures to have the bill published in the New York papers, with a view of injuring the credit of the company and interfering with its financial arrangements. In that proceeding David B. Stuart, the then comptroller of the company, was called as a witness, and in his deposition he affected to entertain doubts as to the solvency of the company. . . . I have reason to believe, and expect to be able to prove, that Stuart was holding private correspondence with one or more officers of the Standard Oil. . . .

Though superficially the Tidewater seemed to have triumphed over its opponents without and within, its position was still very difficult. During 1882 it had been hard pressed to maintain profitable operations. About 22,000,000 barrels of crude oil were shipped from the Regions that year, of which approximately 20,000,000 were moved by the Standard combination, and about 2,000,000 by the Tidewater. That is, its pipes did not average a daily flow of 6000 barrels. The high charges exacted by George F. Baker for his financial help placed a heavy strain upon the company finances. Until the pipe line was driven clear through to New York Bay it would not be safe—and even then it could not be sure of enough refineries for a market. Benson, apprehensive of the future, sent Hopkins abroad in 1883 to drum up European buyers of crude oil.[55] Every one knew that the stockholders hostile to the Benson-McKelvy-Hopkins policy of absolute independence might increase. The Taylor-Satterfield "crowd" was working in close harmony with the Standard, which was always determined and relentless in pushing its policies. The company's situation still inspired uneasiness.

v

The result was a compromise. Rockefeller's determination to bring the Tidewater under control never faltered. His practical mo-

[55]W. S. Benson to the author, May 14, 1938.

nopoly, which to him meant order and security for the whole industry, would be ruined if the pipe line fed a growing array of independent refineries. But he did not need to insist upon a merger; a rigid quota-arrangement would suffice. As for Benson, McKelvy, and Hopkins, they knew that the Standard Oil combination far outmatched them in resources and staying-power. The Taylor-Satterfield coup showed that continual turmoil lay ahead if the management clung to a stubbornly defiant stand. Would they not do better to reach a friendly agreement with the Standard? Both camps, as 1883 wore on, displayed a more conciliatory temper.

Other factors also made for a treaty of peace. The basic conditions of oil transportation had changed with amazing velocity. The Standard, moving swiftly to build long-distance pipe lines, had far outstripped the Tidewater. Whereas Benson's pipe did not reach the Atlantic Coast at Bayonne until 1887,[56] Rockefeller had rapidly laid very superior pipe lines to New York Bay, to Buffalo, and to Cleveland. Distance had been half annihilated; the oil was scarcely pumped from the ground before it was at the point of refining or export—all except that part of it which had to be stored for lack of a market. So far as crude petroleum was concerned, the railroads were largely out of the picture. For years the principal trading points for crude had been Titusville and Oil City, and as late as 1882 Bradford was the leading center. But in December, 1882, the National Petroleum Exchange, with five hundred members, was formally opened at 57 Broadway in New York. President C. G. Wilson rapped with his gavel; a member shouted, "I'll give 94¾ for 5000 barrels," and another responded, "I'll sell 5000 for 94⅞"; and thus was inaugurated an exchange expected to surpass any in the Oil Regions.[57]

In the spring of 1883 the Pennsylvania legislature at last passed the long-sought free pipe-line bill. It went through with an amendment which has often been ascribed to the railroads or the Standard Oil, but which actually had a simpler origin. A group of super-patriots offered a proviso that all pipe-line companies organized under the act should have their termini within Pennsylvania. The purpose was to encourage refining within State borders and keep as much oil as possible from going outside. This, urged its advocates,

[56]*Short History of the Tidewater*, 29.
[57]N. Y. *Tribune*, Dec. 19, 1882.

was a fair compensation for Pennsylvania to require for the right of eminent domain. The House voted the amendment 82 to 77.[58] Verily, the legislature in these years was an astonishing body! Yet defective as the bill was, it seemed likely to encourage more pipe lines. The railroads had agreed in 1875 and again in 1877 upon a systematic division of the oil traffic. Would it not be wise for the Tidewater and Standard Oil now to do the same, and close the door against new pipe-line competitors?

Spokesmen for the Standard took the lead in proposing a settlement. Since they had acquired considerable stock in the Tidewater, they had a voice in its meetings. It was agreed to divide the pipe-line business from the Pennsylvania fields eastward, the Standard taking 88.5 per cent, the Tidewater 11.5. Charges were to be kept uniform at 40 cents a barrel to Philadelphia and 45 cents to New York. Local pipe lines in the Regions were allowed 20 cents a barrel for collecting oil from the wells.[59] This compact, signed October 8, 1883, was hailed by both sides as a victory. The Tidewater regarded it as a final recognition of independence, while the Standard saw in it a much-needed guarantee that the Tidewater would not attempt to build up a great new refining interest.

It is pleasant to record that under this arrangement the Tidewater prospered. It continued operations as before until its line reached Bayonne in 1887. Then the Chester Refinery was consolidated with the Ocean Refinery at Bayonne; and when 1888 opened the Tidewater Oil Company was formed, absorbing the Ocean Oil Company, Polar Oil Company, and Lombard, Ayres. Important Bradford wells owned by Satterfield and Taylor were bought by the Tidewater when it went into oil production. George F. Baker and James R. Keene meanwhile profited hugely from their loan certificates. By 1911 their investment had paid more than 2000 per cent in dividends, and the certificates, having been merged with the stock, were worth about fifteen times what they had cost. These figures are a measure of the gains made by all concerned in the company. As a combined producing, transporting, refining, and exporting corporation, the Tidewater was in a position to do one tenth of the whole American

[58]Harrisburg *Independent*, May 17, 1883.
[59]These were at any rate the charges maintained in 1888; *House Trust Investigation, 1888*, p. 781.

business in petroleum, and its existence gave the Standard some ground for denying that it held an absolute monopoly.[60]

VI

When this compact was signed, the technological revolution wrought by the pipe lines was nearing completion. The tooting and clanking of long trains of tank cars filled with crude oil ceased to be a familiar sight in the Regions. Mountain valleys that had been noisy with traffic now seldom heard the locomotive's wail; the busy crude-oil terminals at seaport cities were left empty and desolate. It was a change of the first importance. And though the Tidewater had initiated the revolution, the Standard did most of the hard work of carrying it through.

Rockefeller gave orders in the summer of 1879 for a five-inch pipe from the Regions to Cleveland, which was completed that fall. It pumped 10,000 barrels a day directly into the refineries. Almost simultaneously new four-inch pipes were laid to Buffalo and Pittsburgh, the small Hostetter line soon being discarded. A six-inch pipe line was quickly driven to New York and another of the same size to Philadelphia. This work was directed by the Standard unit called the American Transfer Company. But on April 14, 1881, Rockefeller organized the National Transit Company, with a broad charter and a capital of $5,000,000, increased ere long to $30,000,000. The new company took over nearly all the stock of the United Pipe-Lines, the properties of the American Transfer Company, the stock of the National Storage Company, and various other pipe-line and tank properties; and it completed the lines to Philadelphia and New York Bay. Before many years passed a second line was laid to New York, and one to Baltimore. As oil production moved westward, the pipe lines went with it; and in 1888 an eight-inch pipe was laid from the Ohio-Lima field to Chicago. The two New York lines, with powerful pumps, were particularly efficient. Where altitude or other impediments had to be overcome, "loop lines" were added to equalize the flow between pumping stations.

When the Standard ran its pipes into Philadelphia, it had to buy most of its way. Apparently it treated the landowners with liberality. One farmer later described its methods. The Standard agents, he

[60]See *Short History of the Tidewater Company,* 16, 29, 32.

wrote, offered to pay for a route under his land. " 'Where do you want to go?' I asked. 'Let me see your plans.' They showed them to me, and I found they were making a bee-line to the seaboard, and that they had designed to lay their pipe straight across my property between my residence and my spring-house, close to my well, and right through my kitchen-garden. Now it stood to reason that I couldn't allow that. . . . Their pipes are liable to burst or leak. Petroleum is very insidious. Once it finds a means of escape it works its way through the ground into the wells, springs, and streams. It ruins the water and poisons the soil. . . . I explained this and they saw the force of my argument. 'Lay down the line yourself, then,' they said, and I marked out a course for them as far distant from my dwelling and barn and garden as I could make it. It was round-about, but they accepted my offer and paid me for the right."[61]

Naturally, the railroads did not give up their crude-oil traffic without a struggle. When the Standard tried to carry its pipe line through Bayonne, the Central of New Jersey prepared to give battle. The Bayonne common council, obedient to the Standard's wishes, granted a franchise for a pipe line under the streets. The mayor, equally obedient to railroad pressure, vetoed the grant. A city election shortly took place, and the Standard exerted itself in behalf of friendly candidates for mayor and council, who were successful. Thereupon the Central prepared to stop the first pipe-laying gang by an injunction. For a time all was quiet. The Standard contented itself with surveying a route. But it was secretly assembling the men, materials, drays, and tools needed for excavating, laying the pipes, and repairing the streets; and on the night of September 22, 1880, it struck a sudden blow.

Early that evening the council passed an ordinance granting a right of way through Thirtieth Street. The mayor immediately signed a ready-engrossed copy. Some 300 engineers, mechanics, and laborers were waiting in the Standard's yards, divided into squads with specific duties. A messenger dashed up from city hall; the

[61]*Arguments Against the Free Pipe-Line Bill Recently Published in Leading Newspapers.* This 54-page pamphlet contains editorials and articles from *The Railway World,* Philadelphia *Times,* Philadelphia Evening *Bulletin,* and many local newspapers of Pennsylvania opposing the eminent-domain feature of the free pipe-line bill. Many farmers opposed the bill. The Philadelphia *Times,* and *Railway World* were reputed organs of the Pennsylvania Railroad.

gates swung open; out swarmed the hundreds of workers; and in a few minutes, under the red glare of lanterns, the pavements were being ripped up in dozens of spots. Before dawn the trenches had been dug, the pipes laid, and the streets repaired. The pipe line was a reality before the Central of New Jersey knew that the ordinance had even been passed![62] At the point where it crossed the Centreville bridge, the Standard garrisoned it by a large force of men till all danger of an attack had ended.

The Standard followed a different course in dealing with the Pennsylvania. For some time now it had been on fairly amicable terms with that powerful railroad, while it was always Rockefeller's wise instinct to avoid conflicts when possible. Tom Scott was at first obstructive, and some stormy meetings occurred. At one, Warden completely lost his temper. "I was never so angry in my life," he said later.[63] But an arrangement was finally made by which the Standard pipe lines were allowed free passage under all Pennsylvania tracks, the 40–45-cent rate to the seaboard was maintained by railroad and pipes alike, and the Pennsylvania was credited with 26 per cent of all the oil traffic from the Regions eastward. It might actually carry very little of the crude oil, and the Standard could certainly have transported it all by pipe line for less than 20 cents a barrel. Nevertheless, in order to preserve harmony the railroad was allowed the regular tariff on 26 per cent of the traffic. Thus the payment of the drawback was reversed, the railroad now being the recipient![64]

Few Americans realized in 1882 what a gigantic network of pipe lines had already been laid down. They ran underground, and men who would have exclaimed over railroads or bridges never saw them; even the largest lacked the spectacular quality of the huge waterpipes later laid to Coolgardie in Australia, or across the desert to Los Angeles. Yet by the beginning of 1882, when it had bought a

[62]N. Y. *Tribune,* Sept. 23, 1880. For an account of the Standard's acquisition of a right of way across New Jersey, see N. Y. *Times,* Sept. 30, 1880.

[63]Mr. Clarence Warden to the author, April 10, 1938. Application of the Pennsylvania Railroad for an injunction to restrain the Standard from laying a pipe under its tracks or across its Hackensack River bridge was denied by the Chancellor at Trenton on Jan. 4, 1881. The pipes were then already down. N. Y. *Times,* Jan. 5, 1881.

[64]*House Trust Investigation, 1888,* pp. 324, 779. The railroad, apparently ashamed of this contract, never permitted it to become public. At different times 1885–88 it protested that the business was not profitable.

competing line from Olean, N. Y., to Buffalo,[65] the Standard owned some 13,000 miles of pipe, capable of running 80,000 barrels of oil daily from the Pennsylvania wells. Its seaboard line was the greatest artery of the kind in the world. Nearly 400 miles in length, it carried 15,000 barrels a day from the great tanks at Bradford to the refineries at Bayonne. Following for the most part the route of the Erie Railroad, it had cost a dollar a foot above right-of-way charges; and it required 12 pumping stations, some 30 miles apart, each of which, with its machinery, had cost about $50,000. The pipe was patrolled night and day by "walkers." An integral part of this system was the company's imposing array of tanks, which on May 1, 1883, held more than 33,000,000 barrels of oil. At one point on the Buffalo & McKeesport Railroad clustered 250 of them, the biggest containing 35,000 barrels each, while another large tank-farm stood at Garfield, N. J. In all, the Standard owned more than 1600 tanks. The pipe lines leading to and from them radiated in all directions, and night and day solid streams of petroleum were in circulation.[66] Only a company of giant strength could have provided this system of pipes and tanks, for as the fields were drained property costing millions sometimes had to be abandoned within a year or two of its construction.[67]

By the spring of 1882 more than three fourths of the crude oil that left the Pennsylvania fields was being moved by pipe line, and the proportion was steadily advancing. It was then roughly accurate to say that 25 per cent of the raw petroleum was shipped by rail to the seaboard; that 35 per cent was piped thither by the Standard and Tidewater lines; and that the remaining 35 per cent was nearly all piped to inland refining centers—Buffalo, Pittsburgh, and above all, Cleveland—by the Standard.[68] The railroads, so long a dominant factor in the industry, had ceased to be important save for the car-

[65]The Buffalo Pipe-Line Company (later Buffalo & Rock City Pipe-Line Company) had laid a four-inch pipe about 65 or 70 miles long from Cattaraugus County to Buffalo. The plan was to feed at least three independent refineries in Buffalo with it; and the Standard acted at once to take it over. See N. Y. *Times*, March 4, 1880, for the plans; July 14, 1881, for their progress.

[66]*Railroad Gazette*, Jan. 27, 1882; report of United Pipe-Lines for May 1, 1883, quoted in Harrisburg *Independent*, May 11, 1883.

[67]*House Trust Investigation, 1888*, p. 325. Archbold testified: "We have spent in one year several hundred thousands of dollars, and within that year it was an abandoned investment." Later the risks grew larger.

[68]*Railroad Gazette*, April 14, 1882.

riage of refined oil. All of them, but especially the Pennsylvania, felt heavily the loss of so lucrative a part of their freight.

This revolutionary change, which might easily have turned the flank of the Standard combination, had been quickly mastered by that great organization. Rockefeller, alert to the necessity for crushing the Empire when it challenged him, had felled that giant with a blow. But he had dealt with the Tidewater more gently. If two or three such pipe lines had sprung up in 1875, while there were still many independent refineries, his control of the industry would have been seriously threatened. But by 1879 the Tidewater found so few outlets available that its competition was never formidable, and it was easily brought under control by bargaining rather than coercion. Having limited its activities, Rockefeller and his associates at once proceeded to build their own enormous pipe-line system. They systematized the rates at a lower level. When the revolution ended they were in as strong a position as ever—even stronger, for their costs had been cheapened, and they stood more completely independent of the railroad magnates.

"Strictly confidential," wrote Rockefeller to a friend on December 16, 1884, "I am happy to state to you as a shareholder of the Standard Trust, that its affairs were never in as good a condition as today; and this affords the greater encouragement as all other business interests seem so prostrated."[69]

[69]Rockefeller Papers.

XXV

The First Great Trust

IN ALL the great manufacturing nations of the world the movement toward industrial concentration was rapidly becoming
irresistible. As the years passed it was to produce stronger and
stronger combinations in Germany, Austria, and France. The
most prominent form of organization in continental Europe was the
cartel, based on a contract among independent establishments fixing
the amount of production for each, and frequently establishing a
central selling-bureau to control prices as well. In Germany the
government showed distinct friendliness to these combinations,
which were for the most part managed conservatively. Though contracts against the public interest were non-enforceable, the courts
were on the whole not hostile, leading government officers gave their
encouragement, and in several industries in which the state was itself
a producer, as in soda-manufacture, it joined the cartel. In Austria
the movement became still more sweeping, covering nearly all
branches of industry in which competition had gravely injured
manufacturers; but there the courts were more frequently antagonistic. France had a stringent penal law against any monopoly effected
by unfair means, with the result that agreements to control production and prices were generally kept secret. Nevertheless, monopolistic
combinations—including one among the petroleum refiners—in time
grew fairly numerous.[1]

But it was in the United States that combinations became most

[1]F. W. Hirst, *Monopolies, Trusts, and Kartells,* is especially useful; see also
H. W. Macrosty, *The Trust Movement in British Industry;* L. Liefmann, *Die
Unternemerverbande;* L. Duchesne, *L'Avènement du régime syndical à Ver-
viers;* C. W. Baker, *Monopolies and the People;* C. Genart, *Les syndicats indus-
triels;* and E. von Halle, *Trusts in the United States.*

numerous, most powerful, and most undisciplined. Competition had been more lawless and destructive in America than elsewhere, and the reaction against it was proportionately strong. The building of a magnificent railroad system, opening the richest national market in the world, encouraged the rise of great national industries in place of the old local manufactories. The high protective tariff, excluding foreign competition, helped to foster concentration. And the United States more than any other nation produced genuine captains of industry, men who thought and operated on the grand scale, and were content with nothing less than absolute sway; in the industrial sphere, with its ceaseless and often relentless conflict——

"Augusti girt with war's paludament."

The pioneer in the American movement toward industrial consolidation was the Standard, and its Augustan leader was Rockefeller. We have narrated the steps by which he conquered the domain of oil refining; we must now examine the means by which he organized what we have hitherto called simply the Standard Oil "combination."

II

Whenever the heads of this combination met in the years 1872–78, whether in the crowded Cleveland offices, or the more spacious Pearl Street quarters in New York, they were troubled at least subconsciously by the question of legal status and organization. Rockefeller and Flagler spent long hours discussing it with their attorneys. In essence the question was simple. They were building up a huge interstate combination of numerous companies and properties, all under one direction; and while such far-spreading organizations were soon to become numerous in America, State laws as yet threw grave impediments in their way.

"Listen to me, Henry," we can imagine Rockefeller saying to Flagler as they paced up Euclid Avenue early in 1872. "The Standard Oil of Ohio is the nucleus around which we must build our structure. But it has been chartered simply to manufacture, ship, and sell petroleum products. It is an Ohio company, and has no legal right to hold a plant in New York or Pennsylvania. It is not authorized to hold stock in another company, and very probably has no legal right to do it. It certainly has no legal right to be a partner in another company. We're surrounded by a stone wall—we can't get out of the State or into another corporation. Yet we've got to expand. In some way we must establish our right to participate in manufacturing and marketing enterprises in other States; and it must be a way that will not unnecessarily advertise every purchase we make, every alliance we effect. How? We are going to get into deep water if we are not careful. You know a little law—tell me how!"[2]

In buying the New York properties of Jabez A. Bostwick & Co. in 1872, Rockefeller and Flagler took merely a stop-gap action. Paying for Bostwick's holdings with Standard Oil stock and cash, they made an agreement by which he carried on the business under his own firm name, but for the account of the Standard and under its direction. That is, although the Bostwick Company was acquired and its profits at the end of the year went to the Standard, legally it remained a separate unit. This was a loose arrangement. It would not prove a satisfactory model for extensive acquisitions, and would not serve at all for the purchase of small properties with a view to their amalgamation with one another. Accordingly, in the second New York purchase a new and significant arrangement was made. The Long Island Oil Company received a certain sum in Standard Oil stock and cash, which was distributed to its stockholders. In return, all the securities of the Long Island were transferred to Henry M. Flagler, Secretary of the Standard, as *trustee*.[3]

This was of course a radically different procedure from that followed in the Cleveland acquisitions. These had represented tangible properties in Ohio; the separate companies soon disappeared, and the properties were scrapped, or were welded into Plants No. 1, 2, 3, 4, 5, and 6. But the Standard had no legal right to take physical possession of manufactories in New York and operate them. Nor, as the law was generally interpreted in America and had been interpreted in England up to 1870, did it have any right to hold stock in another company. Railroads had controlled subsidiary lines in this way, but in general only by special statute. It was not until 1889 that

[2]Walter F. Taylor, of the Standard's counsel (a member of Carter, Ledyard & Milburn), treats the legal question in his MS History of the Standard Oil, 68 ff. See also the interesting testimony of the New York attorney John R. Dos Passos in Volume I of the *Hearings of the United States Industrial Commission* (1900).

[3]Taylor, *op. cit.*, 21, 22.

New Jersey began legalizing the practice of inter-corporation stock-holding by general statute, and so ushered in the day of the great holding company.[4] The Standard would be open to perhaps ruinous attack if it asserted stock ownership in companies outside Ohio. The obvious way out was for some officer to take personal possession of the stock, denominating himself a trustee.

But a trustee for what? Up to 1879, so far as the Standard's archives show, the various trustees holding stocks did not execute any papers in the nature of declarations of trust. No statement was recorded on the stock-books or elsewhere to show who was the beneficiary of the trust. The strongest hint on the subject, given for example in the arrangement made with Charles Pratt & Company, was the declaration that the stock was put in the name of "H. M. Flagler, Secretary, Trustee." Later this question was explored in the courts. Standard officials then declared that the stocks standing in the names of trustees had not been held for the Standard Oil of Ohio, but for its stockholders just as though equitable interests in the various stocks had been distributed in dividends.[5] That is, they were held for individuals, not for a company. Rockefeller himself was always emphatic on this point.[6] The argument is not convincing. Who had paid for the stocks and partnerships? The Standard Oil of Ohio. Who held physical possession of the stocks? The Standard Oil of Ohio.

This device of placing new properties outside Ohio in the hands of a trustee was followed for some years. The Devoe Manufacturing Co., the Vandergrift & Forman Pipe-Line purchases, and the interest in the Chess, Carley concern of Louisville, lying in three different states, were handled in the same way as the Long Island Oil Company. So were subsequent purchases. Flagler was usually the trustee, which was natural, for Rockefeller said later that "he and the attorneys worked out the method for the protection of the enterprise."[7] But Bostwick, William G. Warden, William Rockefeller, Vandergrift, Charles Lockhart, and others also represented the Standard in

---

[4]W. Z. Ripley, *Trusts, Pools, and Corporations,* 703 ff.; J. B. Clark, *The Control of Trusts* (1901) and *The Problem of Monopoly* (1904).

[5]*U. S. vs. The Standard Oil Company,* XVII, 3637 ff.; XVI, 3170 ff.

[6]*Cf.* Rockefeller's comments on Taylor's MS History, Nov., 1922; Rockefeller Papers.

[7]*Ibid.*

this capacity. The device at first seemed effective. It partially protected the company under State laws. It maintained a veil of secrecy
about the Standard's expansion; even on the witness stand the leading officers, from Rockefeller down, could flatly deny the Standard's
ownership or control of purchased corporations. It did something
to weld a large number of properties into an effective alliance. The
trustee for each company could see that it was operated in great
measure as the Standard desired, and agree with the trustee-owner
of other companies (sometimes with himself) to suppress, combine,
or enlarge facilities.[8]

Nevertheless, as the Standard absorbed competitor after competitor, it became clear that this system of individual trustees had
grave defects. If one of the important partners—Rockefeller, Flagler,
or Pratt—died, and his executors wished to sell his Standard Oil
property, they might find the market controlled by the other partners. Moreover, a proper unification of the *management* of the
mighty congeries of plants, pipe lines, and marketing agencies was
difficult. Many of the companies remained essentially separate in
their workings. The single trustee who held the majority-stock of
a unit could sometimes control its active operation only with difficulty, particularly when the managers were men of stubborn force.
The interests of separate companies thus sometimes conflicted with
the interests of the whole organization. Consultations among both
trustees and active plant-managers upon policy were difficult to
arrange; Trustee Flagler was too far away from Trustee Lockhart
in Pittsburgh, and the latter from Trustee Bostwick in New York.
And finally, on the legal side the system was disturbingly weak.
That troublesome question, "Trustee for whom?" would not down.

Rockefeller said later that when the Adnah Neyhart business was
sold to Charles Pratt, representing the Standard, in 1875, the need
for a stronger and closer form of organization began to impress him
as imperative. "It was apparent now that there must be some way
of expanding business and having it under one control, even though
it reached beyond the confines of one State; and as this was rather
of a worldwide proposition, the Standard Oil representatives were
forced to study, and the study was continued year after year."[9]

[8]Taylor, MS History of the Standard Oil, 70.
[9]Inglis, Conversations with Rockefeller.

By "representatives" he meant not only the principal officers but their attorneys. In the early years of the Standard, the able Myron Keith of Cleveland had been Rockefeller's principal legal adviser. "Rockefeller never made a decision without consulting that man," said a shrewd Standard official who worked in the Cleveland office in the seventies.[10] "Mr. Rockefeller would write a letter or draft an agreement and hand it to Flagler. Henry would rewrite it, often interlining. He wrote a beautiful hand. Then, if important, it would go to Keith. When it was finished, it was a *document*." But Keith was soon to be supplanted as leading counsel. As early as 1873 Rockefeller had become acquainted with the Regions man who was later to be head of his legal staff, to brood over the gloomy abyss of American corporation law, and to evolve from it an idea which not only gave unity and power to the Standard, but which profoundly influenced an entire era of American business.

III

This man was Samuel C. T. Dodd. Sturdy Levi Dodd had been the town carpenter of Franklin, Pa., when that backwoods village suddenly boomed with the oil excitement of 1859–60. His son Samuel had been graduated from Jefferson College a few years earlier, and had just passed his bar examinations when the news of Drake's well flashed upon the astounded farmers of Venango County.[11]

With characteristic foresight Dodd had decided to stay in Franklin, established an office, and was soon drawing deeds and organizing companies for oil men. One of his clients was "Coal-Oil Johnny" Steele, who told Dodd that the lawyers stole more from him than the gamblers. Physically Dodd was short and squarely built, and in middle life became so portly that he was described as being of the same dimensions in every direction; intellectually he was quiet, studious, and genial. Markedly religious, he was gifted with a love for literature and a flair for the pen;[12] it was with good reason that his son Lee Wilson Dodd became highly esteemed as a dramatist and novelist. For a time he turned to politics. As a Democrat in a Republican county he was defeated for the legislature, but went to the

---

[10]Charles M. Higgins to the author, Nov. 11, 1936.
[11]*Memoirs of S. C. T. Dodd*, 17.
[12]McLaurin, *Sketches in Crude Oil*, 368.

State Constitutional Convention of 1872, and, as a member of its committee on corporations, raised a vehement voice against railroad rebates.[13] This attitude he always maintained. But he never evinced any hostility toward combination. On the contrary, he was impressed in the Convention by the views of the venerable economist Henry C. Carey, a fellow delegate, who had declared that "the more perfect the power of association, the greater the power of production and the larger the proportion of the product which falls to the laborer's share." There is good evidence that even before he joined the Standard he was convinced that, as he later put it,[14] "just in proportion as combination and concentration of capital have taken place, have prices decreased, wages increased, wealth been created, and the individual been benefited."

By 1873 Dodd was one of the prominent attorneys of the Regions. Vandergrift & Forman were among his clients; and he particularly admired Vandergrift, whom he describes as "uneducated but a thorough gentleman," with "gentle unassuming manners."[15] In 1878 Taylor and Satterfield instructed him to prepare a bill in equity against the Standard, which grew into a suit of some magnitude. But it was no sooner given public notice than Vandergrift walked into Dodd's office, and revealed to him that the United Pipe-Line, nominally a Vandergrift & Forman company, now really belonged to the Standard Oil. Dodd, greatly astonished, realized that he must withdraw, for he wished to retain Vandergrift's business.[16] However, the equity suit shortly terminated in a compromise. Vandergrift at once telegraphed Dodd to meet him in Cleveland, while at the same time a telegram from Taylor summoned him to the same city. Arriving there, Dodd found that the litigants wished him to act for them jointly in drawing up the final settlement. He agreed:[17]

Here, for the first time, I met John D. Rockefeller, a very pleasant, gentlemanly, unassuming man, but slow in his deliberations and particular as possible at every point of negotiation. Being a little vexed one day at my objection to some clause he desired in the contract which was being drawn, he said in a sarcastic tone: "Mr. Dodd, do you often act

[13]John Brooks Leavitt, *Memorial of S. C. T. Dodd*, 8.
[14]S. C. T. Dodd, *Trusts, An Address*, 11.
[15]*Memoirs of S. C. T. Dodd*, 28.
[16]*Ibid.*   [17]*Ibid.*

for both sides in a case?" I said, "Not often, Mr. Rockefeller, but I am always ready to do so when both sides want an honest lawyer." This seemed to amuse him and we soon brought the matter to a settlement.

The Standard leaders then asked Dodd to join their legal staff, but he refused. Doubtless he was still too much in sympathy with the Regions producers to hire himself to the corporation which they most hated. But he believed that the Standard was right in the immediate-shipment quarrel; and when in April, 1879, the grand jury of Clarion County indicted nine Standard officials for criminal conspiracy, Dodd's sympathies were thoroughly enlisted with the defendants, of whom his friend Vandergrift was one. "I had personal knowledge of all these matters, and knew that the Standard was wrongfully accused of fraudulent intent," he tells us.[18] The upshot was that he consented to take charge of the Standard's legal affairs, and after some delay went to New York in 1881 as its general solicitor.

First, however, he made his position clear on a vital point. "I am bitterly opposed to the whole system of railway rebates and discriminations," he told Rockefeller and Flagler, "and shall use my influence against them to the utmost." They assured him that they understood his feeling, and had long been willing to forego rebates if the railroads would only discontinue them universally. "We ask only to be treated the same as our competitors," they said. From that date until his retirement in 1905, on a pension, the amount of which he was asked to fix for himself, he remained in charge of the increasing staff of Standard lawyers. He believed that to give the best legal advice he should maintain an independent position, unswayed by financial considerations. He therefore refused to let Rockefeller place in his name, for gradual purchase, an amount of Standard Oil stock which would have made him a multimillionaire; and he never took more than $25,000 a year in salary. Though cordial in his relations with the Standard executives, he never became an intimate friend of any of them.[19] When need required, he employed the ablest men available: in New York, for example, Elihu Root, James C. Carter, and Joseph H. Choate; in Buffalo, Cleveland's old partner, Wilson H. Bissell.

[18]*Idem,* 29.
[19]*Dictionary of American Biography,* V, 341, 342.

IV

Dodd was no sooner hired, apparently in 1879, than he agreed with Rockefeller and Flagler that something must be done to give the great Standard organization as a whole a clearer legal status. The attorney had a lucid mind, and like Rockefeller, a powerful instinct for simplification and co-ordination. He realized that the principal contrivance thus far tried for uniting corporations in different States, the pool, had proved highly defective. Since partnerships between corporations were illegal, all pool contracts were unenforceable. He also perceived that the expedient of transferring stock to a trustee, already invented by Flagler, offered great possibilities. The word trust, as then used in law, referred almost exclusively to an instrument under which one person held property for the benefit of another. A court might assign the properties of a minor in trust to a guardian; several partners who felt more confidence in a bank or some other agent than in each other might assign their property to it. Dodd believed that the Standard's procedure in using individual trustees to attain its end was legal and proper. However, Rockefeller had no difficulty in showing him that the system was too loose and cumbersome; and he set himself to better it.

Whether just before or just after Dodd's coming, a step was taken which contributed to a solution. Some one, perhaps Flagler, prepared a trust agreement, which, dated April 8, 1879, tentatively met the difficulty. Instead of a single trustee for every company, it was agreed to set up a small body of trustees for all of them; instead of naming men scattered at random from Cleveland to New York, it was agreed to select a little group inside the head office. The new trust agreement was duly executed by the Standard Oil Company, its thirty-seven stockholders, and all the former individual trustees; and it constituted a noteworthy step in advance. Under it they pooled all the stocks acquired in subsidiaries—though not the Standard's own stock—and "all other interests of every kind and description held by the Standard Oil Company or in which it has an interest, which can or by right ought to be divided and distributed among the parties entitled thereto without affecting its proper, legitimate and efficient operations as a corporation." All this pooled property was transferred to three men in the Cleveland office, Myron P. Keith,

George P. Chester, and George H. Vilas, as trustees. They were to manage the stocks and other interests, as Taylor has written, "for the exclusive use and benefit of specified persons in specified proportions"—that is, for the Standard's stockholders.[20]

The thirty-seven stockholders received dividends from not only the Standard of Ohio, but all the subsidiary and allied corporations. This gave every Standard share an enormously greater value than its face. Of the owners, Rockefeller with 8984 shares was much the most important. At face value, his Standard holdings were worth $898,400; but the actual value in 1879, capitalized upon dividends from the controlled companies, was estimated by Standard men at almost $18,000,000, and by outsiders at much more. He was therefore among the richest men in the country, though nobody yet suspected the fact. The next largest holders of stock were Flagler, with 3000 shares; Stephen V. Harkness, with 2925; Charles Pratt, with 2800; and Oliver H. Payne, with 2637. Thereafter, when any Standard Oil stock was sold, it was accompanied by an assignment of the equitable interest of the transfer in all the stocks and other properties that were held by Vilas, Keith, and Chester.

The veil of secrecy about the Standard's acquisitions was still impermeable by any legal searchlight. Rockefeller, in a Cleveland suit in 1880, made solemn affidavit: "It is not true, as stated by Mr. Teagle in his affidavit, that the Standard Oil Company, directly or indirectly through its officers and agents, owns or controls the works of Warden, Frew & Company, Lockhart, Frew & Company, J. A. Bostwick & Company, C. Pratt & Company, Acme Refining Company, Imperial Refining Company, Camden Consolidated Company, and the Devoe Manufacturing Company. . . ."[21] Legally this statement was water-tight. Three trustees held ownership or control; Rockefeller maintained that they acted not for the Standard Oil Company but for its stockholders. Actually, to call the statement disingenuous would be putting it mildly.

But while the action just taken was a step in advance, it was only a short step. It did much to clarify the ownership of the Standard-controlled properties; it furnished a surer and clearer legal status;

---

[20]Taylor, MS History of the Standard Oil, 71.
[21]*Standard Oil Company vs. William C. Scofield, et al., Court of Common Pleas, Cuyahoga County;* cf. Tarbell, *Standard Oil Company,* I, 230.

and it facilitated the distribution of receipts from the properties. But it did nothing to unify and centralize the management, and from the practical point of view this was much the greatest need facing the Standard organization. The still loose and shackling arrangement of companies was likely to run out of gear, with no proper co-ordination of parts. Keith, Vilas, and Chester had no power in any way to control the operations of the subsidiaries. They existed, as trustees, merely to apportion property and profits. Even the former function they discharged only indirectly. The trust agreement instructed them to divide up the shares of the Standard-controlled companies among the Standard stockholders, but this was a difficult thing to do, and was doubtless never seriously expected of them.

Unity, indeed, was being maintained only at the expense of increasingly cumbersome and informal action. The Executive Committees of leaders met occasionally to exchange opinions and guide the course of their huge fleet of manufacturing, transporting, and marketing units; but not frequently enough, and not without great difficulty. The Standard now faced the necessity of establishing a clear-cut centralized control in New York, for the Cleveland office was on the periphery of affairs. Along with the practical concentration of authority, legal steps must be taken to give it permanence and safeguard it against attack. This was the problem with which Rockefeller, Flagler, and Dodd wrestled, and before 1882 they had solved it.

v

The new trust agreement, signed January 2, 1882 (with a supplementary agreement executed two days later),[22] marked a new departure in the history not only of the Standard Oil, but of industrial organizations in the United States. Dodd is generally credited with its authorship. The signers were the stockholders of the Standard, now forty-two in number, and Messrs. Keith, Chester, and Vilas. They agreed to set up a board of trustees of the Standard Oil Trust,

[22]The original Standard Oil Trust agreement contemplated that there would be a Standard Oil Company in each State to which the properties, situated in that State, of the different companies, would be transferred. The supplementary agreement executed two days later gave the Trustees a large discretion in continuing existing companies, if they saw fit. The Trustees did in fact continue a great many of the existing companies.

nine in number, and to place in their hands all the properties owned or controlled by the Standard. That is, they were to take not only the stocks and bonds of the subsidiary and allied companies, but the 35,000 shares of the Standard Oil of Ohio, which had never been held by Keith, Chester, and Vilas. Every stockholder was to receive for each Standard Oil share twenty trust certificates, representing his slice of the whole cake. The profits of all the component companies were to be sent to the nine trustees, and the certificate-holders were to receive dividends as often and in such amounts as the trustees might deem expedient.

In effect, though not in law, one great company—the Standard Oil Trust—was set up which the new certificates represented, and the new trustees managed. The birth of this unprecedented entity was an epochal event in business organization; and as soon as the public became aware of its existence, it showed its grasp of the fact by utterly changing the meaning attached to a venerable English word. A trust had hitherto meant a trusteeship, or something confided to another. But now it quickly came to mean a great monopolistic or semi-monopolistic corporation, and that meaning it has retained ever since. Legally, this corporation did not exist. It had no legal name and no charter. When questioned, Rockefeller, Flagler, and Dodd could say—with literal truth—that there was no all-comprehending company; that they knew only of the Standard and its allied and subsidiary corporations, all separate. But actually the grand unifying company was a fact, of which there existed two symbols: the trust certificates, and the new highly centralized management of the Standard-controlled properties.

The first trustees were designated by the trust agreement itself, three serving for one year, three for two, and three for a triennium. They were John D. Rockefeller, Oliver H. Payne, William Rockefeller, Jabez A. Bostwick, H. M. Flagler, William G. Warden, Charles Pratt, Benjamin Brewster, and John D. Archbold. Power to elect successors was vested in the certificate-holders. The trustees were to have their "principal office in New York" and keep their securities there. They were charged with the formation, "as soon as practicable," of Standard Oil companies in New York and New Jersey. Of course the Standard Oil of Ohio and the Standard Oil of Pennsylvania already existed. Additional companies with similar names might be organized in other States and Territories whenever the trustees felt that the time was ripe. Finally, a tremendous new grant of authority was made to the trustees. They were to "exercise general supervision over the affairs of the said several Standard Oil companies, and, as far as practicable, over the other companies or partnerships, any portion of whose stock is held in such trust." They were to elect the directors and officers of all the companies.[23]

Thus what had still been a fairly loose confederation was transformed into a unitary state, with the nine men at its head possessing full means for industrial control. As soon as the new offices were established in New York early in 1883, and a majority of the trustees began to gather almost daily at the same table, the concentration of power became effective. Creating a State-by-State organization, naming the directors and officers of various companies, they held complete authority over the subsidiaries. The last vestiges of the period of chaos had disappeared, and the dream of John D. Rockefeller had been converted into a reality grander than he had imagined, and more magnificently compact. The nine trustees were all in the prime of life, with their enthusiasm at its height, and their confidence backed by twenty years of successful experience.

It is evident from the facts which we have recited that the "trust" was an evolution, and not a creation snatched from thin air. Its germ had lain in the trusteeship vested in Flagler when the Long Island Oil Company was purchased in 1872; it had reached a new stage of growth in the trust agreement of 1879, though that went little beyond a stock-holding device; finally it had become a highly centralized organism, controlling from one office the oil-refining industry of the country. Its nine trustees held absolute authority. The trust certificates made it possible to buy and sell shares in the trust, even though this was a semi-secret body having no legal existence; they also made possible a regular machinery of elections. At last the industrial necessities of the Standard Oil system had been met. Unquestionably Rockefeller grasped the full significance and possibilities of the trust. We may doubt if Dodd, whose view was more narrowly legal, did so. He always declared in later years that his intention had been merely to set up an effective trusteeship in the old sense, and not to aid in creating a centralized monopoly. He so wrote

[23]Taylor, MS History of the Standard Oil, 177–180.

in his pamphlet on "Combinations: Their Use and Abuses."[24]

All the purposes of the trust might equally have been accomplished in two other ways. Rockefeller and his associates might have created a voluntary unincorporated association like the old American Express Company or Adams Express Company; or they might have arranged a complete consolidation of properties in one corporation, like the American Sugar Refining Company set up in 1891. But the first plan would not have differed vitally from that followed. The second would have required a new charter, cost money and trouble in buying out minority stockholders of various companies, and involved much publicity. As long as possible the nature of the trust was kept secret from the American public. The trust agreement was not published until it was dragged to light by the New York Senate Investigation of 1888; the full facts were not brought out until later still. To be sure, the existence of the trust in the old-time sense, a trusteeship, was openly admitted from the outset. On December 27, 1882, a Senate Committee which was investigating speculative "corners" examined Flagler. He explained the successive creation of, the Standard Oil of Ohio, of Pennsylvania, of New Jersey, and of New York—the last two of which had been established about August 1, 1882.[25] He then remarked: "The Standard Trust Company is an agreement of individuals who have created a trust and placed it in the hands of trustees. It holds bonds and stocks for individuals." But he refused to give any information whatever upon the relations among the various Standard companies.[26] As for the trust in the new sense of a great combination of monopolistic tendency, the officers simply denied its existence—and in fact, legally it had none.

They long maintained, with how much honesty the reader can judge for himself, that the companies were still essentially separate and still largely competitive. In 1888 Rockefeller even told a com-

[24]Dodd, *Combinations*, 22–24.

[25]Philadelphia *Press*, N. Y. *Tribune, Herald*, Dec. 28, 1882.

[26]"Witness then successively declined to say whether a large proportion of the profits were allowed to accumulate; what dividends had been made; if the officers in all the companies are not the same; why the New Jersey and New York companies were organized, and what the capital stock of the latter is; whether the Standard does not absorb all the competing lines; if the company did not refine 90 per cent of the oil in the United States; if it does not control transportation rates and the price of oil in the United States." Philadelphia *Press*, Dec. 28, 1882.

mittee of the Federal House that the trust kept no books—"We have no system of bookkeeping."[27]

VI

The years 1879–1882 inclusive had witnessed a steady continuance of the Standard's acquisitions. As a result, no fewer than fourteen organizations joined as complete units in executing the trust agreement, while twenty-six more became parties through a portion of the stockholders and members.[28] Of course many of these forty companies represented previous consolidations. Like the cannibalistic seaman in the *Bab Ballads*, the National Transit Company, for example, embodied a long list of extinct entities in the pipe-line field.

Never before in history had such an imposing array of industrial units been banded together in a single organization. Never before had any really great industry come under so nearly complete a control, for the new trust comprised probably 90 per cent of the refining capacity of the nation, and almost as large a proportion of the pipe lines. Indeed, there was hardly a refinery in 1882 really worth acquisition that was not incorporated in the trust, or kept in control by some arrangement with it.[29]

The trust was first capitalized at $70,000,000—that is, the trust certificates represented that amount. We have seen that as early as 1874 the $3,500,000 capital stock of the Standard of Ohio was really valued, in exchanges of that year, at about $10,000,000. Enormously valuable refineries in all the main centers had since been added. More than a million had been paid for Hostetter's property; nearly three and a half millions for the Empire holdings. The trust's great pipe-line company alone was now capitalized at $30,000,000. Farms of tanks, fleets of oil cars, squadrons of tank ships, had steadily grown. We shall shortly explain just how vast the Standard Oil

[27]*House Trust Investigation, 1888,* p. 391.

[28]Taylor, MS History of the Standard Oil, 177, 178; see Appendix VII.

[29]Rockefeller said in 1922: "I should say that at this time the Standard Oil Company had 80 per cent of the business or a little more, and that from then to the present day the numbers and power of competing companies have steadily increased." Comment on Taylor's History. This is too low an estimate. In 1879 both H. H. Rogers and Bostwick testified before the Hepburn Committee that the combination owned or controlled 90–95 per cent of the refining industry of America. See *Industrial Commission Report,* I, 95, for this and Lewis Emery's testimony that at one time he did not know of a single independent refiner.

principality was. Beginning in 1883 we have explicit statements of assets and earnings which show the conservative nature of the capitalization:[30]

	Net Assets	Total Net Earnings	Total Dividends
1883	$72,869,596	$11,231,790	$4,268,086
1884	75,858,960	7,778,205	4,288,842
1885	76,762,672	8,382,935	7,479,223
1886	87,012,107	15,350,787	7,226,452
1887	94,377,970	14,026,590	8,463,327
1888	97,005,621	16,226,955	13,705,505
1889	101,281,192	14,845,201	10,620,630
1890	115,810,074	19,131,470	11,200,089

The earnings of the trust in 1883 would have justified a capitalization of two hundred millions, and in 1886 of three hundred millions. In 1890 they would have justified a capitalization of nearly four hundred millions. It is fair to say that the Standard in the eighties was the largest and richest of American industrial organizations— the largest and richest in the world. The fact that there was not a drop of water in the capital was much to Rockefeller's credit in an era of atrocious stock-watering. Jay Gould and "Jim" Fisk had so watered the stock of the Erie between 1868 and 1872 as to increase its par value from $17,000,000 to $78,000,000, chiefly to manipulate Wall Street. The Central Pacific Railroad was capitalized by Huntington, Stanford, and Crocker at $139,000,000, although a Federal Commission reported that $58,000,000 would have been a generous price for the road. William H. Vanderbilt's South Pennsylvania Railroad was actually worth about $6,500,000, the sum for which a responsible contractor had offered to build it; but a construction company made up of Vanderbilt's clerks received $15,000,000 to complete it, while a syndicate of capitalists which supplied this money got $40,000,000 in bonds and shares![31]

The nine trustees comprised the whole group, with one exception, which had done most to build up the Standard combination. Charles Lockhart alone was omitted, probably because the variety of his in-

[30]Taylor, MS History of the Standard Oil, 127.
[31]Van Oss, American Railroads as Investments, 126. One trust, the American Tobacco Company, by various reorganizations between 1890 and 1894 capitalized its good will alone in stock by more than $110,000,000. Report of Bureau of Corporations, "Tobacco Industry," Part 2, p. 13.

terests—banking, mining, lumbering, iron and glass manufacturing —made it impossible for him to leave Pittsburgh or give the Standard a sufficient amount of time.[32] Together, the nine men represented as much in material power as in past achievement. Of the 35,000 shares of the Standard of Ohio, they controlled 23,314, or almost five sevenths. Rockefeller alone, with 9585 shares in 1882, had more than a third of the trustees' holdings, and more than a fourth of the entire capital stock; while he, William, Flagler, Payne, and Harkness—the Cleveland group—held very nearly four sevenths of the whole.[33]

The fact must be emphasized that the trust was not, as many people in later years carelessly supposed, a great unitary organization with Rockefeller as its despotic head. It was rather an association of companies and executives, with Rockefeller, by virtue of his greater abilities, greater personal force, and greater holdings, the chieftain. He was *primus inter pares.* There was no reason inherent in the organization of the trust why Flagler, or Pratt, or Warden should obey his orders. Actually he did not work by orders, but by obtaining an agreement, often after protracted argument; in a letter to Flagler in the early eighties he speaks of having a hard time "holding my own" in the Executive Committee. Sometimes his views were rejected. In short, the trust was not a dictatorship, but an oligarchy. Rockefeller occupied a somewhat different position from Carnegie. The ironmaster became head of by far the strongest steel company in the Pittsburgh area, just as Rockefeller became head of the all-important refining company in the Cleveland area. But Carnegie did not go on to associate the other eminent ironmasters of the land—Abram S. Hewitt, Daniel Morrell, Henry Oliver, and so on—with himself in a great federation of companies. Rockefeller did go on to gather about him the most powerful figures in the oil industry. Carnegie always held a majority of the stock in his company; Rockefeller never had a majority of the trust certificates.

What the new giant would mean to the United States was not even dimly comprehended in 1882 by the outsiders who knew something of the combination. But in perspective we can easily define its primary significance. After the long depression of 1873–79, the country was at last emerging again into the broad sunlight of prosperity;

[32]Boyle, *Derrick's Handbook,* 991.
[33]Figures given in Taylor, MS History of the Standard Oil.

old industries were soon flourishing, new industries like electricity were springing up, immigration was increasing, investments were expanding. The better times continued until 1893. But because of improved transportation facilities, the development of power machinery, the progress of invention, and other factors, industry was tending more and more strongly toward concentration. Particularly was this true of certain fields. During the eighties, the number of iron and steel manufactories rose by only 9.2 per cent, but their capital increased by 97.3 per cent, and the tonnage they produced by 117.3 per cent! That is, the average size of the plants was almost doubled. In shipbuilding during that decade the number of establishments was more than cut in half, while the capital invested grew by almost one third (29.9 per cent). In the manufacture of farm implements, the number of establishments was again reduced by more than half, while the capital increased by 134 per cent. The number of establishments making boots and shoes grew by only 6.3 per cent, but the capital employed rose by 121.6 per cent. Thus the story went.[34] The small manufactory in the little town, save for certain specialties and patent-protected articles, was going bankrupt or being merged with others; the large manufactory was rising to undisputed lordship.

Ever since the Civil War, industrialists had been searching for a mode of interstate combination which would be at once legal and workable. Leaders in various businesses had seen as early as Rockefeller that the savage price-cutting and other practices characteristic of reckless competition must be abated. They had likewise realized how valuable were the advantages which might be achieved by large-scale concentration. Great manufactories could make larger use of cost-saving machinery; could arrange for the subdivision and specialization of labor; could buy materials at wholesale prices; could set up branch plants, making specialized goods for specialized markets, at advantageous points; could save by utilizing by-products; and could establish research departments that were quite beyond the reach of small companies. But how were numerous widely separated units to be combined? In the railroad field, under a masterful figure like Albert Fink, the pool had achieved some successes, but elsewhere it was usually a failure. It was essentially a

[34] See C. R. Van Hise, *Concentration and Control*, 37–52.

partnership of corporations, and as such illegal; and no matter how strictly its agreements were drawn, no matter how definitely its members pledged themselves to pay certain penalties for violation, the compacts were unenforceable.

In numerous industries the excesses of competition constantly held prices at an unremunerative level. Evidence was later collected by the government that in sugar-manufacture, with about forty refineries madly striving to run full time and undersell their rivals, the margin between the prices of raw sugar and refined sugar for the three years 1884–86 was kept close to seven tenths of a cent a pound. The plants lost so much money at that level that eighteen—nearly half the whole number—failed. In self-defense, sugar manufacturers turned to combination. The whiskey-distilling business presented a close parallel to the early phases of the oil-refining industry. The cost of establishing a distillery was small, and when prices were good the profits were large. The natural result was heavy overbuilding, a ghastly excess of production over market demand, and an alternation of brief periods of boom with long intervals of loss and prostration. Beginning in 1882, the distillers made frantic but unsuccessful efforts to control the situation by forming pools and restricting output to one half of capacity. Like the sugar refiners, they found that a stronger form of organization than the pool was indispensable. The situation was much the same in tobacco manufacturing and various other fields.[35] All over the industrial map, manufacturers were searching for an effective means of combination.

In the "trust" Rockefeller, Flagler, and Dodd found the answer. Organizing one industry completely, they pointed the way for others. To be sure, the legal position of the device was vulnerable; but it took years to prove that, and meanwhile imitators became numerous. The distillers of the country, long on the verge of bankruptcy through price wars, soon set up another "trust." The sugar refiners followed suit; and then, near the close of the eighties, came a host of other businesses. The leaders of the Standard had fashioned the

[35]The best summary treatment of disorganization, overcompetition, and losses in the sugar-refining, whiskey-distilling, and other industries is to be found in Volume I of the *Reports of the United States Industrial Commission* (1900), which presents the testimony of Havemeyer, Rockefeller, and numerous other combination leaders. The review of evidence on the trusts, written by Jeremiah W. Jenks, has a section headed "competition the chief cause" (p. 9 ff.).

mould in which much of American business was reshaped until New Jersey passed her holding company law.[36]

The new instrumentality having been created, it was now imperative that the headquarters of combination be removed from Cleveland to New York. This was effected by a series of steps in 1883–85. One after another, Rockefeller, Flagler, and most of the other important partners became legal residents of the metropolis. At one time, early in 1883, a special car was hired to transport about a score of subordinate Standard officers to New York. Rockefeller met them and breakfasted with them at a hotel. Then he arranged for carriages and guides to help them hunt up homes for their families.

Rockefeller himself, in looking upon the trust, never felt any doubt that this creation was good. He had been passionately convinced, as his letters to his wife show, of the necessity for a general combination to save the oil industry from competitive chaos. During the harsh struggle for unification he had never wavered in his faith. And in later life he believed that the accomplishment loomed larger and larger in the perspective of time. "This movement was the origin of the whole system of modern economic administration," he declared with a natural touch of pride.[37] "It has revolutionized the way of doing business all over the world. The time was ripe for it. It had to come, though all we saw at the moment was the need to save ourselves from wasteful conditions. . . . The day of combination is here to stay. Individualism has gone, never to return."

[36]The New Jersey law was passed 1889. The American Cotton Oil Company in that year and the United States Rubber Company in 1893 were apparently the pioneer holding companies. W. Z. Ripley, *Trusts, Pools, and Corporations,* XX. For some of the legal questions involved, see W. W. Cook, *The Corporation Problem,* published in 1891, and J. P. Davis, *Corporations: A Study of the Origin and Development of Great Business Combination* (1905). See also the volume by J. R. Dos Passos on Commercial Trusts.

[37]Inglis, Conversations with Rockefeller.

XXVI

Citizen of Cleveland

O N July 8, 1879, Rockefeller celebrated his fortieth birthday. Already possibly one of the twenty richest Americans, and the leader who had guided the most revolutionary of American experiments in business organization to practical completion, he was little known to the country at
large; and he continued to lead a quiet, unassuming life in Cleveland, a city now of about 160,000 people.[1]

In the business world, of course, his reputation was great and
rapidly increasing. In 1873 he bid against Cornelius Vanderbilt of
the New York Central for control of the Vandergrift & Forman
pipe lines. After the negotiations ended, he obtaining a one-third
interest and Vanderbilt only one-sixth, the railroad magnate exclaimed: "That Rockefeller! He will be the richest man in the country!" A little later Rockefeller saw a good deal of the powerful
Pittsburgh capitalist William H. Thaw, interested in banks, railroads, iron, and oil. Even his general support of the scheme for a
great Standard combination would be helpful, and Rockefeller
tried to convince him. As he recalled later, the process was difficult.
"He was for a time quite opposed to our plan. 'It isn't in the books,
John,' he said. 'It can't be done.' But finally I persuaded him. On the
way home to Cleveland I was a guest in his car from Philadelphia
to Pittsburgh. Years afterward a clergyman from Iowa introduced
himself and told me that he, too, was Mr. Thaw's guest on that ride.
He said that after I left the car Mr. Thaw turned to him and said:

[1]Edmund Kirke, "The City of Cleveland," *Harper's Magazine*, LXXII, 561
ff. (1886), mentions Leonard Case, Henry Chisholm, Amasa Stone, John Hay,
and other prominent citizens, but not Rockefeller.

'That young man will either make a stupendous failure—or a wonderful success!' " And every one was struck in 1879 by the testimony of William H. Vanderbilt in the Hepburn Investigation upon Rockefeller and his associates: "These men are smarter than I am a great deal. They are very enterprising and smart men. I never came into contact with any class of men so smart and able as they are in their business."[2]

As year by year he became better known to the public, a sharp division of opinion about him appeared and grew. Among oil men in Cleveland, Pittsburgh, New York, and above all the Regions, many in 1879 regarded him as a wicked desolater of homes, a Goliath trampling out small businesses, a ruthless embodiment of greed. Many others looked upon him as the architect who had saved the refining industry from utter ruin, and used its elements to build an imposing and durable structure, benefiting the whole country. This disagreement upon his business policy was natural. Much more remarkable was the violent difference as to his personal traits. To distant observers he seemed cold, hard, humorless, self-sufficient, and grasping. They told stories of the "I'm bound to be rich" variety, and anecdotes which illustrated his "slyness." Somebody concocted the fable that when in 1876 he signed the profit-sharing contracts with Scofield, Shurmer & Teagle at his Euclid Avenue house, he told the three men that they should not inform even their wives, and that if they made money they must not drive fast horses or put on style— that would invite competition![3] Many talked as if his piety were hypocrisy. But others, including his closest associates, regarded him with warm admiration. They maintained that, apart from his great intellectual power, his dominant traits were patience, serenity, humor, kindliness, and generosity; and that while he might be outwardly cold, he was just and sincere.

As a matter of fact, men who saw Rockefeller only rarely and judged him by his exterior utterly failed to penetrate to his real character. He was self-contained to an enigmatic and disconcerting degree. Maturing early, laden with business burdens from his late teens, and driven in upon himself by family responsibilities, he had

[2]Inglis, MS Biography, 197, for Cornelius Vanderbilt; Inglis, Conversations with Rockefeller, for Thaw.
[3]Obviously a fable because he himself drove fast horses, had a fine house, and never concealed his wealth.

A Rockefeller family group at Forest Hill.

The time is the late seventies or early eighties. On Rockefeller's right is his wife; on his left is his mother, the strength and fineness of whose face are striking.

Rockefeller on vacation.

Two photographs taken in the Far West. One shows him eating a picnic lunch; the other with Mrs. Rockefeller, Doctor Biggar, and some friends in California.

formed a protective covering. It was thickened by his business battles. Defending an idea of industrial concentration which he knew was instinctively reprobated by nine Americans in ten, he cultivated reticence and made it his rule to "expose as little surface as possible." While his subtle, ruminative mind solved his problems by an acid process of thought, he presented a front of chilled steel to the world. But behind this armor-plate a small number of intimates saw a very different personality, while a much larger number caught transient glimpses of it.

II

At forty Rockefeller had reached his prime, physically and mentally. His figure had filled out so that he impressed most people as a large man. He had grown a heavy reddish mustache, and his light-colored hair was still thick. He bore himself with calm dignity, but with a quiet glint of humor in his keen blue eyes; eyes that could be very friendly, or could drill a visitor or associate with penetrating intensity. An independent Titusville refiner told Ida M. Tarbell how Rockefeller and some associates once met him and other refiners at an office in the Regions to discuss the plan of the Standard combination. Every one talked except Rockefeller. He remained silently attentive, his hands masking his eyes as he softly swung back and forth in a rocking-chair. The narrator made a belligerent speech against the Standard project. "Well, right in the middle of it, John Rockefeller stopped rocking and took down his hands and looked at me. You never saw such eyes. He took me all in, saw just how much fight he could expect from me, and I knew it, and then up went his hands and back and forth went his chair."[4]

In one respect his business traits had undergone an essential change. Whereas early in his career he had given minute and unsleeping attention to details, now he concentrated only upon the larger outlines of his affairs, the major problems. It is one proof of his business genius that fast as the Standard Oil had grown, he had grown still faster. This sudden shift in his attention may be dated in 1872, when the Standard swallowed up the Cleveland industry and turned to conquest in other centers. Till then he had known every warehouse and every ledger. Thereafter he observed the rule

[4]Tarbell, *Standard Oil Company*, I, 105, 106.

that he should do nothing himself that others could do equally well or better. As his son has put it, he was never again "a detail man." "I remained in the background," he said later, "became what you might call a fifth wheel; we had a good organization, an excellent organization."[5] It was the one feasible course, for he would have succumbed under his burden had he not possessed a talent for finding able lieutenants and delegating responsibility. He tried to leave himself free to think, in his deliberate, searching way, a little further ahead than anybody else in American industry. He trained his principal subordinates to do this, and Charles J. Woodbury records that in 1879 he came into the laboratory in suite 28 of the Standard Building to say:[6]

Has any one given you the law of these offices? No? It is this: nobody does anything if he can get anybody else to do it. You smile; but think it over. Your department is the testing of oils. You are responsible; but as soon as you can, get some one whom you can rely on, train him in the work, sit down, cock up your heels, and think out some way for the Standard Oil to make some money.

Even so, the burden he carried was sometimes almost crushing. His was always the planning brain and the central responsibility in the ceaseless advance of the Standard. In conquering and consolidating his industrial principality; in fighting the endless series of battles with producers, independent refiners, railroads, and pipe-line companies; in facing Federal and State investigations; in conducting important litigation; in raising and disbursing money; in working out intricate problems of administration, he was continuously harassed and busy. Business crises would often force him to labor frenziedly for weeks at a time. In the intervals he had to catch up with church affairs, private investments, and the thickening requests for charitable aid. He had family troubles, also, for in 1878 his sister Lucy died, while his strained relations with his brother Frank greatly distressed him.

Both he and Mrs. Rockefeller felt the travail. "Those were days of worry," sighed his wife many years later to William Hoster. And Rockefeller agreed. "I don't know how we came through them," he

[5]Inglis, Conversations with Rockefeller.
[6]Woodbury, "Rockefeller and His Standard," *Saturday Evening Post,* Oct. 21, 1911.

said. "You know how seldom I had an unbroken night's sleep, worrying about how it all was coming out. All the fortune I have made has not served to compensate me for the anxiety of that period. Work by day and worry by night, week in and week out, month after month. If I had foreseen the future I doubt whether I would have had the courage to go on. . . . I had no ambition to make a fortune. Mere money-making has never been my goal. I had an ambition to build."[7]

But he bore his pyramiding burdens with patience and calmness. Despite what he says of his early temper, no associate has recorded a single instance of petulance, excitement, or flurry. On the contrary, many have set down anecdotes of his serenity. "Mr. Rockefeller was always the quietest, most retiring, and modest man," said one of his oil-buyers, Thomas H. Wheeler. "And the bigger he grew the more modest he became. . . . I have never heard of his equal in getting together a lot of the very best men in one team and inspiring each man to do his best for the enterprise. . . . He was so big, so broad, so patient; I don't believe a man like him comes to this world oftener than once in five or six hundred years."[8]

He systematically sought time for relaxation. At thirty he had established certain helpful habits; not to eat hurriedly at breakfast or rush off from the table; to take a short nap, if only for three minutes, after lunch; to drive regularly. He persisted in this regimen although it lengthened his business hours. "It is not good to keep the forces at tension all the time," he remarked. "Men used to laugh at me when I left a railroad eating-room because the boss with the lantern on his arm shouted 'All aboard!' But before going I'd stuff my cheeks with food (I always had a good big mouth), then spend a long time after I got aboard the train eating what I had carried away."[9] He snatched rest in the midst of business. Woodbury writes that he kept a wood-and-rubber contrivance in one room and came in every day to pull and haul it for exercise. A new accountant moved into that suite, decided that the apparatus was a nuisance, and not knowing who Rockefeller was, peremptorily ordered him to remove it. "All right!" said Rockefeller, and had it placed elsewhere. At a

[7]Hoster was a young newspaperman who covered Rockefeller's trip to Europe in 1906; an envelope of materials by him is in the Rockefeller Papers.
[8]Inglis, Conversation with T. H. Wheeler.
[9]Inglis, Conversations with Rockefeller.

committee meeting near the close of a hard day he might stretch out on a couch, announcing:[9] "I am a little tired, but go right on, gentlemen, for I know you want to make a decision." But he never failed to interject searching questions, or grasp the essential points better than his colleagues. The result of his care for his health was that his ailments were few and trifling.

He brought to his office burdens a quiet touch of humor, as his scanty surviving correspondence shows. "Enclosed is a letter from Lewis Meredith," he writes Warden in 1877. "I did not know there was as wise a man as that in Philadelphia. You had better have him come to your office and see if you can make out something."[10] In writing William Rockefeller about a minor matter, he playfully added: "Mind, this is strictly confidential, except to Mira. She can only tell a few friends, in a very confidential way, six or seven hundred."[11] A little later he condoled with Archbold over the Lake Shore's refusal to use the Standard's lubricants. "It seems almost an unfriendly disposition, although we do not want to cherish such a thought, and must persevere in some kindly way to bring them back to their first love."[12]

No less characteristic was his constant concern for the health of his associates. He repeatedly urged Standard executives to take indefinite vacations on full salary. "I trust you will not worry about the business," he writes a Titusville oil-buyer who had been ill. "Your health is more important to you and to us than the business." He was often troubled about Warden's strength, while we find him praising Benjamin Brewster for a trip abroad. During 1877 Camden exhausted himself in the heavy work of consolidating the West Virginia and Maryland refineries. "We cannot have you prejudice your health by any attention to business," Rockefeller exhorted. "Please feel at perfect liberty to break away three, six, nine, twelve, fifteen months, more or less, and it will afford us the greatest pleasure to undertake to come and fill the gap in your absence, knowing how cheerfully and earnestly you would do the same for any of us. . . . Your salary will not cease, however long you decide

[10]Rockefeller to Warden, Oct. 30, 1877; Rockefeller Papers.
[11]Rockefeller to William Rockefeller, Dec. 30, 1879; Rockefeller Papers.
[12]Rockefeller to Archbold, Aug. 26, 1884; Rockefeller Papers.

to remain away from business." In further notes he urged a European tour and expressed the "deepest interest in your welfare." This Camden correspondence shows how quickly he established a cordial relationship with his aides; and a similar friendliness animates his letters to Colonel W. P. Thompson, a Confederate veteran who joined the Standard when it purchased the Parkersburg refineries.[13]

He seems to have been invariably courteous to all members of the staff. The accountant who ordered him to remove his rubber exerciser expected to be discharged or reprimanded, but Rockefeller never said a word. Woodbury came into the office with a strong prejudice against him. Rockefeller had swallowed up his little plant. He had taken over first the customers, then the whole refinery. But "the graces of courtesy, gentleness, and good nature won me to Mr. Rockefeller at our first meeting."[14] The wage policy of the Standard was generous. It consistently paid workmen a little more than the ruling rate, after the first years never had a strike or any dissatisfied working groups, and set up one of the most liberal pension systems in American industry.[15]

In his calm, vigilant way he kept in touch with every branch of the expanding Standard. He became intimate with all the company leaders from Cleveland to Long Island, from Baltimore to Boston, and his letters show him constantly wrestling with their problems. Now it was Archbold whom he advised upon the Regions refineries; now Camden upon the building of tanks in Baltimore; now Warden upon shipments from Point Breeze; and now F. Q. Barstow upon the export trade. While some of his colleagues were ruthless enough, his own instinct in business dealings seems always to have been generous. We find more than one letter like the following to Colonel Payne early in 1878:[16]

In reference to the negotiations with Scofield, Shurmer & Teagle and the Pioneer Oil Company about their paraffine.

Have thought more since you left, and we want to be extra careful not to give them any possible chance of complaint that we have not done all in this matter they have any right to ask, and the same holds

---

[13]Camden Papers.   [14]*Saturday Evening Post,* Oct. 21, 1911.
[15]For the labor record of the Standard, see Appendix V.
[16]April 8, 1878; Rockefeller Papers.

true in our negotiation with Merriam in view of all our past record with him. You know and fully appreciate what I mean as also does Mr. McGregor, for I have personally urged upon him the importance of the greatest care on our part that Merriam should have no just reason to complain that we had in any way deviated from the spirit of the conversations of the past few years pertaining to this matter.

And we have more than one anecdote like that told by his buyer, T. H. Wheeler:[17]

Back in the early eighties I was in the market for twenty thousand tons of hoop-iron to use on oil barrels. That was a big order even for those days; Mr. Carnegie has said that iron men were either princes or paupers as the market fluctuated, and just then they were in the pauper state. A concern at Pittsburgh and another at Youngstown, O., were bidding for our order. I told Mr. Rockefeller why it was likely we'd get very low bids.

"Don't rub 'em against each other, Wheeler," he said to me. "Don't rub them against each other! They must have a chance to live. Give them both a chance to make money. Divide the order between them."

I couldn't give a better idea of Mr. Rockefeller if I talked all day. How many businessmen would have given their purchasing agent such an order as that? He always had that principle in mind: wanted every one who dealt with him to make a profit and be satisfied. And he had a mind that looked far ahead, saw all the possibilities in a situation and provided for them before others thought of them.

"We must be patient" is a frequent phrase in his letters, and Standard men knew well his equanimity in the face of adversity. John Becka, a veteran workman of No. 1 Plant in Cleveland, long afterward recalled a destructive fire of about 1880. Flagler and Rockefeller walked over and stood on a trestle that had run beside the burnt-out building. Rockefeller gazed sadly at the debris, and remarked: "It's pretty bad, but I'm happy that nobody lost his life."[18]

In his various disagreements with producers, refiners, and railroads he always maintained his poise, seeking peaceable adjudication where possible, and sometimes obtaining it; but meanwhile fighting hard to hold his position and lift the Standard to new efficiency. Particularly, and very mistakenly, he yielded nothing to those who urged that the Standard should publicize its side of important disputes. He considered this an undignified waste of energy.

[17]Inglis, Notes of Conversation with T. H. Wheeler.
[18]Becka to the author, Nov. 20, 1936.

It was better to "keep sawing wood," as he later put it. "A man cannot concentrate his faculties at the same time on two opposite things; and I was concentrated upon extending and developing and perfecting our business, rather than on stopping by the wayside to squabble with slanderers." Other Standard men would often wince. "John, you must have a hide like a rhinoceros!" Flagler once exclaimed. But Rockefeller was imperturbable. "No, I will not engage in controversy," he would reply, although he confessed in old age how much the attacks had sometimes hurt him. "I can wait; the trust will justify me."[19] He agreed with Lincoln's remark: "Life is too short to spend half of it in quarrelling."

III

For a man under such heavy strain, the beautiful Forest Hill estate just east of Cleveland was a happy accident. It was well that he stumbled upon it, for it enabled him to develop his love of horses, tree-planting, and landscape-gardening into adequate diversions. During most of the seventies the family lived in the plain, roomy, comfortable house on Euclid Avenue, numbered first 424 and then 997. But after 1878 Forest Hill became the center of their Cleveland life, and the Euclid Avenue house was pushed into the background until they used it for little except Sunday dinners and short spring and autumn stays.

Rockefeller took his first step in acquiring the estate as early as 1873. On June 5 he bought a tract of 79.247 acres of partly wooded land, with a broad hilltop commanding fine views of Lake Erie, from the Doan family at $1000 an acre.[20] "I thought it a good investment," he said later. He then had no intention of building a country house. In the spring of 1875 he and three other men incorporated the Euclid Avenue-Forest Hill Association, with the purpose of establishing a hydropathic sanitarium;[21] and this body, capitalized at $250,000, bought the land from him and began erecting a large building. But times continued so hard that the corporation failed before the nearly completed building had been put into operation. That is, apparently, his associates lost heart, and he had to repurchase

[19]Inglis, Conversations with Rockefeller.
[20]Office records, Rockefeller Estate, Cleveland.
[21]Cleveland *Leader*, April 17, 1875.

the land with the white-elephant structure on the crest of the hill. The ravines, lawns, and wooded slopes were beautiful; from the piazzas the summer blue of Lake Erie was entrancing; but what could he do with the property?

First, in the summer of 1878, he and Mrs. Rockefeller tried to run it as a club hotel.[22] A manager and servants were hired, and friends were invited to bring their families. John D. Rockefeller, Jr., recalls how as a small boy he sat in the large dining-room and wonderingly received his food from colored waiters. But, as Rockefeller subsequently told his son, "I found that the guests expected Mother to entertain them and act as hostess. Therefore, we discontinued the club at the end of the first year."[23]

The next step was to create a summer home. He had quickly fallen in love with the wooded hillsides and rolling patches of open, which reminded him of the western New York of his childhood. If the passionate delight he later felt in planning roads and paths, in planting and moving trees, had not stirred in him when he bought the tract, the new residence quickly brought it to life. He began purchasing more acres. In 1878–79 the building was remodelled, and barns and stables were provided for the horses, machinery, and vehicles which thereafter furnished so much of his recreation.[24]

Here he had the woods and quiet he loved. Here he had also a modest problem in organization, a relaxation after the fatigues of his complex business labors; buildings to be erected, roads and paths laid out, trees planted, vistas opened. His growing family invested the life at Forest Hill with a bubbling energy and gaiety. The four children in 1880 ranged from six to fourteen, with John the youngest. They flung themselves into the activities of the estate with happy abandon. They climbed on stoneboats, sat on plow-tongues, piled into the backs of empty wagons, and gathered chips where the men were felling trees. They were paid for pulling weeds. When they grew old enough for velocipedes, Rockefeller proposed giving a machine to each. "No," said Mrs. Rockefeller, "we will get only one—that will teach them to give up to one another." As John be-

[22]Mrs. John D. Rockefeller wrote her son, Aug. 10, 1909: "In 1877, we came to Forest Hill for the summer"; Rockefeller Papers. But Mr. John D. Rockefeller, Jr., says this seems a mistake and that it was probably 1878.

[23]Mr. John D. Rockefeller, Jr., to the author.

[24]George Sambrook to the author, Nov. 24, 1936.

Rockefeller at Forest Hill.

Swimming in the lake with Mrs. Rockefeller (note the straw hat worn to protect himself from the sun); and bicycling.

Forest Hill.

These photographs show the house itself, one of the drives, and the great hallway
on the first floor.

came strong he insisted on actual work, and swung an axe with skill, proudly selecting the biggest trees. But in these early years it was mostly play, and the frolics of his children gladdened Rockefeller's heart. Friends came for long visits, and the place became almost an asylum for superannuated Baptist ministers.

Rockefeller's parents also spent much time here. The old "doctor" was now away for long periods in the West, nobody knows where, apparently peddling medicines and giving treatments. Indeed, he was so little in Cleveland that not many years after the marriage of their daughter Mary Ann in October, 1872, Eliza Rockefeller spent most of the summers with John, and most of the winters with William. But we have some random glimpses of the man. Charles M. Higgins, who had joined the Standard as an office-boy, recalled that in the seventies he was walking down Euclid Avenue one spring morning when a phaeton drawn by two spirited horses and driven by a robust though elderly gentleman, finely dressed, pulled up at the curb. It was "Doctor" Rockefeller. He leaned over the seat-rail and said in a deep but kindly voice: "I would like to have you ride downtown with me." The youth climbed in. When they reached the Standard Oil offices the driver, his reddish beard flecked with gray, but his vigor apparently as great as when he had shot turkeys at a quarter mile and jumped over fences backward, sprang from the carriage, tied his team, and mounted the stairs to his son's office.[25] An employee at the Forest Hill estate also recalls "Doctor" Rockefeller on summer visits. About seventy, but as robust, cheery, and handsomely dressed as ever, he would stroll over the grounds, barking questions at the workmen or cracking jokes with them. He would set up a target, and soon have the children busy with bow and arrow. Edith was his favorite. He would dance about as she took the bow, shouting delightedly: "I'll bet you! Bet you she hits it eight times out of ten!"[26]

As for Eliza, Higgins remembered seeking her out one bitterly cold Christmas eve with a note from her son John. She was pleased by the note, but distressed to think that the boy was abroad in such weather. She made him sit down by the fire, and brought him a piece of pie and glass of milk. He recalled her as a lively old lady,

[25]Charles M. Higgins to the author, May 10, 1936.
[26]George Sambrook to the author, Nov. 24, 1936.

with hair so evenly parted that he instantly saw she was wearing a wig; for disliking her red hair, she covered it with a gray toupee. One of Rockefeller's letters to her, written apparently from New York on December 22, 1877, expresses concern over news of her illness. "We regret much not to be with you at this time, though we might not be able to nurse you as well as you have often cared for us. I fear you have been working too hard this fall, and when you are well again we must insist upon your visiting more and taking less care and responsibility."[27] We have also a letter of hers, apparently to the Van Duynes of Moravia, dated November 2, 1882, from 33 Cheshire Street, speaking of a visit she had recently paid them, and stating that she had been staying at "fores hill." The ill-spelled, ill-punctuated note concludes with a pathetic sentence: "I cant make a good k and pleas excuse it you may laught at my grammar and spelling all you pleas it does one good to laugh Some times and I am so far I cant hear you."[28]

Whenever he could, Rockefeller spent half a day at the estate overseeing improvements—building roads, clearing land for gardens, and preparing a small lake and race-track. He never performed any manual labor himself, but carefully oversaw the work. George Sambrook, a bright young fellow of English parentage who worked on the place, gives us a vivid snapshot of him at this time.

It was a drizzly spring day, and under a German foreman the men were building a log abutment for a road. Teams were dragging the heavy timbers from the bottom of a deep ravine. Rockefeller stood on a stump at the top of the slope, holding an umbrella above his head and intently watching the work. The German managed it badly. He hitched teams by slipknots to both ends of the log; the horses at the light end constantly got ahead of the other pair, the log swung around endwise, and it soon caught fast. Though four teams and eight or nine men toiled laboriously, in half an hour they did not bring up a single log.

"Too bad, too bad," Rockefeller exclaimed at each failure. Finally, losing patience, he expostulated: "Now, this is a very expensive way of doing the work. We can't go on in this style. There must be a

[27]Rockefeller Papers; he sent $50 as a Christmas gift.
[28]Copy furnished the author by the Van Duyne family.

better method." At which Sambrook, who was near him, remarked with a grin: "That's a Dutch way of logging."

"Do you think you could do any better?" demanded Rockefeller severely.

"I think I can," said Sambrook. He briefly explained what he would try to do. "Let me have two men and two teams and I'll show you," he concluded. Sinclair, the superintendent, who had now arrived on the scene, certified that Sambrook was ingenious, and the German foreman gave his consent. Sambrook accordingly brought the two teams near the middle of the log, one on each side of the center of gravity; attached them both by a rolling hitch, so that the log could revolve a little; and started them slowly. The timber moved up the hill steadily and easily.

Rockefeller was enormously pleased. He continued watching from the stump until the first log cleared the lip of the ravine. Then he waved his umbrella jubilantly, and with a kindly smile at the German foreman cried: "Bravo! Bravo! Let the Yankees do the work!"[29]

Slowly the estate grew. To lay out his race-track properly, Rockefeller needed some land belonging to John Hicks, a Cornish farmer near by. Sambrook, who knew him, volunteered to go with Rockefeller and Superintendent Sinclair to discuss the purchase. "What kind of a man is he?" the oil magnate asked. "A little peppery," replied the young teamster. They found Hicks with a scythe in one of his fields. He listened coldly as they stated their errand.

"Certainly, Mr. Rockefeller," he responded. "You can have the land you need. The price will be $150 an acre."

"What, $150 an acre?" demurred Rockefeller. "Mr. Hicks, that's a lot of money." "Well, damn it," replied Hicks with asperity, gazing westward toward the smoke of Cleveland, "if *you* have any to sell at that price I'll take it all—and pay cash, too." He turned abruptly away.

As Rockefeller led the way back to Forest Hill he looked drolly at Sambrook, and exclaimed: "Peppery, George? Did you say a little peppery? I guess you were right!" He chuckled at the recollection. Years later he bought the land, paying $450 for it.

Discipline on the estate was strict. Tippling was never tolerated

[29]This and other anecdotes were given me by Sambrook, Nov. 24, 25, 1936.

among the employees. Mrs. Rockefeller was a temperance worker. He himself wrote early in 1884, in reference to a plan for a prohibition amendment to the Constitution: "I am very much in favor of these efforts."[30] Habitual profanity among the workmen was not permitted. "He might let it go unmentioned the first time—especially if there was provocation," recalled Sambrook. "But the second time he would warn the man, and if it happened several times more he'd say—he was always very courteous: 'We can't use you here.'" In similar fashion he objected to any unnecessary noise or work on Sunday. When the family, after attending church, took its Sabbath dinner in the Euclid Avenue house, it fared as far as possible on food prepared the day before; they always had cold rice pudding for dessert!

Sambrook for a time left Rockefeller's employ to carry on a horse-selling business. Several hundred prospective buyers would gather on Sunday afternoons in the young man's stable-yard, not far from Forest Hill, and the shouts of the men and whinnying of the horses were audible to the Rockefellers. One day Rockefeller drove up to suggest that Sambrook should cease these Sunday activities. They were a breach of the decalogue, he remarked. "But, Mr. Rockefeller," explained Sambrook, "most of my customers can't come on a week-day. And Sunday seems to be convenient even for those who can. Why, your superintendent, Mr. Sinclair, has often been here on Sunday." "Been here and bought horses?" demanded Rockefeller in dismay. "Well, not exactly bought 'em; but picked 'em out and come next day to pay for 'em," grinned Sambrook. "And he had your assistant superintendent, Mr. Corbett, with him when he did it." "Really?" inquired Rockefeller, half-amused, half-outraged. "Yes, sir," replied Sambrook; "and Mr. Rudd's man has come to pick them out, too." This was Rockefeller's brother-in-law. "Mr. Rudd's man, too?" Rockefeller echoed. Then, turning to his driver with a rueful smile, he exclaimed: "Well, I guess we'd better go! I guess we'd better go!"

Mrs. Rockefeller, who exercised complete authority over the house, expected prompt, careful, and sober behavior on the part of the small staff of servants, but she was gentle in manner and considerate in her acts. When young Sambrook first came to Forest

[30]Rockefeller to L. H. Severance, Feb. 7, 1884; Rockefeller Papers.

Hill, he ate with the maids. His ruddy English cheeks and lively manner made him a good subject for jokes and horseplay by the staff. Once four or five girls set upon him good-naturedly, and he retaliated with spirit by piling them atop each other on the kitchen floor. The rumpus brought in the whole family. Rockefeller and the children were delighted, though the former kept a discreet silence; Mrs. Rockefeller was shocked. She received George's explanation judiciously, but warned him that he would be held responsible for any repetitions of the battle. "If it happens again," she declared, "you will have to eat at home or in a restaurant." Rockefeller afterward winked at Sambrook with a boyish glee. "You had them all in a pile, George," he said appreciatively. Nevertheless, when a second good-natured affray developed, George was sent to get his meals outside.

IV

Horses, always one of Rockefeller's favorite recreations, soon became almost a passion. On summer mornings, sometimes taking Sambrook along, he would drive from Forest Hill to the Standard Block, covering the six miles at a smart trot. There he would hand the team over to the young man to be brought back at a stated hour that afternoon. He was punctilious in keeping these appointments, and when tardy would apologize: "George, I am sorry to be late—there were important matters to attend to." Then he would don goggles to protect his eyes, take the reins, and once out of the congested part of town urge the horses to a burst of speed, perhaps picking up a friendly race with somebody. In those years most wealthy Americans delighted in fast horses; white-haired, ruddy-cheeked Commodore Vanderbilt snapped the whip above his trotters in Central Park, other rich New Yorkers crowded the Speedway to Jerome Park in Westchester, and as Henry Cabot Lodge writes, the solid men of Boston filled the Charles River drive with their equipages. Rockefeller later recalled that whenever he was worn out, an hour's fast driving—"trot, pace, gallop, everything," with a rest and dinner, would rejuvenate him: "I was able to take up the evening's mail and get the letters off."[31]

The Standard Block at 43 Euclid Avenue occupied about seventy-

[31]Inglis, Conversations with Rockefeller.

five feet of frontage. Visitors coming in the main entrance from the Public Square faced a large central staircase, which led up to the Standard quarters, occupying the greater part of the three upper floors. On the street-floor were a number of shops, among which the tailoring establishment of Alfred Eyears was conspicuous. In 1876 two stories were added, and an elevator was installed.[32] Eyears, as Rockefeller's old friend, a member of the Euclid Avenue Church, and his and Payne's tailor, had been especially invited to take space in the building. Born in England, well-read, and fond of outdoor sports, he was very companionable.[33] He owned good horses, and often competed with Rockefeller on the plank-road of outer Euclid Avenue, or the smooth sandy stretch of East Prospect Street, now Carnegie Avenue. Once Rockefeller, driving a favorite pair, was racing pell-mell on Euclid with Eyears when a heavy dray loaded with scrap-iron loomed in sight. Without hesitating, he plunged by it. Sambrook, who was seated beside him, recalled years later that they had so little room that Rockefeller's hub-caps grazed in rapid succession those of the dray, giving two sharp reports: "Tzing! tzing!" The president of the Standard, drawing ahead of Eyears, was delighted with his bold exploit. "George," he said with a happy smile, "did you hear that *Tzing?* That was pret-t-y clo-o-se!"

On another occasion the two were driving home when they drew abreast of a farmer smartly spanking along in a buckboard. The farmer glanced at Rockefeller with a sportsman's challenging gleam. "George," exclaimed the latter, "he's got a pacer. I'll bet she can step!" He spoke to his horses, the farmer with a grin lashed his mare, and off they dashed. Rockefeller's team broke stride several times, and the farmer pushed into the van. The oil magnate waved his acknowledgment of defeat, but was gratified by the race. "George, that must be a fine-bred mare," he remarked delightedly. "Didn't she step? Didn't she step?"

Early in the eighties he owned more than a dozen horses, some of them costly. Many other Clevelanders had blooded animals, and he raced with them or his brother Frank. The latter possessed a roan mare which was a fast trotter, and one of John's ambitions was to own several horses of equal speed. He succeeded, though the

[32]Charles M. Higgins to the author, Oct. 4, 1936.
[33]*Cf.* Ella Grant Wilson, *Famous Old Euclid Avenue,* 276.

fortunes of war were not always predictable. When he had won a race he would come in jubilantly, exclaiming:

"I beat Frank! I've beat his roan mare again! What a heat it was! George, go and hitch up Gentle Annie, and Mrs. Rockefeller and I will take a quiet drive!"

He bargained warily for his horses, inquiring about each as carefully as he investigated any refinery he wished to purchase. A letter which he sent Frank in March, 1880, gives an amusing picture of the pains he took in such matters. Being in New York at the time, he wished his brother to act as his agent. The horse he had in view, Duke, had been owned by the millionaire Leonard Case, founder of the Case School of Applied Science, and was now in the hands of one Kerr. After describing him—not more than twelve years old, perfectly sound, and able with training to trot well under 2.26— Rockefeller went on:[34]

If you please, I desire you to call upon Mr. Kerr immediately upon receiving this. If, however, you find he is not in, would not leave your name, as he may construe it as an anxiety to buy the horse. If he is not in tomorrow, he will be on Wednesday sure, at the Case office.

Now, if the horse is sound and he will warrant him so, I am *very desirous* to buy him (this is confidential to you) and do not wish to let him slip, and believe Kerr is friendly to me, and would rather sell him to me at private sale than to any one else. He intimated to me on Saturday that McKinney advised him that he was worth for a road horse, say a thousand, or perhaps fifteen hundred, or possibly two thousand.

If he is sound, or if Mr. Kerr will warrant him sound or no sale, please do not leave the office without buying him at $1000 or even twelve or fifteen hundred, or get his refusal at the lowest price to submit to me. I may be too much in earnest about the matter, but from what Alexander says, I want him sure; but. . . . I believe that you can buy him at a thousand, and it may be the best way to say to him that it was a matter I left with you, and relied upon your judgment for, and that you would be willing to buy him for me if he offered him to you at a thousand dollars; but please, in no event leave the matter open so that other parties could dicker with him. I do not want to lose the horse if he is sound.

If you give Mr. Kerr the impression that I thought he would sell the horse for a thousand dollars, from what he said to me, I think it might help you to buy him at that price; but in all this matter you know best how to make a horse trade, and I will not presume to instruct you. . . .

I think it is a rare opportunity. Alexander [Rockefeller's trainer] says

[34]March 8, 1880; Rockefeller Papers.

Case would not have sold him during his lifetime for $20,000, and says further that if he can be bought for anything like a thousand dollars not to fail to buy him. My fear is that other people will come in and buy him when they know he is for sale. Excuse my pressing you so hard in this matter, but my anxiety to make the trade is my apology.

Please telegraph me after your interview, without mentioning names, and I will know what you refer to. . . .

As a psychological document, this letter, with its mingled determination, caution, anxiety for a tactful approach, and regard for secrecy (he added, "please burn this letter when you have read it") is eloquent. But it also indicates the importance that horses then held in Rockefeller's life. A closing sentence runs: "My horse Somerset Knox showed better Saturday than ever before. He could just play with Independence all the way down the road and made him run several times though he never left his feet." Besides these two, Midnight, Sir George, Gentle Annie, Tom, Towanda, Jemima, and old Harry, were each a distinct personality to him; they were boon companions in his hours of relaxation, and it is evident that he loved them.

Mrs. Rockefeller never shared this passionate fondness for horses. She liked a leisurely drive, and thought horses a splendid diversion for her husband, but that was all. "George, he's crazy, that's all," she would say humorously to Sambrook. "He's crazy." A woman of decided views, she was more severe in matters of religious doctrine and personal conduct than her husband. Like most women of that day, she did not care for strenuous outdoor pursuits. Yet she loved Forest Hill, and after the family went to New York, turned each spring as delightedly as he to the thought of their return. Gradually various features were developed in which she took great pleasure. She had her carriage and riding-horse. She developed a corps of efficient servants, and managed the house with a smoothness which realized her husband's early wish that she become an excellent business woman. In wide circles in Cleveland, religious and charitable, she never wearied of doing good.

Both, as the busy years wore on, failed to develop many new interests, and Rockefeller in particular showed little versatility of taste or mind. Always a narrow man, he remained narrow. He was never deeply interested in politics, though a staunch Republican.

They never went to the theatre; good stock companies and famous stars played in Cleveland, but they did not attend. They seldom if ever listened to lectures except at the church. Of first-rate music by distinguished artists they heard little or none before they removed to New York; but all the children were taught to play some instrument well—Edith the 'cello and piano, Bessie the violin and piano, Alta the piano, John the violin—and the whole family sang a great deal, Rockefeller with a fair baritone voice. While Mrs. Rockefeller and her sister bought and used a good many books, the husband cared little for any literature outside the Bible. To be sure, he sometimes listened in the evening while others read aloud approved novelists like Scott, Dickens, or Harriet Beecher Stowe, new books like *Ramona,* and some biography and history. Later his son recalled with what avidity he read *Ben Hur,* published in 1880. Taking it on his first trip abroad, he devoured it even as he walked the streets of Paris; and he manifested an equal interest in the *Last Days of Pompeii,* urged upon him when he visited Vesuvius. But these were almost his only secular books in these busy years, as *The Sorrows of Satan* was the only book of Edward VII. He of course regularly looked through the Cleveland *Leader,* the Baptist *Standard,* other church periodicals, and perhaps some magazines. But as he got adventure from business, spiritual sustenance from religion, and society from church and home, so he fed his mind by personal contacts.

"Father increased his education chiefly by talking with people," his son later said. "Wherever he went, on railroad trains, among farmers, with oil men or in business circles, he was constantly asking questions and absorbing information." It should be noted that in these conversations his curiosity was for facts, and not at all for ideas.[35] But while he listened, he thought.

v

Despite his burdens, he remained a devoted religious worker. He was still the principal trustee of the Euclid Avenue Baptist Church, superintendent of its Sunday school, and in business matters its dominant figure. Mrs. Rockefeller continued to teach the infant class, and as the children grew up, they all played in the Sunday

[35] I have received much information from both Mr. John D. Rockefeller, Jr., and Mrs. E. Parmalee Prentice, formerly Alta Rockefeller.

school orchestra. When in town, Rockefeller never missed a service.[36] He was always to be seen at church suppers and picnics, and still felt a special fellowship with other members of the congregation. He would sometimes speak frankly to the young men of his position as an employer. "You know we hire a great many people, and some of you are constantly applying for positions. I mark your conduct in Sunday school, and judge from that whether you would be the right sort of boys to work for me." His Bible class, and the classes of his friends—not forgetting Flagler's in the Presbyterian Church— gave the Standard a number of trusted workers.

Yet already he had to guard himself against those who used the church or some charity as cover for a selfish approach. Mrs. Rocke- feller preserved in her scrapbook a press-cutting which referred to this period. It stated that Rockefeller had two sets of friends, tem- poral and spiritual. When he was out of town, two assistant super- intendents took his place in the Sunday school. One was wily:[37]

Some time ago he found himself in possession of considerable crude oil, which he had bought on a margin at $1.09 a barrel. He . . . was undecided what to do with it. . . . After thinking the matter over he concluded to call on Rockefeller. He did so, and after speaking of the Sunday school . . . and the steady growth of membership, he incidentally spoke of the market. "I see that oil is $1.09," he said by way of an open- ing, "and I have about decided to buy a little." This was addressed as an inquiry more than it was spoken as a statement of fact. Mr. Rocke- feller immediately changed the expression of his face. He crossed his knees and then uncrossed them. He bent his body forward and proceeded to cross his knees again. But he never said a word. The assistant superin- tendent grew restless and a little embarrassed. . . . Finally the assistant superintendent asked: "If you were me, what would you do?" Rocke- feller replied: "I would do as I thought best."

By the later seventies his charities were causing him much worry

[36]Mr. William J. Richards of Cleveland wrote John D. Rockefeller, Jr., early in 1940: "I remember a little infants' class in the old Second Baptist Sunday School up in the corner near the door of old Huntington Street, and your mother was the teacher of it; probably a dozen or so of children. You were one of her pupils, and so was I. I can never forget your mother, so kind and gracious, and how she used to try and make me feel as though I was the equal of anybody there, because I was very self-conscious, and knew I was not dressed as well as the other children, coming from the poor district and owning prob- ably one good suit in a year."

[37]Scrapbook, Rockefeller Papers.

and labor. As his wealth multiplied and his gifts grew proportionately larger, his love of efficiency rendered him anxious to make the best possible use of his money. He knew that his gifts might easily do more harm than good. Probably he never felt the same zest in disbursing money as in amassing it, for the one task was duty, the other adventure. Nevertheless, the ability to promote religious and philanthropic causes that he loved gave him warm satisfaction, while his acquaintance with a growing roster of able ministers and educators was stimulating.

In 1870, probably because all his capital was needed to help launch the Standard Oil, his gifts fell to the low level, as compared with previous years, of $2635.79. The next year they rose again to $6860.86, and in 1872 to $6930.68. Those who accused him of scrimping in every direction to put more money into his business should have seen these figures. In 1873 came the panic and depression, and his recorded gifts for that year and 1874 were $4770.58 and $4841.06 respectively. But these sums may not include many small benefactions—they cover only the church and Denison University. Then in the middle seventies come a series of years in which, so far as available papers show, his contributions seem unaccountably small —$460.08 in 1875; $608 in 1876; and $200 in 1877. It seems certain that he kept no record of numerous donations in these three years, particularly as only $10.08 all told is set down for the church. We may be sure that he was giving to it as generously as ever. But as the depression ended we have full bookkeeping again, with the following totals:

In 1878	$23,485.65
In 1879	29,280.16
In 1880	32,865.64
In 1881	61,070.96
In 1882	61,261.75
In 1883	66,722.97
In 1884	119,109.48

It is clear that as Rockefeller's wealth increased, his giving kept pace with it. As he once said, many men in becoming rich fail to develop any sense of trusteeship for their money, and think of it as entirely their own; he, on the contrary, always regarded giving as a plain duty. His benefactions in the early eighties were becoming highly varied. He gave to "colored students for ministry"; to various colleges; to the C. O. S., newsboys' homes, old ladies' homes, hospitals, the Y. M. C. A.; to missions, temperance societies, and day nurseries; to a school in Italy, and repeatedly and generously to a theological seminary in Hamburg, Germany; to immigrant societies and Indians. The items in 1884 varied from $31,800 for the Baptist Union Theological Seminary to $10 "for poor family" and $5 for a poor man's medicine.

From an early date he adopted two policies in giving which were destined to take on a large significance. Both appear in a letter which he wrote in 1879 in relation to a grant of $600 for the Ohio Baptist State Convention. He informed Doctor Duncan, formerly his Cleveland pastor: "Please do not feel disappointed because I do not promise all you desire. I hope others may contribute the balance, and if so, it will be better for the cause."[38] This reflects what was to become a deep conviction—that it was not good for any cause or organization to depend upon the generosity of one giver. Wherever it was desirable that many should unite to promote a purpose, many should contribute money to it. In no other fashion could men gain a sense of something co-operatively achieved; in no other way could they effect a really large object. Writing one Thomas Jones, a fellow member of the Euclid Avenue Church, early in 1880, Rockefeller remarked: "I am waiting for some advice as to what others did last year. My desire is to do my whole share and at the same time not to do what others ought to do."[39] This insistence that support should be distributed had become a fixed principle by 1883. "I expect all who pledge will pay as they are called upon," he wrote of several gifts which he had made contingent upon other contributions: "and I do not expect to pay my percentage any faster than the balance is paid."[40]

He also wrote Doctor Duncan with reference to the above-mentioned gift of $600: "I am disposed to be conservative in reference to establishing new interests without very satisfactory evidence that within themselves there is the stickative qualities necessary." This, a corollary to his demand for co-operative giving, also rapidly be-

[38]Dec. 30, 1879; Rockefeller Papers.
[39]March 3, 1880; Rockefeller Papers.
[40]Dec. 14, 1883; Rockefeller Papers.

came a fixed principle. How could he justify himself in offering money to those who could not use it well? He felt an obligation to employ his wealth efficiently, and was sometimes sharply businesslike in demanding that power to work as well as abstract merit be shown by those who sought his help. "I am not willing to be a party to failure in this undertaking," he curtly informed a Baptist leader in 1883, "and have many other places where I can surely hit the nail on the head by putting money there, and want to make the best trades I can for our common cause."[41] And later he wrote a fellow church-member: "I think mistakes are made by organizing too many feeble interests—rather consolidate and have good, strong, working church organizations."

These attitudes foreshadow the spirit of Rockefeller's later and larger gifts. They were forced upon him by circumstance. The demands were becoming incessant and confusingly numerous; at first he merely picked as wisely as he could from a medley of importunities, and even by 1879 they left him with a haunting sense of uncertainty as to the wisdom of his benevolences. By 1886, when he had become a resident of New York, he was insisting that all doubt must be dispelled in advance. In that year we find him writing about a request: "I haven't a farthing to give to this or any other interest unless I am perfectly satisfied it is the *very best* I can do with the money."[42]

It is important to understand how crowding and insistent were these demands upon Rockefeller in the late seventies and early eighties, for he was soon to apply his mind to the confusion of his charities just as he applied it to the chaos of the oil industry, and with results quite as striking. In sending $3500 to Doctor George W. Goodspeed, of the Baptist Union Theological Seminary, in 1881, he wrote: "I must shut down brakes for a time, having made so many other promises of like character." This was no empty profession; Rockefeller was never given to exaggeration. "I have numerous calls from all over the country," he writes in another letter.[43] In sending $1000 to Doctor Duncan, doubtless for the Ohio organization of the Baptist Church, he remarks: "I wish I had money enough

[41]Dec. 20, 1883; Rockefeller Papers.
[42]To the Rev. Edward Bright, Oct. 1, 1886; Rockefeller Papers.
[43]Nov. 29, 1882; Rockefeller Papers.

to give to all of the good objects presented. It would be a most delightful occupation." He adds: "I am prepared to do as I stated in respect to the Chicago Seminary, providing they raise One Hundred Thousand Dollars there." This sentence is an interesting indication that even in 1882 the germ of the future University of Chicago was showing life. Later that year we find Rockefeller paying the last part of a $20,000 pledge to Denison University. The extent of his donations is suggested by a letter in which he speaks of having exceeded his gift-budget by "some thirty or $40,000."[44]

However, even as he moved toward systematizing his benefactions he by no means failed to make highly personal contributions; and he plainly took especial pleasure in gifts to organizations or individuals with which or whom he had an intimate acquaintance. By 1881 he was apparently paying almost half the expenses of the large Euclid Avenue Church. A letter of 1883 to a collector for some minor church fund shows with what care he approached even small matters. He wrote that he enclosed cards "signed as follows":[45]

Mrs. Rockefeller ....$10   each week
Self 30   each week
Each of our four children........ 00.20 each week

"My family are all much interested in the work," he declared, "and the 20¢ from each child will be earned by the sweat of their brows, pulling weeds, etc."

His gifts to individuals gave him great enjoyment. We have letters of this period to several ministers whom he admired, proposing vacations at his expense or tactfully offering to help educate their children; while in other letters he speaks of money remittances. In 1882 he sent the Reverend George T. Dowling to Europe. The spirit in which he made these benefactions is happily indicated in a note to John Trevor, of the Fifth Avenue Baptist Church in New York, in which he remarks: "I have been thinking I ought personally to do something for Doctor Clough. He is a great and good man . . . I had thought to hand Doctor Clough $500, but I have gotten up to $1000 this morning, and think I will reach $2000 by night."[46]

[44]To Dr. G. O. King, Sept. 30, 1884; Rockefeller Papers.
[45]To C. A. Davidson, Jan. 3, 1883.
[46]March 20, 1884; Rockefeller Papers.

VI

Puritanical was the word which best described the Rockefeller household; a Puritanism not of New England but of the Baptist West. With its moral austerity, its religious fervor, and its abiding interest in good work, went a certain intellectual and æsthetic aridity. It was not a household of ideas, enthusiasms, artistic impulses, or many of the graces of living. However comfortable and cheerful, Forest Hill struck most visitors as a rather ugly house. The big rooms had a gaunt look. Rockefeller, who liked sunshine, kept many of the windows without curtains or hangings. The furniture was not always harmonious. He and Mrs. Rockefeller cared much for utility; not so much for beauty. Neither of them ever showed any taste for collecting, any touch of the connoisseur's impulse. In its strength and its stiffness, its elevation and its angularity, it was a Puritanical home.

Rockefeller's character presented much that was admirable, while his intimates in church and office as well as home found his personality really lovable. But to the world at large he did not seem an amiable figure. Most businessmen regarded him much as most politicians regarded the aloof and glacial Benjamin Harrison or the serious, austere John Sherman; these men were impressive, but not likeable. For all Rockefeller's piety and conscientiousness, for all his generous acts, he did not possess the great gift of being personally appealing to large and varied groups. His self-containment, his avoidance of outward emotion, his ingrained reserve, had much to do with this deficiency. If he could have bubbled over with child-like good humor like Carnegie; if he could have carried with him the bluff, homely, folksy air of James J. Hill; if he had possessed the histrionic dash, glitter, and wit of H. H. Rogers!—but he had to be his grave, aloof, austere self. And perhaps the explanation of his inability to kindle others goes deeper than his protective shell. There was a certain lack of breadth, richness, and zest in the man; he had genius, but it was essentially narrow, without fire or gusto. For another reason, he was too reticent in expressing his warm human interest in people, both in the mass and as individuals. The interest was there, but he could seldom show it; he was the most democratic of men, but his democracy had no taint of affability.

Of a kindling fraternal concern for people casually met, of that challenging sympathy for others which men like Lincoln and Whitman radiated like a great aura, he had nothing. This want of general likeability was to cost him dear, for it made the public unwilling to recognize his real merits and his many and varied virtues. It remains for later generations, with fuller knowledge, to do his personal qualities a justice that his contemporaries failed to give.

XXVII

The Great Machine

CRUDE right-angled triangle drawn upon the map of the United States, with Boston at its apex, the eastern leg running southward through New York and Philadelphia to Baltimore, the base west from that city through Pittsburgh to Cleveland, and the hypotenuse from Cleveland back through Buffalo to Boston—this as late as 1885 would have circumscribed the American territory intensively concerned with the production, refining, and transport of oil.

The triangle would soon be bulged quite out of shape. For many years there had been a considerable production of oil in West Virginia, southern Ohio, and Ontario; and by 1885 the Lima field in western Ohio and eastern Indiana was rapidly opening. Some petroleum was being produced in the Santa Clara Valley in California, and a little in Kentucky. The Standard had large depots in Louisville, St. Louis, and San Francisco, while it was busy marketing oil in Chicago and dozens of other cities. But the area between the seaboard, Pittsburgh, and Cleveland still contained the main sources of supply, the pipe-line network, the storage tanks, the great manufactories, and the shipping centers. The Bradford field was still by far the richest single fountain of oil, though it had reached its peak of nearly 25,000,000 barrels in 1881.[1] We may think of Rockefeller's great oil-combination as holding this triangle until the later eighties, and then a quadrangle extending westward over Ohio and Indiana. The region was at once the wellspring, the factory, and the chief domestic mart of American oil, where the activities of the Briareus-armed organization were incessant, and from which its agents sallied forth in cohorts to conquer the oil trade of the world.

[1] *House Trust Investigation, 1888*, 54; Boyle, *Derrick's Handbook*, 805.

By 1885 the Standard had acquired a number of wells and an impressive amount of potential oil-producing territory. This was a defensive and not an aggressive move. The lands were bought or leased partly to insure a future supply, partly to limit the number of active wells and reduce the overproduction of crude oil. Having once begun to acquire oil deposits, the Standard was bound to press rapidly forward. While its original holdings were in Pennsylvania and West Virginia, in the middle eighties it began to buy largely in the new Lima field of Ohio. Most of the Standard trustees objected vigorously, for whereas the base of the Pennsylvania crude was paraffin, that of the Lima oil (like Ontario's) was sulphur. "If you got a drop on you, you smelled like a rotten egg!" said a Standard official. The smell was not important—all crude oil had an unpleasant odor; but the kerosene made from this oil rapidly coated lamp chimneys with an intolerable film of soot. Yet the oil was produced in such quantities that it was "almost a miracle" the way it gushed from the earth. Rockefeller insisted that the trust must send its pipe lines to all producing districts, and provide adequate tankage. "We are committed to standing by the producers," he said. He also insisted on extensive leases even before Herman Frasch, the chemical genius employed by the Standard, had discovered how to utilize the crude. Joseph Seep has told the story dramatically:[2]

The Lima oil was sour, had a great deal of sulphur in it, and they could not make it up into a suitable product. Yet Mr. Rockefeller insisted upon buying all that was offered. Even after his fellow-directors in the Standard Oil Company had grown tired of the Lima oil, he insisted on buying. He said that if nature had put the oil there we ought to be able to find a way of using it. Henry Fleming used to go out to Ohio to report on the situation. He came back one day and spread out before Mr. Rockefeller a big blue map of the Lima field, pointing out various leases he could buy. Mr. Rockefeller spread his left hand over a lot of these leases and said, "You'd better take this." Then he spread his right hand over as many more as he could cover, and said, "Take all this." Then he moved it over to another side of the map and said, "If you think well of it, don't miss this." Mr. Rockefeller went on buying leases in the

[2]Inglis, Conversation with Seep. The same story has been told in a memorandum for the author by E. R. Brown, chairman of the board of the Magnolia Petroleum Company, dated Dec. 2, 1937. He obtained his information from C. N. Payne, who attended meetings in New York which discussed the purchase of more Lima field land. According to Payne, nearly every one strongly opposed Rockefeller's desire for additional investments.

Lima field in spite of the coolness of the rest of the directors, until he had accumulated more than forty million barrels of that sulphurous oil in tanks. He must have invested millions of dollars in buying and storing and holding the sour oil for two years, when every one else thought it was no good. The dealers had no use for it; they could not even burn it for fuel. The price of that oil ran down to fifteen cents a barrel of forty-two gallons. I heard of a few thousand barrels going as low as ten cents.

Then, after two years, Frasch found out how to refine it.

Had it not been for the purchase of this supply of Lima crude, which bridged over the long period between the heavy decline of Pennsylvania oil and the development of the Mid-Continent field, the Standard would have been badly pinched for raw materials. Nobody ever felt sure in these years that the industry would endure a decade longer, while many believed that the Regions would soon be drained and it would totally collapse. Early in the eighties some of the Standard trustees grew uneasy, and Archbold lightened his holdings of stock. Nobody then foresaw the great new fields across the Mississippi, and few dreamed of the automobile. Rockefeller had set up a manufacturing empire, but it seemed environed by perils which might overthrow it within a few years. The supply of crude oil might rapidly slacken, or Europe might suddenly discover her own fields, or an industry centering in the East might shift within a short time to the Gulf. Those electric lights which were twinkling more and more numerously in America might be improved until they drove kerosene lamps to the remoter villages and farms. Rockefeller showed both courage and vision when he acted to guarantee the Standard a great supply of crude oil.

II

From the wells ran the local network of pipe lines, emptying into the great trunk systems; both steadily increasing in extent and importance. Gangs of men trenched the earth and brought a line to every important derrick; carpenters and mechanics tossed up enormous steel storage tanks; officers directed the swift construction of warehouses and offices. Expert Standard agents measured the incoming oil, and issued certificates that passed almost like paper money. Under the direction of Standard superintendents the streams of green crude pulsed steadily under the surface of the earth to the refineries.

This enormous pipeage system was one of the principal segments of the great machine. The units bound together in 1885 under the National Transit Company represented a capitalization of $31,495,-733.84, or more than a third of the trust's holdings.[3] To comprehend the complexity of the pipe service we must recall how many old companies had been merged to make up even the nexus in the Regions: the American Transfer Company, O'Day's creation to feed the New York Central; the Union system, once the pride of the Empire; the Pennsylvania Transportation Company, once controlled by the Erie; the Columbia Conduit; the Karns, Grant, Relief, and other lines. The trunk lines were a great web connecting the oil fields with Cleveland, 160 miles; Pittsburgh, 60; Philadelphia, 280; Baltimore, a 70-mile extension of the Philadelphia pipe; and Bayonne, 300 miles. Pipes ran under the Hudson, Manhattan Island, and the East River to the Long Island refineries.[4] Moreover, the system steadily lengthened. In 1889 a large pipe was laid from Lima, O., to the Chicago area; in 1890-91 the Eureka Pipe was thrown from the Kentucky border through West Virginia to Pennsylvania, and the Southern Pipe from the West Virginia border through Pennsylvania to the coast; while in 1893 the Standard purchased the Crescent Pipe-Line from Pittsburgh to New York Bay. These systems, with their tanks, pumping stations, supply yards, and city offices, were an imperial industry in themselves.

So constantly did the situation change that it is always difficult to enumerate the refineries. But in 1885 the Standard had fully fifty of them in the hands of more than twenty component companies. In Pittsburgh there were fifteen or sixteen works; in the New York area twenty-three or twenty-four; in Cleveland and Philadelphia a half-dozen each. Others were scattered from Portland to Titusville, from Buffalo to Louisville.[5] The greatest single refineries in 1885 were the No. 1 Plant in Cleveland, with a capacity of fully 150,000

[3]Taylor, MS History of the Standard Oil, 76.

[4]The New York City government in 1877 gave the New York Central permission to lay a pipe line across Manhattan on the line of 65th Street, and under the East River connecting with the Standard Oil refineries at Hunter's Point. N. Y. *Tribune*, July 2, 1877. Another set of pipes ran from the Weehawken terminals of the Pennsylvania and Erie Railroads under the Hudson, Manhattan Island, and East River to the Standard plants. N. Y. *Herald*, Aug. 30, 1878.

[5]*House Trust Investigation, 1888*, pp. 232-235; Taylor, *passim.*

barrels of crude a week; the Kings County, the Long Island, and the Charles Pratt works on Long Island, with a combined capacity of more than 100,000 barrels; and the Bayonne plant, with a capacity of about 75,000. Many people first grasped the size of a Standard establishment when they read in 1878 of the fire which ravaged the Atlantic Refining works just below Philadelphia. This was not one of the largest Standard units; yet when lightning struck, the flames raged for three days, burned out sixty acres crowded with buildings and tanks, destroyed ships of five different nationalities loading with kerosene, and caused a loss estimated by the press at not less than $1,600,000.[6] Like the pipe lines, the refineries made up a complicated mechanism, with dozens of able executives, a growing corps of engineers, chemists, and other technicians, and an army of office-workers and laborers.

By this time the Standard plants manufactured a wide variety of products. Illuminants were the staple, but naphtha and gasolene grew increasingly important, the best-known brand of the latter being "Pratt's Spirit." In 1878 the combination also began to manufacture lubricants on a large scale. It had acquired a refinery at Franklin, Pa., which used the heavy crudes pumped there and made excellent machine oil, but Rockefeller decided that the independent plants operating in Cleveland were needed to help round out his empire. In rapid succession he bought the Backus Company, the Republic Company, and the American Lubricating Oil Company. The last named had made its products by refining under steam pressure, the two former by taking residuum from other refineries and mixing various oils. In combining these manufactories with his existing plants, Rockefeller once more showed his powers of organization. The equipment of the Backus plant and the American Company was poor—little more than some sheds, stills, and tanks. Most of this material was scrapped, and the remainder hauled to the Republic works, at 65th Street and Erie Road, which were thenceforth operated as part of Plant No. 2 of the Cleveland system.

This system, temporarily the largest in the world, was now fairly complete, and a brief glance at it may be interesting. Plant No. 1 had been expanded to cover about sixty acres, and Plant No. 2, at the head of Kingsbury Run, about forty. No. 1 did the bulk of the

[6]Philadelphia *Press*, N. Y. *Tribune*, June 12-14, 1878.

Standard's Cleveland refining, while at No. 2 the residual materials were turned into engine oils, greases, paints, and other products. M. G. Vilas, who went to work at No. 2 late in the seventies, tells us that it comprised storage tanks; re-running stills; a battery of boilers; a filtering plant; a huge lubricating plant; paraffin and candle works; cooperage shops; can-manufacturing works; shipping sheds; and warehouses for storage of the various products.[7] Plants No. 3 and No. 4 were used for refining. No. 5 was employed chiefly in manufacturing waxes, varnish, and paint, while No. 6 turned out paraffin. McGregor, with the aid of another efficient Scot, Duncan McIntosh, directed these six plants with unfailing skill until early in the eighties he was called to New York. Until telephones were installed, the head office had telegraph wires to every unit.[8]

Within a short time the Standard was making some of the best lubricants in America. It purchased control of the Galena Oil Works (1879), and a minority interest in the Signal Oil Works, with other plants in the New York district.[9] It developed a dozen grand divisions—engine oil, valve oil, cylinder oil, spindle oil, harness oil, and so on—with no fewer than a hundred and fifty varieties. Much of the credit for the growth was due to Orville T. Waring in the New York office. This tall, thin, ascetic-loking executive, when asked by Rockefeller at the outset what had to be done to develop the trade in lubricants, replied, "Everything!" As chairman of the Lubricants Committee, he made a remarkable record. Employing trained men, he found out just what oils what industry needed; he learned to eliminate deleterious substances and make better grades; he cheapened the price by quantity production; and he marketed the wares all over the globe.[10] Perhaps the most remarkable of the Standard products was the No. 23 Red Oil, pressed out of paraffin. Its peculiar combination of qualities, including a high flash-point, made it invaluable for engines of great inner heat.

[7]I had a long talk with Vilas in Cleveland, Nov. 27, 1936.
[8]Charles M. Higgins to the author, Oct. 22, 1936.
[9]In 1879 Archbold, McGregor, and Rogers, in behalf of the Standard, bought from Hiram P. Everest and Charles P. Everest a three-fourths interest in the Vacuum Oil Company of Buffalo, paying $200,000. Everest was a capable lubrication specialist, and developed a number of heavy lubricating products which were much used in the internal oiling of steam engines.
[10]D. R. Crum, *Romance of American Petroleum and Gas,* 302. The Rockefeller Papers contain notes of a brief conversation of Mr. Inglis with Waring.

A long list of by-products was being developed by the Standard. From the oil works came an increasing array of greases—axle-grease, gear-grease, cup-grease, graphite, and others. Vaseline was one of the finer products made from the residuum left after the manufacture of kerosene and naphtha. The Chesebrough Manufacturing Company, which was organized in 1880, with the Standard holding a majority of the stock, specialized in this article.[11] Soon few American households were without it. Nor were many homes without paraffin, though for years the Standard found it difficult to dispose of the huge stocks. Much of it, mixed with stearic acid to impart firmness under heat, was made into wax candles. A Cleveland manufacturer named White bought large quantities of it to make chewing gum. Some went into matches, and some into candles. The Standard soon learned to produce anthracine, component of beautiful aniline dyes, and rhigolene, used in ice manufacture. It made a variety of paints, varnishes, and wood-fillers. It turned out paint-remover and polishes. Before many years passed, it was selling about three hundred by-products, many of which no smaller organization could have made;[12] and it pushed their distribution through the same channels used to market illuminants and fuel oil. Rockefeller, enumerating the most important of these products years later, remarked: "Every one of the articles I have named to you represents a separate industry founded on crude petroleum. And we made a good profit from each industry."[13]

By 1885 the Standard was boasting that its entrance into the lubricating field had improved the economy of oil manufacturing; had bettered the quality of oils; and had drastically cut the lubricating costs of the fast-expanding machine industry of America. The trust had introduced new and improved methods of extracting lubricants. After the lighter illuminants had been distilled away, the residual fluid could not be raised to high temperatures under the old system (as it had been to get the maximum yield of kerosene) without impairing the viscosity essential to good lubrication. Heating in stills

[11]Taylor writes that the company took over a vaseline business already established; the original owners had a minority of the stock, and their men continued as active managers. MS History of the Standard Oil, 40.

[12]Victor S. Clark, *History of Manufacturing in the United States, 1860–1893*, II, 518, 519. See the Census of 1880 for an early list of products.

[13]Inglis, Conversations with Rockefeller.

under powerful steam pressure prevented dissociation of the oil; and the Standard greatly improved upon this method, previously employed by the American Lubricating Oil Company.[14] In acquiring the American it also obtained the services of P. S. Jennings, whose practical skill in helping manage the lubricating department was of great importance. The Standard had vigorous competitors in this field, like the Valveoline Company, who deserve much credit. But Rockefeller claimed that by making lubricants alongside illuminants, by operating on a scale previously unknown, and by using the same salesmen for all wares, he did more than anybody else to halve the charges. "And when customers found," he said, "that they could buy for twenty or thirty or thirty-five cents a gallon products that they had been made to believe were difficult to produce at seventy or eighty, they were not slow to avail themselves of the advantages offered by the Standard Oil Company."

Another field rapidly opened up by Standard enterprise was the piping of natural gas from its Pennsylvania and Ohio holdings to neighboring cities. By 1888 it supplied not fewer than twenty-five important centers in western New York, Pennsylvania, and Ohio, including many towns of the Allegheny Valley, and Buffalo, Erie, and Toledo. The consumers in some of these cities would have been astonished to learn that they were patronizing the Standard, for it had bought control of local companies quietly, and left the management to their old officers. The Standard's principal source of gas was then in northern Pennsylvania; but as its purchases of oil lands moved west into Indiana, it carried the natural gas business with it.[15]

Meanwhile, it was Rockefeller's object to make his great combination as nearly self-contained as possible. For some time the Standard had been manufacturing its own sulphuric acid in Cleveland. As the organization grew, chemical products were needed in the East, and the Elizabethport Acid Works were established in 1882 to furnish them. By 1885 the Standard made its own pumps at Oil City; its own tank cars in Buffalo. It produced its own glue for making barrels oil-tight. It had steadily enlarged its fabrication of barrels, boxes, and tin cans. It soon controlled more than 125 patents, partly for by-products, partly for machines in making containers, and partly

[14]John W. Van Dyke to the author, Oct. 4, 1936.
[15]N. Y. *Tribune,* Feb. 28, 1888.

for processes and apparatus used in manufacturing, distributing, and burning oil—and some of these patents were highly valuable.[16]

III

Rockefeller's ideal was a complete organization of the industry; and even before the combination gained full control of refining he had resolved to suppress the independent wholesaler and jobber. By 1885 one of the trust's strongest departments, the swift growth of which met with angry opposition and aroused violent resentment, was devoted to marketing. Throughout the seventies the Standard had been engrossed in the struggle to combine all the manufacturers. But Rockefeller was keenly aware that the distributing agencies constituted an equal problem, and when he entered the field of domestic sales by the purchase of Chess, Carley & Co., he was determined to dominate it as soon as possible.

His motives were undoubtedly mixed. He wished to share in the profits of distribution. He was anxious to maintain retail prices, and strengthen his general grip upon the industry. But he also alleged, and beyond doubt correctly, that his action was prompted by the disorder then rife in marketing. Many jobbers were buying poor kerosene of independent refiners, representing it to be the Standard's, and selling it at cut rates through grocers and hardware men. Many jobbers also liked to speculate and adulterate. They would purchase large cargoes at low prices, and then smash the market as soon as kerosene rose a little; they would buy good oil and mix it with naphtha, producing a compound likely to explode in the lamp. A Standard employee long afterward spoke emphatically of the unhappy situation in the Middle West. "Sometime in the middle seventies Rockefeller and McGregor became anxious to get the big Chicago dealers into the Standard. They were cutting the life out of us. They had bought bad oil—off color, off fire-test—and undersold us. The public didn't discriminate between good and bad; it was oil, wasn't it? We built tankage at Englewood to bring Chicago dealers into line." The results came immediately. Chicago's principal distributors were Charles Hanford & Co. and Kennedy & Jenkins. "The Standard

---

[16]Ernst von Halle, *Trusts and Industrial Combinations in the United States,* 66, 67; Victor S. Clark, *op. cit.;* Harold F. Howland, "The Standard Oil," *Outlook,* Sept. 28, 1907.

brought Hanford east and performed the operation. He had just returned from a European trip—I think to see the Pope. They locked him in a room and signed him up. I never saw such a happy gang in my life as the officers after they closed with him."[17]

In the Boston area the Maverick Oil Co. was made the principal distributor. This corporation was organized in 1877, on the basis of a business previously done by Carter, Windsor & Co., 70 per cent of the stock being taken by the Standard and 30 per cent by Carter, Windsor. Its leading competitor was Kidder, Vaughn & Co., which the Standard shortly bought out and incorporated in the new Beacon Oil Co.[18] We have already seen how the Standard obtained a foothold in Maine, Maryland, and Virginia.

The marketing area in the Ohio and Mississippi valleys was invaded in 1878, when the Standard built important new firms upon two companies already well established. One, Alexander McDonald & Co., had marketed oil all the way from Cincinnati to Cairo, and was reaching out beyond the Mississippi. The other was Waters, Pierce & Co., with headquarters in St. Louis, which sold oil throughout the Southwest. The former gave up its name and was replaced by the Consolidated Tank Line Company, in which the Standard was of course dominant. Members of the old McDonald firm continued in active charge until 1890. As for the latter, it gave way to the Waters-Pierce Company, 40 per cent of its stock held by the Standard, 20 per cent by Chess, Carley as a Standard subsidiary, and 40 per cent by members of the old firm. In this instance the minority interest was never extinguished, and Henry Clay Pierce remained the active manager until the Standard Oil stocks were distributed in 1911. The Waters-Pierce Company did an immense business in marketing Standard products throughout Missouri, Arkansas, Louisiana, Oklahoma, and Texas, a fast-growing country.

It was not a happy day for the Standard when it added Henry Clay Pierce to its organization. A man of great executive force and incisive personality, he was self-willed, brutal, domineering, and lawless. Born the son of a country doctor in upper New York, he had left school at sixteen to fend for himself, and was soon clerking in a St. Louis bank. But he was too able and independent to relish

[17]Charles M. Higgins to the author, Feb. 2, 1936.
[18]Taylor, MS History of the Standard Oil.

laboring for other men, and set up a brick business. When shortly after the Civil War tales of the golden fortunes made in oil began to fill the newspapers, he determined to tap this Pactolian stream for himself. Beginning as a distributor of oil sold by his father-in-law, John R. Finley, owner of the first refinery built west of the Mississippi, he was so successful that in 1871, at the age of twenty-two, he bought Finley out. Two years later he joined with W. H. Waters, a wealthy St. Louis businessman, to found Waters, Pierce, which proved more successful still. The Southwest was thirsty for kerosene, and he saw that it was furnished.

Before Pierce lay great and picturesque achievements. He was destined to make the sale of all oil products flourish mightily from the Missouri to the Brazos; destined to be one of the greatest (and the most hated) figures in developing the rich Texas oil fields. But much as his gifts benefited the Standard, his faults kept him distrusted by its heads and always injured its reputation. Numerous Standard Oil veterans have spoken of him to the author in scathing terms.[19] "He was a brilliant man," said one. "There was no equal to him. But he wouldn't play ball with a crowd, and he liked to pull fast ones. He wouldn't do a thing straight if it could be done crooked. He was cordial and polite enough, but when he got into a jam with people he became nasty. Then they knew they were fighting a Tartar. He was the meanest fighter you ever saw."[20] Like a few others, he showed that it was impossible to build up a mighty organization without taking in some men with dangerous flaws of character.

The process by which the Standard obtained its earliest sales-organizations was steadily extended during the eighties. For example, the principal Northwestern distributors were P. H. Kelly & Co., of Minneapolis. They had always been friendly to Rockefeller, and had mailed him in 1873 some evidence that one of his clerks was selling secrets to Squire & Teagle. Now the Standard took them over. On the Pacific Coast the biggest share of the oil trade had been held by Alvinza Howard, who brought his supplies by boat around Cape Horn. The Standard in 1878 sent Bostwick's protégé, Wesley Hunt Tilford, out to the coast to organize its sales, and shortly purchased Howard's business. It then arranged to send most of the oil westward

[19]One man confidentially called him "a blackleg."
[20]Another confidential source.

over the Union Pacific by tank cars.[21] In the Rocky Mountain States the leading distributor was the Continental Oil Co. Tilford also looked into the situation there, and in 1884 the Continental became an arm of the Standard, taking over a number of jobbers.[22] Early in the eighties Rockefeller also organized the Standard Oil Company of Iowa, which distributed oil all the way from the Mississippi to Colorado. An arrangement was presently made between it and the Continental for sharing the disputed mountain territory.[23]

Thus the Standard rapidly erected a great distributing system reaching into almost every corner of the land. Either old companies were taken over or new ones set up as fast as the growth of the marketing system required them.[24] None of the old marketing companies absorbed by the trust seems to have complained of the terms offered it, but they numbered only sixteen or seventeen in all. For the most part, the Standard created its own system. Into one city after another, from Portland to Los Angeles, it threw a distribution unit, with a little garrison of energetic salesmen who could furnish oil to local dealers on generally better terms than any competitor. Each of these garrisons had its supply base in a "bulk distributing station"—that is, a storage plant of tanks and warehouses holding large quantities of oil and by-products. Chicago's bulk station, for example, was set up as early as 1876 in Englewood. By 1882 the Standard had 130 bulk stations, each with a marketing system built about it; by 1886 the number had increased to 313; and soon it went first above one thousand, then two thousand.[25] Nothing like this elaborate mechanism for the nationwide wholesaling and jobbing of an industrial product had previously been known in America. Gustavus F. Swift had shown the meat packers how to establish a similar organization, but it did not compare with the Standard's.

Inevitably, much public hostility was aroused by the rapid emergence of this powerful system. As independent refiners had com-

---

[21]*House Trust Investigation, 1888,* pp. 717, 718; N. Y. *Times,* article on Tilford, March 3, 1909.

[22]*House Trust Investigation, 1888,* p. 718.

[23]Taylor, MS History of the Standard Oil, 88, 89.

[24]The old companies acquired included the Republic Oil Co. of Cleveland; the Eureka Oil Co. operating in Virginia and North Carolina; the Argand Refining Co. of Richmond, Va.; and the Eagle Oil Co. of Baltimore.

[25]*United States vs. The Standard Oil,* XVII, 3242 ff., 3467 ff., deals with the growth of this system.

Rockefeller's New York house, No. 4 West 54th Street.

Above: Photograph taken in 1865, looking southward, with Fifth Avenue on the left.
Below: The house as it looked when Rockefeller occupied it.

Rockefeller in informal attitudes.

Above: Jesting with the boyish-looking John D. Archbold. *Below:* In the next to the last seat on an Adirondacks sledge.

plained in the seventies that the Standard took over plants secretly, so that nobody knew which firms were really free and which were masquerading, so now independent jobbers complained that the Continental, the Waters-Pierce, the Eureka, and others posed as "outside" houses long after the Standard took control. This was done, they said, so that price-cutting could be carried on without arousing violent hostility. The Standard replied that the old company names were used to get the benefit of their good will and established brands, and that it was under no obligation to advertise its purchases.[26] Of course this was an inadequate answer; and once more it could be said of Rockefeller, as John Randolph of Roanoke said of Van Buren, that "he rowed to his objective with muffled oars."

While the Standard thus multiplied its central marketing units, it was organizing new methods for reaching every petty dealer's door. Delivery by barrels or cases was not satisfactory in thickly populated areas. Early in the eighties experiments were made in the regular delivery of variable quantities by wagon. One of the first trials was carried out in 1882 in New York, partly because of the strength of the Pratt brands there, and proved a success. Rockefeller wrote Colonel Payne on May 3, 1883:[27] "I have been reviewing the tank wagon business of New York, with Mr. Gregory. He is greatly encouraged. I think we should have tank wagons in Cincinnati, Pittsburgh, and Chicago. I assume that a city like Cleveland is not compactly built enough to make so good a success."

In accordance with this letter, the trust immediately began establishing a similar service in other large cities. Indeed, within a short time the Standard drays and carts were familiar in small cities too. Cleveland had her wagons, in spite of Rockefeller's doubt; so did Buffalo, Omaha, Atlanta, Denver, San Francisco, and a hundred other points. Before many years even most small towns and villages heard the regular clatter of the oil cart. By the end of 1904 nearly four fifths of the towns were thus served, while by 1906 the bulk distributing stations numbered no fewer than 3573.[28] This figure alone affords a clear indication of the broad front upon which the

[26]Usually the concealment was negative—nothing was said about the Standard purchase; but sometimes it was positive—ciphers were used, and reports mailed to a post office box instead of to Standard Oil headquarters.

[27]Rockefeller Papers.

[28]Taylor, MS History of the Standard Oil, 88.

marketing activities of the trust moved, for it meant a good deal more than one bulk station of the Standard Oil for every county in the United States. In sparsely settled areas, of course, oil was still delivered by barrels or cases.

The marketing field, when the system was fairly established, was broken into provinces, all well-articulated, in each of which some company, old or new, was held responsible for results; and each province was divided into districts under the charge of an agent. The Catholic Church did not have a more careful organization! For several simple reasons, the progress of this great distributing organization was almost irresistible. One lay in the trust's practical control of oil supplies. A prominent railroad official testified in 1887:[29] "The Standard Oil Company ships about 95 per cent of the total oil distributed in this country." The dealers who co-operated with it naturally had security and profits, while those who did not were dependent on the scanty and uncertain shipments of the few independent refiners. Outside dealers had to inconvenience themselves by ordering far in advance; Standard dealers could count on prompt and regular deliveries. The customers of a stubborn jobber were often kept alarmed by rumors that the few surviving independent refineries might not much longer be able to supply oil. Finally, the Standard companies seem to have had a free hand to cut prices in competitive territory—they certainly often did so; and while the competitors cut too, they were at a disadvantage. Evidence that the Standard maintained a widespread espionage system in the marketing field, and expected its agents to learn all about shipments of competitive oil, is quite conclusive. The systematic extinction of scores of jobbers and hundreds of small retail dealers all over the American map because they dared to handle independent oil was one of the chief reasons behind the growth of popular antagonism to the Standard; for it aroused a violent local resentment in unnumbered communities.

This was the dark side of a marketing-service which, by 1890, Rockefeller had given an efficiency that possessed a kind of beauty. Long trains of staunchly built tank cars carried the refined oil all over North America. Steel storage tanks, sprinkled thickly from ocean to ocean, were protected from fire by proper spacing and ex-

[29]T. M. Kimball before the Pacific Railroad Commission, June 21, 1887.

cellent fire-fighting apparatus. The familiar blue barrels were of the best quality. At the bulk stations a meticulous neatness was evident. Pumps, buckets, pipes, and tools were all clean, and under constant inspection; no litter was tolerated. The horses were young, well-fed, and well-stabled; the wagons were strong, brightly painted, and smooth-running; the grounds were carefully tended. Ample stocks were carried for instant delivery to all customers. Agents from the central office constantly toured the districts to see that the service met the highest standards of promptness, accuracy, and courtesy. The oil itself was in general of the best character.[30] Nothing was left undone, in accordance with Rockefeller's long-standing policy, to make the Standard products and the Standard ministrations attractive to the customer..

Much more important than the domestic trade, of course, was the export business, for in 1885 about seven tenths of the American oil found its way abroad. Until the early eighties export-organization was in a somewhat rudimentary stage. The Standard naturally had important Asiatic and Latin-American representatives. In 1882 it organized the West India Oil Refining Company, while it soon built up a distributing system in the Far East. By 1885 activities in Canada were well launched, and Waters-Pierce had begun a first abortive

[30]Nearly all the principal investigations and prosecutions of the Standard brought out evidence upon its espionage system, some of which will be summarized later. Charles J. Woodbury in *The Saturday Evening Post,* Oct. 21, 1911, tells how it was applied to the lubricating branch. Agents were supplied with forms for a monthly statement upon all oil sold by competitors as well as by their own dealers. Opposite the columns asking for addresses of oil consumers were others headed: "Their present sources of supply?" "Amounts and brands?" Agents were expected to account for all oil products appearing in their territory, and trace their origin, destination, and history, so far as possible, from shipper to consumer. Woodbury, when asked to take charge of the system, protested. "But this is espionage," he said, "I cannot stand over these men and make them go after these details." It was made clear to him that the system was part of the Standard's permanent policy. He then resigned. His conversation was not with Rockefeller, nor did he know that Rockefeller approved of the requisitions. "They, with other ophidian methods," he writes, "may have been employed under the ægis of the company, of which its president did not approve." See Tarbell, *Standard Oil Company,* II, Chapter X, "Cutting to Kill," for details of both price-cutting and espionage.

Woodbury accuses Rockefeller of failing to take steps in the winter of 1879–80 to improve the quality of lubricating oil that had proved unsatisfactory. When cold weather set in numerous customers complained that oil certified to be fluid at zero really congealed at a much higher temperature. Woodbury found the reason for the bad quality of the oil. The works did not have an

invasion of Mexico.[31] Its efforts to make the most of the European field, dating back to William Rockefeller's arrival in New York in 1865, had been intensified in the middle seventies after the acquisition of good harbor terminals and of Charles Pratt & Co., a firm which had specialized in exporting oil in tins—"case oil." But the selling in Europe and most of Asia was long done by independent agents, not by the Standard's own representatives. Some of them were slack and inefficient, and Rockefeller and his associates resolved to go into the field themselves. First, however, beginning in 1879, they sent quick-witted men abroad to study the situation. These reconnaissances threw a brilliant searchlight upon many obstacles —tariff barriers, taxes, red tape, and popular prejudices. As opportunity offered, the Standard prepared the ground by purchasing wharves, warehouses, tankage facilities, and distributing stations. By 1885 it was ready for a tremendous frontal attack with its own forces upon the Old World market—and ready in the nick of time, for Russia was pouring amazingly cheap oil into Central Europe.[32]

Within a few years the Standard's sales force had some romantic stories to tell. In England they encountered trouble in selling kerosene because the lamp wicks were not adapted to their product. So the Standard helped finance a new lamp-wick factory there, and, as Rockefeller said, "that sold the oil."

Or take the experience of A. P. Coombe in Mexico. He was sent thither by the Waters-Pierce branch of the Standard to help find a sale for its products. His task presented many vexations, for the oil

---

adequate amount of good cold-resisting oil from Franklin, Pa., on hand, and therefore combined it with low-grade kerosene and even naphtha, which served very well for a time, but soon vaporized. He went to Rockefeller and explained the matter. "This is interesting," said Rockefeller. "I will have it looked into." But the discreditable products nevertheless continued to be sold until warm weather rendered the admixture of objectionable oils no longer necessary. The following year, writes Woodbury, the same well-justified complaints arose; and when he remonstrated, Rockefeller pleasantly remarked: "I don't think I would bother about this any more." But Woodbury praises the company's kerosene. He writes of the trade-name Standard: "At the time of its adoption the United States government and the States had various standards of gravity, fire-test, color, and so forth, for the illuminating oils manufactured from petroleum. The new company chose a name by which it guaranteed satisfaction of all these various demands in the oils it marketed. No one denies that from the beginning it has made good this assurance."

[31]C. M. Higgins to the author.

[32]Taylor, MS History; various Standard men to the author.

was imported in cases, and most of it was taken from the railheads inland on burro-back or mule-back. Worn out by his labors, he presently stole a short vacation in Puebla. As he sat one sunny morning opposite the cathedral, watching the colorful scene, his attention was arrested by a procession of donkeys wending their way up to the square from the neighboring country. Each bore a heavy burden roped to his back. "Juan," demanded Coombe of his Mexican servant, "what do all those donkeys have lashed to their backs?" "That, señor," answered Juan, "is a herd of donkeys bringing down beeswax from the farms in the hills. The farmers sell it to the priests; the priests make it into candles, and sell them to raise revenue. These candles are used in the cathedral and churches, and before sacred images in all the houses."

Coombe gazed a moment, lost in a wild surmise.

"Juan," he exclaimed, excitedly slapping his servant's back, "here's where the business of selling paraffin in Mexico gets a flying start."[33]

The demand for candles in the republic proved tremendous. Paraffin was soon a large element in them; it sold readily to the candlemakers, who mixed it with their beeswax and other materials. Mexico lightened the Standard's surplus of paraffin, and South America took still more.

IV

The Standard Oil Trust always prided itself upon its economies, for if necessary it could work upon very narrow margins. The huge volume of oil which it handled gave it enough material to produce by-products in quantity even if the amount yielded for a particular purpose—making varnishes, for example—by each tankful was small. Its financial strength and far-stretching sales-organization furnished ample resources for undertaking new enterprises, buying the latest machinery, hiring the best technicians, and marketing the product extensively. All this was a form of economy. But there was another form which the average man found even more striking. This was the magnification of small savings by their application to an immense output—to mass production.

Rockefeller, as we have seen, had taken pride from the first in

[33]Coombe told me in detail of his experiences, Nov. 26, 1936.

this form of saving. His suggestion for shortening the iron on barrel-hoops was made in the early seventies; his suggestion for using one drop less solder on each oil can came later in that decade. He and his associates tried constantly to economize in more expensive materials, and constantly did so. If their ingenuity returned handsome profits in the million-dollar corporation of 1870, it offered far larger gains in the seventy-million-dollar corporation of 1883.

"We had vision," Rockefeller later said of this period.[34] "We saw the vast possibilities of the oil industry, stood at the center of it, and brought our knowledge and imagination and business experience to bear in a dozen, in twenty, in thirty directions." Quantity-purchasing became of greater importance than ever, and wood, iron, coal, machinery, could all be had at quantity discounts. But going beyond such discounts, the Standard frequently discovered cheaper or better materials than most firms used. "We made a tremendous saving on coal," Rockefeller afterward recalled.[35] "What is the name of the fine stuff, refuse from the mines, that they have standing in mountains around the coal breakers? Culm. It was for many years a drug on their hands. . . . We found a way to use it. The coal men were glad to let us have the stuff at any figure, to get it out of their way. We bought that by the millions of tons and made great savings."

A similar economy was effected in the wood used for the cases holding two five-gallon oil cans each. The original practice had been to buy perfect wood, probably because perfect wood had been sought for the barrel—there, of course, with good reason. But Paul Babcock, a Standard official who had caught Rockefeller's passion for saving, questioned the employment of flawless planks. "What's the matter with wood having a few knots?" he inquired. "If a can leaks, the case won't hold the oil. And the wood holds and protects the can just as well whether it is perfect or not." Rockefeller accepted the suggestion, and although some of his colleagues held out for perfection, saw that it was adopted. "We saved many thousands of dollars a year," he recalled later.[36] Since the boxes ran into tens of millions annually, this may well be believed. Indeed, in the five years 1894–98 inclusive the Standard Oil manufactured 223,116,660 tin cans, which required

[34]Inglis, Conversations with Rockefeller.
[35]Idem.   [36]Various Standard men to the author.

well over a hundred million wooden cases in addition to almost five million tin cases.

Babcock advocated the purchase of pine-tracts in Canada, and the erection of a $50,000 lumbering outfit there. Rockefeller supported this measure also, and in a letter to Payne early in 1884 expressed pleasure that the trustees had endorsed the plan. "An aggressive, forward movement," he wrote,[37] "which we hope will result in a large saving in the cost of our boxes." For some time the Standard bought its own forests for barrels. Thomas Wheeler, who had helped Rockefeller, Andrews & Flagler bring down the price of barrels from $2.50 each to 80 or 90 cents, has told the story:[38]

After the Pittsburgh and Philadelphia refiners came in I was sent to Pittsburgh to install our system of barrel-making. It was the hardest thing in the world to convince Mr. Warden that we could do any better than he. They used to buy their staves and heads from a man named Gibson, who bought the wood from the West Virginia mountaineers who brought it down in barges from the forests. Gibson would pay them almost any old price—then play poker and win most of it back from them. The mountaineers didn't care; they had a good time and they could bring down plenty more staves and heads.

Mr. Rockefeller sent us after our own wood. We bought the lumber as it stood in the forests, in Michigan, Kentucky, everywhere, and made contracts with men to lumber it off in our way. First it was air-dried in sheds; then it was dried in kilns to get the last of the sap out of it. If we had kiln-dried it at first the sap would have exploded inside the green wood and honeycombed it. As it was we saved all the expense of hauling sap out of the woods, and we got the very finest possible wood for oil barrels. It would be hard to estimate the amount of money saved by having barrels as perfect as human skill could make them.

Results in the various refineries were regularly exchanged, and the reports had to be studied by all executives. Each establishment was kept on its mettle to do better than its neighbor, and whenever an advance was made in one, the news was circulated in all. Some interesting stories are told of this practice. In 1879 J. W. Van Dyke had taken over the management of the old Sone & Fleming refinery, renamed the Kings County Oil Works, a large establishment. He discovered that the superintendent of the can factory had been sell-

[37]Feb. 6, 1884; Rockefeller Papers.
[38]Inglis, Conversation with Thomas Wheeler.

ing the dross accumulated in soldering, and discharged the man. Having no can expert available, and possessing wide experience as an engineer, he quietly took over the direction of the factory himself. He found that tremendous quantities of solder were being used to cement the seams, and that by slightly changing the pattern of the can and using more pressure, little need be employed. Fearful that his processes might be unreasonably challenged if he disclosed them, he continued his manufacturing until the Standard officials saw from his reports that he was using far less material than their other factories. They were alarmed lest the cans should prove leaky, but by this time Van Dyke was fully equipped to meet any criticism. He was able to show that the returns of his cans because of leakage were only one eighth of one per cent, far less than figures previously considered normal! Of course he was also saving money on solder. His discovery was immediately applied to all the Standard manufacture, and reduced its costs about $10,000 a month.[39]

Van Dyke was responsible for two more important innovations, one in manufacturing and one in transportation. The first was his invention of the "tower" still, which made it possible to hold oil in the same distilling apparatus while taking from it a considerable list of products. Previously, after distilling for kerosene, refiners had gone through a costly process of draining out the residuum and treating it separately to obtain further distillates. Technicians at the Whiting refinery estimated that the change saved about $17,000,000 a year for the Standard organization. The stills in use down to the invention of Dr. Burton's "cracking" process (by another Standard employee) differed but little from those which Van Dyke had developed. His other improvement was a stronger type of tank car. The wooden undercarriage used in the seventies had become too weak to withstand the shocks it received when switched about with the heavier boxcars and hopper cars that had come into use. Van Dyke perfected an all-steel tank car which, regarded with amazement and doubt at first, quickly proved its superiority, and a quarter century later had come into general use. It protected the oil against accidents, and conserved, in the aggregate, huge quantities of kerosene.[40]

[39]Mr. Van Dyke to the author; see also *Short History of the Atlantic Refining Company.*
[40]*Idem.*

Every one in the organization became infected by this zeal for economy and efficiency. Sometimes an executive could make a useful suggestion to Rockefeller himself, or at least prompt him to an idea. Plant-expansion in Cleveland rendered it necessary to buy barrels as well as fabricate them, and Orville T. Waring tells of an incident a few years later:[41]

On a high hill some miles outside Cleveland stood a large and handsome house, dark green with white trimmings, which could be seen for miles. It was built by George Hooper, who furnished barrels to the Company. Passing in the train, I pointed it out to Mr. Rockefeller.
"You wish to know who owns that house?" he asked. "It's our Mr. Hooper, who makes barrels for us. Whew! That's an expensive house, isn't it? I wonder if Hooper isn't making altogether *too much* money? Let's look into it. When we get back we'll go over the contracts."
It was found that the profits were out of proportion. Mr. Hooper accepted a proposition made to him, his business was appraised, and he received full value in stock of the Standard Oil Company. He was put in charge of the Company's barrel-making business. He grew wealthy; did far better than if he had remained in business for himself, even at excessive profits.

The total effect of this constant drive for economy, applied by the best technologists and managers procurable, can readily be imagined. Even by 1879 it had done much to place the Standard in advance of all competitors. We have referred to the letter which Rockefeller sent his brother Frank that year to explain that his works in Cleveland could refine oil for half of what it was costing Frank's Pioneer Oil Company, and this is worth quoting in full. Apparently the Pioneer had sent cost-sheets to the Standard, for Rockefeller wrote:[42]

Gentlemen:
I see by the reports that have been forwarded me from Cleveland, that your cost of manufacturing for the last year was 1.82 per gall.
We have often spoken in reference to the importance of the most careful economy in the manufacturing department, and this report shows that you are not down as low as other concerns of the same size and not nearly as low as our own.
We desire very much to reduce this cost of manufacturing and make you the following proposition: We will refine your allotment for one year, giving you the same kind, quantity, and quality of goods, subject to your most rigid and careful inspection from day to day, and charge

[41]Inglis, Conversation with Waring.
[42]March 3, 1879; Rockefeller Papers.

for the manufacturing one half of what your sheet shows for the past year; in other words we will charge 91/100ths of a cent per gallon, and if, at any time, you desire to take the contract off our hands, you can do so by giving us a notice of a very few days. The object we have in view in this is to make a saving between us of the extra cost under your administration, giving you the right at any time to come in and do the work by simply doing it as cheap as we offer.

Yours truly,

John D. Rockefeller.

We notice that your yield (74.78) is several per cent less than that obtained by our company.

J. D. R.

The Pioneer Oil Company was doubtless less enterprising than some other competitors, although Frank and his partner John Fawcett bore a good reputation as refiners. A barrel of refined oil contained fifty gallons. Rockefeller was offering them slightly more than 45 cents a barrel out of his manufacturing superiority, a greater amount, year in and year out, than the Standard was supposed by its enemies to be receiving from rebates; especially when it is considered that from 1875 to 1879 inclusive the Standard rendered expensive services as an "evener" for the reduction in freight rates that it obtained. If the Standard enjoyed a manufacturing superiority of 45 cents a barrel over an average competitor, it also drew great advantages from its better facilities in transportation and marketing. All in all, the decisive importance of its industrial efficiency in the achievement of success cannot well be doubted.

But to what end were these economies directed? Simply to piling up greater profits for the Standard Oil Company? This is a crucial question, for the stabilization of an industry by monopolistic steps can be justified only if it lowers prices to the consumer. Whether the Standard Oil prices were excessive, and if so by what margin, are complex questions. Prices did fall, but largely because of cheaper crude oil and technological advances. Apologists for the Standard maintained that it made illuminants cheaper than they would otherwise have been, while critics declared that it kept them higher. James Ford Rhodes agreed with Gilbert H. Montague that "the vexed question of the effect of the Standard Oil combination on the price of refined oil will probably never be settled."[43] The Bureau of Corpora-

[43]Rhodes, *The McKinley and Roosevelt Administrations, 1897–1907*, p. 165; Montague, *Rise and Progress of the Standard Oil Company*, 136.

tions in its report to Roosevelt on the petroleum industry concluded that for the great decline in the margin between the price of crude oil and the price of refined oil down to 1879 the Standard could claim "little if any" credit; and for the further decline after 1879 it deserved "no credit whatever." The same conclusion had been reached by Miss Tarbell in her chapter on "The Price of Oil."[44] But Rockefeller, Archbold, and other Standard men declared, with an array of figures as bewildering as their assailants', that it *had* been responsible for price-reduction. The question involves many obscure factors—for invention, changes in transportation, develop- ment of by-products, marketing arrangements, fluctuations in sup- ply, investment-figures, and other items affected the price trend. But it is clear that even if the Standard did lower prices, it failed to lower them as much as it should have done. The Bureau of Cor- porations found that in three typical American towns, kerosene sold in the years 1885–1905 at an unreasonable margin per gallon over the cost of crude oil. From 1885 to 1891, inclusive, the average margin was 7.6 cents; from 1892 to 1899 it was 5.9 cents; and from 1899 to 1905 it was 6.9 cents. It appears that the trend was downward under Rockefeller, and that Archbold, taking control about 1897, reversed it; but even under Rockefeller the margin was excessively high.[45]

Considerable evidence exists that Rockefeller was more interested than some associates in reducing prices. To be sure, he never dis- avowed the profit motive. "The Standard Oil Company did not claim that they were a benevolent missionary institution," he dryly re- marked.[46] "They boldly claimed they were in the business to make money." But this was not the whole story.

William G. Warden told his sons that at meetings of the execu- tive committee the strongest voice for low prices was always Rocke- feller's. "We should cut the charge, and then find means of manu-

[44]Tarbell, *History of the Standard Oil Company*, II, Ch. XVI; *Report of the Commissioner of Corporations on the Petroleum Industry: Part II, Prices and Profits, 1907*, pp. 47–52.

[45]*Report of Commissioner of Corporations, ut supra*, 196 ff., 295 ff. The three towns were Lawrence, Mass., Tecumseh, Mich., and Paola, Kans. The Bureau reports, p. 225: "It is certain that there was a considerable decline in the margin between the price of crude oil and the true average domestic price of illuminating oil from the eighties to the middle nineties." Rockefeller turned his control over to Archbold soon after the middle nineties. But profits on by-products increased largely in this period.

[46]*Cf.* Rockefeller, *Random Reminiscences*.

facturing more cheaply," he would say.[47] Joseph Seep recalled once standing with Rockefeller, Bostwick, Warden, and other men beside a well that had just been opened in Butler County late in the seventies. Rockefeller remarked: "This is the poor man's light."[48] The same philosophy cropped out in a letter which Rockefeller sent to H. C. Folger in the New York office in 1885. He had received a statement summarizing some notable reductions in manufacturing costs, and replied: "I am much gratified. Let the good work go on. We must ever remember we are refining oil for the poor man and he must have it cheap and good."[49] At about the same time he expressed the idea more casually in a letter to Archbold: "Hope we can continue to hold out with the best illuminator in the world at the *lowest* price."[50] And in old age he remarked that the Standard had three good reasons for keeping prices low: first, it proved that it was doing a good job; second, it kept the business from competitors; and third, it benefited the poor.

The fact remains that profits were extremely high, and they were closely held. We have previously given the net earnings or profits of the trust through 1890. For 1891 they were $16,331,826, and for 1892 they rose to $19,174,878. Then came the panic of 1893; and both that year and the next the net profits were a mere fifteen and a half millions. In 1895, however, they rose again to $24,078,076, and in 1896 they reached $34,077,519. Official figures are lacking for the three subsequent years, but we possess evidence that the net profits were between thirty and forty millions annually. In 1900 we have a sworn statement that they reached $55,501,774. Very large sums were used for reserves and expansion, but the dividend rate after 1890 was never less than 8.5 per cent of the net assets, and in 1900 reached 22.7 per cent.[51]

Of course the Standard heads could justly argue that the real value of the investment was much above the $71,116,000 in trust certificates outstanding in 1882, and the $96,941,000 outstanding in 1890. In 1900 they computed the net assets at $205,480,000, and this was conservative. We must also remember that Carnegie's steel com-

[47]Mr. Clarence Warden repeated this to me.
[48]Inglis, Notes of Conversation with Mr. Seep.
[49]Sept. 21, 1885; Rockefeller Papers.
[50]Aug. 23, 1884; Rockefeller Papers.
[51]*Report of Commissioner of Corporations, ut supra,* 39 ff.

pany made about $40,000,000 net in 1900, and that Henry Ford's profits have been colossal. But these Standard profits were a good deal higher than if regard for the poor man's light had been a paramount consideration. The most cogent excuse for their size in these years was that huge sums were being used as a surplus for absolutely essential reserves and expansion. Rockefeller, even more than Carnegie and Ford, was wisely determined to be independent of finance bankers. Moreover, the oil business was long regarded as highly speculative, and down to 1895 many believed that half the vast investment mightly shortly prove a dead loss. Rockefeller later spoke scornfully of William H. Vanderbilt. Although he bought some Standard Oil Stock, he was always careful to say, "I don't want the Commodore to know about this." The Commodore would have thought it unsafe! When the stock advanced a little, the nervous Vanderbilt sold it, and Rockefeller was glad to see him and his like go. "They took their nimble sixpence and got out."[52]

V

No picture of the combination would be complete without a sketch of the executive agency which bound its parts together and managed them as an organic whole. Even before the creation of the trust a unitary control had been operating with fair effectiveness. Headquarters were at first in Cleveland, but more and more of the combination's business came to be transacted in the handsome Pearl Street offices. By 1882, when the New York offices were moved to 44 Broadway, the central controlling machinery was taking finished shape. Early in 1884 the Standard bought for $450,000 the properties at Nos. 24-28 Broadway,[53] and erected there a massive building of which the trust became the best-known tenant. Although its existence was little known publicly, in 1885, the name appeared in the New York Directory—"Standard Oil Trust, 26 Broadway." This building was the brain from which peremptory orders were flashed to every department and agency of the intricate organization.

The trustees designated in 1882—John and William Rockefeller, Payne, Bostwick, Flagler, Warden, Pratt, Brewster, and Archbold —were of course the supreme authority in the organization. Hand

[52]Rockefeller's comment on the Taylor history, Nov., 1922.
[53]*The Lamp,* Oct., 1923, "Menus and Men."

in hand with them operated the powerful proxy committee controlling the subsidiary companies. After Rockefeller removed to New York an Executive Committee, set up because some trustees could not always be in town, gave continuous supervision. It drafted general policies, and directed the management of wells, pipe lines, refineries, by-products, manufactories, marketing organizations, and export units. Every non-routine transaction involving $5000 or more had to go before this body. Among other affairs, it dealt with the buying of crude, the purchase of chemicals, lumber, and piping, arrangements with railroads, the provisions of shipping, the acceptance of orders, and financial problems. It pressed into service important subordinates who were needed in New York for expert advice or drafting detailed plans. Below this supreme authority was a group of specialized committees, each made up of one or several trustees and some additional experts, and each entrusted with some important branch of the Standard's activities. Usually there were eight or nine of these bodies. At 26 Broadway the leaders received a steady flow of reports from refineries, jobbing companies, pipe lines, buying agencies, and other units; they had thousands of messages every month from the petroleum fields, the centers of manufacture, and the far-scattered and fast-multiplying selling agencies. They assembled the data in its proper categories, and with judgment trained by long experience decided upon policies. Never before had a group of men presided over an activity so many-sided, far-reaching, and crowded with detail.

The Executive Committee usually met five days a week, and its deliberations were secret and unrecorded. Obviously it could not carry on detailed administrative work for the fifty refineries, the twenty thousand miles of pipe line, the producing wells, and the vast marketing system. A single subsidiary like the Consolidated Tank Line Company was a little world in itself. This marketing agency sold its lubricating oil to hardware stores scattered among the wheatfields of the Dakotas; it supplied light to the bustling towns of Illinois and Indiana; its wagons rumbled through the streets of Memphis and Paducah. Sometimes its annual account with the Standard Oil Company of Ohio ran to $5,000,000, and Jim and Alex McDonald, its immediate heads, were millionaires.[54] Yet the Con-

[54]Charles M. Higgins to the author, Jan. 13, 1937.

Left: Rockefeller with his son John (in derby hat) and other young people on the steps of William Rockefeller's house; and, *right:* on a mountain-climbing jaunt in Switzerland.

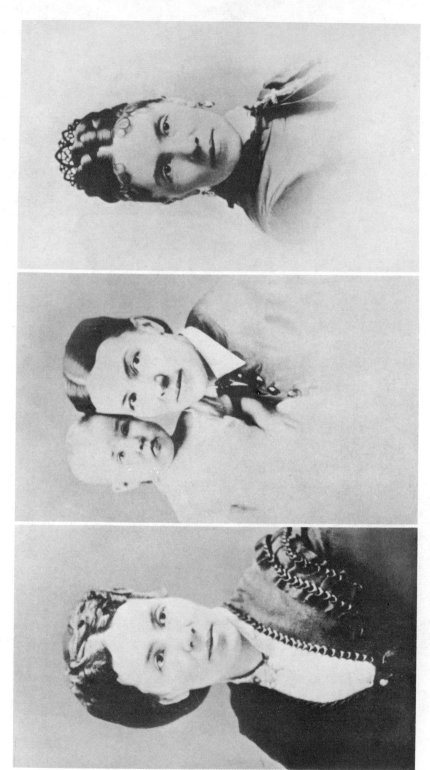

Mrs. John D. Rockefeller.

Left: About 1872. *Center:* With her oldest daughter Bessie, in 1867. *Right:* About 1882.

solidated was merely one of a hundred units, some of them far more powerful and important. Their direction had to be delegated to the special committees.

Perhaps the most important of these was the Manufacturing Committee, which concerned itself with refining, by-products, and materials for shipping. It examined processes, noted costs and profits, gave advice and information, and imposed definite practices where it felt they ought to be generally adopted. H. H. Rogers was chairman for a time, and later Ambrose McGregor. Almost an equivalent position was rapidly assumed by the Committee on Domestic Trade. The first men active in this group included Horace Hutchins, Wesley H. Tilford, Colonel W. P. Thompson, Charles M. Pratt, and C. M. Coburn. This committee studied the whole field of selling and distribution in the United States, and, as the Standard developed marketing, kept in close touch with it. The other committees active in 1885–90 were those on Foreign Trade, with T. C. Bushnell as leader; Shipping, in which R. G. Veit was prominent; Cooperage, with Thomas H. Wheeler as the outstanding figure; Lubricating, with E. T. Bedford acting as executive and Silas H. Paine as technical expert; Pipe Lines, with first Daniel O'Day and then H. H. Rogers as presiding spirit; and the Case and Can Committee.[55]

These bodies threshed out exigent problems, and presented recommendations which were approved or rejected by the Executive Committee. A basis for their work was furnished by the detailed reports from each unit, supplemented by data from travelling auditors and experts. By 1885 officers from 26 Broadway were consulting steadily with managers called to New York, sending specialists to works where new processes were being tried, and otherwise seeing that information and skills were pooled. Statements upon all plants and companies were quickly made avaliable to Standard managers wherever situated, so that each might see how his accomplishments compared with those of others. But the names of the various establishments were never given; the cost and profit sheets were presented simply by number.[56] Nothing was done to humiliate or penalize any one group of men. The great object was to foster a healthy spirit of

[55]Full information on the committees has been furnished me by Charles M. Higgins, Charles T. White, and other Standard Oil veterans.
[56]So J. W. Van Dyke assured me.

emulation, loyalty, and zeal—the "Standard spirit"—by personal attention, praise where deserved, and tangible rewards.

It need not be said that the trustees and their aides had to stick to the job day in and day out, with no truancies and no relaxation. The labor was intense and sustained. But at one hour of the day the leaders met in a more relaxed mood—at lunch.

The noonday table for officers had its beginnings in 1876. At that time the Standard's quarters were at 140 Pearl Street, but the lunch room was situated at 128 Pearl, above the offices of Charles Pratt & Co. In 1882 it removed with the Standard itself to 44 Broadway, and in 1885 to No. 26.[57] Before long it became an important agency in centralizing the activities of the Company. Here the trustees met informally with other officers, exchanged news and opinions, and discussed problems and plans. The men, arriving in the stiff business dress of that day—high silk hats, long coats, gloves—had regular seats. Rockefeller had courteously given the head of the table to his senior, Charles Pratt. On Pratt's right was Flagler, on his left H. H. Rogers. Next to Flagler sat John D. Rockefeller, then Archbold, Bostwick, A. J. Pouch, John Bushnell, and Paul Babcock. Next to Rogers sat William Rockefeller, and then Thomas Bushnell, Benjamin Brewster, F. Q. Barstow, J. Crowell, and J. H. Alexander. At the far end of the Board was James McGee.[58]

Membership in the group naturally changed as the years passed. It was never in any sense an official unit—it was not, for example, limited to the trustees of the Standard Oil Trust; but all who lunched in the room were of high consequence in the organization. To be asked to join the table was the highest honor a rising executive could win. The great function of the gatherings was to provide the cordial relationship, flow of ideas, and opportunity for friendly persuasion which Rockefeller desired, and which fitted in with his way of conducting business.

All these administrative activities were pervaded by the unquestioned personal influence of John D. Rockefeller. He was no autocrat; he often differed with individuals on the Board and off it, and sometimes their ideas and not his were followed. But when he took a

[57]N. Y. *Herald*, Feb. 8, March 16, 1884, says $300,000 was paid for Nos. 24 and 26, and $150,000 for No. 28.

[58]Flagler came east to live in 1882, Payne in 1884; see Flagler obituary, N. Y. *Times*, Nov. 20, 1917; Payne obituary, N. Y. *Sun*, June 28, 1917.

position it represented such a careful examination of the facts, and was supported by so sound a judgment, that in most instances it was accepted. He was successful too in bringing into harmonious co-operation a group of powerful men whose individualities might have seemed too stubborn for unification. It was evidence of his patience, masterful force, and fairness that he could harness to-gether such diverse leaders as the aggressive Rogers, the cautious Pratt, the frosty Lockhart, the aristocratic Payne, the cool but daring Flagler, and the explosive Pierce. As we have suggested, he was assisted by Warden's geniality and Archbold's gaiety. But Rocke-feller's was the compelling touch; he seemed to bring out the best in these men, and under his quiet guidance each found full scope for his activity. They criticized each other, but him they always admired and trusted.

This does not mean that the great organization operated without some inner friction, which in one instance became rather sharp. A definite faction formed in later years about Charles M. Pratt and H. H. Rogers, and was regarded by some Standard men with dis-tinct animosity. This was after the death of the elder Pratt, and Rockefeller's virtual retirement. It was not unnatural that Western and Eastern men should feel some mutual jealousy. The Pratt firm had dominated the New York trade, and Charles Pratt had been for a time the largest stockholder next to Rockefeller himself. He reared several important protégés, such as E. T. Bedford, who had left a Connecticut farm to begin work with Pratt at eighteen.[59] His son C. M. Pratt was regarded by many Standard men as inclined to subordinate the Company's welfare at times to a desire for greater authority. He brought into the Standard Oil of New York a number of Amherst graduates who made up a distinctly marked group. "The Pratt-Rogers element made a dividing line in our company," said Charles M. Higgins bitterly. "Rogers was never our type of man. It would have been better if that crowd had never come in." Higgins told of a long-standing feud between C. M. Pratt and David S. Cowles, president of the Standard Oil of Minnesota. Both were on the Committee for Domestic Trade until Pratt finally shouldered Cowles out of it. That very evening Higgins, who had just been transferred to New York, met Cowles in the elevator going down

[59]See N. Y. *World-Telegram* obituary of Bedford, May 21, 1931.

at 26 Broadway, and they walked over to take the elevated train uptown. As they stood on the platform, Cowles remarked with deep feeling:

"Did you ever look at the building from here? You are just entering, and I am forever leaving that whited sepulchre of blasted hopes and ambitions!"

Rogers was much more aggressive, outspoken, and belligerent than the elder Pratt. Even before 1890 he was interesting himself in outside financial schemes, a fact which some more single-minded associates resented. He and William Rockefeller became partners in various undertakings, among which was the development of certain gas companies. Since naphtha was used for making water-gas, Rogers and William Rockefeller were in a good position to push into this novel and lucrative field. Moreover, they had plenty of capital. They presently went into the business in Boston, buying a franchise and underselling J. Edward Addicks, who had enjoyed green pastures there until his New York rivals appeared. "They took Mr. Addicks's trousers down and patted him plenty," was the way Higgins later expressed it.[60] "They took his business completely away—robbed him of it, that's what they did." Addicks, in retaliation, bought a franchise in Brooklyn, where Rogers and William Rockefeller held control of the Consolidated Gas Company. What then occurred illustrated the possibilities for friction in a great organization like the Standard.

Addicks came to New York, and from the Fifth Avenue Hotel sent for Higgins. "I'm in trouble," remarked Addicks, "and you can help me out. I need 50,000 barrels of oil badly, and I want it delivered by tankboat as soon as possible in Brooklyn." Higgins knew all about Addicks's troubles in Boston and about his new Brooklyn company. He knew also that Rogers would wish to prevent any sale of oil to Addicks, and to starve him out. On the other hand, the Standard would profit by so large an order. Higgins was courageous: "Perhaps we can help you," he said encouragingly.[61]

Going back to 26 Broadway, he explained Addicks's proposal to John D. Archbold, who called in W. H. Tilford. The three agreed to sell the oil at a certain figure. Higgins then obtained a down pay-

[60]Charles M. Higgins to the author, Nov. 4, 11, 1936.
[61]Charles M. Higgins to the author, Jan. 13, 17, 1937.

ment of $25,000, and that same day laid it on Archbold's desk. The latter looked at it, ran his hands through his hair several times, smiled, and said in a humorous drawl: "I think it is a—very good—deal you have made." Undoubtedly Archbold had a shrewd anticipation of just what Rogers's attitude would be.

Naturally, Rogers did not think it a good deal at all. At this time he was in the very prime of life, his splendid vitality at its height; "tall, muscular, fit with the clear skin and bright eye of an athlete in training," said Nick Ewers, manager of the Standard's private restaurant. Higgins himself has described his irresistible force and attraction.[62] "He looked at you and he owned you! A vital, magnetic man, and altogether charming and affable—unless you trod on his little toe!" That was precisely what Higgins had now done.

Rogers sent for him early the next morning. As Higgins entered he looked up from some papers, his face black as a storm cloud. "Didn't you know that William Rockefeller and I were in the gas business in Brooklyn?" he demanded.

Higgins tried to explain. "I heard you were interested—" he began.

"Then I don't understand your making this fool transaction. What is the meaning of it anyhow?"

"If you will examine the price paid the Standard for this oil I think you will agree that it was a very profitable transaction," answered Higgins calmly.

Rogers comprehended the point. The Standard could not turn away good business because it interfered with the private interests of one or more of its partners. He stared at Higgins a long minute, swung about with a grunt, and the interview was over.

Rogers also had a sharp skirmish in the purely internal affairs of the Standard.[63] At the outset he dominated the Manufacturing Committee, but Ambrose McGregor, probably at Rockefeller's desire, began to come from Cleveland ten days in every month to attend its deliberations. A sharp jealousy arose between the two men. As a practical manufacturer, McGregor could give Rogers hearts and spades, and still worst him by his unassailable facts and shrewd discernment. But as a stockholder and the major officer, Rogers held a stronger position. Since it would not do to put him down, he was kicked upstairs; that is, he was appointed a trustee, while McGregor

[62]*Idem.*   [63]*Idem.*

was brought permanently to New York to take the principal super-vision of manufacturing. Rogers accepted this shift with good grace, and busied himself with the pipe lines.[64]

Naturally, Rockefeller never permitted himself to be involved in any company quarrel. He preserved an Olympian position, quite above petty disputes, and had his way of enforcing his wishes with-out personal friction. He was perhaps most frequently at odds on policy with Charles Pratt, whose extreme caution recoiled from some of his bold proposals. Pratt, for example, vehemently opposed the acquisition of Ohio oil lands. Rockefeller's own moderate state-ment on this controversy, dictated in 1918—a statement which char-acteristically omits all mention of Pratt by name—is full of illumi-nation on his quiet, persistent method of attaining a goal.

He told how, after the Lima field was first vigorously opened in 1885, oil was produced in what seemed enormous and fast-increas-ing quantities. He insisted that the Standard should provide pipes and tankage for it all; that it should buy and store large quantities; and that it should obtain new oil acreage of great extent. He and his adherents fought a continuous battle with Pratt and other timid officers who "held up their hands in holy horror" at the large ex-penditures necessary for all this and for Herman Frasch's experi-ments. Finally, after arguing his case fully at an unusually stormy meeting, Rockefeller lost patience with the conservatives and said with quiet finality:

"Very well, gentlemen. At my own personal risk I will put up the money to care for this product—two million—three million dol-lars, if necessary."

And he described the result:[65]

This ended the discussion, and we carried the Board with us and con-tinued to use the funds of the Company in what was regarded as a very hazardous investment of money. But we persevered, and two or three of our practical men stood firmly with me and constantly occupied them-selves with the chemists until at last, after millions of dollars had been expended in the tankage and buying the oil and constructing the pipe lines and tank cars to draw it away to the markets where we could sell it for fuel, one of our German chemists cried "Eureka!" We insisted upon repeated demonstrations, and at last found ourselves able to clarify the oil.

[64]"Sundries Envelope," Rockefeller Papers.
[65]Inglis, Conversations with Rockefeller.

Rockefeller had a way also of anticipating and averting potential clashes between members of the Board. Whenever differences of opinion appeared, he insisted on having all the facts presented, and all the tenable views lucidly set forth. Thus we find him writing Warden in 1885 about an issue which had caused a disagreement:[66] "We want to have our Executive Committee hear the representative of Cleveland, Pittsburgh, Titusville, and New York local trade departments. Then I trust we shall be able to arrive at some equitable, reasonable, fair solution of this question. We certainly must not reach a decision without giving everybody the opportunity to be heard. I trust that the conclusions, when reached, will meet with your approval and that of our good friends in Pittsburgh." Other letters indicate that he was careful to procure the opinion of every important executive on any issue of magnitude, and, if uncertainty remained, was likely to urge a delay for more study. This deference to others had a happy effect.

Yet his leadership was never questioned. Every one who has had occasion to sit in conferences of a dozen able men, where the discussion grows hot and arguments are exchanged with unflinching directness, knows that they afford the best possible test of intellectual superiority. The man who thinks most clearly and sees furthest into the future soon asserts his ascendancy; for as Pascal said, foresight is the mark of a great commander. Weight of character also tells. In such conferences the best mind emerges even more quickly than a Burke or Gladstone comes to the front in Parliament, a Webster or Calhoun in Congress. If, in the conferences of the Standard executives, dealing with the most intricate problems, Warden or Archbold or Pratt had possessed a keener mind and riper sagacity than Rockefeller's, he would soon have established his primacy. But the testimony is unanimous that Rockefeller, by virtue of his intellectual force and shrewdness, his equanimity and wisdom, was always the head. He ruled by agreement, and his view was sometimes rejected, but by and large he was the master.

Abraham Flexner once asked him the secret of the Standard's uninterrupted march to power.[67] The answer was modest. "We had a group of strong men from the outset," said Rockefeller. "There were Flagler, Harkness, Colonel Payne, Andrews, my brother—

---

[66]May 2, 1885, Rockefeller Papers.　　　　[67]Mr. Flexner to the author.

later others. Our general rule was to take no important action till all of us were convinced of its wisdom. We made sure that we were right and had planned for every contingency before we went ahead." Yet Rockefeller's personal strength, for good or ill, penetrated every corner of the organization. His spirit became the Standard's spirit. A generation after this period a retired Standard executive remarked: "I was never trained by Mr. Rockefeller in my business relationships, but I came in contact with men whom he trained, and who knew perfectly how to train me." He believed that he was a direct inheritor of some essential quality from the Standard's builder, even though he had no immediate relationship to him. The Standard would have been held together by the grip of this powerful spirit and tenacious mind, even if common investments and prosperity had operated far less strongly.

VI

It was a mighty creation, this Standard Oil Trust of 1885, and would soon become far more powerful, complex, and far-reaching still. It was to be vehemently denounced throughout most of the next generation, and in part with good cause. But its success was not built upon dishonesty. The rebate contracts of 1877 were deplorable; the "massacre" of independent refineries had indefensible features. But so severe a critic of the trust as Charles J. Woodbury, who stated that its business ethics showed grave flaws, added that "on some of the indictments injustice has been done." The practices by which it earned its merited castigation were fairly congenial to its contemporaries, and "men of business at large have not disapproved of them because they are American." To have been ultra-moral would have invited catastrophe. Rockefeller had probably heard of the bruised urchin who reported to his teacher that the street was just full of boys looking for the one who wouldn't strike back. The companies the Standard competed with, large and small, writes Woodbury, "kept down production, sought partial and discriminating rates and rebates, appropriated processes of manufacture, exercised an elastic scale of prices, gave commissions to purchasers, were down to all the tricks of the trade. The number of them who would not have done much of what the Standard has been arraigned for is minute." In internal administration the Standard was faultless. Its management was as safe and steady as the government itself, it met every business obligation, it benefited every investor, and it treated its labor with generosity. "Chicane," concluded Woodbury, "still taints the ways of the Standard, but its main foundation and business structure are of better material. Tricks may build a small business—never a large one."

Quite apart from this issue of ethics, the time was to come when the Standard would be praised for its pioneering qualities and for its demonstration of the useful possibilities of large-scale organization; when men of discernment would point to it as one of the most impressive industrial fabrics ever erected in any part of the globe. When Nathaniel S. Shaler published his three volumes on the United States in 1894, Charles Francis Adams contributed a chapter on the new rôle of corporate organization. Instancing three great businesses, the Union Pacific, the Mutual Life, and the Standard Oil, he paid tribute to the last-named as a magnificent achievement in the large-scale integration of industry for efficiency and expansion. A little later Miss Tarbell included in her history a long chapter on the Standard's "legitimate greatness," ungrudging in praise of its feats.[68] Walter Hines Page wrote early in the new century: "Now one of the best pieces of constructive practical work ever done to accomplish its purposes . . . was done by John D. Rockefeller when he organized the Standard Oil Company."[69] And in 1915, Charles W. Eliot published an essay on "National Efficiency Best Developed under Free Governments."[70] He chose various illustrations, but when he turned to industry he used the Standard Oil. "The great inventions in business organizations have, of course, proceeded from the freer countries," he wrote. "The organization of the great business of taking petroleum out of the earth, piping the oil over great distances, distilling and refining it, and distributing it in tank steamers, tank wagons, and cans all over the earth, was an American invention." For the power of that huge creation impartial observers had come to feel admiration.

[68]*Standard Oil Company,* II, 231–255.
[69]Burton J. Hendrick, *The Training of An American: Earlier Life and Letters of Walter Hines Page,* 380.
[70]*Atlantic Monthly,* Vol. CXV, April, 1915.